# Hot Wh

# 1968-1972

Includes Gran Toros™
History and Pictures

Bob Parker

4880 Lower Valley Road, Atglen, PA 19310 USA

# DEDICATION

To my dad; I am forever grateful for all of his help and support.

---

"Hot Wheels®," "Spectraflame™," "Gran Toros®," "Matchbox®," "Superfast®,"and many of the names of the various models pictured are trademarks of Mattel Inc., El Segundo CA. 90245 U.S.A.

The names of makes and models of actual vehicles are trademarks of the manufacturers of those vehicles.

Mattel, Inc. did not authorize this book nor furnish or approve of any of the information contained herein. This book was derived from the author's independent research.

Library of Congress-in-Publication Data

Parker, Bob, 1967-
Hot wheels, 1968-1972 / Bob Parker.
p. cm.
ISBN 0-7643-1480-7 (pbk.)
1. Hot Wheels toys--Collectors and collecting--Catalogs. 2. Hot Wheels toys--Prices--Catalogs. 3. Automobiles--Models--Collectors and collecting--Catalogs. I. Title: Hot Wheels. II. Title.
TL237.2.P3722 2002
629.22'1'075--dc21
2001005064

Copyright © 2002 by Bob Parker

All rights reserved. No part of this work may be reproduced or used in any form or by any means—graphic, electronic, or mechanical, including photocopying or information storage and retrieval systems—without written permission from the copyright holder.
"Schiffer," "Schiffer Publishing Ltd. & Design," and the "Design of pen and ink well" are registered trademarks of Schiffer Publishing Ltd.

Designed by Bonnie M. Hensley
Cover design by Bruce M. Waters
Type set in Dutch801 Rm BT

ISBN: 0-7643-1480-7
Printed in China
1 2 3 4

Published by Schiffer Publishing Ltd.
4880 Lower Valley Road
Atglen, PA 19310
Phone: (610) 593-1777; Fax: (610) 593-2002
E-mail: Schifferbk@aol.com
Please visit our web site catalog at **www.schifferbooks.com**
We are always looking for people to write books on new and related subjects. If you have an idea for a book please contact us at the above address.

This book may be purchased from the publisher.
Include $3.95 for shipping.
Please try your bookstore first.
You may write for a free catalog.

In Europe, Schiffer books are distributed by
Bushwood Books
6 Marksbury Ave.
Kew Gardens
Surrey TW9 4JF England
Phone: 44 (0) 20 8392-8585; Fax: 44 (0) 20 8392-9876
E-mail: Bushwd@aol.com
Free postage in the U.K., Europe; air mail at cost.

# CONTENTS

ACKNOWLEDGMENTS _____ 4

INTRODUCTION _____ 5

THE HISTORY OF HOT WHEELS _____ 6

THE ORIGINAL HOT WHEELS DESIGNERS _____ 7

1968 – 1972 SPECTRAFLAME™ COLORS _____ 8

1968-1972 OTHER HOT WHEELS® COLORS _____ 9

1968 _____ 10

1969 _____ 16

1970 _____ 22

1971 _____ 31

1972 _____ 41

MISCELLANEOUS _____ 44

GRAN TOROS™, HOT WHEELS® SUPER RACERS _____ 57

HOT WHEELS 1968-1972 VARIATION / PRICE GUIDE _____ 62

BIBLIOGRAPHY _____ 64

# ACKNOWLEDGMENTS

I am very grateful to the following people for their support, encouragement, and assistance with this book. Thank you to Frank Veres for the fantastic photography work and the brilliant color slides, Charles Kitson for the detailed variation guide, Fran Fried for his help with editing, Jesse Thompson of Milford Photo, Inc., C.J. Aresco for the Gran Toros information and photographs, and Bruce Pascal for the use of pictures including some of the rarest Hot Wheels® models. Special thanks to Randy Price for sharing his knowledge and his unique collection at "Randy's Wooster Street Pizza Shop."

# INTRODUCTION

Mattel Inc., a leading toy manufacturer based in California, introduced the Hot Wheels® toy car line in 1968 and this brand quickly dominated the 1:64 scale toy car market. In 1991, Mattel celebrated the production of the one-billionth Hot Wheels vehicle and that number continues to grow. Toy vehicles are often produced with many interior and exterior variations, and these changes are the driving force of collecting the miniature models. Every year new models are added to the line. These new castings will be produced in a random number of variations. The attraction of collecting is to seek out and obtain as many of these variations as possible. Some castings are produced for many years, while others are discontinued after a short period of time. This is what makes the collecting of variations very interesting. It is estimated that there have been more than 25,000 variations produced in the three decades since the inception of the toy car line.

The toys pictured and described in this book provide an extensive guide to collectors of these dynamic die-cast toys. This book explores the Hot Wheels models produced between 1968 and 1972. While the basic idea of a Hot Wheels car has not changed, some major marketing and design changes have been made to the line over the years. The first four years represent the "Vintage Years" and the models produced during this time period will always have a special place in the heart of a Hot Wheels collector. The color pictures represent all of the various castings produced from the first car in 1968 through the 1972 model year. A complete variation and price guide is included along with a complete listing of all sets and related accessories that were available each year. A special bonus section provides a guide to Hot Wheels Gran Toros®, a line of 1:43 scale die-cast models produced by Mattel in 1970.

# THE HISTORY OF HOT WHEELS

Throughout the 1950s and '60s Lesney's Matchbox® cars were the most well-known and collectible die-cast cars. Elliot and Ruth Handler, the founders of Mattel, are credited with the birth of Hot Wheels cars. In 1966, under the direction of Elliot, Mattel began research and development on a line of die-cast cars that would be unique from other brands currently available. There was much work that needed to be done before a new product could be added to the list of quality toys produced by the company. It was two years before the first Hot Wheels® car rolled off the production line. A design team was formed and began to work on creating the "fastest metal cars in the world."

California styling, raked bodies, torsion-bar suspensions, mag style wheels with a red stripe around the tires, and bright new Spectraflame™ paint colors are what made Hot Wheels cars so unique. A total of 12 different Spectraflame® colors were originally selected to be used on the cars and included purple, lavender, red, orange, gold, brown, olive, lime, green, aqua, light blue and blue. Sixteen vehicles were designed and each was to be available in all of the Spectraflame® colors. All of these new features established Mattel's competitive edge in the die-cast market. Lesney soon changed the style of the Matchbox® line from regular wheels to new Superfast® wheels to compete with the new low-friction wheel bearings used on the Mattel cars. Hot Wheels cars were born and soon earned the nickname "redlines."

Marketing was just as important to the success of the Hot Wheels line. A special bright colored blister pack was designed with flames and a metal collector button was included in each package. A four digit numbering system was developed to identify the individual models. The cars were sold in major retail stores for about $1.00 and sales were better than projected. The Mattel cars had a great visual appeal and were faster than any other brand on the market. Soon many new sets and accessories were produced to enhance the line. The sets included orange plastic track that was unique to the Hot Wheels brand and is still recognized today. Millions of Hot Wheels vehicles were produced during 1968. This was only the beginning of the very successful Hot Wheels product line.

# THE ORIGINAL HOT WHEELS DESIGNERS

It takes many people to move a Hot Wheels® model from an original idea through the design and production process to a finished product sold at a retail store. Several names are recognized by collectors because of their contributions to the unique design and development of the original Hot Wheels models. The idea for the line was born at Mattel in 1966, and many talented designers were hired to make the line a reality.

Harry Bradley was the original Hot Wheels designer. Originally a top designer for General Motors, Harry joined Mattel in 1967. He was with Mattel for a short time but designed many of the models in the original 1968 line.

Ira Gilford, also a designer from General Motors, joined Mattel in 1967. As part of the original staff, Ira designed some of the 1968 line, many of the 1969 line, and some of the models introduced in 1970. He designed the 1969 Spoilers™ line and also worked on models in the Grand Prix™ and Heavyweights™ series.

Rick Irons was responsible for the design of the original Hot Wheels blister pack and special metal collector buttons.

Howard Rees was the lead Hot Wheels designer in 1969. He convinced Larry Wood to work for Mattel's design team.

Larry Wood is by far the best-known Hot Wheels designer, earning the nickname "Mr. Hot Wheels." Larry was a interior aircraft designer at Lockheed before joining Mattel. His first design was the Tri Baby, but he has designed many vehicles over the years and continues to work for the company.

Darryl Starbird designed The Demon, and many of his other designs contributed to the Monograms plastic model kits.

Bob Rosas designed the Classic '32 Ford Vicky casting while working for an outside vendor that was contracted by Mattel. Bob worked on the 1969 and 1970 design molds. He officially joined Mattel in 1972 and worked as a design engineer until 1987.

Tom Daniel was a Monogram model designer but some of his ideas including the Red Baron, Paddy Wagon, and S' Cool Bus became part of the Hot Wheels line.

# 1968 – 1972 SPECTRAFLAME™ COLORS

Mattel wanted the new Hot Wheels models to be painted with special colors that would give the toy cars a look similar to the real hot rod "candy apple" paints which were the rage in the 1960s. Spectraflame™ paint colors were used on most of the Hot Wheels models produced between 1968-1972. These translucent paints were very bright and appealing and 12 colors including purple, lavender (pink), red, orange, gold, brown, olive, lime, green, aqua, light blue and blue were chosen for the first Hot Wheels models. While the original intent was to produce each model in every color, it was not planned to have color shades on the models. However there are many shades that exist today. There are various reasons why collectors today find a model coated with Spectraflame™ paint in many shades of the same color. Hot Wheels vehicles were produced and marketed for children in the late 60s and minor paint variations were not as important as standards set by the American Toy Manufacturers regarding the content of lead and arsenic in the paint. There was a range of acceptability for quality as these toy cars were spray painted and assembled at mass production factories in the United States and Hong Kong. During production an inexpensive metal casting is tumbled in a soft abrasive such as ground walnut shells to prepare the model for painting. The condition of the metal finish determined the color shade when these special paints were used, as there was no primer used in this process. The metal of the model reflects through the paint to produce the bright metallic color. The computer technology of today was not available to help with the production and often a model would be over-or under-sprayed. A model slightly over-sprayed with the candy-color paint would appear as a darker shade, and if under-sprayed, a lighter shade would be apparent. The electrostatic painting system produced a brilliant color, but often many shades of the same color. Each original Hot Wheels model was produced over at least a three-year period, and with millions of cars manufactured, it is easy to understand why so many color shades do exist. These models are now more than 30 years old, and time will have an effect on every color. It is likely that some form of toning, fading, or oxidation has occurred on the models over the past three decades.

Even if packaged, other factors such as light and humidity affect the paint and most of the toy cars have not been stored in a completely clean, dry, and light-free environment.

This leads to different opinions about colors. Is a shade of color a legitimate variation? Many collectors enjoy all of the various shades while others argue a shade is the same paint and not a collectible variation. It all comes down to personal preference. In addition to the original colors, magenta was also used. Due to factors mentioned above, several shades of the same color have become recognized as collectible color shades. These colors include rose red, yellow, pale brown, emerald green, plum, and ice blue. In addition mildly fluorescent versions of the lavender (hot pink) and lime (lime-yellow) were produced. Due to the effect of time some lavender models have become what is called salmon pink. This book recognizes twenty-two different Spectraflame™ color shades and all appear as unique colors.

- Metallic Aqua
- Metallic Blue
- Metallic Ice Blue
- Metallic Pale Blue
- Metallic Pale Brown
- Metallic Dark Brown
- Metallic Gold
- Metallic Green
- Metallic Emerald Green
- Metallic Lime Green
- Metallic Olive Green
- Metallic Orange
- Metallic Magenta
- Metallic Pink
- Metallic Hot Pink
- Metallic Salmon Pink
- Metallic Plum
- Metallic Purple
- Metallic Red
- Metallic Rose Red
- Metallic Yellow
- Metallic Lime Yellow

# 1968-1972 OTHER HOT WHEELS® COLORS

While Spectraflame™ colors were the primary paints used in the early Hot Wheels®, other enamel paints were used on some models. The enamel colors were based on many of the popular racing colors. The eight colors used included British Racing Green, Ford Racing Red, McLaren orange, gray, magenta, white, blue and yellow. These paints are much different than the Spectraflame™ colors and did not produce shades on the models. In addition chrome was used on three models but these finishes were only available in Club Kits.

# 1968

The first Hot Wheels car to come off the production line in 1968 was the Custom Camaro. Harry Bradley and Ira Gilford, both former Chevrolet design team members, are responsible for the design of the 1968 line of Hot Wheels vehicles. Many of the original 16 models in the 1968 line featured detailed engines, moveable parts, and simulated vinyl tops. There were 10 custom cars and 6 models based on actual and experimental show cars. The popular toy cars were first manufactured in the United States, but to keep up with consumer demand, models were also produced in Hong Kong before the end of the year. There are minor variations between the cars produced in the two different countries. The most recognizable difference is that U.S. versions have less detailed chassis than the models made in Hong Kong. The concept of Hot Wheels was an instant success, and soon, many television commercials helped promote the new line of cars. Sales were much better than originally projected, and Mattel began to produce track sets and Accessory Paks to supplement the cars. Several styles of carrying cases were also available, the most popular being the famous, wheel-shaped Rally Case.

## TRACK SETS
#6200 Strip Action Set
#6201 Stunt Action Set
#6202 Drag Race Action Set
#6223 Hot Curves Race Action Set

## POP-UP SETS
#5134 Service Station
#5135 Speed Shop
#5136 House and Car Port
#5141 Speedway Action Set

## FOLD-DOWN SETS
#5013 Service Station
#5014 Construction Company

## ACCESSORIES
#6224 Hot Strip Track Pak
#6225 Full Curve Pak
#6226 Daredevil Loop Pak
#6227 Half Curve Pak
#6475 Hot Strip Super Pak

## CASES
#5137 12 Car Rally Case
#5138 24 Car Case
#5139 12 Car Pop-Up Case

# 1968 MODELS QUICK REFERENCE

### #6205 Custom Cougar
'67 Mercury Cougar
Hood opens, available with or without black painted roof
U.S.A. – has dashboard with small steering wheel, small taillights, clear windows
Hong Kong – no dashboard with separate large black steering wheel, large taillights, blue-tinted windows

### #6206 Custom Mustang
'67 Ford Mustang
Hood opens
U.S.A. – raised dashboard with small steering wheel, front grille is ribbed and painted black, available with or without ribbed rear windows, clear windows
Hong Kong – flat dashboard with separate large black steering wheel, front grille is non-ribbed and unpainted, available with or without open hood scoop, blue-tinted windows

### #6207 Custom T-Bird
'67 Ford Thunderbird
Hood opens, available with or without black painted roof
U.S.A. – has dashboard with small steering wheel, black front grille, clear windows
Hong Kong – no dashboard with separate large black steering wheel, unpainted front grille, blue-tinted windows

### #6208 Custom Camaro
'67 Chevrolet Camaro
Hood opens, available with or without black painted roof

U.S.A. – raised dashboard with small steering wheel, clear windows

Hong Kong – flat dashboard with separate large black steering wheel, blue-tinted windows

**Note:** this model was also produced in white enamel and magenta enamel. Very few models exist in these colors.

### #6209 Silhouette

Custom Show Car

U.S.A. – small steering wheel, clear windows

Hong Kong – separate large black steering wheel, blue-tinted wheels

### #6210 Deora

Custom Dodge Surfing Truck

Model has removable plastic surfboards

U.S.A. – has dashboard, small steering wheel, small front bumper, clear windows

Hong Kong – no dashboard, separate large black steering wheel, large front bumper, blue-tinted windows

### #6211 Custom Barracuda

'67 Plymouth Barracuda

Hood opens

U.S.A. – raised dashboard with small steering wheel, small hood scoops, clear windows

Hong Kong – flat dashboard with separate large black steering wheel, large hood scoops, blue-tinted windows

### #6212 Custom Firebird

'68 Pontiac Firebird Convertible

Hood opens

U.S.A. – small steering wheel, side doors outlined, clear windows

Hong Kong – separate large black steering wheel, no door outline, blue-tinted windows

### #6213 Custom Fleetside

Custom Chevrolet El Camino Pickup

U.S.A. – raised dashboard with small steering wheel, black plastic cover not smooth, clear windows

Hong Kong – flat dashboard with separate black plastic steering wheel, smooth black plastic cover, blue-tinted windows

### #6214 Ford J-Car

Experimental Ford Grand Prix Race Car

Rear hood opens

U.S.A. – small steering wheel, vents on rear fenders, unpainted base, clear windows

Hong Kong – large black steering wheel, no vents, white enamel base, blue-tinted windows

**Note:** this model was also produced in blue enamel, magenta enamel, and white enamel

### #6215 Custom Corvette

'68 Chevrolet Corvette

Hood opens

U.S.A. – raised dashboard with small steering wheel, clear windows

Hong Kong – flat dashboard with separate large black steering wheel, blue-tinted windows

### #6216 Python

Custom Show Car

U.S.A. – has dashboard with small steering wheel, small front grill, clear windows

Hong Kong – no dashboard, separate large black steering wheel, large front grill, blue-tinted windows

**Note:** this model was originally called "Cheetah". Very few models exist with the name "Cheetah" on the base.

### #6217 Beatnik Bandit

Custom Show Car – designed by Ed "Big Daddy" Roth

U.S.A.- has steering rod, clear windows

Hong Kong – has steering wheel, blue-tinted windows

### #6218 Custom Eldorado

'67 Cadillac Eldorado Coupe de Ville

Hood opens

U.S.A. – raised dashboard with small steering wheel, clear windows

Hong Kong – flat dashboard with separate large black steering wheel, blue- tinted windows

### #6219 Hot Heap

Custom Street Rod Show Car – 2 door Ford Model T Roadster

U.S.A. – small steering wheel, clear windows

Hong Kong – large steering wheel, blue tinted windows

### #6220 Custom Volkswagen

'67 Volkswagen Beetle

Plastic sliding sunroof

U.S.A. – has dashboard with small steering wheel, clear windows

Hong Kong – no dashboard with separate large black steering wheel, blue-tinted windows, available with or without sunroof

**Note:** this model was also produced in green enamel, magenta enamel and red enamel.

#6205 Custom Cougar

#6206 Custom Mustang

#6206 Custom Mustang – open hood scoop

#6206 Custom Mustang – ribbed rear window

#6207 Custom T-Bird

#6208 Custom Camaro

#6209 Silhouette

#6210 Deora

 #6211 Custom Barracuda

#6212 Custom Firebird

 #6213 Custom Fleetside

#6214 Ford J-Car

 #6215 Custom Corvette

#6216 Python (original name: Cheetah)

#6219 Hot Heap

#6217 Beatnik Bandit

#6220 Custom Volkswagen

#6218 Custom Eldorado

#6220 Custom Volkswagen – no sunroof

15

# 1969

Sales of Hot Wheels increased and so did the number of new models added to the 1969 line. There were 24 new castings added, bringing the total to 40. Ira Gilford continued to design Hot Wheels for the 1969 line and was joined by Howard Rees. The most famous designer, Larry Wood, also joined the Hot Wheels design team. Decals that could be applied to the vehicles were included in the blister packs. Several new custom cars and 3 classic street rods were included. A new Grand Prix Series, featuring 8 new cars, was also introduced to the expanding line. The Volkswagen Beach Bomb was a popular model that was produced in two different castings; the rare version had plastic surfboards mounted through the back window. Very few of these models are in existence, as the more common model featured the surfboards mounted on the side of the vehicle. Collectors question if the rear-mounted version of this model is a pre-production prototype. Only about 15 of this variation are known to exist, and none are blister packed. It was important to Mattel that all of the early Hot Wheels models were compatible with the track and accessories. The original design of the Beach Bomb was changed to include the side pockets to ensure that the model would work with the Super Chargers and a heavier base changed the center of gravity on the model. Regardless whether or not the original rear-boarded Beach Bomb was a regular production model, it will always be a very rare and collectible item. Models continued to be produced in both the United States and Hong Kong. Many new sets, accessories and cases were marketed in 1969.

### TRACK SETS
#6279 Stunt Action Set
#6280 Double Dare Race Set
#6281 Hot Curves Race Action Set
#6290 Super-Charger Sprint Set
#6291 Super-Charger Speedway-Freeway Set
#6292 Super Charger Grand Prix Race Set

### ACCESSORIES
#6283 Jump Ram Pak
#6284 Trestle Pak
#6285 Competition Pak

### CASES
#5142 24 Car Super Rally Case
#5143 12 Car Adjustable Case
#5144 24 Car Adjustable Case
#5145 48 Car Adjustable Case

### OTHER HOT WHEELS ITEMS
#5146 Custom Shop Showcase Plaque
#5147 Car Carrier Showcase Plaque
#5158 Action City
#5159 Talking Service Center
#5439 Hot Wheels Wipe-Out Race Game

## 1969 MODELS
## QUICK REFERENCE

### #6250 Classic '32 Ford Vicky
'32 Ford Victoria
Available with smooth or rough roof
U.S.A. only

### #6251 Classic '31 Ford Woody
'31 Ford Woody
Aailable with smooth or rough roof
U.S.A. only

### #6252 Classic '57 T-Bird
'57 Ford Thunderbird Convertible
Hood opens
U.S.A. only
**Note:** this model was also produced in yellow enamel

### #6253 Classic '36 Ford Coupe
Custom '36 Ford
Rumble seat opens
U.S.A. only

### #6254 Lola GT70 (Grand Prix Series)
Grand Prix Racer
Rear hood opens
U.S.A. – small taillights, clear windows
Hong Kong – large taillights, blue-tinted windows
**Note:** this model was also produced in dark green
  enamel and red enamel

### #6255 McLaren M6A (Grand Prix Series)
Can-Am Racer
Rear hood opens

U.S.A. – large taillights, clear windows
Hong Kong – small taillights, blue-tinted windows
**Note:** this model was also produced in orange enamel and red enamel

### #6256 Chapparal 2G (Grand Prix Series)
Can-Am Racer
Rear hood opens
U.S.A. – clear windows
Hong Kong – blue-tinted windows
**Note:** this model was also produced in white enamel

### #6257 Ford MK IV (Grand Prix Series)
Grand Prix Racer
Rear hood opens
U.S.A. – clear windows
Hong Kong – blue-tinted windows

### #6258 Twinmill
Concept Car
U.S.A. only

### #6259 Turbofire
Concept Car
Rear hood opens
U.S.A. only

### #6260 Torero
Concept Car
Hood opens
U.S.A. only
**Note:** this model was also produced in green enamel

### #6261 Splittin' Image
Concept Car
U.S.A. only

### #6262 Lotus Turbine (Grand Prix Series)
Indy Style Racer
Plastic detachable fuel tanks were available for this model but are very rare
Hong Kong only
**Note:** model was also produced in chrome

### #6263 Indy Eagle (Grand Prix Series)
Indy Style Racer
Plastic detachable fuel tanks were available for this model but are very rare
Hong Kong only
**Note:** this model was also produced in gold-chrome.

### #6264 Brabham-Repco F1 (Grand Prix Series)
Formula 1 Racer
Plastic detachable fuel tanks were available for this model but are very rare
Hong Kong only

**Note:** this model was also produced in dark green enamel and chrome

### #6265 Shelby Turbine (Grand Prix Series)
Turbine Racer
Plastic detachable fuel tanks were available for this model but are very rare
Hong Kong only
**Note:** this model was also produced in chrome

### #6266 Custom Continental Mark III
'68 Lincoln
Hood opens
U.S.A. only

### #6267 Custom AMX
'68 American Motors Corporation AMX
hood opens
U.S.A. only

### #6268 Custom Charger
'68 Dodge Charger
Hood opens
U.S.A. only
**Note:** this model was also produced in orange enamel

### #6269 Custom Police Cruiser
Plymouth Grand Fury
**Note:** this model was produced in white only

### #6274 Volkswagen Beach Bomb
Custom Volkswagen Bus
Model has 2 removable side mounted plastic surfboards
Hong Kong only
**Note:** very rare casting has 2 removable rear mounted plastic surfboards

### #6275 Mercedes-Benz 280SL
2 Seat German Sports Car
Hood opens, available with or without black painted roof
Hong Kong only

### #6276 Rolls Royce Silver Shadow
Hood opens, available with or without black painted roof
Hong Kong only
**Note:** this model was also produced in gray enamel

### #6277 Maserati Mistral
Hood opens, available with or without a black painted roof
Hong Kong only

#6250 Classic '32 Ford Vicky

#6253 Classic '36 Ford Coupe

#6251 Classic '31 Ford Woody

#6254 Lola GT70

#6252 Classic '57 T-Bird

#6255 McLaren M6A

#6256 Chapparal 2G

#6259 Turbofire

#6257 Ford MK IV

#6260 Torero

#6258 Twinmill

#6261 Splittin' Image

#6262 Lotus Turbine

#6265 Shelby Turbine

#6263 Indy Eagle

#6266 Custom Continental Mark III

#6264 Brabham-Repco F1

#6267 Custom AMX

#6288 Custom Charger

#6275 Mercedes-Benz 280SL

#6269 Custom Police Cruiser

#6276 Rolls-Royce Silver Shadow

#6274 Volkswagen Beach Bomb

#6277 Maserati Mistral

#6274 Volkswagen Beach Bomb – rear mounted surf boards

# 1970

In 1970, production of Hot Wheels continued in both the U.S. and Hong Kong, and 33 new castings were added, along with several new series. The Grand Prix series expanded with the addition of 2 new models. Mattel added new excitement to the line with 6 Heavyweights™ and 6 Spoilers™. The Heavyweights were a line of futuristic trucks designed by Ira Gilford. The Spoilers were a group of cars with front and rear spoilers and exposed engines. A drag racing rivalry developed between Don "The Snake" Prudhomme and Tom "The Mongoose" McEwen. Mattel sponsored the two popular drivers and produced the first in a series of Snake and Mongoose vehicles. The Sky Show Fleetside was unique, as it was sold only in a special set with small plastic airplanes that would launch from a ramp attached to the vehicle. The Heavy Chevy, Boss Hoss, and King Kuda with special chrome paint finishes could be found only in Club Kits that were offered to collectors through the mail. The Club Kits also contained a collector's book, Hot Wheels decal, and membership certificate. The Jack "Rabbit" Special was the first Hot Wheels vehicle to be used in a promotion, and a special version of this model was issued for the Jack-in-the Box restaurant chain. In the late '60s Mattel purchased the Monogram Model Company, and some of the more popular plastic model designs were produced as Hot Wheels vehicles in 1970.

Mattel began to experiment with a larger scale of toy vehicles and in Italy produced a line of 1:43 scale die-cast cars called Gran Toros™. Sold under the Hot Wheels name, there were a total of 25 of these detailed cars manufactured through 1972.

**SETS**
#4355 Hot Wheels Factory
#4952 Action Set Gear Box
#6248 Hazzard Hill
#6429 Super-Charger Race Set
#6430 Super-Charger Rally' n Freeway Set
#6431 Sizzlin' Six Set
#6436 Sky Show Set
#6437 Drag Chute Stunt Set
#6438 Mongoose vs. Snake Drag Race Set
#6439 Rod Runner Speedway Set
#6440 Dual-Lane Rod Runner Race Set
#6641 Super-Charger Speed Test Set
#6442 Road Trials Set
#6443 Hi-Performance Set
#6446 Dual-Lane Rod Runner Drag Set
#6447 Indy Team Gift Set
#6599 Club Kit

**ACCESSORIES**
#6270 Lap Counter
#6278 Strip Action Set
#6284 Trestle 5-Pack
#6294 Super-Charger
#6295 2-Way Super-Charger
#6297 Racing Stickers Pak
#6473 Decal Pak
#6475 Hot Strip Track Super Pak
#6476 Dual-Lane Lap Counter
#6477 Dual-Lane Curve Pak
#6479 Rod Runner
#6480 Dual-Lane Rod Runner
#6481 Tune-Up Tower
#6482 Bridge Pak
#6483 Speedometer

**CASES**
#4975 12 Car Collector's Race Case
#4976 24 Car Collector's Race Case
#4977 48 Car Collector's Race Case
#4978 72 Car Collector's Race Case
#4979 Speed Shop

# 1970 MODELS

# QUICK REFERENCE

**#6400 Red Baron**
Based on Monogram plastic model
Hong Kong only
**Note:** this model was produced in metallic red only

**#6401 The Demon**
"Lil Coffin" Show Car
Hong Kong only

**#6402 Paddy Wagon**
Based on Monogram plastic model

U.S.A. only
**Note:** this model produced in dark blue only

### #6403 Sand Crab
Based on Monogram plastic model
U.S.A. only

### #6404 Classic Nomad
'55 Chevrolet Nomad Wagon
Hood opens
U.S.A. only

### #6405 Nitty Gritty Kitty (The Spoilers)
Mercury Cougar
Available with # 1 through #9 stickers on doors
Hong Kong only

### #6407 TNT-Bird (The Spoilers)
Ford Thunderbird
Available with #1 through #9 stickers on doors
Hong Kong only

### #6408 Heavy Chevy (The Spoilers)
Chevrolet Camaro
Available with #1 through #9 stickers on doors
Hong Kong only
**Note:** #6189 chrome model available in Club Kit only

### #6409 Snake
Plymouth Barracuda Funny Car (Don Prudhomme)
Pop-up body
U.S.A. – clear windows
Hong Kong – blue-tinted windows
**Note:** this model was produced in yellow enamel only

### #6410 Mongoose
Plymouth Duster Funny Car (Tom McEwen)
Pop-up body
USA and Hong Kong
**Note:** this model was produced in red enamel only

### #6411 King Kuda (The Spoilers)
Plymouth Barracuda
Available with #1 through #9 stickers on doors
Hong Kong only
**Note:** #6190 chrome model available in Club Kit only

### #6412 Light My Firebird (The Spoilers)
Pontiac Firebird Convertible
Available with #1 through #9 stickers on the doors
Hong Kong only

### #6413 Seasider
Chevrolet Fleetside Pick-Up
Includes removable plastic boat
U.S.A. only

### #6414 Mighty Maverick
Ford Maverick
Hood opens
U.S.A. – think stripe on roof, black headlights
Hong Kong – thin stripe on roof, unpainted headlights

### #6416 Porsche 917 (Grand Prix Series)
Rear hood opens
U.S.A. – clear windows, small headlights
Hong Kong – blue-tinted windows, large headlights
**Note:** this model was also produced in gray enamel

### #6417 Ferrari 312P (Grand Prix Series)
'69 Ferrari
Rear hood opens
U.S.A. – clear windshield
Hong Kong – blue-tinted windshield
**Note:** this model was also produced in red enamel

### #6419 Peepin' Bomb
Concept Car
Available with silver or orange headlights
U.S.A. and Hong Kong

### #6420 Carabo
Show Car
Opening doors
U.S.A. – clear windows
Hong Kong – blue-tinted windows

### #6421 Jack "Rabbit" Special
Concept Car
U.S.A. only
**Note:** this model was produced in white enamel only

### #6422 Swingin' Wing
Concept Car
U.S.A. – clear windows
Hong Kong – blue-tinted windows

### #6423 Mantis
Concept Car
Windows open
U.S.A. and Hong Kong

### #6424 Tri Baby
Concept Car
Rear hood opens
U.S.A. – clear windows
Hong Kong – blue-tinted windows

### #6436 Sky Show Fleetside
Chevrolet Pick-Up Truck
U.S.A. only
**Note:** this model was only available in the #6436 Sky Show Set and included a plastic launcher and 3 plastic planes

#### #6436 Sky Show Deora
Custom Dodge Truck
U.S.A. only
**Note:** this model was only available in the #6493 Flyin' Circus Set and included a plastic launcher and plastic helicopter

#### #6450 Tow Truck (The Heavyweights)
Concept Model
Hong Kong only

#### #6451 Ambulance (The Heavyweights)
Concept Model
Hong Kong only
**Note:** this model was also produced in white enamel

#### #6452 Cement Mixer (The Heavyweights)
Concept Model
Hong Kong only
**Note:** this model was also produced in white enamel

#### #6453 Dump Tuck (The Heavyweights)
Concept Model
Hong Kong only
**Note:** this model was also produced in white enamel

#### #6454 Fire Engine (The Heavyweights)
Concept Model
Hong Kong only
**Note:** this model was produced in metallic red and red enamel only

#### #6455 Moving Van (The Heavyweights)
Concept Model
Hong Kong only
**Note:** the cab of this model was also produced in red enamel and white enamel.

#### #6456 Mod Quad
Concept Model
Canopy opens
U.S.A. – clear windows
Hong Kong – blue-tinted windows

#### #6457 Whip Creamer
Concept Car
U.S.A. – clear windows
Hong Kong – blue-tinted windows

#### #6459 Power Pad
Custom Pick-Up Truck
U.S.A. only

#### #6469 Fire Chief Cruiser
Plymouth Grand Fury
U.S.A. only
**Note:** model was produced in metallic red or dark red only

#### #6499 Boss Hoss (The Spoilers)
Available with #1 through #9 stickers on doors
Hong Kong only
**Note:** this chrome model was available in Club Kit only

#6400 Red Baron

#6403 Sand Crab

#6401 The Demon

#6404 Classic Nomad

#6402 Paddy Wagon

#6405 Nitty Gritty Kitty

#6407 TNT-Bird

#6409 Snake

#5408 Heavy Chevy

#6410 Mongoose

#6189 Heavy Chevy – chrome (Club Kit)

#6411 King Kuda

#6190 King Kuda – chrome (Club Kit)

#6414 Mighty Maverick

#6412 Light My Firebired

#6413 Seasider

#6416 Porsche 917

#6417 Ferrari 312P

#6419 Peepin' Bomb

#6422 Swingin' Wing

#6420 Carabo

#6423 Mantis

#6421 Jack "Rabbit" Special

#6424 Tri Baby

#6436 Sky Show Fleetside

#6436 Sky Show Deora

#6450 Tow Truck

#6451 Ambulance

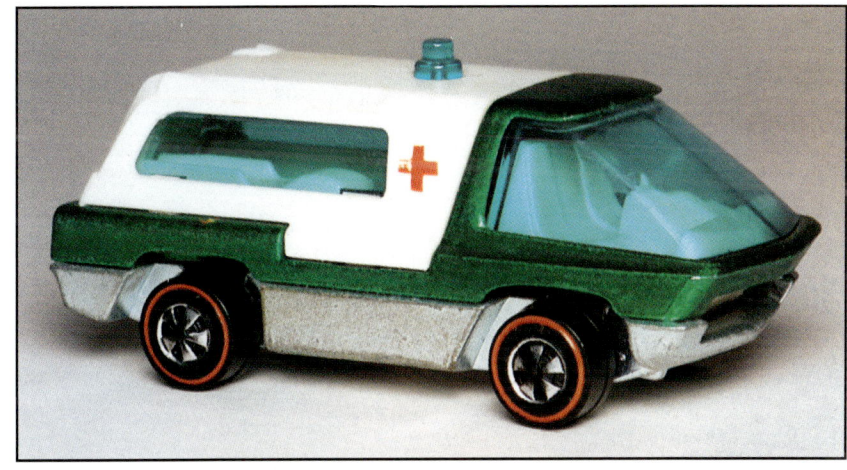

#6452 Cement Mixer

#6453 Dump Truck

#6454 Fire Engine

#6455 Moving Van

**Above:** #6456 Mod Quad

**Center right (1st):** #6457 Whip Creamer

**Above:** #6459 Power Pad

**Center right (2nd):** #6469 Fire Chief Cruiser

#6499 Boss Hoss – chrome (Club Kit)

# 1971

In 1971, 35 new Hot Wheels castings were introduced. More vehicles were added to the Heavyweights and Spoilers series. The Snake and Mongoose lines were also expanded with two front-engine dragsters and two funny cars. The dragsters were only available in unique two-packs or in the Wild Wheelie Set. This was the last year collector's buttons were sold with the cars; however some plastic buttons were made before this practice was discontinued. This was also the last year that Hot Wheels were manufactured in the United States. A Hot Wheels television cartoon show aired late in 1971. Mattel purchased the Monogram model company. Several model designs by Tom Daniel were used in the Hot Wheels line.

**TRACK AND OTHER SETS**
   #5953 Mongoose and Snake Dragster Pak (2 Pack)
   #6037 Mongoose and Snake Wild Wheelie Set
   #6107 Ontario Trio
   #6427 Show Team (4 Pack)
   #6428 Go Team (4 Pack)
   #6429 Ontario Team (4 Pack)
   #6490 Great Getaway Set
   #6493 Flyin' Circus Set

**ACCESSORIES**
   #6013 Victory Pak
   #6015 Danger Changer
   #6034 Big Belter and Matchmaker
   #6115 Crossover Pak
   #6492 Joiner Pak
   #6494 Racing Posters

## 1971 MODELS
## QUICK REFERENCE

**#5178 Bugeye**
   Concept Car
   Rear hood opens, available with or without air scoops
   U.S.A. – clear windows
   Hong Kong – tinted windows

**#5951 Snake Dragster**
   Front-Engine Dragster (Don Prudhomme)
   U.S.A. only
   **Note:** this model was produced only in white enamel and was sold in a 2-pack with #5952 Mongoose Dragster

**#5952 Mongoose Dragster**
   Front-Engine Dragster (Tom McEwen)
   U.S.A. only
   **Note:** this model was produced only in metallic blue and was sold in a 2-pack with #5951 Snake Dragster

**#5953 Snake 2**
   Funny Car (Don Prudhomme)
   Pop-up body
   U.S.A. – clear windows
   Hong Kong – blue-tinted windows
   **Note:** this model was produced in white enamel only

**#5954 Mongoose 2**
   Funny Car (Tom McEwen)
   Pop-up body
   U.S.A. – clear windows
   Hong Kong – blue-tinted windows
   **Note:** this model was produced in metallic blue only

**#6000 Noodle Head**
   Concept Car
   Hood opens
   U.S.A. – clear windows
   Hong Kong – blue tinted windows

**#6001 What-4**
   Concept Car
   Moveable plastic wing
   Hong Kong only

**#6003 Six Shooter**
   Concept Car
   Hong Kong only

**#6006 Special Delivery**
   Concept Model
   Hong Kong only

**#6018 Fuel Tanker (The Heavyweights)**
   Concept Model
   Two plastic pull-out hoses
   Hong Kong only
   **Note:** this model was produced in white enamel only

**#6019 Team Trailer (The Heavyweights)**
   Concept Model
   Hong Kong only
   **Note:** the cab on this model was also available in white enamel

**#6020 Snorkel (The Heavyweights)**
   Concept Model
   Hong Kong only
   Plastic boom extends
   **Note:** this model was also available in white enamel

**#6175 The Hood**
   Concept Model
   Available with or without a black painted roof
   U.S.A. – clear windows
   Hong Kong – blue-tinted windows

**#6176 Short Order**
   Concept Model
   Hong Kong only

**#6177 T-4-2**
   Concept Model
   Hong Kong only

**#6179 Jet Threat**
   Concept Car
   Hong Kong only
   **Note:** this model was also produced in red enamel

**#6183 Pit Crew Car**
   Concept Car
   Trunk opens
   Hong Kong only
   **Note:** this model was available in white enamel only

**#6184 Ice "T"**
   Monogram model design by Tom Daniels
   Hong Kong only
   **Note:** this model was produced only in yellow

**#6185 Mutt Mobile**
   Concept Car
   Hong Kong only

**#6186 Rocket-Bye-Baby**
   Concept Car
   Plastic pull-out tailpipes, opening side slats
   Hong Kong only

**#6187 Bye-Focal**
   Concept Car
   Hong Kong only

**#6188 Strip Teaser**
   Concept Car
   Hong Kong only

**#6192 Waste Wagon (The Heavyweights)**
   Concept Model
   Moveable plastic dump
   Hong Kong only

**#6193 Scooper (The Heavyweights)**
   Concept Model
   Moveable plastic dump
   Hong Kong only

**#6194 Racer Rig (The Heavyweights)**
   Concept Model
   Box on trailer opens
   Hong Kong only
   **Note:** the cab on this model was produced in enamel white and metallic red only

**#6407 Boss Hoss (The Spoilers)**
   Ford Mustang Boss 302
   Available with black roof or stripe labels on roof, available with #1 through #9 stickers on doors
   Hong Kong only
   **Note:** the chrome version of this model was available in Club Kits in 1970

**#6418 Sugar Caddy (The Spoilers)**
   '67 Cadillac Eldorado
   Hood opens, available with #1 through #9 labels on doors
   Hong Kong only

**#6458 Hairy Hauler**
   Concept Car
   Canopy opens
   U.S.A. only

**#6460 AMX/2**
   American Motors Show Car
   Plastic engine covers open
   U.S.A. only

**#6461 Grass Hopper**
   Concept Car
   U.S.A. only

**#6466 Cockney Cab**
English Taxi Cab
U.S.A. – clear windows
Hong Kong – tinted windows

**#6467 Olds 442**
'68 Oldsmobile 442
Hood opens
U.S.A. only

**#6468 S'Cool Bus (The Heavyweights)**
Monogram model design by Tom Daniel
Pop-up body
Hong Kong only
**Note:** this model was produced in yellow enamel only

**#6471 Evil Weevil (The Spoilers)**
Volkswagen Concept Car
Available with #1 through #9 stickers on doors
Hong Kong only

**#6472 Classic Cord**
1937 Cord
Hood opens
Hong Kong only

 #5178 Bugeye

#5951 Snake Dragster

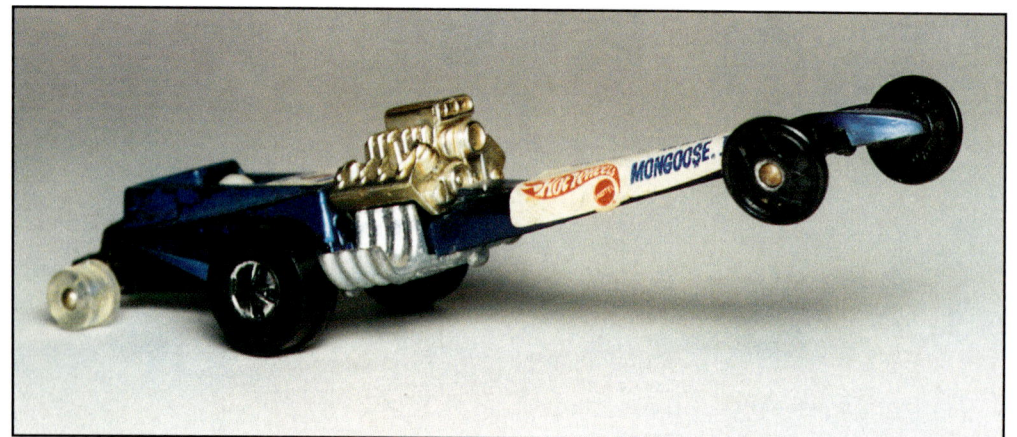 #5952 Mongoose Dragster

#5953 Snake 2

#5954 Mongoose 2

#6003 Six Shooter

#6000 Noodle Head

#6006 Special Delivery

#6001 What-4

#6018 Fuel Tanker

#6019 Team Trailer

#6020 Snorkel

#6175 The Hood

#6176 Short Order

#6177 T-4-2

#6184 Ice "T"

#6179 Jet Threat

#6185 Mutt Mobile

#6186 Rocket-Bye-Baby

#6183 Pit Crew Car

#6187 Bye-Focal

#6188 Strip Teaser

#6192 Waste Wagon

**Top right:** #6193 Scooper

**Center right:** #6194 Racer Rig

**Bottom right:** #6407 Boss Hoss

#6418 Sugar Caddy

#6461 Grass Hopper

#6458 Hairy Hauler

#6466 Cockney Cab

#6467 Olds 442

#6460 AMX/2

#6468 S'Cool Bus

#6471 Evil Weevil

#6472 Classic Cord

# 1972

The first major change to the Hot Wheels line took place in 1972. A new blister pack was designed and the collector buttons were no longer offered with the models. The vehicles were packaged with an attachment that allowed them to be used with an accessory called Drivin' Gear. This accessory could be purchased separately but was not very popular with consumers and the idea was quickly discontinued. The models produced in 1972 were only available for one year.

## 1972 MODELS
## QUICK REFERENCE

**#5699 Rear Engine Mongoose**
Rear-Engine Dragster (Tom McEwen)
Rear engine cover opens
Hong Kong only
**Note:** this model was produced in blue only

**#5856 Rear Engine Snake**
Rear-Engine Dragster (Don Prudhomme)
Rear engine cover opens
Hong Kong only
**Note:** this model was produced in yellow only

**#5881 Open Fire**
American Motors Corporation Gremlin with six wheels
Hong Kong only

**#6005 Funny Money**
Armored Truck
Pop-up body
Hong Kong only
**Note:** this model was produced in gray only

**#6021 Ferrari 512S**
Pininfarina Ferrari 512
Lift-up canopy
Hong Kong only

**#6022 Side Kick**
Slide-out interior
Hong Kong only

**#6169 Mercedes-Benz C-111**
Doors open
Hong Kong only

#5699 Rear Engine Mongoose

#5856 Rear Engine Snake

#5881 Open Fire

#6005 Funny Money

#6021 Ferrari 512S

#6022 Side Kick

#6169 Mercedes-Benz C-111

# MISCELLANEOUS

#6205 Custom Cougar – metallic ice blue

#6208 Custom Camaro – metallic lime yellow

#6208 Custom Camaro – metallic green

#6208 Custom Camaro – metallic red

#6209 Silhouette – metallic purple

#6213 Custom Fleetside – metallic purple

#6214 Ford J-Car – enamel white

#6214 Ford J-Car – metallic dark brown

#6215 Custom Corvette – metallic gold

#6216 Python – metallic blue

#6217 Beatnik Bandit – metallic pale blue

#6218 Custom Eldorado – metallic lime green

#6219 Hot Heap – metallic aqua

#6252 Classic '57 T-Bird – metallic olive green

#6253 Classic '36 Ford Coupe – metallic gold

#6255 McLaren M6A – enamel orange

#6256 Chapparal 2G – metallic blue

#6262 Lotus Turbine – metallic red

#6258 Twinmill – metallic emerald green

#6275 Mercedes-Benz 280SL – metallic green

#6260 Torero – metallic rose red

#6403 Sand Crab – metallic yellow

#6403 Sand Crab – metallic lime green

#6416 Porsche 917 – metallic yellow

#6403 Sand Crab – metallic magenta

#6416 Porsche 917 – metallic hot pink

#6416 Porsche 917 – gray enamel

#6416 Porsche 917 – metallic salmon pink

#6416 Porsche 917 – metallic lime yellow

#6417 Ferrari 312P – enamel red

#6416 Porsche 917 – metallic magenta

#6417 Ferrari 312P – metallic blue

#6416 Porsche 917 – metallic blue

#6417 Ferrari 312P – metallic hot pink

#6423 Mantis – metallic red

#6003 Six Shooter – metallic aqua

#6424 Tri Baby – metallic yellow

#6003 Six Shooter – metallic blue

#6459 Power Pad – metallic hot pink

#6003 Six Shooter – metallic pale blue

#6000 Noodle Head – metallic pale blue

#6021 Ferrari 512S – metallic blue

#6021 Ferrari 512S – metallic lime green

McLaren M6A – enamel orange – Grand Prix Series blister pack

Mercedes-Benz 280SL – metallic olive – in blister pack with metal collector button

Noodle Head – metallic pale blue – in blister pack with plastic collector button

**Opposite page:**
**Top left:** Rear Engine Snake / Rear Engine Mongoose – example of 1972 style blister pack

**Center left:** #6210 Deora – metallic gold, metallic purple  #6274 Volkswagen Beach Bomb – metallic red, metallic purple

**Bottom left:** #6211 Custom Barracuda – metallic blue, metallic aqua, metallic green, metallic pale brown, metallic yellow

**Top right:** #6220 Custom Volkswagen – metallic yellow, metallic pink, metallic hot pink, metallic orange, metallic gold, metallic blue, metallic green

**Center right:** #6212 Custom Firebird – metallic blue with light. brown interior, metallic red with red interior, metallic pale brown with dark brown interior, metallic olive green with pale brown interior, metallic olive green with white interior

**Bottom right:** #6250 Classic '32 Ford Vicky – metallic blue, metallic red, metallic gold, metallic yellow

#6436 Sky Show Fleetside – metallic hot pink with 3 plastic airplanes / plastic helicopter from Flying Circus Set

#6219 Hot Heap – metallic olive green U.S.A. / metallic aqua Hong Kong

1969 #6283 Jump Ramp Accessory Pak

1968 #5136 Pop Up House and Car Port

1968 #6227 Half Curve Accessory Pak

54

**Top left:** 1970 #6294 Super Charger

**Center left:** 1970 #6295 2-Way Super Charger

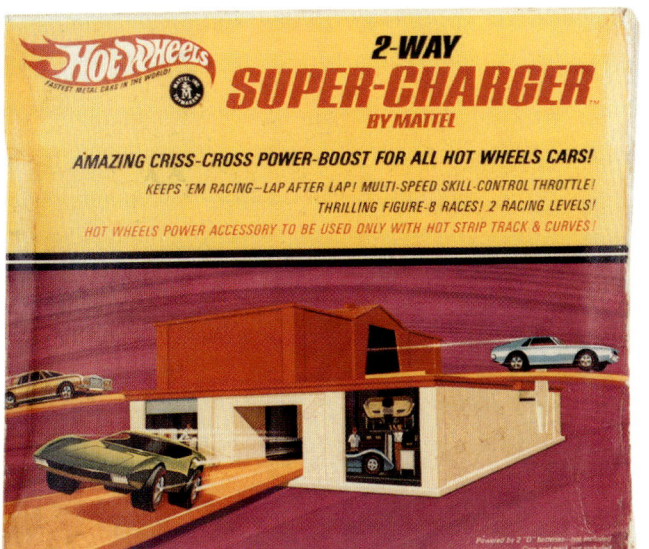

Hot Wheels Club Kit with chrome King Kuda, Mustang Boss Hoss and Heavy Chevy.

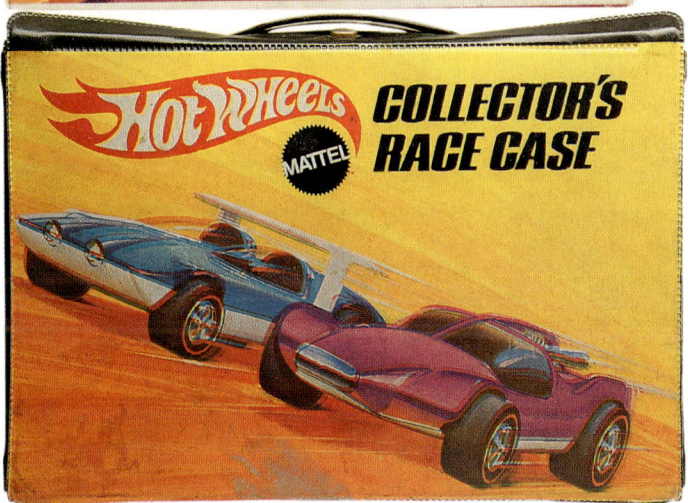

**Above:** 1970 #4975 12 Car Collector's Race Case
**Below:** 1970 #4977 48 Car Collector's Race Case

Custom Camaro (test model) lime green over chrome body

Custom Mustang (test model) gold over chrome body

Custom Cougar (test model) blue over chrome body

Custom Barracuda (test model) aqua over chrome body

Silhouette (test model) purple over chrome body

Custom T-Bird (test model) gold over chrome body

# GRAN TOROS™, HOT WHEELS® SUPER RACERS

By Carmelo J. Aresco, Courtesy of GranToros.com

**The History**

Mario Besana founded the Mebetoys Toy Company in Milan, Italy in 1966. This company issued about forty 1:43 scale model cars before it was sold to Mattel in 1969. Mebetoys became the Italian representative of Mattel as Mattel SpA. Soon after Mattel purchased Mebetoys, they launched the Gran Toros line. Many Gran Toros™ models were remakes of Mebetoys models and had metallic paints and plastic wheels, but many other models were originals. These included the Boss 302 Mustang, Chaparral 2J, and the T'rantula and Torpedo dragsters. The entire line consists of only twenty-five models, but most of the models have been found in more than one color. They were first issued in 1970 and were sold as "Gran Toros" in the U.S.A., Series "Sputafuoco" in Italy, and Series "Heisse Räder Supergross" in Germany. In 1973 the line was discontinued, but the company continued to put the Gran Toros name on the new 1:43 Mebetoys models. Mattel maintained the old Mebetoys name until 1980/81. By 1984, the Italian Mattel die cast model production was over and the Mebetoys factory was closed.

**Identifying a Gran Toros**

So many Mebetoys cars were labeled as Gran Toros that defining a Gran Toros is subject to interpretation. Many people argue about which models are the "true" Gran Toros and there is not a simple, "black and white" answer. Many think that a "true" Gran Toros model must have the "Hot Wheels" logo on the base, however this is not true. To identify a "true" Gran Toros we must first look at the design philosophy of the Hot Wheels. What made Hot Wheels different from the other 1:64 scale die cast cars of its day can help define the Gran Toros line. When Mattel Hot Wheels cars first appeared, the most popular 1:64 die cast cars were Matchbox by Lesney. In comparison, Hot Wheels were radical. Their wheels were very large compared to their bodies. They were mounted on piano wire and were extremely fast. Despite criticism from "scale purists," Hot Wheels were very popular. Mattel decided to apply the Hot Wheels philosophy to 1:43 scale Gran Toros cars made for the American market. Mattel had Mebetoys convert some of their models to Gran Toros and here we can see the criteria for a Gran Toros. The upper left corner of a U.S.A. Gran Toros package lists the Gran Toros features:

Precision moving parts!
Authentic detailing! "Mag" wheels!
Exclusive Spring-Bar™ suspension!
Low-friction wheel bearings!

Mattel had Mebetoys make new models and also convert existing models into Gran Toros. To clearly illustrate the Gran Toros differences we can look at a converted model, the Chaparral (2F). Both Mebetoys and Gran Toros Chaparral models were made simultaneously. Mebetoys had solid metal axles and "true to scale" rubber tires. They were numbered alpha-numerically in an A-XX format (i.e., A-23). The converted Gran Toros had big plastic racing tires and chrome hubs that were mounted on piano wire. They were numbered in a 4-digit numeric series starting with 6601 and ending with 6629. A Mebetoys Chaparral 2F is numbered "A-23" while the Gran Toros version is numbered "6606."

In conclusion, all "true" Gran Toros follow the Hot Wheels philosophy of the time: oversized wheels with Spring Bar™ suspensions, which made them very fast. There are only 25 models which follow this principle. These are the "true" Gran Toros. Just like their 1/64 scale Hot Wheel cousins, these cars were considerably faster than their conventional counterparts.

**Gran Toros Packaging**

Gran Toros first came in cardboard window boxes, then plexi and cardboard boxes, and finally plexi/plastic boxes. All the Gran Toros destined for the USA market were packaged in a "bubble / blister" box, except for the T'rantula dragster which was only found in the "Speed Strip" set.

**Gran Toros Myths**

Much of the history of Gran Toros may never be verified. While myths abound, we do know some facts about the Gran Toros: Every Gran Toros was made in Italy. Gran Toros were never made in the United States or Germany, although the USA and Germany were major target markets as evidenced by the packaging. Not all Gran Toros have the Hot Wheels logo. There were 25 Gran Toros models as listed in this book even though Mebetoys continued to use the Gran Toros name after the Hot Wheels Gran Toros were discontinued.

#6601 Ferrari Can Am

#6604 Torpedo

#6602 Astro II Chevy

#6605 Lamborghini Miura

#6603 T'rantula

#6606 Chaparral 2F

#6607 Ford MK II

#6612 Alpha Romeo 33/3

#6608 Abarth 695 SS

#6613 Porsche Carrera

#6611 Mustang Boss Hoss

#6614 Ferrari P4

#6615 Twinmill

#6618 Lotus Europa

#6616 Silhouette

#6621 Ferrari 512S

#6617 Toyota 2000 GT

#6622 Mercedes C-111

#6623 Porsche 917

#6626 McLaren M8D Can Am

#6624 Abarth 3000

#6627 De Tomasso Pantera

#6625 Mantis

#6628 Chaparral 2J Can Am

#6629 Lola T212 Can Am

# HOT WHEELS 1968-1972 VARIATION / PRICE GUIDE

This variation guide has been developed to assist collectors. The price listed with each model should be used as a guide only. The prices reflect the approximate value for a model in near mint condition but not packaged. Many factors effect prices, including condition and variations of a particular model. With the popularity of computers and online auctions and trading, prices for the highly collectible Hot Wheels models can and will change frequently. The prices shown will help a collector verify a fair price for a model.

Here are some helpful hints for using this guide:
- All of the models are listed in numerical order and are separated by the year when the model was first available.
- The colors of each model are then listed in alphabetical order for ease of use when locating a particular variation.
- First, select the year and name of the vehicle, then use the color column to find the appropriate model. Variations including country, windows, interior, and exterior for that color can be found.

## ABBREVIATION LIST

### COUNTRY

| | |
|---|---|
| United States | USA |
| Hong Kong | HK |

### COLORS

| | |
|---|---|
| Metallic Aqua | M-AQ |
| Metallic Blue | M-BL |
| Metallic Ice Blue | M-BL-I |
| Metallic Pale Blue | M-BL-P |
| Metallic Pale Brown | M-BR-P |
| Metallic Dark Brown | M-BR-D |
| Metallic Gold | M-GD |
| Metallic Green | M-GR |
| Metallic Emerald Green | M-GR-E |
| Metallic Lime Green | M-GR-L |
| Metallic Olive Green | M-GR-O |
| Metallic Magenta | M-MG |
| Metallic Orange | M-OR |
| Metallic Pink | M-PK |
| Metallic Hot Pink | M-PK-H |
| Metallic Salmon Pink | M-PK-S |
| Metallic Plum | M-PL |
| Metallic Purple | M-PR |
| Metallic Red | M-RD |
| Metallic Rose Red | M-RD-RS |
| Metallic Yellow | M-YW |
| Metallic Lime Yellow | M-YW-L |
| | |
| Enamel Blue | E-BL |
| Enamel Gray | E-GY |
| Enamel Dark Green | E-GR-D |
| Enamel Magenta | E-MG |
| Enamel Orange | E-OR |
| Enamel Red | E-RD |
| Enamel White | E-WH |
| Enamel Yellow | E-YW |

### Other Colors Used in Guide

| | |
|---|---|
| Aqua | AQ |
| Black | BK |
| Blue | BL |
| Dark Blue | BL-D |
| Brown | BR |
| Light Brown | BR-L |
| Pale Brown | BR-P |
| Dark Brown | BR-D |
| Chrome | CH |
| Gold | GD |
| Gray | GY |
| Green | GR |
| Magenta | MG |
| Orange | OR |
| Hot Pink | PK-H |
| Salmon Pink | PK-S |
| Plum | PL |
| Purple | PR |
| Red | RD |
| Silver | SL |
| Transparent | Trn |
| White | WH |
| Yellow | YW |

## WINDOWS

| | |
|---|---|
| Blue | BL |
| Blue, clear on trailer | BL/CLT |
| Clear | CL |
| Clear hood | CL-HD |
| Grey Tinted | GY-TNT |
| Tinted | TNT |
| Tinted hood | TNT-HD |
| Tinted roof | TNT-RF |

## INTERIOR

See Color abbreviations above

## PAINT

| | |
|---|---|
| White Trim | WH-TR |
| Blue Stripes | BL-STR |
| Blue & Red Stripes | BL&RD STR |
| Blue/Yellow | BL/YW |
| Blue/Orange | BL/OR |
| Black Stripes | BK-STR |
| Black Roof | BK-RF |
| Black Engine Cover | BK-EC |

# BIBLIOGRAPHY

CB'S Diecast Museum, "Spotlight on Bob Rosas", 2001
http://www.cbsmuseum/Cols/spotlight/
Mace, Scott "The First Hot Wheels", *The Toy Car,* San Jose, California, Vol. 5, No. 1: 3-5, 1978
Mattel, Inc., *Hot Wheels 1968 International Collector's Catalog,* Hawthorne, California, 1967.
Mattel, Inc., *Hot Wheels 1969 International Collector's Catalog,* Hawthorne, California, 1968
Mattel, Inc., *Hot Wheels 1970 International Collector's Catalog,* Hawthorne, California, 1970
Mattel, Inc., *Hot Wheels 1981 Collector's Book, Hawthorne,* California, 1981
Mattel, Inc., *Hot Wheels 1982 Collector's Book, Hawthorne,* California, 1982
Mattel, Inc., *Hot Wheels 1989 Collector's Book, Hawthorne,* California, 1988
Strauss. Mike, *Hot Wheels Newsletter,* volumes 1 through 15, San Carlos, California, November
    1986 through May 2001

## 1968 Variations

| Name | Number | Casting | Country | Color | Windows | Interior | Paint | Other | Value |
|---|---|---|---|---|---|---|---|---|---|
| Custom Cougar | 6205 | | USA | M-AQ | CL | WH | BK-RF | | $130.00 |
| Custom Cougar | 6205 | | USA | M-AQ | CL | WH | | | $115.00 |
| Custom Cougar | 6205 | | HK | M-AQ | BL | WH | BK-RF | | $130.00 |
| Custom Cougar | 6205 | | HK | M-AQ | BL | WH | | | $115.00 |
| Custom Cougar | 6205 | | USA | M-AQ | CL | BK | BK-RF | | $120.00 |
| Custom Cougar | 6205 | | USA | M-AQ | CL | BK | | | $105.00 |
| Custom Cougar | 6205 | | HK | M-AQ | BL | BK | BK-RF | | $120.00 |
| Custom Cougar | 6205 | | HK | M-AQ | BL | BK | | | $105.00 |
| Custom Cougar | 6205 | | USA | M-AQ | CL | GY | BK-RF | | $120.00 |
| Custom Cougar | 6205 | | USA | M-AQ | CL | GY | | | $105.00 |
| Custom Cougar | 6205 | | HK | M-AQ | BL | GY | BK-RF | | $120.00 |
| Custom Cougar | 6205 | | HK | M-AQ | BL | GY | | | $105.00 |
| Custom Cougar | 6205 | | USA | M-AQ | CL | BR-L | BK-RF | | $120.00 |
| Custom Cougar | 6205 | | USA | M-AQ | CL | BR-L | | | $105.00 |
| Custom Cougar | 6205 | | HK | M-AQ | BL | BR-L | BK-RF | | $120.00 |
| Custom Cougar | 6205 | | HK | M-AQ | BL | BR-L | | | $105.00 |
| Custom Cougar | 6205 | | USA | M-AQ | CL | BR-D | BK-RF | | $120.00 |
| Custom Cougar | 6205 | | USA | M-AQ | CL | BR-D | | | $105.00 |
| Custom Cougar | 6205 | | HK | M-AQ | BL | BR-D | BK-RF | | $120.00 |
| Custom Cougar | 6205 | | HK | M-AQ | BL | BR-D | | | $105.00 |
| Custom Cougar | 6205 | | USA | M-BL | CL | WH | BK-RF | | $130.00 |
| Custom Cougar | 6205 | | USA | M-BL | CL | WH | | | $115.00 |
| Custom Cougar | 6205 | | HK | M-BL | BL | WH | BK-RF | | $130.00 |
| Custom Cougar | 6205 | | HK | M-BL | BL | WH | | | $115.00 |
| Custom Cougar | 6205 | | USA | M-BL | CL | BK | BK-RF | | $120.00 |
| Custom Cougar | 6205 | | USA | M-BL | CL | BK | | | $105.00 |
| Custom Cougar | 6205 | | HK | M-BL | BL | BK | BK-RF | | $120.00 |
| Custom Cougar | 6205 | | HK | M-BL | BL | BK | | | $105.00 |
| Custom Cougar | 6205 | | USA | M-BL | CL | GY | BK-RF | | $120.00 |
| Custom Cougar | 6205 | | USA | M-BL | CL | GY | | | $105.00 |
| Custom Cougar | 6205 | | HK | M-BL | BL | GY | BK-RF | | $120.00 |
| Custom Cougar | 6205 | | HK | M-BL | BL | GY | | | $105.00 |
| Custom Cougar | 6205 | | USA | M-BL | CL | BL | BK-RF | | $150.00 |
| Custom Cougar | 6205 | | USA | M-BL | CL | BL | | | $135.00 |
| Custom Cougar | 6205 | | HK | M-BL | BL | BL | BK-RF | | $150.00 |
| Custom Cougar | 6205 | | HK | M-BL | BL | BL | | | $135.00 |
| Custom Cougar | 6205 | | USA | M-BL | CL | BR-L | BK-RF | | $120.00 |
| Custom Cougar | 6205 | | USA | M-BL | CL | BR-L | | | $105.00 |
| Custom Cougar | 6205 | | HK | M-BL | BL | BR-L | BK-RF | | $120.00 |
| Custom Cougar | 6205 | | HK | M-BL | BL | BR-L | | | $105.00 |
| Custom Cougar | 6205 | | USA | M-BL | CL | BR-D | BK-RF | | $120.00 |
| Custom Cougar | 6205 | | USA | M-BL | CL | BR-D | | | $105.00 |
| Custom Cougar | 6205 | | HK | M-BL | BL | BR-D | BK-RF | | $120.00 |
| Custom Cougar | 6205 | | HK | M-BL | BL | BR-D | | | $105.00 |
| Custom Cougar | 6205 | | USA | M-BL-I | CL | WH | BK-RF | | $185.00 |
| Custom Cougar | 6205 | | USA | M-BL-I | CL | WH | | | $170.00 |
| Custom Cougar | 6205 | | HK | M-BL-I | BL | WH | BK-RF | | $185.00 |
| Custom Cougar | 6205 | | HK | M-BL-I | BL | WH | | | $170.00 |
| Custom Cougar | 6205 | | USA | M-BL-I | CL | BK | BK-RF | | $165.00 |
| Custom Cougar | 6205 | | USA | M-BL-I | CL | BK | | | $150.00 |
| Custom Cougar | 6205 | | HK | M-BL-I | BL | BK | BK-RF | | $165.00 |
| Custom Cougar | 6205 | | HK | M-BL-I | BL | BK | | | $150.00 |
| Custom Cougar | 6205 | | USA | M-BL-I | CL | GY | BK-RF | | $165.00 |
| Custom Cougar | 6205 | | USA | M-BL-I | CL | GY | | | $150.00 |
| Custom Cougar | 6205 | | HK | M-BL-I | BL | GY | BK-RF | | $165.00 |
| Custom Cougar | 6205 | | HK | M-BL-I | BL | GY | | | $150.00 |
| Custom Cougar | 6205 | | USA | M-BL-I | CL | BL | BK-RF | | $190.00 |
| Custom Cougar | 6205 | | USA | M-BL-I | CL | BL | | | $175.00 |
| Custom Cougar | 6205 | | HK | M-BL-I | BL | BL | BK-RF | | $190.00 |
| Custom Cougar | 6205 | | HK | M-BL-I | BL | BL | | | $175.00 |
| Custom Cougar | 6205 | | USA | M-BL-I | CL | BR-L | BK-RF | | $165.00 |
| Custom Cougar | 6205 | | USA | M-BL-I | CL | BR-L | | | $150.00 |
| Custom Cougar | 6205 | | HK | M-BL-I | BL | BR-L | BK-RF | | $165.00 |
| Custom Cougar | 6205 | | HK | M-BL-I | BL | BR-L | | | $150.00 |
| Custom Cougar | 6205 | | USA | M-BL-I | CL | BR-D | BK-RF | | $175.00 |
| Custom Cougar | 6205 | | USA | M-BL-I | CL | BR-D | | | $150.00 |
| Custom Cougar | 6205 | | HK | M-BL-I | BL | BR-D | BK-RF | | $175.00 |
| Custom Cougar | 6205 | | HK | M-BL-I | BL | BR-D | | | $150.00 |
| Custom Cougar | 6205 | | USA | M-BL-P | CL | WH | BK-RF | | $150.00 |
| Custom Cougar | 6205 | | USA | M-BL-P | CL | WH | | | $135.00 |
| Custom Cougar | 6205 | | HK | M-BL-P | BL | WH | BK-RF | | $150.00 |
| Custom Cougar | 6205 | | HK | M-BL-P | BL | WH | | | $135.00 |

## 1968 Variations

| Name | Number | Casting | Country | Color | Windows | Interior | Paint | Other | Value |
|---|---|---|---|---|---|---|---|---|---|
| Custom Cougar | 6205 | | USA | M-BL-P | CL | BK | BK-RF | | $140.00 |
| Custom Cougar | 6205 | | USA | M-BL-P | CL | BK | | | $125.00 |
| Custom Cougar | 6205 | | HK | M-BL-P | BL | BK | BK-RF | | $140.00 |
| Custom Cougar | 6205 | | HK | M-BL-P | BL | BK | | | $125.00 |
| Custom Cougar | 6205 | | USA | M-BL-P | CL | GY | BK-RF | | $140.00 |
| Custom Cougar | 6205 | | USA | M-BL-P | CL | GY | | | $125.00 |
| Custom Cougar | 6205 | | HK | M-BL-P | BL | GY | BK-RF | | $140.00 |
| Custom Cougar | 6205 | | HK | M-BL-P | BL | GY | | | $125.00 |
| Custom Cougar | 6205 | | USA | M-BL-P | CL | BL | BK-RF | | $150.00 |
| Custom Cougar | 6205 | | USA | M-BL-P | CL | BL | | | $135.00 |
| Custom Cougar | 6205 | | HK | M-BL-P | BL | BL | BK-RF | | $150.00 |
| Custom Cougar | 6205 | | HK | M-BL-P | BL | BL | | | $135.00 |
| Custom Cougar | 6205 | | USA | M-BL-P | CL | BR-L | BK-RF | | $140.00 |
| Custom Cougar | 6205 | | USA | M-BL-P | CL | BR-L | | | $125.00 |
| Custom Cougar | 6205 | | HK | M-BL-P | BL | BR-L | BK-RF | | $140.00 |
| Custom Cougar | 6205 | | HK | M-BL-P | BL | BR-L | | | $125.00 |
| Custom Cougar | 6205 | | USA | M-BL-P | CL | BR-D | BK-RF | | $140.00 |
| Custom Cougar | 6205 | | USA | M-BL-P | CL | BR-D | | | $125.00 |
| Custom Cougar | 6205 | | HK | M-BL-P | BL | BR-D | BK-RF | | $140.00 |
| Custom Cougar | 6205 | | HK | M-BL-P | BL | BR-D | | | $125.00 |
| Custom Cougar | 6205 | | USA | M-BR-D | CL | WH | BK-RF | | $160.00 |
| Custom Cougar | 6205 | | USA | M-BR-D | CL | WH | | | $155.00 |
| Custom Cougar | 6205 | | HK | M-BR-D | BL | WH | BK-RF | | $160.00 |
| Custom Cougar | 6205 | | HK | M-BR-D | BL | WH | | | $155.00 |
| Custom Cougar | 6205 | | USA | M-BR-D | CL | BK | BK-RF | | $160.00 |
| Custom Cougar | 6205 | | USA | M-BR-D | CL | BK | | | $145.00 |
| Custom Cougar | 6205 | | HK | M-BR-D | BL | BK | BK-RF | | $150.00 |
| Custom Cougar | 6205 | | HK | M-BR-D | BL | BK | | | $145.00 |
| Custom Cougar | 6205 | | USA | M-BR-D | CL | GY | BK-RF | | $150.00 |
| Custom Cougar | 6205 | | USA | M-BR-D | CL | GY | | | $145.00 |
| Custom Cougar | 6205 | | HK | M-BR-D | BL | GY | BK-RF | | $150.00 |
| Custom Cougar | 6205 | | HK | M-BR-D | BL | GY | | | $145.00 |
| Custom Cougar | 6205 | | USA | M-BR-D | CL | BR-L | BK-RF | | $150.00 |
| Custom Cougar | 6205 | | USA | M-BR-D | CL | BR-L | | | $145.00 |
| Custom Cougar | 6205 | | HK | M-BR-D | BL | BR-L | BK-RF | | $150.00 |
| Custom Cougar | 6205 | | HK | M-BR-D | BL | BR-L | | | $145.00 |
| Custom Cougar | 6205 | | USA | M-BR-D | CL | BR-D | BK-RF | | $150.00 |
| Custom Cougar | 6205 | | USA | M-BR-D | CL | BR-D | | | $145.00 |
| Custom Cougar | 6205 | | HK | M-BR-D | BL | BR-D | BK-RF | | $150.00 |
| Custom Cougar | 6205 | | HK | M-BR-D | BL | BR-D | | | $145.00 |
| Custom Cougar | 6205 | | USA | M-BR-P | CL | WH | BK-RF | | $195.00 |
| Custom Cougar | 6205 | | USA | M-BR-P | CL | WH | | | $180.00 |
| Custom Cougar | 6205 | | HK | M-BR-P | BL | WH | BK-RF | | $195.00 |
| Custom Cougar | 6205 | | HK | M-BR-P | BL | WH | | | $180.00 |
| Custom Cougar | 6205 | | USA | M-BR-P | CL | BK | BK-RF | | $175.00 |
| Custom Cougar | 6205 | | USA | M-BR-P | CL | BK | | | $160.00 |
| Custom Cougar | 6205 | | HK | M-BR-P | BL | BK | BK-RF | | $175.00 |
| Custom Cougar | 6205 | | HK | M-BR-P | BL | BK | | | $160.00 |
| Custom Cougar | 6205 | | USA | M-BR-P | CL | GY | BK-RF | | $175.00 |
| Custom Cougar | 6205 | | USA | M-BR-P | CL | GY | | | $160.00 |
| Custom Cougar | 6205 | | HK | M-BR-P | BL | GY | BK-RF | | $175.00 |
| Custom Cougar | 6205 | | HK | M-BR-P | BL | GY | | | $160.00 |
| Custom Cougar | 6205 | | USA | M-BR-P | CL | BR-L | BK-RF | | $175.00 |
| Custom Cougar | 6205 | | USA | M-BR-P | CL | BR-L | | | $160.00 |
| Custom Cougar | 6205 | | HK | M-BR-P | BL | BR-L | BK-RF | | $175.00 |
| Custom Cougar | 6205 | | HK | M-BR-P | BL | BR-L | | | $160.00 |
| Custom Cougar | 6205 | | USA | M-BR-P | CL | BR-D | BK-RF | | $175.00 |
| Custom Cougar | 6205 | | USA | M-BR-P | CL | BR-D | | | $160.00 |
| Custom Cougar | 6205 | | HK | M-BR-P | BL | BR-D | BK-RF | | $175.00 |
| Custom Cougar | 6205 | | HK | M-BR-P | BL | BR-D | | | $160.00 |
| Custom Cougar | 6205 | | USA | M-GD | CL | WH | BK-RF | | $160.00 |
| Custom Cougar | 6205 | | USA | M-GD | CL | WH | | | $145.00 |
| Custom Cougar | 6205 | | HK | M-GD | BL | WH | BK-RF | | $160.00 |
| Custom Cougar | 6205 | | HK | M-GD | BL | WH | | | $145.00 |
| Custom Cougar | 6205 | | USA | M-GD | CL | BK | BK-RF | | $150.00 |
| Custom Cougar | 6205 | | USA | M-GD | CL | BK | | | $135.00 |
| Custom Cougar | 6205 | | HK | M-GD | BL | BK | BK-RF | | $150.00 |
| Custom Cougar | 6205 | | HK | M-GD | BL | BK | | | $135.00 |
| Custom Cougar | 6205 | | USA | M-GD | CL | GY | BK-RF | | $150.00 |
| Custom Cougar | 6205 | | USA | M-GD | CL | GY | | | $135.00 |
| Custom Cougar | 6205 | | HK | M-GD | BL | GY | BK-RF | | $150.00 |
| Custom Cougar | 6205 | | HK | M-GD | BL | GY | | | $135.00 |

## 1968 Variations

| Name | Number | Casting | Country | Color | Windows | Interior | Paint | Other | Value |
|---|---|---|---|---|---|---|---|---|---|
| Custom Cougar | 6205 | | USA | M-GD | CL | BR-L | BK-RF | | $100.00 |
| Custom Cougar | 6205 | | USA | M-GD | CL | BR-L | | | $135.00 |
| Custom Cougar | 6205 | | HK | M-GD | BL | BR-L | BK-RF | | $150.00 |
| Custom Cougar | 6205 | | HK | M-GD | BL | BR-L | | | $135.00 |
| Custom Cougar | 6205 | | USA | M-GD | CL | BR-D | BK-RF | | $150.00 |
| Custom Cougar | 6205 | | USA | M-GD | CL | BR-D | | | $135.00 |
| Custom Cougar | 6205 | | HK | M-GD | BL | BR-D | BK-RF | | $150.00 |
| Custom Cougar | 6205 | | HK | M-GD | BL | BR-D | | | $135.00 |
| Custom Cougar | 6205 | | USA | M-GR | CL | WH | BK-RF | | $130.00 |
| Custom Cougar | 6205 | | USA | M-GR | CL | WH | | | $115.00 |
| Custom Cougar | 6205 | | HK | M-GR | BL | WH | BK-RF | | $130.00 |
| Custom Cougar | 6205 | | HK | M-GR | BL | WH | | | $115.00 |
| Custom Cougar | 6205 | | USA | M-GR | CL | BK | BK-RF | | $120.00 |
| Custom Cougar | 6205 | | USA | M-GR | CL | BK | | | $105.00 |
| Custom Cougar | 6205 | | HK | M-GR | BL | BK | BK-RF | | $120.00 |
| Custom Cougar | 6205 | | HK | M-GR | BL | BK | | | $105.00 |
| Custom Cougar | 6205 | | USA | M-GR | CL | GY | BK-RF | | $120.00 |
| Custom Cougar | 6205 | | USA | M-GR | CL | GY | | | $105.00 |
| Custom Cougar | 6205 | | HK | M-GR | BL | GY | BK-RF | | $120.00 |
| Custom Cougar | 6205 | | HK | M-GR | BL | GY | | | $105.00 |
| Custom Cougar | 6205 | | USA | M-GR | CL | BR-L | BK-RF | | $120.00 |
| Custom Cougar | 6205 | | USA | M-GR | CL | BR-L | | | $105.00 |
| Custom Cougar | 6205 | | HK | M-GR | BL | BR-L | BK-RF | | $120.00 |
| Custom Cougar | 6205 | | HK | M-GR | BL | BR-L | | | $105.00 |
| Custom Cougar | 6205 | | USA | M-GR | CL | BR-D | BK-RF | | $120.00 |
| Custom Cougar | 6205 | | USA | M-GR | CL | BR-D | | | $105.00 |
| Custom Cougar | 6205 | | HK | M-GR | BL | BR-D | BK-RF | | $120.00 |
| Custom Cougar | 6205 | | HK | M-GR | BL | BR-D | | | $105.00 |
| Custom Cougar | 6205 | | USA | M-GR-E | CL | WH | BK-RF | | $130.00 |
| Custom Cougar | 6205 | | USA | M-GR-E | CL | WH | | | $115.00 |
| Custom Cougar | 6205 | | HK | M-GR-E | BL | WH | BK-RF | | $130.00 |
| Custom Cougar | 6205 | | HK | M-GR-E | BL | WH | | | $115.00 |
| Custom Cougar | 6205 | | USA | M-GR-E | CL | BK | BK-RF | | $120.00 |
| Custom Cougar | 6205 | | USA | M-GR-E | CL | BK | | | $105.00 |
| Custom Cougar | 6205 | | HK | M-GR-E | BL | BK | BK-RF | | $120.00 |
| Custom Cougar | 6205 | | HK | M-GR-E | BL | BK | | | $105.00 |
| Custom Cougar | 6205 | | USA | M-GR-E | CL | GY | BK-RF | | $120.00 |
| Custom Cougar | 6205 | | USA | M-GR-E | CL | GY | | | $105.00 |
| Custom Cougar | 6205 | | HK | M-GR-E | BL | GY | BK-RF | | $120.00 |
| Custom Cougar | 6205 | | HK | M-GR-E | BL | GY | | | $105.00 |
| Custom Cougar | 6205 | | USA | M-GR-E | CL | BR-L | BK-RF | | $120.00 |
| Custom Cougar | 6205 | | USA | M-GR-E | CL | BR-L | | | $105.00 |
| Custom Cougar | 6205 | | HK | M-GR-E | BL | BR-L | BK-RF | | $120.00 |
| Custom Cougar | 6205 | | HK | M-GR-E | BL | BR-L | | | $105.00 |
| Custom Cougar | 6205 | | USA | M-GR-E | CL | BR-D | BK-RF | | $120.00 |
| Custom Cougar | 6205 | | USA | M-GR-E | CL | BR-D | | | $105.00 |
| Custom Cougar | 6205 | | HK | M-GR-E | BL | BR-D | BK-RF | | $120.00 |
| Custom Cougar | 6205 | | HK | M-GR-E | BL | BR-D | | | $105.00 |
| Custom Cougar | 6205 | | USA | M-GR-L | CL | WH | BK-RF | | $160.00 |
| Custom Cougar | 6205 | | USA | M-GR-L | CL | WH | | | $145.00 |
| Custom Cougar | 6205 | | HK | M-GR-L | BL | WH | BK-RF | | $160.00 |
| Custom Cougar | 6205 | | HK | M-GR-L | BL | WH | | | $145.00 |
| Custom Cougar | 6205 | | USA | M-GR-L | CL | BK | BK-RF | | $150.00 |
| Custom Cougar | 6205 | | USA | M-GR-L | CL | BK | | | $135.00 |
| Custom Cougar | 6205 | | HK | M-GR-L | BL | BK | BK-RF | | $150.00 |
| Custom Cougar | 6205 | | HK | M-GR-L | BL | BK | | | $145.00 |
| Custom Cougar | 6205 | | USA | M-GR-L | CL | GY | BK-RF | | $150.00 |
| Custom Cougar | 6205 | | USA | M-GR-L | CL | GY | | | $145.00 |
| Custom Cougar | 6205 | | HK | M-GR-L | BL | GY | BK-RF | | $150.00 |
| Custom Cougar | 6205 | | HK | M-GR-L | BL | GY | | | $145.00 |
| Custom Cougar | 6205 | | USA | M-GR-L | CL | BR-L | BK-RF | | $150.00 |
| Custom Cougar | 6205 | | USA | M-GR-L | CL | BR-L | | | $145.00 |
| Custom Cougar | 6205 | | HK | M-GR-L | BL | BR-L | BK-RF | | $150.00 |
| Custom Cougar | 6205 | | HK | M-GR-L | BL | BR-L | | | $145.00 |
| Custom Cougar | 6205 | | USA | M-GR-L | CL | BR-D | BK-RF | | $150.00 |
| Custom Cougar | 6205 | | USA | M-GR-L | CL | BR-D | | | $145.00 |
| Custom Cougar | 6205 | | HK | M-GR-L | BL | BR-D | BK-RF | | $150.00 |
| Custom Cougar | 6205 | | HK | M-GR-L | BL | BR-D | | | $145.00 |
| Custom Cougar | 6205 | | USA | M-GR-O | CL | WH | BK-RF | | $150.00 |
| Custom Cougar | 6205 | | USA | M-GR-O | CL | WH | | | $145.00 |
| Custom Cougar | 6205 | | HK | M-GR-O | BL | WH | BK-RF | | $150.00 |
| Custom Cougar | 6205 | | HK | M-GR-O | BL | WH | | | $145.00 |

## 1968 Variations

| Name | Number | Casting | Country | Color | Windows | Interior | Paint | Other | Value |
|---|---|---|---|---|---|---|---|---|---|
| Custom Cougar | 6205 | | USA | M-GR-O | CL | BK | BK-RF | | $150.00 |
| Custom Cougar | 6205 | | USA | M-GR-O | CL | BK | | | $125.00 |
| Custom Cougar | 6205 | | HK | M-GR-O | BL | BK | BK-RF | | $150.00 |
| Custom Cougar | 6205 | | HK | M-GR-O | BL | BK | | | $135.00 |
| Custom Cougar | 6205 | | USA | M-GR-O | CL | GY | BK-RF | | $150.00 |
| Custom Cougar | 6205 | | USA | M-GR-O | CL | GY | | | $135.00 |
| Custom Cougar | 6205 | | HK | M-GR-O | BL | GY | BK-RF | | $150.00 |
| Custom Cougar | 6205 | | HK | M-GR-O | BL | GY | | | $135.00 |
| Custom Cougar | 6205 | | USA | M-GR-O | CL | BR-L | BK-RF | | $150.00 |
| Custom Cougar | 6205 | | USA | M-GR-O | CL | BR-L | | | $135.00 |
| Custom Cougar | 6205 | | HK | M-GR-O | BL | BR-L | BK-RF | | $150.00 |
| Custom Cougar | 6205 | | HK | M-GR-O | BL | BR-L | | | $135.00 |
| Custom Cougar | 6205 | | USA | M-GR-O | CL | BR-D | BK-RF | | $150.00 |
| Custom Cougar | 6205 | | USA | M-GR-O | CL | BR-D | | | $135.00 |
| Custom Cougar | 6205 | | HK | M-GR-O | BL | BR-D | BK-RF | | $150.00 |
| Custom Cougar | 6205 | | HK | M-GR-O | BL | BR-D | | | $125.00 |
| Custom Cougar | 6205 | | USA | M-OR | CL | WH | BK-RF | | $150.00 |
| Custom Cougar | 6205 | | USA | M-OR | CL | WH | | | $145.00 |
| Custom Cougar | 6205 | | HK | M-OR | BL | WH | BK-RF | | $150.00 |
| Custom Cougar | 6205 | | HK | M-OR | BL | WH | | | $145.00 |
| Custom Cougar | 6205 | | USA | M-OR | CL | BK | BK-RF | | $150.00 |
| Custom Cougar | 6205 | | USA | M-OR | CL | BK | | | $125.00 |
| Custom Cougar | 6205 | | HK | M-OR | BL | BK | BK-RF | | $150.00 |
| Custom Cougar | 6205 | | HK | M-OR | BL | BK | | | $125.00 |
| Custom Cougar | 6205 | | USA | M-OR | CL | GY | BK-RF | | $150.00 |
| Custom Cougar | 6205 | | USA | M-OR | CL | GY | | | $125.00 |
| Custom Cougar | 6205 | | HK | M-OR | BL | GY | BK-RF | | $150.00 |
| Custom Cougar | 6205 | | HK | M-OR | BL | GY | | | $125.00 |
| Custom Cougar | 6205 | | USA | M-OR | CL | BR-L | BK-RF | | $150.00 |
| Custom Cougar | 6205 | | USA | M-OR | CL | BR-L | | | $125.00 |
| Custom Cougar | 6205 | | HK | M-OR | BL | BR-L | BK-RF | | $150.00 |
| Custom Cougar | 6205 | | HK | M-OR | BL | BR-L | | | $125.00 |
| Custom Cougar | 6205 | | USA | M-OR | CL | BR-D | BK-RF | | $150.00 |
| Custom Cougar | 6205 | | USA | M-OR | CL | BR-D | | | $125.00 |
| Custom Cougar | 6205 | | HK | M-OR | BL | BR-D | BK-RF | | $150.00 |
| Custom Cougar | 6205 | | HK | M-OR | BL | BR-D | | | $125.00 |
| Custom Cougar | 6205 | | USA | M-PR | CL | WH | BK-RF | | $200.00 |
| Custom Cougar | 6205 | | USA | M-PR | CL | WH | | | $185.00 |
| Custom Cougar | 6205 | | HK | M-PR | BL | WH | BK-RF | | $200.00 |
| Custom Cougar | 6205 | | HK | M-PR | BL | WH | | | $185.00 |
| Custom Cougar | 6205 | | USA | M-PR | CL | BK | BK-RF | | $185.00 |
| Custom Cougar | 6205 | | USA | M-PR | CL | BK | | | $170.00 |
| Custom Cougar | 6205 | | HK | M-PR | BL | BK | BK-RF | | $185.00 |
| Custom Cougar | 6205 | | HK | M-PR | BL | BK | | | $170.00 |
| Custom Cougar | 6205 | | USA | M-PR | CL | GY | BK-RF | | $185.00 |
| Custom Cougar | 6205 | | USA | M-PR | CL | GY | | | $170.00 |
| Custom Cougar | 6205 | | HK | M-PR | BL | GY | BK-RF | | $185.00 |
| Custom Cougar | 6205 | | HK | M-PR | BL | GY | | | $170.00 |
| Custom Cougar | 6205 | | USA | M-PR | CL | BR-L | BK-RF | | $185.00 |
| Custom Cougar | 6205 | | USA | M-PR | CL | BR-L | | | $170.00 |
| Custom Cougar | 6205 | | HK | M-PR | BL | BR-L | BK-RF | | $185.00 |
| Custom Cougar | 6205 | | HK | M-PR | BL | BR-L | | | $170.00 |
| Custom Cougar | 6205 | | USA | M-PR | CL | BR-D | BK-RF | | $185.00 |
| Custom Cougar | 6205 | | USA | M-PR | CL | BR-D | | | $170.00 |
| Custom Cougar | 6205 | | HK | M-PR | BL | BR-D | BK-RF | | $185.00 |
| Custom Cougar | 6205 | | HK | M-PR | BL | BR-D | | | $170.00 |
| Custom Cougar | 6205 | | USA | M-RD | CL | WH | BK-RF | | $180.00 |
| Custom Cougar | 6205 | | USA | M-RD | CL | WH | | | $165.00 |
| Custom Cougar | 6205 | | HK | M-RD | BL | WH | BK-RF | | $180.00 |
| Custom Cougar | 6205 | | HK | M-RD | BL | WH | | | $165.00 |
| Custom Cougar | 6205 | | USA | M-RD | CL | BK | BK-RF | | $160.00 |
| Custom Cougar | 6205 | | USA | M-RD | CL | BK | | | $145.00 |
| Custom Cougar | 6205 | | HK | M-RD | BL | BK | BK-RF | | $150.00 |
| Custom Cougar | 6205 | | HK | M-RD | BL | BK | | | $145.00 |
| Custom Cougar | 6205 | | USA | M-RD | CL | GY | BK-RF | | $160.00 |
| Custom Cougar | 6205 | | USA | M-RD | CL | GY | | | $145.00 |
| Custom Cougar | 6205 | | HK | M-RD | BL | GY | BK-RF | | $160.00 |
| Custom Cougar | 6205 | | HK | M-RD | BL | GY | | | $145.00 |
| Custom Cougar | 6205 | | USA | M-RD | CL | BR-L | BK-RF | | $160.00 |
| Custom Cougar | 6205 | | USA | M-RD | CL | BR-L | | | $145.00 |
| Custom Cougar | 6205 | | HK | M-RD | BL | BR-L | BK-RF | | $160.00 |
| Custom Cougar | 6205 | | HK | M-RD | BL | BR-L | | | $145.00 |

## 1968 Variations

| Name | Number | Casting | Country | Color | Windows | Interior | Paint | Other | Value |
|---|---|---|---|---|---|---|---|---|---|
| Custom Cougar | 6205 | | USA | M-RD | CL | BR-D | BK-RF | | $160.00 |
| Custom Cougar | 6205 | | USA | M-RD | CL | BR-D | | | $145.00 |
| Custom Cougar | 6205 | | HK | M-RD | BL | BR-D | BK-RF | | $160.00 |
| Custom Cougar | 6205 | | HK | M-RD | BL | BR-D | | | $145.00 |
| Custom Cougar | 6205 | | USA | M-RD-R | CL | WH | BK-RF | | $195.00 |
| Custom Cougar | 6205 | | USA | M-RD-R | CL | WH | | | $180.00 |
| Custom Cougar | 6205 | | HK | M-RD-R | BL | WH | BK-RF | | $195.00 |
| Custom Cougar | 6205 | | HK | M-RD-R | BL | WH | | | $180.00 |
| Custom Cougar | 6205 | | USA | M-RD-R | CL | BK | BK-RF | | $175.00 |
| Custom Cougar | 6205 | | USA | M-RD-R | CL | BK | | | $160.00 |
| Custom Cougar | 6205 | | HK | M-RD-R | BL | BK | BK-RF | | $175.00 |
| Custom Cougar | 6205 | | HK | M-RD-R | BL | BK | | | $160.00 |
| Custom Cougar | 6205 | | USA | M-RD-R | CL | GY | BK-RF | | $175.00 |
| Custom Cougar | 6205 | | USA | M-RD-R | CL | GY | | | $160.00 |
| Custom Cougar | 6205 | | HK | M-RD-R | BL | GY | BK-RF | | $175.00 |
| Custom Cougar | 6205 | | HK | M-RD-R | BL | GY | | | $160.00 |
| Custom Cougar | 6205 | | USA | M-RD-R | CL | BR-L | BK-RF | | $175.00 |
| Custom Cougar | 6205 | | USA | M-RD-R | CL | BR-L | | | $160.00 |
| Custom Cougar | 6205 | | HK | M-RD-R | BL | BR-L | BK-RF | | $175.00 |
| Custom Cougar | 6205 | | HK | M-RD-R | BL | BR-L | | | $160.00 |
| Custom Cougar | 6205 | | USA | M-RD-R | CL | BR-D | BK-RF | | $175.00 |
| Custom Cougar | 6205 | | USA | M-RD-R | CL | BR-D | | | $160.00 |
| Custom Cougar | 6205 | | HK | M-RD-R | BL | BR-D | BK-RF | | $175.00 |
| Custom Cougar | 6205 | | HK | M-RD-R | BL | BR-D | | | $160.00 |
| Custom Cougar | 6205 | | USA | M-YW | CL | WH | BK-RF | | $140.00 |
| Custom Cougar | 6205 | | USA | M-YW | CL | WH | | | $125.00 |
| Custom Cougar | 6205 | | HK | M-YW | BL | WH | BK-RF | | $140.00 |
| Custom Cougar | 6205 | | HK | M-YW | BL | WH | | | $125.00 |
| Custom Cougar | 6205 | | USA | M-YW | CL | BK | BK-RF | | $120.00 |
| Custom Cougar | 6205 | | USA | M-YW | CL | BK | | | $105.00 |
| Custom Cougar | 6205 | | HK | M-YW | BL | BK | BK-RF | | $120.00 |
| Custom Cougar | 6205 | | HK | M-YW | BL | BK | | | $105.00 |
| Custom Cougar | 6205 | | USA | M-YW | CL | GY | BK-RF | | $120.00 |
| Custom Cougar | 6205 | | USA | M-YW | CL | GY | | | $105.00 |
| Custom Cougar | 6205 | | HK | M-YW | BL | GY | BK-RF | | $120.00 |
| Custom Cougar | 6205 | | HK | M-YW | BL | GY | | | $105.00 |
| Custom Cougar | 6205 | | USA | M-YW | CL | BR-L | BK-RF | | $120.00 |
| Custom Cougar | 6205 | | USA | M-YW | CL | BR-L | | | $105.00 |
| Custom Cougar | 6205 | | HK | M-YW | BL | BR-L | BK-RF | | $120.00 |
| Custom Cougar | 6205 | | HK | M-YW | BL | BR-L | | | $105.00 |
| Custom Cougar | 6205 | | USA | M-YW | CL | BR-D | BK-RF | | $120.00 |
| Custom Cougar | 6205 | | USA | M-YW | CL | BR-D | | | $105.00 |
| Custom Cougar | 6205 | | HK | M-YW | BL | BR-D | BK-RF | | $120.00 |
| Custom Cougar | 6205 | | HK | M-YW | BL | BR-D | | | $105.00 |
| Custom Cougar | 6205 | | USA | M-YW-L | CL | WH | BK-RF | | $145.00 |
| Custom Cougar | 6205 | | USA | M-YW-L | CL | WH | | | $130.00 |
| Custom Cougar | 6205 | | HK | M-YW-L | BL | WH | BK-RF | | $145.00 |
| Custom Cougar | 6205 | | HK | M-YW-L | BL | WH | | | $130.00 |
| Custom Cougar | 6205 | | USA | M-YW-L | CL | BK | BK-RF | | $125.00 |
| Custom Cougar | 6205 | | USA | M-YW-L | CL | BK | | | $110.00 |
| Custom Cougar | 6205 | | HK | M-YW-L | BL | BK | BK-RF | | $125.00 |
| Custom Cougar | 6205 | | HK | M-YW-L | BL | BK | | | $110.00 |
| Custom Cougar | 6205 | | USA | M-YW-L | CL | GY | BK-RF | | $125.00 |
| Custom Cougar | 6205 | | USA | M-YW-L | CL | GY | | | $110.00 |
| Custom Cougar | 6205 | | HK | M-YW-L | BL | GY | BK-RF | | $125.00 |
| Custom Cougar | 6205 | | HK | M-YW-L | BL | GY | | | $110.00 |
| Custom Cougar | 6205 | | USA | M-YW-L | CL | BR-L | BK-RF | | $125.00 |
| Custom Cougar | 6205 | | USA | M-YW-L | CL | BR-L | | | $110.00 |
| Custom Cougar | 6205 | | HK | M-YW-L | BL | BR-L | BK-RF | | $125.00 |
| Custom Cougar | 6205 | | HK | M-YW-L | BL | BR-L | | | $110.00 |
| Custom Cougar | 6205 | | USA | M-YW-L | CL | BR-D | BK-RF | | $125.00 |
| Custom Cougar | 6205 | | USA | M-YW-L | CL | BR-D | | | $110.00 |
| Custom Cougar | 6205 | | HK | M-YW-L | BL | BR-D | BK-RF | | $125.00 |
| Custom Cougar | 6205 | | HK | M-YW-L | BL | BR-D | | | $110.00 |
| | | | | | | | | | |
| Custom Mustang | 6206 | | USA | M-AQ | CL | WH | | | $145.00 |
| Custom Mustang | 6206 | | HK | M-AQ | BL | WH | | | $145.00 |
| Custom Mustang | 6206 | | USA | M-AQ | CL | BK | | | $135.00 |
| Custom Mustang | 6206 | | HK | M-AQ | BL | BK | | | $135.00 |
| Custom Mustang | 6206 | | USA | M-AQ | CL | GY | | | $135.00 |
| Custom Mustang | 6206 | | HK | M-AQ | BL | GY | | | $135.00 |

## 1968 Variations

| Name | Number | Casting | Country | Color | Windows | Interior | Paint | Other | Value |
|---|---|---|---|---|---|---|---|---|---|
| Custom Mustang | 6206 | | USA | M-AQ | CL | BR-L | | | $135.00 |
| Custom Mustang | 6206 | | HK | M-AQ | BL | BR-L | | | $135.00 |
| Custom Mustang | 6206 | | USA | M-AQ | CL | BR-D | | | $135.00 |
| Custom Mustang | 6206 | | HK | M-AQ | BL | BR-D | | | $135.00 |
| Custom Mustang | 6206 | | USA | M-BL | CL | WH | | | $155.00 |
| Custom Mustang | 6206 | | HK | M-BL | BL | WH | | | $155.00 |
| Custom Mustang | 6206 | | USA | M-BL | CL | BK | | | $145.00 |
| Custom Mustang | 6206 | | HK | M-BL | BL | BK | | | $145.00 |
| Custom Mustang | 6206 | | USA | M-BL | CL | GY | | | $145.00 |
| Custom Mustang | 6206 | | HK | M-BL | BL | GY | | | $125.00 |
| Custom Mustang | 6206 | | USA | M-BL | CL | BR-L | | | $145.00 |
| Custom Mustang | 6206 | | HK | M-BL | BL | BR-L | | | $145.00 |
| Custom Mustang | 6206 | | USA | M-BL | CL | BR-D | | | $145.00 |
| Custom Mustang | 6206 | | HK | M-BL | BL | BR-D | | | $145.00 |
| Custom Mustang | 6206 | Ribbed rear window | USA | M-BL | BL | WH | | | $550.00 |
| Custom Mustang | 6206 | Ribbed rear window | USA | M-BL | BL | BK | | | $550.00 |
| Custom Mustang | 6206 | Ribbed rear window | USA | M-BL | BL | GY | | | $550.00 |
| Custom Mustang | 6206 | Ribbed rear window | USA | M-BL | BL | BR-L | | | $550.00 |
| Custom Mustang | 6206 | Ribbed rear window | USA | M-BL | BL | BR-D | | | $550.00 |
| Custom Mustang | 6206 | | USA | M-BL-I | CL | WH | | | $180.00 |
| Custom Mustang | 6206 | | HK | M-BL-I | BL | WH | | | $180.00 |
| Custom Mustang | 6206 | | USA | M-BL-I | CL | BK | | | $170.00 |
| Custom Mustang | 6206 | | HK | M-BL-I | BL | BK | | | $170.00 |
| Custom Mustang | 6206 | | USA | M-BL-I | CL | GY | | | $170.00 |
| Custom Mustang | 6206 | | HK | M-BL-I | BL | GY | | | $170.00 |
| Custom Mustang | 6206 | | USA | M-BL-I | CL | BR-L | | | $170.00 |
| Custom Mustang | 6206 | | HK | M-BL-I | BL | BR-L | | | $170.00 |
| Custom Mustang | 6206 | | USA | M-BL-I | CL | BR-D | | | $170.00 |
| Custom Mustang | 6206 | | HK | M-BL-I | BL | BR-D | | | $170.00 |
| Custom Mustang | 6206 | | USA | M-BL-P | CL | WH | | | $160.00 |
| Custom Mustang | 6206 | | HK | M-BL-P | BL | WH | | | $160.00 |
| Custom Mustang | 6206 | | USA | M-BL-P | CL | BK | | | $150.00 |
| Custom Mustang | 6206 | | HK | M-BL-P | BL | BK | | | $150.00 |
| Custom Mustang | 6206 | | USA | M-BL-P | CL | GY | | | $150.00 |
| Custom Mustang | 6206 | | HK | M-BL-P | BL | GY | | | $150.00 |
| Custom Mustang | 6206 | | USA | M-BL-P | CL | BR-L | | | $150.00 |
| Custom Mustang | 6206 | | HK | M-BL-P | BL | BR-L | | | $150.00 |
| Custom Mustang | 6206 | | USA | M-BL-P | CL | BR-D | | | $150.00 |
| Custom Mustang | 6206 | | HK | M-BL-P | BL | BR-D | | | $150.00 |
| Custom Mustang | 6206 | | USA | M-BR-D | CL | WH | | | $155.00 |
| Custom Mustang | 6206 | | HK | M-BR-D | BL | WH | | | $155.00 |
| Custom Mustang | 6206 | | USA | M-BR-D | CL | BK | | | $145.00 |
| Custom Mustang | 6206 | | HK | M-BR-D | BL | BK | | | $145.00 |
| Custom Mustang | 6206 | | USA | M-BR-D | CL | GY | | | $145.00 |
| Custom Mustang | 6206 | | HK | M-BR-D | BL | GY | | | $145.00 |
| Custom Mustang | 6206 | | USA | M-BR-D | CL | BR-L | | | $145.00 |
| Custom Mustang | 6206 | | HK | M-BR-D | BL | BR-L | | | $145.00 |
| Custom Mustang | 6206 | | USA | M-BR-D | CL | BR-D | | | $145.00 |
| Custom Mustang | 6206 | | HK | M-BR-D | BL | BR-D | | | $145.00 |
| Custom Mustang | 6206 | | USA | M-BR-P | CL | WH | | | $135.00 |
| Custom Mustang | 6206 | | HK | M-BR-P | BL | WH | | | $135.00 |
| Custom Mustang | 6206 | | USA | M-BR-P | CL | BK | | | $125.00 |
| Custom Mustang | 6206 | | HK | M-BR-P | BL | BK | | | $125.00 |
| Custom Mustang | 6206 | | USA | M-BR-P | CL | GY | | | $125.00 |
| Custom Mustang | 6206 | | HK | M-BR-P | BL | GY | | | $125.00 |
| Custom Mustang | 6206 | | USA | M-BR-P | CL | BR-L | | | $125.00 |
| Custom Mustang | 6206 | | HK | M-BR-P | BL | BR-L | | | $125.00 |
| Custom Mustang | 6206 | | USA | M-BR-P | CL | BR-D | | | $125.00 |
| Custom Mustang | 6206 | | HK | M-BR-P | BL | BR-D | | | $125.00 |
| Custom Mustang | 6206 | | USA | M-GD | CL | WH | | | $135.00 |
| Custom Mustang | 6206 | | HK | M-GD | BL | WH | | | $135.00 |
| Custom Mustang | 6206 | | USA | M-GD | CL | BK | | | $125.00 |
| Custom Mustang | 6206 | | HK | M-GD | BL | BK | | | $125.00 |
| Custom Mustang | 6206 | | USA | M-GD | CL | GY | | | $125.00 |
| Custom Mustang | 6206 | | HK | M-GD | BL | GY | | | $125.00 |
| Custom Mustang | 6206 | | USA | M-GD | CL | BR-L | | | $125.00 |
| Custom Mustang | 6206 | | HK | M-GD | BL | BR-L | | | $135.00 |
| Custom Mustang | 6206 | | USA | M-GD | CL | BR-D | | | $135.00 |
| Custom Mustang | 6206 | | HK | M-GD | BL | BR-D | | | $125.00 |
| Custom Mustang | 6206 | Open hood scoops | HK | M-GD | BL | WH | | | $600.00 |
| Custom Mustang | 6206 | Open hood scoops | HK | M-GD | BL | BK | | | $600.00 |
| Custom Mustang | 6206 | Open hood scoops | HK | M-GD | BL | GY | | | $600.00 |

## 1968 Variations

| Name | Number | Casting | Country | Color | Windows | Interior | Paint | Other | Value |
|---|---|---|---|---|---|---|---|---|---|
| Custom Mustang | 6206 | Open hood scoops | HK | M-GD | BL | BR-L | | | $600.00 |
| Custom Mustang | 6206 | Open hood scoops | HK | M-GD | BL | BR-D | | | $600.00 |
| Custom Mustang | 6206 | | USA | M-GR | CL | WH | | | $160.00 |
| Custom Mustang | 6206 | | HK | M-GR | BL | WH | | | $160.00 |
| Custom Mustang | 6206 | | USA | M-GR | CL | BK | | | $150.00 |
| Custom Mustang | 6206 | | HK | M-GR | BL | BK | | | $150.00 |
| Custom Mustang | 6206 | | USA | M-GR | CL | GY | | | $150.00 |
| Custom Mustang | 6206 | | HK | M-GR | BL | GY | | | $150.00 |
| Custom Mustang | 6206 | | USA | M-GR | CL | BR-L | | | $150.00 |
| Custom Mustang | 6206 | | HK | M-GR | BL | BR-L | | | $150.00 |
| Custom Mustang | 6206 | | USA | M-GR | CL | BR-D | | | $150.00 |
| Custom Mustang | 6206 | | HK | M-GR | BL | BR-D | | | $150.00 |
| Custom Mustang | 6206 | | USA | M-GR-E | CL | WH | | | $160.00 |
| Custom Mustang | 6206 | | HK | M-GR-E | BL | WH | | | $160.00 |
| Custom Mustang | 6206 | | USA | M-GR-E | CL | BK | | | $150.00 |
| Custom Mustang | 6206 | | HK | M-GR-E | BL | BK | | | $150.00 |
| Custom Mustang | 6206 | | USA | M-GR-E | CL | GY | | | $150.00 |
| Custom Mustang | 6206 | | HK | M-GR-E | BL | GY | | | $150.00 |
| Custom Mustang | 6206 | | USA | M-GR-E | CL | BR-L | | | $150.00 |
| Custom Mustang | 6206 | | HK | M-GR-E | BL | BR-L | | | $150.00 |
| Custom Mustang | 6206 | | USA | M-GR-E | CL | BR-D | | | $150.00 |
| Custom Mustang | 6206 | | HK | M-GR-E | BL | BR-D | | | $150.00 |
| Custom Mustang | 6206 | | USA | M-GR-L | CL | WH | | | $180.00 |
| Custom Mustang | 6206 | | HK | M-GR-L | BL | WH | | | $180.00 |
| Custom Mustang | 6206 | | USA | M-GR-L | CL | BK | | | $160.00 |
| Custom Mustang | 6206 | | HK | M-GR-L | BL | BK | | | $160.00 |
| Custom Mustang | 6206 | | USA | M-GR-L | CL | GY | | | $160.00 |
| Custom Mustang | 6206 | | HK | M-GR-L | BL | GY | | | $160.00 |
| Custom Mustang | 6206 | | USA | M-GR-L | CL | BR-L | | | $160.00 |
| Custom Mustang | 6206 | | HK | M-GR-L | BL | BR-L | | | $160.00 |
| Custom Mustang | 6206 | | USA | M-GR-L | CL | BR-D | | | $160.00 |
| Custom Mustang | 6206 | | HK | M-GR-L | BL | BR-D | | | $160.00 |
| Custom Mustang | 6206 | | USA | M-GR-O | CL | WH | | | $180.00 |
| Custom Mustang | 6206 | | HK | M-GR-O | BL | WH | | | $180.00 |
| Custom Mustang | 6206 | | USA | M-GR-O | CL | BK | | | $170.00 |
| Custom Mustang | 6206 | | HK | M-GR-O | BL | BK | | | $170.00 |
| Custom Mustang | 6206 | | USA | M-GR-O | CL | GY | | | $170.00 |
| Custom Mustang | 6206 | | HK | M-GR-O | BL | GY | | | $170.00 |
| Custom Mustang | 6206 | | USA | M-GR-O | CL | BR-L | | | $170.00 |
| Custom Mustang | 6206 | | HK | M-GR-O | BL | BR-L | | | $170.00 |
| Custom Mustang | 6206 | | USA | M-GR-O | CL | BR-D | | | $170.00 |
| Custom Mustang | 6206 | | HK | M-GR-O | BL | BR-D | | | $170.00 |
| Custom Mustang | 6206 | | USA | M-MG | CL | WH | | | $290.00 |
| Custom Mustang | 6206 | | HK | M-MG | BL | WH | | | $290.00 |
| Custom Mustang | 6206 | | USA | M-MG | CL | BK | | | $280.00 |
| Custom Mustang | 6206 | | HK | M-MG | BL | BK | | | $280.00 |
| Custom Mustang | 6206 | | USA | M-MG | CL | GY | | | $280.00 |
| Custom Mustang | 6206 | | HK | M-MG | BL | GY | | | $280.00 |
| Custom Mustang | 6206 | | USA | M-MG | CL | BR-L | | | $280.00 |
| Custom Mustang | 6206 | | HK | M-MG | BL | BR-L | | | $280.00 |
| Custom Mustang | 6206 | | USA | M-MG | CL | BR-D | | | $280.00 |
| Custom Mustang | 6206 | | HK | M-MG | BL | BR-D | | | $280.00 |
| Custom Mustang | 6206 | | USA | M-OR | CL | WH | | | $120.00 |
| Custom Mustang | 6206 | | HK | M-OR | BL | WH | | | $120.00 |
| Custom Mustang | 6206 | | USA | M-OR | CL | BK | | | $110.00 |
| Custom Mustang | 6206 | | HK | M-OR | BL | BK | | | $110.00 |
| Custom Mustang | 6206 | | USA | M-OR | CL | GY | | | $110.00 |
| Custom Mustang | 6206 | | HK | M-OR | BL | GY | | | $110.00 |
| Custom Mustang | 6206 | | USA | M-OR | CL | BR-L | | | $110.00 |
| Custom Mustang | 6206 | | HK | M-OR | BL | BR-L | | | $110.00 |
| Custom Mustang | 6206 | | USA | M-OR | CL | BR-D | | | $110.00 |
| Custom Mustang | 6206 | | HK | M-OR | BL | BR-D | | | $110.00 |
| Custom Mustang | 6206 | Ribbed rear window | USA | M-OR | BL | WH | | | $550.00 |
| Custom Mustang | 6206 | Ribbed rear window | USA | M-OR | BL | BK | | | $550.00 |
| Custom Mustang | 6206 | Ribbed rear window | USA | M-OR | BL | GY | | | $550.00 |
| Custom Mustang | 6206 | Ribbed rear window | USA | M-OR | BL | BR-L | | | $550.00 |
| Custom Mustang | 6206 | Ribbed rear window | USA | M-OR | BL | BR-D | | | $550.00 |
| Custom Mustang | 6206 | | USA | M-PK | CL | WH | | | $700.00 |
| Custom Mustang | 6206 | | HK | M-PK | BL | WH | | | $700.00 |
| Custom Mustang | 6206 | | USA | M-PK | CL | BK | | | $700.00 |
| Custom Mustang | 6206 | | HK | M-PK | BL | BK | | | $650.00 |
| Custom Mustang | 6206 | | USA | M-PK | CL | GY | | | $650.00 |

## 1968 Variations

| Name | Number | Casting | Country | Color | Windows | Interior | Paint | Other | Value |
|---|---|---|---|---|---|---|---|---|---|
| Custom Mustang | 6206 | | HK | M-PK | BL | GY | | | $650.00 |
| Custom Mustang | 6206 | | USA | M-PK | CL | BR-L | | | $650.00 |
| Custom Mustang | 6206 | | HK | M-PK | BL | BR-L | | | $650.00 |
| Custom Mustang | 6206 | | USA | M-PK | CL | BR-D | | | $650.00 |
| Custom Mustang | 6206 | | HK | M-PK | BL | BR-D | | | $650.00 |
| Custom Mustang | 6206 | | USA | M-PK-H | CL | WH | | | $700.00 |
| Custom Mustang | 6206 | | HK | M-PK-H | BL | WH | | | $700.00 |
| Custom Mustang | 6206 | | USA | M-PK-H | CL | BK | | | $650.00 |
| Custom Mustang | 6206 | | HK | M-PK-H | BL | BK | | | $650.00 |
| Custom Mustang | 6206 | | USA | M-PK-H | CL | GY | | | $650.00 |
| Custom Mustang | 6206 | | HK | M-PK-H | BL | GY | | | $650.00 |
| Custom Mustang | 6206 | | USA | M-PK-H | CL | BR-L | | | $650.00 |
| Custom Mustang | 6206 | | HK | M-PK-H | BL | BR-L | | | $650.00 |
| Custom Mustang | 6206 | | USA | M-PK-H | CL | BR-D | | | $650.00 |
| Custom Mustang | 6206 | | HK | M-PK-H | BL | BR-D | | | $650.00 |
| Custom Mustang | 6206 | | USA | M-PK-S | CL | WH | | | $700.00 |
| Custom Mustang | 6206 | | HK | M-PK-S | BL | WH | | | $700.00 |
| Custom Mustang | 6206 | | USA | M-PK-S | CL | BK | | | $650.00 |
| Custom Mustang | 6206 | | HK | M-PK-S | BL | BK | | | $650.00 |
| Custom Mustang | 6206 | | USA | M-PK-S | CL | GY | | | $650.00 |
| Custom Mustang | 6206 | | HK | M-PK-S | BL | GY | | | $650.00 |
| Custom Mustang | 6206 | | USA | M-PK-S | CL | BR-L | | | $650.00 |
| Custom Mustang | 6206 | | HK | M-PK-S | BL | BR-L | | | $650.00 |
| Custom Mustang | 6206 | | USA | M-PK-S | CL | BR-D | | | $650.00 |
| Custom Mustang | 6206 | | HK | M-PK-S | BL | BR-D | | | $650.00 |
| Custom Mustang | 6206 | | USA | M-PR | CL | WH | | | $210.00 |
| Custom Mustang | 6206 | | HK | M-PR | BL | WH | | | $210.00 |
| Custom Mustang | 6206 | | USA | M-PR | CL | BK | | | $200.00 |
| Custom Mustang | 6206 | | HK | M-PR | BL | BK | | | $200.00 |
| Custom Mustang | 6206 | | USA | M-PR | CL | GY | | | $200.00 |
| Custom Mustang | 6206 | | HK | M-PR | BL | GY | | | $200.00 |
| Custom Mustang | 6206 | | USA | M-PR | CL | BR-L | | | $200.00 |
| Custom Mustang | 6206 | | HK | M-PR | BL | BR-L | | | $200.00 |
| Custom Mustang | 6206 | | USA | M-PR | CL | BR-D | | | $200.00 |
| Custom Mustang | 6206 | | HK | M-PR | BL | BR-D | | | $200.00 |
| Custom Mustang | 6206 | | USA | M-RD | CL | WH | | | $120.00 |
| Custom Mustang | 6206 | | HK | M-RD | BL | WH | | | $120.00 |
| Custom Mustang | 6206 | | USA | M-RD | CL | BK | | | $110.00 |
| Custom Mustang | 6206 | | HK | M-RD | BL | BK | | | $110.00 |
| Custom Mustang | 6206 | | USA | M-RD | CL | GY | | | $110.00 |
| Custom Mustang | 6206 | | HK | M-RD | BL | GY | | | $110.00 |
| Custom Mustang | 6206 | | USA | M-RD | CL | RD | | | $120.00 |
| Custom Mustang | 6206 | | HK | M-RD | BL | RD | | | $120.00 |
| Custom Mustang | 6206 | | USA | M-RD | CL | BR-L | | | $110.00 |
| Custom Mustang | 6206 | | HK | M-RD | BL | BR-L | | | $110.00 |
| Custom Mustang | 6206 | | USA | M-RD | CL | BR-D | | | $110.00 |
| Custom Mustang | 6206 | | HK | M-RD | BL | BR-D | | | $110.00 |
| Custom Mustang | 6206 | Open hood scoops | HK | M-RD | BL | WH | | | $700.00 |
| Custom Mustang | 6206 | Open hood scoops | HK | M-RD | BL | BK | | | $700.00 |
| Custom Mustang | 6206 | Open hood scoops | HK | M-RD | BL | GY | | | $700.00 |
| Custom Mustang | 6206 | Open hood scoops | HK | M-RD | BL | RD | | | $700.00 |
| Custom Mustang | 6206 | Open hood scoops | HK | M-RD | BL | BR-L | | | $700.00 |
| Custom Mustang | 6206 | Open hood scoops | HK | M-RD | BL | BR-D | | | $700.00 |
| Custom Mustang | 6206 | Ribbed rear window | USA | M-RD | BL | WH | | | $550.00 |
| Custom Mustang | 6206 | Ribbed rear window | USA | M-RD | BL | BK | | | $550.00 |
| Custom Mustang | 6206 | Ribbed rear window | USA | M-RD | BL | GY | | | $550.00 |
| Custom Mustang | 6206 | Ribbed rear window | USA | M-RD | BL | RD | | | $550.00 |
| Custom Mustang | 6206 | Ribbed rear window | USA | M-RD | BL | BR-L | | | $550.00 |
| Custom Mustang | 6206 | Ribbed rear window | USA | M-RD | BL | BR-D | | | $550.00 |
| Custom Mustang | 6206 | | USA | M-RD-R | CL | WH | | | $140.00 |
| Custom Mustang | 6206 | | HK | M-RD-R | BL | WH | | | $140.00 |
| Custom Mustang | 6206 | | USA | M-RD-R | CL | BK | | | $130.00 |
| Custom Mustang | 6206 | | HK | M-RD-R | BL | BK | | | $130.00 |
| Custom Mustang | 6206 | | USA | M-RD-R | CL | GY | | | $130.00 |
| Custom Mustang | 6206 | | HK | M-RD-R | BL | GY | | | $130.00 |
| Custom Mustang | 6206 | | USA | M-RD-R | CL | RD | | | $140.00 |
| Custom Mustang | 6206 | | HK | M-RD-R | BL | RD | | | $140.00 |
| Custom Mustang | 6206 | | USA | M-RD-R | CL | BR-L | | | $130.00 |
| Custom Mustang | 6206 | | HK | M-RD-R | BL | BR-L | | | $130.00 |
| Custom Mustang | 6206 | | USA | M-RD-R | CL | BR-D | | | $130.00 |
| Custom Mustang | 6206 | | HK | M-RD-R | BL | BR-D | | | $130.00 |
| Custom Mustang | 6206 | Open hood scoops | HK | M-RD-R | BL | WH | | | $750.00 |

## 1968 Variations

| Name | Number | Casting | Country | Color | Windows | Interior | Paint | Other | Value |
|---|---|---|---|---|---|---|---|---|---|
| Custom Mustang | 6206 | Open hood scoops | HK | M-RD-R | BL | BK | | | $750.00 |
| Custom Mustang | 6206 | Open hood scoops | HK | M-RD-R | BL | GY | | | $750.00 |
| Custom Mustang | 6206 | Open hood scoops | HK | M-RD-R | BL | RD | | | $750.00 |
| Custom Mustang | 6206 | Open hood scoops | HK | M-RD-R | BL | BR-L | | | $750.00 |
| Custom Mustang | 6206 | Open hood scoops | HK | M-RD-R | BL | BR-D | | | $750.00 |
| Custom Mustang | 6206 | Ribbed rear window | USA | M-RD-R | BL | WH | | | $600.00 |
| Custom Mustang | 6206 | Ribbed rear window | USA | M-RD-R | BL | BK | | | $600.00 |
| Custom Mustang | 6206 | Ribbed rear window | USA | M-RD-R | BL | GY | | | $600.00 |
| Custom Mustang | 6206 | Ribbed rear window | USA | M-RD-R | BL | RD | | | $600.00 |
| Custom Mustang | 6206 | Ribbed rear window | USA | M-RD-R | BL | BR-L | | | $600.00 |
| Custom Mustang | 6206 | Ribbed rear window | USA | M-RD-R | BL | BR-D | | | $600.00 |
| Custom Mustang | 6206 | | USA | M-YW | CL | WH | | | $155.00 |
| Custom Mustang | 6206 | | HK | M-YW | BL | WH | | | $155.00 |
| Custom Mustang | 6206 | | USA | M-YW | CL | BK | | | $140.00 |
| Custom Mustang | 6206 | | HK | M-YW | BL | BK | | | $140.00 |
| Custom Mustang | 6206 | | USA | M-YW | CL | GY | | | $140.00 |
| Custom Mustang | 6206 | | HK | M-YW | BL | GY | | | $140.00 |
| Custom Mustang | 6206 | | USA | M-YW | CL | BR-L | | | $140.00 |
| Custom Mustang | 6206 | | HK | M-YW | BL | BR-L | | | $140.00 |
| Custom Mustang | 6206 | | USA | M-YW | CL | BR-D | | | $140.00 |
| Custom Mustang | 6206 | | HK | M-YW | BL | BR-D | | | $140.00 |
| Custom Mustang | 6206 | Open hood scoops | USA | M-YW | BL | WH | | | $700.00 |
| Custom Mustang | 6206 | Open hood scoops | USA | M-YW | BL | BK | | | $700.00 |
| Custom Mustang | 6206 | Open hood scoops | USA | M-YW | BL | GY | | | $700.00 |
| Custom Mustang | 6206 | Open hood scoops | USA | M-YW | BL | BR-L | | | $700.00 |
| Custom Mustang | 6206 | Open hood scoops | USA | M-YW | BL | BR-D | | | $700.00 |
| Custom Mustang | 6206 | Ribbed rear window | USA | M-YW | BL | WH | | | $550.00 |
| Custom Mustang | 6206 | Ribbed rear window | USA | M-YW | BL | BK | | | $550.00 |
| Custom Mustang | 6206 | Ribbed rear window | USA | M-YW | BL | GY | | | $550.00 |
| Custom Mustang | 6206 | Ribbed rear window | USA | M-YW | BL | BR-L | | | $550.00 |
| Custom Mustang | 6206 | Ribbed rear window | USA | M-YW | BL | BR-D | | | $550.00 |
| Custom Mustang | 6206 | | USA | M-YW-L | CL | WH | | | $200.00 |
| Custom Mustang | 6206 | | HK | M-YW-L | BL | WH | | | $200.00 |
| Custom Mustang | 6206 | | USA | M-YW-L | CL | BK | | | $180.00 |
| Custom Mustang | 6206 | | HK | M-YW-L | BL | BK | | | $180.00 |
| Custom Mustang | 6206 | | USA | M-YW-L | CL | GY | | | $180.00 |
| Custom Mustang | 6206 | | HK | M-YW-L | BL | GY | | | $180.00 |
| Custom Mustang | 6206 | | USA | M-YW-L | CL | BR-L | | | $180.00 |
| Custom Mustang | 6206 | | HK | M-YW-L | BL | BR-L | | | $180.00 |
| Custom Mustang | 6206 | | USA | M-YW-L | CL | BR-D | | | $180.00 |
| Custom Mustang | 6206 | | HK | M-YW-L | BL | BR-D | | | $180.00 |
| | | | | | | | | | |
| Custom T-Bird | 6207 | | USA | M-AQ | CL | WH | | | $80.00 |
| Custom T-Bird | 6207 | | USA | M-AQ | CL | WH | BK-RF | | $100.00 |
| Custom T-Bird | 6207 | | HK | M-AQ | BL | WH | | | $80.00 |
| Custom T-Bird | 6207 | | HK | M-AQ | BL | WH | BK-RF | | $100.00 |
| Custom T-Bird | 6207 | | USA | M-AQ | CL | BK | | | $70.00 |
| Custom T-Bird | 6207 | | USA | M-AQ | CL | BK | BK-RF | | $90.00 |
| Custom T-Bird | 6207 | | HK | M-AQ | BL | BK | | | $70.00 |
| Custom T-Bird | 6207 | | HK | M-AQ | BL | BK | BK-RF | | $90.00 |
| Custom T-Bird | 6207 | | USA | M-AQ | CL | GY | | | $70.00 |
| Custom T-Bird | 6207 | | USA | M-AQ | CL | GY | BK-RF | | $90.00 |
| Custom T-Bird | 6207 | | HK | M-AQ | BL | GY | | | $70.00 |
| Custom T-Bird | 6207 | | HK | M-AQ | BL | GY | BK-RF | | $90.00 |
| Custom T-Bird | 6207 | | USA | M-AQ | CL | BR-L | | | $70.00 |
| Custom T-Bird | 6207 | | USA | M-AQ | CL | BR-L | BK-RF | | $90.00 |
| Custom T-Bird | 6207 | | HK | M-AQ | BL | BR-L | | | $70.00 |
| Custom T-Bird | 6207 | | HK | M-AQ | BL | BR-L | BK-RF | | $90.00 |
| Custom T-Bird | 6207 | | USA | M-AQ | CL | BR-D | | | $70.00 |
| Custom T-Bird | 6207 | | USA | M-AQ | CL | BR-D | BK-RF | | $90.00 |
| Custom T-Bird | 6207 | | HK | M-AQ | BL | BR-D | | | $70.00 |
| Custom T-Bird | 6207 | | HK | M-AQ | BL | BR-D | BK-RF | | $90.00 |
| Custom T-Bird | 6207 | | USA | M-BL | CL | WH | | | $80.00 |
| Custom T-Bird | 6207 | | USA | M-BL | CL | WH | BK-RF | | $100.00 |
| Custom T-Bird | 6207 | | HK | M-BL | BL | WH | | | $80.00 |
| Custom T-Bird | 6207 | | HK | M-BL | BL | WH | BK-RF | | $100.00 |
| Custom T-Bird | 6207 | | USA | M-BL | CL | BK | | | $70.00 |
| Custom T-Bird | 6207 | | USA | M-BL | CL | BK | BK-RF | | $90.00 |
| Custom T-Bird | 6207 | | HK | M-BL | BL | BK | | | $70.00 |
| Custom T-Bird | 6207 | | HK | M-BL | BL | BK | BK-RF | | $90.00 |
| Custom T-Bird | 6207 | | USA | M-BL | CL | GY | | | $70.00 |

## 1968 Variations

| Name | Number | Casting | Country | Color | Windows | Interior | Paint | Other | Value |
|---|---|---|---|---|---|---|---|---|---|
| Custom T-Bird | 6207 | | USA | M-BL | CL | GY | BK-RF | | $90.00 |
| Custom T-Bird | 6207 | | HK | M-BL | BL | GY | | | $70.00 |
| Custom T-Bird | 6207 | | HK | M-BL | BL | GY | BK-RF | | $90.00 |
| Custom T-Bird | 6207 | | USA | M-BL | CL | BR-L | | | $70.00 |
| Custom T-Bird | 6207 | | USA | M-BL | CL | BR-L | BK-RF | | $90.00 |
| Custom T-Bird | 6207 | | HK | M-BL | BL | BR-L | | | $70.00 |
| Custom T-Bird | 6207 | | HK | M-BL | BL | BR-L | BK-RF | | $90.00 |
| Custom T-Bird | 6207 | | USA | M-BL | CL | BR-D | | | $70.00 |
| Custom T-Bird | 6207 | | USA | M-BL | CL | BR-D | BK-RF | | $90.00 |
| Custom T-Bird | 6207 | | HK | M-BL | BL | BR-D | | | $70.00 |
| Custom T-Bird | 6207 | | HK | M-BL | BL | BR-D | BK-RF | | $90.00 |
| Custom T-Bird | 6207 | | USA | M-BL-I | CL | WH | | | $130.00 |
| Custom T-Bird | 6207 | | USA | M-BL-I | CL | WH | BK-RF | | $150.00 |
| Custom T-Bird | 6207 | | HK | M-BL-I | BL | WH | | | $130.00 |
| Custom T-Bird | 6207 | | HK | M-BL-I | BL | WH | BK-RF | | $150.00 |
| Custom T-Bird | 6207 | | USA | M-BL-I | CL | BK | | | $120.00 |
| Custom T-Bird | 6207 | | USA | M-BL-I | CL | BK | BK-RF | | $140.00 |
| Custom T-Bird | 6207 | | HK | M-BL-I | BL | BK | | | $120.00 |
| Custom T-Bird | 6207 | | HK | M-BL-I | BL | BK | BK-RF | | $140.00 |
| Custom T-Bird | 6207 | | USA | M-BL-I | CL | GY | | | $120.00 |
| Custom T-Bird | 6207 | | USA | M-BL-I | CL | GY | BK-RF | | $140.00 |
| Custom T-Bird | 6207 | | HK | M-BL-I | BL | GY | | | $120.00 |
| Custom T-Bird | 6207 | | HK | M-BL-I | BL | GY | BK-RF | | $140.00 |
| Custom T-Bird | 6207 | | USA | M-BL-I | CL | BR-L | | | $120.00 |
| Custom T-Bird | 6207 | | USA | M-BL-I | CL | BR-L | BK-RF | | $140.00 |
| Custom T-Bird | 6207 | | HK | M-BL-I | BL | BR-L | | | $120.00 |
| Custom T-Bird | 6207 | | HK | M-BL-I | BL | BR-L | BK-RF | | $140.00 |
| Custom T-Bird | 6207 | | USA | M-BL-I | CL | BR-D | | | $120.00 |
| Custom T-Bird | 6207 | | USA | M-BL-I | CL | BR-D | BK-RF | | $140.00 |
| Custom T-Bird | 6207 | | HK | M-BL-I | BL | BR-D | | | $120.00 |
| Custom T-Bird | 6207 | | HK | M-BL-I | BL | BR-D | BK-RF | | $140.00 |
| Custom T-Bird | 6207 | | USA | M-BL-P | CL | WH | | | $110.00 |
| Custom T-Bird | 6207 | | USA | M-BL-P | CL | WH | BK-RF | | $130.00 |
| Custom T-Bird | 6207 | | HK | M-BL-P | BL | WH | | | $110.00 |
| Custom T-Bird | 6207 | | HK | M-BL-P | BL | WH | BK-RF | | $130.00 |
| Custom T-Bird | 6207 | | USA | M-BL-P | CL | BK | | | $100.00 |
| Custom T-Bird | 6207 | | USA | M-BL-P | CL | BK | BK-RF | | $120.00 |
| Custom T-Bird | 6207 | | HK | M-BL-P | BL | BK | | | $100.00 |
| Custom T-Bird | 6207 | | HK | M-BL-P | BL | BK | BK-RF | | $120.00 |
| Custom T-Bird | 6207 | | USA | M-BL-P | CL | GY | | | $100.00 |
| Custom T-Bird | 6207 | | USA | M-BL-P | CL | GY | BK-RF | | $120.00 |
| Custom T-Bird | 6207 | | HK | M-BL-P | BL | GY | | | $100.00 |
| Custom T-Bird | 6207 | | HK | M-BL-P | BL | GY | BK-RF | | $120.00 |
| Custom T-Bird | 6207 | | USA | M-BL-P | CL | BR-L | | | $100.00 |
| Custom T-Bird | 6207 | | USA | M-BL-P | CL | BR-L | BK-RF | | $120.00 |
| Custom T-Bird | 6207 | | HK | M-BL-P | BL | BR-L | | | $100.00 |
| Custom T-Bird | 6207 | | HK | M-BL-P | BL | BR-L | BK-RF | | $120.00 |
| Custom T-Bird | 6207 | | USA | M-BL-P | CL | BR-D | | | $100.00 |
| Custom T-Bird | 6207 | | USA | M-BL-P | CL | BR-D | BK-RF | | $120.00 |
| Custom T-Bird | 6207 | | HK | M-BL-P | BL | BR-D | | | $100.00 |
| Custom T-Bird | 6207 | | HK | M-BL-P | BL | BR-D | BK-RF | | $120.00 |
| Custom T-Bird | 6207 | | USA | M-BR-D | CL | WH | | | $100.00 |
| Custom T-Bird | 6207 | | USA | M-BR-D | CL | WH | BK-RF | | $120.00 |
| Custom T-Bird | 6207 | | HK | M-BR-D | BL | WH | | | $100.00 |
| Custom T-Bird | 6207 | | HK | M-BR-D | BL | WH | BK-RF | | $120.00 |
| Custom T-Bird | 6207 | | USA | M-BR-D | CL | BK | | | $90.00 |
| Custom T-Bird | 6207 | | USA | M-BR-D | CL | BK | BK-RF | | $110.00 |
| Custom T-Bird | 6207 | | HK | M-BR-D | BL | BK | | | $90.00 |
| Custom T-Bird | 6207 | | HK | M-BR-D | BL | BK | BK-RF | | $110.00 |
| Custom T-Bird | 6207 | | USA | M-BR-D | CL | GY | | | $90.00 |
| Custom T-Bird | 6207 | | USA | M-BR-D | CL | GY | BK-RF | | $110.00 |
| Custom T-Bird | 6207 | | HK | M-BR-D | BL | GY | | | $90.00 |
| Custom T-Bird | 6207 | | HK | M-BR-D | BL | GY | BK-RF | | $110.00 |
| Custom T-Bird | 6207 | | USA | M-BR-D | CL | BR-L | | | $90.00 |
| Custom T-Bird | 6207 | | USA | M-BR-D | CL | BR-L | BK-RF | | $110.00 |
| Custom T-Bird | 6207 | | HK | M-BR-D | BL | BR-L | | | $90.00 |
| Custom T-Bird | 6207 | | HK | M-BR-D | BL | BR-L | BK-RF | | $110.00 |
| Custom T-Bird | 6207 | | USA | M-BR-D | CL | BR-D | | | $90.00 |
| Custom T-Bird | 6207 | | USA | M-BR-D | CL | BR-D | BK-RF | | $110.00 |
| Custom T-Bird | 6207 | | HK | M-BR-D | BL | BR-D | | | $90.00 |
| Custom T-Bird | 6207 | | HK | M-BR-D | BL | BR-D | BK-RF | | $110.00 |
| Custom T-Bird | 6207 | | USA | M-BR-P | CL | WH | | | $90.00 |

## 1968 Variations

| Name | Number | Casting | Country | Color | Windows | Interior | Paint | Other | Value |
|---|---|---|---|---|---|---|---|---|---|
| Custom T-Bird | 6207 | | USA | M-BR-P | CL | WH | BK-RF | | $110.00 |
| Custom T-Bird | 6207 | | HK | M-BR-P | BL | WH | | | $90.00 |
| Custom T-Bird | 6207 | | HK | M-BR-P | BL | WH | BK-RF | | $110.00 |
| Custom T-Bird | 6207 | | USA | M-BR-P | CL | BK | | | $80.00 |
| Custom T-Bird | 6207 | | USA | M-BR-P | CL | BK | BK-RF | | $100.00 |
| Custom T-Bird | 6207 | | HK | M-BR-P | BL | BK | | | $80.00 |
| Custom T-Bird | 6207 | | HK | M-BR-P | BL | BK | BK-RF | | $100.00 |
| Custom T-Bird | 6207 | | USA | M-BR-P | CL | GY | | | $80.00 |
| Custom T-Bird | 6207 | | USA | M-BR-P | CL | GY | BK-RF | | $100.00 |
| Custom T-Bird | 6207 | | HK | M-BR-P | BL | GY | | | $80.00 |
| Custom T-Bird | 6207 | | HK | M-BR-P | BL | GY | BK-RF | | $100.00 |
| Custom T-Bird | 6207 | | USA | M-BR-P | CL | BR-L | | | $80.00 |
| Custom T-Bird | 6207 | | USA | M-BR-P | CL | BR-L | BK-RF | | $100.00 |
| Custom T-Bird | 6207 | | HK | M-BR-P | BL | BR-L | | | $80.00 |
| Custom T-Bird | 6207 | | HK | M-BR-P | BL | BR-L | BK-RF | | $100.00 |
| Custom T-Bird | 6207 | | USA | M-BR-P | CL | BR-D | | | $80.00 |
| Custom T-Bird | 6207 | | USA | M-BR-P | CL | BR-D | BK-RF | | $100.00 |
| Custom T-Bird | 6207 | | HK | M-BR-P | BL | BR-D | | | $80.00 |
| Custom T-Bird | 6207 | | HK | M-BR-P | BL | BR-D | BK-RF | | $100.00 |
| Custom T-Bird | 6207 | | USA | M-GD | CL | WH | | | $85.00 |
| Custom T-Bird | 6207 | | USA | M-GD | CL | WH | BK-RF | | $105.00 |
| Custom T-Bird | 6207 | | HK | M-GD | BL | WH | | | $85.00 |
| Custom T-Bird | 6207 | | HK | M-GD | BL | WH | BK-RF | | $105.00 |
| Custom T-Bird | 6207 | | USA | M-GD | CL | BK | | | $75.00 |
| Custom T-Bird | 6207 | | USA | M-GD | CL | BK | BK-RF | | $95.00 |
| Custom T-Bird | 6207 | | HK | M-GD | BL | BK | | | $75.00 |
| Custom T-Bird | 6207 | | HK | M-GD | BL | BK | BK-RF | | $95.00 |
| Custom T-Bird | 6207 | | USA | M-GD | CL | GY | | | $75.00 |
| Custom T-Bird | 6207 | | USA | M-GD | CL | GY | BK-RF | | $95.00 |
| Custom T-Bird | 6207 | | HK | M-GD | BL | GY | | | $75.00 |
| Custom T-Bird | 6207 | | HK | M-GD | BL | GY | BK-RF | | $95.00 |
| Custom T-Bird | 6207 | | USA | M-GD | CL | BR-L | | | $75.00 |
| Custom T-Bird | 6207 | | USA | M-GD | CL | BR-L | BK-RF | | $95.00 |
| Custom T-Bird | 6207 | | HK | M-GD | BL | BR-L | | | $75.00 |
| Custom T-Bird | 6207 | | HK | M-GD | BL | BR-L | BK-RF | | $95.00 |
| Custom T-Bird | 6207 | | USA | M-GD | CL | BR-D | | | $75.00 |
| Custom T-Bird | 6207 | | USA | M-GD | CL | BR-D | BK-RF | | $95.00 |
| Custom T-Bird | 6207 | | HK | M-GD | BL | BR-D | | | $75.00 |
| Custom T-Bird | 6207 | | HK | M-GD | BL | BR-D | BK-RF | | $95.00 |
| Custom T-Bird | 6207 | | USA | M-GR | CL | WH | | | $95.00 |
| Custom T-Bird | 6207 | | USA | M-GR | CL | WH | BK-RF | | $100.00 |
| Custom T-Bird | 6207 | | HK | M-GR | BL | WH | | | $80.00 |
| Custom T-Bird | 6207 | | HK | M-GR | BL | WH | BK-RF | | $100.00 |
| Custom T-Bird | 6207 | | USA | M-GR | CL | BK | | | $70.00 |
| Custom T-Bird | 6207 | | USA | M-GR | CL | BK | BK-RF | | $90.00 |
| Custom T-Bird | 6207 | | HK | M-GR | BL | BK | | | $70.00 |
| Custom T-Bird | 6207 | | HK | M-GR | BL | BK | BK-RF | | $90.00 |
| Custom T-Bird | 6207 | | USA | M-GR | CL | GY | | | $70.00 |
| Custom T-Bird | 6207 | | USA | M-GR | CL | GY | BK-RF | | $90.00 |
| Custom T-Bird | 6207 | | HK | M-GR | BL | GY | | | $70.00 |
| Custom T-Bird | 6207 | | HK | M-GR | BL | GY | BK-RF | | $90.00 |
| Custom T-Bird | 6207 | | USA | M-GR | CL | BR-L | | | $70.00 |
| Custom T-Bird | 6207 | | USA | M-GR | CL | BR-L | BK-RF | | $90.00 |
| Custom T-Bird | 6207 | | HK | M-GR | BL | BR-L | | | $70.00 |
| Custom T-Bird | 6207 | | HK | M-GR | BL | BR-L | BK-RF | | $90.00 |
| Custom T-Bird | 6207 | | USA | M-GR | CL | BR-D | | | $70.00 |
| Custom T-Bird | 6207 | | USA | M-GR | CL | BR-D | BK-RF | | $90.00 |
| Custom T-Bird | 6207 | | HK | M-GR | BL | BR-D | | | $70.00 |
| Custom T-Bird | 6207 | | HK | M-GR | BL | BR-D | BK-RF | | $90.00 |
| Custom T-Bird | 6207 | | USA | M-GR-E | CL | WH | | | $80.00 |
| Custom T-Bird | 6207 | | USA | M-GR-E | CL | WH | BK-RF | | $100.00 |
| Custom T-Bird | 6207 | | HK | M-GR-E | BL | WH | | | $80.00 |
| Custom T-Bird | 6207 | | HK | M-GR-E | BL | WH | BK-RF | | $100.00 |
| Custom T-Bird | 6207 | | USA | M-GR-E | CL | BK | | | $70.00 |
| Custom T-Bird | 6207 | | USA | M-GR-E | CL | BK | BK-RF | | $90.00 |
| Custom T-Bird | 6207 | | HK | M-GR-E | BL | BK | | | $70.00 |
| Custom T-Bird | 6207 | | HK | M-GR-E | BL | BK | BK-RF | | $90.00 |
| Custom T-Bird | 6207 | | USA | M-GR-E | CL | GY | | | $70.00 |
| Custom T-Bird | 6207 | | USA | M-GR-E | CL | GY | BK-RF | | $90.00 |
| Custom T-Bird | 6207 | | HK | M-GR-E | BL | GY | | | $70.00 |
| Custom T-Bird | 6207 | | HK | M-GR-E | BL | GY | BK-RF | | $90.00 |
| Custom T-Bird | 6207 | | USA | M-GR-E | CL | BR-L | | | $70.00 |

## 1968 Variations

| Name | Number | Casting | Country | Color | Windows | Interior | Paint | Other | Value |
|---|---|---|---|---|---|---|---|---|---|
| Custom T-Bird | 6207 | | USA | M-GR-E | CL | BR-L | BK-RF | | $90.00 |
| Custom T-Bird | 6207 | | HK | M-GR-E | BL | BR-L | | | $70.00 |
| Custom T-Bird | 6207 | | HK | M-GR-E | BL | BR-L | BK-RF | | $90.00 |
| Custom T-Bird | 6207 | | USA | M-GR-E | CL | BR-D | | | $70.00 |
| Custom T-Bird | 6207 | | USA | M-GR-E | CL | BR-D | BK-RF | | $90.00 |
| Custom T-Bird | 6207 | | HK | M-GR-E | BL | BR-D | | | $70.00 |
| Custom T-Bird | 6207 | | HK | M-GR-E | BL | BR-D | BK-RF | | $90.00 |
| Custom T-Bird | 6207 | | USA | M-GR-L | CL | WH | | | $140.00 |
| Custom T-Bird | 6207 | | USA | M-GR-L | CL | WH | BK-RF | | $160.00 |
| Custom T-Bird | 6207 | | HK | M-GR-L | BL | WH | | | $140.00 |
| Custom T-Bird | 6207 | | HK | M-GR-L | BL | WH | BK-RF | | $160.00 |
| Custom T-Bird | 6207 | | USA | M-GR-L | CL | BK | | | $130.00 |
| Custom T-Bird | 6207 | | USA | M-GR-L | CL | BK | BK-RF | | $150.00 |
| Custom T-Bird | 6207 | | HK | M-GR-L | BL | BK | | | $130.00 |
| Custom T-Bird | 6207 | | HK | M-GR-L | BL | BK | BK-RF | | $150.00 |
| Custom T-Bird | 6207 | | USA | M-GR-L | CL | GY | | | $130.00 |
| Custom T-Bird | 6207 | | USA | M-GR-L | CL | GY | BK-RF | | $150.00 |
| Custom T-Bird | 6207 | | HK | M-GR-L | BL | GY | | | $130.00 |
| Custom T-Bird | 6207 | | HK | M-GR-L | BL | GY | BK-RF | | $150.00 |
| Custom T-Bird | 6207 | | USA | M-GR-L | CL | BR-L | | | $130.00 |
| Custom T-Bird | 6207 | | USA | M-GR-L | CL | BR-L | BK-RF | | $150.00 |
| Custom T-Bird | 6207 | | HK | M-GR-L | BL | BR-L | | | $130.00 |
| Custom T-Bird | 6207 | | HK | M-GR-L | BL | BR-L | BK-RF | | $150.00 |
| Custom T-Bird | 6207 | | USA | M-GR-L | CL | BR-D | | | $130.00 |
| Custom T-Bird | 6207 | | USA | M-GR-L | CL | BR-D | BK-RF | | $150.00 |
| Custom T-Bird | 6207 | | HK | M-GR-L | BL | BR-D | | | $130.00 |
| Custom T-Bird | 6207 | | HK | M-GR-L | BL | BR-D | BK-RF | | $150.00 |
| Custom T-Bird | 6207 | | USA | M-GR-O | CL | WH | | | $90.00 |
| Custom T-Bird | 6207 | | USA | M-GR-O | CL | WH | BK-RF | | $110.00 |
| Custom T-Bird | 6207 | | HK | M-GR-O | BL | WH | | | $90.00 |
| Custom T-Bird | 6207 | | HK | M-GR-O | BL | WH | BK-RF | | $110.00 |
| Custom T-Bird | 6207 | | USA | M-GR-O | CL | BK | | | $80.00 |
| Custom T-Bird | 6207 | | USA | M-GR-O | CL | BK | BK-RF | | $100.00 |
| Custom T-Bird | 6207 | | HK | M-GR-O | BL | BK | | | $80.00 |
| Custom T-Bird | 6207 | | HK | M-GR-O | BL | BK | BK-RF | | $100.00 |
| Custom T-Bird | 6207 | | USA | M-GR-O | CL | GY | | | $80.00 |
| Custom T-Bird | 6207 | | USA | M-GR-O | CL | GY | BK-RF | | $100.00 |
| Custom T-Bird | 6207 | | HK | M-GR-O | BL | GY | | | $80.00 |
| Custom T-Bird | 6207 | | HK | M-GR-O | BL | GY | BK-RF | | $100.00 |
| Custom T-Bird | 6207 | | USA | M-GR-O | CL | BR-L | | | $80.00 |
| Custom T-Bird | 6207 | | USA | M-GR-O | CL | BR-L | BK-RF | | $100.00 |
| Custom T-Bird | 6207 | | HK | M-GR-O | BL | BR-L | | | $80.00 |
| Custom T-Bird | 6207 | | HK | M-GR-O | BL | BR-L | BK-RF | | $100.00 |
| Custom T-Bird | 6207 | | USA | M-GR-O | CL | BR-D | | | $80.00 |
| Custom T-Bird | 6207 | | USA | M-GR-O | CL | BR-D | BK-RF | | $100.00 |
| Custom T-Bird | 6207 | | HK | M-GR-O | BL | BR-D | | | $80.00 |
| Custom T-Bird | 6207 | | HK | M-GR-O | BL | BR-D | BK-RF | | $100.00 |
| Custom T-Bird | 6207 | | USA | M-MG | CL | WH | | | $130.00 |
| Custom T-Bird | 6207 | | USA | M-MG | CL | WH | BK-RF | | $150.00 |
| Custom T-Bird | 6207 | | HK | M-MG | BL | WH | | | $130.00 |
| Custom T-Bird | 6207 | | HK | M-MG | BL | WH | BK-RF | | $150.00 |
| Custom T-Bird | 6207 | | USA | M-MG | CL | BK | | | $120.00 |
| Custom T-Bird | 6207 | | USA | M-MG | CL | BK | BK-RF | | $140.00 |
| Custom T-Bird | 6207 | | HK | M-MG | BL | BK | | | $120.00 |
| Custom T-Bird | 6207 | | HK | M-MG | BL | BK | BK-RF | | $140.00 |
| Custom T-Bird | 6207 | | USA | M-MG | CL | GY | | | $120.00 |
| Custom T-Bird | 6207 | | USA | M-MG | CL | GY | BK-RF | | $140.00 |
| Custom T-Bird | 6207 | | HK | M-MG | BL | GY | | | $120.00 |
| Custom T-Bird | 6207 | | HK | M-MG | BL | GY | BK-RF | | $140.00 |
| Custom T-Bird | 6207 | | USA | M-MG | CL | BR-L | | | $120.00 |
| Custom T-Bird | 6207 | | USA | M-MG | CL | BR-L | BK-RF | | $140.00 |
| Custom T-Bird | 6207 | | HK | M-MG | BL | BR-L | | | $120.00 |
| Custom T-Bird | 6207 | | HK | M-MG | BL | BR-L | BK-RF | | $140.00 |
| Custom T-Bird | 6207 | | USA | M-MG | CL | BR-D | | | $120.00 |
| Custom T-Bird | 6207 | | USA | M-MG | CL | BR-D | BK-RF | | $140.00 |
| Custom T-Bird | 6207 | | HK | M-MG | BL | BR-D | | | $120.00 |
| Custom T-Bird | 6207 | | HK | M-MG | BL | BR-D | BK-RF | | $140.00 |
| Custom T-Bird | 6207 | | USA | M-OR | CL | WH | | | $80.00 |
| Custom T-Bird | 6207 | | USA | M-OR | CL | WH | BK-RF | | $100.00 |
| Custom T-Bird | 6207 | | HK | M-OR | BL | WH | | | $80.00 |
| Custom T-Bird | 6207 | | HK | M-OR | BL | WH | BK-RF | | $100.00 |
| Custom T-Bird | 6207 | | USA | M-OR | CL | BK | | | $70.00 |

## 1968 Variations

| Name | Number | Casting | Country | Color | Windows | Interior | Paint | Other | Value |
|---|---|---|---|---|---|---|---|---|---|
| Custom T-Bird | 6207 | | USA | M-OR | CL | BK | BK-RF | | $90.00 |
| Custom T-Bird | 6207 | | HK | M-OR | BL | BK | | | $70.00 |
| Custom T-Bird | 6207 | | HK | M-OR | BL | BK | BK-RF | | $90.00 |
| Custom T-Bird | 6207 | | USA | M-OR | CL | GY | | | $70.00 |
| Custom T-Bird | 6207 | | USA | M-OR | CL | GY | BK-RF | | $90.00 |
| Custom T-Bird | 6207 | | HK | M-OR | BL | GY | | | $70.00 |
| Custom T-Bird | 6207 | | HK | M-OR | BL | GY | BK-RF | | $90.00 |
| Custom T-Bird | 6207 | | USA | M-OR | CL | BR-L | | | $70.00 |
| Custom T-Bird | 6207 | | USA | M-OR | CL | BR-L | BK-RF | | $90.00 |
| Custom T-Bird | 6207 | | HK | M-OR | BL | BR-L | | | $70.00 |
| Custom T-Bird | 6207 | | HK | M-OR | BL | BR-L | BK-RF | | $90.00 |
| Custom T-Bird | 6207 | | USA | M-OR | CL | BR-D | | | $70.00 |
| Custom T-Bird | 6207 | | USA | M-OR | CL | BR-D | BK-RF | | $90.00 |
| Custom T-Bird | 6207 | | HK | M-OR | BL | BR-D | | | $70.00 |
| Custom T-Bird | 6207 | | HK | M-OR | BL | BR-D | BK-RF | | $90.00 |
| Custom T-Bird | 6207 | | USA | M-PK | CL | WH | | | $360.00 |
| Custom T-Bird | 6207 | | USA | M-PK | CL | WH | BK-RF | | $400.00 |
| Custom T-Bird | 6207 | | HK | M-PK | BL | WH | | | $360.00 |
| Custom T-Bird | 6207 | | HK | M-PK | BL | WH | BK-RF | | $400.00 |
| Custom T-Bird | 6207 | | USA | M-PK | CL | BK | | | $340.00 |
| Custom T-Bird | 6207 | | USA | M-PK | CL | BK | BK-RF | | $380.00 |
| Custom T-Bird | 6207 | | HK | M-PK | BL | BK | | | $340.00 |
| Custom T-Bird | 6207 | | HK | M-PK | BL | BK | BK-RF | | $380.00 |
| Custom T-Bird | 6207 | | USA | M-PK | CL | GY | | | $340.00 |
| Custom T-Bird | 6207 | | USA | M-PK | CL | GY | BK-RF | | $380.00 |
| Custom T-Bird | 6207 | | HK | M-PK | BL | GY | | | $340.00 |
| Custom T-Bird | 6207 | | HK | M-PK | BL | GY | BK-RF | | $380.00 |
| Custom T-Bird | 6207 | | USA | M-PK | CL | BR-L | | | $340.00 |
| Custom T-Bird | 6207 | | USA | M-PK | CL | BR-L | BK-RF | | $380.00 |
| Custom T-Bird | 6207 | | HK | M-PK | BL | BR-L | | | $340.00 |
| Custom T-Bird | 6207 | | HK | M-PK | BL | BR-L | BK-RF | | $380.00 |
| Custom T-Bird | 6207 | | USA | M-PK | CL | BR-D | | | $340.00 |
| Custom T-Bird | 6207 | | USA | M-PK | CL | BR-D | BK-RF | | $380.00 |
| Custom T-Bird | 6207 | | HK | M-PK | BL | BR-D | | | $340.00 |
| Custom T-Bird | 6207 | | HK | M-PK | BL | BR-D | BK-RF | | $380.00 |
| Custom T-Bird | 6207 | | USA | M-PK-H | CL | WH | | | $360.00 |
| Custom T-Bird | 6207 | | USA | M-PK-H | CL | WH | BK-RF | | $400.00 |
| Custom T-Bird | 6207 | | HK | M-PK-H | BL | WH | | | $360.00 |
| Custom T-Bird | 6207 | | HK | M-PK-H | BL | WH | BK-RF | | $400.00 |
| Custom T-Bird | 6207 | | USA | M-PK-H | CL | BK | | | $340.00 |
| Custom T-Bird | 6207 | | USA | M-PK-H | CL | BK | BK-RF | | $380.00 |
| Custom T-Bird | 6207 | | HK | M-PK-H | BL | BK | | | $340.00 |
| Custom T-Bird | 6207 | | HK | M-PK-H | BL | BK | BK-RF | | $380.00 |
| Custom T-Bird | 6207 | | USA | M-PK-H | CL | GY | | | $340.00 |
| Custom T-Bird | 6207 | | USA | M-PK-H | CL | GY | BK-RF | | $380.00 |
| Custom T-Bird | 6207 | | HK | M-PK-H | BL | GY | | | $340.00 |
| Custom T-Bird | 6207 | | HK | M-PK-H | BL | GY | BK-RF | | $380.00 |
| Custom T-Bird | 6207 | | USA | M-PK-H | CL | BR-L | | | $340.00 |
| Custom T-Bird | 6207 | | USA | M-PK-H | CL | BR-L | BK-RF | | $380.00 |
| Custom T-Bird | 6207 | | HK | M-PK-H | BL | BR-L | | | $340.00 |
| Custom T-Bird | 6207 | | HK | M-PK-H | BL | BR-L | BK-RF | | $380.00 |
| Custom T-Bird | 6207 | | USA | M-PK-H | CL | BR-D | | | $340.00 |
| Custom T-Bird | 6207 | | USA | M-PK-H | CL | BR-D | BK-RF | | $380.00 |
| Custom T-Bird | 6207 | | HK | M-PK-H | BL | BR-D | | | $340.00 |
| Custom T-Bird | 6207 | | HK | M-PK-H | BL | BR-D | BK-RF | | $380.00 |
| Custom T-Bird | 6207 | | USA | M-PK-S | CL | WH | | | $360.00 |
| Custom T-Bird | 6207 | | USA | M-PK-S | CL | WH | BK-RF | | $400.00 |
| Custom T-Bird | 6207 | | HK | M-PK-S | BL | WH | | | $360.00 |
| Custom T-Bird | 6207 | | HK | M-PK-S | BL | WH | BK-RF | | $400.00 |
| Custom T-Bird | 6207 | | USA | M-PK-S | CL | BK | | | $340.00 |
| Custom T-Bird | 6207 | | USA | M-PK-S | CL | BK | BK-RF | | $380.00 |
| Custom T-Bird | 6207 | | HK | M-PK-S | BL | BK | | | $340.00 |
| Custom T-Bird | 6207 | | HK | M-PK-S | BL | BK | BK-RF | | $380.00 |
| Custom T-Bird | 6207 | | USA | M-PK-S | CL | GY | | | $340.00 |
| Custom T-Bird | 6207 | | USA | M-PK-S | CL | GY | BK-RF | | $380.00 |
| Custom T-Bird | 6207 | | HK | M-PK-S | BL | GY | | | $340.00 |
| Custom T-Bird | 6207 | | HK | M-PK-S | BL | GY | BK-RF | | $380.00 |
| Custom T-Bird | 6207 | | USA | M-PK-S | CL | BR-L | | | $340.00 |
| Custom T-Bird | 6207 | | USA | M-PK-S | CL | BR-L | BK-RF | | $380.00 |
| Custom T-Bird | 6207 | | HK | M-PK-S | BL | BR-L | | | $340.00 |
| Custom T-Bird | 6207 | | HK | M-PK-S | BL | BR-L | BK-RF | | $380.00 |
| Custom T-Bird | 6207 | | USA | M-PK-S | CL | BR-D | | | $340.00 |

## 1968 Variations

| Name | Number | Casting | Country | Color | Windows | Interior | Paint | Other | Value |
|---|---|---|---|---|---|---|---|---|---|
| Custom T-Bird | 6207 | | USA | M-PK-S | CL | BR-D | BK-RF | | $380.00 |
| Custom T-Bird | 6207 | | HK | M-PK-S | BL | BR-D | | | $340.00 |
| Custom T-Bird | 6207 | | HK | M-PK-S | BL | BR-D | BK-RF | | $380.00 |
| Custom T-Bird | 6207 | | USA | M-PR | CL | WH | | | $240.00 |
| Custom T-Bird | 6207 | | USA | M-PR | CL | WH | BK-RF | | $280.00 |
| Custom T-Bird | 6207 | | HK | M-PR | BL | WH | | | $240.00 |
| Custom T-Bird | 6207 | | HK | M-PR | BL | WH | BK-RF | | $280.00 |
| Custom T-Bird | 6207 | | USA | M-PR | CL | BK | | | $220.00 |
| Custom T-Bird | 6207 | | USA | M-PR | CL | BK | BK-RF | | $260.00 |
| Custom T-Bird | 6207 | | HK | M-PR | BL | BK | | | $220.00 |
| Custom T-Bird | 6207 | | HK | M-PR | BL | BK | BK-RF | | $260.00 |
| Custom T-Bird | 6207 | | USA | M-PR | CL | GY | | | $220.00 |
| Custom T-Bird | 6207 | | USA | M-PR | CL | GY | BK-RF | | $260.00 |
| Custom T-Bird | 6207 | | HK | M-PR | BL | GY | | | $220.00 |
| Custom T-Bird | 6207 | | HK | M-PR | BL | GY | BK-RF | | $260.00 |
| Custom T-Bird | 6207 | | USA | M-PR | CL | BR-L | | | $220.00 |
| Custom T-Bird | 6207 | | USA | M-PR | CL | BR-L | BK-RF | | $260.00 |
| Custom T-Bird | 6207 | | HK | M-PR | BL | BR-L | | | $220.00 |
| Custom T-Bird | 6207 | | HK | M-PR | BL | BR-L | BK-RF | | $260.00 |
| Custom T-Bird | 6207 | | USA | M-PR | CL | BR-D | | | $220.00 |
| Custom T-Bird | 6207 | | USA | M-PR | CL | BR-D | BK-RF | | $260.00 |
| Custom T-Bird | 6207 | | HK | M-PR | BL | BR-D | | | $220.00 |
| Custom T-Bird | 6207 | | HK | M-PR | BL | BR-D | BK-RF | | $260.00 |
| Custom T-Bird | 6207 | | USA | M-RD | CL | WH | | | $80.00 |
| Custom T-Bird | 6207 | | USA | M-RD | CL | WH | BK-RF | | $100.00 |
| Custom T-Bird | 6207 | | HK | M-RD | BL | WH | | | $80.00 |
| Custom T-Bird | 6207 | | HK | M-RD | BL | WH | BK-RF | | $100.00 |
| Custom T-Bird | 6207 | | USA | M-RD | CL | BK | | | $70.00 |
| Custom T-Bird | 6207 | | USA | M-RD | CL | BK | BK-RF | | $90.00 |
| Custom T-Bird | 6207 | | HK | M-RD | BL | BK | | | $70.00 |
| Custom T-Bird | 6207 | | HK | M-RD | BL | BK | BK-RF | | $90.00 |
| Custom T-Bird | 6207 | | USA | M-RD | CL | GY | | | $70.00 |
| Custom T-Bird | 6207 | | USA | M-RD | CL | GY | BK-RF | | $90.00 |
| Custom T-Bird | 6207 | | HK | M-RD | BL | GY | | | $70.00 |
| Custom T-Bird | 6207 | | HK | M-RD | BL | GY | BK-RF | | $90.00 |
| Custom T-Bird | 6207 | | USA | M-RD | CL | BR-L | | | $70.00 |
| Custom T-Bird | 6207 | | USA | M-RD | CL | BR-L | BK-RF | | $90.00 |
| Custom T-Bird | 6207 | | HK | M-RD | BL | BR-L | | | $70.00 |
| Custom T-Bird | 6207 | | HK | M-RD | BL | BR-L | BK-RF | | $90.00 |
| Custom T-Bird | 6207 | | USA | M-RD | CL | BR-D | | | $70.00 |
| Custom T-Bird | 6207 | | USA | M-RD | CL | BR-D | BK-RF | | $90.00 |
| Custom T-Bird | 6207 | | HK | M-RD | BL | BR-D | | | $70.00 |
| Custom T-Bird | 6207 | | HK | M-RD | BL | BR-D | BK-RF | | $90.00 |
| Custom T-Bird | 6207 | | USA | M-RD-R | CL | WH | | | $100.00 |
| Custom T-Bird | 6207 | | USA | M-RD-R | CL | WH | BK-RF | | $120.00 |
| Custom T-Bird | 6207 | | HK | M-RD-R | BL | WH | | | $100.00 |
| Custom T-Bird | 6207 | | HK | M-RD-R | BL | WH | BK-RF | | $120.00 |
| Custom T-Bird | 6207 | | USA | M-RD-R | CL | BK | | | $90.00 |
| Custom T-Bird | 6207 | | USA | M-RD-R | CL | BK | BK-RF | | $110.00 |
| Custom T-Bird | 6207 | | HK | M-RD-R | BL | BK | | | $90.00 |
| Custom T-Bird | 6207 | | HK | M-RD-R | BL | BK | BK-RF | | $110.00 |
| Custom T-Bird | 6207 | | USA | M-RD-R | CL | GY | | | $90.00 |
| Custom T-Bird | 6207 | | USA | M-RD-R | CL | GY | BK-RF | | $110.00 |
| Custom T-Bird | 6207 | | HK | M-RD-R | BL | GY | | | $90.00 |
| Custom T-Bird | 6207 | | HK | M-RD-R | BL | GY | BK-RF | | $110.00 |
| Custom T-Bird | 6207 | | USA | M-RD-R | CL | BR-L | | | $90.00 |
| Custom T-Bird | 6207 | | USA | M-RD-R | CL | BR-L | BK-RF | | $110.00 |
| Custom T-Bird | 6207 | | HK | M-RD-R | BL | BR-L | | | $90.00 |
| Custom T-Bird | 6207 | | HK | M-RD-R | BL | BR-L | BK-RF | | $110.00 |
| Custom T-Bird | 6207 | | USA | M-RD-R | CL | BR-D | | | $90.00 |
| Custom T-Bird | 6207 | | USA | M-RD-R | CL | BR-D | BK-RF | | $110.00 |
| Custom T-Bird | 6207 | | HK | M-RD-R | BL | BR-D | | | $90.00 |
| Custom T-Bird | 6207 | | HK | M-RD-R | BL | BR-D | BK-RF | | $110.00 |
| Custom T-Bird | 6207 | | USA | M-YW | CL | WH | | | $100.00 |
| Custom T-Bird | 6207 | | USA | M-YW | CL | WH | BK-RF | | $120.00 |
| Custom T-Bird | 6207 | | HK | M-YW | BL | WH | | | $100.00 |
| Custom T-Bird | 6207 | | HK | M-YW | BL | WH | BK-RF | | $120.00 |
| Custom T-Bird | 6207 | | USA | M-YW | CL | BK | | | $90.00 |
| Custom T-Bird | 6207 | | USA | M-YW | CL | BK | BK-RF | | $110.00 |
| Custom T-Bird | 6207 | | HK | M-YW | BL | BK | | | $90.00 |
| Custom T-Bird | 6207 | | HK | M-YW | BL | BK | BK-RF | | $110.00 |
| Custom T-Bird | 6207 | | USA | M-YW | CL | GY | | | $90.00 |

## 1968 Variations

| Name | Number | Casting | Country | Color | Windows | Interior | Paint | Other | Value |
|---|---|---|---|---|---|---|---|---|---|
| Custom T-Bird | 6207 | | USA | M-YW | CL | GY | BK-RF | | $110.00 |
| Custom T-Bird | 6207 | | HK | M-YW | BL | GY | | | $90.00 |
| Custom T-Bird | 6207 | | HK | M-YW | BL | GY | BK-RF | | $110.00 |
| Custom T-Bird | 6207 | | USA | M-YW | CL | BR-L | | | $90.00 |
| Custom T-Bird | 6207 | | USA | M-YW | CL | BR-L | BK-RF | | $110.00 |
| Custom T-Bird | 6207 | | HK | M-YW | BL | BR-L | | | $90.00 |
| Custom T-Bird | 6207 | | HK | M-YW | BL | BR-L | BK-RF | | $110.00 |
| Custom T-Bird | 6207 | | USA | M-YW | CL | BR-D | | | $90.00 |
| Custom T-Bird | 6207 | | USA | M-YW | CL | BR-D | BK-RF | | $110.00 |
| Custom T-Bird | 6207 | | HK | M-YW | BL | BR-D | | | $90.00 |
| Custom T-Bird | 6207 | | HK | M-YW | BL | BR-D | BK-RF | | $110.00 |
| Custom T-Bird | 6207 | | USA | M-YW-L | CL | WH | | | $160.00 |
| Custom T-Bird | 6207 | | USA | M-YW-L | CL | WH | BK-RF | | $180.00 |
| Custom T-Bird | 6207 | | HK | M-YW-L | BL | WH | | | $160.00 |
| Custom T-Bird | 6207 | | HK | M-YW-L | BL | WH | BK-RF | | $180.00 |
| Custom T-Bird | 6207 | | USA | M-YW-L | CL | BK | | | $150.00 |
| Custom T-Bird | 6207 | | USA | M-YW-L | CL | BK | BK-RF | | $170.00 |
| Custom T-Bird | 6207 | | HK | M-YW-L | BL | BK | | | $150.00 |
| Custom T-Bird | 6207 | | HK | M-YW-L | BL | BK | BK-RF | | $170.00 |
| Custom T-Bird | 6207 | | USA | M-YW-L | CL | GY | | | $150.00 |
| Custom T-Bird | 6207 | | USA | M-YW-L | CL | GY | BK-RF | | $170.00 |
| Custom T-Bird | 6207 | | HK | M-YW-L | BL | GY | | | $150.00 |
| Custom T-Bird | 6207 | | HK | M-YW-L | BL | GY | BK-RF | | $170.00 |
| Custom T-Bird | 6207 | | USA | M-YW-L | CL | BR-L | | | $150.00 |
| Custom T-Bird | 6207 | | USA | M-YW-L | CL | BR-L | BK-RF | | $170.00 |
| Custom T-Bird | 6207 | | HK | M-YW-L | BL | BR-L | | | $150.00 |
| Custom T-Bird | 6207 | | HK | M-YW-L | BL | BR-L | BK-RF | | $170.00 |
| Custom T-Bird | 6207 | | USA | M-YW-L | CL | BR-D | | | $150.00 |
| Custom T-Bird | 6207 | | USA | M-YW-L | CL | BR-D | BK-RF | | $170.00 |
| Custom T-Bird | 6207 | | HK | M-YW-L | BL | BR-D | | | $150.00 |
| Custom T-Bird | 6207 | | HK | M-YW-L | BL | BR-D | BK-RF | | $170.00 |
| Custom Camaro | 6208 | | USA | E-MG | CL | WH | | | $1,800.00 |
| Custom Camaro | 6208 | | HK | E-MG | BL | WH | | | $1,800.00 |
| Custom Camaro | 6208 | | USA | E-MG | CL | BK | | | $1,600.00 |
| Custom Camaro | 6208 | | HK | E-MG | BL | BK | | | $1,600.00 |
| Custom Camaro | 6208 | | USA | E-MG | CL | GY | | | $1,600.00 |
| Custom Camaro | 6208 | | HK | E-MG | BL | GY | | | $1,600.00 |
| Custom Camaro | 6208 | | USA | E-MG | CL | BR-L | | | $1,600.00 |
| Custom Camaro | 6208 | | HK | E-MG | BL | BR-L | | | $1,600.00 |
| Custom Camaro | 6208 | | USA | E-MG | CL | BR-D | | | $1,600.00 |
| Custom Camaro | 6208 | | HK | E-MG | BL | BR-D | | | $1,600.00 |
| Custom Camaro | 6208 | | USA | E-WH | CL | WH | | | $2,500.00 |
| Custom Camaro | 6208 | | HK | E-WH | BL | WH | | | $2,500.00 |
| Custom Camaro | 6208 | | USA | E-WH | CL | BK | | | $2,000.00 |
| Custom Camaro | 6208 | | HK | E-WH | BL | BK | | | $2,000.00 |
| Custom Camaro | 6208 | | USA | E-WH | CL | GY | | | $2,000.00 |
| Custom Camaro | 6208 | | HK | E-WH | BL | GY | | | $2,000.00 |
| Custom Camaro | 6208 | | USA | E-WH | CL | BR-L | | | $2,000.00 |
| Custom Camaro | 6208 | | HK | E-WH | BL | BR-L | | | $2,000.00 |
| Custom Camaro | 6208 | | USA | E-WH | CL | BR-D | | | $2,000.00 |
| Custom Camaro | 6208 | | HK | E-WH | BL | BR-D | | | $2,000.00 |
| Custom Camaro | 6208 | | USA | M-AQ | CL | WH | | | $120.00 |
| Custom Camaro | 6208 | | USA | M-AQ | CL | WH | BK-RF | | $140.00 |
| Custom Camaro | 6208 | | HK | M-AQ | BL | WH | | | $120.00 |
| Custom Camaro | 6208 | | HK | M-AQ | BL | WH | BK-RF | | $140.00 |
| Custom Camaro | 6208 | | USA | M-AQ | CL | BK | | | $110.00 |
| Custom Camaro | 6208 | | USA | M-AQ | CL | BK | BK-RF | | $130.00 |
| Custom Camaro | 6208 | | HK | M-AQ | BL | BK | | | $110.00 |
| Custom Camaro | 6208 | | HK | M-AQ | BL | BK | BK-RF | | $130.00 |
| Custom Camaro | 6208 | | USA | M-AQ | CL | GY | | | $110.00 |
| Custom Camaro | 6208 | | USA | M-AQ | CL | GY | BK-RF | | $130.00 |
| Custom Camaro | 6208 | | HK | M-AQ | BL | GY | | | $110.00 |
| Custom Camaro | 6208 | | HK | M-AQ | BL | GY | BK-RF | | $130.00 |
| Custom Camaro | 6208 | | USA | M-AQ | CL | BR-L | | | $110.00 |
| Custom Camaro | 6208 | | USA | M-AQ | CL | BR-L | BK-RF | | $130.00 |
| Custom Camaro | 6208 | | HK | M-AQ | BL | BR-L | | | $110.00 |
| Custom Camaro | 6208 | | HK | M-AQ | BL | BR-L | BK-RF | | $130.00 |
| Custom Camaro | 6208 | | USA | M-AQ | CL | BR-D | | | $110.00 |
| Custom Camaro | 6208 | | USA | M-AQ | CL | BR-D | BK-RF | | $130.00 |
| Custom Camaro | 6208 | | HK | M-AQ | BL | BR-D | | | $110.00 |

## 1968 Variations

| Name | Number | Casting | Country | Color | Windows | Interior | Paint | Other | Value |
|---|---|---|---|---|---|---|---|---|---|
| Custom Camaro | 6208 | | HK | M-AQ | BL | BR-D | BK-RF | | $130.00 |
| Custom Camaro | 6208 | | USA | M-BL | CL | WH | | | $85.00 |
| Custom Camaro | 6208 | | USA | M-BL | CL | WH | BK-RF | | $105.00 |
| Custom Camaro | 6208 | | HK | M-BL | BL | WH | | | $85.00 |
| Custom Camaro | 6208 | | HK | M-BL | BL | WH | BK-RF | | $105.00 |
| Custom Camaro | 6208 | | USA | M-BL | CL | BK | | | $75.00 |
| Custom Camaro | 6208 | | USA | M-BL | CL | BK | BK-RF | | $95.00 |
| Custom Camaro | 6208 | | HK | M-BL | BL | BK | | | $75.00 |
| Custom Camaro | 6208 | | HK | M-BL | BL | BK | BK-RF | | $95.00 |
| Custom Camaro | 6208 | | USA | M-BL | CL | GY | | | $75.00 |
| Custom Camaro | 6208 | | USA | M-BL | CL | GY | BK-RF | | $95.00 |
| Custom Camaro | 6208 | | HK | M-BL | BL | GY | | | $75.00 |
| Custom Camaro | 6208 | | HK | M-BL | BL | GY | BK-RF | | $95.00 |
| Custom Camaro | 6208 | | USA | M-BL | CL | BL | | | $75.00 |
| Custom Camaro | 6208 | | USA | M-BL | CL | BL | BK-RF | | $95.00 |
| Custom Camaro | 6208 | | HK | M-BL | BL | BL | | | $75.00 |
| Custom Camaro | 6208 | | HK | M-BL | BL | BL | BK-RF | | $95.00 |
| Custom Camaro | 6208 | | USA | M-BL | CL | BR-L | | | $75.00 |
| Custom Camaro | 6208 | | USA | M-BL | CL | BR-L | BK-RF | | $95.00 |
| Custom Camaro | 6208 | | HK | M-BL | BL | BR-L | | | $75.00 |
| Custom Camaro | 6208 | | HK | M-BL | BL | BR-L | BK-RF | | $95.00 |
| Custom Camaro | 6208 | | USA | M-BL | CL | BR-D | | | $75.00 |
| Custom Camaro | 6208 | | USA | M-BL | CL | BR-D | BK-RF | | $95.00 |
| Custom Camaro | 6208 | | HK | M-BL | BL | BR-D | | | $75.00 |
| Custom Camaro | 6208 | | HK | M-BL | BL | BR-D | BK-RF | | $95.00 |
| Custom Camaro | 6208 | | USA | M-BL-I | CL | WH | | | $140.00 |
| Custom Camaro | 6208 | | USA | M-BL-I | CL | WH | BK-RF | | $160.00 |
| Custom Camaro | 6208 | | HK | M-BL-I | BL | WH | | | $140.00 |
| Custom Camaro | 6208 | | HK | M-BL-I | BL | WH | BK-RF | | $160.00 |
| Custom Camaro | 6208 | | USA | M-BL-I | CL | BK | | | $130.00 |
| Custom Camaro | 6208 | | USA | M-BL-I | CL | BK | BK-RF | | $150.00 |
| Custom Camaro | 6208 | | HK | M-BL-I | BL | BK | | | $130.00 |
| Custom Camaro | 6208 | | HK | M-BL-I | BL | BK | BK-RF | | $150.00 |
| Custom Camaro | 6208 | | USA | M-BL-I | CL | GY | | | $130.00 |
| Custom Camaro | 6208 | | USA | M-BL-I | CL | GY | BK-RF | | $150.00 |
| Custom Camaro | 6208 | | HK | M-BL-I | BL | GY | | | $130.00 |
| Custom Camaro | 6208 | | HK | M-BL-I | BL | GY | BK-RF | | $150.00 |
| Custom Camaro | 6208 | | USA | M-BL-I | CL | BR-L | | | $130.00 |
| Custom Camaro | 6208 | | USA | M-BL-I | CL | BR-L | BK-RF | | $150.00 |
| Custom Camaro | 6208 | | HK | M-BL-I | BL | BR-L | | | $130.00 |
| Custom Camaro | 6208 | | HK | M-BL-I | BL | BR-L | BK-RF | | $150.00 |
| Custom Camaro | 6208 | | USA | M-BL-I | CL | BR-D | | | $130.00 |
| Custom Camaro | 6208 | | USA | M-BL-I | CL | BR-D | BK-RF | | $150.00 |
| Custom Camaro | 6208 | | HK | M-BL-I | BL | BR-D | | | $130.00 |
| Custom Camaro | 6208 | | HK | M-BL-I | BL | BR-D | BK-RF | | $150.00 |
| Custom Camaro | 6208 | | USA | M-BL-P | CL | WH | | | $120.00 |
| Custom Camaro | 6208 | | USA | M-BL-P | CL | WH | BK-RF | | $140.00 |
| Custom Camaro | 6208 | | HK | M-BL-P | BL | WH | | | $120.00 |
| Custom Camaro | 6208 | | HK | M-BL-P | BL | WH | BK-RF | | $140.00 |
| Custom Camaro | 6208 | | USA | M-BL-P | CL | BK | | | $110.00 |
| Custom Camaro | 6208 | | USA | M-BL-P | CL | BK | BK-RF | | $130.00 |
| Custom Camaro | 6208 | | HK | M-BL-P | BL | BK | | | $110.00 |
| Custom Camaro | 6208 | | HK | M-BL-P | BL | BK | BK-RF | | $130.00 |
| Custom Camaro | 6208 | | USA | M-BL-P | CL | GY | | | $110.00 |
| Custom Camaro | 6208 | | USA | M-BL-P | CL | GY | BK-RF | | $130.00 |
| Custom Camaro | 6208 | | HK | M-BL-P | BL | GY | | | $110.00 |
| Custom Camaro | 6208 | | HK | M-BL-P | BL | GY | BK-RF | | $130.00 |
| Custom Camaro | 6208 | | USA | M-BL-P | CL | BR-L | | | $110.00 |
| Custom Camaro | 6208 | | USA | M-BL-P | CL | BR-L | BK-RF | | $130.00 |
| Custom Camaro | 6208 | | HK | M-BL-P | BL | BR-L | | | $110.00 |
| Custom Camaro | 6208 | | HK | M-BL-P | BL | BR-L | BK-RF | | $130.00 |
| Custom Camaro | 6208 | | USA | M-BL-P | CL | BR-D | | | $110.00 |
| Custom Camaro | 6208 | | USA | M-BL-P | CL | BR-D | BK-RF | | $130.00 |
| Custom Camaro | 6208 | | HK | M-BL-P | BL | BR-D | | | $110.00 |
| Custom Camaro | 6208 | | HK | M-BL-P | BL | BR-D | BK-RF | | $130.00 |
| Custom Camaro | 6208 | | USA | M-BR-D | CL | WH | | | $120.00 |
| Custom Camaro | 6208 | | USA | M-BR-D | CL | WH | BK-RF | | $140.00 |
| Custom Camaro | 6208 | | HK | M-BR-D | BL | WH | | | $120.00 |
| Custom Camaro | 6208 | | HK | M-BR-D | BL | WH | BK-RF | | $140.00 |
| Custom Camaro | 6208 | | USA | M-BR-D | CL | BK | | | $110.00 |
| Custom Camaro | 6208 | | USA | M-BR-D | CL | BK | BK-RF | | $130.00 |
| Custom Camaro | 6208 | | HK | M-BR-D | BL | BK | | | $110.00 |

## 1968 Variations

| Name | Number | Casting | Country | Color | Windows | Interior | Paint | Other | Value |
|---|---|---|---|---|---|---|---|---|---|
| Custom Camaro | 6208 | | HK | M-BR-D | BL | BK | BK-RF | | $130.00 |
| Custom Camaro | 6208 | | USA | M-BR-D | CL | GY | | | $110.00 |
| Custom Camaro | 6208 | | USA | M-BR-D | CL | GY | BK-RF | | $130.00 |
| Custom Camaro | 6208 | | HK | M-BR-D | BL | GY | | | $110.00 |
| Custom Camaro | 6208 | | HK | M-BR-D | BL | GY | BK-RF | | $130.00 |
| Custom Camaro | 6208 | | USA | M-BR-D | CL | BR-L | | | $110.00 |
| Custom Camaro | 6208 | | USA | M-BR-D | CL | BR-L | BK-RF | | $130.00 |
| Custom Camaro | 6208 | | HK | M-BR-D | BL | BR-L | | | $110.00 |
| Custom Camaro | 6208 | | HK | M-BR-D | BL | BR-L | BK-RF | | $130.00 |
| Custom Camaro | 6208 | | USA | M-BR-D | CL | BR-D | | | $110.00 |
| Custom Camaro | 6208 | | USA | M-BR-D | CL | BR-D | BK-RF | | $130.00 |
| Custom Camaro | 6208 | | HK | M-BR-D | BL | BR-D | | | $110.00 |
| Custom Camaro | 6208 | | HK | M-BR-D | BL | BR-D | BK-RF | | $130.00 |
| Custom Camaro | 6208 | | USA | M-BR-P | CL | WH | | | $95.00 |
| Custom Camaro | 6208 | | USA | M-BR-P | CL | WH | BK-RF | | $100.00 |
| Custom Camaro | 6208 | | HK | M-BR-P | BL | WH | | | $95.00 |
| Custom Camaro | 6208 | | HK | M-BR-P | BL | WH | BK-RF | | $115.00 |
| Custom Camaro | 6208 | | USA | M-BR-P | CL | BK | | | $85.00 |
| Custom Camaro | 6208 | | USA | M-BR-P | CL | BK | BK-RF | | $105.00 |
| Custom Camaro | 6208 | | HK | M-BR-P | BL | BK | | | $85.00 |
| Custom Camaro | 6208 | | HK | M-BR-P | BL | BK | BK-RF | | $105.00 |
| Custom Camaro | 6208 | | USA | M-BR-P | CL | GY | | | $85.00 |
| Custom Camaro | 6208 | | USA | M-BR-P | CL | GY | BK-RF | | $105.00 |
| Custom Camaro | 6208 | | HK | M-BR-P | BL | GY | | | $85.00 |
| Custom Camaro | 6208 | | HK | M-BR-P | BL | GY | BK-RF | | $105.00 |
| Custom Camaro | 6208 | | USA | M-BR-P | CL | BR-L | | | $85.00 |
| Custom Camaro | 6208 | | USA | M-BR-P | CL | BR-L | BK-RF | | $105.00 |
| Custom Camaro | 6208 | | HK | M-BR-P | BL | BR-L | | | $85.00 |
| Custom Camaro | 6208 | | HK | M-BR-P | BL | BR-L | BK-RF | | $105.00 |
| Custom Camaro | 6208 | | USA | M-BR-P | CL | BR-D | | | $85.00 |
| Custom Camaro | 6208 | | USA | M-BR-P | CL | BR-D | BK-RF | | $105.00 |
| Custom Camaro | 6208 | | HK | M-BR-P | BL | BR-D | | | $85.00 |
| Custom Camaro | 6208 | | HK | M-BR-P | BL | BR-D | BK-RF | | $105.00 |
| Custom Camaro | 6208 | | USA | M-GD | CL | WH | | | $95.00 |
| Custom Camaro | 6208 | | USA | M-GD | CL | WH | BK-RF | | $115.00 |
| Custom Camaro | 6208 | | HK | M-GD | BL | WH | | | $95.00 |
| Custom Camaro | 6208 | | HK | M-GD | BL | WH | BK-RF | | $115.00 |
| Custom Camaro | 6208 | | USA | M-GD | CL | BK | | | $85.00 |
| Custom Camaro | 6208 | | USA | M-GD | CL | BK | BK-RF | | $105.00 |
| Custom Camaro | 6208 | | HK | M-GD | BL | BK | | | $85.00 |
| Custom Camaro | 6208 | | HK | M-GD | BL | BK | BK-RF | | $105.00 |
| Custom Camaro | 6208 | | USA | M-GD | CL | GY | | | $85.00 |
| Custom Camaro | 6208 | | USA | M-GD | CL | GY | BK-RF | | $105.00 |
| Custom Camaro | 6208 | | HK | M-GD | BL | GY | | | $85.00 |
| Custom Camaro | 6208 | | HK | M-GD | BL | GY | BK-RF | | $105.00 |
| Custom Camaro | 6208 | | USA | M-GD | CL | BR-L | | | $85.00 |
| Custom Camaro | 6208 | | USA | M-GD | CL | BR-L | BK-RF | | $105.00 |
| Custom Camaro | 6208 | | HK | M-GD | BL | BR-L | | | $85.00 |
| Custom Camaro | 6208 | | HK | M-GD | BL | BR-L | BK-RF | | $105.00 |
| Custom Camaro | 6208 | | USA | M-GD | CL | BR-D | | | $85.00 |
| Custom Camaro | 6208 | | USA | M-GD | CL | BR-D | BK-RF | | $105.00 |
| Custom Camaro | 6208 | | HK | M-GD | BL | BR-D | | | $85.00 |
| Custom Camaro | 6208 | | HK | M-GD | BL | BR-D | BK-RF | | $105.00 |
| Custom Camaro | 6208 | | USA | M-GR | CL | WH | | | $85.00 |
| Custom Camaro | 6208 | | USA | M-GR | CL | WH | BK-RF | | $105.00 |
| Custom Camaro | 6208 | | HK | M-GR | BL | WH | | | $85.00 |
| Custom Camaro | 6208 | | HK | M-GR | BL | WH | BK-RF | | $105.00 |
| Custom Camaro | 6208 | | USA | M-GR | CL | BK | | | $75.00 |
| Custom Camaro | 6208 | | USA | M-GR | CL | BK | BK-RF | | $95.00 |
| Custom Camaro | 6208 | | HK | M-GR | BL | BK | | | $75.00 |
| Custom Camaro | 6208 | | HK | M-GR | BL | BK | BK-RF | | $95.00 |
| Custom Camaro | 6208 | | USA | M-GR | CL | GY | | | $75.00 |
| Custom Camaro | 6208 | | USA | M-GR | CL | GY | BK-RF | | $95.00 |
| Custom Camaro | 6208 | | HK | M-GR | BL | GY | | | $75.00 |
| Custom Camaro | 6208 | | HK | M-GR | BL | GY | BK-RF | | $95.00 |
| Custom Camaro | 6208 | | USA | M-GR | CL | BR-L | | | $75.00 |
| Custom Camaro | 6208 | | USA | M-GR | CL | BR-L | BK-RF | | $95.00 |
| Custom Camaro | 6208 | | HK | M-GR | BL | BR-L | | | $75.00 |
| Custom Camaro | 6208 | | HK | M-GR | BL | BR-L | BK-RF | | $95.00 |
| Custom Camaro | 6208 | | USA | M-GR | CL | BR-D | | | $75.00 |
| Custom Camaro | 6208 | | USA | M-GR | CL | BR-D | BK-RF | | $95.00 |
| Custom Camaro | 6208 | | HK | M-GR | BL | BR-D | | | $75.00 |

## 1968 Variations

| Name | Number | Casting | Country | Color | Windows | Interior | Paint | Other | Value |
|---|---|---|---|---|---|---|---|---|---|
| Custom Camaro | 6208 | | HK | M-GR | BL | BR-D | BK-RF | | $95.00 |
| Custom Camaro | 6208 | | USA | M-GR-E | CL | WH | | | $100.00 |
| Custom Camaro | 6208 | | USA | M-GR-E | CL | WH | BK-RF | | $110.00 |
| Custom Camaro | 6208 | | HK | M-GR-E | BL | WH | | | $90.00 |
| Custom Camaro | 6208 | | HK | M-GR-E | BL | WH | BK-RF | | $110.00 |
| Custom Camaro | 6208 | | USA | M-GR-E | CL | BK | | | $80.00 |
| Custom Camaro | 6208 | | USA | M-GR-E | CL | BK | BK-RF | | $100.00 |
| Custom Camaro | 6208 | | HK | M-GR-E | BL | BK | | | $80.00 |
| Custom Camaro | 6208 | | HK | M-GR-E | BL | BK | BK-RF | | $100.00 |
| Custom Camaro | 6208 | | USA | M-GR-E | CL | GY | | | $80.00 |
| Custom Camaro | 6208 | | USA | M-GR-E | CL | GY | BK-RF | | $100.00 |
| Custom Camaro | 6208 | | HK | M-GR-E | BL | GY | | | $80.00 |
| Custom Camaro | 6208 | | HK | M-GR-E | BL | GY | BK-RF | | $100.00 |
| Custom Camaro | 6208 | | USA | M-GR-E | CL | BR-L | | | $80.00 |
| Custom Camaro | 6208 | | USA | M-GR-E | CL | BR-L | BK-RF | | $100.00 |
| Custom Camaro | 6208 | | HK | M-GR-E | BL | BR-L | | | $80.00 |
| Custom Camaro | 6208 | | HK | M-GR-E | BL | BR-L | BK-RF | | $100.00 |
| Custom Camaro | 6208 | | USA | M-GR-E | CL | BR-D | | | $80.00 |
| Custom Camaro | 6208 | | USA | M-GR-E | CL | BR-D | BK-RF | | $100.00 |
| Custom Camaro | 6208 | | HK | M-GR-E | BL | BR-D | | | $80.00 |
| Custom Camaro | 6208 | | HK | M-GR-E | BL | BR-D | BK-RF | | $100.00 |
| Custom Camaro | 6208 | | USA | M-GR-L | CL | WH | | | $140.00 |
| Custom Camaro | 6208 | | USA | M-GR-L | CL | WH | BK-RF | | $160.00 |
| Custom Camaro | 6208 | | HK | M-GR-L | BL | WH | | | $140.00 |
| Custom Camaro | 6208 | | HK | M-GR-L | BL | WH | BK-RF | | $160.00 |
| Custom Camaro | 6208 | | USA | M-GR-L | CL | BK | | | $130.00 |
| Custom Camaro | 6208 | | USA | M-GR-L | CL | BK | BK-RF | | $150.00 |
| Custom Camaro | 6208 | | HK | M-GR-L | BL | BK | | | $130.00 |
| Custom Camaro | 6208 | | HK | M-GR-L | BL | BK | BK-RF | | $150.00 |
| Custom Camaro | 6208 | | USA | M-GR-L | CL | GY | | | $130.00 |
| Custom Camaro | 6208 | | USA | M-GR-L | CL | GY | BK-RF | | $150.00 |
| Custom Camaro | 6208 | | HK | M-GR-L | BL | GY | | | $130.00 |
| Custom Camaro | 6208 | | HK | M-GR-L | BL | GY | BK-RF | | $150.00 |
| Custom Camaro | 6208 | | USA | M-GR-L | CL | BR-L | | | $130.00 |
| Custom Camaro | 6208 | | USA | M-GR-L | CL | BR-L | BK-RF | | $150.00 |
| Custom Camaro | 6208 | | HK | M-GR-L | BL | BR-L | | | $130.00 |
| Custom Camaro | 6208 | | HK | M-GR-L | BL | BR-L | BK-RF | | $150.00 |
| Custom Camaro | 6208 | | USA | M-GR-L | CL | BR-D | | | $130.00 |
| Custom Camaro | 6208 | | USA | M-GR-L | CL | BR-D | BK-RF | | $150.00 |
| Custom Camaro | 6208 | | HK | M-GR-L | BL | BR-D | | | $130.00 |
| Custom Camaro | 6208 | | HK | M-GR-L | BL | BR-D | BK-RF | | $150.00 |
| Custom Camaro | 6208 | | USA | M-GR-O | CL | WH | | | $160.00 |
| Custom Camaro | 6208 | | USA | M-GR-O | CL | WH | BK-RF | | $200.00 |
| Custom Camaro | 6208 | | HK | M-GR-O | BL | WH | | | $160.00 |
| Custom Camaro | 6208 | | HK | M-GR-O | BL | WH | BK-RF | | $200.00 |
| Custom Camaro | 6208 | | USA | M-GR-O | CL | BK | | | $140.00 |
| Custom Camaro | 6208 | | USA | M-GR-O | CL | BK | BK-RF | | $180.00 |
| Custom Camaro | 6208 | | HK | M-GR-O | BL | BK | | | $140.00 |
| Custom Camaro | 6208 | | HK | M-GR-O | BL | BK | BK-RF | | $180.00 |
| Custom Camaro | 6208 | | USA | M-GR-O | CL | GY | | | $140.00 |
| Custom Camaro | 6208 | | USA | M-GR-O | CL | GY | BK-RF | | $180.00 |
| Custom Camaro | 6208 | | HK | M-GR-O | BL | GY | | | $140.00 |
| Custom Camaro | 6208 | | HK | M-GR-O | BL | GY | BK-RF | | $180.00 |
| Custom Camaro | 6208 | | USA | M-GR-O | CL | BR-L | | | $140.00 |
| Custom Camaro | 6208 | | USA | M-GR-O | CL | BR-L | BK-RF | | $180.00 |
| Custom Camaro | 6208 | | HK | M-GR-O | BL | BR-L | | | $140.00 |
| Custom Camaro | 6208 | | HK | M-GR-O | BL | BR-L | BK-RF | | $180.00 |
| Custom Camaro | 6208 | | USA | M-GR-O | CL | BR-D | | | $140.00 |
| Custom Camaro | 6208 | | USA | M-GR-O | CL | BR-D | BK-RF | | $180.00 |
| Custom Camaro | 6208 | | HK | M-GR-O | BL | BR-D | | | $140.00 |
| Custom Camaro | 6208 | | HK | M-GR-O | BL | BR-D | BK-RF | | $180.00 |
| Custom Camaro | 6208 | | USA | M-OR | CL | WH | | | $160.00 |
| Custom Camaro | 6208 | | USA | M-OR | CL | WH | BK-RF | | $200.00 |
| Custom Camaro | 6208 | | HK | M-OR | BL | WH | | | $160.00 |
| Custom Camaro | 6208 | | HK | M-OR | BL | WH | BK-RF | | $200.00 |
| Custom Camaro | 6208 | | USA | M-OR | CL | BK | | | $140.00 |
| Custom Camaro | 6208 | | USA | M-OR | CL | BK | BK-RF | | $180.00 |
| Custom Camaro | 6208 | | HK | M-OR | BL | BK | | | $140.00 |
| Custom Camaro | 6208 | | HK | M-OR | BL | BK | BK-RF | | $180.00 |
| Custom Camaro | 6208 | | USA | M-OR | CL | GY | | | $140.00 |
| Custom Camaro | 6208 | | USA | M-OR | CL | GY | BK-RF | | $180.00 |
| Custom Camaro | 6208 | | HK | M-OR | BL | GY | | | $140.00 |

## 1968 Variations

| Name | Number | Casting | Country | Color | Windows | Interior | Paint | Other | Value |
|---|---|---|---|---|---|---|---|---|---|
| Custom Camaro | 6208 | | HK | M-OR | BL | GY | BK-RF | | $180.00 |
| Custom Camaro | 6208 | | USA | M-OR | CL | BR-L | | | $140.00 |
| Custom Camaro | 6208 | | USA | M-OR | CL | BR-L | BK-RF | | $180.00 |
| Custom Camaro | 6208 | | HK | M-OR | BL | BR-L | | | $140.00 |
| Custom Camaro | 6208 | | HK | M-OR | BL | BR-L | BK-RF | | $180.00 |
| Custom Camaro | 6208 | | USA | M-OR | CL | BR-D | | | $140.00 |
| Custom Camaro | 6208 | | USA | M-OR | CL | BR-D | BK-RF | | $180.00 |
| Custom Camaro | 6208 | | HK | M-OR | BL | BR-D | | | $140.00 |
| Custom Camaro | 6208 | | HK | M-OR | BL | BR-D | BK-RF | | $180.00 |
| Custom Camaro | 6208 | | USA | M-PR | CL | WH | | | $200.00 |
| Custom Camaro | 6208 | | USA | M-PR | CL | WH | BK-RF | | $240.00 |
| Custom Camaro | 6208 | | HK | M-PR | BL | WH | | | $200.00 |
| Custom Camaro | 6208 | | HK | M-PR | BL | WH | BK-RF | | $240.00 |
| Custom Camaro | 6208 | | USA | M-PR | CL | BK | | | $180.00 |
| Custom Camaro | 6208 | | USA | M-PR | CL | BK | BK-RF | | $210.00 |
| Custom Camaro | 6208 | | HK | M-PR | BL | BK | | | $180.00 |
| Custom Camaro | 6208 | | HK | M-PR | BL | BK | BK-RF | | $220.00 |
| Custom Camaro | 6208 | | USA | M-PR | CL | GY | | | $180.00 |
| Custom Camaro | 6208 | | USA | M-PR | CL | GY | BK-RF | | $220.00 |
| Custom Camaro | 6208 | | HK | M-PR | BL | GY | | | $180.00 |
| Custom Camaro | 6208 | | HK | M-PR | BL | GY | BK-RF | | $220.00 |
| Custom Camaro | 6208 | | USA | M-PR | CL | BR-L | | | $180.00 |
| Custom Camaro | 6208 | | USA | M-PR | CL | BR-L | BK-RF | | $220.00 |
| Custom Camaro | 6208 | | HK | M-PR | BL | BR-L | | | $180.00 |
| Custom Camaro | 6208 | | HK | M-PR | BL | BR-L | BK-RF | | $220.00 |
| Custom Camaro | 6208 | | USA | M-PR | CL | BR-D | | | $180.00 |
| Custom Camaro | 6208 | | USA | M-PR | CL | BR-D | BK-RF | | $220.00 |
| Custom Camaro | 6208 | | HK | M-PR | BL | BR-D | | | $180.00 |
| Custom Camaro | 6208 | | HK | M-PR | BL | BR-D | BK-RF | | $220.00 |
| Custom Camaro | 6208 | | USA | M-RD | CL | WH | | | $160.00 |
| Custom Camaro | 6208 | | USA | M-RD | CL | WH | BK-RF | | $200.00 |
| Custom Camaro | 6208 | | HK | M-RD | BL | WH | | | $160.00 |
| Custom Camaro | 6208 | | HK | M-RD | BL | WH | BK-RF | | $200.00 |
| Custom Camaro | 6208 | | USA | M-RD | CL | BK | | | $140.00 |
| Custom Camaro | 6208 | | USA | M-RD | CL | BK | BK-RF | | $180.00 |
| Custom Camaro | 6208 | | HK | M-RD | BL | BK | | | $140.00 |
| Custom Camaro | 6208 | | HK | M-RD | BL | BK | BK-RF | | $180.00 |
| Custom Camaro | 6208 | | USA | M-RD | CL | GY | | | $140.00 |
| Custom Camaro | 6208 | | USA | M-RD | CL | GY | BK-RF | | $180.00 |
| Custom Camaro | 6208 | | HK | M-RD | BL | GY | | | $140.00 |
| Custom Camaro | 6208 | | HK | M-RD | BL | GY | BK-RF | | $180.00 |
| Custom Camaro | 6208 | | USA | M-RD | CL | BR-L | | | $140.00 |
| Custom Camaro | 6208 | | USA | M-RD | CL | BR-L | BK-RF | | $180.00 |
| Custom Camaro | 6208 | | HK | M-RD | BL | BR-L | | | $140.00 |
| Custom Camaro | 6208 | | HK | M-RD | BL | BR-L | BK-RF | | $180.00 |
| Custom Camaro | 6208 | | USA | M-RD | CL | BR-D | | | $140.00 |
| Custom Camaro | 6208 | | USA | M-RD | CL | BR-D | BK-RF | | $180.00 |
| Custom Camaro | 6208 | | HK | M-RD | BL | BR-D | | | $140.00 |
| Custom Camaro | 6208 | | HK | M-RD | BL | BR-D | BK-RF | | $180.00 |
| Custom Camaro | 6208 | | USA | M-RD-R | CL | WH | | | $200.00 |
| Custom Camaro | 6208 | | USA | M-RD-R | CL | WH | BK-RF | | $240.00 |
| Custom Camaro | 6208 | | HK | M-RD-R | BL | WH | | | $200.00 |
| Custom Camaro | 6208 | | HK | M-RD-R | BL | WH | BK-RF | | $240.00 |
| Custom Camaro | 6208 | | USA | M-RD-R | CL | BK | | | $180.00 |
| Custom Camaro | 6208 | | USA | M-RD-R | CL | BK | BK-RF | | $220.00 |
| Custom Camaro | 6208 | | HK | M-RD-R | BL | BK | | | $180.00 |
| Custom Camaro | 6208 | | HK | M-RD-R | BL | BK | BK-RF | | $220.00 |
| Custom Camaro | 6208 | | USA | M-RD-R | CL | GY | | | $180.00 |
| Custom Camaro | 6208 | | USA | M-RD-R | CL | GY | BK-RF | | $220.00 |
| Custom Camaro | 6208 | | HK | M-RD-R | BL | GY | | | $180.00 |
| Custom Camaro | 6208 | | HK | M-RD-R | BL | GY | BK-RF | | $220.00 |
| Custom Camaro | 6208 | | USA | M-RD-R | CL | BR-L | | | $180.00 |
| Custom Camaro | 6208 | | USA | M-RD-R | CL | BR-L | BK-RF | | $220.00 |
| Custom Camaro | 6208 | | HK | M-RD-R | BL | BR-L | | | $180.00 |
| Custom Camaro | 6208 | | HK | M-RD-R | BL | BR-L | BK-RF | | $220.00 |
| Custom Camaro | 6208 | | USA | M-RD-R | CL | BR-D | | | $180.00 |
| Custom Camaro | 6208 | | USA | M-RD-R | CL | BR-D | BK-RF | | $220.00 |
| Custom Camaro | 6208 | | HK | M-RD-R | BL | BR-D | | | $180.00 |
| Custom Camaro | 6208 | | HK | M-RD-R | BL | BR-D | BK-RF | | $220.00 |
| Custom Camaro | 6208 | | USA | M-YW | CL | WH | | | $70.00 |
| Custom Camaro | 6208 | | USA | M-YW | CL | WH | BK-RF | | $90.00 |
| Custom Camaro | 6208 | | HK | M-YW | BL | WH | | | $90.00 |

## 1968 Variations

| Name | Number | Casting | Country | Color | Windows | Interior | Paint | Other | Value |
|---|---|---|---|---|---|---|---|---|---|
| Custom Camaro | 6208 | | HK | M-YW | BL | WH | BK-RF | | $110.00 |
| Custom Camaro | 6208 | | USA | M-YW | CL | BK | | | $80.00 |
| Custom Camaro | 6208 | | USA | M-YW | CL | BK | BK-RF | | $100.00 |
| Custom Camaro | 6208 | | HK | M-YW | BL | BK | | | $80.00 |
| Custom Camaro | 6208 | | HK | M-YW | BL | BK | BK-RF | | $100.00 |
| Custom Camaro | 6208 | | USA | M-YW | CL | GY | | | $80.00 |
| Custom Camaro | 6208 | | USA | M-YW | CL | GY | BK-RF | | $100.00 |
| Custom Camaro | 6208 | | HK | M-YW | BL | GY | | | $80.00 |
| Custom Camaro | 6208 | | HK | M-YW | BL | GY | BK-RF | | $100.00 |
| Custom Camaro | 6208 | | USA | M-YW | CL | BR-L | | | $80.00 |
| Custom Camaro | 6208 | | USA | M-YW | CL | BR-L | BK-RF | | $100.00 |
| Custom Camaro | 6208 | | HK | M-YW | BL | BR-L | | | $80.00 |
| Custom Camaro | 6208 | | HK | M-YW | BL | BR-L | BK-RF | | $100.00 |
| Custom Camaro | 6208 | | USA | M-YW | CL | BR-D | | | $80.00 |
| Custom Camaro | 6208 | | USA | M-YW | CL | BR-D | BK-RF | | $100.00 |
| Custom Camaro | 6208 | | HK | M-YW | BL | BR-D | | | $80.00 |
| Custom Camaro | 6208 | | HK | M-YW | BL | BR-D | BK-RF | | $100.00 |
| Custom Camaro | 6208 | | USA | M-YW-L | CL | WH | | | $170.00 |
| Custom Camaro | 6208 | | USA | M-YW-L | CL | WH | BK-RF | | $190.00 |
| Custom Camaro | 6208 | | HK | M-YW-L | BL | WH | | | $170.00 |
| Custom Camaro | 6208 | | HK | M-YW-L | BL | WH | BK-RF | | $190.00 |
| Custom Camaro | 6208 | | USA | M-YW-L | CL | BK | | | $160.00 |
| Custom Camaro | 6208 | | USA | M-YW-L | CL | BK | BK-RF | | $180.00 |
| Custom Camaro | 6208 | | HK | M-YW-L | BL | BK | | | $160.00 |
| Custom Camaro | 6208 | | HK | M-YW-L | BL | BK | BK-RF | | $180.00 |
| Custom Camaro | 6208 | | USA | M-YW-L | CL | GY | | | $160.00 |
| Custom Camaro | 6208 | | USA | M-YW-L | CL | GY | BK-RF | | $180.00 |
| Custom Camaro | 6208 | | HK | M-YW-L | BL | GY | | | $160.00 |
| Custom Camaro | 6208 | | HK | M-YW-L | BL | GY | BK-RF | | $180.00 |
| Custom Camaro | 6208 | | USA | M-YW-L | CL | BR-L | | | $160.00 |
| Custom Camaro | 6200 | | USA | M-YW-L | CL | BR-L | BK-RF | | $180.00 |
| Custom Camaro | 6208 | | HK | M-YW-L | BL | BR-L | | | $160.00 |
| Custom Camaro | 6208 | | HK | M-YW-L | BL | BR-L | BK-RF | | $180.00 |
| Custom Camaro | 6208 | | USA | M-YW-L | CL | BR-D | | | $160.00 |
| Custom Camaro | 6208 | | USA | M-YW-L | CL | BR-D | BK-RF | | $180.00 |
| Custom Camaro | 6208 | | HK | M-YW-L | BL | BR-D | | | $160.00 |
| Custom Camaro | 6208 | | HK | M-YW-L | BL | BR-D | BK-RF | | $180.00 |
| | | | | | | | | | |
| Silhouette | 6209 | | USA | M-AQ | CL | WH | | | $60.00 |
| Silhouette | 6209 | | HK | M-AQ | BL | WH | | | $60.00 |
| Silhouette | 6209 | | USA | M-AQ | CL | BK | | | $50.00 |
| Silhouette | 6209 | | HK | M-AQ | BL | BK | | | $50.00 |
| Silhouette | 6209 | | USA | M-AQ | CL | GY | | | $50.00 |
| Silhouette | 6209 | | HK | M-AQ | BL | GY | | | $50.00 |
| Silhouette | 6209 | | USA | M-AQ | CL | BR-L | | | $50.00 |
| Silhouette | 6209 | | HK | M-AQ | BL | BR-L | | | $50.00 |
| Silhouette | 6209 | | USA | M-AQ | CL | BR-D | | | $50.00 |
| Silhouette | 6209 | | HK | M-AQ | BL | BR-D | | | $50.00 |
| Silhouette | 6209 | | USA | M-BL | CL | WH | | | $45.00 |
| Silhouette | 6209 | | HK | M-BL | BL | WH | | | $45.00 |
| Silhouette | 6209 | | USA | M-BL | CL | BK | | | $40.00 |
| Silhouette | 6209 | | HK | M-BL | BL | BK | | | $40.00 |
| Silhouette | 6209 | | USA | M-BL | CL | GY | | | $40.00 |
| Silhouette | 6209 | | HK | M-BL | BL | GY | | | $40.00 |
| Silhouette | 6209 | | USA | M-BL | CL | BR-L | | | $40.00 |
| Silhouette | 6209 | | HK | M-BL | BL | BR-L | | | $40.00 |
| Silhouette | 6209 | | USA | M-BL | CL | BR-D | | | $40.00 |
| Silhouette | 6209 | | HK | M-BL | BL | BR-D | | | $40.00 |
| Silhouette | 6209 | | USA | M-BL-I | CL | WH | | | $90.00 |
| Silhouette | 6209 | | HK | M-BL-I | BL | WH | | | $90.00 |
| Silhouette | 6209 | | USA | M-BL-I | CL | BK | | | $80.00 |
| Silhouette | 6209 | | HK | M-BL-I | BL | BK | | | $80.00 |
| Silhouette | 6209 | | USA | M-BL-I | CL | GY | | | $80.00 |
| Silhouette | 6209 | | HK | M-BL-I | BL | GY | | | $80.00 |
| Silhouette | 6209 | | USA | M-BL-I | CL | BR-L | | | $80.00 |
| Silhouette | 6209 | | HK | M-BL-I | BL | BR-L | | | $80.00 |
| Silhouette | 6209 | | USA | M-BL-I | CL | BR-D | | | $80.00 |
| Silhouette | 6209 | | HK | M-BL-I | BL | BR-D | | | $80.00 |
| Silhouette | 6209 | | USA | M-BL-P | CL | WH | | | $60.00 |
| Silhouette | 6209 | | HK | M-BL-P | BL | WH | | | $60.00 |
| Silhouette | 6209 | | USA | M-BL-P | CL | BK | | | $50.00 |

## 1968 Variations

| Name | Number | Casting | Country | Color | Windows | Interior | Paint | Other | Value |
|---|---|---|---|---|---|---|---|---|---|
| Silhouette | 6209 | | HK | M-BL-P | BL | BK | | | $50.00 |
| Silhouette | 6209 | | USA | M-BL-P | CL | GY | | | $50.00 |
| Silhouette | 6209 | | HK | M-BL-P | BL | GY | | | $50.00 |
| Silhouette | 6209 | | USA | M-BL-P | CL | BR-L | | | $50.00 |
| Silhouette | 6209 | | HK | M-BL-P | BL | BR-L | | | $50.00 |
| Silhouette | 6209 | | USA | M-BL-P | CL | BR-D | | | $50.00 |
| Silhouette | 6209 | | HK | M-BL-P | BL | BR-D | | | $50.00 |
| Silhouette | 6209 | | USA | M-BR-D | CL | WH | | | $130.00 |
| Silhouette | 6209 | | HK | M-BR-D | BL | WH | | | $130.00 |
| Silhouette | 6209 | | USA | M-BR-D | CL | BK | | | $110.00 |
| Silhouette | 6209 | | HK | M-BR-D | BL | BK | | | $110.00 |
| Silhouette | 6209 | | USA | M-BR-D | CL | GY | | | $110.00 |
| Silhouette | 6209 | | HK | M-BR-D | BL | GY | | | $110.00 |
| Silhouette | 6209 | | USA | M-BR-D | CL | BR-L | | | $110.00 |
| Silhouette | 6209 | | HK | M-BR-D | BL | BR-L | | | $110.00 |
| Silhouette | 6209 | | USA | M-BR-D | CL | BR-D | | | $110.00 |
| Silhouette | 6209 | | HK | M-BR-D | BL | BR-D | | | $110.00 |
| Silhouette | 6209 | | USA | M-BR-P | CL | WH | | | $140.00 |
| Silhouette | 6209 | | HK | M-BR-P | BL | WH | | | $140.00 |
| Silhouette | 6209 | | USA | M-BR-P | CL | BK | | | $120.00 |
| Silhouette | 6209 | | HK | M-BR-P | BL | BK | | | $120.00 |
| Silhouette | 6209 | | USA | M-BR-P | CL | GY | | | $120.00 |
| Silhouette | 6209 | | HK | M-BR-P | BL | GY | | | $120.00 |
| Silhouette | 6209 | | USA | M-BR-P | CL | BR-L | | | $120.00 |
| Silhouette | 6209 | | HK | M-BR-P | BL | BR-L | | | $120.00 |
| Silhouette | 6209 | | USA | M-BR-P | CL | BR-D | | | $120.00 |
| Silhouette | 6209 | | HK | M-BR-P | BL | BR-D | | | $120.00 |
| Silhouette | 6209 | | USA | M-GD | CL | WH | | | $45.00 |
| Silhouette | 6209 | | HK | M-GD | BL | WH | | | $45.00 |
| Silhouette | 6209 | | USA | M-GD | CL | BK | | | $40.00 |
| Silhouette | 6209 | | HK | M-GD | BL | BK | | | $40.00 |
| Silhouette | 6209 | | USA | M-GD | CL | GY | | | $40.00 |
| Silhouette | 6209 | | HK | M-GD | BL | GY | | | $40.00 |
| Silhouette | 6209 | | USA | M-GD | CL | BR-L | | | $40.00 |
| Silhouette | 6209 | | HK | M-GD | BL | BR-L | | | $40.00 |
| Silhouette | 6209 | | USA | M-GD | CL | BR-D | | | $40.00 |
| Silhouette | 6209 | | HK | M-GD | BL | BR-D | | | $40.00 |
| Silhouette | 6209 | | USA | M-GR | CL | WH | | | $45.00 |
| Silhouette | 6209 | | HK | M-GR | BL | WH | | | $45.00 |
| Silhouette | 6209 | | USA | M-GR | CL | BK | | | $40.00 |
| Silhouette | 6209 | | HK | M-GR | BL | BK | | | $40.00 |
| Silhouette | 6209 | | USA | M-GR | CL | GY | | | $40.00 |
| Silhouette | 6209 | | HK | M-GR | BL | GY | | | $40.00 |
| Silhouette | 6209 | | USA | M-GR | CL | BR-L | | | $40.00 |
| Silhouette | 6209 | | HK | M-GR | BL | BR-L | | | $40.00 |
| Silhouette | 6209 | | USA | M-GR | CL | BR-D | | | $40.00 |
| Silhouette | 6209 | | HK | M-GR | BL | BR-D | | | $40.00 |
| Silhouette | 6209 | | USA | M-GR-E | CL | WH | | | $45.00 |
| Silhouette | 6209 | | HK | M-GR-E | BL | WH | | | $45.00 |
| Silhouette | 6209 | | USA | M-GR-E | CL | BK | | | $40.00 |
| Silhouette | 6209 | | HK | M-GR-E | BL | BK | | | $40.00 |
| Silhouette | 6209 | | USA | M-GR-E | CL | GY | | | $40.00 |
| Silhouette | 6209 | | HK | M-GR-E | BL | GY | | | $40.00 |
| Silhouette | 6209 | | USA | M-GR-E | CL | BR-L | | | $40.00 |
| Silhouette | 6209 | | HK | M-GR-E | BL | BR-L | | | $40.00 |
| Silhouette | 6209 | | USA | M-GR-E | CL | BR-D | | | $40.00 |
| Silhouette | 6209 | | HK | M-GR-E | BL | BR-D | | | $40.00 |
| Silhouette | 6209 | | USA | M-GR-L | CL | WH | | | $75.00 |
| Silhouette | 6209 | | HK | M-GR-L | BL | WH | | | $75.00 |
| Silhouette | 6209 | | USA | M-GR-L | CL | BK | | | $65.00 |
| Silhouette | 6209 | | HK | M-GR-L | BL | BK | | | $65.00 |
| Silhouette | 6209 | | USA | M-GR-L | CL | GY | | | $65.00 |
| Silhouette | 6209 | | HK | M-GR-L | BL | GY | | | $65.00 |
| Silhouette | 6209 | | USA | M-GR-L | CL | BR-L | | | $65.00 |
| Silhouette | 6209 | | HK | M-GR-L | BL | BR-L | | | $65.00 |
| Silhouette | 6209 | | USA | M-GR-L | CL | BR-D | | | $65.00 |
| Silhouette | 6209 | | HK | M-GR-L | BL | BR-D | | | $65.00 |
| Silhouette | 6209 | | USA | M-GR-O | CL | WH | | | $45.00 |
| Silhouette | 6209 | | HK | M-GR-O | BL | WH | | | $45.00 |
| Silhouette | 6209 | | USA | M-GR-O | CL | BK | | | $40.00 |
| Silhouette | 6209 | | HK | M-GR-O | BL | BK | | | $40.00 |
| Silhouette | 6209 | | USA | M-GR-O | CL | GY | | | $40.00 |

## 1968 Variations

| Name | Number | Casting | Country | Color | Windows | Interior | Paint | Other | Value |
|---|---|---|---|---|---|---|---|---|---|
| Silhouette | 6209 | | HK | M-GR-O | BL | GY | | | $40.00 |
| Silhouette | 6209 | | USA | M-GR-O | CL | BR-L | | | $40.00 |
| Silhouette | 6209 | | HK | M-GR-O | BL | BR-L | | | $40.00 |
| Silhouette | 6209 | | USA | M-GR-O | CL | BR-D | | | $40.00 |
| Silhouette | 6209 | | HK | M-GR-O | BL | BR-D | | | $40.00 |
| Silhouette | 6209 | | USA | M-MG | CL | WH | | | $100.00 |
| Silhouette | 6209 | | HK | M-MG | BL | WH | | | $100.00 |
| Silhouette | 6209 | | USA | M-MG | CL | BK | | | $90.00 |
| Silhouette | 6209 | | HK | M-MG | BL | BK | | | $90.00 |
| Silhouette | 6209 | | USA | M-MG | CL | GY | | | $90.00 |
| Silhouette | 6209 | | HK | M-MG | BL | GY | | | $90.00 |
| Silhouette | 6209 | | USA | M-MG | CL | BR-L | | | $90.00 |
| Silhouette | 6209 | | HK | M-MG | BL | BR-L | | | $90.00 |
| Silhouette | 6209 | | USA | M-MG | CL | BR-D | | | $90.00 |
| Silhouette | 6209 | | HK | M-MG | BL | BR-D | | | $90.00 |
| Silhouette | 6209 | | USA | M-OR | CL | WH | | | $45.00 |
| Silhouette | 6209 | | HK | M-OR | BL | WH | | | $45.00 |
| Silhouette | 6209 | | USA | M-OR | CL | BK | | | $40.00 |
| Silhouette | 6209 | | HK | M-OR | BL | BK | | | $40.00 |
| Silhouette | 6209 | | USA | M-OR | CL | GY | | | $40.00 |
| Silhouette | 6209 | | HK | M-OR | BL | GY | | | $40.00 |
| Silhouette | 6209 | | USA | M-OR | CL | BR-L | | | $40.00 |
| Silhouette | 6209 | | HK | M-OR | BL | BR-L | | | $40.00 |
| Silhouette | 6209 | | USA | M-OR | CL | BR-D | | | $40.00 |
| Silhouette | 6209 | | HK | M-OR | BL | BR-D | | | $40.00 |
| Silhouette | 6209 | | USA | M-PK | CL | WH | | | $360.00 |
| Silhouette | 6209 | | HK | M-PK | BL | WH | | | $360.00 |
| Silhouette | 6209 | | USA | M-PK | CL | BK | | | $330.00 |
| Silhouette | 6209 | | HK | M-PK | BL | BK | | | $330.00 |
| Silhouette | 6209 | | USA | M-PK | CL | GY | | | $330.00 |
| Silhouette | 6209 | | HK | M-PK | BL | GY | | | $330.00 |
| Silhouette | 6209 | | USA | M-PK | CL | BR-L | | | $330.00 |
| Silhouette | 6209 | | HK | M-PK | BL | BR-L | | | $330.00 |
| Silhouette | 6209 | | USA | M-PK | CL | BR-D | | | $330.00 |
| Silhouette | 6209 | | HK | M-PK | BL | BR-D | | | $330.00 |
| Silhouette | 6209 | | USA | M-PK-H | CL | WH | | | $360.00 |
| Silhouette | 6209 | | HK | M-PK-H | BL | WH | | | $360.00 |
| Silhouette | 6209 | | USA | M-PK-H | CL | BK | | | $330.00 |
| Silhouette | 6209 | | HK | M-PK-H | BL | BK | | | $330.00 |
| Silhouette | 6209 | | USA | M-PK-H | CL | GY | | | $330.00 |
| Silhouette | 6209 | | HK | M-PK-H | BL | GY | | | $330.00 |
| Silhouette | 6209 | | USA | M-PK-H | CL | BR-L | | | $330.00 |
| Silhouette | 6209 | | HK | M-PK-H | BL | BR-L | | | $330.00 |
| Silhouette | 6209 | | USA | M-PK-H | CL | BR-D | | | $330.00 |
| Silhouette | 6209 | | HK | M-PK-H | BL | BR-D | | | $330.00 |
| Silhouette | 6209 | | USA | M-PK-S | CL | WH | | | $360.00 |
| Silhouette | 6209 | | HK | M-PK-S | BL | WH | | | $360.00 |
| Silhouette | 6209 | | USA | M-PK-S | CL | BK | | | $330.00 |
| Silhouette | 6209 | | HK | M-PK-S | BL | BK | | | $330.00 |
| Silhouette | 6209 | | USA | M-PK-S | CL | GY | | | $330.00 |
| Silhouette | 6209 | | HK | M-PK-S | BL | GY | | | $330.00 |
| Silhouette | 6209 | | USA | M-PK-S | CL | BR-L | | | $330.00 |
| Silhouette | 6209 | | HK | M-PK-S | BL | BR-L | | | $330.00 |
| Silhouette | 6209 | | USA | M-PK-S | CL | BR-D | | | $330.00 |
| Silhouette | 6209 | | HK | M-PK-S | BL | BR-D | | | $330.00 |
| Silhouette | 6209 | | USA | M-PR | CL | WH | | | $50.00 |
| Silhouette | 6209 | | HK | M-PR | BL | WH | | | $50.00 |
| Silhouette | 6209 | | USA | M-PR | CL | BK | | | $40.00 |
| Silhouette | 6209 | | HK | M-PR | BL | BK | | | $40.00 |
| Silhouette | 6209 | | USA | M-PR | CL | GY | | | $40.00 |
| Silhouette | 6209 | | HK | M-PR | BL | GY | | | $40.00 |
| Silhouette | 6209 | | USA | M-PR | CL | BR-L | | | $40.00 |
| Silhouette | 6209 | | HK | M-PR | BL | BR-L | | | $40.00 |
| Silhouette | 6209 | | USA | M-PR | CL | BR-D | | | $40.00 |
| Silhouette | 6209 | | HK | M-PR | BL | BR-D | | | $40.00 |
| Silhouette | 6209 | | USA | M-RD | CL | WH | | | $45.00 |
| Silhouette | 6209 | | HK | M-RD | BL | WH | | | $45.00 |
| Silhouette | 6209 | | USA | M-RD | CL | BK | | | $40.00 |
| Silhouette | 6209 | | HK | M-RD | BL | BK | | | $40.00 |
| Silhouette | 6209 | | USA | M-RD | CL | GY | | | $40.00 |
| Silhouette | 6209 | | HK | M-RD | BL | GY | | | $40.00 |
| Silhouette | 6209 | | USA | M-RD | CL | BR-L | | | $40.00 |

## 1968 Variations

| Name | Number | Casting | Country | Color | Windows | Interior | Paint | Other | Value |
|---|---|---|---|---|---|---|---|---|---|
| Silhouette | 6209 | | HK | M-RD | BL | BR-L | | | $40.00 |
| Silhouette | 6209 | | USA | M-RD | CL | BR-D | | | $40.00 |
| Silhouette | 6209 | | HK | M-RD | BL | BR-D | | | $40.00 |
| Silhouette | 6209 | | USA | M-RD-R | CL | WH | | | $55.00 |
| Silhouette | 6209 | | HK | M-RD-R | BL | WH | | | $55.00 |
| Silhouette | 6209 | | USA | M-RD-R | CL | BK | | | $50.00 |
| Silhouette | 6209 | | HK | M-RD-R | BL | BK | | | $50.00 |
| Silhouette | 6209 | | USA | M-RD-R | CL | GY | | | $50.00 |
| Silhouette | 6209 | | HK | M-RD-R | BL | GY | | | $50.00 |
| Silhouette | 6209 | | USA | M-RD-R | CL | BR-L | | | $50.00 |
| Silhouette | 6209 | | HK | M-RD-R | BL | BR-L | | | $50.00 |
| Silhouette | 6209 | | USA | M-RD-R | CL | BR-D | | | $50.00 |
| Silhouette | 6209 | | HK | M-RD-R | BL | BR-D | | | $50.00 |
| Silhouette | 6209 | | USA | M-YW | CL | WH | | | $45.00 |
| Silhouette | 6209 | | HK | M-YW | BL | WH | | | $45.00 |
| Silhouette | 6209 | | USA | M-YW | CL | BK | | | $40.00 |
| Silhouette | 6209 | | HK | M-YW | BL | BK | | | $40.00 |
| Silhouette | 6209 | | USA | M-YW | CL | GY | | | $40.00 |
| Silhouette | 6209 | | HK | M-YW | BL | GY | | | $40.00 |
| Silhouette | 6209 | | USA | M-YW | CL | BR-L | | | $40.00 |
| Silhouette | 6209 | | HK | M-YW | BL | BR-L | | | $40.00 |
| Silhouette | 6209 | | USA | M-YW | CL | BR-D | | | $40.00 |
| Silhouette | 6209 | | HK | M-YW | BL | BR-D | | | $40.00 |
| Silhouette | 6209 | | USA | M-YW-L | CL | WH | | | $100.00 |
| Silhouette | 6209 | | HK | M-YW-L | BL | WH | | | $100.00 |
| Silhouette | 6209 | | USA | M-YW-L | CL | BK | | | $90.00 |
| Silhouette | 6209 | | HK | M-YW-L | BL | BK | | | $90.00 |
| Silhouette | 6209 | | USA | M-YW-L | CL | GY | | | $90.00 |
| Silhouette | 6209 | | HK | M-YW-L | BL | GY | | | $90.00 |
| Silhouette | 6209 | | USA | M-YW-L | CL | BR-L | | | $90.00 |
| Silhouette | 6209 | | HK | M-YW-L | BL | BR-L | | | $90.00 |
| Silhouette | 6209 | | USA | M-YW-L | CL | BR-D | | | $90.00 |
| Silhouette | 6209 | | HK | M-YW-L | BL | BR-D | | | $90.00 |
| | | | | | | | | | |
| Deora | 6210 | | USA | M-AQ | CL | WH | | | $100.00 |
| Deora | 6210 | | HK | M-AQ | BL | WH | | | $100.00 |
| Deora | 6210 | | USA | M-AQ | CL | BK | | | $90.00 |
| Deora | 6210 | | HK | M-AQ | BL | BK | | | $90.00 |
| Deora | 6210 | | USA | M-AQ | CL | GY | | | $90.00 |
| Deora | 6210 | | HK | M-AQ | BL | GY | | | $90.00 |
| Deora | 6210 | | USA | M-AQ | CL | BR-L | | | $90.00 |
| Deora | 6210 | | HK | M-AQ | BL | BR-L | | | $90.00 |
| Deora | 6210 | | USA | M-AQ | CL | BR-D | | | $90.00 |
| Deora | 6210 | | HK | M-AQ | BL | BR-D | | | $90.00 |
| Deora | 6210 | | USA | M-BL | CL | WH | | | $440.00 |
| Deora | 6210 | | HK | M-BL | BL | WH | | | $440.00 |
| Deora | 6210 | | USA | M-BL | CL | BK | | | $400.00 |
| Deora | 6210 | | HK | M-BL | BL | BK | | | $400.00 |
| Deora | 6210 | | USA | M-BL | CL | GY | | | $400.00 |
| Deora | 6210 | | HK | M-BL | BL | GY | | | $400.00 |
| Deora | 6210 | | USA | M-BL | CL | BR-L | | | $400.00 |
| Deora | 6210 | | HK | M-BL | BL | BR-L | | | $400.00 |
| Deora | 6210 | | USA | M-BL | CL | BR-D | | | $400.00 |
| Deora | 6210 | | HK | M-BL | BL | BR-D | | | $400.00 |
| Deora | 6210 | | USA | M-BL-I | CL | WH | | | $380.00 |
| Deora | 6210 | | HK | M-BL-I | BL | WH | | | $380.00 |
| Deora | 6210 | | USA | M-BL-I | CL | BK | | | $340.00 |
| Deora | 6210 | | HK | M-BL-I | BL | BK | | | $340.00 |
| Deora | 6210 | | USA | M-BL-I | CL | GY | | | $340.00 |
| Deora | 6210 | | HK | M-BL-I | BL | GY | | | $340.00 |
| Deora | 6210 | | USA | M-BL-I | CL | BR-L | | | $340.00 |
| Deora | 6210 | | HK | M-BL-I | BL | BR-L | | | $340.00 |
| Deora | 6210 | | USA | M-BL-I | CL | BR-D | | | $340.00 |
| Deora | 6210 | | HK | M-BL-I | BL | BR-D | | | $340.00 |
| Deora | 6210 | | USA | M-BL-P | CL | WH | | | $300.00 |
| Deora | 6210 | | HK | M-BL-P | BL | WH | | | $300.00 |
| Deora | 6210 | | USA | M-BL-P | CL | BK | | | $170.00 |
| Deora | 6210 | | HK | M-BL-P | BL | BK | | | $170.00 |
| Deora | 6210 | | USA | M-BL-P | CL | GY | | | $170.00 |
| Deora | 6210 | | HK | M-BL-P | BL | GY | | | $170.00 |
| Deora | 6210 | | USA | M-BL-P | CL | BR-L | | | $170.00 |

## 1968 Variations

| Name | Number | Casting | Country | Color | Windows | Interior | Paint | Other | Value |
|---|---|---|---|---|---|---|---|---|---|
| Deora | 6210 | | HK | M-BL-P | BL | BR-L | | | $170.00 |
| Deora | 6210 | | USA | M-BL-P | CL | BR-D | | | $170.00 |
| Deora | 6210 | | HK | M-BL-P | BL | BR-D | | | $170.00 |
| Deora | 6210 | | USA | M-BR-D | CL | WH | | | $320.00 |
| Deora | 6210 | | HK | M-BR-D | BL | WH | | | $320.00 |
| Deora | 6210 | | USA | M-BR-D | CL | BK | | | $290.00 |
| Deora | 6210 | | HK | M-BR-D | BL | BK | | | $290.00 |
| Deora | 6210 | | USA | M-BR-D | CL | GY | | | $290.00 |
| Deora | 6210 | | HK | M-BR-D | BL | GY | | | $290.00 |
| Deora | 6210 | | USA | M-BR-D | CL | BR-L | | | $290.00 |
| Deora | 6210 | | HK | M-BR-D | BL | BR-L | | | $290.00 |
| Deora | 6210 | | USA | M-BR-D | CL | BR-D | | | $290.00 |
| Deora | 6210 | | HK | M-BR-D | BL | BR-D | | | $290.00 |
| Deora | 6210 | | USA | M-BR-P | CL | WH | | | $300.00 |
| Deora | 6210 | | HK | M-BR-P | BL | WH | | | $300.00 |
| Deora | 6210 | | USA | M-BR-P | CL | BK | | | $270.00 |
| Deora | 6210 | | HK | M-BR-P | BL | BK | | | $270.00 |
| Deora | 6210 | | USA | M-BR-P | CL | GY | | | $270.00 |
| Deora | 6210 | | HK | M-BR-P | BL | GY | | | $270.00 |
| Deora | 6210 | | USA | M-BR-P | CL | BR-L | | | $270.00 |
| Deora | 6210 | | HK | M-BR-P | BL | BR-L | | | $270.00 |
| Deora | 6210 | | USA | M-BR-P | CL | BR-D | | | $270.00 |
| Deora | 6210 | | HK | M-BR-P | BL | BR-D | | | $270.00 |
| Deora | 6210 | | USA | M-GD | CL | WH | | | $90.00 |
| Deora | 6210 | | HK | M-GD | BL | WH | | | $90.00 |
| Deora | 6210 | | USA | M-GD | CL | BK | | | $80.00 |
| Deora | 6210 | | HK | M-GD | BL | BK | | | $80.00 |
| Deora | 6210 | | USA | M-GD | CL | GY | | | $80.00 |
| Deora | 6210 | | HK | M-GD | BL | GY | | | $80.00 |
| Deora | 6210 | | USA | M-GD | CL | BR-L | | | $80.00 |
| Deora | 6210 | | HK | M-GD | BL | BR-L | | | $80.00 |
| Deora | 6210 | | USA | M-GD | CL | BR-D | | | $80.00 |
| Deora | 6210 | | HK | M-GD | BL | BR-D | | | $80.00 |
| Deora | 6210 | | USA | M-GR | CL | WH | | | $210.00 |
| Deora | 6210 | | HK | M-GR | BL | WH | | | $210.00 |
| Deora | 6210 | | USA | M-GR | CL | BK | | | $190.00 |
| Deora | 6210 | | HK | M-GR | BL | BK | | | $190.00 |
| Deora | 6210 | | USA | M-GR | CL | GY | | | $190.00 |
| Deora | 6210 | | HK | M-GR | BL | GY | | | $190.00 |
| Deora | 6210 | | USA | M-GR | CL | BR-L | | | $190.00 |
| Deora | 6210 | | HK | M-GR | BL | BR-L | | | $190.00 |
| Deora | 6210 | | USA | M-GR | CL | BR-D | | | $190.00 |
| Deora | 6210 | | HK | M-GR | BL | BR-D | | | $190.00 |
| Deora | 6210 | | USA | M-GR-E | CL | WH | | | $230.00 |
| Deora | 6210 | | HK | M-GR-E | BL | WH | | | $230.00 |
| Deora | 6210 | | USA | M-GR-E | CL | BK | | | $210.00 |
| Deora | 6210 | | HK | M-GR-E | BL | BK | | | $210.00 |
| Deora | 6210 | | USA | M-GR-E | CL | GY | | | $210.00 |
| Deora | 6210 | | HK | M-GR-E | BL | GY | | | $210.00 |
| Deora | 6210 | | USA | M-GR-E | CL | BR-L | | | $210.00 |
| Deora | 6210 | | HK | M-GR-E | BL | BR-L | | | $210.00 |
| Deora | 6210 | | USA | M-GR-E | CL | BR-D | | | $210.00 |
| Deora | 6210 | | HK | M-GR-E | BL | BR-D | | | $210.00 |
| Deora | 6210 | | USA | M-GR-L | CL | WH | | | $160.00 |
| Deora | 6210 | | HK | M-GR-L | BL | WH | | | $160.00 |
| Deora | 6210 | | USA | M-GR-L | CL | BK | | | $145.00 |
| Deora | 6210 | | HK | M-GR-L | BL | BK | | | $145.00 |
| Deora | 6210 | | USA | M-GR-L | CL | GY | | | $145.00 |
| Deora | 6210 | | HK | M-GR-L | BL | GY | | | $145.00 |
| Deora | 6210 | | USA | M-GR-L | CL | BR-L | | | $145.00 |
| Deora | 6210 | | HK | M-GR-L | BL | BR-L | | | $145.00 |
| Deora | 6210 | | USA | M-GR-L | CL | BR-D | | | $145.00 |
| Deora | 6210 | | HK | M-GR-L | BL | BR-D | | | $145.00 |
| Deora | 6210 | | USA | M-GR-O | CL | WH | | | $170.00 |
| Deora | 6210 | | HK | M-GR-O | BL | WH | | | $170.00 |
| Deora | 6210 | | USA | M-GR-O | CL | BK | | | $160.00 |
| Deora | 6210 | | HK | M-GR-O | BL | BK | | | $160.00 |
| Deora | 6210 | | USA | M-GR-O | CL | GY | | | $160.00 |
| Deora | 6210 | | HK | M-GR-O | BL | GY | | | $160.00 |
| Deora | 6210 | | USA | M-GR-O | CL | BR-L | | | $160.00 |
| Deora | 6210 | | HK | M-GR-O | BL | BR-L | | | $160.00 |
| Deora | 6210 | | USA | M-GR-O | CL | BR-D | | | $160.00 |

## 1968 Variations

| Name | Number | Casting | Country | Color | Windows | Interior | Paint | Other | Value |
|---|---|---|---|---|---|---|---|---|---|
| Deora | 6210 | | HK | M-GR-O | BL | BR-D | | | $160.00 |
| Deora | 6210 | | USA | M-OR | CL | WH | | | $85.00 |
| Deora | 6210 | | HK | M-OR | BL | WH | | | $85.00 |
| Deora | 6210 | | USA | M-OR | CL | BK | | | $75.00 |
| Deora | 6210 | | HK | M-OR | BL | BK | | | $75.00 |
| Deora | 6210 | | USA | M-OR | CL | GY | | | $75.00 |
| Deora | 6210 | | HK | M-OR | BL | GY | | | $75.00 |
| Deora | 6210 | | USA | M-OR | CL | BR-L | | | $75.00 |
| Deora | 6210 | | HK | M-OR | BL | BR-L | | | $75.00 |
| Deora | 6210 | | USA | M-OR | CL | BR-D | | | $75.00 |
| Deora | 6210 | | HK | M-OR | BL | BR-D | | | $75.00 |
| Deora | 6210 | | USA | M-PR | CL | WH | | | $85.00 |
| Deora | 6210 | | HK | M-PR | BL | WH | | | $85.00 |
| Deora | 6210 | | USA | M-PR | CL | BK | | | $75.00 |
| Deora | 6210 | | HK | M-PR | BL | BK | | | $75.00 |
| Deora | 6210 | | USA | M-PR | CL | GY | | | $75.00 |
| Deora | 6210 | | HK | M-PR | BL | GY | | | $75.00 |
| Deora | 6210 | | USA | M-PR | CL | BR-L | | | $75.00 |
| Deora | 6210 | | HK | M-PR | BL | BR-L | | | $75.00 |
| Deora | 6210 | | USA | M-PR | CL | BR-D | | | $75.00 |
| Deora | 6210 | | HK | M-PR | BL | BR-D | | | $75.00 |
| Deora | 6210 | | USA | M-RD | CL | WH | | | $145.00 |
| Deora | 6210 | | HK | M-RD | BL | WH | | | $145.00 |
| Deora | 6210 | | USA | M-RD | CL | BK | | | $135.00 |
| Deora | 6210 | | HK | M-RD | BL | BK | | | $135.00 |
| Deora | 6210 | | USA | M-RD | CL | GY | | | $135.00 |
| Deora | 6210 | | HK | M-RD | BL | GY | | | $135.00 |
| Deora | 6210 | | USA | M-RD | CL | BR-L | | | $135.00 |
| Deora | 6210 | | HK | M-RD | BL | BR-L | | | $135.00 |
| Deora | 6210 | | USA | M-RD | CL | BR-D | | | $135.00 |
| Deora | 6210 | | HK | M-RD | BL | BR-D | | | $135.00 |
| Deora | 6210 | | USA | M-RD-R | CL | WH | | | $170.00 |
| Deora | 6210 | | HK | M-RD-R | BL | WH | | | $170.00 |
| Deora | 6210 | | USA | M-RD-R | CL | BK | | | $160.00 |
| Deora | 6210 | | HK | M-RD-R | BL | BK | | | $160.00 |
| Deora | 6210 | | USA | M-RD-R | CL | GY | | | $160.00 |
| Deora | 6210 | | HK | M-RD-R | BL | GY | | | $160.00 |
| Deora | 6210 | | USA | M-RD-R | CL | BR-L | | | $160.00 |
| Deora | 6210 | | HK | M-RD-R | BL | BR-L | | | $160.00 |
| Deora | 6210 | | USA | M-RD-R | CL | BR-D | | | $160.00 |
| Deora | 6210 | | HK | M-RD-R | BL | BR-D | | | $160.00 |
| Deora | 6210 | | USA | M-YW | CL | WH | | | $85.00 |
| Deora | 6210 | | HK | M-YW | BL | WH | | | $85.00 |
| Deora | 6210 | | USA | M-YW | CL | BK | | | $75.00 |
| Deora | 6210 | | HK | M-YW | BL | BK | | | $75.00 |
| Deora | 6210 | | USA | M-YW | CL | GY | | | $75.00 |
| Deora | 6210 | | HK | M-YW | BL | GY | | | $75.00 |
| Deora | 6210 | | USA | M-YW | CL | BR-L | | | $75.00 |
| Deora | 6210 | | HK | M-YW | BL | BR-L | | | $75.00 |
| Deora | 6210 | | USA | M-YW | CL | BR-D | | | $75.00 |
| Deora | 6210 | | HK | M-YW | BL | BR-D | | | $75.00 |
| Deora | 6210 | | USA | M-YW-L | CL | WH | | | $190.00 |
| Deora | 6210 | | HK | M-YW-L | BL | WH | | | $190.00 |
| Deora | 6210 | | USA | M-YW-L | CL | BK | | | $170.00 |
| Deora | 6210 | | HK | M-YW-L | BL | BK | | | $170.00 |
| Deora | 6210 | | USA | M-YW-L | CL | GY | | | $170.00 |
| Deora | 6210 | | HK | M-YW-L | BL | GY | | | $170.00 |
| Deora | 6210 | | USA | M-YW-L | CL | BR-L | | | $170.00 |
| Deora | 6210 | | HK | M-YW-L | BL | BR-L | | | $170.00 |
| Deora | 6210 | | USA | M-YW-L | CL | BR-D | | | $170.00 |
| Deora | 6210 | | HK | M-YW-L | BL | BR-D | | | $170.00 |
| | | | | | | | | | |
| Custom Barracuda | 6211 | | USA | M-AQ | CL | WH | | | $90.00 |
| Custom Barracuda | 6211 | | HK | M-AQ | BL | WH | | | $90.00 |
| Custom Barracuda | 6211 | | USA | M-AQ | CL | BK | | | $80.00 |
| Custom Barracuda | 6211 | | HK | M-AQ | BL | BK | | | $80.00 |
| Custom Barracuda | 6211 | | USA | M-AQ | CL | GY | | | $80.00 |
| Custom Barracuda | 6211 | | HK | M-AQ | BL | GY | | | $80.00 |
| Custom Barracuda | 6211 | | USA | M-AQ | CL | BR-L | | | $80.00 |
| Custom Barracuda | 6211 | | HK | M-AQ | BL | BR-L | | | $80.00 |
| Custom Barracuda | 6211 | | USA | M-AQ | CL | BR-D | | | $80.00 |

## 1968 Variations

| Name | Number | Casting | Country | Color | Windows | Interior | Paint | Other | Value |
|---|---|---|---|---|---|---|---|---|---|
| Custom Barracuda | 6211 | | HK | M-AQ | BL | BR-D | | | $80.00 |
| Custom Barracuda | 6211 | | USA | M-BL | CL | WH | | | $125.00 |
| Custom Barracuda | 6211 | | HK | M-BL | BL | WH | | | $125.00 |
| Custom Barracuda | 6211 | | USA | M-BL | CL | BK | | | $115.00 |
| Custom Barracuda | 6211 | | HK | M-BL | BL | BK | | | $115.00 |
| Custom Barracuda | 6211 | | USA | M-BL | CL | GY | | | $115.00 |
| Custom Barracuda | 6211 | | HK | M-BL | BL | GY | | | $115.00 |
| Custom Barracuda | 6211 | | USA | M-BL | CL | BR-L | | | $115.00 |
| Custom Barracuda | 6211 | | HK | M-BL | BL | BR-L | | | $115.00 |
| Custom Barracuda | 6211 | | USA | M-BL | CL | BR-D | | | $115.00 |
| Custom Barracuda | 6211 | | HK | M-BL | BL | BR-D | | | $115.00 |
| Custom Barracuda | 6211 | | USA | M-BL-I | CL | WH | | | $145.00 |
| Custom Barracuda | 6211 | | HK | M-BL-I | BL | WH | | | $145.00 |
| Custom Barracuda | 6211 | | USA | M-BL-I | CL | BK | | | $135.00 |
| Custom Barracuda | 6211 | | HK | M-BL-I | BL | BK | | | $135.00 |
| Custom Barracuda | 6211 | | USA | M-BL-I | CL | GY | | | $135.00 |
| Custom Barracuda | 6211 | | HK | M-BL-I | BL | GY | | | $135.00 |
| Custom Barracuda | 6211 | | USA | M-BL-I | CL | BR-L | | | $135.00 |
| Custom Barracuda | 6211 | | HK | M-BL-I | BL | BR-L | | | $135.00 |
| Custom Barracuda | 6211 | | USA | M-BL-I | CL | BR-D | | | $135.00 |
| Custom Barracuda | 6211 | | HK | M-BL-I | BL | BR-D | | | $135.00 |
| Custom Barracuda | 6211 | | USA | M-BL-P | CL | WH | | | $135.00 |
| Custom Barracuda | 6211 | | HK | M-BL-P | BL | WH | | | $135.00 |
| Custom Barracuda | 6211 | | USA | M-BL-P | CL | BK | | | $125.00 |
| Custom Barracuda | 6211 | | HK | M-BL-P | BL | BK | | | $125.00 |
| Custom Barracuda | 6211 | | USA | M-BL-P | CL | GY | | | $125.00 |
| Custom Barracuda | 6211 | | HK | M-BL-P | BL | GY | | | $125.00 |
| Custom Barracuda | 6211 | | USA | M-BL-P | CL | BR-L | | | $125.00 |
| Custom Barracuda | 6211 | | HK | M-BL-P | BL | BR-L | | | $125.00 |
| Custom Barracuda | 6211 | | USA | M-BL-P | CL | BR-D | | | $125.00 |
| Custom Barracuda | 6211 | | HK | M-BL-P | BL | BR-D | | | $125.00 |
| Custom Barracuda | 6211 | | USA | M-BR-D | CL | WH | | | $95.00 |
| Custom Barracuda | 6211 | | HK | M-BR-D | BL | WH | | | $95.00 |
| Custom Barracuda | 6211 | | USA | M-BR-D | CL | BK | | | $85.00 |
| Custom Barracuda | 6211 | | HK | M-BR-D | BL | BK | | | $85.00 |
| Custom Barracuda | 6211 | | USA | M-BR-D | CL | GY | | | $85.00 |
| Custom Barracuda | 6211 | | HK | M-BR-D | BL | GY | | | $85.00 |
| Custom Barracuda | 6211 | | USA | M-BR-D | CL | PR | | | $105.00 |
| Custom Barracuda | 6211 | | HK | M-BR-D | BL | PR | | | $105.00 |
| Custom Barracuda | 6211 | | USA | M-BR-D | CL | BR-L | | | $85.00 |
| Custom Barracuda | 6211 | | HK | M-BR-D | BL | BR-L | | | $85.00 |
| Custom Barracuda | 6211 | | USA | M-BR-D | CL | BR-D | | | $85.00 |
| Custom Barracuda | 6211 | | HK | M-BR-D | BL | BR-D | | | $85.00 |
| Custom Barracuda | 6211 | | USA | M-BR-P | CL | WH | | | $85.00 |
| Custom Barracuda | 6211 | | HK | M-BR-P | BL | WH | | | $85.00 |
| Custom Barracuda | 6211 | | USA | M-BR-P | CL | BK | | | $75.00 |
| Custom Barracuda | 6211 | | HK | M-BR-P | BL | BK | | | $75.00 |
| Custom Barracuda | 6211 | | USA | M-BR-P | CL | GY | | | $75.00 |
| Custom Barracuda | 6211 | | HK | M-BR-P | BL | GY | | | $75.00 |
| Custom Barracuda | 6211 | | USA | M-BR-P | CL | PR | | | $105.00 |
| Custom Barracuda | 6211 | | HK | M-BR-P | BL | PR | | | $105.00 |
| Custom Barracuda | 6211 | | USA | M-BR-P | CL | BR-L | | | $75.00 |
| Custom Barracuda | 6211 | | HK | M-BR-P | BL | BR-L | | | $75.00 |
| Custom Barracuda | 6211 | | USA | M-BR-P | CL | BR-D | | | $75.00 |
| Custom Barracuda | 6211 | | HK | M-BR-P | BL | BR-D | | | $75.00 |
| Custom Barracuda | 6211 | | USA | M-GD | CL | WH | | | $115.00 |
| Custom Barracuda | 6211 | | HK | M-GD | BL | WH | | | $115.00 |
| Custom Barracuda | 6211 | | USA | M-GD | CL | BK | | | $105.00 |
| Custom Barracuda | 6211 | | HK | M-GD | BL | BK | | | $105.00 |
| Custom Barracuda | 6211 | | USA | M-GD | CL | GY | | | $105.00 |
| Custom Barracuda | 6211 | | HK | M-GD | BL | GY | | | $105.00 |
| Custom Barracuda | 6211 | | USA | M-GD | CL | BR-L | | | $105.00 |
| Custom Barracuda | 6211 | | HK | M-GD | BL | BR-L | | | $105.00 |
| Custom Barracuda | 6211 | | USA | M-GD | CL | BR-D | | | $105.00 |
| Custom Barracuda | 6211 | | HK | M-GD | BL | BR-D | | | $105.00 |
| Custom Barracuda | 6211 | | USA | M-GR | CL | WH | | | $115.00 |
| Custom Barracuda | 6211 | | HK | M-GR | BL | WH | | | $115.00 |
| Custom Barracuda | 6211 | | USA | M-GR | CL | BK | | | $105.00 |
| Custom Barracuda | 6211 | | HK | M-GR | BL | BK | | | $105.00 |
| Custom Barracuda | 6211 | | USA | M-GR | CL | GY | | | $105.00 |
| Custom Barracuda | 6211 | | HK | M-GR | BL | GY | | | $105.00 |
| Custom Barracuda | 6211 | | USA | M-GR | CL | BR-L | | | $105.00 |

## 1968 Variations

| Name | Number | Casting | Country | Color | Windows | Interior | Paint | Other | Value |
|---|---|---|---|---|---|---|---|---|---|
| Custom Barracuda | 6211 | | HK | M-GR | BL | BR-L | | | $105.00 |
| Custom Barracuda | 6211 | | USA | M-GR | CL | BR-D | | | $105.00 |
| Custom Barracuda | 6211 | | HK | M-GR | BL | BR-D | | | $105.00 |
| Custom Barracuda | 6211 | | USA | M-GR-E | CL | WH | | | $125.00 |
| Custom Barracuda | 6211 | | HK | M-GR-E | BL | WH | | | $125.00 |
| Custom Barracuda | 6211 | | USA | M-GR-E | CL | BK | | | $115.00 |
| Custom Barracuda | 6211 | | HK | M-GR-E | BL | BK | | | $115.00 |
| Custom Barracuda | 6211 | | USA | M-GR-E | CL | GY | | | $115.00 |
| Custom Barracuda | 6211 | | HK | M-GR-E | BL | GY | | | $115.00 |
| Custom Barracuda | 6211 | | USA | M-GR-E | CL | BR-L | | | $115.00 |
| Custom Barracuda | 6211 | | HK | M-GR-E | BL | BR-L | | | $115.00 |
| Custom Barracuda | 6211 | | USA | M-GR-E | CL | BR-D | | | $115.00 |
| Custom Barracuda | 6211 | | HK | M-GR-E | BL | BR-D | | | $115.00 |
| Custom Barracuda | 6211 | | USA | M-GR-L | CL | WH | | | $155.00 |
| Custom Barracuda | 6211 | | HK | M-GR-L | BL | WH | | | $155.00 |
| Custom Barracuda | 6211 | | USA | M-GR-L | CL | BK | | | $145.00 |
| Custom Barracuda | 6211 | | HK | M-GR-L | BL | BK | | | $145.00 |
| Custom Barracuda | 6211 | | USA | M-GR-L | CL | GY | | | $145.00 |
| Custom Barracuda | 6211 | | HK | M-GR-L | BL | GY | | | $145.00 |
| Custom Barracuda | 6211 | | USA | M-GR-L | CL | BR-L | | | $145.00 |
| Custom Barracuda | 6211 | | HK | M-GR-L | BL | BR-L | | | $145.00 |
| Custom Barracuda | 6211 | | USA | M-GR-L | CL | BR-D | | | $145.00 |
| Custom Barracuda | 6211 | | HK | M-GR-L | BL | BR-D | | | $145.00 |
| Custom Barracuda | 6211 | | USA | M-GR-O | CL | WH | | | $180.00 |
| Custom Barracuda | 6211 | | HK | M-GR-O | BL | WH | | | $180.00 |
| Custom Barracuda | 6211 | | USA | M-GR-O | CL | BK | | | $160.00 |
| Custom Barracuda | 6211 | | HK | M-GR-O | BL | BK | | | $160.00 |
| Custom Barracuda | 6211 | | USA | M-GR-O | CL | GY | | | $160.00 |
| Custom Barracuda | 6211 | | HK | M-GR-O | BL | GY | | | $160.00 |
| Custom Barracuda | 6211 | | USA | M-GR-O | CL | BR-L | | | $160.00 |
| Custom Barracuda | 6211 | | HK | M-GR-O | BL | BR-L | | | $160.00 |
| Custom Barracuda | 6211 | | USA | M-GR-O | CL | BR-D | | | $160.00 |
| Custom Barracuda | 6211 | | HK | M-GR-O | BL | BR-D | | | $160.00 |
| Custom Barracuda | 6211 | | USA | M-MG | CL | WH | | | $240.00 |
| Custom Barracuda | 6211 | | HK | M-MG | BL | WH | | | $240.00 |
| Custom Barracuda | 6211 | | USA | M-MG | CL | BK | | | $220.00 |
| Custom Barracuda | 6211 | | HK | M-MG | BL | BK | | | $220.00 |
| Custom Barracuda | 6211 | | USA | M-MG | CL | GY | | | $220.00 |
| Custom Barracuda | 6211 | | HK | M-MG | BL | GY | | | $220.00 |
| Custom Barracuda | 6211 | | USA | M-MG | CL | BR-L | | | $220.00 |
| Custom Barracuda | 6211 | | HK | M-MG | BL | BR-L | | | $220.00 |
| Custom Barracuda | 6211 | | USA | M-MG | CL | BR-D | | | $220.00 |
| Custom Barracuda | 6211 | | HK | M-MG | BL | BR-D | | | $220.00 |
| Custom Barracuda | 6211 | | USA | M-OR | CL | WH | | | $170.00 |
| Custom Barracuda | 6211 | | HK | M-OR | BL | WH | | | $170.00 |
| Custom Barracuda | 6211 | | USA | M-OR | CL | BK | | | $150.00 |
| Custom Barracuda | 6211 | | HK | M-OR | BL | BK | | | $150.00 |
| Custom Barracuda | 6211 | | USA | M-OR | CL | GY | | | $150.00 |
| Custom Barracuda | 6211 | | HK | M-OR | BL | GY | | | $150.00 |
| Custom Barracuda | 6211 | | USA | M-OR | CL | BR-L | | | $150.00 |
| Custom Barracuda | 6211 | | HK | M-OR | BL | BR-L | | | $150.00 |
| Custom Barracuda | 6211 | | USA | M-OR | CL | BR-D | | | $150.00 |
| Custom Barracuda | 6211 | | HK | M-OR | BL | BR-D | | | $150.00 |
| Custom Barracuda | 6211 | | USA | M-PK | CL | WH | | | $300.00 |
| Custom Barracuda | 6211 | | HK | M-PK | BL | WH | | | $300.00 |
| Custom Barracuda | 6211 | | USA | M-PK | CL | BK | | | $260.00 |
| Custom Barracuda | 6211 | | HK | M-PK | BL | BK | | | $260.00 |
| Custom Barracuda | 6211 | | USA | M-PK | CL | GY | | | $260.00 |
| Custom Barracuda | 6211 | | HK | M-PK | BL | GY | | | $260.00 |
| Custom Barracuda | 6211 | | USA | M-PK | CL | BR-L | | | $260.00 |
| Custom Barracuda | 6211 | | HK | M-PK | BL | BR-L | | | $260.00 |
| Custom Barracuda | 6211 | | USA | M-PK | CL | BR-D | | | $260.00 |
| Custom Barracuda | 6211 | | HK | M-PK | BL | BR-D | | | $260.00 |
| Custom Barracuda | 6211 | | USA | M-PK-H | CL | WH | | | $300.00 |
| Custom Barracuda | 6211 | | HK | M-PK-H | BL | WH | | | $300.00 |
| Custom Barracuda | 6211 | | USA | M-PK-H | CL | BK | | | $260.00 |
| Custom Barracuda | 6211 | | HK | M-PK-H | BL | BK | | | $260.00 |
| Custom Barracuda | 6211 | | USA | M-PK-H | CL | GY | | | $260.00 |
| Custom Barracuda | 6211 | | HK | M-PK-H | BL | GY | | | $260.00 |
| Custom Barracuda | 6211 | | USA | M-PK-H | CL | BR-L | | | $260.00 |
| Custom Barracuda | 6211 | | HK | M-PK-H | BL | BR-L | | | $260.00 |
| Custom Barracuda | 6211 | | USA | M-PK-H | CL | BR-D | | | $260.00 |

## 1968 Variations

| Name | Number | Casting | Country | Color | Windows | Interior | Paint | Other | Value |
|---|---|---|---|---|---|---|---|---|---|
| Custom Barracuda | 6211 | | HK | M-PK-H | BL | BR-D | | | $260.00 |
| Custom Barracuda | 6211 | | USA | M-PK-S | CL | WH | | | $300.00 |
| Custom Barracuda | 6211 | | HK | M-PK-S | BL | WH | | | $300.00 |
| Custom Barracuda | 6211 | | USA | M-PK-S | CL | BK | | | $260.00 |
| Custom Barracuda | 6211 | | HK | M-PK-S | BL | BK | | | $260.00 |
| Custom Barracuda | 6211 | | USA | M-PK-S | CL | GY | | | $260.00 |
| Custom Barracuda | 6211 | | HK | M-PK-S | BL | GY | | | $260.00 |
| Custom Barracuda | 6211 | | USA | M-PK-S | CL | BR-L | | | $260.00 |
| Custom Barracuda | 6211 | | HK | M-PK-S | BL | BR-L | | | $260.00 |
| Custom Barracuda | 6211 | | USA | M-PK-S | CL | BR-D | | | $260.00 |
| Custom Barracuda | 6211 | | HK | M-PK-S | BL | BR-D | | | $260.00 |
| Custom Barracuda | 6211 | | USA | M-PR | CL | WH | | | $270.00 |
| Custom Barracuda | 6211 | | HK | M-PR | BL | WH | | | $270.00 |
| Custom Barracuda | 6211 | | USA | M-PR | CL | BK | | | $240.00 |
| Custom Barracuda | 6211 | | HK | M-PR | BL | BK | | | $240.00 |
| Custom Barracuda | 6211 | | USA | M-PR | CL | GY | | | $240.00 |
| Custom Barracuda | 6211 | | HK | M-PR | BL | GY | | | $240.00 |
| Custom Barracuda | 6211 | | USA | M-PR | CL | PR | | | $270.00 |
| Custom Barracuda | 6211 | | HK | M-PR | BL | PR | | | $270.00 |
| Custom Barracuda | 6211 | | USA | M-PR | CL | BR-L | | | $240.00 |
| Custom Barracuda | 6211 | | HK | M-PR | BL | BR-L | | | $240.00 |
| Custom Barracuda | 6211 | | USA | M-PR | CL | BR-D | | | $240.00 |
| Custom Barracuda | 6211 | | HK | M-PR | BL | BR-D | | | $240.00 |
| Custom Barracuda | 6211 | | USA | M-RD | CL | WH | | | $225.00 |
| Custom Barracuda | 6211 | | HK | M-RD | BL | WH | | | $225.00 |
| Custom Barracuda | 6211 | | USA | M-RD | CL | BK | | | $195.00 |
| Custom Barracuda | 6211 | | HK | M-RD | BL | BK | | | $195.00 |
| Custom Barracuda | 6211 | | USA | M-RD | CL | GY | | | $195.00 |
| Custom Barracuda | 6211 | | HK | M-RD | BL | GY | | | $195.00 |
| Custom Barracuda | 6211 | | USA | M-RD | CL | BR-L | | | $195.00 |
| Custom Barracuda | 6211 | | HK | M-RD | BL | BR-L | | | $195.00 |
| Custom Barracuda | 6211 | | USA | M-RD | CL | BR-D | | | $195.00 |
| Custom Barracuda | 6211 | | HK | M-RD | BL | BR-D | | | $195.00 |
| Custom Barracuda | 6211 | | USA | M-RD-R | CL | WH | | | $285.00 |
| Custom Barracuda | 6211 | | HK | M-RD-R | BL | WH | | | $285.00 |
| Custom Barracuda | 6211 | | USA | M-RD-R | CL | BK | | | $255.00 |
| Custom Barracuda | 6211 | | HK | M-RD-R | BL | BK | | | $255.00 |
| Custom Barracuda | 6211 | | USA | M-RD-R | CL | GY | | | $255.00 |
| Custom Barracuda | 6211 | | HK | M-RD-R | BL | GY | | | $255.00 |
| Custom Barracuda | 6211 | | USA | M-RD-R | CL | BR-L | | | $255.00 |
| Custom Barracuda | 6211 | | HK | M-RD-R | BL | BR-L | | | $255.00 |
| Custom Barracuda | 6211 | | USA | M-RD-R | CL | BR-D | | | $255.00 |
| Custom Barracuda | 6211 | | HK | M-RD-R | BL | BR-D | | | $255.00 |
| Custom Barracuda | 6211 | | USA | M-YW | CL | WH | | | $95.00 |
| Custom Barracuda | 6211 | | HK | M-YW | BL | WH | | | $95.00 |
| Custom Barracuda | 6211 | | USA | M-YW | CL | BK | | | $85.00 |
| Custom Barracuda | 6211 | | HK | M-YW | BL | BK | | | $85.00 |
| Custom Barracuda | 6211 | | USA | M-YW | CL | GY | | | $85.00 |
| Custom Barracuda | 6211 | | HK | M-YW | BL | GY | | | $85.00 |
| Custom Barracuda | 6211 | | USA | M-YW | CL | BR-L | | | $85.00 |
| Custom Barracuda | 6211 | | HK | M-YW | BL | BR-L | | | $85.00 |
| Custom Barracuda | 6211 | | USA | M-YW | CL | BR-D | | | $85.00 |
| Custom Barracuda | 6211 | | HK | M-YW | BL | BR-D | | | $85.00 |
| Custom Barracuda | 6211 | | USA | M-YW-L | CL | WH | | | $130.00 |
| Custom Barracuda | 6211 | | HK | M-YW-L | BL | WH | | | $130.00 |
| Custom Barracuda | 6211 | | USA | M-YW-L | CL | BK | | | $120.00 |
| Custom Barracuda | 6211 | | HK | M-YW-L | BL | BK | | | $120.00 |
| Custom Barracuda | 6211 | | USA | M-YW-L | CL | GY | | | $120.00 |
| Custom Barracuda | 6211 | | HK | M-YW-L | BL | GY | | | $120.00 |
| Custom Barracuda | 6211 | | USA | M-YW-L | CL | BR-L | | | $120.00 |
| Custom Barracuda | 6211 | | HK | M-YW-L | BL | BR-L | | | $120.00 |
| Custom Barracuda | 6211 | | USA | M-YW-L | CL | BR-D | | | $120.00 |
| Custom Barracuda | 6211 | | HK | M-YW-L | BL | BR-D | | | $120.00 |
| | | | | | | | | | |
| Custom Firebird | 6212 | Doors | USA | M-AQ | CL | WH | | | $75.00 |
| Custom Firebird | 6212 | Doors | USA | M-AQ | CL | BK | | | $75.00 |
| Custom Firebird | 6212 | Doors | USA | M-AQ | CL | GY | | | $75.00 |
| Custom Firebird | 6212 | Doors | USA | M-AQ | CL | BR-L | | | $75.00 |
| Custom Firebird | 6212 | Doors | USA | M-AQ | CL | BR-D | | | $75.00 |
| Custom Firebird | 6212 | No doors | USA | M-AQ | CL | WH | | | $75.00 |
| Custom Firebird | 6212 | No doors | HK | M-AQ | BL | WH | | | $75.00 |

## 1968 Variations

| Name | Number | Casting | Country | Color | Windows | Interior | Paint | Other | Value |
|---|---|---|---|---|---|---|---|---|---|
| Custom Firebird | 6212 | No doors | USA | M-AQ | CL | BK | | | $75.00 |
| Custom Firebird | 6212 | No doors | HK | M-AQ | BL | BK | | | $75.00 |
| Custom Firebird | 6212 | No doors | USA | M-AQ | CL | GY | | | $75.00 |
| Custom Firebird | 6212 | No doors | HK | M-AQ | BL | GY | | | $75.00 |
| Custom Firebird | 6212 | No doors | USA | M-AQ | CL | BR-L | | | $75.00 |
| Custom Firebird | 6212 | No doors | HK | M-AQ | BL | BR-L | | | $75.00 |
| Custom Firebird | 6212 | No doors | USA | M-AQ | CL | BR-D | | | $75.00 |
| Custom Firebird | 6212 | No doors | HK | M-AQ | BL | BR-D | | | $75.00 |
| Custom Firebird | 6212 | Doors | USA | M-BL | CL | WH | | | $60.00 |
| Custom Firebird | 6212 | Doors | USA | M-BL | CL | BK | | | $60.00 |
| Custom Firebird | 6212 | Doors | USA | M-BL | CL | GY | | | $60.00 |
| Custom Firebird | 6212 | Doors | USA | M-BL | CL | BL | | | $75.00 |
| Custom Firebird | 6212 | Doors | USA | M-BL | CL | BR-L | | | $60.00 |
| Custom Firebird | 6212 | Doors | USA | M-BL | CL | BR-D | | | $60.00 |
| Custom Firebird | 6212 | No doors | USA | M-BL | CL | WH | | | $60.00 |
| Custom Firebird | 6212 | No doors | HK | M-BL | BL | WH | | | $60.00 |
| Custom Firebird | 6212 | No doors | USA | M-BL | CL | BK | | | $60.00 |
| Custom Firebird | 6212 | No doors | HK | M-BL | BL | BK | | | $60.00 |
| Custom Firebird | 6212 | No doors | USA | M-BL | CL | GY | | | $60.00 |
| Custom Firebird | 6212 | No doors | HK | M-BL | BL | GY | | | $60.00 |
| Custom Firebird | 6212 | No doors | USA | M-BL | CL | BL | | | $75.00 |
| Custom Firebird | 6212 | No doors | HK | M-BL | BL | BL | | | $75.00 |
| Custom Firebird | 6212 | No doors | USA | M-BL | CL | BR-L | | | $60.00 |
| Custom Firebird | 6212 | No doors | HK | M-BL | BL | BR-L | | | $60.00 |
| Custom Firebird | 6212 | No doors | USA | M-BL | CL | BR-D | | | $60.00 |
| Custom Firebird | 6212 | No doors | HK | M-BL | BL | BR-D | | | $60.00 |
| Custom Firebird | 6212 | Doors | USA | M-BL-I | CL | WH | | | $80.00 |
| Custom Firebird | 6212 | Doors | USA | M-BL-I | CL | BK | | | $80.00 |
| Custom Firebird | 6212 | Doors | USA | M-BL-I | CL | GY | | | $80.00 |
| Custom Firebird | 6212 | Doors | USA | M-BL-I | CL | BL | | | $100.00 |
| Custom Firebird | 6212 | Doors | USA | M-BL-I | CL | BR-L | | | $80.00 |
| Custom Firebird | 6212 | Doors | USA | M-BL-I | CL | BR-D | | | $80.00 |
| Custom Firebird | 6212 | No doors | USA | M-BL-I | CL | WH | | | $80.00 |
| Custom Firebird | 6212 | No doors | HK | M-BL-I | BL | WH | | | $80.00 |
| Custom Firebird | 6212 | No doors | USA | M-BL-I | CL | BK | | | $80.00 |
| Custom Firebird | 6212 | No doors | HK | M-BL-I | BL | BK | | | $80.00 |
| Custom Firebird | 6212 | No doors | USA | M-BL-I | CL | GY | | | $80.00 |
| Custom Firebird | 6212 | No doors | HK | M-BL-I | BL | GY | | | $80.00 |
| Custom Firebird | 6212 | No doors | USA | M-BL-I | CL | BL | | | $100.00 |
| Custom Firebird | 6212 | No doors | HK | M-BL-I | BL | BL | | | $100.00 |
| Custom Firebird | 6212 | No doors | USA | M-BL-I | CL | BR-L | | | $80.00 |
| Custom Firebird | 6212 | No doors | HK | M-BL-I | BL | BR-L | | | $80.00 |
| Custom Firebird | 6212 | No doors | USA | M-BL-I | CL | BR-D | | | $80.00 |
| Custom Firebird | 6212 | No doors | HK | M-BL-I | BL | BR-D | | | $80.00 |
| Custom Firebird | 6212 | Doors | USA | M-BL-P | CL | WH | | | $60.00 |
| Custom Firebird | 6212 | Doors | USA | M-BL-P | CL | BK | | | $60.00 |
| Custom Firebird | 6212 | Doors | USA | M-BL-P | CL | GY | | | $60.00 |
| Custom Firebird | 6212 | Doors | USA | M-BL-P | CL | BL | | | $80.00 |
| Custom Firebird | 6212 | Doors | USA | M-BL-P | CL | BR-L | | | $60.00 |
| Custom Firebird | 6212 | Doors | USA | M-BL-P | CL | BR-D | | | $60.00 |
| Custom Firebird | 6212 | No doors | USA | M-BL-P | CL | WH | | | $60.00 |
| Custom Firebird | 6212 | No doors | HK | M-BL-P | BL | WH | | | $60.00 |
| Custom Firebird | 6212 | No doors | USA | M-BL-P | CL | BK | | | $60.00 |
| Custom Firebird | 6212 | No doors | HK | M-BL-P | BL | BK | | | $60.00 |
| Custom Firebird | 6212 | No doors | USA | M-BL-P | CL | GY | | | $60.00 |
| Custom Firebird | 6212 | No doors | HK | M-BL-P | BL | GY | | | $60.00 |
| Custom Firebird | 6212 | No doors | USA | M-BL-P | CL | BL | | | $80.00 |
| Custom Firebird | 6212 | No doors | HK | M-BL-P | BL | BL | | | $80.00 |
| Custom Firebird | 6212 | No doors | USA | M-BL-P | CL | BR-L | | | $60.00 |
| Custom Firebird | 6212 | No doors | HK | M-BL-P | BL | BR-L | | | $60.00 |
| Custom Firebird | 6212 | No doors | USA | M-BL-P | CL | BR-D | | | $60.00 |
| Custom Firebird | 6212 | No doors | HK | M-BL-P | BL | BR-D | | | $60.00 |
| Custom Firebird | 6212 | Doors | USA | M-BR-D | CL | WH | | | $100.00 |
| Custom Firebird | 6212 | Doors | USA | M-BR-D | CL | BK | | | $100.00 |
| Custom Firebird | 6212 | Doors | USA | M-BR-D | CL | GY | | | $100.00 |
| Custom Firebird | 6212 | Doors | USA | M-BR-D | CL | BR-L | | | $100.00 |
| Custom Firebird | 6212 | Doors | USA | M-BR-D | CL | BR-D | | | $100.00 |
| Custom Firebird | 6212 | No doors | USA | M-BR-D | CL | WH | | | $100.00 |
| Custom Firebird | 6212 | No doors | HK | M-BR-D | BL | WH | | | $100.00 |
| Custom Firebird | 6212 | No doors | USA | M-BR-D | CL | BK | | | $100.00 |
| Custom Firebird | 6212 | No doors | HK | M-BR-D | BL | BK | | | $100.00 |
| Custom Firebird | 6212 | No doors | USA | M-BR-D | CL | GY | | | $100.00 |

## 1968 Variations

| Name | Number | Casting | Country | Color | Windows | Interior | Paint | Other | Value |
|---|---|---|---|---|---|---|---|---|---|
| Custom Firebird | 6212 | No doors | HK | M-BR-D | BL | GY | | | $100.00 |
| Custom Firebird | 6212 | No doors | USA | M-BR-D | CL | BR-L | | | $100.00 |
| Custom Firebird | 6212 | No doors | HK | M-BR-D | BL | BR-L | | | $100.00 |
| Custom Firebird | 6212 | No doors | USA | M-BR-D | CL | BR-D | | | $100.00 |
| Custom Firebird | 6212 | No doors | HK | M-BR-D | BL | BR-D | | | $100.00 |
| Custom Firebird | 6212 | Doors | USA | M-BR-P | CL | WH | | | $90.00 |
| Custom Firebird | 6212 | Doors | USA | M-BR-P | CL | BK | | | $90.00 |
| Custom Firebird | 6212 | Doors | USA | M-BR-P | CL | GY | | | $90.00 |
| Custom Firebird | 6212 | Doors | USA | M-BR-P | CL | BR-L | | | $90.00 |
| Custom Firebird | 6212 | Doors | USA | M-BR-P | CL | BR-D | | | $90.00 |
| Custom Firebird | 6212 | No doors | USA | M-BR-P | CL | WH | | | $90.00 |
| Custom Firebird | 6212 | No doors | HK | M-BR-P | BL | WH | | | $90.00 |
| Custom Firebird | 6212 | No doors | USA | M-BR-P | CL | BK | | | $90.00 |
| Custom Firebird | 6212 | No doors | HK | M-BR-P | BL | BK | | | $90.00 |
| Custom Firebird | 6212 | No doors | USA | M-BR-P | CL | GY | | | $90.00 |
| Custom Firebird | 6212 | No doors | HK | M-BR-P | BL | GY | | | $90.00 |
| Custom Firebird | 6212 | No doors | USA | M-BR-P | CL | BR-L | | | $90.00 |
| Custom Firebird | 6212 | No doors | HK | M-BR-P | BL | BR-L | | | $90.00 |
| Custom Firebird | 6212 | No doors | USA | M-BR-P | CL | BR-D | | | $90.00 |
| Custom Firebird | 6212 | No doors | HK | M-BR-P | BL | BR-D | | | $90.00 |
| Custom Firebird | 6212 | Doors | USA | M-GD | CL | WH | | | $60.00 |
| Custom Firebird | 6212 | Doors | USA | M-GD | CL | BK | | | $60.00 |
| Custom Firebird | 6212 | Doors | USA | M-GD | CL | GY | | | $60.00 |
| Custom Firebird | 6212 | Doors | USA | M-GD | CL | BR-L | | | $60.00 |
| Custom Firebird | 6212 | Doors | USA | M-GD | CL | BR-D | | | $60.00 |
| Custom Firebird | 6212 | No doors | USA | M-GD | CL | WH | | | $60.00 |
| Custom Firebird | 6212 | No doors | HK | M-GD | BL | WH | | | $60.00 |
| Custom Firebird | 6212 | No doors | USA | M-GD | CL | BK | | | $60.00 |
| Custom Firebird | 6212 | No doors | HK | M-GD | BL | BK | | | $60.00 |
| Custom Firebird | 6212 | No doors | USA | M-GD | CL | GY | | | $60.00 |
| Custom Firebird | 6212 | No doors | HK | M-GD | BL | GY | | | $60.00 |
| Custom Firebird | 6212 | No doors | USA | M-GD | CL | BR-L | | | $60.00 |
| Custom Firebird | 6212 | No doors | HK | M-GD | BL | BR-L | | | $60.00 |
| Custom Firebird | 6212 | No doors | USA | M-GD | CL | BR-D | | | $60.00 |
| Custom Firebird | 6212 | No doors | HK | M-GD | BL | BR-D | | | $60.00 |
| Custom Firebird | 6212 | Doors | USA | M-GR | CL | WH | | | $60.00 |
| Custom Firebird | 6212 | Doors | USA | M-GR | CL | BK | | | $60.00 |
| Custom Firebird | 6212 | Doors | USA | M-GR | CL | GY | | | $60.00 |
| Custom Firebird | 6212 | Doors | USA | M-GR | CL | BR-L | | | $60.00 |
| Custom Firebird | 6212 | Doors | USA | M-GR | CL | BR-D | | | $60.00 |
| Custom Firebird | 6212 | No doors | USA | M-GR | CL | WH | | | $60.00 |
| Custom Firebird | 6212 | No doors | HK | M-GR | BL | WH | | | $60.00 |
| Custom Firebird | 6212 | No doors | USA | M-GR | CL | BK | | | $60.00 |
| Custom Firebird | 6212 | No doors | HK | M-GR | BL | BK | | | $60.00 |
| Custom Firebird | 6212 | No doors | USA | M-GR | CL | GY | | | $60.00 |
| Custom Firebird | 6212 | No doors | HK | M-GR | BL | GY | | | $60.00 |
| Custom Firebird | 6212 | No doors | USA | M-GR | CL | BR-L | | | $60.00 |
| Custom Firebird | 6212 | No doors | HK | M-GR | BL | BR-L | | | $60.00 |
| Custom Firebird | 6212 | No doors | USA | M-GR | CL | BR-D | | | $60.00 |
| Custom Firebird | 6212 | No doors | HK | M-GR | BL | BR-D | | | $60.00 |
| Custom Firebird | 6212 | Doors | USA | M-GR-E | CL | WH | | | $75.00 |
| Custom Firebird | 6212 | Doors | USA | M-GR-E | CL | BK | | | $75.00 |
| Custom Firebird | 6212 | Doors | USA | M-GR-E | CL | GY | | | $75.00 |
| Custom Firebird | 6212 | Doors | USA | M-GR-E | CL | BR-L | | | $75.00 |
| Custom Firebird | 6212 | Doors | USA | M-GR-E | CL | BR-D | | | $75.00 |
| Custom Firebird | 6212 | No doors | USA | M-GR-E | CL | WH | | | $75.00 |
| Custom Firebird | 6212 | No doors | HK | M-GR-E | BL | WH | | | $75.00 |
| Custom Firebird | 6212 | No doors | USA | M-GR-E | CL | BK | | | $75.00 |
| Custom Firebird | 6212 | No doors | HK | M-GR-E | BL | BK | | | $75.00 |
| Custom Firebird | 6212 | No doors | USA | M-GR-E | CL | GY | | | $75.00 |
| Custom Firebird | 6212 | No doors | HK | M-GR-E | BL | GY | | | $75.00 |
| Custom Firebird | 6212 | No doors | USA | M-GR-E | CL | BR-L | | | $75.00 |
| Custom Firebird | 6212 | No doors | HK | M-GR-E | BL | BR-L | | | $75.00 |
| Custom Firebird | 6212 | No doors | USA | M-GR-E | CL | BR-D | | | $75.00 |
| Custom Firebird | 6212 | No doors | HK | M-GR-E | BL | BR-D | | | $75.00 |
| Custom Firebird | 6212 | Doors | USA | M-GR-L | CL | WH | | | $80.00 |
| Custom Firebird | 6212 | Doors | USA | M-GR-L | CL | BK | | | $80.00 |
| Custom Firebird | 6212 | Doors | USA | M-GR-L | CL | GY | | | $80.00 |
| Custom Firebird | 6212 | Doors | USA | M-GR-L | CL | BR-L | | | $80.00 |
| Custom Firebird | 6212 | Doors | USA | M-GR-L | CL | BR-D | | | $80.00 |
| Custom Firebird | 6212 | No doors | USA | M-GR-L | CL | WH | | | $80.00 |
| Custom Firebird | 6212 | No doors | HK | M-GR-L | BL | WH | | | $80.00 |

**1968 Variations**

| Name | Number | Casting | Country | Color | Windows | Interior | Paint | Other | Value |
|---|---|---|---|---|---|---|---|---|---|
| Custom Firebird | 6212 | No doors | USA | M-GR-L | CL | BK | | | $80.00 |
| Custom Firebird | 6212 | No doors | HK | M-GR-L | BL | BK | | | $80.00 |
| Custom Firebird | 6212 | No doors | USA | M-GR-L | CL | GY | | | $80.00 |
| Custom Firebird | 6212 | No doors | HK | M-GR-L | BL | GY | | | $80.00 |
| Custom Firebird | 6212 | No doors | USA | M-GR-L | CL | BR-L | | | $80.00 |
| Custom Firebird | 6212 | No doors | HK | M-GR-L | BL | BR-L | | | $80.00 |
| Custom Firebird | 6212 | No doors | USA | M-GR-L | CL | BR-D | | | $80.00 |
| Custom Firebird | 6212 | No doors | HK | M-GR-L | BL | BR-D | | | $80.00 |
| Custom Firebird | 6212 | Doors | USA | M-GR-O | CL | WH | | | $90.00 |
| Custom Firebird | 6212 | Doors | USA | M-GR-O | CL | BK | | | $90.00 |
| Custom Firebird | 6212 | Doors | USA | M-GR-O | CL | GY | | | $90.00 |
| Custom Firebird | 6212 | Doors | USA | M-GR-O | CL | BR-L | | | $90.00 |
| Custom Firebird | 6212 | Doors | USA | M-GR-O | CL | BR-D | | | $90.00 |
| Custom Firebird | 6212 | No doors | USA | M-GR-O | CL | WH | | | $90.00 |
| Custom Firebird | 6212 | No doors | HK | M-GR-O | BL | WH | | | $90.00 |
| Custom Firebird | 6212 | No doors | USA | M-GR-O | CL | BK | | | $90.00 |
| Custom Firebird | 6212 | No doors | HK | M-GR-O | BL | BK | | | $90.00 |
| Custom Firebird | 6212 | No doors | USA | M-GR-O | CL | GY | | | $90.00 |
| Custom Firebird | 6212 | No doors | HK | M-GR-O | BL | GY | | | $90.00 |
| Custom Firebird | 6212 | No doors | USA | M-GR-O | CL | BR-L | | | $90.00 |
| Custom Firebird | 6212 | No doors | HK | M-GR-O | BL | BR-L | | | $90.00 |
| Custom Firebird | 6212 | No doors | USA | M-GR-O | CL | BR-D | | | $90.00 |
| Custom Firebird | 6212 | No doors | HK | M-GR-O | BL | BR-D | | | $90.00 |
| Custom Firebird | 6212 | Doors | USA | M-MG | CL | WH | | | $150.00 |
| Custom Firebird | 6212 | Doors | USA | M-MG | CL | BK | | | $140.00 |
| Custom Firebird | 6212 | Doors | USA | M-MG | CL | GY | | | $140.00 |
| Custom Firebird | 6212 | Doors | USA | M-MG | CL | BR-L | | | $140.00 |
| Custom Firebird | 6212 | Doors | USA | M-MG | CL | BR-D | | | $140.00 |
| Custom Firebird | 6212 | No doors | USA | M-MG | CL | WH | | | $150.00 |
| Custom Firebird | 6212 | No doors | HK | M-MG | BL | WH | | | $140.00 |
| Custom Firebird | 6212 | No doors | USA | M-MG | CL | BK | | | $140.00 |
| Custom Firebird | 6212 | No doors | HK | M-MG | BL | BK | | | $140.00 |
| Custom Firebird | 6212 | No doors | USA | M-MG | CL | GY | | | $140.00 |
| Custom Firebird | 6212 | No doors | HK | M-MG | BL | GY | | | $140.00 |
| Custom Firebird | 6212 | No doors | USA | M-MG | CL | BR-L | | | $140.00 |
| Custom Firebird | 6212 | No doors | HK | M-MG | BL | BR-L | | | $140.00 |
| Custom Firebird | 6212 | No doors | USA | M-MG | CL | BR-D | | | $140.00 |
| Custom Firebird | 6212 | No doors | HK | M-MG | BL | BR-D | | | $140.00 |
| Custom Firebird | 6212 | Doors | USA | M-OR | CL | WH | | | $75.00 |
| Custom Firebird | 6212 | Doors | USA | M-OR | CL | BK | | | $75.00 |
| Custom Firebird | 6212 | Doors | USA | M-OR | CL | GY | | | $75.00 |
| Custom Firebird | 6212 | Doors | USA | M-OR | CL | BR-L | | | $75.00 |
| Custom Firebird | 6212 | Doors | USA | M-OR | CL | BR-D | | | $75.00 |
| Custom Firebird | 6212 | No doors | USA | M-OR | CL | WH | | | $75.00 |
| Custom Firebird | 6212 | No doors | HK | M-OR | BL | WH | | | $75.00 |
| Custom Firebird | 6212 | No doors | USA | M-OR | CL | BK | | | $75.00 |
| Custom Firebird | 6212 | No doors | HK | M-OR | BL | BK | | | $75.00 |
| Custom Firebird | 6212 | No doors | USA | M-OR | CL | GY | | | $75.00 |
| Custom Firebird | 6212 | No doors | HK | M-OR | BL | GY | | | $75.00 |
| Custom Firebird | 6212 | No doors | USA | M-OR | CL | BR-L | | | $75.00 |
| Custom Firebird | 6212 | No doors | HK | M-OR | BL | BR-L | | | $75.00 |
| Custom Firebird | 6212 | No doors | USA | M-OR | CL | BR-D | | | $75.00 |
| Custom Firebird | 6212 | No doors | HK | M-OR | BL | BR-D | | | $75.00 |
| Custom Firebird | 6212 | Doors | USA | M-PR | CL | WH | | | $200.00 |
| Custom Firebird | 6212 | Doors | USA | M-PR | CL | BK | | | $200.00 |
| Custom Firebird | 6212 | Doors | USA | M-PR | CL | GY | | | $200.00 |
| Custom Firebird | 6212 | Doors | USA | M-PR | CL | BR-L | | | $200.00 |
| Custom Firebird | 6212 | Doors | USA | M-PR | CL | BR-D | | | $200.00 |
| Custom Firebird | 6212 | No doors | USA | M-PR | CL | WH | | | $200.00 |
| Custom Firebird | 6212 | No doors | HK | M-PR | BL | WH | | | $200.00 |
| Custom Firebird | 6212 | No doors | USA | M-PR | CL | BK | | | $200.00 |
| Custom Firebird | 6212 | No doors | HK | M-PR | BL | BK | | | $200.00 |
| Custom Firebird | 6212 | No doors | USA | M-PR | CL | GY | | | $200.00 |
| Custom Firebird | 6212 | No doors | HK | M-PR | BL | GY | | | $200.00 |
| Custom Firebird | 6212 | No doors | USA | M-PR | CL | BR-L | | | $200.00 |
| Custom Firebird | 6212 | No doors | HK | M-PR | BL | BR-L | | | $200.00 |
| Custom Firebird | 6212 | No doors | USA | M-PR | CL | BR-D | | | $200.00 |
| Custom Firebird | 6212 | No doors | HK | M-PR | BL | BR-D | | | $200.00 |
| Custom Firebird | 6212 | Doors | USA | M-RD | CL | WH | | | $95.00 |
| Custom Firebird | 6212 | Doors | USA | M-RD | CL | BK | | | $95.00 |
| Custom Firebird | 6212 | Doors | USA | M-RD | CL | GY | | | $95.00 |
| Custom Firebird | 6212 | Doors | USA | M-RD | CL | RD | | | $100.00 |

## 1968 Variations

| Name | Number | Casting | Country | Color | Windows | Interior | Paint | Other | Value |
|---|---|---|---|---|---|---|---|---|---|
| Custom Firebird | 6212 | Doors | USA | M-RD | CL | BR-L | | | $95.00 |
| Custom Firebird | 6212 | Doors | USA | M-RD | CL | BR-D | | | $95.00 |
| Custom Firebird | 6212 | No doors | USA | M-RD | CL | WH | | | $95.00 |
| Custom Firebird | 6212 | No doors | HK | M-RD | BL | WH | | | $95.00 |
| Custom Firebird | 6212 | No doors | USA | M-RD | CL | BK | | | $95.00 |
| Custom Firebird | 6212 | No doors | HK | M-RD | BL | BK | | | $95.00 |
| Custom Firebird | 6212 | No doors | USA | M-RD | CL | GY | | | $95.00 |
| Custom Firebird | 6212 | No doors | HK | M-RD | BL | GY | | | $95.00 |
| Custom Firebird | 6212 | No doors | USA | M-RD | CL | RD | | | $100.00 |
| Custom Firebird | 6212 | No doors | HK | M-RD | BL | RD | | | $100.00 |
| Custom Firebird | 6212 | No doors | USA | M-RD | CL | BR-L | | | $95.00 |
| Custom Firebird | 6212 | No doors | HK | M-RD | BL | BR-L | | | $95.00 |
| Custom Firebird | 6212 | No doors | USA | M-RD | CL | BR-D | | | $95.00 |
| Custom Firebird | 6212 | No doors | HK | M-RD | BL | BR-D | | | $95.00 |
| Custom Firebird | 6212 | Doors | USA | M-RD-R | CL | WH | | | $100.00 |
| Custom Firebird | 6212 | Doors | USA | M-RD-R | CL | BK | | | $100.00 |
| Custom Firebird | 6212 | Doors | USA | M-RD-R | CL | GY | | | $100.00 |
| Custom Firebird | 6212 | Doors | USA | M-RD-R | CL | RD | | | $110.00 |
| Custom Firebird | 6212 | Doors | USA | M-RD-R | CL | BR-L | | | $100.00 |
| Custom Firebird | 6212 | Doors | USA | M-RD-R | CL | BR-D | | | $100.00 |
| Custom Firebird | 6212 | No doors | USA | M-RD-R | CL | WH | | | $100.00 |
| Custom Firebird | 6212 | No doors | HK | M-RD-R | BL | WH | | | $100.00 |
| Custom Firebird | 6212 | No doors | USA | M-RD-R | CL | BK | | | $100.00 |
| Custom Firebird | 6212 | No doors | HK | M-RD-R | BL | BK | | | $100.00 |
| Custom Firebird | 6212 | No doors | USA | M-RD-R | CL | GY | | | $100.00 |
| Custom Firebird | 6212 | No doors | HK | M-RD-R | BL | GY | | | $100.00 |
| Custom Firebird | 6212 | No doors | USA | M-RD-R | CL | RD | | | $110.00 |
| Custom Firebird | 6212 | No doors | HK | M-RD-R | BL | RD | | | $110.00 |
| Custom Firebird | 6212 | No doors | USA | M-RD-R | CL | BR-L | | | $100.00 |
| Custom Firebird | 6212 | No doors | HK | M-RD-R | BL | BR-L | | | $100.00 |
| Custom Firebird | 6212 | No doors | USA | M-RD-R | CL | BR-D | | | $100.00 |
| Custom Firebird | 6212 | No doors | HK | M-RD-R | BL | BR-D | | | $100.00 |
| Custom Firebird | 6212 | Doors | USA | M-YW | CL | WH | | | $75.00 |
| Custom Firebird | 6212 | Doors | USA | M-YW | CL | BK | | | $75.00 |
| Custom Firebird | 6212 | Doors | USA | M-YW | CL | GY | | | $75.00 |
| Custom Firebird | 6212 | Doors | USA | M-YW | CL | BR-L | | | $75.00 |
| Custom Firebird | 6212 | Doors | USA | M-YW | CL | BR-D | | | $75.00 |
| Custom Firebird | 6212 | No doors | USA | M-YW | CL | WH | | | $75.00 |
| Custom Firebird | 6212 | No doors | HK | M-YW | BL | WH | | | $75.00 |
| Custom Firebird | 6212 | No doors | USA | M-YW | CL | BK | | | $75.00 |
| Custom Firebird | 6212 | No doors | HK | M-YW | BL | BK | | | $75.00 |
| Custom Firebird | 6212 | No doors | USA | M-YW | CL | GY | | | $75.00 |
| Custom Firebird | 6212 | No doors | HK | M-YW | BL | GY | | | $75.00 |
| Custom Firebird | 6212 | No doors | USA | M-YW | CL | BR-L | | | $75.00 |
| Custom Firebird | 6212 | No doors | HK | M-YW | BL | BR-L | | | $75.00 |
| Custom Firebird | 6212 | No doors | USA | M-YW | CL | BR-D | | | $75.00 |
| Custom Firebird | 6212 | No doors | HK | M-YW | BL | BR-D | | | $75.00 |
| Custom Firebird | 6212 | Doors | USA | M-YW-L | CL | WH | | | $80.00 |
| Custom Firebird | 6212 | Doors | USA | M-YW-L | CL | BK | | | $80.00 |
| Custom Firebird | 6212 | Doors | USA | M-YW-L | CL | GY | | | $80.00 |
| Custom Firebird | 6212 | Doors | USA | M-YW-L | CL | BR-L | | | $80.00 |
| Custom Firebird | 6212 | Doors | USA | M-YW-L | CL | BR-D | | | $80.00 |
| Custom Firebird | 6212 | No doors | USA | M-YW-L | CL | WH | | | $80.00 |
| Custom Firebird | 6212 | No doors | HK | M-YW-L | BL | WH | | | $80.00 |
| Custom Firebird | 6212 | No doors | USA | M-YW-L | CL | BK | | | $80.00 |
| Custom Firebird | 6212 | No doors | HK | M-YW-L | BL | BK | | | $80.00 |
| Custom Firebird | 6212 | No doors | USA | M-YW-L | CL | GY | | | $80.00 |
| Custom Firebird | 6212 | No doors | HK | M-YW-L | BL | GY | | | $80.00 |
| Custom Firebird | 6212 | No doors | USA | M-YW-L | CL | BR-L | | | $80.00 |
| Custom Firebird | 6212 | No doors | HK | M-YW-L | BL | BR-L | | | $80.00 |
| Custom Firebird | 6212 | No doors | USA | M-YW-L | CL | BR-D | | | $80.00 |
| Custom Firebird | 6212 | No doors | HK | M-YW-L | BL | BR-D | | | $80.00 |
| | | | | | | | | | |
| Custom Fleetside | 6213 | | USA | M-AQ | CL | WH | | | $75.00 |
| Custom Fleetside | 6213 | | HK | M-AQ | BL | WH | | | $75.00 |
| Custom Fleetside | 6213 | | USA | M-AQ | CL | BK | | | $65.00 |
| Custom Fleetside | 6213 | | HK | M-AQ | BL | BK | | | $65.00 |
| Custom Fleetside | 6213 | | USA | M-AQ | CL | GY | | | $65.00 |
| Custom Fleetside | 6213 | | HK | M-AQ | BL | GY | | | $65.00 |
| Custom Fleetside | 6213 | | USA | M-AQ | CL | BR-L | | | $65.00 |
| Custom Fleetside | 6213 | | HK | M-AQ | BL | BR-L | | | $65.00 |

## 1968 Variations

| Name | Number | Casting | Country | Color | Windows | Interior | Paint | Other | Value |
|---|---|---|---|---|---|---|---|---|---|
| Custom Fleetside | 6213 | | USA | M-AQ | CL | BR-D | | | $65.00 |
| Custom Fleetside | 6213 | | HK | M-AQ | BL | BR-D | | | $65.00 |
| Custom Fleetside | 6213 | | USA | M-BL | CL | WH | | | $90.00 |
| Custom Fleetside | 6213 | | HK | M-BL | BL | WH | | | $90.00 |
| Custom Fleetside | 6213 | | USA | M-BL | CL | BK | | | $80.00 |
| Custom Fleetside | 6213 | | HK | M-BL | BL | BK | | | $80.00 |
| Custom Fleetside | 6213 | | USA | M-BL | CL | GY | | | $80.00 |
| Custom Fleetside | 6213 | | HK | M-BL | BL | GY | | | $80.00 |
| Custom Fleetside | 6213 | | USA | M-BL | CL | BR-L | | | $80.00 |
| Custom Fleetside | 6213 | | HK | M-BL | BL | BR-L | | | $80.00 |
| Custom Fleetside | 6213 | | USA | M-BL | CL | BR-D | | | $80.00 |
| Custom Fleetside | 6213 | | HK | M-BL | BL | BR-D | | | $80.00 |
| Custom Fleetside | 6213 | | USA | M-BL-I | CL | WH | | | $140.00 |
| Custom Fleetside | 6213 | | HK | M-BL-I | BL | WH | | | $140.00 |
| Custom Fleetside | 6213 | | USA | M-BL-I | CL | BK | | | $130.00 |
| Custom Fleetside | 6213 | | HK | M-BL-I | BL | BK | | | $130.00 |
| Custom Fleetside | 6213 | | USA | M-BL-I | CL | GY | | | $130.00 |
| Custom Fleetside | 6213 | | HK | M-BL-I | BL | GY | | | $130.00 |
| Custom Fleetside | 6213 | | USA | M-BL-I | CL | BR-L | | | $130.00 |
| Custom Fleetside | 6213 | | HK | M-BL-I | BL | BR-L | | | $130.00 |
| Custom Fleetside | 6213 | | USA | M-BL-I | CL | BR-D | | | $130.00 |
| Custom Fleetside | 6213 | | HK | M-BL-I | BL | BR-D | | | $130.00 |
| Custom Fleetside | 6213 | | USA | M-BL-P | CL | WH | | | $120.00 |
| Custom Fleetside | 6213 | | HK | M-BL-P | BL | WH | | | $120.00 |
| Custom Fleetside | 6213 | | USA | M-BL-P | CL | BK | | | $110.00 |
| Custom Fleetside | 6213 | | HK | M-BL-P | BL | BK | | | $110.00 |
| Custom Fleetside | 6213 | | USA | M-BL-P | CL | GY | | | $110.00 |
| Custom Fleetside | 6213 | | HK | M-BL-P | BL | GY | | | $110.00 |
| Custom Fleetside | 6213 | | USA | M-BL-P | CL | BR-L | | | $110.00 |
| Custom Fleetside | 6213 | | HK | M-BL-P | BL | BR-L | | | $110.00 |
| Custom Fleetside | 6213 | | USA | M-BL-P | CL | BR-D | | | $110.00 |
| Custom Fleetside | 6213 | | HK | M-BL-P | BL | BR-D | | | $110.00 |
| Custom Fleetside | 6213 | | USA | M-BR-D | CL | WH | | | $110.00 |
| Custom Fleetside | 6213 | | HK | M-BR-D | BL | WH | | | $110.00 |
| Custom Fleetside | 6213 | | USA | M-BR-D | CL | BK | | | $100.00 |
| Custom Fleetside | 6213 | | HK | M-BR-D | BL | BK | | | $100.00 |
| Custom Fleetside | 6213 | | USA | M-BR-D | CL | GY | | | $100.00 |
| Custom Fleetside | 6213 | | HK | M-BR-D | BL | GY | | | $100.00 |
| Custom Fleetside | 6213 | | USA | M-BR-D | CL | BR-L | | | $100.00 |
| Custom Fleetside | 6213 | | HK | M-BR-D | BL | BR-L | | | $100.00 |
| Custom Fleetside | 6213 | | USA | M-BR-D | CL | BR-D | | | $100.00 |
| Custom Fleetside | 6213 | | HK | M-BR-D | BL | BR-D | | | $100.00 |
| Custom Fleetside | 6213 | | USA | M-BR-P | CL | WH | | | $100.00 |
| Custom Fleetside | 6213 | | HK | M-BR-P | BL | WH | | | $100.00 |
| Custom Fleetside | 6213 | | USA | M-BR-P | CL | BK | | | $90.00 |
| Custom Fleetside | 6213 | | HK | M-BR-P | BL | BK | | | $90.00 |
| Custom Fleetside | 6213 | | USA | M-BR-P | CL | GY | | | $90.00 |
| Custom Fleetside | 6213 | | HK | M-BR-P | BL | GY | | | $90.00 |
| Custom Fleetside | 6213 | | USA | M-BR-P | CL | BR-L | | | $90.00 |
| Custom Fleetside | 6213 | | HK | M-BR-P | BL | BR-L | | | $90.00 |
| Custom Fleetside | 6213 | | USA | M-BR-P | CL | BR-D | | | $90.00 |
| Custom Fleetside | 6213 | | HK | M-BR-P | BL | BR-D | | | $90.00 |
| Custom Fleetside | 6213 | | USA | M-GD | CL | WH | | | $75.00 |
| Custom Fleetside | 6213 | | HK | M-GD | BL | WH | | | $75.00 |
| Custom Fleetside | 6213 | | USA | M-GD | CL | BK | | | $65.00 |
| Custom Fleetside | 6213 | | HK | M-GD | BL | BK | | | $65.00 |
| Custom Fleetside | 6213 | | USA | M-GD | CL | GY | | | $65.00 |
| Custom Fleetside | 6213 | | HK | M-GD | BL | GY | | | $65.00 |
| Custom Fleetside | 6213 | | USA | M-GD | CL | BR-L | | | $65.00 |
| Custom Fleetside | 6213 | | HK | M-GD | BL | BR-L | | | $65.00 |
| Custom Fleetside | 6213 | | USA | M-GD | CL | BR-D | | | $65.00 |
| Custom Fleetside | 6213 | | HK | M-GD | BL | BR-D | | | $65.00 |
| Custom Fleetside | 6213 | | USA | M-GR | CL | WH | | | $75.00 |
| Custom Fleetside | 6213 | | HK | M-GR | BL | WH | | | $75.00 |
| Custom Fleetside | 6213 | | USA | M-GR | CL | BK | | | $65.00 |
| Custom Fleetside | 6213 | | HK | M-GR | BL | BK | | | $65.00 |
| Custom Fleetside | 6213 | | USA | M-GR | CL | GY | | | $65.00 |
| Custom Fleetside | 6213 | | HK | M-GR | BL | GY | | | $65.00 |
| Custom Fleetside | 6213 | | USA | M-GR | CL | BR-L | | | $65.00 |
| Custom Fleetside | 6213 | | HK | M-GR | BL | BR-L | | | $65.00 |
| Custom Fleetside | 6213 | | USA | M-GR | CL | BR-D | | | $65.00 |
| Custom Fleetside | 6213 | | HK | M-GR | BL | BR-D | | | $65.00 |

## 1968 Variations

| Name | Number | Casting | Country | Color | Windows | Interior | Paint | Other | Value |
|---|---|---|---|---|---|---|---|---|---|
| Custom Fleetside | 6213 | | USA | M-GR-E | CL | WH | | | $85.00 |
| Custom Fleetside | 6213 | | HK | M-GR-E | BL | WH | | | $85.00 |
| Custom Fleetside | 6213 | | USA | M-GR-E | CL | BK | | | $75.00 |
| Custom Fleetside | 6213 | | HK | M-GR-E | BL | BK | | | $75.00 |
| Custom Fleetside | 6213 | | USA | M-GR-E | CL | GY | | | $75.00 |
| Custom Fleetside | 6213 | | HK | M-GR-E | BL | GY | | | $75.00 |
| Custom Fleetside | 6213 | | USA | M-GR-E | CL | BR-L | | | $75.00 |
| Custom Fleetside | 6213 | | HK | M-GR-E | BL | BR-L | | | $75.00 |
| Custom Fleetside | 6213 | | USA | M-GR-E | CL | BR-D | | | $75.00 |
| Custom Fleetside | 6213 | | HK | M-GR-E | BL | BR-D | | | $75.00 |
| Custom Fleetside | 6213 | | USA | M-GR-L | CL | WH | | | $120.00 |
| Custom Fleetside | 6213 | | HK | M-GR-L | BL | WH | | | $120.00 |
| Custom Fleetside | 6213 | | USA | M-GR-L | CL | BK | | | $110.00 |
| Custom Fleetside | 6213 | | HK | M-GR-L | BL | BK | | | $110.00 |
| Custom Fleetside | 6213 | | USA | M-GR-L | CL | GY | | | $110.00 |
| Custom Fleetside | 6213 | | HK | M-GR-L | BL | GY | | | $110.00 |
| Custom Fleetside | 6213 | | USA | M-GR-L | CL | BR-L | | | $110.00 |
| Custom Fleetside | 6213 | | HK | M-GR-L | BL | BR-L | | | $110.00 |
| Custom Fleetside | 6213 | | USA | M-GR-L | CL | BR-D | | | $110.00 |
| Custom Fleetside | 6213 | | HK | M-GR-L | BL | BR-D | | | $110.00 |
| Custom Fleetside | 6213 | | USA | M-OR | CL | WH | | | $75.00 |
| Custom Fleetside | 6213 | | HK | M-OR | BL | WH | | | $75.00 |
| Custom Fleetside | 6213 | | USA | M-OR | CL | BK | | | $65.00 |
| Custom Fleetside | 6213 | | HK | M-OR | BL | BK | | | $65.00 |
| Custom Fleetside | 6213 | | USA | M-OR | CL | GY | | | $65.00 |
| Custom Fleetside | 6213 | | HK | M-OR | BL | GY | | | $65.00 |
| Custom Fleetside | 6213 | | USA | M-OR | CL | BR-L | | | $65.00 |
| Custom Fleetside | 6213 | | HK | M-OR | BL | BR-L | | | $65.00 |
| Custom Fleetside | 6213 | | USA | M-OR | CL | BR-D | | | $65.00 |
| Custom Fleetside | 6213 | | HK | M-OR | BL | BR-D | | | $65.00 |
| Custom Fleetside | 6213 | | USA | M-PH | CL | WH | | | $130.00 |
| Custom Fleetside | 6213 | | HK | M-PR | BL | WH | | | $130.00 |
| Custom Fleetside | 6213 | | USA | M-PR | CL | BK | | | $110.00 |
| Custom Fleetside | 6213 | | HK | M-PR | BL | BK | | | $110.00 |
| Custom Fleetside | 6213 | | USA | M-PR | CL | GY | | | $110.00 |
| Custom Fleetside | 6213 | | HK | M-PR | BL | GY | | | $110.00 |
| Custom Fleetside | 6213 | | USA | M-PR | CL | BR-L | | | $110.00 |
| Custom Fleetside | 6213 | | HK | M-PR | BL | BR-L | | | $110.00 |
| Custom Fleetside | 6213 | | USA | M-PR | CL | BR-D | | | $110.00 |
| Custom Fleetside | 6213 | | HK | M-PR | BL | BR-D | | | $110.00 |
| Custom Fleetside | 6213 | | USA | M-RD | CL | WH | | | $85.00 |
| Custom Fleetside | 6213 | | HK | M-RD | BL | WH | | | $85.00 |
| Custom Fleetside | 6213 | | USA | M-RD | CL | BK | | | $75.00 |
| Custom Fleetside | 6213 | | HK | M-RD | BL | BK | | | $75.00 |
| Custom Fleetside | 6213 | | USA | M-RD | CL | GY | | | $75.00 |
| Custom Fleetside | 6213 | | HK | M-RD | BL | GY | | | $75.00 |
| Custom Fleetside | 6213 | | USA | M-RD | CL | BR-L | | | $75.00 |
| Custom Fleetside | 6213 | | HK | M-RD | BL | BR-L | | | $75.00 |
| Custom Fleetside | 6213 | | USA | M-RD | CL | BR-D | | | $75.00 |
| Custom Fleetside | 6213 | | HK | M-RD | BL | BR-D | | | $75.00 |
| Custom Fleetside | 6213 | | USA | M-RD-R | CL | WH | | | $95.00 |
| Custom Fleetside | 6213 | | HK | M-RD-R | BL | WH | | | $95.00 |
| Custom Fleetside | 6213 | | USA | M-RD-R | CL | BK | | | $85.00 |
| Custom Fleetside | 6213 | | HK | M-RD-R | BL | BK | | | $85.00 |
| Custom Fleetside | 6213 | | USA | M-RD-R | CL | GY | | | $85.00 |
| Custom Fleetside | 6213 | | HK | M-RD-R | BL | GY | | | $85.00 |
| Custom Fleetside | 6213 | | USA | M-RD-R | CL | BR-L | | | $85.00 |
| Custom Fleetside | 6213 | | HK | M-RD-R | BL | BR-L | | | $85.00 |
| Custom Fleetside | 6213 | | USA | M-RD-R | CL | BR-D | | | $85.00 |
| Custom Fleetside | 6213 | | HK | M-RD-R | BL | BR-D | | | $85.00 |
| Custom Fleetside | 6213 | | USA | M-YW | CL | WH | | | $70.00 |
| Custom Fleetside | 6213 | | HK | M-YW | BL | WH | | | $70.00 |
| Custom Fleetside | 6213 | | USA | M-YW | CL | BK | | | $60.00 |
| Custom Fleetside | 6213 | | HK | M-YW | BL | BK | | | $60.00 |
| Custom Fleetside | 6213 | | USA | M-YW | CL | GY | | | $60.00 |
| Custom Fleetside | 6213 | | HK | M-YW | BL | GY | | | $60.00 |
| Custom Fleetside | 6213 | | USA | M-YW | CL | BR-L | | | $60.00 |
| Custom Fleetside | 6213 | | HK | M-YW | BL | BR-L | | | $60.00 |
| Custom Fleetside | 6213 | | USA | M-YW | CL | BR-D | | | $60.00 |
| Custom Fleetside | 6213 | | HK | M-YW | BL | BR-D | | | $60.00 |
| Custom Fleetside | 6213 | | USA | M-YW-L | CL | WH | | | $140.00 |
| Custom Fleetside | 6213 | | HK | M-YW-L | BL | WH | | | $140.00 |

## 1968 Variations

| Name | Number | Casting | Country | Color | Windows | Interior | Paint | Other | Value |
|---|---|---|---|---|---|---|---|---|---|
| Custom Fleetside | 6213 | | USA | M-YW-L | CL | BK | | | $130.00 |
| Custom Fleetside | 6213 | | HK | M-YW-L | BL | BK | | | $130.00 |
| Custom Fleetside | 6213 | | USA | M-YW-L | CL | GY | | | $130.00 |
| Custom Fleetside | 6213 | | HK | M-YW-L | BL | GY | | | $130.00 |
| Custom Fleetside | 6213 | | USA | M-YW-L | CL | BR-L | | | $130.00 |
| Custom Fleetside | 6213 | | HK | M-YW-L | BL | BR-L | | | $130.00 |
| Custom Fleetside | 6213 | | USA | M-YW-L | CL | BR-D | | | $130.00 |
| Custom Fleetside | 6213 | | HK | M-YW-L | BL | BR-D | | | $130.00 |
| | | | | | | | | | |
| Ford J Car | 6214 | Rear vents | USA | E-BL | CL | WH | | | $550.00 |
| Ford J Car | 6214 | Rear vents | USA | E-BL | CL | BK | | | $550.00 |
| Ford J Car | 6214 | Rear vents | USA | E-BL | CL | GY | | | $550.00 |
| Ford J Car | 6214 | Rear vents | USA | E-BL | CL | BR-L | | | $550.00 |
| Ford J Car | 6214 | Rear vents | USA | E-BL | CL | BR-D | | | $550.00 |
| Ford J Car | 6214 | Rear vents | USA | E-MG | CL | WH | | | $500.00 |
| Ford J Car | 6214 | Rear vents | USA | E-MG | CL | BK | | | $500.00 |
| Ford J Car | 6214 | Rear vents | USA | E-MG | CL | GY | | | $500.00 |
| Ford J Car | 6214 | Rear vents | USA | E-MG | CL | BR-L | | | $500.00 |
| Ford J Car | 6214 | Rear vents | USA | E-MG | CL | BR-D | | | $500.00 |
| Ford J Car | 6214 | | HK | E-WH | BL | WH | | | $75.00 |
| Ford J Car | 6214 | | HK | E-WH | BL | BK | | | $70.00 |
| Ford J Car | 6214 | | HK | E-WH | BL | GY | | | $70.00 |
| Ford J Car | 6214 | | HK | E-WH | BL | BR-L | | | $70.00 |
| Ford J Car | 6214 | | HK | E-WH | BL | BR-D | | | $70.00 |
| Ford J Car | 6214 | Rear vents | USA | E-WH | CL | WH | | | $90.00 |
| Ford J Car | 6214 | Rear vents | USA | E-WH | CL | BK | | | $75.00 |
| Ford J Car | 6214 | Rear vents | USA | E-WH | CL | GY | | | $75.00 |
| Ford J Car | 6214 | Rear vents | USA | E-WH | CL | BR-L | | | $75.00 |
| Ford J Car | 6214 | Rear vents | USA | E-WH | CL | BR-D | | | $75.00 |
| Ford J Car | 6214 | Rear vents | USA | M-AQ | CL | WH | | | $40.00 |
| Ford J Car | 6214 | Rear vents | USA | M-AQ | CL | BK | | | $35.00 |
| Ford J Car | 6214 | Rear vents | USA | M-AQ | CL | GY | | | $35.00 |
| Ford J Car | 6214 | Rear vents | USA | M-AQ | CL | BR-L | | | $35.00 |
| Ford J Car | 6214 | Rear vents | USA | M-AQ | CL | BR-D | | | $35.00 |
| Ford J Car | 6214 | Rear vents | USA | M-BL | CL | WH | | | $40.00 |
| Ford J Car | 6214 | Rear vents | USA | M-BL | CL | BK | | | $35.00 |
| Ford J Car | 6214 | Rear vents | USA | M-BL | CL | GY | | | $35.00 |
| Ford J Car | 6214 | Rear vents | USA | M-BL | CL | BR-L | | | $35.00 |
| Ford J Car | 6214 | Rear vents | USA | M-BL | CL | BR-D | | | $35.00 |
| Ford J Car | 6214 | Rear vents | USA | M-BL-I | CL | WH | | | $55.00 |
| Ford J Car | 6214 | Rear vents | USA | M-BL-I | CL | BK | | | $50.00 |
| Ford J Car | 6214 | Rear vents | USA | M-BL-I | CL | GY | | | $50.00 |
| Ford J Car | 6214 | Rear vents | USA | M-BL-I | CL | BR-L | | | $50.00 |
| Ford J Car | 6214 | Rear vents | USA | M-BL-I | CL | BR-D | | | $50.00 |
| Ford J Car | 6214 | Rear vents | USA | M-BL-P | CL | WH | | | $45.00 |
| Ford J Car | 6214 | Rear vents | USA | M-BL-P | CL | BK | | | $40.00 |
| Ford J Car | 6214 | Rear vents | USA | M-BL-P | CL | GY | | | $40.00 |
| Ford J Car | 6214 | Rear vents | USA | M-BL-P | CL | BR-L | | | $40.00 |
| Ford J Car | 6214 | Rear vents | USA | M-BL-P | CL | BR-D | | | $40.00 |
| Ford J Car | 6214 | Rear vents | USA | M-BR-D | CL | WH | | | $35.00 |
| Ford J Car | 6214 | Rear vents | USA | M-BR-D | CL | BK | | | $35.00 |
| Ford J Car | 6214 | Rear vents | USA | M-BR-D | CL | GY | | | $35.00 |
| Ford J Car | 6214 | Rear vents | USA | M-BR-D | CL | BR-L | | | $35.00 |
| Ford J Car | 6214 | Rear vents | USA | M-BR-D | CL | BR-D | | | $35.00 |
| Ford J Car | 6214 | Rear vents | USA | M-BR-P | CL | WH | | | $35.00 |
| Ford J Car | 6214 | Rear vents | USA | M-BR-P | CL | BK | | | $35.00 |
| Ford J Car | 6214 | Rear vents | USA | M-BR-P | CL | GY | | | $35.00 |
| Ford J Car | 6214 | Rear vents | USA | M-BR-P | CL | BR-L | | | $35.00 |
| Ford J Car | 6214 | Rear vents | USA | M-BR-P | CL | BR-D | | | $35.00 |
| Ford J Car | 6214 | Rear vents | USA | M-GD | CL | WH | | | $45.00 |
| Ford J Car | 6214 | Rear vents | USA | M-GD | CL | BK | | | $35.00 |
| Ford J Car | 6214 | Rear vents | USA | M-GD | CL | GY | | | $35.00 |
| Ford J Car | 6214 | Rear vents | USA | M-GD | CL | BR-L | | | $35.00 |
| Ford J Car | 6214 | Rear vents | USA | M-GD | CL | BR-D | | | $35.00 |
| Ford J Car | 6214 | Rear vents | USA | M-GR | CL | WH | | | $40.00 |
| Ford J Car | 6214 | Rear vents | USA | M-GR | CL | BK | | | $40.00 |
| Ford J Car | 6214 | Rear vents | USA | M-GR | CL | GY | | | $35.00 |
| Ford J Car | 6214 | Rear vents | USA | M-GR | CL | BR-L | | | $35.00 |
| Ford J Car | 6214 | Rear vents | USA | M-GR | CL | BR-D | | | $35.00 |
| Ford J Car | 6214 | Rear vents | USA | M-GR-E | CL | WH | | | $45.00 |
| Ford J Car | 6214 | Rear vents | USA | M-GR-E | CL | BK | | | $40.00 |

## 1968 Variations

| Name | Number | Casting | Country | Color | Windows | Interior | Paint | Other | Value |
|---|---|---|---|---|---|---|---|---|---|
| Ford J Car | 6214 | Rear vents | USA | M-GR-E | CL | GY | | | $40.00 |
| Ford J Car | 6214 | Rear vents | USA | M-GR-E | CL | BR-L | | | $40.00 |
| Ford J Car | 6214 | Rear vents | USA | M-GR-E | CL | BR-D | | | $40.00 |
| Ford J Car | 6214 | Rear vents | USA | M-GR-L | CL | WH | | | $45.00 |
| Ford J Car | 6214 | Rear vents | USA | M-GR-L | CL | BK | | | $40.00 |
| Ford J Car | 6214 | Rear vents | USA | M-GR-L | CL | GY | | | $40.00 |
| Ford J Car | 6214 | Rear vents | USA | M-GR-L | CL | BR-L | | | $40.00 |
| Ford J Car | 6214 | Rear vents | USA | M-GR-L | CL | BR-D | | | $40.00 |
| Ford J Car | 6214 | Rear vents | USA | M-GR-O | CL | WH | | | $40.00 |
| Ford J Car | 6214 | Rear vents | USA | M-GR-O | CL | BK | | | $35.00 |
| Ford J Car | 6214 | Rear vents | USA | M-GR-O | CL | GY | | | $35.00 |
| Ford J Car | 6214 | Rear vents | USA | M-GR-O | CL | BR-L | | | $35.00 |
| Ford J Car | 6214 | Rear vents | USA | M-GR-O | CL | BR-D | | | $35.00 |
| Ford J Car | 6214 | Rear vents | USA | M-MG | CL | WH | | | $70.00 |
| Ford J Car | 6214 | Rear vents | USA | M-MG | CL | BK | | | $60.00 |
| Ford J Car | 6214 | Rear vents | USA | M-MG | CL | GY | | | $60.00 |
| Ford J Car | 6214 | Rear vents | USA | M-MG | CL | BR-L | | | $60.00 |
| Ford J Car | 6214 | Rear vents | USA | M-MG | CL | BR-D | | | $60.00 |
| Ford J Car | 6214 | Rear vents | USA | M-OR | CL | WH | | | $40.00 |
| Ford J Car | 6214 | Rear vents | USA | M-OR | CL | BK | | | $35.00 |
| Ford J Car | 6214 | Rear vents | USA | M-OR | CL | GY | | | $35.00 |
| Ford J Car | 6214 | Rear vents | USA | M-OR | CL | BR-L | | | $35.00 |
| Ford J Car | 6214 | Rear vents | USA | M-OR | CL | BR-D | | | $35.00 |
| Ford J Car | 6214 | Rear vents | USA | M-PK | CL | WH | | | $220.00 |
| Ford J Car | 6214 | Rear vents | USA | M-PK | CL | BK | | | $200.00 |
| Ford J Car | 6214 | Rear vents | USA | M-PK | CL | GY | | | $200.00 |
| Ford J Car | 6214 | Rear vents | USA | M-PK | CL | BR-L | | | $200.00 |
| Ford J Car | 6214 | Rear vents | USA | M-PK | CL | BR-D | | | $200.00 |
| Ford J Car | 6214 | Rear vents | USA | M-PK-H | CL | WH | | | $220.00 |
| Ford J Car | 6214 | Rear vents | USA | M-PK-H | CL | BK | | | $200.00 |
| Ford J Car | 6214 | Rear vents | USA | M-PK-H | CL | GY | | | $200.00 |
| Ford J Car | 6214 | Rear vents | USA | M-PK-H | CL | BR-L | | | $200.00 |
| Ford J Car | 6214 | Rear vents | USA | M-PK-H | CL | BR-D | | | $200.00 |
| Ford J Car | 6214 | Rear vents | USA | M-PK-S | CL | WH | | | $220.00 |
| Ford J Car | 6214 | Rear vents | USA | M-PK-S | CL | BK | | | $200.00 |
| Ford J Car | 6214 | Rear vents | USA | M-PK-S | CL | GY | | | $200.00 |
| Ford J Car | 6214 | Rear vents | USA | M-PK-S | CL | BR-L | | | $200.00 |
| Ford J Car | 6214 | Rear vents | USA | M-PK-S | CL | BR-D | | | $200.00 |
| Ford J Car | 6214 | Rear vents | USA | M-PR | CL | WH | | | $70.00 |
| Ford J Car | 6214 | Rear vents | USA | M-PR | CL | BK | | | $65.00 |
| Ford J Car | 6214 | Rear vents | USA | M-PR | CL | GY | | | $65.00 |
| Ford J Car | 6214 | Rear vents | USA | M-PR | CL | BR-L | | | $65.00 |
| Ford J Car | 6214 | Rear vents | USA | M-PR | CL | BR-D | | | $65.00 |
| Ford J Car | 6214 | Rear vents | USA | M-RD | CL | WH | | | $40.00 |
| Ford J Car | 6214 | Rear vents | USA | M-RD | CL | BK | | | $35.00 |
| Ford J Car | 6214 | Rear vents | USA | M-RD | CL | GY | | | $35.00 |
| Ford J Car | 6214 | Rear vents | USA | M-RD | CL | BR-L | | | $35.00 |
| Ford J Car | 6214 | Rear vents | USA | M-RD | CL | BR-D | | | $35.00 |
| Ford J Car | 6214 | Rear vents | USA | M-RD-R | CL | WH | | | $45.00 |
| Ford J Car | 6214 | Rear vents | USA | M-RD-R | CL | BK | | | $40.00 |
| Ford J Car | 6214 | Rear vents | USA | M-RD-R | CL | GY | | | $40.00 |
| Ford J Car | 6214 | Rear vents | USA | M-RD-R | CL | BR-L | | | $40.00 |
| Ford J Car | 6214 | Rear vents | USA | M-RD-R | CL | BR-D | | | $40.00 |
| Ford J Car | 6214 | Rear vents | USA | M-YW | CL | WH | | | $40.00 |
| Ford J Car | 6214 | Rear vents | USA | M-YW | CL | BK | | | $35.00 |
| Ford J Car | 6214 | Rear vents | USA | M-YW | CL | GY | | | $35.00 |
| Ford J Car | 6214 | Rear vents | USA | M-YW | CL | BR-L | | | $35.00 |
| Ford J Car | 6214 | Rear vents | USA | M-YW | CL | BR-D | | | $35.00 |
| Ford J Car | 6214 | Rear vents | USA | M-YW-L | CL | WH | | | $55.00 |
| Ford J Car | 6214 | Rear vents | USA | M-YW-L | CL | BK | | | $50.00 |
| Ford J Car | 6214 | Rear vents | USA | M-YW-L | CL | GY | | | $50.00 |
| Ford J Car | 6214 | Rear vents | USA | M-YW-L | CL | BR-L | | | $50.00 |
| Ford J Car | 6214 | Rear vents | USA | M-YW-L | CL | BR-D | | | $50.00 |
| | | | | | | | | | |
| Custom Corvette | 6215 | Custom Corvette | USA | M-AQ | CL | WH | | | $120.00 |
| Custom Corvette | 6215 | Corvette | USA | M-AQ | CL | WH | | | $130.00 |
| Custom Corvette | 6215 | Custom Corvette | HK | M-AQ | BL | WH | | | $120.00 |
| Custom Corvette | 6215 | Corvette | HK | M-AQ | BL | WH | | | $130.00 |
| Custom Corvette | 6215 | Custom Corvette | USA | M-AQ | CL | BK | | | $110.00 |
| Custom Corvette | 6215 | Corvette | USA | M-AQ | CL | BK | | | $120.00 |
| Custom Corvette | 6215 | Custom Corvette | HK | M-AQ | BL | BK | | | $110.00 |

## 1968 Variations

| Name | Number | Casting | Country | Color | Windows | Interior | Paint | Other | Value |
|---|---|---|---|---|---|---|---|---|---|
| Custom Corvette | 6215 | Corvette | HK | M-AQ | BL | BK | | | $120.00 |
| Custom Corvette | 6215 | Custom Corvette | USA | M-AQ | CL | GY | | | $110.00 |
| Custom Corvette | 6215 | Corvette | USA | M-AQ | CL | GY | | | $120.00 |
| Custom Corvette | 6215 | Custom Corvette | HK | M-AQ | BL | GY | | | $110.00 |
| Custom Corvette | 6215 | Corvette | HK | M-AQ | BL | GY | | | $120.00 |
| Custom Corvette | 6215 | Custom Corvette | USA | M-AQ | CL | BR-L | | | $110.00 |
| Custom Corvette | 6215 | Corvette | USA | M-AQ | CL | BR-L | | | $120.00 |
| Custom Corvette | 6215 | Custom Corvette | HK | M-AQ | BL | BR-L | | | $110.00 |
| Custom Corvette | 6215 | Corvette | HK | M-AQ | BL | BR-L | | | $120.00 |
| Custom Corvette | 6215 | Custom Corvette | USA | M-AQ | CL | BR-D | | | $110.00 |
| Custom Corvette | 6215 | Corvette | USA | M-AQ | CL | BR-D | | | $120.00 |
| Custom Corvette | 6215 | Custom Corvette | HK | M-AQ | BL | BR-D | | | $110.00 |
| Custom Corvette | 6215 | Corvette | HK | M-AQ | BL | BR-D | | | $120.00 |
| Custom Corvette | 6215 | Custom Corvette | USA | M-BL | CL | WH | | | $120.00 |
| Custom Corvette | 6215 | Corvette | USA | M-BL | CL | WH | | | $130.00 |
| Custom Corvette | 6215 | Custom Corvette | HK | M-BL | BL | WH | | | $120.00 |
| Custom Corvette | 6215 | Corvette | HK | M-BL | BL | WH | | | $130.00 |
| Custom Corvette | 6215 | Custom Corvette | USA | M-BL | CL | BK | | | $110.00 |
| Custom Corvette | 6215 | Corvette | USA | M-BL | CL | BK | | | $120.00 |
| Custom Corvette | 6215 | Custom Corvette | HK | M-BL | BL | BK | | | $110.00 |
| Custom Corvette | 6215 | Corvette | HK | M-BL | BL | BK | | | $120.00 |
| Custom Corvette | 6215 | Custom Corvette | USA | M-BL | CL | GY | | | $110.00 |
| Custom Corvette | 6215 | Corvette | USA | M-BL | CL | GY | | | $120.00 |
| Custom Corvette | 6215 | Custom Corvette | HK | M-BL | BL | GY | | | $110.00 |
| Custom Corvette | 6215 | Corvette | HK | M-BL | BL | GY | | | $120.00 |
| Custom Corvette | 6215 | Custom Corvette | USA | M-BL | CL | BR-L | | | $110.00 |
| Custom Corvette | 6215 | Corvette | USA | M-BL | CL | BR-L | | | $120.00 |
| Custom Corvette | 6215 | Custom Corvette | HK | M-BL | BL | BR-L | | | $110.00 |
| Custom Corvette | 6215 | Corvette | HK | M-BL | BL | BR-L | | | $120.00 |
| Custom Corvette | 6215 | Custom Corvette | USA | M-BL | CL | BR-D | | | $110.00 |
| Custom Corvette | 6215 | Corvette | USA | M-BL | CL | BR-D | | | $120.00 |
| Custom Corvette | 6215 | Custom Corvette | HK | M-BL | BL | BR-D | | | $110.00 |
| Custom Corvette | 6215 | Corvette | HK | M-BL | BL | BR-D | | | $120.00 |
| Custom Corvette | 6215 | Custom Corvette | USA | M-BL-I | CL | WH | | | $140.00 |
| Custom Corvette | 6215 | Corvette | USA | M-BL-I | CL | WH | | | $150.00 |
| Custom Corvette | 6215 | Custom Corvette | HK | M-BL-I | BL | WH | | | $140.00 |
| Custom Corvette | 6215 | Corvette | HK | M-BL-I | BL | WH | | | $150.00 |
| Custom Corvette | 6215 | Custom Corvette | USA | M-BL-I | CL | BK | | | $130.00 |
| Custom Corvette | 6215 | Corvette | USA | M-BL-I | CL | BK | | | $140.00 |
| Custom Corvette | 6215 | Custom Corvette | HK | M-BL-I | BL | BK | | | $130.00 |
| Custom Corvette | 6215 | Corvette | HK | M-BL-I | BL | BK | | | $140.00 |
| Custom Corvette | 6215 | Custom Corvette | USA | M-BL-I | CL | GY | | | $130.00 |
| Custom Corvette | 6215 | Corvette | USA | M-BL-I | CL | GY | | | $140.00 |
| Custom Corvette | 6215 | Custom Corvette | HK | M-BL-I | BL | GY | | | $130.00 |
| Custom Corvette | 6215 | Corvette | HK | M-BL-I | BL | GY | | | $140.00 |
| Custom Corvette | 6215 | Custom Corvette | USA | M-BL-I | CL | BR-L | | | $130.00 |
| Custom Corvette | 6215 | Corvette | USA | M-BL-I | CL | BR-L | | | $140.00 |
| Custom Corvette | 6215 | Custom Corvette | HK | M-BL-I | BL | BR-L | | | $130.00 |
| Custom Corvette | 6215 | Corvette | HK | M-BL-I | BL | BR-L | | | $140.00 |
| Custom Corvette | 6215 | Custom Corvette | USA | M-BL-I | CL | BR-D | | | $130.00 |
| Custom Corvette | 6215 | Corvette | USA | M-BL-I | CL | BR-D | | | $140.00 |
| Custom Corvette | 6215 | Custom Corvette | HK | M-BL-I | BL | BR-D | | | $130.00 |
| Custom Corvette | 6215 | Corvette | HK | M-BL-I | BL | BR-D | | | $140.00 |
| Custom Corvette | 6215 | Custom Corvette | USA | M-BL-P | CL | WH | | | $120.00 |
| Custom Corvette | 6215 | Corvette | USA | M-BL-P | CL | WH | | | $130.00 |
| Custom Corvette | 6215 | Custom Corvette | HK | M-BL-P | BL | WH | | | $120.00 |
| Custom Corvette | 6215 | Corvette | HK | M-BL-P | BL | WH | | | $130.00 |
| Custom Corvette | 6215 | Custom Corvette | USA | M-BL-P | CL | BK | | | $110.00 |
| Custom Corvette | 6215 | Corvette | USA | M-BL-P | CL | BK | | | $120.00 |
| Custom Corvette | 6215 | Custom Corvette | HK | M-BL-P | BL | BK | | | $110.00 |
| Custom Corvette | 6215 | Corvette | HK | M-BL-P | BL | BK | | | $120.00 |
| Custom Corvette | 6215 | Custom Corvette | USA | M-BL-P | CL | GY | | | $110.00 |
| Custom Corvette | 6215 | Corvette | USA | M-BL-P | CL | GY | | | $120.00 |
| Custom Corvette | 6215 | Custom Corvette | HK | M-BL-P | BL | GY | | | $110.00 |
| Custom Corvette | 6215 | Corvette | HK | M-BL-P | BL | GY | | | $120.00 |
| Custom Corvette | 6215 | Custom Corvette | USA | M-BL-P | CL | BR-L | | | $110.00 |
| Custom Corvette | 6215 | Corvette | USA | M-BL-P | CL | BR-L | | | $120.00 |
| Custom Corvette | 6215 | Custom Corvette | HK | M-BL-P | BL | BR-L | | | $110.00 |
| Custom Corvette | 6215 | Corvette | HK | M-BL-P | BL | BR-L | | | $120.00 |
| Custom Corvette | 6215 | Custom Corvette | USA | M-BL-P | CL | BR-D | | | $110.00 |
| Custom Corvette | 6215 | Corvette | USA | M-BL-P | CL | BR-D | | | $120.00 |
| Custom Corvette | 6215 | Custom Corvette | HK | M-BL-P | BL | BR-D | | | $110.00 |

## 1968 Variations

| Name | Number | Casting | Country | Color | Windows | Interior | Paint | Other | Value |
|---|---|---|---|---|---|---|---|---|---|
| Custom Corvette | 6215 | Corvette | HK | M-BL-P | BL | BR-D | | | $120.00 |
| Custom Corvette | 6215 | Custom Corvette | USA | M-BR-D | CL | WH | | | $240.00 |
| Custom Corvette | 6215 | Corvette | USA | M-BR-D | CL | WH | | | $260.00 |
| Custom Corvette | 6215 | Custom Corvette | HK | M-BR-D | BL | WH | | | $240.00 |
| Custom Corvette | 6215 | Corvette | HK | M-BR-D | BL | WH | | | $260.00 |
| Custom Corvette | 6215 | Custom Corvette | USA | M-BR-D | CL | BK | | | $220.00 |
| Custom Corvette | 6215 | Corvette | USA | M-BR-D | CL | BK | | | $240.00 |
| Custom Corvette | 6215 | Custom Corvette | HK | M-BR-D | BL | BK | | | $220.00 |
| Custom Corvette | 6215 | Corvette | HK | M-BR-D | BL | BK | | | $240.00 |
| Custom Corvette | 6215 | Custom Corvette | USA | M-BR-D | CL | GY | | | $220.00 |
| Custom Corvette | 6215 | Corvette | USA | M-BR-D | CL | GY | | | $240.00 |
| Custom Corvette | 6215 | Custom Corvette | HK | M-BR-D | BL | GY | | | $220.00 |
| Custom Corvette | 6215 | Corvette | HK | M-BR-D | BL | GY | | | $240.00 |
| Custom Corvette | 6215 | Custom Corvette | USA | M-BR-D | CL | BR-L | | | $220.00 |
| Custom Corvette | 6215 | Corvette | USA | M-BR-D | CL | BR-L | | | $240.00 |
| Custom Corvette | 6215 | Custom Corvette | HK | M-BR-D | BL | BR-L | | | $220.00 |
| Custom Corvette | 6215 | Corvette | HK | M-BR-D | BL | BR-L | | | $240.00 |
| Custom Corvette | 6215 | Custom Corvette | USA | M-BR-D | CL | BR-D | | | $220.00 |
| Custom Corvette | 6215 | Corvette | USA | M-BR-D | CL | BR-D | | | $240.00 |
| Custom Corvette | 6215 | Custom Corvette | HK | M-BR-D | BL | BR-D | | | $220.00 |
| Custom Corvette | 6215 | Corvette | HK | M-BR-D | BL | BR-D | | | $240.00 |
| Custom Corvette | 6215 | Custom Corvette | USA | M-BR-P | CL | WH | | | $220.00 |
| Custom Corvette | 6215 | Corvette | USA | M-BR-P | CL | WH | | | $240.00 |
| Custom Corvette | 6215 | Custom Corvette | HK | M-BR-P | BL | WH | | | $220.00 |
| Custom Corvette | 6215 | Corvette | HK | M-BR-P | BL | WH | | | $240.00 |
| Custom Corvette | 6215 | Custom Corvette | USA | M-BR-P | CL | BK | | | $200.00 |
| Custom Corvette | 6215 | Corvette | USA | M-BR-P | CL | BK | | | $220.00 |
| Custom Corvette | 6215 | Custom Corvette | HK | M-BR-P | BL | BK | | | $200.00 |
| Custom Corvette | 6215 | Corvette | HK | M-BR-P | BL | BK | | | $220.00 |
| Custom Corvette | 6215 | Custom Corvette | USA | M-BR-P | CL | GY | | | $200.00 |
| Custom Corvette | 6215 | Corvette | USA | M-BR-P | CL | GY | | | $220.00 |
| Custom Corvette | 6215 | Custom Corvette | HK | M-BR-P | BL | GY | | | $200.00 |
| Custom Corvette | 6215 | Corvette | HK | M-BR-P | BL | GY | | | $220.00 |
| Custom Corvette | 6215 | Custom Corvette | USA | M-BR-P | CL | BR-L | | | $200.00 |
| Custom Corvette | 6215 | Corvette | USA | M-BR-P | CL | BR-L | | | $220.00 |
| Custom Corvette | 6215 | Custom Corvette | HK | M-BR-P | BL | BR-L | | | $200.00 |
| Custom Corvette | 6215 | Corvette | HK | M-BR-P | BL | BR-L | | | $220.00 |
| Custom Corvette | 6215 | Custom Corvette | USA | M-BR-P | CL | BR-D | | | $200.00 |
| Custom Corvette | 6215 | Corvette | USA | M-BR-P | CL | BR-D | | | $220.00 |
| Custom Corvette | 6215 | Custom Corvette | HK | M-BR-P | BL | BR-D | | | $200.00 |
| Custom Corvette | 6215 | Corvette | HK | M-BR-P | BL | BR-D | | | $220.00 |
| Custom Corvette | 6215 | Custom Corvette | USA | M-GD | CL | WH | | | $120.00 |
| Custom Corvette | 6215 | Corvette | USA | M-GD | CL | WH | | | $130.00 |
| Custom Corvette | 6215 | Custom Corvette | HK | M-GD | BL | WH | | | $120.00 |
| Custom Corvette | 6215 | Corvette | HK | M-GD | BL | WH | | | $130.00 |
| Custom Corvette | 6215 | Custom Corvette | USA | M-GD | CL | BK | | | $110.00 |
| Custom Corvette | 6215 | Corvette | USA | M-GD | CL | BK | | | $120.00 |
| Custom Corvette | 6215 | Custom Corvette | HK | M-GD | BL | BK | | | $110.00 |
| Custom Corvette | 6215 | Corvette | HK | M-GD | BL | BK | | | $120.00 |
| Custom Corvette | 6215 | Custom Corvette | USA | M-GD | CL | GY | | | $110.00 |
| Custom Corvette | 6215 | Corvette | USA | M-GD | CL | GY | | | $120.00 |
| Custom Corvette | 6215 | Custom Corvette | HK | M-GD | BL | GY | | | $110.00 |
| Custom Corvette | 6215 | Corvette | HK | M-GD | BL | GY | | | $120.00 |
| Custom Corvette | 6215 | Custom Corvette | USA | M-GD | CL | BR-L | | | $110.00 |
| Custom Corvette | 6215 | Corvette | USA | M-GD | CL | BR-L | | | $120.00 |
| Custom Corvette | 6215 | Custom Corvette | HK | M-GD | BL | BR-L | | | $110.00 |
| Custom Corvette | 6215 | Corvette | HK | M-GD | BL | BR-L | | | $120.00 |
| Custom Corvette | 6215 | Custom Corvette | USA | M-GD | CL | BR-D | | | $110.00 |
| Custom Corvette | 6215 | Corvette | USA | M-GD | CL | BR-D | | | $120.00 |
| Custom Corvette | 6215 | Custom Corvette | HK | M-GD | BL | BR-D | | | $110.00 |
| Custom Corvette | 6215 | Corvette | HK | M-GD | BL | BR-D | | | $120.00 |
| Custom Corvette | 6215 | Custom Corvette | USA | M-GR | CL | WH | | | $120.00 |
| Custom Corvette | 6215 | Corvette | USA | M-GR | CL | WH | | | $130.00 |
| Custom Corvette | 6215 | Custom Corvette | HK | M-GR | BL | WH | | | $120.00 |
| Custom Corvette | 6215 | Corvette | HK | M-GR | BL | WH | | | $130.00 |
| Custom Corvette | 6215 | Custom Corvette | USA | M-GR | CL | BK | | | $110.00 |
| Custom Corvette | 6215 | Corvette | USA | M-GR | CL | BK | | | $120.00 |
| Custom Corvette | 6215 | Custom Corvette | HK | M-GR | BL | BK | | | $110.00 |
| Custom Corvette | 6215 | Corvette | HK | M-GR | BL | BK | | | $120.00 |
| Custom Corvette | 6215 | Custom Corvette | USA | M-GR | CL | GY | | | $110.00 |
| Custom Corvette | 6215 | Corvette | USA | M-GR | CL | GY | | | $120.00 |
| Custom Corvette | 6215 | Custom Corvette | HK | M-GR | BL | GY | | | $110.00 |

## 1968 Variations

| Name | Number | Casting | Country | Color | Windows | Interior | Paint | Other | Value |
|---|---|---|---|---|---|---|---|---|---|
| Custom Corvette | 6215 | Corvette | HK | M-GR | BL | GY | | | $120.00 |
| Custom Corvette | 6215 | Custom Corvette | USA | M-GR | CL | BR-L | | | $110.00 |
| Custom Corvette | 6215 | Corvette | USA | M-GR | CL | BR-L | | | $120.00 |
| Custom Corvette | 6215 | Custom Corvette | HK | M-GR | BL | BR-L | | | $110.00 |
| Custom Corvette | 6215 | Corvette | HK | M-GR | BL | BR-L | | | $120.00 |
| Custom Corvette | 6215 | Custom Corvette | USA | M-GR | CL | BR-D | | | $110.00 |
| Custom Corvette | 6215 | Corvette | USA | M-GR | CL | BR-D | | | $120.00 |
| Custom Corvette | 6215 | Custom Corvette | HK | M-GR | BL | BR-D | | | $110.00 |
| Custom Corvette | 6215 | Corvette | HK | M-GR | BL | BR-D | | | $120.00 |
| Custom Corvette | 6215 | Custom Corvette | USA | M-GR-E | CL | WH | | | $120.00 |
| Custom Corvette | 6215 | Corvette | USA | M-GR-E | CL | WH | | | $130.00 |
| Custom Corvette | 6215 | Custom Corvette | HK | M-GR-E | BL | WH | | | $120.00 |
| Custom Corvette | 6215 | Corvette | HK | M-GR-E | BL | WH | | | $130.00 |
| Custom Corvette | 6215 | Custom Corvette | USA | M-GR-E | CL | BK | | | $110.00 |
| Custom Corvette | 6215 | Corvette | USA | M-GR-E | CL | BK | | | $120.00 |
| Custom Corvette | 6215 | Custom Corvette | HK | M-GR-E | BL | BK | | | $110.00 |
| Custom Corvette | 6215 | Corvette | HK | M-GR-E | BL | BK | | | $120.00 |
| Custom Corvette | 6215 | Custom Corvette | USA | M-GR-E | CL | GY | | | $110.00 |
| Custom Corvette | 6215 | Corvette | USA | M-GR-E | CL | GY | | | $120.00 |
| Custom Corvette | 6215 | Custom Corvette | HK | M-GR-E | BL | GY | | | $110.00 |
| Custom Corvette | 6215 | Corvette | HK | M-GR-E | BL | GY | | | $120.00 |
| Custom Corvette | 6215 | Custom Corvette | USA | M-GR-E | CL | BR-L | | | $110.00 |
| Custom Corvette | 6215 | Corvette | USA | M-GR-E | CL | BR-L | | | $120.00 |
| Custom Corvette | 6215 | Custom Corvette | HK | M-GR-E | BL | BR-L | | | $110.00 |
| Custom Corvette | 6215 | Corvette | HK | M-GR-E | BL | BR-L | | | $120.00 |
| Custom Corvette | 6215 | Custom Corvette | USA | M-GR-E | CL | BR-D | | | $110.00 |
| Custom Corvette | 6215 | Corvette | USA | M-GR-E | CL | BR-D | | | $120.00 |
| Custom Corvette | 6215 | Custom Corvette | HK | M-GR-E | BL | BR-D | | | $110.00 |
| Custom Corvette | 6215 | Corvette | HK | M-GR-E | BL | BR-D | | | $120.00 |
| Custom Corvette | 6215 | Custom Corvette | USA | M-GR-L | CL | WH | | | $120.00 |
| Custom Corvette | 6215 | Corvette | USA | M-GR-L | CL | WH | | | $130.00 |
| Custom Corvette | 6215 | Custom Corvette | HK | M-GR-L | BL | WH | | | $120.00 |
| Custom Corvette | 6215 | Corvette | HK | M-GR-L | BL | WH | | | $130.00 |
| Custom Corvette | 6215 | Custom Corvette | USA | M-GR-L | CL | BK | | | $110.00 |
| Custom Corvette | 6215 | Corvette | USA | M-GR-L | CL | BK | | | $120.00 |
| Custom Corvette | 6215 | Custom Corvette | HK | M-GR-L | BL | BK | | | $110.00 |
| Custom Corvette | 6215 | Corvette | HK | M-GR-L | BL | BK | | | $120.00 |
| Custom Corvette | 6215 | Custom Corvette | USA | M-GR-L | CL | GY | | | $110.00 |
| Custom Corvette | 6215 | Corvette | USA | M-GR-L | CL | GY | | | $120.00 |
| Custom Corvette | 6215 | Custom Corvette | HK | M-GR-L | BL | GY | | | $110.00 |
| Custom Corvette | 6215 | Corvette | HK | M-GR-L | BL | GY | | | $120.00 |
| Custom Corvette | 6215 | Custom Corvette | USA | M-GR-L | CL | BR-L | | | $110.00 |
| Custom Corvette | 6215 | Corvette | USA | M-GR-L | CL | BR-L | | | $120.00 |
| Custom Corvette | 6215 | Custom Corvette | HK | M-GR-L | BL | BR-L | | | $110.00 |
| Custom Corvette | 6215 | Corvette | HK | M-GR-L | BL | BR-L | | | $120.00 |
| Custom Corvette | 6215 | Custom Corvette | USA | M-GR-L | CL | BR-D | | | $110.00 |
| Custom Corvette | 6215 | Corvette | USA | M-GR-L | CL | BR-D | | | $120.00 |
| Custom Corvette | 6215 | Custom Corvette | HK | M-GR-L | BL | BR-D | | | $110.00 |
| Custom Corvette | 6215 | Corvette | HK | M-GR-L | BL | BR-D | | | $120.00 |
| Custom Corvette | 6215 | Custom Corvette | USA | M-GR-O | CL | WH | | | $200.00 |
| Custom Corvette | 6215 | Corvette | USA | M-GR-O | CL | WH | | | $210.00 |
| Custom Corvette | 6215 | Custom Corvette | HK | M-GR-O | BL | WH | | | $200.00 |
| Custom Corvette | 6215 | Corvette | HK | M-GR-O | BL | WH | | | $210.00 |
| Custom Corvette | 6215 | Custom Corvette | USA | M-GR-O | CL | BK | | | $190.00 |
| Custom Corvette | 6215 | Corvette | USA | M-GR-O | CL | BK | | | $200.00 |
| Custom Corvette | 6215 | Custom Corvette | HK | M-GR-O | BL | BK | | | $190.00 |
| Custom Corvette | 6215 | Corvette | HK | M-GR-O | BL | BK | | | $200.00 |
| Custom Corvette | 6215 | Custom Corvette | USA | M-GR-O | CL | GY | | | $190.00 |
| Custom Corvette | 6215 | Corvette | USA | M-GR-O | CL | GY | | | $200.00 |
| Custom Corvette | 6215 | Custom Corvette | HK | M-GR-O | BL | GY | | | $190.00 |
| Custom Corvette | 6215 | Corvette | HK | M-GR-O | BL | GY | | | $200.00 |
| Custom Corvette | 6215 | Custom Corvette | USA | M-GR-O | CL | BR-L | | | $190.00 |
| Custom Corvette | 6215 | Corvette | USA | M-GR-O | CL | BR-L | | | $200.00 |
| Custom Corvette | 6215 | Custom Corvette | HK | M-GR-O | BL | BR-L | | | $190.00 |
| Custom Corvette | 6215 | Corvette | HK | M-GR-O | BL | BR-L | | | $200.00 |
| Custom Corvette | 6215 | Custom Corvette | USA | M-GR-O | CL | BR-D | | | $190.00 |
| Custom Corvette | 6215 | Corvette | USA | M-GR-O | CL | BR-D | | | $200.00 |
| Custom Corvette | 6215 | Custom Corvette | HK | M-GR-O | BL | BR-D | | | $190.00 |
| Custom Corvette | 6215 | Corvette | HK | M-GR-O | BL | BR-D | | | $200.00 |
| Custom Corvette | 6215 | Custom Corvette | USA | M-MG | CL | WH | | | $240.00 |
| Custom Corvette | 6215 | Corvette | USA | M-MG | CL | WH | | | $260.00 |
| Custom Corvette | 6215 | Custom Corvette | HK | M-MG | BL | WH | | | $240.00 |

## 1968 Variations

| Name | Number | Casting | Country | Color | Windows | Interior | Paint | Other | Value |
|---|---|---|---|---|---|---|---|---|---|
| Custom Corvette | 6215 | Corvette | HK | M-MG | BL | WH | | | $260.00 |
| Custom Corvette | 6215 | Custom Corvette | USA | M-MG | CL | DK | | | $220.00 |
| Custom Corvette | 6215 | Corvette | USA | M-MG | CL | BK | | | $240.00 |
| Custom Corvette | 6215 | Custom Corvette | HK | M-MG | BL | BK | | | $220.00 |
| Custom Corvette | 6215 | Corvette | HK | M-MG | BL | BK | | | $240.00 |
| Custom Corvette | 6215 | Custom Corvette | USA | M-MG | CL | GY | | | $220.00 |
| Custom Corvette | 6215 | Corvette | USA | M-MG | CL | GY | | | $240.00 |
| Custom Corvette | 6215 | Custom Corvette | HK | M-MG | BL | GY | | | $220.00 |
| Custom Corvette | 6215 | Corvette | HK | M-MG | BL | GY | | | $240.00 |
| Custom Corvette | 6215 | Custom Corvette | USA | M-MG | CL | BR-L | | | $220.00 |
| Custom Corvette | 6215 | Corvette | USA | M-MG | CL | BR-L | | | $240.00 |
| Custom Corvette | 6215 | Custom Corvette | HK | M-MG | BL | BR-L | | | $220.00 |
| Custom Corvette | 6215 | Corvette | HK | M-MG | BL | BR-L | | | $240.00 |
| Custom Corvette | 6215 | Custom Corvette | USA | M-MG | CL | BR-D | | | $220.00 |
| Custom Corvette | 6215 | Corvette | USA | M-MG | CL | BR-D | | | $240.00 |
| Custom Corvette | 6215 | Custom Corvette | HK | M-MG | BL | BR-D | | | $220.00 |
| Custom Corvette | 6215 | Corvette | HK | M-MG | BL | BR-D | | | $240.00 |
| Custom Corvette | 6215 | Custom Corvette | USA | M-OR | CL | WH | | | $180.00 |
| Custom Corvette | 6215 | Corvette | USA | M-OR | CL | WH | | | $190.00 |
| Custom Corvette | 6215 | Custom Corvette | HK | M-OR | BL | WH | | | $180.00 |
| Custom Corvette | 6215 | Corvette | HK | M-OR | BL | WH | | | $190.00 |
| Custom Corvette | 6215 | Custom Corvette | USA | M-OR | CL | BK | | | $170.00 |
| Custom Corvette | 6215 | Corvette | USA | M-OR | CL | BK | | | $180.00 |
| Custom Corvette | 6215 | Custom Corvette | HK | M-OR | BL | BK | | | $170.00 |
| Custom Corvette | 6215 | Corvette | HK | M-OR | BL | BK | | | $180.00 |
| Custom Corvette | 6215 | Custom Corvette | USA | M-OR | CL | GY | | | $170.00 |
| Custom Corvette | 6215 | Corvette | USA | M-OR | CL | GY | | | $180.00 |
| Custom Corvette | 6215 | Custom Corvette | HK | M-OR | BL | GY | | | $170.00 |
| Custom Corvette | 6215 | Corvette | HK | M-OR | BL | GY | | | $180.00 |
| Custom Corvette | 6215 | Custom Corvette | USA | M-OR | CL | BR-L | | | $170.00 |
| Custom Corvette | 6215 | Corvette | USA | M-OR | CL | BR-L | | | $180.00 |
| Custom Corvette | 6215 | Custom Corvette | HK | M-OR | BL | BR-L | | | $170.00 |
| Custom Corvette | 6215 | Corvette | HK | M-OR | BL | BR-L | | | $180.00 |
| Custom Corvette | 6215 | Custom Corvette | USA | M-OR | CL | BR-D | | | $170.00 |
| Custom Corvette | 6215 | Corvette | USA | M-OR | CL | BR-D | | | $180.00 |
| Custom Corvette | 6215 | Custom Corvette | HK | M-OR | BL | BR-D | | | $170.00 |
| Custom Corvette | 6215 | Corvette | HK | M-OR | BL | BR-D | | | $180.00 |
| Custom Corvette | 6215 | Custom Corvette | USA | M-PR | CL | WH | | | $200.00 |
| Custom Corvette | 6215 | Corvette | USA | M-PR | CL | WH | | | $210.00 |
| Custom Corvette | 6215 | Custom Corvette | HK | M-PR | BL | WH | | | $200.00 |
| Custom Corvette | 6215 | Corvette | HK | M-PR | BL | WH | | | $210.00 |
| Custom Corvette | 6215 | Custom Corvette | USA | M-PR | CL | BK | | | $190.00 |
| Custom Corvette | 6215 | Corvette | USA | M-PR | CL | BK | | | $200.00 |
| Custom Corvette | 6215 | Custom Corvette | HK | M-PR | BL | BK | | | $190.00 |
| Custom Corvette | 6215 | Corvette | HK | M-PR | BL | BK | | | $200.00 |
| Custom Corvette | 6215 | Custom Corvette | USA | M-PR | CL | GY | | | $190.00 |
| Custom Corvette | 6215 | Corvette | USA | M-PR | CL | GY | | | $200.00 |
| Custom Corvette | 6215 | Custom Corvette | HK | M-PR | BL | GY | | | $190.00 |
| Custom Corvette | 6215 | Corvette | HK | M-PR | BL | GY | | | $200.00 |
| Custom Corvette | 6215 | Custom Corvette | USA | M-PR | CL | BR-L | | | $190.00 |
| Custom Corvette | 6215 | Corvette | USA | M-PR | CL | BR-L | | | $200.00 |
| Custom Corvette | 6215 | Custom Corvette | HK | M-PR | BL | BR-L | | | $190.00 |
| Custom Corvette | 6215 | Corvette | HK | M-PR | BL | BR-L | | | $200.00 |
| Custom Corvette | 6215 | Custom Corvette | USA | M-PR | CL | BR-D | | | $190.00 |
| Custom Corvette | 6215 | Corvette | USA | M-PR | CL | BR-D | | | $200.00 |
| Custom Corvette | 6215 | Custom Corvette | HK | M-PR | BL | BR-D | | | $190.00 |
| Custom Corvette | 6215 | Corvette | HK | M-PR | BL | BR-D | | | $200.00 |
| Custom Corvette | 6215 | Custom Corvette | USA | M-RD | CL | WH | | | $110.00 |
| Custom Corvette | 6215 | Corvette | USA | M-RD | CL | WH | | | $120.00 |
| Custom Corvette | 6215 | Custom Corvette | HK | M-RD | BL | WH | | | $110.00 |
| Custom Corvette | 6215 | Corvette | HK | M-RD | BL | WH | | | $120.00 |
| Custom Corvette | 6215 | Custom Corvette | USA | M-RD | CL | BK | | | $100.00 |
| Custom Corvette | 6215 | Corvette | USA | M-RD | CL | BK | | | $110.00 |
| Custom Corvette | 6215 | Custom Corvette | HK | M-RD | BL | BK | | | $100.00 |
| Custom Corvette | 6215 | Corvette | HK | M-RD | BL | BK | | | $110.00 |
| Custom Corvette | 6215 | Custom Corvette | USA | M-RD | CL | GY | | | $100.00 |
| Custom Corvette | 6215 | Corvette | USA | M-RD | CL | GY | | | $110.00 |
| Custom Corvette | 6215 | Custom Corvette | HK | M-RD | BL | GY | | | $100.00 |
| Custom Corvette | 6215 | Corvette | HK | M-RD | BL | GY | | | $110.00 |
| Custom Corvette | 6215 | Custom Corvette | USA | M-RD | CL | BR-L | | | $100.00 |
| Custom Corvette | 6215 | Corvette | USA | M-RD | CL | BR-L | | | $110.00 |
| Custom Corvette | 6215 | Custom Corvette | HK | M-RD | BL | BR-L | | | $100.00 |

## 1968 Variations

| Name | Number | Casting | Country | Color | Windows | Interior | Paint | Other | Value |
|---|---|---|---|---|---|---|---|---|---|
| Custom Corvette | 6215 | Corvette | HK | M-RD | BL | BR-L | | | $110.00 |
| Custom Corvette | 6215 | Custom Corvette | USA | M-RD | CL | BR-D | | | $100.00 |
| Custom Corvette | 6215 | Corvette | USA | M-RD | CL | BR-D | | | $110.00 |
| Custom Corvette | 6215 | Custom Corvette | HK | M-RD | BL | BR-D | | | $100.00 |
| Custom Corvette | 6215 | Corvette | HK | M-RD | BL | BR-D | | | $110.00 |
| Custom Corvette | 6215 | Custom Corvette | USA | M-RD-R | CL | WH | | | $110.00 |
| Custom Corvette | 6215 | Corvette | USA | M-RD-R | CL | WH | | | $120.00 |
| Custom Corvette | 6215 | Custom Corvette | HK | M-RD-R | BL | WH | | | $110.00 |
| Custom Corvette | 6215 | Corvette | HK | M-RD-R | BL | WH | | | $120.00 |
| Custom Corvette | 6215 | Custom Corvette | USA | M-RD-R | CL | BK | | | $100.00 |
| Custom Corvette | 6215 | Corvette | USA | M-RD-R | CL | BK | | | $110.00 |
| Custom Corvette | 6215 | Custom Corvette | HK | M-RD-R | BL | BK | | | $100.00 |
| Custom Corvette | 6215 | Corvette | HK | M-RD-R | BL | BK | | | $110.00 |
| Custom Corvette | 6215 | Custom Corvette | USA | M-RD-R | CL | GY | | | $100.00 |
| Custom Corvette | 6215 | Corvette | USA | M-RD-R | CL | GY | | | $110.00 |
| Custom Corvette | 6215 | Custom Corvette | HK | M-RD-R | BL | GY | | | $100.00 |
| Custom Corvette | 6215 | Corvette | HK | M-RD-R | BL | GY | | | $110.00 |
| Custom Corvette | 6215 | Custom Corvette | USA | M-RD-R | CL | BR-L | | | $100.00 |
| Custom Corvette | 6215 | Corvette | USA | M-RD-R | CL | BR-L | | | $110.00 |
| Custom Corvette | 6215 | Custom Corvette | HK | M-RD-R | BL | BR-L | | | $100.00 |
| Custom Corvette | 6215 | Corvette | HK | M-RD-R | BL | BR-L | | | $110.00 |
| Custom Corvette | 6215 | Custom Corvette | USA | M-RD-R | CL | BR-D | | | $100.00 |
| Custom Corvette | 6215 | Corvette | USA | M-RD-R | CL | BR-D | | | $110.00 |
| Custom Corvette | 6215 | Custom Corvette | HK | M-RD-R | BL | BR-D | | | $100.00 |
| Custom Corvette | 6215 | Corvette | HK | M-RD-R | BL | BR-D | | | $110.00 |
| Custom Corvette | 6215 | Custom Corvette | USA | M-YW | CL | WH | | | $120.00 |
| Custom Corvette | 6215 | Corvette | USA | M-YW | CL | WH | | | $130.00 |
| Custom Corvette | 6215 | Custom Corvette | HK | M-YW | BL | WH | | | $120.00 |
| Custom Corvette | 6215 | Corvette | HK | M-YW | BL | WH | | | $130.00 |
| Custom Corvette | 6215 | Custom Corvette | USA | M-YW | CL | BK | | | $110.00 |
| Custom Corvette | 6215 | Corvette | USA | M-YW | CL | BK | | | $120.00 |
| Custom Corvette | 6215 | Custom Corvette | HK | M-YW | BL | BK | | | $110.00 |
| Custom Corvette | 6215 | Corvette | HK | M-YW | BL | BK | | | $120.00 |
| Custom Corvette | 6215 | Custom Corvette | USA | M-YW | CL | GY | | | $110.00 |
| Custom Corvette | 6215 | Corvette | USA | M-YW | CL | GY | | | $120.00 |
| Custom Corvette | 6215 | Custom Corvette | HK | M-YW | BL | GY | | | $110.00 |
| Custom Corvette | 6215 | Corvette | HK | M-YW | BL | GY | | | $120.00 |
| Custom Corvette | 6215 | Custom Corvette | USA | M-YW | CL | BR-L | | | $110.00 |
| Custom Corvette | 6215 | Corvette | USA | M-YW | CL | BR-L | | | $120.00 |
| Custom Corvette | 6215 | Custom Corvette | HK | M-YW | BL | BR-L | | | $110.00 |
| Custom Corvette | 6215 | Corvette | HK | M-YW | BL | BR-L | | | $120.00 |
| Custom Corvette | 6215 | Custom Corvette | USA | M-YW | CL | BR-D | | | $110.00 |
| Custom Corvette | 6215 | Corvette | USA | M-YW | CL | BR-D | | | $120.00 |
| Custom Corvette | 6215 | Custom Corvette | HK | M-YW | BL | BR-D | | | $110.00 |
| Custom Corvette | 6215 | Corvette | HK | M-YW | BL | BR-D | | | $120.00 |
| Custom Corvette | 6215 | Custom Corvette | USA | M-YW-L | CL | WH | | | $140.00 |
| Custom Corvette | 6215 | Corvette | USA | M-YW-L | CL | WH | | | $150.00 |
| Custom Corvette | 6215 | Custom Corvette | HK | M-YW-L | BL | WH | | | $140.00 |
| Custom Corvette | 6215 | Corvette | HK | M-YW-L | BL | WH | | | $150.00 |
| Custom Corvette | 6215 | Custom Corvette | USA | M-YW-L | CL | BK | | | $130.00 |
| Custom Corvette | 6215 | Corvette | USA | M-YW-L | CL | BK | | | $140.00 |
| Custom Corvette | 6215 | Custom Corvette | HK | M-YW-L | BL | BK | | | $130.00 |
| Custom Corvette | 6215 | Corvette | HK | M-YW-L | BL | BK | | | $140.00 |
| Custom Corvette | 6215 | Custom Corvette | USA | M-YW-L | CL | GY | | | $130.00 |
| Custom Corvette | 6215 | Corvette | USA | M-YW-L | CL | GY | | | $140.00 |
| Custom Corvette | 6215 | Custom Corvette | HK | M-YW-L | BL | GY | | | $130.00 |
| Custom Corvette | 6215 | Corvette | HK | M-YW-L | BL | GY | | | $140.00 |
| Custom Corvette | 6215 | Custom Corvette | USA | M-YW-L | CL | BR-L | | | $130.00 |
| Custom Corvette | 6215 | Corvette | USA | M-YW-L | CL | BR-L | | | $140.00 |
| Custom Corvette | 6215 | Custom Corvette | HK | M-YW-L | BL | BR-L | | | $130.00 |
| Custom Corvette | 6215 | Corvette | HK | M-YW-L | BL | BR-L | | | $140.00 |
| Custom Corvette | 6215 | Custom Corvette | USA | M-YW-L | CL | BR-D | | | $130.00 |
| Custom Corvette | 6215 | Corvette | USA | M-YW-L | CL | BR-D | | | $140.00 |
| Custom Corvette | 6215 | Custom Corvette | HK | M-YW-L | BL | BR-D | | | $130.00 |
| Custom Corvette | 6215 | Corvette | HK | M-YW-L | BL | BR-D | | | $140.00 |
| | | | | | | | | | |
| Cheetah | 6216 | | HK | M-OR | BL | | | | $1,200.00 |
| Cheetah | 6216 | | HK | M-RD | BL | | | | $1,200.00 |
| Python | 6216 | | HK | M-AQ | BL | WH | | | $45.00 |
| Python | 6216 | | HK | M-AQ | BL | BK | | | $40.00 |
| Python | 6216 | | HK | M-AQ | BL | GY | | | $40.00 |

## 1968 Variations

| Name | Number | Casting | Country | Color | Windows | Interior | Paint | Other | Value |
|---|---|---|---|---|---|---|---|---|---|
| Python | 6216 | | HK | M-AQ | BL | BR-L | | | $40.00 |
| Python | 6216 | | HK | M-AQ | BL | BR-D | | | $40.00 |
| Python | 6216 | Large rear window | USA | M-AQ | CL | WH | | | $45.00 |
| Python | 6216 | Large rear window | USA | M-AQ | CL | BK | | | $40.00 |
| Python | 6216 | Large rear window | USA | M-AQ | CL | GY | | | $40.00 |
| Python | 6216 | Large rear window | USA | M-AQ | CL | BR-L | | | $40.00 |
| Python | 6216 | Large rear window | USA | M-AQ | CL | BR-D | | | $40.00 |
| Python | 6216 | | HK | M-BL | BL | WH | | | $50.00 |
| Python | 6216 | | HK | M-BL | BL | BK | | | $45.00 |
| Python | 6216 | | HK | M-BL | BL | GY | | | $45.00 |
| Python | 6216 | | HK | M-BL | BL | BR-L | | | $45.00 |
| Python | 6216 | | HK | M-BL | BL | BR-D | | | $45.00 |
| Python | 6216 | Large rear window | USA | M-BL | CL | WH | | | $50.00 |
| Python | 6216 | Large rear window | USA | M-BL | CL | BK | | | $45.00 |
| Python | 6216 | Large rear window | USA | M-BL | CL | GY | | | $45.00 |
| Python | 6216 | Large rear window | USA | M-BL | CL | BR-L | | | $45.00 |
| Python | 6216 | Large rear window | USA | M-BL | CL | BR-D | | | $45.00 |
| Python | 6216 | | HK | M-BL-I | BL | WH | | | $70.00 |
| Python | 6216 | | HK | M-BL-I | BL | BK | | | $60.00 |
| Python | 6216 | | HK | M-BL-I | BL | GY | | | $60.00 |
| Python | 6216 | | HK | M-BL-I | BL | BR-L | | | $60.00 |
| Python | 6216 | | HK | M-BL-I | BL | BR-D | | | $60.00 |
| Python | 6216 | Large rear window | USA | M-BL-I | CL | WH | | | $70.00 |
| Python | 6216 | Large rear window | USA | M-BL-I | CL | BK | | | $60.00 |
| Python | 6216 | Large rear window | USA | M-BL-I | CL | GY | | | $60.00 |
| Python | 6216 | Large rear window | USA | M-BL-I | CL | BR-L | | | $60.00 |
| Python | 6216 | Large rear window | USA | M-BL-I | CL | BR-D | | | $60.00 |
| Python | 6216 | | HK | M-BL-P | BL | WH | | | $60.00 |
| Python | 6216 | | HK | M-BL-P | BL | BK | | | $50.00 |
| Python | 6216 | | HK | M-BL-P | BL | GY | | | $50.00 |
| Python | 6216 | | HK | M-BL-P | BL | BR-L | | | $50.00 |
| Python | 6216 | | HK | M-BL-P | BL | BR-D | | | $50.00 |
| Python | 6216 | Large rear window | USA | M-BL-P | CL | WH | | | $60.00 |
| Python | 6216 | Large rear window | USA | M-BL-P | CL | BK | | | $50.00 |
| Python | 6216 | Large rear window | USA | M-BL-P | CL | GY | | | $50.00 |
| Python | 6216 | Large rear window | USA | M-BL-P | CL | BR-L | | | $50.00 |
| Python | 6216 | Large rear window | USA | M-BL-P | CL | BR-D | | | $50.00 |
| Python | 6216 | | HK | M-BR-D | BL | WH | | | $120.00 |
| Python | 6216 | | HK | M-BR-D | BL | BK | | | $110.00 |
| Python | 6216 | | HK | M-BR-D | BL | GY | | | $110.00 |
| Python | 6216 | | HK | M-BR-D | BL | BR-L | | | $110.00 |
| Python | 6216 | | HK | M-BR-D | BL | BR-D | | | $110.00 |
| Python | 6216 | Large rear window | USA | M-BR-D | CL | WH | | | $120.00 |
| Python | 6216 | Large rear window | USA | M-BR-D | CL | BK | | | $110.00 |
| Python | 6216 | Large rear window | USA | M-BR-D | CL | GY | | | $110.00 |
| Python | 6216 | Large rear window | USA | M-BR-D | CL | BR-L | | | $110.00 |
| Python | 6216 | Large rear window | USA | M-BR-D | CL | BR-D | | | $110.00 |
| Python | 6216 | | HK | M-BR-P | BL | WH | | | $120.00 |
| Python | 6216 | | HK | M-BR-P | BL | BK | | | $110.00 |
| Python | 6216 | | HK | M-BR-P | BL | GY | | | $110.00 |
| Python | 6216 | | HK | M-BR-P | BL | BR-L | | | $110.00 |
| Python | 6216 | | HK | M-BR-P | BL | BR-D | | | $110.00 |
| Python | 6216 | Large rear window | USA | M-BR-P | CL | WH | | | $120.00 |
| Python | 6216 | Large rear window | USA | M-BR-P | CL | BK | | | $100.00 |
| Python | 6216 | Large rear window | USA | M-BR-P | CL | GY | | | $100.00 |
| Python | 6216 | Large rear window | USA | M-BR-P | CL | BR-L | | | $100.00 |
| Python | 6216 | Large rear window | USA | M-BR-P | CL | BR-D | | | $100.00 |
| Python | 6216 | | HK | M-GD | BL | WH | | | $45.00 |
| Python | 6216 | | HK | M-GD | BL | BK | | | $40.00 |
| Python | 6216 | | HK | M-GD | BL | GY | | | $40.00 |
| Python | 6216 | | HK | M-GD | BL | BR-L | | | $40.00 |
| Python | 6216 | | HK | M-GD | BL | BR-D | | | $40.00 |
| Python | 6216 | Large rear window | USA | M-GD | CL | WH | | | $45.00 |
| Python | 6216 | Large rear window | USA | M-GD | CL | BK | | | $40.00 |
| Python | 6216 | Large rear window | USA | M-GD | CL | GY | | | $40.00 |
| Python | 6216 | Large rear window | USA | M-GD | CL | BR-L | | | $40.00 |
| Python | 6216 | Large rear window | USA | M-GD | CL | BR-D | | | $40.00 |
| Python | 6216 | | HK | M-GR | BL | WH | | | $45.00 |
| Python | 6216 | | HK | M-GR | BL | BK | | | $40.00 |
| Python | 6216 | | HK | M-GR | BL | GY | | | $40.00 |
| Python | 6216 | | HK | M-GR | BL | BR-L | | | $40.00 |
| Python | 6216 | | HK | M-GR | BL | BR-D | | | $40.00 |

## 1968 Variations

| Name | Number | Casting | Country | Color | Windows | Interior | Paint | Other | Value |
|---|---|---|---|---|---|---|---|---|---|
| Python | 6216 | Large rear window | USA | M-GR | CL | WH | | | $45.00 |
| Python | 6216 | Large rear window | USA | M-GR | CL | BK | | | $40.00 |
| Python | 6216 | Large rear window | USA | M-GR | CL | GY | | | $40.00 |
| Python | 6216 | Large rear window | USA | M-GR | CL | BR-L | | | $40.00 |
| Python | 6216 | Large rear window | USA | M-GR | CL | BR-D | | | $40.00 |
| Python | 6216 | | HK | M-GR-E | BL | WH | | | $50.00 |
| Python | 6216 | | HK | M-GR-E | BL | BK | | | $45.00 |
| Python | 6216 | | HK | M-GR-E | BL | GY | | | $45.00 |
| Python | 6216 | | HK | M-GR-E | BL | BR-L | | | $45.00 |
| Python | 6216 | | HK | M-GR-E | BL | BR-D | | | $45.00 |
| Python | 6216 | Large rear window | USA | M-GR-E | CL | WH | | | $50.00 |
| Python | 6216 | Large rear window | USA | M-GR-E | CL | BK | | | $45.00 |
| Python | 6216 | Large rear window | USA | M-GR-E | CL | GY | | | $45.00 |
| Python | 6216 | Large rear window | USA | M-GR-E | CL | BR-L | | | $45.00 |
| Python | 6216 | Large rear window | USA | M-GR-E | CL | BR-D | | | $45.00 |
| Python | 6216 | | HK | M-GR-L | BL | WH | | | $120.00 |
| Python | 6216 | | HK | M-GR-L | BL | BK | | | $110.00 |
| Python | 6216 | | HK | M-GR-L | BL | GY | | | $110.00 |
| Python | 6216 | | HK | M-GR-L | BL | BR-L | | | $110.00 |
| Python | 6216 | | HK | M-GR-L | BL | BR-D | | | $110.00 |
| Python | 6216 | Large rear window | USA | M-GR-L | CL | WH | | | $120.00 |
| Python | 6216 | Large rear window | USA | M-GR-L | CL | BK | | | $110.00 |
| Python | 6216 | Large rear window | USA | M-GR-L | CL | GY | | | $110.00 |
| Python | 6216 | Large rear window | USA | M-GR-L | CL | BR-L | | | $110.00 |
| Python | 6216 | Large rear window | USA | M-GR-L | CL | BR-D | | | $110.00 |
| Python | 6216 | | HK | M-GR-O | BL | WH | | | $75.00 |
| Python | 6216 | | HK | M-GR-O | BL | BK | | | $70.00 |
| Python | 6216 | | HK | M-GR-O | BL | GY | | | $70.00 |
| Python | 6216 | | HK | M-GR-O | BL | BR-L | | | $70.00 |
| Python | 6216 | | HK | M-GR-O | BL | BR-D | | | $70.00 |
| Python | 6216 | Large rear window | USA | M-GR-O | CL | WH | | | $75.00 |
| Python | 6216 | Large rear window | USA | M-GR-O | CL | BK | | | $70.00 |
| Python | 6216 | Large rear window | USA | M-GR-O | CL | GY | | | $70.00 |
| Python | 6216 | Large rear window | USA | M-GR-O | CL | BR-L | | | $70.00 |
| Python | 6216 | Large rear window | USA | M-GR-O | CL | BR-D | | | $70.00 |
| Python | 6216 | | HK | M-MG | BL | WH | | | $80.00 |
| Python | 6216 | | HK | M-MG | BL | BK | | | $70.00 |
| Python | 6216 | | HK | M-MG | BL | GY | | | $70.00 |
| Python | 6216 | | HK | M-MG | BL | BR-L | | | $70.00 |
| Python | 6216 | | HK | M-MG | BL | BR-D | | | $70.00 |
| Python | 6216 | Large rear window | USA | M-MG | CL | WH | | | $80.00 |
| Python | 6216 | Large rear window | USA | M-MG | CL | BK | | | $70.00 |
| Python | 6216 | Large rear window | USA | M-MG | CL | GY | | | $70.00 |
| Python | 6216 | Large rear window | USA | M-MG | CL | BR-L | | | $70.00 |
| Python | 6216 | Large rear window | USA | M-MG | CL | BR-D | | | $70.00 |
| Python | 6216 | | HK | M-OR | BL | WH | | | $45.00 |
| Python | 6216 | | HK | M-OR | BL | BK | | | $40.00 |
| Python | 6216 | | HK | M-OR | BL | GY | | | $40.00 |
| Python | 6216 | | HK | M-OR | BL | BR-L | | | $40.00 |
| Python | 6216 | | HK | M-OR | BL | BR-D | | | $40.00 |
| Python | 6216 | Large rear window | USA | M-OR | CL | WH | | | $45.00 |
| Python | 6216 | Large rear window | USA | M-OR | CL | BK | | | $40.00 |
| Python | 6216 | Large rear window | USA | M-OR | CL | GY | | | $40.00 |
| Python | 6216 | Large rear window | USA | M-OR | CL | BR-L | | | $40.00 |
| Python | 6216 | Large rear window | USA | M-OR | CL | BR-D | | | $40.00 |
| Python | 6216 | | HK | M-PK | BL | WH | | | $320.00 |
| Python | 6216 | | HK | M-PK | BL | BK | | | $300.00 |
| Python | 6216 | | HK | M-PK | BL | GY | | | $300.00 |
| Python | 6216 | | HK | M-PK | BL | BR-L | | | $300.00 |
| Python | 6216 | | HK | M-PK | BL | BR-D | | | $300.00 |
| Python | 6216 | Large rear window | USA | M-PK | CL | WH | | | $320.00 |
| Python | 6216 | Large rear window | USA | M-PK | CL | BK | | | $300.00 |
| Python | 6216 | Large rear window | USA | M-PK | CL | GY | | | $300.00 |
| Python | 6216 | Large rear window | USA | M-PK | CL | BR-L | | | $300.00 |
| Python | 6216 | Large rear window | USA | M-PK | CL | BR-D | | | $300.00 |
| Python | 6216 | | HK | M-PK-H | BL | WH | | | $320.00 |
| Python | 6216 | | HK | M-PK-H | BL | BK | | | $300.00 |
| Python | 6216 | | HK | M-PK-H | BL | GY | | | $300.00 |
| Python | 6216 | | HK | M-PK-H | BL | BR-L | | | $300.00 |
| Python | 6216 | | HK | M-PK-H | BL | BR-D | | | $300.00 |
| Python | 6216 | Large rear window | USA | M-PK-H | CL | WH | | | $320.00 |
| Python | 6216 | Large rear window | USA | M-PK-H | CL | BK | | | $300.00 |

## 1968 Variations

| Name | Number | Casting | Country | Color | Windows | Interior | Paint | Other | Value |
|---|---|---|---|---|---|---|---|---|---|
| Python | 6216 | Large rear window | USA | M-PK-H | CL | GY | | | $300.00 |
| Python | 6216 | Large rear window | USA | M-PK-H | CL | BR-L | | | $300.00 |
| Python | 6216 | Large rear window | USA | M-PK-H | CL | BR-D | | | $300.00 |
| Python | 6216 | | HK | M-PK-S | BL | WH | | | $320.00 |
| Python | 6216 | | HK | M-PK-S | BL | BK | | | $300.00 |
| Python | 6216 | | HK | M-PK-S | BL | GY | | | $300.00 |
| Python | 6216 | | HK | M-PK-S | BL | BR-L | | | $300.00 |
| Python | 6216 | | HK | M-PK-S | BL | BR-D | | | $300.00 |
| Python | 6216 | Large rear window | USA | M-PK-S | CL | WH | | | $320.00 |
| Python | 6216 | Large rear window | USA | M-PK-S | CL | BK | | | $300.00 |
| Python | 6216 | Large rear window | USA | M-PK-S | CL | GY | | | $300.00 |
| Python | 6216 | Large rear window | USA | M-PK-S | CL | BR-L | | | $300.00 |
| Python | 6216 | Large rear window | USA | M-PK-S | CL | BR-D | | | $300.00 |
| Python | 6216 | | HK | M-PR | BL | WH | | | $75.00 |
| Python | 6216 | | HK | M-PR | BL | BK | | | $65.00 |
| Python | 6216 | | HK | M-PR | BL | GY | | | $65.00 |
| Python | 6216 | | HK | M-PR | BL | BR-L | | | $65.00 |
| Python | 6216 | | HK | M-PR | BL | BR-D | | | $65.00 |
| Python | 6216 | Large rear window | USA | M-PR | CL | WH | | | $75.00 |
| Python | 6216 | Large rear window | USA | M-PR | CL | BK | | | $65.00 |
| Python | 6216 | Large rear window | USA | M-PR | CL | GY | | | $65.00 |
| Python | 6216 | Large rear window | USA | M-PR | CL | BR-L | | | $65.00 |
| Python | 6216 | Large rear window | USA | M-PR | CL | BR-D | | | $65.00 |
| Python | 6216 | | HK | M-RD | BL | WH | | | $45.00 |
| Python | 6216 | | HK | M-RD | BL | BK | | | $40.00 |
| Python | 6216 | | HK | M-RD | BL | GY | | | $40.00 |
| Python | 6216 | | HK | M-RD | BL | BR-L | | | $40.00 |
| Python | 6216 | | HK | M-RD | BL | BR-D | | | $40.00 |
| Python | 6216 | Large rear window | USA | M-RD | CL | WH | | | $45.00 |
| Python | 6216 | Large rear window | USA | M-RD | CL | BK | | | $40.00 |
| Python | 6216 | Large rear window | USA | M-RD | CL | GY | | | $40.00 |
| Python | 6216 | Large rear window | USA | M-RD | CL | BR-L | | | $40.00 |
| Python | 6216 | Large rear window | USA | M-RD | CL | BR-D | | | $40.00 |
| Python | 6216 | | HK | M-RD-R | BL | WH | | | $50.00 |
| Python | 6216 | | HK | M-RD-R | BL | BK | | | $45.00 |
| Python | 6216 | | HK | M-RD-R | BL | GY | | | $45.00 |
| Python | 6216 | | HK | M-RD-R | BL | BR-L | | | $45.00 |
| Python | 6216 | | HK | M-RD-R | BL | BR-D | | | $45.00 |
| Python | 6216 | Large rear window | USA | M-RD-R | CL | WH | | | $50.00 |
| Python | 6216 | Large rear window | USA | M-RD-R | CL | BK | | | $45.00 |
| Python | 6216 | Large rear window | USA | M-RD-R | CL | GY | | | $45.00 |
| Python | 6216 | Large rear window | USA | M-RD-R | CL | BR-L | | | $45.00 |
| Python | 6216 | Large rear window | USA | M-RD-R | CL | BR-D | | | $45.00 |
| Python | 6216 | | HK | M-YW | BL | WH | | | $45.00 |
| Python | 6216 | | HK | M-YW | BL | BK | | | $40.00 |
| Python | 6216 | | HK | M-YW | BL | GY | | | $40.00 |
| Python | 6216 | | HK | M-YW | BL | BR-L | | | $40.00 |
| Python | 6216 | | HK | M-YW | BL | BR-D | | | $40.00 |
| Python | 6216 | Large rear window | USA | M-YW | CL | WH | | | $45.00 |
| Python | 6216 | Large rear window | USA | M-YW | CL | BK | | | $40.00 |
| Python | 6216 | Large rear window | USA | M-YW | CL | GY | | | $40.00 |
| Python | 6216 | Large rear window | USA | M-YW | CL | BR-L | | | $40.00 |
| Python | 6216 | Large rear window | USA | M-YW | CL | BR-D | | | $40.00 |
| Python | 6216 | | HK | M-YW-L | BL | WH | | | $140.00 |
| Python | 6216 | | HK | M-YW-L | BL | BK | | | $130.00 |
| Python | 6216 | | HK | M-YW-L | BL | GY | | | $130.00 |
| Python | 6216 | | HK | M-YW-L | BL | BR-L | | | $130.00 |
| Python | 6216 | | HK | M-YW-L | BL | BR-D | | | $130.00 |
| Python | 6216 | Large rear window | USA | M-YW-L | CL | WH | | | $140.00 |
| Python | 6216 | Large rear window | USA | M-YW-L | CL | BK | | | $130.00 |
| Python | 6216 | Large rear window | USA | M-YW-L | CL | GY | | | $130.00 |
| Python | 6216 | Large rear window | USA | M-YW-L | CL | BR-L | | | $130.00 |
| Python | 6216 | Large rear window | USA | M-YW-L | CL | BR-D | | | $130.00 |
| | | | | | | | | | |
| Beatnik Bandit | 6217 | | USA | M-AQ | CL | WH | | | $60.00 |
| Beatnik Bandit | 6217 | | HK | M-AQ | BL | WH | | | $60.00 |
| Beatnik Bandit | 6217 | | USA | M-AQ | CL | BK | | | $50.00 |
| Beatnik Bandit | 6217 | | HK | M-AQ | BL | BK | | | $50.00 |
| Beatnik Bandit | 6217 | | USA | M-AQ | CL | GY | | | $50.00 |
| Beatnik Bandit | 6217 | | HK | M-AQ | BL | GY | | | $50.00 |
| Beatnik Bandit | 6217 | | USA | M-AQ | CL | BR-L | | | $50.00 |

## 1968 Variations

| Name | Number | Casting | Country | Color | Windows | Interior | Paint | Other | Value |
|---|---|---|---|---|---|---|---|---|---|
| Beatnik Bandit | 6217 | | HK | M-AQ | BL | BR-L | | | $50.00 |
| Beatnik Bandit | 6217 | | USA | M-AQ | CL | BR-D | | | $50.00 |
| Beatnik Bandit | 6217 | | HK | M-AQ | BL | BR-D | | | $50.00 |
| Beatnik Bandit | 6217 | | USA | M-BL | CL | WH | | | $50.00 |
| Beatnik Bandit | 6217 | | HK | M-BL | BL | WH | | | $50.00 |
| Beatnik Bandit | 6217 | | USA | M-BL | CL | BK | | | $40.00 |
| Beatnik Bandit | 6217 | | HK | M-BL | BL | BK | | | $40.00 |
| Beatnik Bandit | 6217 | | USA | M-BL | CL | GY | | | $40.00 |
| Beatnik Bandit | 6217 | | HK | M-BL | BL | GY | | | $40.00 |
| Beatnik Bandit | 6217 | | USA | M-BL | CL | BR-L | | | $40.00 |
| Beatnik Bandit | 6217 | | HK | M-BL | BL | BR-L | | | $40.00 |
| Beatnik Bandit | 6217 | | USA | M-BL | CL | BR-D | | | $40.00 |
| Beatnik Bandit | 6217 | | HK | M-BL | BL | BR-D | | | $40.00 |
| Beatnik Bandit | 6217 | | USA | M-BL-I | CL | WH | | | $55.00 |
| Beatnik Bandit | 6217 | | HK | M-BL-I | BL | WH | | | $55.00 |
| Beatnik Bandit | 6217 | | USA | M-BL-I | CL | BK | | | $45.00 |
| Beatnik Bandit | 6217 | | HK | M-BL-I | BL | BK | | | $45.00 |
| Beatnik Bandit | 6217 | | USA | M-BL-I | CL | GY | | | $45.00 |
| Beatnik Bandit | 6217 | | HK | M-BL-I | BL | GY | | | $45.00 |
| Beatnik Bandit | 6217 | | USA | M-BL-I | CL | BR-L | | | $45.00 |
| Beatnik Bandit | 6217 | | HK | M-BL-I | BL | BR-L | | | $45.00 |
| Beatnik Bandit | 6217 | | USA | M-BL-I | CL | BR-D | | | $45.00 |
| Beatnik Bandit | 6217 | | HK | M-BL-I | BL | BR-D | | | $45.00 |
| Beatnik Bandit | 6217 | | USA | M-BL-P | CL | WH | | | $50.00 |
| Beatnik Bandit | 6217 | | HK | M-BL-P | BL | WH | | | $50.00 |
| Beatnik Bandit | 6217 | | USA | M-BL-P | CL | BK | | | $40.00 |
| Beatnik Bandit | 6217 | | HK | M-BL-P | BL | BK | | | $40.00 |
| Beatnik Bandit | 6217 | | USA | M-BL-P | CL | GY | | | $40.00 |
| Beatnik Bandit | 6217 | | HK | M-BL-P | BL | GY | | | $40.00 |
| Beatnik Bandit | 6217 | | USA | M-BL-P | CL | BR-L | | | $40.00 |
| Beatnik Bandit | 6217 | | HK | M-BL-P | BL | BR-L | | | $40.00 |
| Beatnik Bandit | 6217 | | USA | M-BL-P | CL | BR-D | | | $40.00 |
| Beatnik Bandit | 6217 | | HK | M-BL-P | BL | BR-D | | | $40.00 |
| Beatnik Bandit | 6217 | | USA | M-BR-D | CL | WH | | | $65.00 |
| Beatnik Bandit | 6217 | | HK | M-BR-D | BL | WH | | | $65.00 |
| Beatnik Bandit | 6217 | | USA | M-BR-D | CL | BK | | | $55.00 |
| Beatnik Bandit | 6217 | | HK | M-BR-D | BL | BK | | | $55.00 |
| Beatnik Bandit | 6217 | | USA | M-BR-D | CL | GY | | | $55.00 |
| Beatnik Bandit | 6217 | | HK | M-BR-D | BL | GY | | | $55.00 |
| Beatnik Bandit | 6217 | | USA | M-BR-D | CL | BR-L | | | $55.00 |
| Beatnik Bandit | 6217 | | HK | M-BR-D | BL | BR-L | | | $55.00 |
| Beatnik Bandit | 6217 | | USA | M-BR-D | CL | BR-D | | | $55.00 |
| Beatnik Bandit | 6217 | | HK | M-BR-D | BL | BR-D | | | $55.00 |
| Beatnik Bandit | 6217 | | USA | M-BR-P | CL | WH | | | $55.00 |
| Beatnik Bandit | 6217 | | HK | M-BR-P | BL | WH | | | $55.00 |
| Beatnik Bandit | 6217 | | USA | M-BR-P | CL | BK | | | $45.00 |
| Beatnik Bandit | 6217 | | HK | M-BR-P | BL | BK | | | $45.00 |
| Beatnik Bandit | 6217 | | USA | M-BR-P | CL | GY | | | $45.00 |
| Beatnik Bandit | 6217 | | HK | M-BR-P | BL | GY | | | $45.00 |
| Beatnik Bandit | 6217 | | USA | M-BR-P | CL | BR-L | | | $45.00 |
| Beatnik Bandit | 6217 | | HK | M-BR-P | BL | BR-L | | | $45.00 |
| Beatnik Bandit | 6217 | | USA | M-BR-P | CL | BR-D | | | $45.00 |
| Beatnik Bandit | 6217 | | HK | M-BR-P | BL | BR-D | | | $45.00 |
| Beatnik Bandit | 6217 | | USA | M-GD | CL | WH | | | $45.00 |
| Beatnik Bandit | 6217 | | HK | M-GD | BL | WH | | | $45.00 |
| Beatnik Bandit | 6217 | | USA | M-GD | CL | BK | | | $35.00 |
| Beatnik Bandit | 6217 | | HK | M-GD | BL | BK | | | $35.00 |
| Beatnik Bandit | 6217 | | USA | M-GD | CL | GY | | | $35.00 |
| Beatnik Bandit | 6217 | | HK | M-GD | BL | GY | | | $35.00 |
| Beatnik Bandit | 6217 | | USA | M-GD | CL | BR-L | | | $35.00 |
| Beatnik Bandit | 6217 | | HK | M-GD | BL | BR-L | | | $35.00 |
| Beatnik Bandit | 6217 | | USA | M-GD | CL | BR-D | | | $35.00 |
| Beatnik Bandit | 6217 | | HK | M-GD | BL | BR-D | | | $35.00 |
| Beatnik Bandit | 6217 | | USA | M-GR | CL | WH | | | $45.00 |
| Beatnik Bandit | 6217 | | HK | M-GR | BL | WH | | | $45.00 |
| Beatnik Bandit | 6217 | | USA | M-GR | CL | BK | | | $35.00 |
| Beatnik Bandit | 6217 | | HK | M-GR | BL | BK | | | $35.00 |
| Beatnik Bandit | 6217 | | USA | M-GR | CL | GY | | | $35.00 |
| Beatnik Bandit | 6217 | | HK | M-GR | BL | GY | | | $35.00 |
| Beatnik Bandit | 6217 | | USA | M-GR | CL | BR-L | | | $35.00 |
| Beatnik Bandit | 6217 | | HK | M-GR | BL | BR-L | | | $35.00 |
| Beatnik Bandit | 6217 | | USA | M-GR | CL | BR-D | | | $35.00 |

## 1968 Variations

| Name | Number | Casting | Country | Color | Windows | Interior | Paint | Other | Value |
|---|---|---|---|---|---|---|---|---|---|
| Beatnik Bandit | 6217 | | HK | M-GR | BL | BR-D | | | $35.00 |
| Beatnik Bandit | 6217 | | USA | M-GR-E | CL | WH | | | $50.00 |
| Beatnik Bandit | 6217 | | HK | M-GR-E | BL | WH | | | $50.00 |
| Beatnik Bandit | 6217 | | USA | M-GR-E | CL | BK | | | $40.00 |
| Beatnik Bandit | 6217 | | HK | M-GR-E | BL | BK | | | $40.00 |
| Beatnik Bandit | 6217 | | USA | M-GR-E | CL | GY | | | $40.00 |
| Beatnik Bandit | 6217 | | HK | M-GR-E | BL | GY | | | $40.00 |
| Beatnik Bandit | 6217 | | USA | M-GR-E | CL | BR-L | | | $40.00 |
| Beatnik Bandit | 6217 | | HK | M-GR-E | BL | BR-L | | | $40.00 |
| Beatnik Bandit | 6217 | | USA | M-GR-E | CL | BR-D | | | $40.00 |
| Beatnik Bandit | 6217 | | HK | M-GR-E | BL | BR-D | | | $40.00 |
| Beatnik Bandit | 6217 | | USA | M-GR-L | CL | WH | | | $55.00 |
| Beatnik Bandit | 6217 | | HK | M-GR-L | BL | WH | | | $55.00 |
| Beatnik Bandit | 6217 | | USA | M-GR-L | CL | BK | | | $45.00 |
| Beatnik Bandit | 6217 | | HK | M-GR-L | BL | BK | | | $45.00 |
| Beatnik Bandit | 6217 | | USA | M-GR-L | CL | GY | | | $45.00 |
| Beatnik Bandit | 6217 | | HK | M-GR-L | BL | GY | | | $45.00 |
| Beatnik Bandit | 6217 | | USA | M-GR-L | CL | BR-L | | | $45.00 |
| Beatnik Bandit | 6217 | | HK | M-GR-L | BL | BR-L | | | $45.00 |
| Beatnik Bandit | 6217 | | USA | M-GR-L | CL | BR-D | | | $45.00 |
| Beatnik Bandit | 6217 | | HK | M-GR-L | BL | BR-D | | | $45.00 |
| Beatnik Bandit | 6217 | | USA | M-GR-O | CL | WH | | | $60.00 |
| Beatnik Bandit | 6217 | | HK | M-GR-O | BL | WH | | | $60.00 |
| Beatnik Bandit | 6217 | | USA | M-GR-O | CL | BK | | | $50.00 |
| Beatnik Bandit | 6217 | | HK | M-GR-O | BL | BK | | | $50.00 |
| Beatnik Bandit | 6217 | | USA | M-GR-O | CL | GY | | | $50.00 |
| Beatnik Bandit | 6217 | | HK | M-GR-O | BL | GY | | | $50.00 |
| Beatnik Bandit | 6217 | | USA | M-GR-O | CL | BR-L | | | $50.00 |
| Beatnik Bandit | 6217 | | HK | M-GR-O | BL | BR-L | | | $50.00 |
| Beatnik Bandit | 6217 | | USA | M-GR-O | CL | BR-D | | | $50.00 |
| Beatnik Bandit | 6217 | | HK | M-GR-O | BL | BR-D | | | $50.00 |
| Beatnik Bandit | 6217 | | USA | M-MG | CL | WH | | | $60.00 |
| Beatnik Bandit | 6217 | | HK | M-MG | BL | WH | | | $60.00 |
| Beatnik Bandit | 6217 | | USA | M-MG | CL | BK | | | $50.00 |
| Beatnik Bandit | 6217 | | HK | M-MG | BL | BK | | | $50.00 |
| Beatnik Bandit | 6217 | | USA | M-MG | CL | GY | | | $50.00 |
| Beatnik Bandit | 6217 | | HK | M-MG | BL | GY | | | $50.00 |
| Beatnik Bandit | 6217 | | USA | M-MG | CL | BR-L | | | $50.00 |
| Beatnik Bandit | 6217 | | HK | M-MG | BL | BR-L | | | $50.00 |
| Beatnik Bandit | 6217 | | USA | M-MG | CL | BR-D | | | $50.00 |
| Beatnik Bandit | 6217 | | HK | M-MG | BL | BR-D | | | $50.00 |
| Beatnik Bandit | 6217 | | USA | M-OR | CL | WH | | | $50.00 |
| Beatnik Bandit | 6217 | | HK | M-OR | BL | WH | | | $50.00 |
| Beatnik Bandit | 6217 | | USA | M-OR | CL | BK | | | $40.00 |
| Beatnik Bandit | 6217 | | HK | M-OR | BL | BK | | | $40.00 |
| Beatnik Bandit | 6217 | | USA | M-OR | CL | GY | | | $40.00 |
| Beatnik Bandit | 6217 | | HK | M-OR | BL | GY | | | $40.00 |
| Beatnik Bandit | 6217 | | USA | M-OR | CL | BR-L | | | $40.00 |
| Beatnik Bandit | 6217 | | HK | M-OR | BL | BR-L | | | $40.00 |
| Beatnik Bandit | 6217 | | USA | M-OR | CL | BR-D | | | $40.00 |
| Beatnik Bandit | 6217 | | HK | M-OR | BL | BR-D | | | $40.00 |
| Beatnik Bandit | 6217 | | USA | M-PK | CL | WH | | | $270.00 |
| Beatnik Bandit | 6217 | | HK | M-PK | BL | WH | | | $270.00 |
| Beatnik Bandit | 6217 | | USA | M-PK | CL | BK | | | $240.00 |
| Beatnik Bandit | 6217 | | HK | M-PK | BL | BK | | | $240.00 |
| Beatnik Bandit | 6217 | | USA | M-PK | CL | GY | | | $240.00 |
| Beatnik Bandit | 6217 | | HK | M-PK | BL | GY | | | $240.00 |
| Beatnik Bandit | 6217 | | USA | M-PK | CL | BR-L | | | $240.00 |
| Beatnik Bandit | 6217 | | HK | M-PK | BL | BR-L | | | $240.00 |
| Beatnik Bandit | 6217 | | USA | M-PK | CL | BR-D | | | $240.00 |
| Beatnik Bandit | 6217 | | HK | M-PK | BL | BR-D | | | $240.00 |
| Beatnik Bandit | 6217 | | USA | M-PK-H | CL | WH | | | $270.00 |
| Beatnik Bandit | 6217 | | HK | M-PK-H | BL | WH | | | $270.00 |
| Beatnik Bandit | 6217 | | USA | M-PK-H | CL | BK | | | $240.00 |
| Beatnik Bandit | 6217 | | HK | M-PK-H | BL | BK | | | $240.00 |
| Beatnik Bandit | 6217 | | USA | M-PK-H | CL | GY | | | $240.00 |
| Beatnik Bandit | 6217 | | HK | M-PK-H | BL | GY | | | $240.00 |
| Beatnik Bandit | 6217 | | USA | M-PK-H | CL | BR-L | | | $240.00 |
| Beatnik Bandit | 6217 | | HK | M-PK-H | BL | BR-L | | | $240.00 |
| Beatnik Bandit | 6217 | | USA | M-PK-H | CL | BR-D | | | $240.00 |
| Beatnik Bandit | 6217 | | HK | M-PK-H | BL | BR-D | | | $240.00 |
| Beatnik Bandit | 6217 | | USA | M-PK-S | CL | WH | | | $270.00 |

## 1968 Variations

| Name | Number | Casting | Country | Color | Windows | Interior | Paint | Other | Value |
|---|---|---|---|---|---|---|---|---|---|
| Beatnik Bandit | 6217 | | HK | M-PK-S | BL | WH | | | $270.00 |
| Beatnik Bandit | 6217 | | USA | M-PK-S | CL | BK | | | $240.00 |
| Beatnik Bandit | 6217 | | HK | M-PK-S | BL | BK | | | $240.00 |
| Beatnik Bandit | 6217 | | USA | M-PK-S | CL | GY | | | $240.00 |
| Beatnik Bandit | 6217 | | HK | M-PK-S | BL | GY | | | $240.00 |
| Beatnik Bandit | 6217 | | USA | M-PK-S | CL | BR-L | | | $240.00 |
| Beatnik Bandit | 6217 | | HK | M-PK-S | BL | BR-L | | | $240.00 |
| Beatnik Bandit | 6217 | | USA | M-PK-S | CL | BR-D | | | $240.00 |
| Beatnik Bandit | 6217 | | HK | M-PK-S | BL | BR-D | | | $240.00 |
| Beatnik Bandit | 6217 | | USA | M-PR | CL | WH | | | $60.00 |
| Beatnik Bandit | 6217 | | HK | M-PR | BL | WH | | | $60.00 |
| Beatnik Bandit | 6217 | | USA | M-PR | CL | BK | | | $50.00 |
| Beatnik Bandit | 6217 | | HK | M-PR | BL | BK | | | $50.00 |
| Beatnik Bandit | 6217 | | USA | M-PR | CL | GY | | | $50.00 |
| Beatnik Bandit | 6217 | | HK | M-PR | BL | GY | | | $50.00 |
| Beatnik Bandit | 6217 | | USA | M-PR | CL | BR-L | | | $50.00 |
| Beatnik Bandit | 6217 | | HK | M-PR | BL | BR-L | | | $50.00 |
| Beatnik Bandit | 6217 | | USA | M-PR | CL | BR-D | | | $50.00 |
| Beatnik Bandit | 6217 | | HK | M-PR | BL | BR-D | | | $50.00 |
| Beatnik Bandit | 6217 | | USA | M-RD | CL | WH | | | $50.00 |
| Beatnik Bandit | 6217 | | HK | M-RD | BL | WH | | | $50.00 |
| Beatnik Bandit | 6217 | | USA | M-RD | CL | BK | | | $40.00 |
| Beatnik Bandit | 6217 | | HK | M-RD | BL | BK | | | $40.00 |
| Beatnik Bandit | 6217 | | USA | M-RD | CL | GY | | | $40.00 |
| Beatnik Bandit | 6217 | | HK | M-RD | BL | GY | | | $40.00 |
| Beatnik Bandit | 6217 | | USA | M-RD | CL | BR-L | | | $40.00 |
| Beatnik Bandit | 6217 | | HK | M-RD | BL | BR-L | | | $40.00 |
| Beatnik Bandit | 6217 | | USA | M-RD | CL | BR-D | | | $40.00 |
| Beatnik Bandit | 6217 | | HK | M-RD | BL | BR-D | | | $40.00 |
| Beatnik Bandit | 6217 | | USA | M-RD-R | CL | WH | | | $55.00 |
| Beatnik Bandit | 6217 | | HK | M-RD-R | BL | WH | | | $55.00 |
| Beatnik Bandit | 6217 | | USA | M-RD-R | CL | BK | | | $45.00 |
| Beatnik Bandit | 6217 | | HK | M-RD-R | BL | BK | | | $45.00 |
| Beatnik Bandit | 6217 | | USA | M-RD-R | CL | GY | | | $45.00 |
| Beatnik Bandit | 6217 | | HK | M-RD-R | BL | GY | | | $45.00 |
| Beatnik Bandit | 6217 | | USA | M-RD-R | CL | BR-L | | | $45.00 |
| Beatnik Bandit | 6217 | | HK | M-RD-R | BL | BR-L | | | $45.00 |
| Beatnik Bandit | 6217 | | USA | M-RD-R | CL | BR-D | | | $45.00 |
| Beatnik Bandit | 6217 | | HK | M-RD-R | BL | BR-D | | | $45.00 |
| Beatnik Bandit | 6217 | | USA | M-YW | CL | WH | | | $45.00 |
| Beatnik Bandit | 6217 | | HK | M-YW | BL | WH | | | $45.00 |
| Beatnik Bandit | 6217 | | USA | M-YW | CL | BK | | | $35.00 |
| Beatnik Bandit | 6217 | | HK | M-YW | BL | BK | | | $35.00 |
| Beatnik Bandit | 6217 | | USA | M-YW | CL | GY | | | $35.00 |
| Beatnik Bandit | 6217 | | HK | M-YW | BL | GY | | | $35.00 |
| Beatnik Bandit | 6217 | | USA | M-YW | CL | BR-L | | | $35.00 |
| Beatnik Bandit | 6217 | | HK | M-YW | BL | BR-L | | | $35.00 |
| Beatnik Bandit | 6217 | | USA | M-YW | CL | BR-D | | | $35.00 |
| Beatnik Bandit | 6217 | | HK | M-YW | BL | BR-D | | | $35.00 |
| Beatnik Bandit | 6217 | | USA | M-YW-L | CL | WH | | | $65.00 |
| Beatnik Bandit | 6217 | | HK | M-YW-L | BL | WH | | | $65.00 |
| Beatnik Bandit | 6217 | | USA | M-YW-L | CL | BK | | | $55.00 |
| Beatnik Bandit | 6217 | | HK | M-YW-L | BL | BK | | | $55.00 |
| Beatnik Bandit | 6217 | | USA | M-YW-L | CL | GY | | | $55.00 |
| Beatnik Bandit | 6217 | | HK | M-YW-L | BL | GY | | | $55.00 |
| Beatnik Bandit | 6217 | | USA | M-YW-L | CL | BR-L | | | $55.00 |
| Beatnik Bandit | 6217 | | HK | M-YW-L | BL | BR-L | | | $55.00 |
| Beatnik Bandit | 6217 | | USA | M-YW-L | CL | BR-D | | | $55.00 |
| Beatnik Bandit | 6217 | | HK | M-YW-L | BL | BR-D | | | $55.00 |
| | | | | | | | | | |
| Custom Eldorado | 6218 | | USA | M-AQ | CL | WH | | | $65.00 |
| Custom Eldorado | 6218 | | HK | M-AQ | BL | WH | | | $65.00 |
| Custom Eldorado | 6218 | | USA | M-AQ | CL | BK | | | $60.00 |
| Custom Eldorado | 6218 | | HK | M-AQ | BL | BK | | | $60.00 |
| Custom Eldorado | 6218 | | USA | M-AQ | CL | GY | | | $60.00 |
| Custom Eldorado | 6218 | | HK | M-AQ | BL | GY | | | $60.00 |
| Custom Eldorado | 6218 | | USA | M-AQ | CL | BR-L | | | $60.00 |
| Custom Eldorado | 6218 | | HK | M-AQ | BL | BR-L | | | $60.00 |
| Custom Eldorado | 6218 | | USA | M-AQ | CL | BR-D | | | $60.00 |
| Custom Eldorado | 6218 | | HK | M-AQ | BL | BR-D | | | $60.00 |
| Custom Eldorado | 6218 | | USA | M-BL | CL | WH | | | $60.00 |

## 1968 Variations

| Name | Number | Casting | Country | Color | Windows | Interior | Paint | Other | Value |
|---|---|---|---|---|---|---|---|---|---|
| Custom Eldorado | 6218 | | HK | M-BL | BL | WH | | | $60.00 |
| Custom Eldorado | 6218 | | USA | M-BL | CL | BK | | | $55.00 |
| Custom Eldorado | 6218 | | HK | M-BL | BL | BK | | | $55.00 |
| Custom Eldorado | 6218 | | USA | M-BL | CL | GY | | | $55.00 |
| Custom Eldorado | 6218 | | HK | M-BL | BL | GY | | | $55.00 |
| Custom Eldorado | 6218 | | USA | M-BL | CL | BR-L | | | $55.00 |
| Custom Eldorado | 6218 | | HK | M-BL | BL | BR-L | | | $55.00 |
| Custom Eldorado | 6218 | | USA | M-BL | CL | BR-D | | | $55.00 |
| Custom Eldorado | 6218 | | HK | M-BL | BL | BR-D | | | $55.00 |
| Custom Eldorado | 6218 | | USA | M-BL-I | CL | WH | | | $90.00 |
| Custom Eldorado | 6218 | | HK | M-BL-I | BL | WH | | | $90.00 |
| Custom Eldorado | 6218 | | USA | M-BL-I | CL | BK | | | $80.00 |
| Custom Eldorado | 6218 | | HK | M-BL-I | BL | BK | | | $80.00 |
| Custom Eldorado | 6218 | | USA | M-BL-I | CL | GY | | | $80.00 |
| Custom Eldorado | 6218 | | HK | M-BL-I | BL | GY | | | $80.00 |
| Custom Eldorado | 6218 | | USA | M-BL-I | CL | BR-L | | | $80.00 |
| Custom Eldorado | 6218 | | HK | M-BL-I | BL | BR-L | | | $80.00 |
| Custom Eldorado | 6218 | | USA | M-BL-I | CL | BR-D | | | $80.00 |
| Custom Eldorado | 6218 | | HK | M-BL-I | BL | BR-D | | | $80.00 |
| Custom Eldorado | 6218 | | USA | M-BL-P | CL | WH | | | $80.00 |
| Custom Eldorado | 6218 | | HK | M-BL-P | BL | WH | | | $80.00 |
| Custom Eldorado | 6218 | | USA | M-BL-P | CL | BK | | | $70.00 |
| Custom Eldorado | 6218 | | HK | M-BL-P | BL | BK | | | $70.00 |
| Custom Eldorado | 6218 | | USA | M-BL-P | CL | GY | | | $70.00 |
| Custom Eldorado | 6218 | | HK | M-BL-P | BL | GY | | | $70.00 |
| Custom Eldorado | 6218 | | USA | M-BL-P | CL | BR-L | | | $70.00 |
| Custom Eldorado | 6218 | | HK | M-BL-P | BL | BR-L | | | $70.00 |
| Custom Eldorado | 6218 | | USA | M-BL-P | CL | BR-D | | | $70.00 |
| Custom Eldorado | 6218 | | HK | M-BL-P | BL | BR-D | | | $70.00 |
| Custom Eldorado | 6218 | | USA | M-BR-D | CL | WH | | | $75.00 |
| Custom Eldorado | 6218 | | HK | M-BR-D | BL | WH | | | $75.00 |
| Custom Eldorado | 6218 | | USA | M-BR-D | CL | BK | | | $65.00 |
| Custom Eldorado | 6218 | | HK | M-BR-D | BL | BK | | | $65.00 |
| Custom Eldorado | 6218 | | USA | M-BR-D | CL | GY | | | $65.00 |
| Custom Eldorado | 6218 | | HK | M-BR-D | BL | GY | | | $65.00 |
| Custom Eldorado | 6218 | | USA | M-BR-D | CL | BR-L | | | $65.00 |
| Custom Eldorado | 6218 | | HK | M-BR-D | BL | BR-L | | | $65.00 |
| Custom Eldorado | 6218 | | USA | M-BR-D | CL | BR-D | | | $65.00 |
| Custom Eldorado | 6218 | | HK | M-BR-D | BL | BR-D | | | $65.00 |
| Custom Eldorado | 6218 | | USA | M-BR-P | CL | WH | | | $65.00 |
| Custom Eldorado | 6218 | | HK | M-BR-P | BL | WH | | | $65.00 |
| Custom Eldorado | 6218 | | USA | M-BR-P | CL | BK | | | $55.00 |
| Custom Eldorado | 6218 | | HK | M-BR-P | BL | BK | | | $55.00 |
| Custom Eldorado | 6218 | | USA | M-BR-P | CL | GY | | | $55.00 |
| Custom Eldorado | 6218 | | HK | M-BR-P | BL | GY | | | $55.00 |
| Custom Eldorado | 6218 | | USA | M-BR-P | CL | BR-L | | | $55.00 |
| Custom Eldorado | 6218 | | HK | M-BR-P | BL | BR-L | | | $55.00 |
| Custom Eldorado | 6218 | | USA | M-BR-P | CL | BR-D | | | $55.00 |
| Custom Eldorado | 6218 | | HK | M-BR-P | BL | BR-D | | | $55.00 |
| Custom Eldorado | 6218 | | USA | M-GD | CL | WH | | | $65.00 |
| Custom Eldorado | 6218 | | HK | M-GD | BL | WH | | | $65.00 |
| Custom Eldorado | 6218 | | USA | M-GD | CL | BK | | | $60.00 |
| Custom Eldorado | 6218 | | HK | M-GD | BL | BK | | | $60.00 |
| Custom Eldorado | 6218 | | USA | M-GD | CL | GY | | | $60.00 |
| Custom Eldorado | 6218 | | HK | M-GD | BL | GY | | | $60.00 |
| Custom Eldorado | 6218 | | USA | M-GD | CL | BR-L | | | $60.00 |
| Custom Eldorado | 6218 | | HK | M-GD | BL | BR-L | | | $60.00 |
| Custom Eldorado | 6218 | | USA | M-GD | CL | BR-D | | | $60.00 |
| Custom Eldorado | 6218 | | HK | M-GD | BL | BR-D | | | $60.00 |
| Custom Eldorado | 6218 | | USA | M-GR | CL | WH | | | $65.00 |
| Custom Eldorado | 6218 | | HK | M-GR | BL | WH | | | $65.00 |
| Custom Eldorado | 6218 | | USA | M-GR | CL | BK | | | $55.00 |
| Custom Eldorado | 6218 | | HK | M-GR | BL | BK | | | $55.00 |
| Custom Eldorado | 6218 | | USA | M-GR | CL | GY | | | $55.00 |
| Custom Eldorado | 6218 | | HK | M-GR | BL | GY | | | $55.00 |
| Custom Eldorado | 6218 | | USA | M-GR | CL | BR-L | | | $55.00 |
| Custom Eldorado | 6218 | | HK | M-GR | BL | BR-L | | | $55.00 |
| Custom Eldorado | 6218 | | USA | M-GR | CL | BR-D | | | $55.00 |
| Custom Eldorado | 6218 | | HK | M-GR | BL | BR-D | | | $55.00 |
| Custom Eldorado | 6218 | | USA | M-GR-E | CL | WH | | | $75.00 |
| Custom Eldorado | 6218 | | HK | M-GR-E | BL | WH | | | $75.00 |
| Custom Eldorado | 6218 | | USA | M-GR-E | CL | BK | | | $65.00 |

## 1968 Variations

| Name | Number | Casting | Country | Color | Windows | Interior | Paint | Other | Value |
|---|---|---|---|---|---|---|---|---|---|
| Custom Eldorado | 6218 | | HK | M-GR-E | BL | BK | | | $65.00 |
| Custom Eldorado | 6218 | | USA | M-GR-E | CL | GY | | | $65.00 |
| Custom Eldorado | 6218 | | HK | M-GR-E | BL | GY | | | $65.00 |
| Custom Eldorado | 6218 | | USA | M-GR-E | CL | BR-L | | | $65.00 |
| Custom Eldorado | 6218 | | HK | M-GR-E | BL | BR-L | | | $65.00 |
| Custom Eldorado | 6218 | | USA | M-GR-E | CL | BR-D | | | $65.00 |
| Custom Eldorado | 6218 | | HK | M-GR-E | BL | BR-D | | | $65.00 |
| Custom Eldorado | 6218 | | USA | M-GR-L | CL | WH | | | $85.00 |
| Custom Eldorado | 6218 | | HK | M-GR-L | BL | WH | | | $85.00 |
| Custom Eldorado | 6218 | | USA | M-GR-L | CL | BK | | | $75.00 |
| Custom Eldorado | 6218 | | HK | M-GR-L | BL | BK | | | $75.00 |
| Custom Eldorado | 6218 | | USA | M-GR-L | CL | GY | | | $75.00 |
| Custom Eldorado | 6218 | | HK | M-GR-L | BL | GY | | | $75.00 |
| Custom Eldorado | 6218 | | USA | M-GR-L | CL | BR-L | | | $75.00 |
| Custom Eldorado | 6218 | | HK | M-GR-L | BL | BR-L | | | $75.00 |
| Custom Eldorado | 6218 | | USA | M-GR-L | CL | BR-D | | | $75.00 |
| Custom Eldorado | 6218 | | HK | M-GR-L | BL | BR-D | | | $75.00 |
| Custom Eldorado | 6218 | | USA | M-GR-O | CL | WH | | | $75.00 |
| Custom Eldorado | 6218 | | HK | M-GR-O | BL | WH | | | $75.00 |
| Custom Eldorado | 6218 | | USA | M-GR-O | CL | BK | | | $65.00 |
| Custom Eldorado | 6218 | | HK | M-GR-O | BL | BK | | | $65.00 |
| Custom Eldorado | 6218 | | USA | M-GR-O | CL | GY | | | $65.00 |
| Custom Eldorado | 6218 | | HK | M-GR-O | BL | GY | | | $65.00 |
| Custom Eldorado | 6218 | | USA | M-GR-O | CL | BR-L | | | $65.00 |
| Custom Eldorado | 6218 | | HK | M-GR-O | BL | BR-L | | | $65.00 |
| Custom Eldorado | 6218 | | USA | M-GR-O | CL | BR-D | | | $65.00 |
| Custom Eldorado | 6218 | | HK | M-GR-O | BL | BR-D | | | $65.00 |
| Custom Eldorado | 6218 | | USA | M-MG | CL | WH | | | $75.00 |
| Custom Eldorado | 6218 | | HK | M-MG | BL | WH | | | $75.00 |
| Custom Eldorado | 6218 | | USA | M-MG | CL | BK | | | $65.00 |
| Custom Eldorado | 6218 | | HK | M-MG | BL | BK | | | $65.00 |
| Custom Eldorado | 6218 | | USA | M-MG | CL | GY | | | $65.00 |
| Custom Eldorado | 6218 | | HK | M-MG | BL | GY | | | $65.00 |
| Custom Eldorado | 6218 | | USA | M-MG | CL | BR-L | | | $65.00 |
| Custom Eldorado | 6218 | | HK | M-MG | BL | BR-L | | | $65.00 |
| Custom Eldorado | 6218 | | USA | M-MG | CL | BR-D | | | $65.00 |
| Custom Eldorado | 6218 | | HK | M-MG | BL | BR-D | | | $65.00 |
| Custom Eldorado | 6218 | | USA | M-OR | CL | WH | | | $75.00 |
| Custom Eldorado | 6218 | | HK | M-OR | BL | WH | | | $75.00 |
| Custom Eldorado | 6218 | | USA | M-OR | CL | BK | | | $65.00 |
| Custom Eldorado | 6218 | | HK | M-OR | BL | BK | | | $65.00 |
| Custom Eldorado | 6218 | | USA | M-OR | CL | GY | | | $65.00 |
| Custom Eldorado | 6218 | | HK | M-OR | BL | GY | | | $65.00 |
| Custom Eldorado | 6218 | | USA | M-OR | CL | BR-L | | | $65.00 |
| Custom Eldorado | 6218 | | HK | M-OR | BL | BR-L | | | $65.00 |
| Custom Eldorado | 6218 | | USA | M-OR | CL | BR-D | | | $65.00 |
| Custom Eldorado | 6218 | | HK | M-OR | BL | BR-D | | | $65.00 |
| Custom Eldorado | 6218 | | USA | M-PK | CL | WH | | | $220.00 |
| Custom Eldorado | 6218 | | HK | M-PK | BL | WH | | | $220.00 |
| Custom Eldorado | 6218 | | USA | M-PK | CL | BK | | | $200.00 |
| Custom Eldorado | 6218 | | HK | M-PK | BL | BK | | | $200.00 |
| Custom Eldorado | 6218 | | USA | M-PK | CL | GY | | | $200.00 |
| Custom Eldorado | 6218 | | HK | M-PK | BL | GY | | | $200.00 |
| Custom Eldorado | 6218 | | USA | M-PK | CL | BR-L | | | $200.00 |
| Custom Eldorado | 6218 | | HK | M-PK | BL | BR-L | | | $200.00 |
| Custom Eldorado | 6218 | | USA | M-PK | CL | BR-D | | | $200.00 |
| Custom Eldorado | 6218 | | HK | M-PK | BL | BR-D | | | $200.00 |
| Custom Eldorado | 6218 | | USA | M-PK-H | CL | WH | | | $220.00 |
| Custom Eldorado | 6218 | | HK | M-PK-H | BL | WH | | | $220.00 |
| Custom Eldorado | 6218 | | USA | M-PK-H | CL | BK | | | $200.00 |
| Custom Eldorado | 6218 | | HK | M-PK-H | BL | BK | | | $200.00 |
| Custom Eldorado | 6218 | | USA | M-PK-H | CL | GY | | | $200.00 |
| Custom Eldorado | 6218 | | HK | M-PK-H | BL | GY | | | $200.00 |
| Custom Eldorado | 6218 | | USA | M-PK-H | CL | BR-L | | | $200.00 |
| Custom Eldorado | 6218 | | HK | M-PK-H | BL | BR-L | | | $200.00 |
| Custom Eldorado | 6218 | | USA | M-PK-H | CL | BR-D | | | $200.00 |
| Custom Eldorado | 6218 | | HK | M-PK-H | BL | BR-D | | | $200.00 |
| Custom Eldorado | 6218 | | USA | M-PK-S | CL | WH | | | $220.00 |
| Custom Eldorado | 6218 | | HK | M-PK-S | BL | WH | | | $220.00 |
| Custom Eldorado | 6218 | | USA | M-PK-S | CL | BK | | | $200.00 |
| Custom Eldorado | 6218 | | HK | M-PK-S | BL | BK | | | $200.00 |
| Custom Eldorado | 6218 | | USA | M-PK-S | CL | GY | | | $200.00 |

## 1968 Variations

| Name | Number | Casting | Country | Color | Windows | Interior | Paint | Other | Value |
|---|---|---|---|---|---|---|---|---|---|
| Custom Eldorado | 6218 | | HK | M-PK-S | BL | GY | | | $200.00 |
| Custom Eldorado | 6218 | | USA | M-PK-S | CL | BR-L | | | $200.00 |
| Custom Eldorado | 6218 | | HK | M-PK-S | BL | BR-L | | | $200.00 |
| Custom Eldorado | 6218 | | USA | M-PK-S | CL | BR-D | | | $200.00 |
| Custom Eldorado | 6218 | | HK | M-PK-S | BL | BR-D | | | $200.00 |
| Custom Eldorado | 6218 | | USA | M-PL | CL | WH | | | $75.00 |
| Custom Eldorado | 6218 | | HK | M-PL | BL | WH | | | $75.00 |
| Custom Eldorado | 6218 | | USA | M-PL | CL | BK | | | $75.00 |
| Custom Eldorado | 6218 | | HK | M-PL | BL | BK | | | $75.00 |
| Custom Eldorado | 6218 | | USA | M-PL | CL | GY | | | $75.00 |
| Custom Eldorado | 6218 | | HK | M-PL | BL | GY | | | $75.00 |
| Custom Eldorado | 6218 | | USA | M-PL | CL | BR-L | | | $75.00 |
| Custom Eldorado | 6218 | | HK | M-PL | BL | BR-L | | | $75.00 |
| Custom Eldorado | 6218 | | USA | M-PL | CL | BR-D | | | $75.00 |
| Custom Eldorado | 6218 | | HK | M-PL | BL | BR-D | | | $75.00 |
| Custom Eldorado | 6218 | | USA | M-PR | CL | WH | | | $80.00 |
| Custom Eldorado | 6218 | | HK | M-PR | BL | WH | | | $80.00 |
| Custom Eldorado | 6218 | | USA | M-PR | CL | BK | | | $70.00 |
| Custom Eldorado | 6218 | | HK | M-PR | BL | BK | | | $70.00 |
| Custom Eldorado | 6218 | | USA | M-PR | CL | GY | | | $70.00 |
| Custom Eldorado | 6218 | | HK | M-PR | BL | GY | | | $70.00 |
| Custom Eldorado | 6218 | | USA | M-PR | CL | BR-L | | | $70.00 |
| Custom Eldorado | 6218 | | HK | M-PR | BL | BR-L | | | $70.00 |
| Custom Eldorado | 6218 | | USA | M-PR | CL | BR-D | | | $70.00 |
| Custom Eldorado | 6218 | | HK | M-PR | BL | BR-D | | | $70.00 |
| Custom Eldorado | 6218 | | USA | M-RD | CL | WH | | | $65.00 |
| Custom Eldorado | 6218 | | HK | M-RD | BL | WH | | | $65.00 |
| Custom Eldorado | 6218 | | USA | M-RD | CL | BK | | | $60.00 |
| Custom Eldorado | 6218 | | HK | M-RD | BL | BK | | | $60.00 |
| Custom Eldorado | 6218 | | USA | M-RD | CL | GY | | | $60.00 |
| Custom Eldorado | 6218 | | HK | M-RD | BL | GY | | | $60.00 |
| Custom Eldorado | 6218 | | USA | M-RD | CL | BR-L | | | $60.00 |
| Custom Eldorado | 6218 | | HK | M-RD | BL | BR-L | | | $60.00 |
| Custom Eldorado | 6218 | | USA | M-RD | CL | BR-D | | | $60.00 |
| Custom Eldorado | 6218 | | HK | M-RD | BL | BR-D | | | $60.00 |
| Custom Eldorado | 6218 | | USA | M-RD-R | CL | WH | | | $75.00 |
| Custom Eldorado | 6218 | | HK | M-RD-R | BL | WH | | | $75.00 |
| Custom Eldorado | 6218 | | USA | M-RD-R | CL | BK | | | $65.00 |
| Custom Eldorado | 6218 | | HK | M-RD-R | BL | BK | | | $65.00 |
| Custom Eldorado | 6218 | | USA | M-RD-R | CL | GY | | | $65.00 |
| Custom Eldorado | 6218 | | HK | M-RD-R | BL | GY | | | $65.00 |
| Custom Eldorado | 6218 | | USA | M-RD-R | CL | BR-L | | | $65.00 |
| Custom Eldorado | 6218 | | HK | M-RD-R | BL | BR-L | | | $65.00 |
| Custom Eldorado | 6218 | | USA | M-RD-R | CL | BR-D | | | $65.00 |
| Custom Eldorado | 6218 | | HK | M-RD-R | BL | BR-D | | | $65.00 |
| Custom Eldorado | 6218 | | USA | M-YW | CL | WH | | | $65.00 |
| Custom Eldorado | 6218 | | HK | M-YW | BL | WH | | | $65.00 |
| Custom Eldorado | 6218 | | USA | M-YW | CL | BK | | | $60.00 |
| Custom Eldorado | 6218 | | HK | M-YW | BL | BK | | | $60.00 |
| Custom Eldorado | 6218 | | USA | M-YW | CL | GY | | | $60.00 |
| Custom Eldorado | 6218 | | HK | M-YW | BL | GY | | | $60.00 |
| Custom Eldorado | 6218 | | USA | M-YW | CL | BR-L | | | $60.00 |
| Custom Eldorado | 6218 | | HK | M-YW | BL | BR-L | | | $60.00 |
| Custom Eldorado | 6218 | | USA | M-YW | CL | BR-D | | | $60.00 |
| Custom Eldorado | 6218 | | HK | M-YW | BL | BR-D | | | $60.00 |
| Custom Eldorado | 6218 | | USA | M-YW-L | CL | WH | | | $85.00 |
| Custom Eldorado | 6218 | | HK | M-YW-L | BL | WH | | | $85.00 |
| Custom Eldorado | 6218 | | USA | M-YW-L | CL | BK | | | $75.00 |
| Custom Eldorado | 6218 | | HK | M-YW-L | BL | BK | | | $75.00 |
| Custom Eldorado | 6218 | | USA | M-YW-L | CL | GY | | | $75.00 |
| Custom Eldorado | 6218 | | HK | M-YW-L | BL | GY | | | $75.00 |
| Custom Eldorado | 6218 | | USA | M-YW-L | CL | BR-L | | | $75.00 |
| Custom Eldorado | 6218 | | HK | M-YW-L | BL | BR-L | | | $75.00 |
| Custom Eldorado | 6218 | | USA | M-YW-L | CL | BR-D | | | $75.00 |
| Custom Eldorado | 6218 | | HK | M-YW-L | BL | BR-D | | | $75.00 |
| | | | | | | | | | |
| Hot Heap | 6219 | | USA | M-AQ | CL | WH | | | $50.00 |
| Hot Heap | 6219 | | HK | M-AQ | BL | WH | | | $50.00 |
| Hot Heap | 6219 | | USA | M-AQ | CL | BK | | | $50.00 |
| Hot Heap | 6219 | | HK | M-AQ | BL | BK | | | $50.00 |
| Hot Heap | 6219 | | USA | M-AQ | CL | GY | | | $50.00 |

## 1968 Variations

| Name | Number | Casting | Country | Color | Windows | Interior | Paint | Other | Value |
|---|---|---|---|---|---|---|---|---|---|
| Hot Heap | 6219 | | HK | M-AQ | BL | GY | | | $50.00 |
| Hot Heap | 6219 | | USA | M-AQ | CL | BR-L | | | $50.00 |
| Hot Heap | 6219 | | HK | M-AQ | BL | BR-L | | | $50.00 |
| Hot Heap | 6219 | | USA | M-AQ | CL | BR-D | | | $50.00 |
| Hot Heap | 6219 | | HK | M-AQ | BL | BR-D | | | $50.00 |
| Hot Heap | 6219 | | USA | M-BL | CL | WH | | | $40.00 |
| Hot Heap | 6219 | | HK | M-BL | BL | WH | | | $40.00 |
| Hot Heap | 6219 | | USA | M-BL | CL | BK | | | $40.00 |
| Hot Heap | 6219 | | HK | M-BL | BL | BK | | | $40.00 |
| Hot Heap | 6219 | | USA | M-BL | CL | GY | | | $40.00 |
| Hot Heap | 6219 | | HK | M-BL | BL | GY | | | $40.00 |
| Hot Heap | 6219 | | USA | M-BL | CL | BR-L | | | $40.00 |
| Hot Heap | 6219 | | HK | M-BL | BL | BR-L | | | $40.00 |
| Hot Heap | 6219 | | USA | M-BL | CL | BR-D | | | $40.00 |
| Hot Heap | 6219 | | HK | M-BL | BL | BR-D | | | $40.00 |
| Hot Heap | 6219 | | USA | M-BL-I | CL | WH | | | $180.00 |
| Hot Heap | 6219 | | HK | M-BL-I | BL | WH | | | $180.00 |
| Hot Heap | 6219 | | USA | M-BL-I | CL | BK | | | $180.00 |
| Hot Heap | 6219 | | HK | M-BL-I | BL | BK | | | $180.00 |
| Hot Heap | 6219 | | USA | M-BL-I | CL | GY | | | $180.00 |
| Hot Heap | 6219 | | HK | M-BL-I | BL | GY | | | $180.00 |
| Hot Heap | 6219 | | USA | M-BL-I | CL | BR-L | | | $180.00 |
| Hot Heap | 6219 | | HK | M-BL-I | BL | BR-L | | | $180.00 |
| Hot Heap | 6219 | | USA | M-BL-I | CL | BR-D | | | $180.00 |
| Hot Heap | 6219 | | HK | M-BL-I | BL | BR-D | | | $180.00 |
| Hot Heap | 6219 | | USA | M-BL-P | CL | WH | | | $160.00 |
| Hot Heap | 6219 | | HK | M-BL-P | BL | WH | | | $160.00 |
| Hot Heap | 6219 | | USA | M-BL-P | CL | BK | | | $160.00 |
| Hot Heap | 6219 | | HK | M-BL-P | BL | BK | | | $160.00 |
| Hot Heap | 6219 | | USA | M-BL-P | CL | GY | | | $160.00 |
| Hot Heap | 6219 | | HK | M-BL-P | BL | GY | | | $160.00 |
| Hot Heap | 6219 | | USA | M-BL-P | CL | BR-L | | | $160.00 |
| Hot Heap | 6219 | | HK | M-BL-P | BL | BR-L | | | $160.00 |
| Hot Heap | 6219 | | USA | M-BL-P | CL | BR-D | | | $160.00 |
| Hot Heap | 6219 | | HK | M-BL-P | BL | BR-D | | | $160.00 |
| Hot Heap | 6219 | | USA | M-BR-D | CL | WH | | | $180.00 |
| Hot Heap | 6219 | | HK | M-BR-D | BL | WH | | | $180.00 |
| Hot Heap | 6219 | | USA | M-BR-D | CL | BK | | | $180.00 |
| Hot Heap | 6219 | | HK | M-BR-D | BL | BK | | | $180.00 |
| Hot Heap | 6219 | | USA | M-BR-D | CL | GY | | | $180.00 |
| Hot Heap | 6219 | | HK | M-BR-D | BL | GY | | | $180.00 |
| Hot Heap | 6219 | | USA | M-BR-D | CL | BR-L | | | $180.00 |
| Hot Heap | 6219 | | HK | M-BR-D | BL | BR-L | | | $180.00 |
| Hot Heap | 6219 | | USA | M-BR-D | CL | BR-D | | | $180.00 |
| Hot Heap | 6219 | | HK | M-BR-D | BL | BR-D | | | $180.00 |
| Hot Heap | 6219 | | USA | M-BR-P | CL | WH | | | $160.00 |
| Hot Heap | 6219 | | HK | M-BR-P | BL | WH | | | $160.00 |
| Hot Heap | 6219 | | USA | M-BR-P | CL | BK | | | $160.00 |
| Hot Heap | 6219 | | HK | M-BR-P | BL | BK | | | $160.00 |
| Hot Heap | 6219 | | USA | M-BR-P | CL | GY | | | $160.00 |
| Hot Heap | 6219 | | HK | M-BR-P | BL | GY | | | $160.00 |
| Hot Heap | 6219 | | USA | M-BR-P | CL | BR-L | | | $160.00 |
| Hot Heap | 6219 | | HK | M-BR-P | BL | BR-L | | | $160.00 |
| Hot Heap | 6219 | | USA | M-BR-P | CL | BR-D | | | $160.00 |
| Hot Heap | 6219 | | HK | M-BR-P | BL | BR-D | | | $160.00 |
| Hot Heap | 6219 | | USA | M-GD | CL | WH | | | $40.00 |
| Hot Heap | 6219 | | HK | M-GD | BL | WH | | | $40.00 |
| Hot Heap | 6219 | | USA | M-GD | CL | BK | | | $40.00 |
| Hot Heap | 6219 | | HK | M-GD | BL | BK | | | $40.00 |
| Hot Heap | 6219 | | USA | M-GD | CL | GY | | | $40.00 |
| Hot Heap | 6219 | | HK | M-GD | BL | GY | | | $40.00 |
| Hot Heap | 6219 | | USA | M-GD | CL | BR-L | | | $40.00 |
| Hot Heap | 6219 | | HK | M-GD | BL | BR-L | | | $40.00 |
| Hot Heap | 6219 | | USA | M-GD | CL | BR-D | | | $40.00 |
| Hot Heap | 6219 | | HK | M-GD | BL | BR-D | | | $40.00 |
| Hot Heap | 6219 | | USA | M-GR | CL | WH | | | $40.00 |
| Hot Heap | 6219 | | HK | M-GR | BL | WH | | | $40.00 |
| Hot Heap | 6219 | | USA | M-GR | CL | BK | | | $40.00 |
| Hot Heap | 6219 | | HK | M-GR | BL | BK | | | $40.00 |
| Hot Heap | 6219 | | USA | M-GR | CL | GY | | | $40.00 |
| Hot Heap | 6219 | | HK | M-GR | BL | GY | | | $40.00 |
| Hot Heap | 6219 | | USA | M-GR | CL | BR-L | | | $40.00 |

## 1968 Variations

| Name | Number | Casting | Country | Color | Windows | Interior | Paint | Other | Value |
|---|---|---|---|---|---|---|---|---|---|
| Hot Heap | 6219 | | HK | M-GR | BL | BR-L | | | $40.00 |
| Hot Heap | 6219 | | USA | M-GR | CL | BR-D | | | $40.00 |
| Hot Heap | 6219 | | HK | M-GR | BL | BR-D | | | $40.00 |
| Hot Heap | 6219 | | USA | M-GR-E | CL | WH | | | $45.00 |
| Hot Heap | 6219 | | HK | M-GR-E | BL | WH | | | $45.00 |
| Hot Heap | 6219 | | USA | M-GR-E | CL | BK | | | $45.00 |
| Hot Heap | 6219 | | HK | M-GR-E | BL | BK | | | $45.00 |
| Hot Heap | 6219 | | USA | M-GR-E | CL | GY | | | $45.00 |
| Hot Heap | 6219 | | HK | M-GR-E | BL | GY | | | $45.00 |
| Hot Heap | 6219 | | USA | M-GR-E | CL | BR-L | | | $45.00 |
| Hot Heap | 6219 | | HK | M-GR-E | BL | BR-L | | | $45.00 |
| Hot Heap | 6219 | | USA | M-GR-E | CL | BR-D | | | $45.00 |
| Hot Heap | 6219 | | HK | M-GR-E | BL | BR-D | | | $45.00 |
| Hot Heap | 6219 | | USA | M-GR-L | CL | WH | | | $65.00 |
| Hot Heap | 6219 | | HK | M-GR-L | BL | WH | | | $65.00 |
| Hot Heap | 6219 | | USA | M-GR-L | CL | BK | | | $65.00 |
| Hot Heap | 6219 | | HK | M-GR-L | BL | BK | | | $65.00 |
| Hot Heap | 6219 | | USA | M-GR-L | CL | GY | | | $65.00 |
| Hot Heap | 6219 | | HK | M-GR-L | BL | GY | | | $65.00 |
| Hot Heap | 6219 | | USA | M-GR-L | CL | BR-L | | | $65.00 |
| Hot Heap | 6219 | | HK | M-GR-L | BL | BR-L | | | $65.00 |
| Hot Heap | 6219 | | USA | M-GR-L | CL | BR-D | | | $65.00 |
| Hot Heap | 6219 | | HK | M-GR-L | BL | BR-D | | | $65.00 |
| Hot Heap | 6219 | | USA | M-GR-O | CL | WH | | | $50.00 |
| Hot Heap | 6219 | | HK | M-GR-O | BL | WH | | | $50.00 |
| Hot Heap | 6219 | | USA | M-GR-O | CL | BK | | | $50.00 |
| Hot Heap | 6219 | | HK | M-GR-O | BL | BK | | | $50.00 |
| Hot Heap | 6219 | | USA | M-GR-O | CL | GY | | | $50.00 |
| Hot Heap | 6219 | | HK | M-GR-O | BL | GY | | | $50.00 |
| Hot Heap | 6219 | | USA | M-GR-O | CL | BR-L | | | $50.00 |
| Hot Heap | 6219 | | HK | M-GR-O | BL | BR-L | | | $50.00 |
| Hot Heap | 6219 | | USA | M-GR-O | CL | BR-D | | | $50.00 |
| Hot Heap | 6219 | | HK | M-GR-O | BL | BR-D | | | $50.00 |
| Hot Heap | 6219 | | USA | M-MG | CL | WH | | | $160.00 |
| Hot Heap | 6219 | | HK | M-MG | BL | WH | | | $160.00 |
| Hot Heap | 6219 | | USA | M-MG | CL | BK | | | $160.00 |
| Hot Heap | 6219 | | HK | M-MG | BL | BK | | | $160.00 |
| Hot Heap | 6219 | | USA | M-MG | CL | GY | | | $160.00 |
| Hot Heap | 6219 | | HK | M-MG | BL | GY | | | $160.00 |
| Hot Heap | 6219 | | USA | M-MG | CL | BR-L | | | $160.00 |
| Hot Heap | 6219 | | HK | M-MG | BL | BR-L | | | $160.00 |
| Hot Heap | 6219 | | USA | M-MG | CL | BR-D | | | $160.00 |
| Hot Heap | 6219 | | HK | M-MG | BL | BR-D | | | $160.00 |
| Hot Heap | 6219 | | USA | M-OR | CL | WH | | | $40.00 |
| Hot Heap | 6219 | | HK | M-OR | BL | WH | | | $40.00 |
| Hot Heap | 6219 | | USA | M-OR | CL | BK | | | $40.00 |
| Hot Heap | 6219 | | HK | M-OR | BL | BK | | | $40.00 |
| Hot Heap | 6219 | | USA | M-OR | CL | GY | | | $40.00 |
| Hot Heap | 6219 | | HK | M-OR | BL | GY | | | $40.00 |
| Hot Heap | 6219 | | USA | M-OR | CL | BR-L | | | $40.00 |
| Hot Heap | 6219 | | HK | M-OR | BL | BR-L | | | $40.00 |
| Hot Heap | 6219 | | USA | M-OR | CL | BR-D | | | $40.00 |
| Hot Heap | 6219 | | HK | M-OR | BL | BR-D | | | $40.00 |
| Hot Heap | 6219 | | USA | M-PK | CL | WH | | | $420.00 |
| Hot Heap | 6219 | | HK | M-PK | BL | WH | | | $420.00 |
| Hot Heap | 6219 | | USA | M-PK | CL | BK | | | $420.00 |
| Hot Heap | 6219 | | HK | M-PK | BL | BK | | | $420.00 |
| Hot Heap | 6219 | | USA | M-PK | CL | GY | | | $420.00 |
| Hot Heap | 6219 | | HK | M-PK | BL | GY | | | $420.00 |
| Hot Heap | 6219 | | USA | M-PK | CL | BR-L | | | $420.00 |
| Hot Heap | 6219 | | HK | M-PK | BL | BR-L | | | $420.00 |
| Hot Heap | 6219 | | USA | M-PK | CL | BR-D | | | $420.00 |
| Hot Heap | 6219 | | HK | M-PK | BL | BR-D | | | $420.00 |
| Hot Heap | 6219 | | USA | M-PK-H | CL | WH | | | $420.00 |
| Hot Heap | 6219 | | HK | M-PK-H | BL | WH | | | $420.00 |
| Hot Heap | 6219 | | USA | M-PK-H | CL | BK | | | $420.00 |
| Hot Heap | 6219 | | HK | M-PK-H | BL | BK | | | $420.00 |
| Hot Heap | 6219 | | USA | M-PK-H | CL | GY | | | $420.00 |
| Hot Heap | 6219 | | HK | M-PK-H | BL | GY | | | $420.00 |
| Hot Heap | 6219 | | USA | M-PK-H | CL | BR-L | | | $420.00 |
| Hot Heap | 6219 | | HK | M-PK-H | BL | BR-L | | | $420.00 |
| Hot Heap | 6219 | | USA | M-PK-H | CL | BR-D | | | $420.00 |

## 1968 Variations

| Name | Number | Casting | Country | Color | Windows | Interior | Paint | Other | Value |
|---|---|---|---|---|---|---|---|---|---|
| Hot Heap | 6219 | | HK | M-PK-H | BL | BR-D | | | $420.00 |
| Hot Heap | 6219 | | USA | M-PK-S | CL | WH | | | $420.00 |
| Hot Heap | 6219 | | HK | M-PK-S | BL | WH | | | $420.00 |
| Hot Heap | 6219 | | USA | M-PK-S | CL | BK | | | $420.00 |
| Hot Heap | 6219 | | HK | M-PK-S | BL | BK | | | $420.00 |
| Hot Heap | 6219 | | USA | M-PK-S | CL | GY | | | $420.00 |
| Hot Heap | 6219 | | HK | M-PK-S | BL | GY | | | $420.00 |
| Hot Heap | 6219 | | USA | M-PK-S | CL | BR-L | | | $420.00 |
| Hot Heap | 6219 | | HK | M-PK-S | BL | BR-L | | | $420.00 |
| Hot Heap | 6219 | | USA | M-PK-S | CL | BR-D | | | $420.00 |
| Hot Heap | 6219 | | HK | M-PK-S | BL | BR-D | | | $420.00 |
| Hot Heap | 6219 | | USA | M-PR | CL | WH | | | $100.00 |
| Hot Heap | 6219 | | HK | M-PR | BL | WH | | | $100.00 |
| Hot Heap | 6219 | | USA | M-PR | CL | BK | | | $100.00 |
| Hot Heap | 6219 | | HK | M-PR | BL | BK | | | $100.00 |
| Hot Heap | 6219 | | USA | M-PR | CL | GY | | | $100.00 |
| Hot Heap | 6219 | | HK | M-PR | BL | GY | | | $100.00 |
| Hot Heap | 6219 | | USA | M-PR | CL | BR-L | | | $100.00 |
| Hot Heap | 6219 | | HK | M-PR | BL | BR-L | | | $100.00 |
| Hot Heap | 6219 | | USA | M-PR | CL | BR-D | | | $100.00 |
| Hot Heap | 6219 | | HK | M-PR | BL | BR-D | | | $100.00 |
| Hot Heap | 6219 | | USA | M-RD | CL | WH | | | $40.00 |
| Hot Heap | 6219 | | HK | M-RD | BL | WH | | | $40.00 |
| Hot Heap | 6219 | | USA | M-RD | CL | BK | | | $40.00 |
| Hot Heap | 6219 | | HK | M-RD | BL | BK | | | $40.00 |
| Hot Heap | 6219 | | USA | M-RD | CL | GY | | | $40.00 |
| Hot Heap | 6219 | | HK | M-RD | BL | GY | | | $40.00 |
| Hot Heap | 6219 | | USA | M-RD | CL | BR-L | | | $40.00 |
| Hot Heap | 6219 | | HK | M-RD | BL | BR-L | | | $40.00 |
| Hot Heap | 6219 | | USA | M-RD | CL | BR-D | | | $40.00 |
| Hot Heap | 6219 | | HK | M-RD | BL | BR-D | | | $40.00 |
| Hot Heap | 6219 | | USA | M-RD-R | CL | WH | | | $45.00 |
| Hot Heap | 6219 | | HK | M-RD-R | BL | WH | | | $45.00 |
| Hot Heap | 6219 | | USA | M-RD-R | CL | BK | | | $45.00 |
| Hot Heap | 6219 | | HK | M-RD-R | BL | BK | | | $45.00 |
| Hot Heap | 6219 | | USA | M-RD-R | CL | GY | | | $45.00 |
| Hot Heap | 6219 | | HK | M-RD-R | BL | GY | | | $45.00 |
| Hot Heap | 6219 | | USA | M-RD-R | CL | BR-L | | | $45.00 |
| Hot Heap | 6219 | | HK | M-RD-R | BL | BR-L | | | $45.00 |
| Hot Heap | 6219 | | USA | M-RD-R | CL | BR-D | | | $45.00 |
| Hot Heap | 6219 | | HK | M-RD-R | BL | BR-D | | | $45.00 |
| Hot Heap | 6219 | | USA | M-YW | CL | WH | | | $40.00 |
| Hot Heap | 6219 | | HK | M-YW | BL | WH | | | $40.00 |
| Hot Heap | 6219 | | USA | M-YW | CL | BK | | | $40.00 |
| Hot Heap | 6219 | | HK | M-YW | BL | BK | | | $40.00 |
| Hot Heap | 6219 | | USA | M-YW | CL | GY | | | $40.00 |
| Hot Heap | 6219 | | HK | M-YW | BL | GY | | | $40.00 |
| Hot Heap | 6219 | | USA | M-YW | CL | BR-L | | | $40.00 |
| Hot Heap | 6219 | | HK | M-YW | BL | BR-L | | | $40.00 |
| Hot Heap | 6219 | | USA | M-YW | CL | BR-D | | | $40.00 |
| Hot Heap | 6219 | | HK | M-YW | BL | BR-D | | | $40.00 |
| Hot Heap | 6219 | | USA | M-YW-L | CL | WH | | | $60.00 |
| Hot Heap | 6219 | | HK | M-YW-L | BL | WH | | | $60.00 |
| Hot Heap | 6219 | | USA | M-YW-L | CL | BK | | | $60.00 |
| Hot Heap | 6219 | | HK | M-YW-L | BL | BK | | | $60.00 |
| Hot Heap | 6219 | | USA | M-YW-L | CL | GY | | | $60.00 |
| Hot Heap | 6219 | | HK | M-YW-L | BL | GY | | | $60.00 |
| Hot Heap | 6219 | | USA | M-YW-L | CL | BR-L | | | $60.00 |
| Hot Heap | 6219 | | HK | M-YW-L | BL | BR-L | | | $60.00 |
| Hot Heap | 6219 | | USA | M-YW-L | CL | BR-D | | | $60.00 |
| Hot Heap | 6219 | | HK | M-YW-L | BL | BR-D | | | $60.00 |
| | | | | | | | | | |
| Custom Volkswagen | 6220 | Sunroof | USA | E-GR-D | CL | WH | | | $220.00 |
| Custom Volkswagen | 6220 | Sunroof | HK | E-GR-D | BL | WH | | | $220.00 |
| Custom Volkswagen | 6220 | Sunroof | USA | E-GR-D | CL | BK | | | $200.00 |
| Custom Volkswagen | 6220 | Sunroof | HK | E-GR-D | BL | BK | | | $200.00 |
| Custom Volkswagen | 6220 | Sunroof | USA | E-GR-D | CL | GY | | | $200.00 |
| Custom Volkswagen | 6220 | Sunroof | HK | E-GR-D | BL | GY | | | $200.00 |
| Custom Volkswagen | 6220 | Sunroof | USA | E-GR-D | CL | BR-L | | | $200.00 |
| Custom Volkswagen | 6220 | Sunroof | HK | E-GR-D | BL | BR-L | | | $200.00 |
| Custom Volkswagen | 6220 | Sunroof | USA | E-GR-D | CL | BR-D | | | $200.00 |

## 1968 Variations

| Name | Number | Casting | Country | Color | Windows | Interior | Paint | Other | Value |
|---|---|---|---|---|---|---|---|---|---|
| Custom Volkswagen | 6220 | Sunroof | HK | E-GR-D | BL | BR-D | | | $200.00 |
| Custom Volkswagon | 6220 | Sunroof | USA | E-MG | CL | WH | | | $300.00 |
| Custom Volkswagen | 6220 | Sunroof | HK | E-MG | BL | WH | | | $300.00 |
| Custom Volkswagen | 6220 | Sunroof | USA | E-MG | CL | BK | | | $280.00 |
| Custom Volkswagen | 6220 | Sunroof | HK | E-MG | BL | BK | | | $280.00 |
| Custom Volkswagen | 6220 | Sunroof | USA | E-MG | CL | GY | | | $280.00 |
| Custom Volkswagen | 6220 | Sunroof | HK | E-MG | BL | GY | | | $280.00 |
| Custom Volkswagen | 6220 | Sunroof | USA | E-MG | CL | BR-L | | | $280.00 |
| Custom Volkswagen | 6220 | Sunroof | HK | E-MG | BL | BR-L | | | $280.00 |
| Custom Volkswagen | 6220 | Sunroof | USA | E-MG | CL | BR-D | | | $280.00 |
| Custom Volkswagen | 6220 | Sunroof | HK | E-MG | BL | BR-D | | | $280.00 |
| Custom Volkswagen | 6220 | Sunroof | USA | E-RD | CL | WH | | | $200.00 |
| Custom Volkswagen | 6220 | No sunroof | HK | M-AQ | BL | WH | | | $1,000.00 |
| Custom Volkswagen | 6220 | No sunroof | HK | M-AQ | BL | BK | | | $1,000.00 |
| Custom Volkswagen | 6220 | No sunroof | HK | M-AQ | BL | GY | | | $1,000.00 |
| Custom Volkswagen | 6220 | No sunroof | HK | M-AQ | BL | BR-L | | | $1,000.00 |
| Custom Volkswagen | 6220 | No sunroof | HK | M-AQ | BL | BR-D | | | $1,000.00 |
| Custom Volkswagen | 6220 | Sunroof | USA | M-AQ | CL | WH | | | $40.00 |
| Custom Volkswagen | 6220 | Sunroof | HK | M-AQ | BL | WH | | | $40.00 |
| Custom Volkswagen | 6220 | Sunroof | USA | M-AQ | CL | BK | | | $40.00 |
| Custom Volkswagen | 6220 | Sunroof | HK | M-AQ | BL | BK | | | $35.00 |
| Custom Volkswagen | 6220 | Sunroof | USA | M-AQ | CL | GY | | | $35.00 |
| Custom Volkswagen | 6220 | Sunroof | HK | M-AQ | BL | GY | | | $35.00 |
| Custom Volkswagen | 6220 | Sunroof | USA | M-AQ | CL | BR-L | | | $35.00 |
| Custom Volkswagen | 6220 | Sunroof | HK | M-AQ | BL | BR-L | | | $35.00 |
| Custom Volkswagen | 6220 | Sunroof | USA | M-AQ | CL | BR-D | | | $35.00 |
| Custom Volkswagen | 6220 | Sunroof | HK | M-AQ | BL | BR-D | | | $35.00 |
| Custom Volkswagen | 6220 | No sunroof | HK | M-BL | BL | WH | | | $1,000.00 |
| Custom Volkswagen | 6220 | No sunroof | HK | M-BL | BL | BK | | | $1,000.00 |
| Custom Volkswagen | 6220 | No sunroof | HK | M-BL | BL | GY | | | $1,000.00 |
| Custom Volkswagen | 6220 | No sunroof | HK | M-BL | BL | BR-L | | | $1,000.00 |
| Custom Volkswagen | 6220 | No sunroof | HK | M-BL | BL | BR-D | | | $1,000.00 |
| Custom Volkswagen | 6220 | Sunroof | HK | M-BL | BL | WH | | | $40.00 |
| Custom Volkswagen | 6220 | Sunroof | USA | M-BL | CL | WH | | | $40.00 |
| Custom Volkswagen | 6220 | Sunroof | HK | M-BL | BL | WH | | | $40.00 |
| Custom Volkswagen | 6220 | Sunroof | USA | M-BL | CL | BK | | | $35.00 |
| Custom Volkswagen | 6220 | Sunroof | HK | M-BL | BL | BK | | | $35.00 |
| Custom Volkswagen | 6220 | Sunroof | USA | M-BL | CL | GY | | | $35.00 |
| Custom Volkswagen | 6220 | Sunroof | HK | M-BL | BL | GY | | | $35.00 |
| Custom Volkswagen | 6220 | Sunroof | USA | M-BL | CL | BR-L | | | $35.00 |
| Custom Volkswagen | 6220 | Sunroof | HK | M-BL | BL | BR-L | | | $35.00 |
| Custom Volkswagen | 6220 | Sunroof | USA | M-BL | CL | BR-D | | | $35.00 |
| Custom Volkswagen | 6220 | Sunroof | HK | M-BL | BL | BR-D | | | $35.00 |
| Custom Volkswagen | 6220 | Sunroof | USA | M-BL-I | CL | WH | | | $80.00 |
| Custom Volkswagen | 6220 | Sunroof | HK | M-BL-I | BL | WH | | | $80.00 |
| Custom Volkswagen | 6220 | Sunroof | USA | M-BL-I | CL | BK | | | $70.00 |
| Custom Volkswagen | 6220 | Sunroof | HK | M-BL-I | BL | BK | | | $70.00 |
| Custom Volkswagen | 6220 | Sunroof | USA | M-BL-I | CL | GY | | | $70.00 |
| Custom Volkswagen | 6220 | Sunroof | HK | M-BL-I | BL | GY | | | $70.00 |
| Custom Volkswagen | 6220 | Sunroof | USA | M-BL-I | CL | BR-L | | | $70.00 |
| Custom Volkswagen | 6220 | Sunroof | HK | M-BL-I | BL | BR-L | | | $70.00 |
| Custom Volkswagen | 6220 | Sunroof | USA | M-BL-I | CL | BR-D | | | $70.00 |
| Custom Volkswagen | 6220 | Sunroof | HK | M-BL-I | BL | BR-D | | | $70.00 |
| Custom Volkswagen | 6220 | Sunroof | USA | M-BL-P | CL | WH | | | $65.00 |
| Custom Volkswagen | 6220 | Sunroof | HK | M-BL-P | BL | WH | | | $65.00 |
| Custom Volkswagen | 6220 | Sunroof | USA | M-BL-P | CL | BK | | | $55.00 |
| Custom Volkswagen | 6220 | Sunroof | HK | M-BL-P | BL | BK | | | $55.00 |
| Custom Volkswagen | 6220 | Sunroof | USA | M-BL-P | CL | GY | | | $55.00 |
| Custom Volkswagen | 6220 | Sunroof | HK | M-BL-P | BL | GY | | | $55.00 |
| Custom Volkswagen | 6220 | Sunroof | USA | M-BL-P | CL | BR-L | | | $55.00 |
| Custom Volkswagen | 6220 | Sunroof | HK | M-BL-P | BL | BR-L | | | $55.00 |
| Custom Volkswagen | 6220 | Sunroof | USA | M-BL-P | CL | BR-D | | | $55.00 |
| Custom Volkswagen | 6220 | Sunroof | HK | M-BL-P | BL | BR-D | | | $55.00 |
| Custom Volkswagen | 6220 | Sunroof | USA | M-BR-D | CL | WH | | | $50.00 |
| Custom Volkswagen | 6220 | Sunroof | HK | M-BR-D | BL | WH | | | $50.00 |
| Custom Volkswagen | 6220 | Sunroof | USA | M-BR-D | CL | BK | | | $45.00 |
| Custom Volkswagen | 6220 | Sunroof | HK | M-BR-D | BL | BK | | | $45.00 |
| Custom Volkswagen | 6220 | Sunroof | USA | M-BR-D | CL | GY | | | $45.00 |
| Custom Volkswagen | 6220 | Sunroof | HK | M-BR-D | BL | GY | | | $45.00 |
| Custom Volkswagen | 6220 | Sunroof | USA | M-BR-D | CL | BR-L | | | $45.00 |
| Custom Volkswagen | 6220 | Sunroof | HK | M-BR-D | BL | BR-L | | | $45.00 |
| Custom Volkswagen | 6220 | Sunroof | USA | M-BR-D | CL | BR-D | | | $45.00 |

## 1968 Variations

| Name | Number | Casting | Country | Color | Windows | Interior | Paint | Other | Value |
|---|---|---|---|---|---|---|---|---|---|
| Custom Volkswagen | 6220 | Sunroof | HK | M-BR-D | BL | BR-D | | | $45.00 |
| Custom Volkswagen | 6220 | Sunroof | USA | M-BR-P | CL | WH | | | $40.00 |
| Custom Volkswagen | 6220 | Sunroof | HK | M-BR-P | BL | WH | | | $40.00 |
| Custom Volkswagen | 6220 | Sunroof | USA | M-BR-P | CL | BK | | | $35.00 |
| Custom Volkswagen | 6220 | Sunroof | HK | M-BR-P | BL | BK | | | $35.00 |
| Custom Volkswagen | 6220 | Sunroof | USA | M-BR-P | CL | GY | | | $35.00 |
| Custom Volkswagen | 6220 | Sunroof | HK | M-BR-P | BL | GY | | | $35.00 |
| Custom Volkswagen | 6220 | Sunroof | USA | M-BR-P | CL | BR-L | | | $35.00 |
| Custom Volkswagen | 6220 | Sunroof | HK | M-BR-P | BL | BR-L | | | $35.00 |
| Custom Volkswagen | 6220 | Sunroof | USA | M-BR-P | CL | BR-D | | | $35.00 |
| Custom Volkswagen | 6220 | Sunroof | HK | M-BR-P | BL | BR-D | | | $35.00 |
| Custom Volkswagen | 6220 | Sunroof | USA | M-GD | CL | WH | | | $40.00 |
| Custom Volkswagen | 6220 | Sunroof | HK | M-GD | BL | WH | | | $40.00 |
| Custom Volkswagen | 6220 | Sunroof | USA | M-GD | CL | BK | | | $35.00 |
| Custom Volkswagen | 6220 | Sunroof | HK | M-GD | BL | BK | | | $35.00 |
| Custom Volkswagen | 6220 | Sunroof | USA | M-GD | CL | GY | | | $35.00 |
| Custom Volkswagen | 6220 | Sunroof | HK | M-GD | BL | GY | | | $35.00 |
| Custom Volkswagen | 6220 | Sunroof | USA | M-GD | CL | BR-L | | | $35.00 |
| Custom Volkswagen | 6220 | Sunroof | HK | M-GD | BL | BR-L | | | $35.00 |
| Custom Volkswagen | 6220 | Sunroof | USA | M-GD | CL | BR-D | | | $35.00 |
| Custom Volkswagen | 6220 | Sunroof | HK | M-GD | BL | BR-D | | | $35.00 |
| Custom Volkswagen | 6220 | No sunroof | HK | M-GR | BL | WH | | | $1,000.00 |
| Custom Volkswagen | 6220 | No sunroof | HK | M-GR | BL | BK | | | $1,000.00 |
| Custom Volkswagen | 6220 | No sunroof | HK | M-GR | BL | GY | | | $1,000.00 |
| Custom Volkswagen | 6220 | No sunroof | HK | M-GR | BL | BR-L | | | $1,000.00 |
| Custom Volkswagen | 6220 | No sunroof | HK | M-GR | BL | BR-D | | | $1,000.00 |
| Custom Volkswagen | 6220 | Sunroof | USA | M-GR | CL | WH | | | $40.00 |
| Custom Volkswagen | 6220 | Sunroof | HK | M-GR | BL | WH | | | $40.00 |
| Custom Volkswagen | 6220 | Sunroof | USA | M-GR | CL | BK | | | $35.00 |
| Custom Volkswagen | 6220 | Sunroof | HK | M-GR | BL | BK | | | $35.00 |
| Custom Volkswagen | 6220 | Sunroof | USA | M-GR | CL | GY | | | $35.00 |
| Custom Volkswagen | 6220 | Sunroof | HK | M-GR | BL | GY | | | $35.00 |
| Custom Volkswagen | 6220 | Sunroof | USA | M-GR | CL | BR-L | | | $35.00 |
| Custom Volkswagen | 6220 | Sunroof | HK | M-GR | BL | BR-L | | | $35.00 |
| Custom Volkswagen | 6220 | Sunroof | USA | M-GR | CL | BR-D | | | $35.00 |
| Custom Volkswagen | 6220 | Sunroof | HK | M-GR | BL | BR-D | | | $35.00 |
| Custom Volkswagen | 6220 | No sunroof | HK | M-GR-E | BL | WH | | | $1,100.00 |
| Custom Volkswagen | 6220 | No sunroof | HK | M-GR-E | BL | BK | | | $1,000.00 |
| Custom Volkswagen | 6220 | No sunroof | HK | M-GR-E | BL | GY | | | $1,000.00 |
| Custom Volkswagen | 6220 | No sunroof | HK | M-GR-E | BL | BR-L | | | $1,000.00 |
| Custom Volkswagen | 6220 | No sunroof | HK | M-GR-E | BL | BR-D | | | $1,000.00 |
| Custom Volkswagen | 6220 | Sunroof | USA | M-GR-E | CL | WH | | | $50.00 |
| Custom Volkswagen | 6220 | Sunroof | HK | M-GR-E | BL | WH | | | $50.00 |
| Custom Volkswagen | 6220 | Sunroof | USA | M-GR-E | CL | BK | | | $45.00 |
| Custom Volkswagen | 6220 | Sunroof | HK | M-GR-E | BL | BK | | | $45.00 |
| Custom Volkswagen | 6220 | Sunroof | USA | M-GR-E | CL | GY | | | $45.00 |
| Custom Volkswagen | 6220 | Sunroof | HK | M-GR-E | BL | GY | | | $45.00 |
| Custom Volkswagen | 6220 | Sunroof | USA | M-GR-E | CL | BR-L | | | $45.00 |
| Custom Volkswagen | 6220 | Sunroof | HK | M-GR-E | BL | BR-L | | | $45.00 |
| Custom Volkswagen | 6220 | Sunroof | USA | M-GR-E | CL | BR-D | | | $45.00 |
| Custom Volkswagen | 6220 | Sunroof | HK | M-GR-E | BL | BR-D | | | $45.00 |
| Custom Volkswagen | 6220 | Sunroof | USA | M-GR-L | CL | WH | | | $80.00 |
| Custom Volkswagen | 6220 | Sunroof | HK | M-GR-L | BL | WH | | | $80.00 |
| Custom Volkswagen | 6220 | Sunroof | USA | M-GR-L | CL | BK | | | $70.00 |
| Custom Volkswagen | 6220 | Sunroof | HK | M-GR-L | BL | BK | | | $70.00 |
| Custom Volkswagen | 6220 | Sunroof | USA | M-GR-L | CL | GY | | | $70.00 |
| Custom Volkswagen | 6220 | Sunroof | HK | M-GR-L | BL | GY | | | $70.00 |
| Custom Volkswagen | 6220 | Sunroof | USA | M-GR-L | CL | BR-L | | | $70.00 |
| Custom Volkswagen | 6220 | Sunroof | HK | M-GR-L | BL | BR-L | | | $70.00 |
| Custom Volkswagen | 6220 | Sunroof | USA | M-GR-L | CL | BR-D | | | $70.00 |
| Custom Volkswagen | 6220 | Sunroof | HK | M-GR-L | BL | BR-D | | | $70.00 |
| Custom Volkswagen | 6220 | Sunroof | USA | M-GR-O | CL | WH | | | $55.00 |
| Custom Volkswagen | 6220 | Sunroof | HK | M-GR-O | BL | WH | | | $55.00 |
| Custom Volkswagen | 6220 | Sunroof | USA | M-GR-O | CL | BK | | | $45.00 |
| Custom Volkswagen | 6220 | Sunroof | HK | M-GR-O | BL | BK | | | $45.00 |
| Custom Volkswagen | 6220 | Sunroof | USA | M-GR-O | CL | GY | | | $45.00 |
| Custom Volkswagen | 6220 | Sunroof | HK | M-GR-O | BL | GY | | | $45.00 |
| Custom Volkswagen | 6220 | Sunroof | USA | M-GR-O | CL | BR-L | | | $45.00 |
| Custom Volkswagen | 6220 | Sunroof | HK | M-GR-O | BL | BR-L | | | $45.00 |
| Custom Volkswagen | 6220 | Sunroof | USA | M-GR-O | CL | BR-D | | | $45.00 |
| Custom Volkswagen | 6220 | Sunroof | HK | M-GR-O | BL | BR-D | | | $45.00 |
| Custom Volkswagen | 6220 | Sunroof | USA | M-MG | CL | WH | | | $95.00 |

## 1968 Variations

| Name | Number | Casting | Country | Color | Windows | Interior | Paint | Other | Value |
|---|---|---|---|---|---|---|---|---|---|
| Custom Volkswagen | 6220 | Sunroof | HK | M-MG | BL | WH | | | $95.00 |
| Custom Volkswagen | 6220 | Sunroof | USA | M-MG | CL | BK | | | $90.00 |
| Custom Volkswagen | 6220 | Sunroof | HK | M-MG | BL | BK | | | $90.00 |
| Custom Volkswagen | 6220 | Sunroof | USA | M-MG | CL | GY | | | $90.00 |
| Custom Volkswagen | 6220 | Sunroof | HK | M-MG | BL | GY | | | $90.00 |
| Custom Volkswagen | 6220 | Sunroof | USA | M-MG | CL | BR-L | | | $90.00 |
| Custom Volkswagen | 6220 | Sunroof | HK | M-MG | BL | BR-L | | | $90.00 |
| Custom Volkswagen | 6220 | Sunroof | USA | M-MG | CL | BR-D | | | $90.00 |
| Custom Volkswagen | 6220 | Sunroof | HK | M-MG | BL | BR-D | | | $90.00 |
| Custom Volkswagen | 6220 | No sunroof | HK | M-OR | BL | WH | | | $1,200.00 |
| Custom Volkswagen | 6220 | No sunroof | HK | M-OR | BL | BK | | | $1,200.00 |
| Custom Volkswagen | 6220 | No sunroof | HK | M-OR | BL | GY | | | $1,200.00 |
| Custom Volkswagen | 6220 | No sunroof | HK | M-OR | BL | BR-L | | | $1,100.00 |
| Custom Volkswagen | 6220 | No sunroof | HK | M-OR | BL | BR-D | | | $1,100.00 |
| Custom Volkswagen | 6220 | Sunroof | USA | M-OR | CL | WH | | | $55.00 |
| Custom Volkswagen | 6220 | Sunroof | HK | M-OR | BL | WH | | | $55.00 |
| Custom Volkswagen | 6220 | Sunroof | USA | M-OR | CL | BK | | | $45.00 |
| Custom Volkswagen | 6220 | Sunroof | HK | M-OR | BL | BK | | | $45.00 |
| Custom Volkswagen | 6220 | Sunroof | USA | M-OR | CL | GY | | | $45.00 |
| Custom Volkswagen | 6220 | Sunroof | HK | M-OR | BL | GY | | | $45.00 |
| Custom Volkswagen | 6220 | Sunroof | USA | M-OR | CL | BR-L | | | $45.00 |
| Custom Volkswagen | 6220 | Sunroof | HK | M-OR | BL | BR-L | | | $45.00 |
| Custom Volkswagen | 6220 | Sunroof | USA | M-OR | CL | BR-D | | | $45.00 |
| Custom Volkswagen | 6220 | Sunroof | HK | M-OR | BL | BR-D | | | $45.00 |
| Custom Volkswagen | 6220 | Sunroof | USA | M-PK | CL | WH | | | $390.00 |
| Custom Volkswagen | 6220 | Sunroof | HK | M-PK | BL | WH | | | $390.00 |
| Custom Volkswagen | 6220 | Sunroof | USA | M-PK | CL | BK | | | $360.00 |
| Custom Volkswagen | 6220 | Sunroof | HK | M-PK | BL | BK | | | $360.00 |
| Custom Volkswagen | 6220 | Sunroof | USA | M-PK | CL | GY | | | $360.00 |
| Custom Volkswagen | 6220 | Sunroof | HK | M-PK | BL | GY | | | $360.00 |
| Custom Volkswagen | 6220 | Sunroof | USA | M-PK | CL | BR-L | | | $360.00 |
| Custom Volkswagen | 6220 | Sunroof | HK | M-PK | BL | BR-L | | | $360.00 |
| Custom Volkswagen | 6220 | Sunroof | USA | M-PK | CL | BR-D | | | $360.00 |
| Custom Volkswagen | 6220 | Sunroof | HK | M-PK | BL | BR-D | | | $360.00 |
| Custom Volkswagen | 6220 | Sunroof | USA | M-PK-H | CL | WH | | | $390.00 |
| Custom Volkswagen | 6220 | Sunroof | HK | M-PK-H | BL | WH | | | $390.00 |
| Custom Volkswagen | 6220 | Sunroof | USA | M-PK-H | CL | BK | | | $360.00 |
| Custom Volkswagen | 6220 | Sunroof | HK | M-PK-H | BL | BK | | | $360.00 |
| Custom Volkswagen | 6220 | Sunroof | USA | M-PK-H | CL | GY | | | $360.00 |
| Custom Volkswagen | 6220 | Sunroof | HK | M-PK-H | BL | GY | | | $360.00 |
| Custom Volkswagen | 6220 | Sunroof | USA | M-PK-H | CL | BR-L | | | $360.00 |
| Custom Volkswagen | 6220 | Sunroof | HK | M-PK-H | BL | BR-L | | | $360.00 |
| Custom Volkswagen | 6220 | Sunroof | USA | M-PK-H | CL | BR-D | | | $360.00 |
| Custom Volkswagen | 6220 | Sunroof | HK | M-PK-H | BL | BR-D | | | $360.00 |
| Custom Volkswagen | 6220 | Sunroof | USA | M-PK-S | CL | WH | | | $390.00 |
| Custom Volkswagen | 6220 | Sunroof | HK | M-PK-S | BL | WH | | | $390.00 |
| Custom Volkswagen | 6220 | Sunroof | USA | M-PK-S | CL | BK | | | $360.00 |
| Custom Volkswagen | 6220 | Sunroof | HK | M-PK-S | BL | BK | | | $360.00 |
| Custom Volkswagen | 6220 | Sunroof | USA | M-PK-S | CL | GY | | | $360.00 |
| Custom Volkswagen | 6220 | Sunroof | HK | M-PK-S | BL | GY | | | $360.00 |
| Custom Volkswagen | 6220 | Sunroof | USA | M-PK-S | CL | BR-L | | | $360.00 |
| Custom Volkswagen | 6220 | Sunroof | HK | M-PK-S | BL | BR-L | | | $360.00 |
| Custom Volkswagen | 6220 | Sunroof | USA | M-PK-S | CL | BR-D | | | $360.00 |
| Custom Volkswagen | 6220 | Sunroof | HK | M-PK-S | BL | BR-D | | | $360.00 |
| Custom Volkswagen | 6220 | Sunroof | USA | M-PR | CL | WH | | | $135.00 |
| Custom Volkswagen | 6220 | Sunroof | HK | M-PR | BL | WH | | | $135.00 |
| Custom Volkswagen | 6220 | Sunroof | USA | M-PR | CL | BK | | | $140.00 |
| Custom Volkswagen | 6220 | Sunroof | HK | M-PR | BL | BK | | | $120.00 |
| Custom Volkswagen | 6220 | Sunroof | USA | M-PR | CL | GY | | | $120.00 |
| Custom Volkswagen | 6220 | Sunroof | HK | M-PR | BL | GY | | | $120.00 |
| Custom Volkswagen | 6220 | Sunroof | USA | M-PR | CL | BR-L | | | $120.00 |
| Custom Volkswagen | 6220 | Sunroof | HK | M-PR | BL | BR-L | | | $120.00 |
| Custom Volkswagen | 6220 | Sunroof | USA | M-PR | CL | BR-D | | | $120.00 |
| Custom Volkswagen | 6220 | Sunroof | HK | M-PR | BL | BR-D | | | $120.00 |
| Custom Volkswagen | 6220 | No sunroof | HK | M-RD | BL | WH | | | $1,000.00 |
| Custom Volkswagen | 6220 | No sunroof | HK | M-RD | BL | BK | | | $900.00 |
| Custom Volkswagen | 6220 | No sunroof | HK | M-RD | BL | GY | | | $900.00 |
| Custom Volkswagen | 6220 | No sunroof | HK | M-RD | BL | BR-L | | | $900.00 |
| Custom Volkswagen | 6220 | No sunroof | HK | M-RD | BL | BR-D | | | $900.00 |
| Custom Volkswagen | 6220 | Sunroof | USA | M-RD | CL | WH | | | $40.00 |
| Custom Volkswagen | 6220 | Sunroof | HK | M-RD | BL | WH | | | $40.00 |
| Custom Volkswagen | 6220 | Sunroof | USA | M-RD | CL | BK | | | $35.00 |

## 1968 Variations

| Name | Number | Casting | Country | Color | Windows | Interior | Paint | Other | Value |
|---|---|---|---|---|---|---|---|---|---|
| Custom Volkswagen | 6220 | Sunroof | HK | M-RD | BL | BK | | | $35.00 |
| Custom Volkswagen | 6220 | Sunroof | USA | M-RD | CL | GY | | | $35.00 |
| Custom Volkswagen | 6220 | Sunroof | HK | M-RD | BL | GY | | | $35.00 |
| Custom Volkswagen | 6220 | Sunroof | USA | M-RD | CL | BR-L | | | $35.00 |
| Custom Volkswagen | 6220 | Sunroof | HK | M-RD | BL | BR-L | | | $35.00 |
| Custom Volkswagen | 6220 | Sunroof | USA | M-RD | CL | BR-D | | | $35.00 |
| Custom Volkswagen | 6220 | Sunroof | HK | M-RD | BL | BR-D | | | $35.00 |
| Custom Volkswagen | 6220 | No sunroof | HK | M-RD-R | BL | WH | | | $1,200.00 |
| Custom Volkswagen | 6220 | No sunroof | HK | M-RD-R | BL | BK | | | $1,100.00 |
| Custom Volkswagen | 6220 | No sunroof | HK | M-RD-R | BL | GY | | | $1,100.00 |
| Custom Volkswagen | 6220 | No sunroof | HK | M-RD-R | BL | BR-L | | | $1,100.00 |
| Custom Volkswagen | 6220 | No sunroof | HK | M-RD-R | BL | BR-D | | | $1,100.00 |
| Custom Volkswagen | 6220 | Sunroof | USA | M-RD-R | CL | WH | | | $50.00 |
| Custom Volkswagen | 6220 | Sunroof | HK | M-RD-R | BL | WH | | | $50.00 |
| Custom Volkswagen | 6220 | Sunroof | USA | M-RD-R | CL | BK | | | $45.00 |
| Custom Volkswagen | 6220 | Sunroof | HK | M-RD-R | BL | BK | | | $45.00 |
| Custom Volkswagen | 6220 | Sunroof | USA | M-RD-R | CL | GY | | | $45.00 |
| Custom Volkswagen | 6220 | Sunroof | HK | M-RD-R | BL | GY | | | $45.00 |
| Custom Volkswagen | 6220 | Sunroof | USA | M-RD-R | CL | BR-L | | | $45.00 |
| Custom Volkswagen | 6220 | Sunroof | HK | M-RD-R | BL | BR-L | | | $45.00 |
| Custom Volkswagen | 6220 | Sunroof | USA | M-RD-R | CL | BR-D | | | $45.00 |
| Custom Volkswagen | 6220 | Sunroof | HK | M-RD-R | BL | BR-D | | | $45.00 |
| Custom Volkswagen | 6220 | Sunroof | USA | M-YW | CL | WH | | | $40.00 |
| Custom Volkswagen | 6220 | Sunroof | HK | M-YW | BL | WH | | | $40.00 |
| Custom Volkswagen | 6220 | Sunroof | USA | M-YW | CL | BK | | | $35.00 |
| Custom Volkswagen | 6220 | Sunroof | HK | M-YW | BL | BK | | | $35.00 |
| Custom Volkswagen | 6220 | Sunroof | USA | M-YW | CL | GY | | | $35.00 |
| Custom Volkswagen | 6220 | Sunroof | HK | M-YW | BL | GY | | | $35.00 |
| Custom Volkswagen | 6220 | Sunroof | USA | M-YW | CL | BR-L | | | $35.00 |
| Custom Volkswagen | 6220 | Sunroof | HK | M-YW | BL | BR-L | | | $35.00 |
| Custom Volkswagen | 6220 | Sunroof | USA | M-YW | CL | BR-D | | | $35.00 |
| Custom Volkswagen | 6220 | Sunroof | HK | M-YW | BL | BR-D | | | $35.00 |
| Custom Volkswagen | 6220 | Sunroof | USA | M-YW-L | CL | WH | | | $95.00 |
| Custom Volkswagen | 6220 | Sunroof | HK | M-YW-L | BL | WH | | | $95.00 |
| Custom Volkswagen | 6220 | Sunroof | USA | M-YW-L | CL | BK | | | $85.00 |
| Custom Volkswagen | 6220 | Sunroof | HK | M-YW-L | BL | BK | | | $85.00 |
| Custom Volkswagen | 6220 | Sunroof | USA | M-YW-L | CL | GY | | | $85.00 |
| Custom Volkswagen | 6220 | Sunroof | HK | M-YW-L | BL | GY | | | $85.00 |
| Custom Volkswagen | 6220 | Sunroof | USA | M-YW-L | CL | BR-L | | | $85.00 |
| Custom Volkswagen | 6220 | Sunroof | HK | M-YW-L | BL | BR-L | | | $85.00 |
| Custom Volkswagen | 6220 | Sunroof | USA | M-YW-L | CL | BR-D | | | $85.00 |
| Custom Volkswagen | 6220 | Sunroof | HK | M-YW-L | BL | BR-D | | | $85.00 |

## 1969 Variations

| Name | Number | Casting | Country | Color | Windows | Interior | Paint | Other | Value |
|---|---|---|---|---|---|---|---|---|---|
| Classic '32 Ford Vicky | 6250 | | USA | M-AQ | | WH | | Smooth roof | $50.00 |
| Classic '32 Ford Vicky | 6250 | | USA | M-AQ | | WH | | Rough roof | $55.00 |
| Classic '32 Ford Vicky | 6250 | | USA | M-AQ | | BK | | Smooth roof | $45.00 |
| Classic '32 Ford Vicky | 6250 | | USA | M-AQ | | BK | | Rough roof | $50.00 |
| Classic '32 Ford Vicky | 6250 | | USA | M-AQ | | GY | | Smooth roof | $45.00 |
| Classic '32 Ford Vicky | 6250 | | USA | M-AQ | | GY | | Rough roof | $50.00 |
| Classic '32 Ford Vicky | 6250 | | USA | M-AQ | | BR-L | | Smooth roof | $45.00 |
| Classic '32 Ford Vicky | 6250 | | USA | M-AQ | | BR-L | | Rough roof | $50.00 |
| Classic '32 Ford Vicky | 6250 | | USA | M-AQ | | BR-D | | Smooth roof | $45.00 |
| Classic '32 Ford Vicky | 6250 | | USA | M-AQ | | BR-D | | Rough roof | $50.00 |
| Classic '32 Ford Vicky | 6250 | | USA | M-BL | | WH | | Smooth roof | $50.00 |
| Classic '32 Ford Vicky | 6250 | | USA | M-BL | | WH | | Rough roof | $55.00 |
| Classic '32 Ford Vicky | 6250 | | USA | M-BL | | BK | | Smooth roof | $45.00 |
| Classic '32 Ford Vicky | 6250 | | USA | M-BL | | BK | | Rough roof | $50.00 |
| Classic '32 Ford Vicky | 6250 | | USA | M-BL | | GY | | Smooth roof | $45.00 |
| Classic '32 Ford Vicky | 6250 | | USA | M-BL | | GY | | Rough roof | $50.00 |
| Classic '32 Ford Vicky | 6250 | | USA | M-BL | | BR-L | | Smooth roof | $45.00 |
| Classic '32 Ford Vicky | 6250 | | USA | M-BL | | BR-L | | Rough roof | $50.00 |
| Classic '32 Ford Vicky | 6250 | | USA | M-BL | | BR-D | | Smooth roof | $45.00 |
| Classic '32 Ford Vicky | 6250 | | USA | M-BL | | BR-D | | Rough roof | $50.00 |
| Classic '32 Ford Vicky | 6250 | | USA | M-BL-I | | WH | | Smooth roof | $125.00 |
| Classic '32 Ford Vicky | 6250 | | USA | M-BL-I | | WH | | Rough roof | $120.00 |
| Classic '32 Ford Vicky | 6250 | | USA | M-BL-I | | BK | | Smooth roof | $120.00 |
| Classic '32 Ford Vicky | 6250 | | USA | M-BL-I | | BK | | Rough roof | $110.00 |
| Classic '32 Ford Vicky | 6250 | | USA | M-BL-I | | GY | | Smooth roof | $120.00 |
| Classic '32 Ford Vicky | 6250 | | USA | M-BL-I | | GY | | Rough roof | $110.00 |
| Classic '32 Ford Vicky | 6250 | | USA | M-BL-I | | BR-L | | Smooth roof | $120.00 |
| Classic '32 Ford Vicky | 6250 | | USA | M-BL-I | | BR-L | | Rough roof | $120.00 |
| Classic '32 Ford Vicky | 6250 | | USA | M-BL-I | | BR-D | | Smooth roof | $120.00 |
| Classic '32 Ford Vicky | 6250 | | USA | M-BL-I | | BR-D | | Rough roof | $120.00 |
| Classic '32 Ford Vicky | 6250 | | USA | M-BL-P | | WH | | Smooth roof | $100.00 |
| Classic '32 Ford Vicky | 6250 | | USA | M-BL-P | | WH | | Rough roof | $95.00 |
| Classic '32 Ford Vicky | 6250 | | USA | M-BL-P | | BK | | Smooth roof | $100.00 |
| Classic '32 Ford Vicky | 6250 | | USA | M-BL-P | | BK | | Rough roof | $90.00 |
| Classic '32 Ford Vicky | 6250 | | USA | M-BL-P | | GY | | Smooth roof | $90.00 |
| Classic '32 Ford Vicky | 6250 | | USA | M-BL-P | | GY | | Rough roof | $85.00 |
| Classic '32 Ford Vicky | 6250 | | USA | M-BL-P | | BR-L | | Smooth roof | $90.00 |
| Classic '32 Ford Vicky | 6250 | | USA | M-BL-P | | BR-L | | Rough roof | $85.00 |
| Classic '32 Ford Vicky | 6250 | | USA | M-BL-P | | BR-D | | Smooth roof | $90.00 |
| Classic '32 Ford Vicky | 6250 | | USA | M-BL-P | | BR-D | | Rough roof | $85.00 |
| Classic '32 Ford Vicky | 6250 | | USA | M-BR-D | | WH | | Smooth roof | $60.00 |
| Classic '32 Ford Vicky | 6250 | | USA | M-BR-D | | WH | | Rough roof | $55.00 |
| Classic '32 Ford Vicky | 6250 | | USA | M-BR-D | | BK | | Smooth roof | $55.00 |
| Classic '32 Ford Vicky | 6250 | | USA | M-BR-D | | BK | | Rough roof | $50.00 |
| Classic '32 Ford Vicky | 6250 | | USA | M-BR-D | | GY | | Smooth roof | $55.00 |
| Classic '32 Ford Vicky | 6250 | | USA | M-BR-D | | GY | | Rough roof | $50.00 |
| Classic '32 Ford Vicky | 6250 | | USA | M-BR-D | | BR-L | | Smooth roof | $55.00 |
| Classic '32 Ford Vicky | 6250 | | USA | M-BR-D | | BR-L | | Rough roof | $50.00 |
| Classic '32 Ford Vicky | 6250 | | USA | M-BR-D | | BR-D | | Smooth roof | $55.00 |
| Classic '32 Ford Vicky | 6250 | | USA | M-BR-D | | BR-D | | Rough roof | $50.00 |
| Classic '32 Ford Vicky | 6250 | | USA | M-BR-P | | WH | | Smooth roof | $50.00 |
| Classic '32 Ford Vicky | 6250 | | USA | M-BR-P | | WH | | Rough roof | $55.00 |
| Classic '32 Ford Vicky | 6250 | | USA | M-BR-P | | BK | | Smooth roof | $45.00 |
| Classic '32 Ford Vicky | 6250 | | USA | M-BR-P | | BK | | Rough roof | $50.00 |
| Classic '32 Ford Vicky | 6250 | | USA | M-BR-P | | GY | | Smooth roof | $45.00 |
| Classic '32 Ford Vicky | 6250 | | USA | M-BR-P | | GY | | Rough roof | $50.00 |
| Classic '32 Ford Vicky | 6250 | | USA | M-BR-P | | BR-L | | Smooth roof | $45.00 |
| Classic '32 Ford Vicky | 6250 | | USA | M-BR-P | | BR-L | | Rough roof | $50.00 |
| Classic '32 Ford Vicky | 6250 | | USA | M-BR-P | | BR-D | | Smooth roof | $45.00 |
| Classic '32 Ford Vicky | 6250 | | USA | M-BR-P | | BR-D | | Rough roof | $50.00 |
| Classic '32 Ford Vicky | 6250 | | USA | M-GD | | WH | | Smooth roof | $50.00 |
| Classic '32 Ford Vicky | 6250 | | USA | M-GD | | WH | | Rough roof | $55.00 |
| Classic '32 Ford Vicky | 6250 | | USA | M-GD | | BK | | Smooth roof | $45.00 |
| Classic '32 Ford Vicky | 6250 | | USA | M-GD | | BK | | Rough roof | $50.00 |
| Classic '32 Ford Vicky | 6250 | | USA | M-GD | | GY | | Smooth roof | $45.00 |
| Classic '32 Ford Vicky | 6250 | | USA | M-GD | | GY | | Rough roof | $50.00 |
| Classic '32 Ford Vicky | 6250 | | USA | M-GD | | BR-L | | Smooth roof | $45.00 |
| Classic '32 Ford Vicky | 6250 | | USA | M-GD | | BR-L | | Rough roof | $50.00 |
| Classic '32 Ford Vicky | 6250 | | USA | M-GD | | BR-D | | Smooth roof | $45.00 |
| Classic '32 Ford Vicky | 6250 | | USA | M-GD | | BR-D | | Rough roof | $50.00 |
| Classic '32 Ford Vicky | 6250 | | USA | M-GR | | WH | | Smooth roof | $55.00 |
| Classic '32 Ford Vicky | 6250 | | USA | M-GR | | WH | | Rough roof | $50.00 |

## 1969 Variations

| Name | Number | Casting | Country | Color | Windows | Interior | Paint | Other | Value |
|---|---|---|---|---|---|---|---|---|---|
| Classic '32 Ford Vicky | 6250 | | USA | M-GR | | BK | | Smooth roof | $50.00 |
| Classic '32 Ford Vicky | 6250 | | USA | M-GR | | BK | | Rough roof | $45.00 |
| Classic '32 Ford Vicky | 6250 | | USA | M-GR | | GY | | Smooth roof | $50.00 |
| Classic '32 Ford Vicky | 6250 | | USA | M-GR | | GY | | Rough roof | $45.00 |
| Classic '32 Ford Vicky | 6250 | | USA | M-GR | | BR-L | | Smooth roof | $50.00 |
| Classic '32 Ford Vicky | 6250 | | USA | M-GR | | BR-L | | Rough roof | $45.00 |
| Classic '32 Ford Vicky | 6250 | | USA | M-GR | | BR-D | | Smooth roof | $50.00 |
| Classic '32 Ford Vicky | 6250 | | USA | M-GR | | BR-D | | Rough roof | $45.00 |
| Classic '32 Ford Vicky | 6250 | | USA | M-GR-E | | WH | | Smooth roof | $60.00 |
| Classic '32 Ford Vicky | 6250 | | USA | M-GR-E | | WH | | Rough roof | $55.00 |
| Classic '32 Ford Vicky | 6250 | | USA | M-GR-E | | BK | | Smooth roof | $55.00 |
| Classic '32 Ford Vicky | 6250 | | USA | M-GR-E | | BK | | Rough roof | $50.00 |
| Classic '32 Ford Vicky | 6250 | | USA | M-GR-E | | GY | | Smooth roof | $55.00 |
| Classic '32 Ford Vicky | 6250 | | USA | M-GR-E | | GY | | Rough roof | $50.00 |
| Classic '32 Ford Vicky | 6250 | | USA | M-GR-E | | BR-L | | Smooth roof | $55.00 |
| Classic '32 Ford Vicky | 6250 | | USA | M-GR-E | | BR-L | | Rough roof | $50.00 |
| Classic '32 Ford Vicky | 6250 | | USA | M-GR-E | | BR-D | | Smooth roof | $55.00 |
| Classic '32 Ford Vicky | 6250 | | USA | M-GR-E | | BR-D | | Rough roof | $50.00 |
| Classic '32 Ford Vicky | 6250 | | USA | M-GR-L | | WH | | Smooth roof | $110.00 |
| Classic '32 Ford Vicky | 6250 | | USA | M-GR-L | | WH | | Rough roof | $100.00 |
| Classic '32 Ford Vicky | 6250 | | USA | M-GR-L | | BK | | Smooth roof | $100.00 |
| Classic '32 Ford Vicky | 6250 | | USA | M-GR-L | | BK | | Rough roof | $95.00 |
| Classic '32 Ford Vicky | 6250 | | USA | M-GR-L | | GY | | Smooth roof | $100.00 |
| Classic '32 Ford Vicky | 6250 | | USA | M-GR-L | | GY | | Rough roof | $95.00 |
| Classic '32 Ford Vicky | 6250 | | USA | M-GR-L | | BR-L | | Smooth roof | $100.00 |
| Classic '32 Ford Vicky | 6250 | | USA | M-GR-L | | BR-L | | Rough roof | $95.00 |
| Classic '32 Ford Vicky | 6250 | | USA | M-GR-L | | BR-D | | Smooth roof | $100.00 |
| Classic '32 Ford Vicky | 6250 | | USA | M-GR-L | | BR-D | | Rough roof | $95.00 |
| Classic '32 Ford Vicky | 6250 | | USA | M-GR-O | | WH | | Smooth roof | $50.00 |
| Classic '32 Ford Vicky | 6250 | | USA | M-GR-O | | WH | | Rough roof | $55.00 |
| Classic '32 Ford Vicky | 6250 | | USA | M-GR-O | | BK | | Smooth roof | $45.00 |
| Classic '32 Ford Vicky | 6250 | | USA | M-GR-O | | BK | | Rough roof | $50.00 |
| Classic '32 Ford Vicky | 6250 | | USA | M-GR-O | | GY | | Smooth roof | $45.00 |
| Classic '32 Ford Vicky | 6250 | | USA | M-GR-O | | GY | | Rough roof | $50.00 |
| Classic '32 Ford Vicky | 6250 | | USA | M-GR-O | | BR-L | | Smooth roof | $45.00 |
| Classic '32 Ford Vicky | 6250 | | USA | M-GR-O | | BR-L | | Rough roof | $50.00 |
| Classic '32 Ford Vicky | 6250 | | USA | M-GR-O | | BR-D | | Smooth roof | $45.00 |
| Classic '32 Ford Vicky | 6250 | | USA | M-GR-O | | BR-D | | Rough roof | $50.00 |
| Classic '32 Ford Vicky | 6250 | | USA | M-MG | | WH | | Smooth roof | $95.00 |
| Classic '32 Ford Vicky | 6250 | | USA | M-MG | | WH | | Rough roof | $90.00 |
| Classic '32 Ford Vicky | 6250 | | USA | M-MG | | BK | | Smooth roof | $90.00 |
| Classic '32 Ford Vicky | 6250 | | USA | M-MG | | BK | | Rough roof | $80.00 |
| Classic '32 Ford Vicky | 6250 | | USA | M-MG | | GY | | Smooth roof | $75.00 |
| Classic '32 Ford Vicky | 6250 | | USA | M-MG | | GY | | Rough roof | $70.00 |
| Classic '32 Ford Vicky | 6250 | | USA | M-MG | | BR-L | | Smooth roof | $75.00 |
| Classic '32 Ford Vicky | 6250 | | USA | M-MG | | BR-L | | Rough roof | $70.00 |
| Classic '32 Ford Vicky | 6250 | | USA | M-MG | | BR-D | | Smooth roof | $75.00 |
| Classic '32 Ford Vicky | 6250 | | USA | M-MG | | BR-D | | Rough roof | $70.00 |
| Classic '32 Ford Vicky | 6250 | | USA | M-OR | | WH | | Smooth roof | $55.00 |
| Classic '32 Ford Vicky | 6250 | | USA | M-OR | | WH | | Rough roof | $50.00 |
| Classic '32 Ford Vicky | 6250 | | USA | M-OR | | BK | | Smooth roof | $50.00 |
| Classic '32 Ford Vicky | 6250 | | USA | M-OR | | BK | | Rough roof | $45.00 |
| Classic '32 Ford Vicky | 6250 | | USA | M-OR | | GY | | Smooth roof | $50.00 |
| Classic '32 Ford Vicky | 6250 | | USA | M-OR | | GY | | Rough roof | $60.00 |
| Classic '32 Ford Vicky | 6250 | | USA | M-OR | | BR-L | | Smooth roof | $50.00 |
| Classic '32 Ford Vicky | 6250 | | USA | M-OR | | BR-L | | Rough roof | $45.00 |
| Classic '32 Ford Vicky | 6250 | | USA | M-OR | | BR-D | | Smooth roof | $50.00 |
| Classic '32 Ford Vicky | 6250 | | USA | M-OR | | BR-D | | Rough roof | $45.00 |
| Classic '32 Ford Vicky | 6250 | | USA | M-PK | | WH | | Smooth roof | $520.00 |
| Classic '32 Ford Vicky | 6250 | | USA | M-PK | | WH | | Rough roof | $480.00 |
| Classic '32 Ford Vicky | 6250 | | USA | M-PK | | BK | | Smooth roof | $440.00 |
| Classic '32 Ford Vicky | 6250 | | USA | M-PK | | BK | | Rough roof | $400.00 |
| Classic '32 Ford Vicky | 6250 | | USA | M-PK | | GY | | Smooth roof | $440.00 |
| Classic '32 Ford Vicky | 6250 | | USA | M-PK | | GY | | Rough roof | $400.00 |
| Classic '32 Ford Vicky | 6250 | | USA | M-PK | | BR-L | | Smooth roof | $440.00 |
| Classic '32 Ford Vicky | 6250 | | USA | M-PK | | BR-L | | Rough roof | $400.00 |
| Classic '32 Ford Vicky | 6250 | | USA | M-PK | | BR-D | | Smooth roof | $440.00 |
| Classic '32 Ford Vicky | 6250 | | USA | M-PK | | BR-D | | Rough roof | $400.00 |
| Classic '32 Ford Vicky | 6250 | | USA | M-PK-H | | WH | | Smooth roof | $520.00 |
| Classic '32 Ford Vicky | 6250 | | USA | M-PK-H | | WH | | Rough roof | $480.00 |
| Classic '32 Ford Vicky | 6250 | | USA | M-PK-H | | BK | | Smooth roof | $440.00 |
| Classic '32 Ford Vicky | 6250 | | USA | M-PK-H | | BK | | Rough roof | $400.00 |

## 1969 Variations

| Name | Number | Casting | Country | Color | Windows | Interior | Paint | Other | Value |
|---|---|---|---|---|---|---|---|---|---|
| Classic '32 Ford Vicky | 6250 | | USA | M-PK-H | | GY | | Smooth roof | $440.00 |
| Classic '32 Ford Vicky | 6250 | | USA | M-PK-H | | GY | | Rough roof | $400.00 |
| Classic '32 Ford Vicky | 6250 | | USA | M-PK-H | | BR-L | | Smooth roof | $440.00 |
| Classic '32 Ford Vicky | 6250 | | USA | M-PK-H | | BR-L | | Rough roof | $400.00 |
| Classic '32 Ford Vicky | 6250 | | USA | M-PK-H | | BR-D | | Smooth roof | $440.00 |
| Classic '32 Ford Vicky | 6250 | | USA | M-PK-H | | BR-D | | Rough roof | $400.00 |
| Classic '32 Ford Vicky | 6250 | | USA | M-PK-S | | WH | | Smooth roof | $520.00 |
| Classic '32 Ford Vicky | 6250 | | USA | M-PK-S | | WH | | Rough roof | $480.00 |
| Classic '32 Ford Vicky | 6250 | | USA | M-PK-S | | BK | | Smooth roof | $440.00 |
| Classic '32 Ford Vicky | 6250 | | USA | M-PK-S | | BK | | Rough roof | $400.00 |
| Classic '32 Ford Vicky | 6250 | | USA | M-PK-S | | GY | | Smooth roof | $440.00 |
| Classic '32 Ford Vicky | 6250 | | USA | M-PK-S | | GY | | Rough roof | $400.00 |
| Classic '32 Ford Vicky | 6250 | | USA | M-PK-S | | BR-L | | Smooth roof | $440.00 |
| Classic '32 Ford Vicky | 6250 | | USA | M-PK-S | | BR-L | | Rough roof | $400.00 |
| Classic '32 Ford Vicky | 6250 | | USA | M-PK-S | | BR-D | | Smooth roof | $440.00 |
| Classic '32 Ford Vicky | 6250 | | USA | M-PK-S | | BR-D | | Rough roof | $400.00 |
| Classic '32 Ford Vicky | 6250 | | USA | M-PR | | WH | | Smooth roof | $65.00 |
| Classic '32 Ford Vicky | 6250 | | USA | M-PR | | WH | | Rough roof | $60.00 |
| Classic '32 Ford Vicky | 6250 | | USA | M-PR | | BK | | Smooth roof | $60.00 |
| Classic '32 Ford Vicky | 6250 | | USA | M-PR | | BK | | Rough roof | $55.00 |
| Classic '32 Ford Vicky | 6250 | | USA | M-PR | | GY | | Smooth roof | $60.00 |
| Classic '32 Ford Vicky | 6250 | | USA | M-PR | | GY | | Rough roof | $55.00 |
| Classic '32 Ford Vicky | 6250 | | USA | M-PR | | BR-L | | Smooth roof | $60.00 |
| Classic '32 Ford Vicky | 6250 | | USA | M-PR | | BR-L | | Rough roof | $55.00 |
| Classic '32 Ford Vicky | 6250 | | USA | M-PR | | BR-D | | Smooth roof | $60.00 |
| Classic '32 Ford Vicky | 6250 | | USA | M-PR | | BR-D | | Rough roof | $55.00 |
| Classic '32 Ford Vicky | 6250 | | USA | M-RD | | WH | | Smooth roof | $50.00 |
| Classic '32 Ford Vicky | 6250 | | USA | M-RD | | WH | | Rough roof | $55.00 |
| Classic '32 Ford Vicky | 6250 | | USA | M-RD | | BK | | Smooth roof | $45.00 |
| Classic '32 Ford Vicky | 6250 | | USA | M-RD | | BK | | Rough roof | $50.00 |
| Classic '32 Ford Vicky | 6250 | | USA | M-RD | | GY | | Smooth roof | $45.00 |
| Classic '32 Ford Vicky | 6250 | | USA | M-RD | | GY | | Rough roof | $50.00 |
| Classic '32 Ford Vicky | 6250 | | USA | M-RD | | BR-L | | Smooth roof | $45.00 |
| Classic '32 Ford Vicky | 6250 | | USA | M-RD | | BR-L | | Rough roof | $50.00 |
| Classic '32 Ford Vicky | 6250 | | USA | M-RD | | BR-D | | Smooth roof | $45.00 |
| Classic '32 Ford Vicky | 6250 | | USA | M-RD | | BR-D | | Rough roof | $50.00 |
| Classic '32 Ford Vicky | 6250 | | USA | M-RD-R | | WH | | Smooth roof | $60.00 |
| Classic '32 Ford Vicky | 6250 | | USA | M-RD-R | | WH | | Rough roof | $55.00 |
| Classic '32 Ford Vicky | 6250 | | USA | M-RD-R | | BK | | Smooth roof | $55.00 |
| Classic '32 Ford Vicky | 6250 | | USA | M-RD-R | | BK | | Rough roof | $50.00 |
| Classic '32 Ford Vicky | 6250 | | USA | M-RD-R | | GY | | Smooth roof | $55.00 |
| Classic '32 Ford Vicky | 6250 | | USA | M-RD-R | | GY | | Rough roof | $50.00 |
| Classic '32 Ford Vicky | 6250 | | USA | M-RD-R | | BR-L | | Smooth roof | $55.00 |
| Classic '32 Ford Vicky | 6250 | | USA | M-RD-R | | BR-L | | Rough roof | $50.00 |
| Classic '32 Ford Vicky | 6250 | | USA | M-RD-R | | BR-D | | Smooth roof | $55.00 |
| Classic '32 Ford Vicky | 6250 | | USA | M-RD-R | | BR-D | | Rough roof | $50.00 |
| Classic '32 Ford Vicky | 6250 | | USA | M-YW | | WH | | Smooth roof | $50.00 |
| Classic '32 Ford Vicky | 6250 | | USA | M-YW | | WH | | Rough roof | $55.00 |
| Classic '32 Ford Vicky | 6250 | | USA | M-YW | | BK | | Smooth roof | $45.00 |
| Classic '32 Ford Vicky | 6250 | | USA | M-YW | | BK | | Rough roof | $50.00 |
| Classic '32 Ford Vicky | 6250 | | USA | M-YW | | GY | | Smooth roof | $45.00 |
| Classic '32 Ford Vicky | 6250 | | USA | M-YW | | GY | | Rough roof | $50.00 |
| Classic '32 Ford Vicky | 6250 | | USA | M-YW | | BR-L | | Smooth roof | $45.00 |
| Classic '32 Ford Vicky | 6250 | | USA | M-YW | | BR-L | | Rough roof | $50.00 |
| Classic '32 Ford Vicky | 6250 | | USA | M-YW | | BR-D | | Smooth roof | $45.00 |
| Classic '32 Ford Vicky | 6250 | | USA | M-YW | | BR-D | | Rough roof | $50.00 |
| Classic '32 Ford Vicky | 6250 | | USA | M-YW-L | | WH | | Smooth roof | $90.00 |
| Classic '32 Ford Vicky | 6250 | | USA | M-YW-L | | WH | | Rough roof | $85.00 |
| Classic '32 Ford Vicky | 6250 | | USA | M-YW-L | | BK | | Smooth roof | $85.00 |
| Classic '32 Ford Vicky | 6250 | | USA | M-YW-L | | BK | | Rough roof | $80.00 |
| Classic '32 Ford Vicky | 6250 | | USA | M-YW-L | | GY | | Smooth roof | $85.00 |
| Classic '32 Ford Vicky | 6250 | | USA | M-YW-L | | GY | | Rough roof | $80.00 |
| Classic '32 Ford Vicky | 6250 | | USA | M-YW-L | | BR-L | | Smooth roof | $85.00 |
| Classic '32 Ford Vicky | 6250 | | USA | M-YW-L | | BR-L | | Rough roof | $80.00 |
| Classic '32 Ford Vicky | 6250 | | USA | M-YW-L | | BR-D | | Smooth roof | $85.00 |
| Classic '32 Ford Vicky | 6250 | | USA | M-YW-L | | BR-D | | Rough roof | $80.00 |
| | | | | | | | | | |
| Classic '31 Ford Woody | 6251 | | USA | M-AQ | | WH | | Smooth roof | $50.00 |
| Classic '31 Ford Woody | 6251 | | USA | M-AQ | | WH | | Rough roof | $55.00 |
| Classic '31 Ford Woody | 6251 | | USA | M-AQ | | BK | | Smooth roof | $45.00 |
| Classic '31 Ford Woody | 6251 | | USA | M-AQ | | BK | | Rough roof | $50.00 |

## 1969 Variations

| Name | Number | Casting | Country | Color | Windows | Interior | Paint | Other | Value |
|---|---|---|---|---|---|---|---|---|---|
| Classic '31 Ford Woody | 6251 | | USA | M-AQ | | GY | | Smooth roof | $45.00 |
| Classic '31 Ford Woody | 6251 | | USA | M-AQ | | GY | | Rough roof | $50.00 |
| Classic '31 Ford Woody | 6251 | | USA | M-AQ | | BR-L | | Smooth roof | $45.00 |
| Classic '31 Ford Woody | 6251 | | USA | M-AQ | | BR-L | | Rough roof | $50.00 |
| Classic '31 Ford Woody | 6251 | | USA | M-AQ | | BR-D | | Smooth roof | $45.00 |
| Classic '31 Ford Woody | 6251 | | USA | M-AQ | | BR-D | | Rough roof | $50.00 |
| Classic '31 Ford Woody | 6251 | | USA | M-BL | | WH | | Smooth roof | $40.00 |
| Classic '31 Ford Woody | 6251 | | USA | M-BL | | WH | | Rough roof | $45.00 |
| Classic '31 Ford Woody | 6251 | | USA | M-BL | | BK | | Smooth roof | $35.00 |
| Classic '31 Ford Woody | 6251 | | USA | M-BL | | BK | | Rough roof | $40.00 |
| Classic '31 Ford Woody | 6251 | | USA | M-BL | | GY | | Smooth roof | $35.00 |
| Classic '31 Ford Woody | 6251 | | USA | M-BL | | GY | | Rough roof | $40.00 |
| Classic '31 Ford Woody | 6251 | | USA | M-BL | | BR-L | | Smooth roof | $35.00 |
| Classic '31 Ford Woody | 6251 | | USA | M-BL | | BR-L | | Rough roof | $40.00 |
| Classic '31 Ford Woody | 6251 | | USA | M-BL | | BR-D | | Smooth roof | $35.00 |
| Classic '31 Ford Woody | 6251 | | USA | M-BL | | BR-D | | Rough roof | $40.00 |
| Classic '31 Ford Woody | 6251 | | USA | M-BL-I | | WH | | Smooth roof | $70.00 |
| Classic '31 Ford Woody | 6251 | | USA | M-BL-I | | WH | | Rough roof | $75.00 |
| Classic '31 Ford Woody | 6251 | | USA | M-BL-I | | BK | | Smooth roof | $65.00 |
| Classic '31 Ford Woody | 6251 | | USA | M-BL-I | | BK | | Rough roof | $70.00 |
| Classic '31 Ford Woody | 6251 | | USA | M-BL-I | | GY | | Smooth roof | $65.00 |
| Classic '31 Ford Woody | 6251 | | USA | M-BL-I | | GY | | Rough roof | $70.00 |
| Classic '31 Ford Woody | 6251 | | USA | M-BL-I | | BR-L | | Smooth roof | $65.00 |
| Classic '31 Ford Woody | 6251 | | USA | M-BL-I | | BR-L | | Rough roof | $70.00 |
| Classic '31 Ford Woody | 6251 | | USA | M-BL-I | | BR-D | | Smooth roof | $65.00 |
| Classic '31 Ford Woody | 6251 | | USA | M-BL-I | | BR-D | | Rough roof | $70.00 |
| Classic '31 Ford Woody | 6251 | | USA | M-BL-P | | WH | | Smooth roof | $90.00 |
| Classic '31 Ford Woody | 6251 | | USA | M-BL-P | | WH | | Rough roof | $95.00 |
| Classic '31 Ford Woody | 6251 | | USA | M-BL-P | | BK | | Smooth roof | $85.00 |
| Classic '31 Ford Woody | 6251 | | USA | M-BL-P | | BK | | Rough roof | $90.00 |
| Classic '31 Ford Woody | 6251 | | USA | M-BL-P | | GY | | Smooth roof | $85.00 |
| Classic '31 Ford Woody | 6251 | | USA | M-BL-P | | GY | | Rough roof | $90.00 |
| Classic '31 Ford Woody | 6251 | | USA | M-BL-P | | BR-L | | Smooth roof | $85.00 |
| Classic '31 Ford Woody | 6251 | | USA | M-BL-P | | BR-L | | Rough roof | $90.00 |
| Classic '31 Ford Woody | 6251 | | USA | M-BL-P | | BR-D | | Smooth roof | $85.00 |
| Classic '31 Ford Woody | 6251 | | USA | M-BL-P | | BR-D | | Rough roof | $90.00 |
| Classic '31 Ford Woody | 6251 | | USA | M-BR-D | | WH | | Smooth roof | $100.00 |
| Classic '31 Ford Woody | 6251 | | USA | M-BR-D | | WH | | Rough roof | $110.00 |
| Classic '31 Ford Woody | 6251 | | USA | M-BR-D | | BK | | Smooth roof | $95.00 |
| Classic '31 Ford Woody | 6251 | | USA | M-BR-D | | BK | | Rough roof | $100.00 |
| Classic '31 Ford Woody | 6251 | | USA | M-BR-D | | GY | | Smooth roof | $95.00 |
| Classic '31 Ford Woody | 6251 | | USA | M-BR-D | | GY | | Rough roof | $100.00 |
| Classic '31 Ford Woody | 6251 | | USA | M-BR-D | | BR-L | | Smooth roof | $90.00 |
| Classic '31 Ford Woody | 6251 | | USA | M-BR-D | | BR-L | | Rough roof | $95.00 |
| Classic '31 Ford Woody | 6251 | | USA | M-BR-D | | BR-D | | Smooth roof | $90.00 |
| Classic '31 Ford Woody | 6251 | | USA | M-BR-D | | BR-D | | Rough roof | $100.00 |
| Classic '31 Ford Woody | 6251 | | USA | M-BR-P | | WH | | Smooth roof | $85.00 |
| Classic '31 Ford Woody | 6251 | | USA | M-BR-P | | WH | | Rough roof | $90.00 |
| Classic '31 Ford Woody | 6251 | | USA | M-BR-P | | BK | | Smooth roof | $85.00 |
| Classic '31 Ford Woody | 6251 | | USA | M-BR-P | | BK | | Rough roof | $90.00 |
| Classic '31 Ford Woody | 6251 | | USA | M-BR-P | | GY | | Smooth roof | $85.00 |
| Classic '31 Ford Woody | 6251 | | USA | M-BR-P | | GY | | Rough roof | $90.00 |
| Classic '31 Ford Woody | 6251 | | USA | M-BR-P | | BR-L | | Smooth roof | $85.00 |
| Classic '31 Ford Woody | 6251 | | USA | M-BR-P | | BR-L | | Rough roof | $90.00 |
| Classic '31 Ford Woody | 6251 | | USA | M-BR-P | | BR-D | | Smooth roof | $85.00 |
| Classic '31 Ford Woody | 6251 | | USA | M-BR-P | | BR-D | | Rough roof | $90.00 |
| Classic '31 Ford Woody | 6251 | | USA | M-GD | | WH | | Smooth roof | $40.00 |
| Classic '31 Ford Woody | 6251 | | USA | M-GD | | WH | | Rough roof | $45.00 |
| Classic '31 Ford Woody | 6251 | | USA | M-GD | | BK | | Smooth roof | $35.00 |
| Classic '31 Ford Woody | 6251 | | USA | M-GD | | BK | | Rough roof | $40.00 |
| Classic '31 Ford Woody | 6251 | | USA | M-GD | | GY | | Smooth roof | $35.00 |
| Classic '31 Ford Woody | 6251 | | USA | M-GD | | GY | | Rough roof | $40.00 |
| Classic '31 Ford Woody | 6251 | | USA | M-GD | | BR-L | | Smooth roof | $35.00 |
| Classic '31 Ford Woody | 6251 | | USA | M-GD | | BR-L | | Rough roof | $40.00 |
| Classic '31 Ford Woody | 6251 | | USA | M-GD | | BR-D | | Smooth roof | $35.00 |
| Classic '31 Ford Woody | 6251 | | USA | M-GD | | BR-D | | Rough roof | $40.00 |
| Classic '31 Ford Woody | 6251 | | USA | M-GR | | WH | | Smooth roof | $40.00 |
| Classic '31 Ford Woody | 6251 | | USA | M-GR | | WH | | Rough roof | $45.00 |
| Classic '31 Ford Woody | 6251 | | USA | M-GR | | BK | | Smooth roof | $35.00 |
| Classic '31 Ford Woody | 6251 | | USA | M-GR | | BK | | Rough roof | $40.00 |
| Classic '31 Ford Woody | 6251 | | USA | M-GR | | GY | | Smooth roof | $35.00 |
| Classic '31 Ford Woody | 6251 | | USA | M-GR | | GY | | Rough roof | $40.00 |

## 1969 Variations

| Name | Number | Casting | Country | Color | Windows | Interior | Paint | Other | Value |
|---|---|---|---|---|---|---|---|---|---|
| Classic '31 Ford Woody | 6251 | | USA | M-GR | | BR-L | | Smooth roof | $35.00 |
| Classic '31 Ford Woody | 6251 | | USA | M-GR | | BR-L | | Rough roof | $40.00 |
| Classic '31 Ford Woody | 6251 | | USA | M-GR | | BR-D | | Smooth roof | $35.00 |
| Classic '31 Ford Woody | 6251 | | USA | M-GR | | BR-D | | Rough roof | $40.00 |
| Classic '31 Ford Woody | 6251 | | USA | M-GR-E | | WH | | Smooth roof | $45.00 |
| Classic '31 Ford Woody | 6251 | | USA | M-GR-E | | WH | | Rough roof | $50.00 |
| Classic '31 Ford Woody | 6251 | | USA | M-GR-E | | BK | | Smooth roof | $40.00 |
| Classic '31 Ford Woody | 6251 | | USA | M-GR-E | | BK | | Rough roof | $45.00 |
| Classic '31 Ford Woody | 6251 | | USA | M-GR-E | | GY | | Smooth roof | $40.00 |
| Classic '31 Ford Woody | 6251 | | USA | M-GR-E | | GY | | Rough roof | $45.00 |
| Classic '31 Ford Woody | 6251 | | USA | M-GR-E | | BR-L | | Smooth roof | $40.00 |
| Classic '31 Ford Woody | 6251 | | USA | M-GR-E | | BR-L | | Rough roof | $45.00 |
| Classic '31 Ford Woody | 6251 | | USA | M-GR-E | | BR-D | | Smooth roof | $40.00 |
| Classic '31 Ford Woody | 6251 | | USA | M-GR-E | | BR-D | | Rough roof | $45.00 |
| Classic '31 Ford Woody | 6251 | | USA | M-GR-L | | WH | | Smooth roof | $75.00 |
| Classic '31 Ford Woody | 6251 | | USA | M-GR-L | | WH | | Rough roof | $80.00 |
| Classic '31 Ford Woody | 6251 | | USA | M-GR-L | | BK | | Smooth roof | $70.00 |
| Classic '31 Ford Woody | 6251 | | USA | M-GR-L | | BK | | Rough roof | $75.00 |
| Classic '31 Ford Woody | 6251 | | USA | M-GR-L | | GY | | Smooth roof | $70.00 |
| Classic '31 Ford Woody | 6251 | | USA | M-GR-L | | GY | | Rough roof | $75.00 |
| Classic '31 Ford Woody | 6251 | | USA | M-GR-L | | BR-L | | Smooth roof | $70.00 |
| Classic '31 Ford Woody | 6251 | | USA | M-GR-L | | BR-L | | Rough roof | $75.00 |
| Classic '31 Ford Woody | 6251 | | USA | M-GR-L | | BR-D | | Smooth roof | $70.00 |
| Classic '31 Ford Woody | 6251 | | USA | M-GR-L | | BR-D | | Rough roof | $75.00 |
| Classic '31 Ford Woody | 6251 | | USA | M-GR-O | | WH | | Smooth roof | $55.00 |
| Classic '31 Ford Woody | 6251 | | USA | M-GR-O | | WH | | Rough roof | $60.00 |
| Classic '31 Ford Woody | 6251 | | USA | M-GR-O | | BK | | Smooth roof | $40.00 |
| Classic '31 Ford Woody | 6251 | | USA | M-GR-O | | BK | | Rough roof | $55.00 |
| Classic '31 Ford Woody | 6251 | | USA | M-GR-O | | GY | | Smooth roof | $40.00 |
| Classic '31 Ford Woody | 6251 | | USA | M-GR-O | | GY | | Rough roof | $55.00 |
| Classic '31 Ford Woody | 6251 | | USA | M-GR-O | | BR-L | | Smooth roof | $50.00 |
| Classic '31 Ford Woody | 6251 | | USA | M-GR-O | | BR-L | | Rough roof | $55.00 |
| Classic '31 Ford Woody | 6251 | | USA | M-GR-O | | BR-D | | Smooth roof | $50.00 |
| Classic '31 Ford Woody | 6251 | | USA | M-GR-O | | BR-D | | Rough roof | $55.00 |
| Classic '31 Ford Woody | 6251 | | USA | M-MG | | WH | | Smooth roof | $40.00 |
| Classic '31 Ford Woody | 6251 | | USA | M-MG | | WH | | Rough roof | $45.00 |
| Classic '31 Ford Woody | 6251 | | USA | M-MG | | BK | | Smooth roof | $35.00 |
| Classic '31 Ford Woody | 6251 | | USA | M-MG | | BK | | Rough roof | $40.00 |
| Classic '31 Ford Woody | 6251 | | USA | M-MG | | GY | | Smooth roof | $35.00 |
| Classic '31 Ford Woody | 6251 | | USA | M-MG | | GY | | Rough roof | $40.00 |
| Classic '31 Ford Woody | 6251 | | USA | M-MG | | BR-L | | Smooth roof | $35.00 |
| Classic '31 Ford Woody | 6251 | | USA | M-MG | | BR-L | | Rough roof | $40.00 |
| Classic '31 Ford Woody | 6251 | | USA | M-MG | | BR-D | | Smooth roof | $35.00 |
| Classic '31 Ford Woody | 6251 | | USA | M-MG | | BR-D | | Rough roof | $40.00 |
| Classic '31 Ford Woody | 6251 | | USA | M-OR | | WH | | Smooth roof | $40.00 |
| Classic '31 Ford Woody | 6251 | | USA | M-OR | | WH | | Rough roof | $45.00 |
| Classic '31 Ford Woody | 6251 | | USA | M-OR | | BK | | Smooth roof | $35.00 |
| Classic '31 Ford Woody | 6251 | | USA | M-OR | | BK | | Rough roof | $40.00 |
| Classic '31 Ford Woody | 6251 | | USA | M-OR | | GY | | Smooth roof | $35.00 |
| Classic '31 Ford Woody | 6251 | | USA | M-OR | | GY | | Rough roof | $40.00 |
| Classic '31 Ford Woody | 6251 | | USA | M-OR | | BR-L | | Smooth roof | $35.00 |
| Classic '31 Ford Woody | 6251 | | USA | M-OR | | BR-L | | Rough roof | $40.00 |
| Classic '31 Ford Woody | 6251 | | USA | M-OR | | BR-D | | Smooth roof | $35.00 |
| Classic '31 Ford Woody | 6251 | | USA | M-OR | | BR-D | | Rough roof | $40.00 |
| Classic '31 Ford Woody | 6251 | | USA | M-PK | | WH | | Smooth roof | $270.00 |
| Classic '31 Ford Woody | 6251 | | USA | M-PK | | WH | | Rough roof | $280.00 |
| Classic '31 Ford Woody | 6251 | | USA | M-PK | | BK | | Smooth roof | $250.00 |
| Classic '31 Ford Woody | 6251 | | USA | M-PK | | BK | | Rough roof | $260.00 |
| Classic '31 Ford Woody | 6251 | | USA | M-PK | | GY | | Smooth roof | $250.00 |
| Classic '31 Ford Woody | 6251 | | USA | M-PK | | GY | | Rough roof | $260.00 |
| Classic '31 Ford Woody | 6251 | | USA | M-PK | | BR-L | | Smooth roof | $250.00 |
| Classic '31 Ford Woody | 6251 | | USA | M-PK | | BR-L | | Rough roof | $260.00 |
| Classic '31 Ford Woody | 6251 | | USA | M-PK | | BR-D | | Smooth roof | $250.00 |
| Classic '31 Ford Woody | 6251 | | USA | M-PK | | BR-D | | Rough roof | $260.00 |
| Classic '31 Ford Woody | 6251 | | USA | M-PK-H | | WH | | Smooth roof | $270.00 |
| Classic '31 Ford Woody | 6251 | | USA | M-PK-H | | WH | | Rough roof | $280.00 |
| Classic '31 Ford Woody | 6251 | | USA | M-PK-H | | BK | | Smooth roof | $250.00 |
| Classic '31 Ford Woody | 6251 | | USA | M-PK-H | | BK | | Rough roof | $260.00 |
| Classic '31 Ford Woody | 6251 | | USA | M-PK-H | | GY | | Smooth roof | $250.00 |
| Classic '31 Ford Woody | 6251 | | USA | M-PK-H | | GY | | Rough roof | $260.00 |
| Classic '31 Ford Woody | 6251 | | USA | M-PK-H | | BR-L | | Smooth roof | $250.00 |
| Classic '31 Ford Woody | 6251 | | USA | M-PK-H | | BR-L | | Rough roof | $260.00 |

## 1969 Variations

| Name | Number | Casting | Country | Color | Windows | Interior | Paint | Other | Value |
|---|---|---|---|---|---|---|---|---|---|
| Classic '31 Ford Woody | 6251 | | USA | M-PK-H | | BR-D | | Smooth roof | $250.00 |
| Classic '31 Ford Woody | 6251 | | USA | M-PK-H | | BR-D | | Rough roof | $260.00 |
| Classic '31 Ford Woody | 6251 | | USA | M-PK-S | | WH | | Smooth roof | $270.00 |
| Classic '31 Ford Woody | 6251 | | USA | M-PK-S | | WH | | Rough roof | $280.00 |
| Classic '31 Ford Woody | 6251 | | USA | M-PK-S | | BK | | Smooth roof | $250.00 |
| Classic '31 Ford Woody | 6251 | | USA | M-PK-S | | BK | | Rough roof | $260.00 |
| Classic '31 Ford Woody | 6251 | | USA | M-PK-S | | GY | | Smooth roof | $250.00 |
| Classic '31 Ford Woody | 6251 | | USA | M-PK-S | | GY | | Rough roof | $260.00 |
| Classic '31 Ford Woody | 6251 | | USA | M-PK-S | | BR-L | | Smooth roof | $250.00 |
| Classic '31 Ford Woody | 6251 | | USA | M-PK-S | | BR-L | | Rough roof | $260.00 |
| Classic '31 Ford Woody | 6251 | | USA | M-PK-S | | BR-D | | Smooth roof | $250.00 |
| Classic '31 Ford Woody | 6251 | | USA | M-PK-S | | BR-D | | Rough roof | $260.00 |
| Classic '31 Ford Woody | 6251 | | USA | M-PR | | WH | | Smooth roof | $40.00 |
| Classic '31 Ford Woody | 6251 | | USA | M-PR | | WH | | Rough roof | $45.00 |
| Classic '31 Ford Woody | 6251 | | USA | M-PR | | BK | | Smooth roof | $35.00 |
| Classic '31 Ford Woody | 6251 | | USA | M-PR | | BK | | Rough roof | $40.00 |
| Classic '31 Ford Woody | 6251 | | USA | M-PR | | GY | | Smooth roof | $35.00 |
| Classic '31 Ford Woody | 6251 | | USA | M-PR | | GY | | Rough roof | $40.00 |
| Classic '31 Ford Woody | 6251 | | USA | M-PR | | BR-L | | Smooth roof | $35.00 |
| Classic '31 Ford Woody | 6251 | | USA | M-PR | | BR-L | | Rough roof | $40.00 |
| Classic '31 Ford Woody | 6251 | | USA | M-PR | | BR-D | | Smooth roof | $35.00 |
| Classic '31 Ford Woody | 6251 | | USA | M-PR | | BR-D | | Rough roof | $40.00 |
| Classic '31 Ford Woody | 6251 | | USA | M-RD | | WH | | Smooth roof | $40.00 |
| Classic '31 Ford Woody | 6251 | | USA | M-RD | | WH | | Rough roof | $45.00 |
| Classic '31 Ford Woody | 6251 | | USA | M-RD | | BK | | Smooth roof | $35.00 |
| Classic '31 Ford Woody | 6251 | | USA | M-RD | | BK | | Rough roof | $40.00 |
| Classic '31 Ford Woody | 6251 | | USA | M-RD | | GY | | Smooth roof | $35.00 |
| Classic '31 Ford Woody | 6251 | | USA | M-RD | | GY | | Rough roof | $40.00 |
| Classic '31 Ford Woody | 6251 | | USA | M-RD | | BR-L | | Smooth roof | $35.00 |
| Classic '31 Ford Woody | 6251 | | USA | M-RD | | BR-L | | Rough roof | $40.00 |
| Classic '31 Ford Woody | 6251 | | USA | M-RD | | BR-D | | Smooth roof | $35.00 |
| Classic '31 Ford Woody | 6251 | | USA | M-RD | | BR-D | | Rough roof | $40.00 |
| Classic '31 Ford Woody | 6251 | | USA | M-RD-R | | WH | | Smooth roof | $45.00 |
| Classic '31 Ford Woody | 6251 | | USA | M-RD-R | | WH | | Rough roof | $50.00 |
| Classic '31 Ford Woody | 6251 | | USA | M-RD-R | | BK | | Smooth roof | $40.00 |
| Classic '31 Ford Woody | 6251 | | USA | M-RD-R | | BK | | Rough roof | $45.00 |
| Classic '31 Ford Woody | 6251 | | USA | M-RD-R | | GY | | Smooth roof | $40.00 |
| Classic '31 Ford Woody | 6251 | | USA | M-RD-R | | GY | | Rough roof | $45.00 |
| Classic '31 Ford Woody | 6251 | | USA | M-RD-R | | BR-L | | Smooth roof | $40.00 |
| Classic '31 Ford Woody | 6251 | | USA | M-RD-R | | BR-L | | Rough roof | $45.00 |
| Classic '31 Ford Woody | 6251 | | USA | M-RD-R | | BR-D | | Smooth roof | $40.00 |
| Classic '31 Ford Woody | 6251 | | USA | M-RD-R | | BR-D | | Rough roof | $45.00 |
| Classic '31 Ford Woody | 6251 | | USA | M-YW | | WH | | Smooth roof | $40.00 |
| Classic '31 Ford Woody | 6251 | | USA | M-YW | | WH | | Rough roof | $45.00 |
| Classic '31 Ford Woody | 6251 | | USA | M-YW | | BK | | Smooth roof | $35.00 |
| Classic '31 Ford Woody | 6251 | | USA | M-YW | | BK | | Rough roof | $40.00 |
| Classic '31 Ford Woody | 6251 | | USA | M-YW | | GY | | Smooth roof | $35.00 |
| Classic '31 Ford Woody | 6251 | | USA | M-YW | | GY | | Rough roof | $40.00 |
| Classic '31 Ford Woody | 6251 | | USA | M-YW | | BR-L | | Smooth roof | $35.00 |
| Classic '31 Ford Woody | 6251 | | USA | M-YW | | BR-L | | Rough roof | $40.00 |
| Classic '31 Ford Woody | 6251 | | USA | M-YW | | BR-D | | Smooth roof | $35.00 |
| Classic '31 Ford Woody | 6251 | | USA | M-YW | | BR-D | | Rough roof | $40.00 |
| Classic '31 Ford Woody | 6251 | | USA | M-YW-L | | WH | | Smooth roof | $90.00 |
| Classic '31 Ford Woody | 6251 | | USA | M-YW-L | | WH | | Rough roof | $95.00 |
| Classic '31 Ford Woody | 6251 | | USA | M-YW-L | | BK | | Smooth roof | $85.00 |
| Classic '31 Ford Woody | 6251 | | USA | M-YW-L | | BK | | Rough roof | $90.00 |
| Classic '31 Ford Woody | 6251 | | USA | M-YW-L | | GY | | Smooth roof | $85.00 |
| Classic '31 Ford Woody | 6251 | | USA | M-YW-L | | GY | | Rough roof | $90.00 |
| Classic '31 Ford Woody | 6251 | | USA | M-YW-L | | BR-L | | Smooth roof | $85.00 |
| Classic '31 Ford Woody | 6251 | | USA | M-YW-L | | BR-L | | Rough roof | $90.00 |
| Classic '31 Ford Woody | 6251 | | USA | M-YW-L | | BR-D | | Smooth roof | $85.00 |
| Classic '31 Ford Woody | 6251 | | USA | M-YW-L | | BR-D | | Rough roof | $90.00 |
| | | | | | | | | | |
| Classic '57 T-Bird | 6252 | | USA | E-YW | | WH | | | $300.00 |
| Classic '57 T-Bird | 6252 | | USA | M-AQ | | WH | | | $70.00 |
| Classic '57 T-Bird | 6252 | | USA | M-AQ | | BK | | | $70.00 |
| Classic '57 T-Bird | 6252 | | USA | M-AQ | | GY | | | $70.00 |
| Classic '57 T-Bird | 6252 | | USA | M-AQ | | BR-L | | | $70.00 |
| Classic '57 T-Bird | 6252 | | USA | M-AQ | | BR-D | | | $70.00 |
| Classic '57 T-Bird | 6252 | | USA | M-BL | | WH | | | $50.00 |
| Classic '57 T-Bird | 6252 | | USA | M-BL | | BK | | | $50.00 |

## 1969 Variations

| Name | Number | Casting | Country | Color | Windows | Interior | Paint | Other | Value |
|---|---|---|---|---|---|---|---|---|---|
| Classic '57 T-Bird | 6252 | | USA | M-BL | | GY | | | $50.00 |
| Classic '57 T-Bird | 6252 | | USA | M-BL | | BR-L | | | $50.00 |
| Classic '57 T-Bird | 6252 | | USA | M-BL | | BR-D | | | $50.00 |
| Classic '57 T-Bird | 6252 | | USA | M-BL-I | | WH | | | $70.00 |
| Classic '57 T-Bird | 6252 | | USA | M-BL-I | | BK | | | $70.00 |
| Classic '57 T-Bird | 6252 | | USA | M-BL-I | | GY | | | $70.00 |
| Classic '57 T-Bird | 6252 | | USA | M-BL-I | | BR-L | | | $70.00 |
| Classic '57 T-Bird | 6252 | | USA | M-BL-I | | BR-D | | | $70.00 |
| Classic '57 T-Bird | 6252 | | USA | M-BL-P | | WH | | | $60.00 |
| Classic '57 T-Bird | 6252 | | USA | M-BL-P | | BK | | | $60.00 |
| Classic '57 T-Bird | 6252 | | USA | M-BL-P | | GY | | | $60.00 |
| Classic '57 T-Bird | 6252 | | USA | M-BL-P | | BR-L | | | $60.00 |
| Classic '57 T-Bird | 6252 | | USA | M-BL-P | | BR-D | | | $60.00 |
| Classic '57 T-Bird | 6252 | | USA | M-BR-D | | WH | | | $85.00 |
| Classic '57 T-Bird | 6252 | | USA | M-BR-D | | BK | | | $85.00 |
| Classic '57 T-Bird | 6252 | | USA | M-BR-D | | GY | | | $85.00 |
| Classic '57 T-Bird | 6252 | | USA | M-BR-D | | BR-L | | | $85.00 |
| Classic '57 T-Bird | 6252 | | USA | M-BR-D | | BR-D | | | $85.00 |
| Classic '57 T-Bird | 6252 | | USA | M-BR-P | | WH | | | $75.00 |
| Classic '57 T-Bird | 6252 | | USA | M-BR-P | | BK | | | $75.00 |
| Classic '57 T-Bird | 6252 | | USA | M-BR-P | | GY | | | $75.00 |
| Classic '57 T-Bird | 6252 | | USA | M-BR-P | | BR-L | | | $75.00 |
| Classic '57 T-Bird | 6252 | | USA | M-BR-P | | BR-D | | | $75.00 |
| Classic '57 T-Bird | 6252 | | USA | M-GD | | WH | | | $65.00 |
| Classic '57 T-Bird | 6252 | | USA | M-GD | | BK | | | $65.00 |
| Classic '57 T-Bird | 6252 | | USA | M-GD | | GY | | | $65.00 |
| Classic '57 T-Bird | 6252 | | USA | M-GD | | BR-L | | | $65.00 |
| Classic '57 T-Bird | 6252 | | USA | M-GD | | BR-D | | | $65.00 |
| Classic '57 T-Bird | 6252 | | USA | M-GR | | WH | | | $55.00 |
| Classic '57 T-Bird | 6252 | | USA | M-GR | | BK | | | $55.00 |
| Classic '57 T-Bird | 6252 | | USA | M-GR | | GY | | | $55.00 |
| Classic '57 T-Bird | 6252 | | USA | M-GR | | BR-L | | | $55.00 |
| Classic '57 T-Bird | 6252 | | USA | M-GR | | BR-D | | | $55.00 |
| Classic '57 T-Bird | 6252 | | USA | M-GR-E | | WH | | | $60.00 |
| Classic '57 T-Bird | 6252 | | USA | M-GR-E | | BK | | | $60.00 |
| Classic '57 T-Bird | 6252 | | USA | M-GR-E | | GY | | | $60.00 |
| Classic '57 T-Bird | 6252 | | USA | M-GR-E | | BR-L | | | $60.00 |
| Classic '57 T-Bird | 6252 | | USA | M-GR-E | | BR-D | | | $60.00 |
| Classic '57 T-Bird | 6252 | | USA | M-GR-L | | WH | | | $85.00 |
| Classic '57 T-Bird | 6252 | | USA | M-GR-L | | BK | | | $85.00 |
| Classic '57 T-Bird | 6252 | | USA | M-GR-L | | GY | | | $85.00 |
| Classic '57 T-Bird | 6252 | | USA | M-GR-L | | BR-L | | | $85.00 |
| Classic '57 T-Bird | 6252 | | USA | M-GR-L | | BR-D | | | $85.00 |
| Classic '57 T-Bird | 6252 | | USA | M-GR-O | | WH | | | $75.00 |
| Classic '57 T-Bird | 6252 | | USA | M-GR-O | | BK | | | $75.00 |
| Classic '57 T-Bird | 6252 | | USA | M-GR-O | | GY | | | $75.00 |
| Classic '57 T-Bird | 6252 | | USA | M-GR-O | | BR-L | | | $75.00 |
| Classic '57 T-Bird | 6252 | | USA | M-GR-O | | BR-D | | | $75.00 |
| Classic '57 T-Bird | 6252 | | USA | M-MG | | WH | | | $90.00 |
| Classic '57 T-Bird | 6252 | | USA | M-MG | | BK | | | $90.00 |
| Classic '57 T-Bird | 6252 | | USA | M-MG | | GY | | | $90.00 |
| Classic '57 T-Bird | 6252 | | USA | M-MG | | BR-L | | | $90.00 |
| Classic '57 T-Bird | 6252 | | USA | M-MG | | BR-D | | | $90.00 |
| Classic '57 T-Bird | 6252 | | USA | M-OR | | WH | | | $60.00 |
| Classic '57 T-Bird | 6252 | | USA | M-OR | | BK | | | $60.00 |
| Classic '57 T-Bird | 6252 | | USA | M-OR | | GY | | | $60.00 |
| Classic '57 T-Bird | 6252 | | USA | M-OR | | BR-L | | | $60.00 |
| Classic '57 T-Bird | 6252 | | USA | M-OR | | BR-D | | | $60.00 |
| Classic '57 T-Bird | 6252 | | USA | M-PK | | WH | | | $340.00 |
| Classic '57 T-Bird | 6252 | | USA | M-PK | | BK | | | $340.00 |
| Classic '57 T-Bird | 6252 | | USA | M-PK | | GY | | | $340.00 |
| Classic '57 T-Bird | 6252 | | USA | M-PK | | BR-L | | | $340.00 |
| Classic '57 T-Bird | 6252 | | USA | M-PK | | BR-D | | | $340.00 |
| Classic '57 T-Bird | 6252 | | USA | M-PK-H | | WH | | | $340.00 |
| Classic '57 T-Bird | 6252 | | USA | M-PK-H | | BK | | | $340.00 |
| Classic '57 T-Bird | 6252 | | USA | M-PK-H | | GY | | | $340.00 |
| Classic '57 T-Bird | 6252 | | USA | M-PK-H | | BR-L | | | $340.00 |
| Classic '57 T-Bird | 6252 | | USA | M-PK-H | | BR-D | | | $340.00 |
| Classic '57 T-Bird | 6252 | | USA | M-PK-S | | WH | | | $340.00 |
| Classic '57 T-Bird | 6252 | | USA | M-PK-S | | BK | | | $340.00 |
| Classic '57 T-Bird | 6252 | | USA | M-PK-S | | GY | | | $340.00 |
| Classic '57 T-Bird | 6252 | | USA | M-PK-S | | BR-L | | | $340.00 |

## 1969 Variations

| Name | Number | Casting | Country | Color | Windows | Interior | Paint | Other | Value |
|---|---|---|---|---|---|---|---|---|---|
| Classic '57 T-Bird | 6252 | | USA | M-PK-S | | BR-D | | | $340.00 |
| Classic '57 T-Bird | 6252 | | USA | M-PR | | WH | | | $75.00 |
| Classic '57 T-Bird | 6252 | | USA | M-PR | | BK | | | $75.00 |
| Classic '57 T-Bird | 6252 | | USA | M-PR | | GY | | | $75.00 |
| Classic '57 T-Bird | 6252 | | USA | M-PR | | BR-L | | | $75.00 |
| Classic '57 T-Bird | 6252 | | USA | M-PR | | BR-D | | | $75.00 |
| Classic '57 T-Bird | 6252 | | USA | M-RD | | WH | | | $55.00 |
| Classic '57 T-Bird | 6252 | | USA | M-RD | | BK | | | $55.00 |
| Classic '57 T-Bird | 6252 | | USA | M-RD | | GY | | | $55.00 |
| Classic '57 T-Bird | 6252 | | USA | M-RD | | BR-L | | | $55.00 |
| Classic '57 T-Bird | 6252 | | USA | M-RD | | BR-D | | | $55.00 |
| Classic '57 T-Bird | 6252 | | USA | M-RD-R | | WH | | | $55.00 |
| Classic '57 T-Bird | 6252 | | USA | M-RD-R | | BK | | | $55.00 |
| Classic '57 T-Bird | 6252 | | USA | M-RD-R | | GY | | | $55.00 |
| Classic '57 T-Bird | 6252 | | USA | M-RD-R | | BR-L | | | $55.00 |
| Classic '57 T-Bird | 6252 | | USA | M-RD-R | | BR-D | | | $55.00 |
| Classic '57 T-Bird | 6252 | | USA | M-YW | | WH | | | $50.00 |
| Classic '57 T-Bird | 6252 | | USA | M-YW | | BK | | | $50.00 |
| Classic '57 T-Bird | 6252 | | USA | M-YW | | GY | | | $50.00 |
| Classic '57 T- Bird | 6252 | | USA | M-YW | | BR-L | | | $50.00 |
| Classic '57 T-Bird | 6252 | | USA | M-YW | | BR-D | | | $50.00 |
| Classic '57 T-Bird | 6252 | | USA | M-YW-L | | WH | | | $80.00 |
| Classic '57 T-Bird | 6252 | | USA | M-YW-L | | BK | | | $80.00 |
| Classic '57 T-Bird | 6252 | | USA | M-YW-L | | GY | | | $80.00 |
| Classic '57 T-Bird | 6252 | | USA | M-YW-L | | BR-L | | | $80.00 |
| Classic '57 T-Bird | 6252 | | USA | M-YW-L | | BR-D | | | $80.00 |
| | | | | | | | | | |
| Classic '36 Ford Coupe | 6253 | | USA | M-AQ | | WH | | | $65.00 |
| Classic '36 Ford Coupe | 6253 | | USA | M-AQ | | BK | | | $50.00 |
| Classic '36 Ford Coupe | 6253 | | USA | M-AQ | | GY | | | $50.00 |
| Classic '36 Ford Coupe | 6253 | | USA | M-AQ | | BR-D | | | $50.00 |
| Classic '36 Ford Coupe | 6253 | | USA | M-BL | | WH | | | $40.00 |
| Classic '36 Ford Coupe | 6253 | | USA | M-BL | | BK | | | $35.00 |
| Classic '36 Ford Coupe | 6253 | | USA | M-BL | | GY | | | $35.00 |
| Classic '36 Ford Coupe | 6253 | | USA | M-BL | | BR-D | | | $35.00 |
| Classic '36 Ford Coupe | 6253 | | USA | M-BL-I | | WH | | | $140.00 |
| Classic '36 Ford Coupe | 6253 | | USA | M-BL-I | | BK | | | $105.00 |
| Classic '36 Ford Coupe | 6253 | | USA | M-BL-I | | GY | | | $105.00 |
| Classic '36 Ford Coupe | 6253 | | USA | M-BL-I | | BR-D | | | $105.00 |
| Classic '36 Ford Coupe | 6253 | | USA | M-BL-P | | WH | | | $120.00 |
| Classic '36 Ford Coupe | 6253 | | USA | M-BL-P | | BK | | | $90.00 |
| Classic '36 Ford Coupe | 6253 | | USA | M-BL-P | | GY | | | $90.00 |
| Classic '36 Ford Coupe | 6253 | | USA | M-BL-P | | BR-D | | | $90.00 |
| Classic '36 Ford Coupe | 6253 | | USA | M-BR-D | | WH | | | $70.00 |
| Classic '36 Ford Coupe | 6253 | | USA | M-BR-D | | BK | | | $55.00 |
| Classic '36 Ford Coupe | 6253 | | USA | M-BR-D | | GY | | | $55.00 |
| Classic '36 Ford Coupe | 6253 | | USA | M-BR-D | | BR-D | | | $55.00 |
| Classic '36 Ford Coupe | 6253 | | USA | M-BR-P | | WH | | | $60.00 |
| Classic '36 Ford Coupe | 6253 | | USA | M-BR-P | | BK | | | $45.00 |
| Classic '36 Ford Coupe | 6253 | | USA | M-BR-P | | GY | | | $45.00 |
| Classic '36 Ford Coupe | 6253 | | USA | M-BR-P | | BR-D | | | $45.00 |
| Classic '36 Ford Coupe | 6253 | | USA | M-GD | | WH | | | $50.00 |
| Classic '36 Ford Coupe | 6253 | | USA | M-GD | | BK | | | $50.00 |
| Classic '36 Ford Coupe | 6253 | | USA | M-GD | | GY | | | $50.00 |
| Classic '36 Ford Coupe | 6253 | | USA | M-GD | | BR-D | | | $50.00 |
| Classic '36 Ford Coupe | 6253 | | USA | M-GR | | WH | | | $50.00 |
| Classic '36 Ford Coupe | 6253 | | USA | M-GR | | BK | | | $50.00 |
| Classic '36 Ford Coupe | 6253 | | USA | M-GR | | GY | | | $50.00 |
| Classic '36 Ford Coupe | 6253 | | USA | M-GR | | BR-D | | | $50.00 |
| Classic '36 Ford Coupe | 6253 | | USA | M-GR-E | | WH | | | $60.00 |
| Classic '36 Ford Coupe | 6253 | | USA | M-GR-E | | BK | | | $45.00 |
| Classic '36 Ford Coupe | 6253 | | USA | M-GR-E | | GY | | | $45.00 |
| Classic '36 Ford Coupe | 6253 | | USA | M-GR-E | | BR-D | | | $45.00 |
| Classic '36 Ford Coupe | 6253 | | USA | M-GR-L | | WH | | | $120.00 |
| Classic '36 Ford Coupe | 6253 | | USA | M-GR-L | | BK | | | $120.00 |
| Classic '36 Ford Coupe | 6253 | | USA | M-GR-L | | GY | | | $120.00 |
| Classic '36 Ford Coupe | 6253 | | USA | M-GR-L | | BR-D | | | $120.00 |
| Classic '36 Ford Coupe | 6253 | | USA | M-GR-O | | WH | | | $95.00 |
| Classic '36 Ford Coupe | 6253 | | USA | M-GR-O | | BK | | | $75.00 |
| Classic '36 Ford Coupe | 6253 | | USA | M-GR-O | | GY | | | $75.00 |
| Classic '36 Ford Coupe | 6253 | | USA | M-GR-O | | BR-D | | | $75.00 |

## 1969 Variations

| Name | Number | Casting | Country | Color | Windows | Interior | Paint | Other | Value |
|---|---|---|---|---|---|---|---|---|---|
| Classic '36 Ford Coupe | 6253 | | USA | M-MG | | WH | | | $95.00 |
| Classic '36 Ford Coupe | 6253 | | USA | M-MG | | BK | | | $75.00 |
| Classic '36 Ford Coupe | 6253 | | USA | M-MG | | GY | | | $75.00 |
| Classic '36 Ford Coupe | 6253 | | USA | M-MG | | BR-D | | | $75.00 |
| Classic '36 Ford Coupe | 6253 | | USA | M-OR | | WH | | | $50.00 |
| Classic '36 Ford Coupe | 6253 | | USA | M-OR | | BK | | | $35.00 |
| Classic '36 Ford Coupe | 6253 | | USA | M-OR | | GY | | | $35.00 |
| Classic '36 Ford Coupe | 6253 | | USA | M-OR | | BR-D | | | $35.00 |
| Classic '36 Ford Coupe | 6253 | | USA | M-PK | | WH | | | $440.00 |
| Classic '36 Ford Coupe | 6253 | | USA | M-PK | | BK | | | $340.00 |
| Classic '36 Ford Coupe | 6253 | | USA | M-PK | | GY | | | $340.00 |
| Classic '36 Ford Coupe | 6253 | | USA | M-PK | | BR-D | | | $340.00 |
| Classic '36 Ford Coupe | 6253 | | USA | M-PK-H | | WH | | | $440.00 |
| Classic '36 Ford Coupe | 6253 | | USA | M-PK-H | | BK | | | $340.00 |
| Classic '36 Ford Coupe | 6253 | | USA | M-PK-H | | GY | | | $340.00 |
| Classic '36 Ford Coupe | 6253 | | USA | M-PK-H | | BR-D | | | $340.00 |
| Classic '36 Ford Coupe | 6253 | | USA | M-PK-S | | WH | | | $440.00 |
| Classic '36 Ford Coupe | 6253 | | USA | M-PK-S | | BK | | | $340.00 |
| Classic '36 Ford Coupe | 6253 | | USA | M-PK-S | | GY | | | $340.00 |
| Classic '36 Ford Coupe | 6253 | | USA | M-PK-S | | BR-D | | | $340.00 |
| Classic '36 Ford Coupe | 6253 | | USA | M-PR | | WH | | | $60.00 |
| Classic '36 Ford Coupe | 6253 | | USA | M-PR | | BK | | | $45.00 |
| Classic '36 Ford Coupe | 6253 | | USA | M-PR | | GY | | | $45.00 |
| Classic '36 Ford Coupe | 6253 | | USA | M-PR | | BR-D | | | $45.00 |
| Classic '36 Ford Coupe | 6253 | | USA | M-RD | | WH | | | $60.00 |
| Classic '36 Ford Coupe | 6253 | | USA | M-RD | | BK | | | $60.00 |
| Classic '36 Ford Coupe | 6253 | | USA | M-RD | | GY | | | $60.00 |
| Classic '36 Ford Coupe | 6253 | | USA | M-RD | | BR-D | | | $60.00 |
| Classic '36 Ford Coupe | 6253 | | USA | M-RD-R | | WH | | | $70.00 |
| Classic '36 Ford Coupe | 6253 | | USA | M-RD-R | | BK | | | $55.00 |
| Classic '36 Ford Coupe | 6253 | | USA | M-RD-R | | GY | | | $55.00 |
| Classic '36 Ford Coupe | 6253 | | USA | M-RD-R | | BR-D | | | $55.00 |
| Classic '36 Ford Coupe | 6253 | | USA | M-YW | | WH | | | $65.00 |
| Classic '36 Ford Coupe | 6253 | | USA | M-YW | | BK | | | $50.00 |
| Classic '36 Ford Coupe | 6253 | | USA | M-YW | | GY | | | $50.00 |
| Classic '36 Ford Coupe | 6253 | | USA | M-YW | | BR-D | | | $50.00 |
| Classic '36 Ford Coupe | 6253 | | USA | M-YW-L | | WH | | | $140.00 |
| Classic '36 Ford Coupe | 6253 | | USA | M-YW-L | | BK | | | $105.00 |
| Classic '36 Ford Coupe | 6253 | | USA | M-YW-L | | GY | | | $105.00 |
| Classic '36 Ford Coupe | 6253 | | USA | M-YW-L | | BR-D | | | $105.00 |
| | | | | | | | | | |
| Lola GT70 | 6254 | | USA | E-GR | | BK | | | $35.00 |
| Lola GT70 | 6254 | | HK | E-GR | | BK | | | $35.00 |
| Lola GT70 | 6254 | | USA | E-GR | | BR-D | | | $35.00 |
| Lola GT70 | 6254 | | HK | E-GR | | BR-D | | | $35.00 |
| Lola GT70 | 6254 | | USA | E-RD | | BK | | | $35.00 |
| Lola GT70 | 6254 | | HK | E-RD | | BK | | | $35.00 |
| Lola GT70 | 6254 | | USA | E-RD | | BR-D | | | $35.00 |
| Lola GT70 | 6254 | | HK | E-RD | | BR-D | | | $35.00 |
| Lola GT70 | 6254 | | USA | M-AQ | | BK | | | $35.00 |
| Lola GT70 | 6254 | | HK | M-AQ | | BK | | | $35.00 |
| Lola GT70 | 6254 | | USA | M-AQ | | BR-D | | | $35.00 |
| Lola GT70 | 6254 | | HK | M-AQ | | BR-D | | | $35.00 |
| Lola GT70 | 6254 | | USA | M-BL | | BK | | | $35.00 |
| Lola GT70 | 6254 | | HK | M-BL | | BK | | | $35.00 |
| Lola GT70 | 6254 | | USA | M-BL | | BR-D | | | $35.00 |
| Lola GT70 | 6254 | | HK | M-BL | | BR-D | | | $35.00 |
| Lola GT70 | 6254 | | USA | M-BL-I | | BK | | | $55.00 |
| Lola GT70 | 6254 | | HK | M-BL-I | | BK | | | $55.00 |
| Lola GT70 | 6254 | | USA | M-BL-I | | BR-D | | | $55.00 |
| Lola GT70 | 6254 | | HK | M-BL-I | | BR-D | | | $55.00 |
| Lola GT70 | 6254 | | USA | M-BL-P | | BK | | | $50.00 |
| Lola GT70 | 6254 | | HK | M-BL-P | | BK | | | $50.00 |
| Lola GT70 | 6254 | | USA | M-BL-P | | BR-D | | | $50.00 |
| Lola GT70 | 6254 | | HK | M-BL-P | | BR-D | | | $50.00 |
| Lola GT70 | 6254 | | USA | M-BR-D | | BK | | | $45.00 |
| Lola GT70 | 6254 | | HK | M-BR-D | | BK | | | $45.00 |
| Lola GT70 | 6254 | | USA | M-BR-D | | BR-D | | | $45.00 |
| Lola GT70 | 6254 | | HK | M-BR-D | | BR-D | | | $45.00 |
| Lola GT70 | 6254 | | USA | M-BR-P | | BK | | | $40.00 |
| Lola GT70 | 6254 | | HK | M-BR-P | | BK | | | $40.00 |

## 1969 Variations

| Name | Number | Casting | Country | Color | Windows | Interior | Paint | Other | Value |
|---|---|---|---|---|---|---|---|---|---|
| Lola GT70 | 6254 | | USA | M-BR-P | | BR-D | | | $40.00 |
| Lola GT70 | 6254 | | HK | M-BR-P | | BR-D | | | $40.00 |
| Lola GT70 | 6254 | | USA | M-GD | | BK | | | $35.00 |
| Lola GT70 | 6254 | | HK | M-GD | | BK | | | $35.00 |
| Lola GT70 | 6254 | | USA | M-GD | | BR-D | | | $35.00 |
| Lola GT70 | 6254 | | HK | M-GD | | BR-D | | | $35.00 |
| Lola GT70 | 6254 | | USA | M-GR | | BK | | | $35.00 |
| Lola GT70 | 6254 | | HK | M-GR | | BK | | | $35.00 |
| Lola GT70 | 6254 | | USA | M-GR | | BR-D | | | $35.00 |
| Lola GT70 | 6254 | | HK | M-GR | | BR-D | | | $35.00 |
| Lola GT70 | 6254 | | USA | M-GR-E | | BK | | | $40.00 |
| Lola GT70 | 6254 | | HK | M-GR-E | | BK | | | $40.00 |
| Lola GT70 | 6254 | | USA | M-GR-E | | BR-D | | | $40.00 |
| Lola GT70 | 6254 | | HK | M-GR-E | | BR-D | | | $40.00 |
| Lola GT70 | 6254 | | USA | M-GR-L | | BK | | | $50.00 |
| Lola GT70 | 6254 | | HK | M-GR-L | | BK | | | $50.00 |
| Lola GT70 | 6254 | | USA | M-GR-L | | BR-D | | | $50.00 |
| Lola GT70 | 6254 | | HK | M-GR-L | | BR-D | | | $50.00 |
| Lola GT70 | 6254 | | USA | M-GR-O | | BK | | | $45.00 |
| Lola GT70 | 6254 | | HK | M-GR-O | | BK | | | $45.00 |
| Lola GT70 | 6254 | | USA | M-GR-O | | BR-D | | | $45.00 |
| Lola GT70 | 6254 | | HK | M-GR-O | | BR-D | | | $45.00 |
| Lola GT70 | 6254 | | USA | M-MG | | BK | | | $45.00 |
| Lola GT70 | 6254 | | HK | M-MG | | BK | | | $45.00 |
| Lola GT70 | 6254 | | USA | M-MG | | BR-D | | | $45.00 |
| Lola GT70 | 6254 | | HK | M-MG | | BR-D | | | $45.00 |
| Lola GT70 | 6254 | | USA | M-OR | | BK | | | $20.00 |
| Lola GT70 | 6254 | | HK | M-OR | | BK | | | $35.00 |
| Lola GT70 | 6254 | | USA | M-OR | | BR-D | | | $35.00 |
| Lola GT70 | 6254 | | HK | M-OR | | BR-D | | | $35.00 |
| Lola GT70 | 6254 | | USA | M-PK | | BK | | | $150.00 |
| Lola GT70 | 6254 | | HK | M-PK | | BK | | | $150.00 |
| Lola GT70 | 6254 | | USA | M-PK | | BR-D | | | $150.00 |
| Lola GT70 | 6254 | | HK | M-PK | | BR-D | | | $150.00 |
| Lola GT70 | 6254 | | USA | M-PK-H | | BK | | | $150.00 |
| Lola GT70 | 6254 | | HK | M-PK-H | | BK | | | $150.00 |
| Lola GT70 | 6254 | | USA | M-PK-H | | BR-D | | | $150.00 |
| Lola GT70 | 6254 | | HK | M-PK-H | | BR-D | | | $150.00 |
| Lola GT70 | 6254 | | USA | M-PK-S | | BK | | | $150.00 |
| Lola GT70 | 6254 | | HK | M-PK-S | | BK | | | $150.00 |
| Lola GT70 | 6254 | | USA | M-PK-S | | BR-D | | | $150.00 |
| Lola GT70 | 6254 | | HK | M-PK-S | | BR-D | | | $150.00 |
| Lola GT70 | 6254 | | USA | M-PR | | BK | | | $45.00 |
| Lola GT70 | 6254 | | HK | M-PR | | BK | | | $45.00 |
| Lola GT70 | 6254 | | USA | M-PR | | BR-D | | | $45.00 |
| Lola GT70 | 6254 | | HK | M-PR | | BR-D | | | $45.00 |
| Lola GT70 | 6254 | | USA | M-RD | | BK | | | $35.00 |
| Lola GT70 | 6254 | | HK | M-RD | | BK | | | $35.00 |
| Lola GT70 | 6254 | | USA | M-RD | | BR-D | | | $35.00 |
| Lola GT70 | 6254 | | HK | M-RD | | BR-D | | | $35.00 |
| Lola GT70 | 6254 | | USA | M-RD-R | | BK | | | $40.00 |
| Lola GT70 | 6254 | | HK | M-RD-R | | BK | | | $40.00 |
| Lola GT70 | 6254 | | USA | M-RD-R | | BR-D | | | $40.00 |
| Lola GT70 | 6254 | | HK | M-RD-R | | BR-D | | | $40.00 |
| Lola GT70 | 6254 | | USA | M-YW | | BK | | | $35.00 |
| Lola GT70 | 6254 | | HK | M-YW | | BK | | | $35.00 |
| Lola GT70 | 6254 | | USA | M-YW | | BR-D | | | $35.00 |
| Lola GT70 | 6254 | | HK | M-YW | | BR-D | | | $35.00 |
| Lola GT70 | 6254 | | USA | M-YW-L | | BK | | | $55.00 |
| Lola GT70 | 6254 | | HK | M-YW-L | | BK | | | $55.00 |
| Lola GT70 | 6254 | | USA | M-YW-L | | BR-D | | | $55.00 |
| Lola GT70 | 6254 | | HK | M-YW-L | | BR-D | | | $55.00 |
| | | | | | | | | | |
| McLaren M6A | 6255 | | USA | E-OR | | BK | | | $60.00 |
| McLaren M6A | 6255 | | HK | E-OR | | BK | | | $60.00 |
| McLaren M6A | 6255 | | USA | E-OR | | BR-D | | | $60.00 |
| McLaren M6A | 6255 | | HK | E-OR | | BR-D | | | $60.00 |
| McLaren M6A | 6255 | | HK | E-RD | | BK | | | $300.00 |
| McLaren M6A | 6255 | | USA | M-AQ | | BK | | | $40.00 |
| McLaren M6A | 6255 | | HK | M-AQ | | BK | | | $40.00 |
| McLaren M6A | 6255 | | USA | M-AQ | | BR-D | | | $40.00 |

## 1969 Variations

| Name | Number | Casting | Country | Color | Windows | Interior | Paint | Other | Value |
|---|---|---|---|---|---|---|---|---|---|
| McLaren M6A | 6255 | | HK | M-AQ | | BR-D | | | $40.00 |
| McLaren M6A | 6255 | | USA | M-BL | | BK | | | $40.00 |
| McLaren M6A | 6255 | | HK | M-BL | | BK | | | $40.00 |
| McLaren M6A | 6255 | | USA | M-BL | | BR-D | | | $40.00 |
| McLaren M6A | 6255 | | HK | M-BL | | BR-D | | | $40.00 |
| McLaren M6A | 6255 | | USA | M-BL-I | | BK | | | $55.00 |
| McLaren M6A | 6255 | | HK | M-BL-I | | BK | | | $55.00 |
| McLaren M6A | 6255 | | USA | M-BL-I | | BR-D | | | $55.00 |
| McLaren M6A | 6255 | | HK | M-BL-I | | BR-D | | | $55.00 |
| McLaren M6A | 6255 | | USA | M-BL-P | | BK | | | $50.00 |
| McLaren M6A | 6255 | | HK | M-BL-P | | BK | | | $50.00 |
| McLaren M6A | 6255 | | USA | M-BL-P | | BR-D | | | $50.00 |
| McLaren M6A | 6255 | | HK | M-BL-P | | BR-D | | | $50.00 |
| McLaren M6A | 6255 | | USA | M-BR-D | | BK | | | $45.00 |
| McLaren M6A | 6255 | | HK | M-BR-D | | BK | | | $45.00 |
| McLaren M6A | 6255 | | USA | M-BR-D | | BR-D | | | $45.00 |
| McLaren M6A | 6255 | | HK | M-BR-D | | BR-D | | | $45.00 |
| McLaren M6A | 6255 | | USA | M-BR-P | | BK | | | $40.00 |
| McLaren M6A | 6255 | | HK | M-BR-P | | BK | | | $40.00 |
| McLaren M6A | 6255 | | USA | M-BR-P | | BR-D | | | $40.00 |
| McLaren M6A | 6255 | | HK | M-BR-P | | BR-D | | | $40.00 |
| McLaren M6A | 6255 | | USA | M-GD | | BK | | | $40.00 |
| McLaren M6A | 6255 | | HK | M-GD | | BK | | | $40.00 |
| McLaren M6A | 6255 | | USA | M-GD | | BR-D | | | $40.00 |
| McLaren M6A | 6255 | | HK | M-GD | | BR-D | | | $40.00 |
| McLaren M6A | 6255 | | USA | M-GR | | BK | | | $40.00 |
| McLaren M6A | 6255 | | HK | M-GR | | BK | | | $40.00 |
| McLaren M6A | 6255 | | USA | M-GR | | BR-D | | | $40.00 |
| McLaren M6A | 6255 | | HK | M-GR | | BR-D | | | $40.00 |
| McLaren M6A | 6255 | | USA | M-GR-E | | BK | | | $45.00 |
| McLaren M6A | 6255 | | HK | M-GR-E | | BK | | | $45.00 |
| McLaren M6A | 6255 | | USA | M-GR-E | | BR-D | | | $45.00 |
| McLaren M6A | 6255 | | HK | M-GR-E | | BR-D | | | $45.00 |
| McLaren M6A | 6255 | | USA | M-GR-L | | BK | | | $40.00 |
| McLaren M6A | 6255 | | HK | M-GR-L | | BK | | | $40.00 |
| McLaren M6A | 6255 | | USA | M-GR-L | | BR-D | | | $40.00 |
| McLaren M6A | 6255 | | HK | M-GR-L | | BR-D | | | $40.00 |
| McLaren M6A | 6255 | | USA | M-GR-O | | BK | | | $45.00 |
| McLaren M6A | 6255 | | HK | M-GR-O | | BK | | | $45.00 |
| McLaren M6A | 6255 | | USA | M-GR-O | | BR-D | | | $45.00 |
| McLaren M6A | 6255 | | HK | M-GR-O | | BR-D | | | $45.00 |
| McLaren M6A | 6255 | | USA | M-MG | | BK | | | $45.00 |
| McLaren M6A | 6255 | | HK | M-MG | | BK | | | $45.00 |
| McLaren M6A | 6255 | | USA | M-MG | | BR-D | | | $45.00 |
| McLaren M6A | 6255 | | HK | M-MG | | BR-D | | | $45.00 |
| McLaren M6A | 6255 | | USA | M-OR | | BK | | | $40.00 |
| McLaren M6A | 6255 | | HK | M-OR | | BK | | | $40.00 |
| McLaren M6A | 6255 | | USA | M-OR | | BR-D | | | $40.00 |
| McLaren M6A | 6255 | | HK | M-OR | | BR-D | | | $40.00 |
| McLaren M6A | 6255 | | USA | M-PL | | BK | | | $50.00 |
| McLaren M6A | 6255 | | HK | M-PL | | BK | | | $50.00 |
| McLaren M6A | 6255 | | USA | M-PL | | BR-D | | | $50.00 |
| McLaren M6A | 6255 | | HK | M-PL | | BR-D | | | $50.00 |
| McLaren M6A | 6255 | | USA | M-PR | | BK | | | $45.00 |
| McLaren M6A | 6255 | | HK | M-PR | | BK | | | $45.00 |
| McLaren M6A | 6255 | | USA | M-PR | | BR-D | | | $45.00 |
| McLaren M6A | 6255 | | HK | M-PR | | BR-D | | | $45.00 |
| McLaren M6A | 6255 | | USA | M-RD | | BK | | | $40.00 |
| McLaren M6A | 6255 | | HK | M-RD | | BK | | | $40.00 |
| McLaren M6A | 6255 | | USA | M-RD | | BR-D | | | $40.00 |
| McLaren M6A | 6255 | | HK | M-RD | | BR-D | | | $40.00 |
| McLaren M6A | 6255 | | USA | M-RD-R | | BK | | | $45.00 |
| McLaren M6A | 6255 | | HK | M-RD-R | | BK | | | $45.00 |
| McLaren M6A | 6255 | | USA | M-RD-R | | BR-D | | | $45.00 |
| McLaren M6A | 6255 | | HK | M-RD-R | | BR-D | | | $45.00 |
| McLaren M6A | 6255 | | USA | M-YW | | BK | | | $40.00 |
| McLaren M6A | 6255 | | HK | M-YW | | BK | | | $40.00 |
| McLaren M6A | 6255 | | USA | M-YW | | BR-D | | | $40.00 |
| McLaren M6A | 6255 | | HK | M-YW | | BR-D | | | $40.00 |
| McLaren M6A | 6255 | | USA | M-YW-L | | BK | | | $45.00 |
| McLaren M6A | 6255 | | HK | M-YW-L | | BK | | | $45.00 |
| McLaren M6A | 6255 | | USA | M-YW-L | | BR-D | | | $45.00 |

## 1969 Variations

| Name | Number | Casting | Country | Color | Windows | Interior | Paint | Other | Value |
|---|---|---|---|---|---|---|---|---|---|
| McLaren M6A | 6255 | | HK | M-YW-L | | BR-D | | | $45.00 |
| | | | | | | | | | |
| Chaparral 2G | 6256 | | USA | E-WH | | BK | | | $65.00 |
| Chaparral 2G | 6256 | | HK | E-WH | | BK | | | $65.00 |
| Chaparral 2G | 6256 | | USA | E-WH | | BR-D | | | $65.00 |
| Chaparral 2G | 6256 | | HK | E-WH | | BR-D | | | $65.00 |
| Chaparral 2G | 6256 | | USA | M-AQ | | BK | | | $50.00 |
| Chaparral 2G | 6256 | | HK | M-AQ | | BK | | | $50.00 |
| Chaparral 2G | 6256 | | USA | M-AQ | | BR-D | | | $50.00 |
| Chaparral 2G | 6256 | | HK | M-AQ | | BR-D | | | $50.00 |
| Chaparral 2G | 6256 | | USA | M-BL | | BK | | | $50.00 |
| Chaparral 2G | 6256 | | HK | M-BL | | BK | | | $50.00 |
| Chaparral 2G | 6256 | | USA | M-BL | | BR-D | | | $50.00 |
| Chaparral 2G | 6256 | | HK | M-BL | | BR-D | | | $50.00 |
| Chaparral 2G | 6256 | | USA | M-BL-I | | BK | | | $80.00 |
| Chaparral 2G | 6256 | | HK | M-BL-I | | BK | | | $80.00 |
| Chaparral 2G | 6256 | | USA | M-BL-I | | BR-D | | | $80.00 |
| Chaparral 2G | 6256 | | HK | M-BL-I | | BR-D | | | $80.00 |
| Chaparral 2G | 6256 | | USA | M-BL-P | | BK | | | $70.00 |
| Chaparral 2G | 6256 | | HK | M-BL-P | | BK | | | $70.00 |
| Chaparral 2G | 6256 | | USA | M-BL-P | | BR-D | | | $70.00 |
| Chaparral 2G | 6256 | | HK | M-BL-P | | BR-D | | | $70.00 |
| Chaparral 2G | 6256 | | USA | M-BR-D | | BK | | | $55.00 |
| Chaparral 2G | 6256 | | HK | M-BR-D | | BK | | | $55.00 |
| Chaparral 2G | 6256 | | USA | M-BR-D | | BR-D | | | $55.00 |
| Chaparral 2G | 6256 | | HK | M-BR-D | | BR-D | | | $55.00 |
| Chaparral 2G | 6256 | | USA | M-BR-P | | BK | | | $50.00 |
| Chaparral 2G | 6256 | | HK | M-BR-P | | BK | | | $50.00 |
| Chaparral 2G | 6256 | | USA | M-BR-P | | BR-D | | | $50.00 |
| Chaparral 2G | 6256 | | HK | M-BR-P | | BR-D | | | $50.00 |
| Chaparral 2G | 6256 | | USA | M-GD | | BK | | | $50.00 |
| Chaparral 2G | 6256 | | HK | M-GD | | BK | | | $50.00 |
| Chaparral 2G | 6256 | | USA | M-GD | | BR-D | | | $50.00 |
| Chaparral 2G | 6256 | | HK | M-GD | | BR-D | | | $50.00 |
| Chaparral 2G | 6256 | | USA | M-GR-L | | BK | | | $60.00 |
| Chaparral 2G | 6256 | | HK | M-GR-L | | BK | | | $60.00 |
| Chaparral 2G | 6256 | | USA | M-GR-L | | BR-D | | | $60.00 |
| Chaparral 2G | 6256 | | HK | M-GR-L | | BR-D | | | $60.00 |
| Chaparral 2G | 6256 | | USA | M-GR-O | | BK | | | $85.00 |
| Chaparral 2G | 6256 | | HK | M-GR-O | | BK | | | $85.00 |
| Chaparral 2G | 6256 | | USA | M-GR-O | | BR-D | | | $85.00 |
| Chaparral 2G | 6256 | | HK | M-GR-O | | BR-D | | | $85.00 |
| Chaparral 2G | 6256 | | USA | M-MG | | BK | | | $100.00 |
| Chaparral 2G | 6256 | | HK | M-MG | | BK | | | $100.00 |
| Chaparral 2G | 6256 | | USA | M-MG | | BR-D | | | $100.00 |
| Chaparral 2G | 6256 | | HK | M-MG | | BR-D | | | $100.00 |
| Chaparral 2G | 6256 | | USA | M-OR | | BK | | | $50.00 |
| Chaparral 2G | 6256 | | HK | M-OR | | BK | | | $50.00 |
| Chaparral 2G | 6256 | | USA | M-OR | | BR-D | | | $50.00 |
| Chaparral 2G | 6256 | | HK | M-OR | | BR-D | | | $50.00 |
| Chaparral 2G | 6256 | | USA | M-PK | | BK | | | $320.00 |
| Chaparral 2G | 6256 | | HK | M-PK | | BK | | | $320.00 |
| Chaparral 2G | 6256 | | USA | M-PK | | BR-D | | | $320.00 |
| Chaparral 2G | 6256 | | HK | M-PK | | BR-D | | | $320.00 |
| Chaparral 2G | 6256 | | USA | M-PK-H | | BK | | | $320.00 |
| Chaparral 2G | 6256 | | HK | M-PK-H | | BK | | | $320.00 |
| Chaparral 2G | 6256 | | USA | M-PK-H | | BR-D | | | $320.00 |
| Chaparral 2G | 6256 | | HK | M-PK-H | | BR-D | | | $320.00 |
| Chaparral 2G | 6256 | | USA | M-PK-S | | BK | | | $320.00 |
| Chaparral 2G | 6256 | | HK | M-PK-S | | BK | | | $320.00 |
| Chaparral 2G | 6256 | | USA | M-PK-S | | BR-D | | | $320.00 |
| Chaparral 2G | 6256 | | HK | M-PK-S | | BR-D | | | $320.00 |
| Chaparral 2G | 6256 | | USA | M-PR | | BK | | | $70.00 |
| Chaparral 2G | 6256 | | HK | M-PR | | BK | | | $70.00 |
| Chaparral 2G | 6256 | | USA | M-PR | | BR-D | | | $70.00 |
| Chaparral 2G | 6256 | | HK | M-PR | | BR-D | | | $70.00 |
| Chaparral 2G | 6256 | | USA | M-RD | | BK | | | $50.00 |
| Chaparral 2G | 6256 | | HK | M-RD | | BK | | | $50.00 |
| Chaparral 2G | 6256 | | USA | M-RD | | BR-D | | | $50.00 |
| Chaparral 2G | 6256 | | HK | M-RD | | BR-D | | | $50.00 |
| Chaparral 2G | 6256 | | USA | M-RD-R | | BK | | | $55.00 |

## 1969 Variations

| Name | Number | Casting | Country | Color | Windows | Interior | Paint | Other | Value |
|---|---|---|---|---|---|---|---|---|---|
| Chaparral 2G | 6256 | | HK | M-RD-R | | BK | | | $55.00 |
| Chaparral 2G | 6256 | | USA | M-RD-R | | BR-D | | | $55.00 |
| Chaparral 2G | 6256 | | HK | M-RD-R | | BR-D | | | $55.00 |
| Chaparral 2G | 6256 | | USA | M-YW | | BK | | | $50.00 |
| Chaparral 2G | 6256 | | HK | M-YW | | BK | | | $50.00 |
| Chaparral 2G | 6256 | | USA | M-YW | | BR-D | | | $50.00 |
| Chaparral 2G | 6256 | | HK | M-YW | | BR-D | | | $50.00 |
| Chaparral 2G | 6256 | | USA | M-YW-L | | BK | | | $55.00 |
| Chaparral 2G | 6256 | | HK | M-YW-L | | BK | | | $55.00 |
| Chaparral 2G | 6256 | | USA | M-YW-L | | BR-D | | | $55.00 |
| Chaparral 2G | 6256 | | HK | M-YW-L | | BR-D | | | $55.00 |
| Chaparral 2G | 6256 | | USA | SL | | BR-D | | | $300.00 |
| | | | | | | | | | |
| Ford Mk IV | 6257 | | USA | E-RD | | BK | | | $35.00 |
| Ford Mk IV | 6257 | | HK | E-RD | | BK | | | $35.00 |
| Ford Mk IV | 6257 | | USA | E-RD | | BR-D | | | $35.00 |
| Ford Mk IV | 6257 | | HK | E-RD | | BR-D | | | $35.00 |
| Ford Mk IV | 6257 | | USA | M-AQ | | BK | | | $35.00 |
| Ford Mk IV | 6257 | | HK | M-AQ | | BK | | | $35.00 |
| Ford Mk IV | 6257 | | USA | M-AQ | | BR-D | | | $35.00 |
| Ford Mk IV | 6257 | | HK | M-AQ | | BR-D | | | $35.00 |
| Ford Mk IV | 6257 | | USA | M-BL | | BK | | | $35.00 |
| Ford Mk IV | 6257 | | HK | M-BL | | BK | | | $35.00 |
| Ford Mk IV | 6257 | | USA | M-BL | | BR-D | | | $35.00 |
| Ford Mk IV | 6257 | | HK | M-BL | | BR-D | | | $35.00 |
| Ford Mk IV | 6257 | | USA | M-BL-I | | BK | | | $40.00 |
| Ford Mk IV | 6257 | | HK | M-BL-I | | BK | | | $40.00 |
| Ford Mk IV | 6257 | | USA | M-BL-I | | BR-D | | | $40.00 |
| Ford Mk IV | 6257 | | HK | M-BL-I | | BR-D | | | $40.00 |
| Ford Mk IV | 6257 | | USA | M-BL-P | | BK | | | $35.00 |
| Ford Mk IV | 6257 | | HK | M-BL-P | | BK | | | $35.00 |
| Ford Mk IV | 6257 | | USA | M-BL-P | | BR-D | | | $35.00 |
| Ford Mk IV | 6257 | | HK | M-BL-P | | BR-D | | | $35.00 |
| Ford Mk IV | 6257 | | USA | M-BR-D | | BK | | | $50.00 |
| Ford Mk IV | 6257 | | HK | M-BR-D | | BK | | | $50.00 |
| Ford Mk IV | 6257 | | USA | M-BR-D | | BR-D | | | $50.00 |
| Ford Mk IV | 6257 | | HK | M-BR-D | | BR-D | | | $50.00 |
| Ford Mk IV | 6257 | | USA | M-BR-P | | BK | | | $45.00 |
| Ford Mk IV | 6257 | | HK | M-BR-P | | BK | | | $45.00 |
| Ford Mk IV | 6257 | | USA | M-BR-P | | BR-D | | | $45.00 |
| Ford Mk IV | 6257 | | HK | M-BR-P | | BR-D | | | $45.00 |
| Ford Mk IV | 6257 | | USA | M-GD | | BK | | | $35.00 |
| Ford Mk IV | 6257 | | HK | M-GD | | BK | | | $35.00 |
| Ford Mk IV | 6257 | | USA | M-GD | | BR-D | | | $35.00 |
| Ford Mk IV | 6257 | | HK | M-GD | | BR-D | | | $35.00 |
| Ford Mk IV | 6257 | | USA | M-GR | | BK | | | $35.00 |
| Ford Mk IV | 6257 | | HK | M-GR | | BK | | | $35.00 |
| Ford Mk IV | 6257 | | USA | M-GR | | BR-D | | | $35.00 |
| Ford Mk IV | 6257 | | HK | M-GR | | BR-D | | | $35.00 |
| Ford Mk IV | 6257 | | USA | M-GR-E | | BK | | | $40.00 |
| Ford Mk IV | 6257 | | HK | M-GR-E | | BK | | | $40.00 |
| Ford Mk IV | 6257 | | USA | M-GR-E | | BR-D | | | $40.00 |
| Ford Mk IV | 6257 | | HK | M-GR-E | | BR-D | | | $40.00 |
| Ford Mk IV | 6257 | | USA | M-GR-L | | BK | | | $55.00 |
| Ford Mk IV | 6257 | | HK | M-GR-L | | BK | | | $55.00 |
| Ford Mk IV | 6257 | | USA | M-GR-L | | BR-D | | | $55.00 |
| Ford Mk IV | 6257 | | HK | M-GR-L | | BR-D | | | $55.00 |
| Ford Mk IV | 6257 | | USA | M-GR-O | | BK | | | $35.00 |
| Ford Mk IV | 6257 | | HK | M-GR-O | | BK | | | $35.00 |
| Ford Mk IV | 6257 | | USA | M-GR-O | | BR-D | | | $35.00 |
| Ford Mk IV | 6257 | | HK | M-GR-O | | BR-D | | | $35.00 |
| Ford Mk IV | 6257 | | USA | M-MG | | BK | | | $50.00 |
| Ford Mk IV | 6257 | | HK | M-MG | | BK | | | $50.00 |
| Ford Mk IV | 6257 | | USA | M-MG | | BR-D | | | $50.00 |
| Ford Mk IV | 6257 | | HK | M-MG | | BR-D | | | $50.00 |
| Ford Mk IV | 6257 | | USA | M-OR | | BK | | | $40.00 |
| Ford Mk IV | 6257 | | HK | M-OR | | BK | | | $40.00 |
| Ford Mk IV | 6257 | | USA | M-OR | | BR-D | | | $40.00 |
| Ford Mk IV | 6257 | | HK | M-OR | | BR-D | | | $40.00 |
| Ford Mk IV | 6257 | | USA | M-PL | | BK | | | $40.00 |
| Ford Mk IV | 6257 | | HK | M-PL | | BK | | | $40.00 |

## 1969 Variations

| Name | Number | Casting | Country | Color | Windows | Interior | Paint | Other | Value |
|---|---|---|---|---|---|---|---|---|---|
| Ford Mk IV | 6257 | | USA | M-PL | | BR-D | | | $40.00 |
| Ford Mk IV | 6257 | | HK | M-PL | | BR-D | | | $40.00 |
| Ford Mk IV | 6257 | | USA | M-PR | | BK | | | $35.00 |
| Ford Mk IV | 6257 | | HK | M-PR | | BK | | | $35.00 |
| Ford Mk IV | 6257 | | USA | M-PR | | BR-D | | | $35.00 |
| Ford Mk IV | 6257 | | HK | M-PR | | BR-D | | | $35.00 |
| Ford Mk IV | 6257 | | USA | M-RD | | BK | | | $35.00 |
| Ford Mk IV | 6257 | | HK | M-RD | | BK | | | $35.00 |
| Ford Mk IV | 6257 | | USA | M-RD | | BR-D | | | $35.00 |
| Ford Mk IV | 6257 | | HK | M-RD | | BR-D | | | $35.00 |
| Ford Mk IV | 6257 | | USA | M-RD-R | | BK | | | $40.00 |
| Ford Mk IV | 6257 | | HK | M-RD-R | | BK | | | $40.00 |
| Ford Mk IV | 6257 | | USA | M-RD-R | | BR-D | | | $40.00 |
| Ford Mk IV | 6257 | | HK | M-RD-R | | BR-D | | | $40.00 |
| Ford Mk IV | 6257 | | USA | M-YW | | BK | | | $35.00 |
| Ford Mk IV | 6257 | | HK | M-YW | | BK | | | $35.00 |
| Ford Mk IV | 6257 | | USA | M-YW | | BR-D | | | $35.00 |
| Ford Mk IV | 6257 | | HK | M-YW | | BR-D | | | $35.00 |
| Ford Mk IV | 6257 | | USA | M-YW-L | | BK | | | $60.00 |
| Ford Mk IV | 6257 | | HK | M-YW-L | | BK | | | $60.00 |
| Ford Mk IV | 6257 | | USA | M-YW-L | | BR-D | | | $60.00 |
| Ford Mk IV | 6257 | | HK | M-YW-L | | BR-D | | | $60.00 |
| Twinmill | 6258 | | USA | M-AQ | CL | WH | | | $45.00 |
| Twinmill | 6258 | | USA | M-AQ | CL | BK | | | $40.00 |
| Twinmill | 6258 | | USA | M-AQ | CL | GY | | | $40.00 |
| Twinmill | 6258 | | USA | M-AQ | CL | BR-L | | | $40.00 |
| Twinmill | 6258 | | USA | M-AQ | CL | BR-D | | | $40.00 |
| Twinmill | 6258 | | USA | M-BL | CL | WH | | | $45.00 |
| Twinmill | 6258 | | USA | M-BL | CL | BK | | | $40.00 |
| Twinmill | 6258 | | USA | M-BL | CL | GY | | | $40.00 |
| Twinmill | 6258 | | USA | M-BL | CL | BR-L | | | $40.00 |
| Twinmill | 6258 | | USA | M-BL | CL | BR-D | | | $40.00 |
| Twinmill | 6258 | | USA | M-BL-I | CL | WH | | | $55.00 |
| Twinmill | 6258 | | USA | M-BL-I | CL | BK | | | $45.00 |
| Twinmill | 6258 | | USA | M-BL-I | CL | GY | | | $45.00 |
| Twinmill | 6258 | | USA | M-BL-I | CL | BR-L | | | $45.00 |
| Twinmill | 6258 | | USA | M-BL-I | CL | BR-D | | | $45.00 |
| Twinmill | 6258 | | USA | M-BL-P | CL | WH | | | $45.00 |
| Twinmill | 6258 | | USA | M-BL-P | CL | BK | | | $40.00 |
| Twinmill | 6258 | | USA | M-BL-P | CL | GY | | | $40.00 |
| Twinmill | 6258 | | USA | M-BL-P | CL | BR-L | | | $40.00 |
| Twinmill | 6258 | | USA | M-BL-P | CL | BR-D | | | $40.00 |
| Twinmill | 6258 | | USA | M-BR-D | CL | WH | | | $100.00 |
| Twinmill | 6258 | | USA | M-BR-D | CL | BK | | | $95.00 |
| Twinmill | 6258 | | USA | M-BR-D | CL | GY | | | $95.00 |
| Twinmill | 6258 | | USA | M-BR-D | CL | BR-L | | | $95.00 |
| Twinmill | 6258 | | USA | M-BR-D | CL | BR-D | | | $95.00 |
| Twinmill | 6258 | | USA | M-BR-P | CL | WH | | | $95.00 |
| Twinmill | 6258 | | USA | M-BR-P | CL | BK | | | $80.00 |
| Twinmill | 6258 | | USA | M-BR-P | CL | GY | | | $80.00 |
| Twinmill | 6258 | | USA | M-BR-P | CL | BR-L | | | $80.00 |
| Twinmill | 6258 | | USA | M-BR-P | CL | BR-D | | | $80.00 |
| Twinmill | 6258 | | USA | M-GD | CL | WH | | | $45.00 |
| Twinmill | 6258 | | USA | M-GD | CL | BK | | | $40.00 |
| Twinmill | 6258 | | USA | M-GD | CL | GY | | | $40.00 |
| Twinmill | 6258 | | USA | M-GD | CL | BR-L | | | $40.00 |
| Twinmill | 6258 | | USA | M-GD | CL | BR-D | | | $40.00 |
| Twinmill | 6258 | | USA | M-GR | CL | WH | | | $45.00 |
| Twinmill | 6258 | | USA | M-GR | CL | BK | | | $40.00 |
| Twinmill | 6258 | | USA | M-GR | CL | GY | | | $40.00 |
| Twinmill | 6258 | | USA | M-GR | CL | BR-L | | | $40.00 |
| Twinmill | 6258 | | USA | M-GR | CL | BR-D | | | $40.00 |
| Twinmill | 6258 | | USA | M-GR-E | CL | WH | | | $50.00 |
| Twinmill | 6258 | | USA | M-GR-E | CL | BK | | | $45.00 |
| Twinmill | 6258 | | USA | M-GR-E | CL | GY | | | $45.00 |
| Twinmill | 6258 | | USA | M-GR-E | CL | BR-L | | | $45.00 |
| Twinmill | 6258 | | USA | M-GR-E | CL | BR-D | | | $45.00 |
| Twinmill | 6258 | | USA | M-GR-L | CL | WH | | | $70.00 |
| Twinmill | 6258 | | USA | M-GR-L | CL | BK | | | $60.00 |
| Twinmill | 6258 | | USA | M-GR-L | CL | GY | | | $60.00 |

## 1969 Variations

| Name | Number | Casting | Country | Color | Windows | Interior | Paint | Other | Value |
|---|---|---|---|---|---|---|---|---|---|
| Twinmill | 6258 | | USA | M-GR-L | CL | BR-L | | | $60.00 |
| Twinmill | 6258 | | USA | M-GR-L | CL | BR-D | | | $60.00 |
| Twinmill | 6258 | | USA | M-GR-O | CL | WH | | | $90.00 |
| Twinmill | 6258 | | USA | M-GR-O | CL | BK | | | $80.00 |
| Twinmill | 6258 | | USA | M-GR-O | CL | GY | | | $80.00 |
| Twinmill | 6258 | | USA | M-GR-O | CL | BR-L | | | $80.00 |
| Twinmill | 6258 | | USA | M-GR-O | CL | BR-D | | | $80.00 |
| Twinmill | 6258 | | USA | M-MG | CL | WH | | | $100.00 |
| Twinmill | 6258 | | USA | M-MG | CL | BK | | | $90.00 |
| Twinmill | 6258 | | USA | M-MG | CL | GY | | | $90.00 |
| Twinmill | 6258 | | USA | M-MG | CL | BR-L | | | $90.00 |
| Twinmill | 6258 | | USA | M-MG | CL | BR-D | | | $90.00 |
| Twinmill | 6258 | | USA | M-OR | CL | WH | | | $45.00 |
| Twinmill | 6258 | | USA | M-OR | CL | BK | | | $40.00 |
| Twinmill | 6258 | | USA | M-OR | CL | GY | | | $40.00 |
| Twinmill | 6258 | | USA | M-OR | CL | BR-L | | | $40.00 |
| Twinmill | 6258 | | USA | M-OR | CL | BR-D | | | $40.00 |
| Twinmill | 6258 | | USA | M-PK | CL | WH | | | $220.00 |
| Twinmill | 6258 | | USA | M-PK | CL | BK | | | $200.00 |
| Twinmill | 6258 | | USA | M-PK | CL | GY | | | $200.00 |
| Twinmill | 6258 | | USA | M-PK | CL | BR-L | | | $200.00 |
| Twinmill | 6258 | | USA | M-PK | CL | BR-D | | | $200.00 |
| Twinmill | 6258 | | USA | M-PK-H | CL | WH | | | $220.00 |
| Twinmill | 6258 | | USA | M-PK-H | CL | BK | | | $200.00 |
| Twinmill | 6258 | | USA | M-PK-H | CL | GY | | | $200.00 |
| Twinmill | 6258 | | USA | M-PK-H | CL | BR-L | | | $200.00 |
| Twinmill | 6258 | | USA | M-PK-H | CL | BR-D | | | $200.00 |
| Twinmill | 6258 | | USA | M-PK-S | CL | WH | | | $220.00 |
| Twinmill | 6258 | | USA | M-PK-S | CL | BK | | | $200.00 |
| Twinmill | 6258 | | USA | M-PK-S | CL | GY | | | $200.00 |
| Twinmill | 6258 | | USA | M-PK-S | CL | BR-L | | | $200.00 |
| Twinmill | 6258 | | USA | M-PK-S | CL | BR-D | | | $200.00 |
| Twinmill | 6258 | | USA | M-PR | CL | WH | | | $55.00 |
| Twinmill | 6258 | | USA | M-PR | CL | BK | | | $40.00 |
| Twinmill | 6258 | | USA | M-PR | CL | GY | | | $40.00 |
| Twinmill | 6258 | | USA | M-PR | CL | BR-L | | | $40.00 |
| Twinmill | 6258 | | USA | M-PR | CL | BR-D | | | $40.00 |
| Twinmill | 6258 | | USA | M-RD | CL | WH | | | $45.00 |
| Twinmill | 6258 | | USA | M-RD | CL | BK | | | $40.00 |
| Twinmill | 6258 | | USA | M-RD | CL | GY | | | $40.00 |
| Twinmill | 6258 | | USA | M-RD | CL | BR-L | | | $40.00 |
| Twinmill | 6258 | | USA | M-RD | CL | BR-D | | | $40.00 |
| Twinmill | 6258 | | USA | M-RD-R | CL | WH | | | $50.00 |
| Twinmill | 6258 | | USA | M-RD-R | CL | BK | | | $45.00 |
| Twinmill | 6258 | | USA | M-RD-R | CL | GY | | | $45.00 |
| Twinmill | 6258 | | USA | M-RD-R | CL | BR-L | | | $45.00 |
| Twinmill | 6258 | | USA | M-RD-R | CL | BR-D | | | $45.00 |
| Twinmill | 6258 | | USA | M-YW | CL | WH | | | $45.00 |
| Twinmill | 6258 | | USA | M-YW | CL | BK | | | $40.00 |
| Twinmill | 6258 | | USA | M-YW | CL | GY | | | $40.00 |
| Twinmill | 6258 | | USA | M-YW | CL | BR-L | | | $40.00 |
| Twinmill | 6258 | | USA | M-YW | CL | BR-D | | | $40.00 |
| Twinmill | 6258 | | USA | M-YW-L | CL | WH | | | $80.00 |
| Twinmill | 6258 | | USA | M-YW-L | CL | BK | | | $70.00 |
| Twinmill | 6258 | | USA | M-YW-L | CL | GY | | | $70.00 |
| Twinmill | 6258 | | USA | M-YW-L | CL | BR-L | | | $70.00 |
| Twinmill | 6258 | | USA | M-YW-L | CL | BR-D | | | $70.00 |
| | | | | | | | | | |
| Turbofire | 6259 | | USA | M-AQ | | WH | | | $50.00 |
| Turbofire | 6259 | | USA | M-AQ | | BK | | | $45.00 |
| Turbofire | 6259 | | USA | M-AQ | | GY | | | $45.00 |
| Turbofire | 6259 | | USA | M-AQ | | BR-L | | | $45.00 |
| Turbofire | 6259 | | USA | M-AQ | | BR-D | | | $45.00 |
| Turbofire | 6259 | | USA | M-BL | | WH | | | $45.00 |
| Turbofire | 6259 | | USA | M-BL | | BK | | | $40.00 |
| Turbofire | 6259 | | USA | M-BL | | GY | | | $40.00 |
| Turbofire | 6259 | | USA | M-BL | | BR-L | | | $40.00 |
| Turbofire | 6259 | | USA | M-BL | | BR-D | | | $40.00 |
| Turbofire | 6259 | | USA | M-BL-I | | WH | | | $60.00 |
| Turbofire | 6259 | | USA | M-BL-I | | BK | | | $55.00 |
| Turbofire | 6259 | | USA | M-BL-I | | GY | | | $55.00 |

## 1969 Variations

| Name | Number | Casting | Country | Color | Windows | Interior | Paint | Other | Value |
|------|--------|---------|---------|-------|---------|----------|-------|-------|-------|
| Turbofire | 6259 | | USA | M-BL-I | | BR-L | | | $55.00 |
| Turbofire | 6259 | | USA | M-BL-I | | BR-D | | | $55.00 |
| Turbofire | 6259 | | USA | M-BL-P | | WH | | | $55.00 |
| Turbofire | 6259 | | USA | M-BL-P | | BK | | | $40.00 |
| Turbofire | 6259 | | USA | M-BL-P | | GY | | | $40.00 |
| Turbofire | 6259 | | USA | M-BL-P | | BR-L | | | $40.00 |
| Turbofire | 6259 | | USA | M-BL-P | | BR-D | | | $40.00 |
| Turbofire | 6259 | | USA | M-BR-D | | WH | | | $60.00 |
| Turbofire | 6259 | | USA | M-BR-D | | BK | | | $55.00 |
| Turbofire | 6259 | | USA | M-BR-D | | GY | | | $55.00 |
| Turbofire | 6259 | | USA | M-BR-D | | BR-L | | | $55.00 |
| Turbofire | 6259 | | USA | M-BR-D | | BR-D | | | $55.00 |
| Turbofire | 6259 | | USA | M-BR-P | | WH | | | $55.00 |
| Turbofire | 6259 | | USA | M-BR-P | | BK | | | $50.00 |
| Turbofire | 6259 | | USA | M-BR-P | | GY | | | $50.00 |
| Turbofire | 6259 | | USA | M-BR-P | | BR-L | | | $50.00 |
| Turbofire | 6259 | | USA | M-BR-P | | BR-D | | | $50.00 |
| Turbofire | 6259 | | USA | M-GD | | WH | | | $45.00 |
| Turbofire | 6259 | | USA | M-GD | | BK | | | $40.00 |
| Turbofire | 6259 | | USA | M-GD | | GY | | | $40.00 |
| Turbofire | 6259 | | USA | M-GD | | BR-L | | | $40.00 |
| Turbofire | 6259 | | USA | M-GD | | BR-D | | | $40.00 |
| Turbofire | 6259 | | USA | M-GR | | WH | | | $55.00 |
| Turbofire | 6259 | | USA | M-GR | | BK | | | $40.00 |
| Turbofire | 6259 | | USA | M-GR | | GY | | | $40.00 |
| Turbofire | 6259 | | USA | M-GR | | BR-L | | | $40.00 |
| Turbofire | 6259 | | USA | M-GR | | BR-D | | | $40.00 |
| Turbofire | 6259 | | USA | M-GR-E | | WH | | | $60.00 |
| Turbofire | 6259 | | USA | M-GR-E | | BK | | | $55.00 |
| Turbofire | 6259 | | USA | M-GR-E | | GY | | | $55.00 |
| Turbofire | 6259 | | USA | M-GR-E | | BR-L | | | $55.00 |
| Turbofire | 6259 | | USA | M-GR-E | | BR-D | | | $55.00 |
| Turbofire | 6259 | | USA | M-GR-L | | WH | | | $60.00 |
| Turbofire | 6259 | | USA | M-GR-L | | BK | | | $50.00 |
| Turbofire | 6259 | | USA | M-GR-L | | GY | | | $50.00 |
| Turbofire | 6259 | | USA | M-GR-L | | BR-L | | | $50.00 |
| Turbofire | 6259 | | USA | M-GR-L | | BR-D | | | $50.00 |
| Turbofire | 6259 | | USA | M-GR-O | | WH | | | $50.00 |
| Turbofire | 6259 | | USA | M-GR-O | | BK | | | $45.00 |
| Turbofire | 6259 | | USA | M-GR-O | | GY | | | $45.00 |
| Turbofire | 6259 | | USA | M-GR-O | | BR-L | | | $45.00 |
| Turbofire | 6259 | | USA | M-GR-O | | BR-D | | | $45.00 |
| Turbofire | 6259 | | USA | M-MG | | WH | | | $55.00 |
| Turbofire | 6259 | | USA | M-MG | | BK | | | $50.00 |
| Turbofire | 6259 | | USA | M-MG | | GY | | | $50.00 |
| Turbofire | 6259 | | USA | M-MG | | BR-L | | | $50.00 |
| Turbofire | 6259 | | USA | M-MG | | BR-D | | | $50.00 |
| Turbofire | 6259 | | USA | M-OR | | WH | | | $45.00 |
| Turbofire | 6259 | | USA | M-OR | | BK | | | $40.00 |
| Turbofire | 6259 | | USA | M-OR | | GY | | | $40.00 |
| Turbofire | 6259 | | USA | M-OR | | BR-L | | | $40.00 |
| Turbofire | 6259 | | USA | M-OR | | BR-D | | | $40.00 |
| Turbofire | 6259 | | USA | M-PK | | WH | | | $260.00 |
| Turbofire | 6259 | | USA | M-PK | | BK | | | $240.00 |
| Turbofire | 6259 | | USA | M-PK | | GY | | | $240.00 |
| Turbofire | 6259 | | USA | M-PK | | BR-L | | | $240.00 |
| Turbofire | 6259 | | USA | M-PK | | BR-D | | | $240.00 |
| Turbofire | 6259 | | USA | M-PK-H | | WH | | | $260.00 |
| Turbofire | 6259 | | USA | M-PK-H | | BK | | | $240.00 |
| Turbofire | 6259 | | USA | M-PK-H | | GY | | | $240.00 |
| Turbofire | 6259 | | USA | M-PK-H | | BR-L | | | $240.00 |
| Turbofire | 6259 | | USA | M-PK-H | | BR-D | | | $240.00 |
| Turbofire | 6259 | | USA | M-PK-S | | WH | | | $260.00 |
| Turbofire | 6259 | | USA | M-PK-S | | BK | | | $240.00 |
| Turbofire | 6259 | | USA | M-PK-S | | GY | | | $240.00 |
| Turbofire | 6259 | | USA | M-PK-S | | BR-L | | | $240.00 |
| Turbofire | 6259 | | USA | M-PK-S | | BR-D | | | $240.00 |
| Turbofire | 6259 | | USA | M-PR | | WH | | | $75.00 |
| Turbofire | 6259 | | USA | M-PR | | BK | | | $65.00 |
| Turbofire | 6259 | | USA | M-PR | | GY | | | $65.00 |
| Turbofire | 6259 | | USA | M-PR | | BR-L | | | $65.00 |
| Turbofire | 6259 | | USA | M-PR | | BR-D | | | $65.00 |

## 1969 Variations

| Name | Number | Casting | Country | Color | Windows | Interior | Paint | Other | Value |
|---|---|---|---|---|---|---|---|---|---|
| Turbofire | 6259 | | USA | M-RD | | WH | | | $45.00 |
| Turbofire | 6259 | | USA | M-RD | | BK | | | $40.00 |
| Turbofire | 6259 | | USA | M-RD | | GY | | | $40.00 |
| Turbofire | 6259 | | USA | M-RD | | BR-L | | | $40.00 |
| Turbofire | 6259 | | USA | M-RD | | BR-D | | | $40.00 |
| Turbofire | 6259 | | USA | M-RD-R | | WH | | | $50.00 |
| Turbofire | 6259 | | USA | M-RD-R | | BK | | | $45.00 |
| Turbofire | 6259 | | USA | M-RD-R | | GY | | | $45.00 |
| Turbofire | 6259 | | USA | M-RD-R | | BR-L | | | $45.00 |
| Turbofire | 6259 | | USA | M-RD-R | | BR-D | | | $45.00 |
| Turbofire | 6259 | | USA | M-YW | | WH | | | $45.00 |
| Turbofire | 6259 | | USA | M-YW | | BK | | | $40.00 |
| Turbofire | 6259 | | USA | M-YW | | GY | | | $40.00 |
| Turbofire | 6259 | | USA | M-YW | | BR-L | | | $40.00 |
| Turbofire | 6259 | | USA | M-YW | | BR-D | | | $40.00 |
| Turbofire | 6259 | | USA | M-YW-L | | WH | | | $70.00 |
| Turbofire | 6259 | | USA | M-YW-L | | BK | | | $60.00 |
| Turbofire | 6259 | | USA | M-YW-L | | GY | | | $60.00 |
| Turbofire | 6259 | | USA | M-YW-L | | BR-L | | | $60.00 |
| Turbofire | 6259 | | USA | M-YW-L | | BR-D | | | $60.00 |
| Torero | 6260 | | USA | E-GR | | GY | | | $300.00 |
| Torero | 6260 | | USA | M-AQ | | WH | | | $50.00 |
| Torero | 6260 | | USA | M-AQ | | BK | | | $45.00 |
| Torero | 6260 | | USA | M-AQ | | GY | | | $45.00 |
| Torero | 6260 | | USA | M-AQ | | BR-L | | | $45.00 |
| Torero | 6260 | | USA | M-AQ | | BR-D | | | $45.00 |
| Torero | 6260 | | USA | M-BL | | WH | | | $50.00 |
| Torero | 6260 | | USA | M-BL | | BK | | | $45.00 |
| Torero | 6260 | | USA | M-BL | | GY | | | $45.00 |
| Torero | 6260 | | USA | M-BL | | BR-L | | | $45.00 |
| Torero | 6260 | | USA | M-BL | | BR-D | | | $45.00 |
| Torero | 6260 | | USA | M-BL-I | | WH | | | $60.00 |
| Torero | 6260 | | USA | M-BL-I | | BK | | | $55.00 |
| Torero | 6260 | | USA | M-BL-I | | GY | | | $55.00 |
| Torero | 6260 | | USA | M-BL-I | | BR-L | | | $55.00 |
| Torero | 6260 | | USA | M-BL-I | | BR-D | | | $55.00 |
| Torero | 6260 | | USA | M-BL-P | | WH | | | $55.00 |
| Torero | 6260 | | USA | M-BL-P | | BK | | | $50.00 |
| Torero | 6260 | | USA | M-BL-P | | GY | | | $50.00 |
| Torero | 6260 | | USA | M-BL-P | | BR-L | | | $50.00 |
| Torero | 6260 | | USA | M-BL-P | | BR-D | | | $50.00 |
| Torero | 6260 | | USA | M-BR-D | | WH | | | $60.00 |
| Torero | 6260 | | USA | M-BR-D | | BK | | | $55.00 |
| Torero | 6260 | | USA | M-BR-D | | GY | | | $55.00 |
| Torero | 6260 | | USA | M-BR-D | | BR-L | | | $55.00 |
| Torero | 6260 | | USA | M-BR-D | | BR-D | | | $55.00 |
| Torero | 6260 | | USA | M-BR-P | | WH | | | $55.00 |
| Torero | 6260 | | USA | M-BR-P | | BK | | | $50.00 |
| Torero | 6260 | | USA | M-BR-P | | GY | | | $50.00 |
| Torero | 6260 | | USA | M-BR-P | | BR-L | | | $50.00 |
| Torero | 6260 | | USA | M-BR-P | | BR-D | | | $50.00 |
| Torero | 6260 | | USA | M-GD | | WH | | | $45.00 |
| Torero | 6260 | | USA | M-GD | | BK | | | $40.00 |
| Torero | 6260 | | USA | M-GD | | GY | | | $40.00 |
| Torero | 6260 | | USA | M-GD | | BR-L | | | $40.00 |
| Torero | 6260 | | USA | M-GD | | BR-D | | | $40.00 |
| Torero | 6260 | | USA | M-GR | | WH | | | $65.00 |
| Torero | 6260 | | USA | M-GR | | BK | | | $60.00 |
| Torero | 6260 | | USA | M-GR | | GY | | | $45.00 |
| Torero | 6260 | | USA | M-GR | | BR-L | | | $45.00 |
| Torero | 6260 | | USA | M-GR | | BR-D | | | $45.00 |
| Torero | 6260 | | USA | M-GR-E | | WH | | | $55.00 |
| Torero | 6260 | | USA | M-GR-E | | BK | | | $40.00 |
| Torero | 6260 | | USA | M-GR-E | | GY | | | $50.00 |
| Torero | 6260 | | USA | M-GR-E | | BR-L | | | $50.00 |
| Torero | 6260 | | USA | M-GR-E | | BR-D | | | $50.00 |
| Torero | 6260 | | USA | M-GR-L | | WH | | | $55.00 |
| Torero | 6260 | | USA | M-GR-L | | BK | | | $50.00 |
| Torero | 6260 | | USA | M-GR-L | | GY | | | $50.00 |
| Torero | 6260 | | USA | M-GR-L | | BR-L | | | $50.00 |

**1969 Variations**

| Name | Number | Casting | Country | Color | Windows | Interior | Paint | Other | Value |
|---|---|---|---|---|---|---|---|---|---|
| Torero | 6260 | | USA | M-GR-L | | BR-D | | | $50.00 |
| Torero | 6260 | | USA | M-GR-O | | WH | | | $55.00 |
| Torero | 6260 | | USA | M-GR-O | | BK | | | $50.00 |
| Torero | 6260 | | USA | M-GR-O | | GY | | | $50.00 |
| Torero | 6260 | | USA | M-GR-O | | BR-L | | | $50.00 |
| Torero | 6260 | | USA | M-GR-O | | BR-D | | | $50.00 |
| Torero | 6260 | | USA | M-MG | | WH | | | $55.00 |
| Torero | 6260 | | USA | M-MG | | BK | | | $50.00 |
| Torero | 6260 | | USA | M-MG | | GY | | | $50.00 |
| Torero | 6260 | | USA | M-MG | | BR-L | | | $50.00 |
| Torero | 6260 | | USA | M-MG | | BR-D | | | $50.00 |
| Torero | 6260 | | USA | M-OR | | WH | | | $45.00 |
| Torero | 6260 | | USA | M-OR | | BK | | | $40.00 |
| Torero | 6260 | | USA | M-OR | | GY | | | $40.00 |
| Torero | 6260 | | USA | M-OR | | BR-L | | | $40.00 |
| Torero | 6260 | | USA | M-OR | | BR-D | | | $40.00 |
| Torero | 6260 | | USA | M-PK | | WH | | | $200.00 |
| Torero | 6260 | | USA | M-PK | | BK | | | $180.00 |
| Torero | 6260 | | USA | M-PK | | GY | | | $180.00 |
| Torero | 6260 | | USA | M-PK | | BR-L | | | $180.00 |
| Torero | 6260 | | USA | M-PK | | BR-D | | | $180.00 |
| Torero | 6260 | | USA | M-PK-H | | WH | | | $200.00 |
| Torero | 6260 | | USA | M-PK-H | | BK | | | $180.00 |
| Torero | 6260 | | USA | M-PK-H | | GY | | | $180.00 |
| Torero | 6260 | | USA | M-PK-H | | BR-L | | | $180.00 |
| Torero | 6260 | | USA | M-PK-H | | BR-D | | | $180.00 |
| Torero | 6260 | | USA | M-PK-S | | WH | | | $200.00 |
| Torero | 6260 | | USA | M-PK-S | | BK | | | $180.00 |
| Torero | 6260 | | USA | M-PK-S | | GY | | | $180.00 |
| Torero | 6260 | | USA | M-PK-S | | BR-L | | | $180.00 |
| Torero | 6260 | | USA | M-PK-S | | BR-D | | | $180.00 |
| Torero | 6260 | | USA | M-PR | | WH | | | $65.00 |
| Torero | 6260 | | USA | M-PR | | BK | | | $60.00 |
| Torero | 6260 | | USA | M-PR | | GY | | | $60.00 |
| Torero | 6260 | | USA | M-PR | | BR-L | | | $60.00 |
| Torero | 6260 | | USA | M-PR | | BR-D | | | $60.00 |
| Torero | 6260 | | USA | M-RD | | WH | | | $45.00 |
| Torero | 6260 | | USA | M-RD | | BK | | | $40.00 |
| Torero | 6260 | | USA | M-RD | | GY | | | $40.00 |
| Torero | 6260 | | USA | M-RD | | BR-L | | | $40.00 |
| Torero | 6260 | | USA | M-RD | | BR-D | | | $40.00 |
| Torero | 6260 | | USA | M-RD-R | | WH | | | $50.00 |
| Torero | 6260 | | USA | M-RD-R | | BK | | | $45.00 |
| Torero | 6260 | | USA | M-RD-R | | GY | | | $45.00 |
| Torero | 6260 | | USA | M-RD-R | | BR-L | | | $45.00 |
| Torero | 6260 | | USA | M-RD-R | | BR-D | | | $45.00 |
| Torero | 6260 | | USA | M-YW | | WH | | | $45.00 |
| Torero | 6260 | | USA | M-YW | | BK | | | $40.00 |
| Torero | 6260 | | USA | M-YW | | GY | | | $40.00 |
| Torero | 6260 | | USA | M-YW | | BR-L | | | $40.00 |
| Torero | 6260 | | USA | M-YW | | BR-D | | | $40.00 |
| Torero | 6260 | | USA | M-YW-L | | WH | | | $45.00 |
| Torero | 6260 | | USA | M-YW-L | | BK | | | $40.00 |
| Torero | 6260 | | USA | M-YW-L | | GY | | | $40.00 |
| Torero | 6260 | | USA | M-YW-L | | BR-L | | | $40.00 |
| Torero | 6260 | | USA | M-YW-L | | BR-D | | | $40.00 |
| | | | | | | | | | |
| Splittin' Image | 6261 | | USA | M-AQ | CL | WH | | | $55.00 |
| Splittin' Image | 6261 | | USA | M-AQ | CL | BK | | | $50.00 |
| Splittin' Image | 6261 | | USA | M-AQ | CL | GY | | | $50.00 |
| Splittin' Image | 6261 | | USA | M-AQ | CL | BR-L | | | $50.00 |
| Splittin' Image | 6261 | | USA | M-AQ | CL | BR-D | | | $50.00 |
| Splittin' Image | 6261 | | USA | M-BL | CL | WH | | | $45.00 |
| Splittin' Image | 6261 | | USA | M-BL | CL | BK | | | $40.00 |
| Splittin' Image | 6261 | | USA | M-BL | CL | GY | | | $40.00 |
| Splittin' Image | 6261 | | USA | M-BL | CL | BR-L | | | $40.00 |
| Splittin' Image | 6261 | | USA | M-BL | CL | BR-D | | | $40.00 |
| Splittin' Image | 6261 | | USA | M-BL-I | CL | WH | | | $60.00 |
| Splittin' Image | 6261 | | USA | M-BL-I | CL | BK | | | $55.00 |
| Splittin' Image | 6261 | | USA | M-BL-I | CL | GY | | | $55.00 |
| Splittin' Image | 6261 | | USA | M-BL-I | CL | BR-L | | | $55.00 |

## 1969 Variations

| Name | Number | Casting | Country | Color | Windows | Interior | Paint | Other | Value |
|---|---|---|---|---|---|---|---|---|---|
| Splittin' Image | 6261 | | USA | M-BL-I | CL | BR-D | | | $65.00 |
| Splittin' Image | 6261 | | USA | M-BL-P | CL | WH | | | $55.00 |
| Splittin' Image | 6261 | | USA | M-BL-P | CL | BK | | | $40.00 |
| Splittin' Image | 6261 | | USA | M-BL-P | CL | GY | | | $40.00 |
| Splittin' Image | 6261 | | USA | M-BL-P | CL | BR-L | | | $50.00 |
| Splittin' Image | 6261 | | USA | M-BL-P | CL | BR-D | | | $50.00 |
| Splittin' Image | 6261 | | USA | M-BR-D | CL | WH | | | $50.00 |
| Splittin' Image | 6261 | | USA | M-BR-D | CL | BK | | | $45.00 |
| Splittin' Image | 6261 | | USA | M-BR-D | CL | GY | | | $45.00 |
| Splittin' Image | 6261 | | USA | M-BR-D | CL | BR-L | | | $45.00 |
| Splittin' Image | 6261 | | USA | M-BR-D | CL | BR-D | | | $45.00 |
| Splittin' Image | 6261 | | USA | M-BR-P | CL | WH | | | $45.00 |
| Splittin' Image | 6261 | | USA | M-BR-P | CL | BK | | | $40.00 |
| Splittin' Image | 6261 | | USA | M-BR-P | CL | GY | | | $40.00 |
| Splittin' Image | 6261 | | USA | M-BR-P | CL | BR-L | | | $40.00 |
| Splittin' Image | 6261 | | USA | M-BR-P | CL | BR-D | | | $40.00 |
| Splittin' Image | 6261 | | USA | M-GD | CL | WH | | | $45.00 |
| Splittin' Image | 6261 | | USA | M-GD | CL | BK | | | $40.00 |
| Splittin' Image | 6261 | | USA | M-GD | CL | GY | | | $40.00 |
| Splittin' Image | 6261 | | USA | M-GD | CL | BR-L | | | $40.00 |
| Splittin' Image | 6261 | | USA | M-GD | CL | BR-D | | | $40.00 |
| Splittin' Image | 6261 | | USA | M-GR | CL | WH | | | $45.00 |
| Splittin' Image | 6261 | | USA | M-GR | CL | BK | | | $40.00 |
| Splittin' Image | 6261 | | USA | M-GR | CL | GY | | | $40.00 |
| Splittin' Image | 6261 | | USA | M-GR | CL | BR-L | | | $40.00 |
| Splittin' Image | 6261 | | USA | M-GR | CL | BR-D | | | $40.00 |
| Splittin' Image | 6261 | | USA | M-GR-E | CL | WH | | | $50.00 |
| Splittin' Image | 6261 | | USA | M-GR-E | CL | BK | | | $45.00 |
| Splittin' Image | 6261 | | USA | M-GR-E | CL | GY | | | $45.00 |
| Splittin' Image | 6261 | | USA | M-GR-E | CL | BR-L | | | $45.00 |
| Splittin' Image | 6261 | | USA | M-GR-E | CL | BR-D | | | $45.00 |
| Splittin' Image | 6261 | | USA | M-GR-L | CL | WH | | | $70.00 |
| Splittin' Image | 6261 | | USA | M-GR-L | CL | BK | | | $60.00 |
| Splittin' Image | 6261 | | USA | M-GR-L | CL | GY | | | $60.00 |
| Splittin' Image | 6261 | | USA | M-GR-L | CL | BR-L | | | $60.00 |
| Splittin' Image | 6261 | | USA | M-GR-L | CL | BR-D | | | $60.00 |
| Splittin' Image | 6261 | | USA | M-GR-O | CL | WH | | | $45.00 |
| Splittin' Image | 6261 | | USA | M-GR-O | CL | BK | | | $40.00 |
| Splittin' Image | 6261 | | USA | M-GR-O | CL | GY | | | $40.00 |
| Splittin' Image | 6261 | | USA | M-GR-O | CL | BR-L | | | $40.00 |
| Splittin' Image | 6261 | | USA | M-GR-O | CL | BR-D | | | $40.00 |
| Splittin' Image | 6261 | | USA | M-MG | CL | WH | | | $55.00 |
| Splittin' Image | 6261 | | USA | M-MG | CL | BK | | | $50.00 |
| Splittin' Image | 6261 | | USA | M-MG | CL | GY | | | $50.00 |
| Splittin' Image | 6261 | | USA | M-MG | CL | BR-L | | | $50.00 |
| Splittin' Image | 6261 | | USA | M-MG | CL | BR-D | | | $50.00 |
| Splittin' Image | 6261 | | USA | M-OR | CL | WH | | | $45.00 |
| Splittin' Image | 6261 | | USA | M-OR | CL | BK | | | $40.00 |
| Splittin' Image | 6261 | | USA | M-OR | CL | GY | | | $40.00 |
| Splittin' Image | 6261 | | USA | M-OR | CL | BR-L | | | $40.00 |
| Splittin' Image | 6261 | | USA | M-OR | CL | BR-D | | | $40.00 |
| Splittin' Image | 6261 | | USA | M-PK | CL | WH | | | $240.00 |
| Splittin' Image | 6261 | | USA | M-PK | CL | BK | | | $220.00 |
| Splittin' Image | 6261 | | USA | M-PK | CL | GY | | | $220.00 |
| Splittin' Image | 6261 | | USA | M-PK | CL | BR-L | | | $220.00 |
| Splittin' Image | 6261 | | USA | M-PK | CL | BR-D | | | $220.00 |
| Splittin' Image | 6261 | | USA | M-PK-H | CL | WH | | | $220.00 |
| Splittin' Image | 6261 | | USA | M-PK-H | CL | BK | | | $220.00 |
| Splittin' Image | 6261 | | USA | M-PK-H | CL | GY | | | $220.00 |
| Splittin' Image | 6261 | | USA | M-PK-H | CL | BR-L | | | $220.00 |
| Splittin' Image | 6261 | | USA | M-PK-H | CL | BR-D | | | $220.00 |
| Splittin' Image | 6261 | | USA | M-PK-S | CL | WH | | | $240.00 |
| Splittin' Image | 6261 | | USA | M-PK-S | CL | BK | | | $220.00 |
| Splittin' Image | 6261 | | USA | M-PK-S | CL | GY | | | $220.00 |
| Splittin' Image | 6261 | | USA | M-PK-S | CL | BR-L | | | $220.00 |
| Splittin' Image | 6261 | | USA | M-PK-S | CL | BR-D | | | $220.00 |
| Splittin' Image | 6261 | | USA | M-PR | CL | WH | | | $45.00 |
| Splittin' Image | 6261 | | USA | M-PR | CL | BK | | | $40.00 |
| Splittin' Image | 6261 | | USA | M-PR | CL | GY | | | $40.00 |
| Splittin' Image | 6261 | | USA | M-PR | CL | BR-L | | | $40.00 |
| Splittin' Image | 6261 | | USA | M-PR | CL | BR-D | | | $40.00 |
| Splittin' Image | 6261 | | USA | M-RD | CL | WH | | | $45.00 |

## 1969 Variations

| Name | Number | Casting | Country | Color | Windows | Interior | Paint | Other | Value |
|---|---|---|---|---|---|---|---|---|---|
| Splittin' Image | 6261 | | USA | M-RD | CL | BK | | | $40.00 |
| Splittin' Image | 6261 | | USA | M-RD | CL | GY | | | $40.00 |
| Splittin' Image | 6261 | | USA | M-RD | CL | BR-L | | | $40.00 |
| Splittin' Image | 6261 | | USA | M-RD | CL | BR-D | | | $40.00 |
| Splittin' Image | 6261 | | USA | M-RD-R | CL | WH | | | $50.00 |
| Splittin' Image | 6261 | | USA | M-RD-R | CL | BK | | | $45.00 |
| Splittin' Image | 6261 | | USA | M-RD-R | CL | GY | | | $45.00 |
| Splittin' Image | 6261 | | USA | M-RD-R | CL | BR-L | | | $45.00 |
| Splittin' Image | 6261 | | USA | M-RD-R | CL | BR-D | | | $45.00 |
| Splittin' Image | 6261 | | USA | M-YW | CL | WH | | | $45.00 |
| Splittin' Image | 6261 | | USA | M-YW | CL | BK | | | $40.00 |
| Splittin' Image | 6261 | | USA | M-YW | CL | GY | | | $40.00 |
| Splittin' Image | 6261 | | USA | M-YW | CL | BR-L | | | $40.00 |
| Splittin' Image | 6261 | | USA | M-YW | CL | BR-D | | | $40.00 |
| Splittin' Image | 6261 | | USA | M-YW-L | CL | WH | | | $80.00 |
| Splittin' Image | 6261 | | USA | M-YW-L | CL | BK | | | $70.00 |
| Splittin' Image | 6261 | | USA | M-YW-L | CL | GY | | | $70.00 |
| Splittin' Image | 6261 | | USA | M-YW-L | CL | BR-L | | | $70.00 |
| Splittin' Image | 6261 | | USA | M-YW-L | CL | BR-D | | | $70.00 |
| | | | | | | | | | |
| Lotus Turbine | 6262 | | HK | CH | | WH | | | $400.00 |
| Lotus Turbine | 6262 | | HK | CH | | BK | | | $400.00 |
| Lotus Turbine | 6262 | | HK | M-AQ | | WH | | | $90.00 |
| Lotus Turbine | 6262 | | HK | M-AQ | | BK | | | $25.00 |
| Lotus Turbine | 6262 | | HK | M-BL | | WH | | | $110.00 |
| Lotus Turbine | 6262 | | HK | M-BL | | BK | | | $30.00 |
| Lotus Turbine | 6262 | | HK | M-BR-D | | WH | | | $150.00 |
| Lotus Turbine | 6262 | | HK | M-BR-D | | BK | | | $40.00 |
| Lotus Turbine | 6262 | | HK | M-BR-P | | WH | | | $130.00 |
| Lotus Turbine | 6262 | | HK | M-BR-P | | BK | | | $35.00 |
| Lotus Turbine | 6262 | | HK | M-GR | | WH | | | $90.00 |
| Lotus Turbine | 6262 | | HK | M-GR | | BK | | | $25.00 |
| Lotus Turbine | 6262 | | HK | M-GR-E | | WH | | | $110.00 |
| Lotus Turbine | 6262 | | HK | M-GR-E | | BK | | | $30.00 |
| Lotus Turbine | 6262 | | HK | M-GR-O | | WH | | | $130.00 |
| Lotus Turbine | 6262 | | HK | M-GR-O | | BK | | | $35.00 |
| Lotus Turbine | 6262 | | HK | M-MG | | WH | | | $180.00 |
| Lotus Turbine | 6262 | | HK | M-MG | | BK | | | $45.00 |
| Lotus Turbine | 6262 | | HK | M-OR | | WH | | | $90.00 |
| Lotus Turbine | 6262 | | HK | M-OR | | BK | | | $25.00 |
| Lotus Turbine | 6262 | | HK | M-PR | | WH | | | $90.00 |
| Lotus Turbine | 6262 | | HK | M-PR | | BK | | | $25.00 |
| Lotus Turbine | 6262 | | HK | M-RD | | WH | | | $90.00 |
| Lotus Turbine | 6262 | | HK | M-RD | | BK | | | $25.00 |
| Lotus Turbine | 6262 | | HK | M-RD-R | | WH | | | $110.00 |
| Lotus Turbine | 6262 | | HK | M-RD-R | | BK | | | $30.00 |
| | | | | | | | | | |
| Indy Eagle | 6263 | | HK | GD | BL | WH | | | $300.00 |
| Indy Eagle | 6263 | | HK | GD | BL | BK | | | $80.00 |
| Indy Eagle | 6263 | | HK | M-AQ | BL | WH | | | $90.00 |
| Indy Eagle | 6263 | | HK | M-AQ | BL | BK | | | $25.00 |
| Indy Eagle | 6263 | | HK | M-BL | BL | WH | | | $90.00 |
| Indy Eagle | 6263 | | HK | M-BL | BL | BK | | | $25.00 |
| Indy Eagle | 6263 | | HK | M-BL | CL | WH | | | $300.00 |
| Indy Eagle | 6263 | | HK | M-BR-D | BL | WH | | | $110.00 |
| Indy Eagle | 6263 | | HK | M-BR-D | BL | BK | | | $30.00 |
| Indy Eagle | 6263 | | HK | M-BR-P | BL | WH | | | $130.00 |
| Indy Eagle | 6263 | | HK | M-BR-P | BL | BK | | | $35.00 |
| Indy Eagle | 6263 | | HK | M-GR | BL | WH | | | $90.00 |
| Indy Eagle | 6263 | | HK | M-GR | BL | BK | | | $25.00 |
| Indy Eagle | 6263 | | HK | M-GR-E | BL | WH | | | $110.00 |
| Indy Eagle | 6263 | | HK | M-GR-E | BL | BK | | | $30.00 |
| Indy Eagle | 6263 | | HK | M-GR-O | BL | WH | | | $180.00 |
| Indy Eagle | 6263 | | HK | M-GR-O | BL | BK | | | $45.00 |
| Indy Eagle | 6263 | | HK | M-OR | BL | WH | | | $90.00 |
| Indy Eagle | 6263 | | HK | M-OR | BL | BK | | | $25.00 |
| Indy Eagle | 6263 | | HK | M-PR | BL | WH | | | $130.00 |
| Indy Eagle | 6263 | | HK | M-PR | BL | BK | | | $35.00 |
| Indy Eagle | 6263 | | HK | M-RD | BL | WH | | | $90.00 |
| Indy Eagle | 6263 | | HK | M-RD | BL | BK | | | $25.00 |

## 1969 Variations

| Name | Number | Casting | Country | Color | Windows | Interior | Paint | Other | Value |
|---|---|---|---|---|---|---|---|---|---|
| Indy Eagle | 6263 | | HK | M-RD | CL | WH | | | $300.00 |
| Indy Eagle | 6263 | | HK | M-RD-R | BL | WH | | | $110.00 |
| Indy Eagle | 6263 | | HK | M-RD-R | BL | BK | | | $30.00 |
| | | | | | | | | | |
| Brabham Repco F1 | 6264 | | HK | CH | | WH | | | $450.00 |
| Brabham Repco F1 | 6264 | | HK | CH | | BK | | | $120.00 |
| Brabham Repco F1 | 6264 | | HK | E-GR-D | | WH | | | $130.00 |
| Brabham Repco F1 | 6264 | | HK | E-GR-D | | BK | | | $35.00 |
| Brabham Repco F1 | 6264 | | HK | M-AQ | | WH | | | $90.00 |
| Brabham Repco F1 | 6264 | | HK | M-AQ | | BK | | | $25.00 |
| Brabham Repco F1 | 6264 | | HK | M-BL | | WH | | | $90.00 |
| Brabham Repco F1 | 6264 | | HK | M-BL | | BK | | | $25.00 |
| Brabham Repco F1 | 6264 | | HK | M-BR-D | | WH | | | $110.00 |
| Brabham Repco F1 | 6264 | | HK | M-BR-D | | BK | | | $35.00 |
| Brabham Repco F1 | 6264 | | HK | M-BR-P | | WH | | | $110.00 |
| Brabham Repco F1 | 6264 | | HK | M-BR-P | | BK | | | $30.00 |
| Brabham Repco F1 | 6264 | | HK | M-GR | | WH | | | $90.00 |
| Brabham Repco F1 | 6264 | | HK | M-GR | | BK | | | $25.00 |
| Brabham Repco F1 | 6264 | | HK | M-GR-E | | WH | | | $110.00 |
| Brabham Repco F1 | 6264 | | HK | M-GR-E | | BK | | | $30.00 |
| Brabham Repco F1 | 6264 | | HK | M-GR-O | | WH | | | $90.00 |
| Brabham Repco F1 | 6264 | | HK | M-GR-O | | BK | | | $25.00 |
| Brabham Repco F1 | 6264 | | HK | M-OR | | WH | | | $130.00 |
| Brabham Repco F1 | 6264 | | HK | M-OR | | BK | | | $35.00 |
| Brabham Repco F1 | 6264 | | HK | M-PR | | WH | | | $110.00 |
| Brabham Repco F1 | 6264 | | HK | M-PR | | BK | | | $30.00 |
| Brabham Repco F1 | 6264 | | HK | M-RD | | WH | | | $110.00 |
| Brabham Repco F1 | 6264 | | HK | M-RD | | BK | | | $30.00 |
| Brabham Repco F1 | 6264 | | HK | M-RD-R | | WH | | | $130.00 |
| Brabham Repco F1 | 6264 | | HK | M-RD-R | | BK | | | $35.00 |
| | | | | | | | | | |
| Shelby Turbine | 6265 | | HK | CH | | BK | | | $400.00 |
| Shelby Turbine | 6265 | | HK | CH | | BR-L | | | $400.00 |
| Shelby Turbine | 6265 | | HK | M-AQ | | BK | | | $110.00 |
| Shelby Turbine | 6265 | | HK | M-AQ | | BR-L | | | $30.00 |
| Shelby Turbine | 6265 | | HK | M-BL | | BK | | | $110.00 |
| Shelby Turbine | 6265 | | HK | M-BL | | BR-L | | | $30.00 |
| Shelby Turbine | 6265 | | HK | M-BR-D | | BK | | | $170.00 |
| Shelby Turbine | 6265 | | HK | M-BR-D | | BR-L | | | $45.00 |
| Shelby Turbine | 6265 | | HK | M-BR-P | | BK | | | $150.00 |
| Shelby Turbine | 6265 | | HK | M-BR-P | | BR-L | | | $40.00 |
| Shelby Turbine | 6265 | | HK | M-GD | | BK | | | $170.00 |
| Shelby Turbine | 6265 | | HK | M-GD | | BR-L | | | $45.00 |
| Shelby Turbine | 6265 | | HK | M-GR | | BK | | | $110.00 |
| Shelby Turbine | 6265 | | HK | M-GR | | BR-L | | | $30.00 |
| Shelby Turbine | 6265 | | HK | M-GR-E | | BK | | | $130.00 |
| Shelby Turbine | 6265 | | HK | M-GR-E | | BR-L | | | $35.00 |
| Shelby Turbine | 6265 | | HK | M-GR-L | | BK | | | $150.00 |
| Shelby Turbine | 6265 | | HK | M-GR-L | | BR-L | | | $40.00 |
| Shelby Turbine | 6265 | | HK | M-GR-O | | BK | | | $150.00 |
| Shelby Turbine | 6265 | | HK | M-GR-O | | BR-L | | | $40.00 |
| Shelby Turbine | 6265 | | HK | M-OR | | BK | | | $110.00 |
| Shelby Turbine | 6265 | | HK | M-OR | | BR-L | | | $30.00 |
| Shelby Turbine | 6265 | | HK | M-PR | | BK | | | $150.00 |
| Shelby Turbine | 6265 | | HK | M-PR | | BR-L | | | $40.00 |
| Shelby Turbine | 6265 | | HK | M-RD | | BK | | | $110.00 |
| Shelby Turbine | 6265 | | HK | M-RD | | BR-L | | | $30.00 |
| Shelby Turbine | 6265 | | HK | M-RD-R | | BK | | | $130.00 |
| Shelby Turbine | 6265 | | HK | M-RD-R | | BR-L | | | $35.00 |
| Shelby Turbine | 6265 | | HK | M-YW | | BK | | | $150.00 |
| Shelby Turbine | 6265 | | HK | M-YW | | BR-L | | | $40.00 |
| Shelby Turbine | 6265 | | HK | M-YW-L | | BK | | | $170.00 |
| Shelby Turbine | 6265 | | HK | M-YW-L | | BR-L | | | $45.00 |
| | | | | | | | | | |
| Continental Mark III | 6266 | | USA | M-AQ | | WH | | | $50.00 |
| Continental Mark III | 6266 | | USA | M-AQ | | BK | | | $125.00 |
| Continental Mark III | 6266 | | USA | M-BL | | WH | | | $50.00 |
| Continental Mark III | 6266 | | USA | M-BL | | BK | | | $125.00 |
| Continental Mark III | 6266 | | USA | M-BL-I | | WH | | | $60.00 |
| Continental Mark III | 6266 | | USA | M-BL-I | | BK | | | $150.00 |

## 1969 Variations

| Name | Number | Casting | Country | Color | Windows | Interior | Paint | Other | Value |
|---|---|---|---|---|---|---|---|---|---|
| Continental Mark III | 6266 | | USA | M-BL-P | | WH | | | $50.00 |
| Continental Mark III | 6266 | | USA | M-BL-P | | BK | | | $125.00 |
| Continental Mark III | 6266 | | USA | M-GD | | WH | | | $50.00 |
| Continental Mark III | 6266 | | USA | M-GD | | BK | | | $125.00 |
| Continental Mark III | 6266 | | USA | M-GR | | WH | | | $60.00 |
| Continental Mark III | 6266 | | USA | M-GR | | BK | | | $140.00 |
| Continental Mark III | 6266 | | USA | M-GR-E | | WH | | | $65.00 |
| Continental Mark III | 6266 | | USA | M-GR-E | | BK | | | $150.00 |
| Continental Mark III | 6266 | | USA | M-GR-L | | WH | | | $50.00 |
| Continental Mark III | 6266 | | USA | M-GR-L | | BK | | | $125.00 |
| Continental Mark III | 6266 | | USA | M-GR-O | | WH | | | $140.00 |
| Continental Mark III | 6266 | | USA | M-GR-O | | BK | | | $200.00 |
| Continental Mark III | 6266 | | USA | M-MG | | WH | | | $55.00 |
| Continental Mark III | 6266 | | USA | M-MG | | BK | | | $130.00 |
| Continental Mark III | 6266 | | USA | M-OR | | WH | | | $50.00 |
| Continental Mark III | 6266 | | USA | M-OR | | BK | | | $125.00 |
| Continental Mark III | 6266 | | USA | M-PK | | WH | | | $240.00 |
| Continental Mark III | 6266 | | USA | M-PK | | BK | | | $500.00 |
| Continental Mark III | 6266 | | USA | M-PK-H | | WH | | | $240.00 |
| Continental Mark III | 6266 | | USA | M-PK-H | | BK | | | $500.00 |
| Continental Mark III | 6266 | | USA | M-PK-S | | WH | | | $240.00 |
| Continental Mark III | 6266 | | USA | M-PK-S | | BK | | | $500.00 |
| Continental Mark III | 6266 | | USA | M-PR | | WH | | | $60.00 |
| Continental Mark III | 6266 | | USA | M-PR | | BK | | | $125.00 |
| Continental Mark III | 6266 | | USA | M-RD | | WH | | | $50.00 |
| Continental Mark III | 6266 | | USA | M-RD | | BK | | | $125.00 |
| Continental Mark III | 6266 | | USA | M-RD-R | | WH | | | $55.00 |
| Continental Mark III | 6266 | | USA | M-RD-R | | BK | | | $130.00 |
| Continental Mark III | 6266 | | USA | M-YW | | WH | | | $50.00 |
| Continental Mark III | 6266 | | USA | M-YW | | BK | | | $125.00 |
| Continental Mark III | 6266 | | USA | M-YW-L | | WH | | | $60.00 |
| Continental Mark III | 6266 | | USA | M-YW-L | | BK | | | $150.00 |
| Custom AMX | 6267 | | USA | M-AQ | | WH | | | $85.00 |
| Custom AMX | 6267 | | USA | M-BL | | WH | | | $90.00 |
| Custom AMX | 6267 | | USA | M-BL | | WH | | Ed Shaver Decals | $2,500.00 |
| Custom AMX | 6267 | | USA | M-GD | | WH | | | $85.00 |
| Custom AMX | 6267 | | USA | M-GR | | WH | | | $85.00 |
| Custom AMX | 6267 | | USA | M-GR-E | | WH | | | $90.00 |
| Custom AMX | 6267 | | USA | M-GR-L | | WH | | | $130.00 |
| Custom AMX | 6267 | | USA | M-MG | | WH | | | $140.00 |
| Custom AMX | 6267 | | USA | M-OR | | WH | | | $140.00 |
| Custom AMX | 6267 | | USA | M-PK | | WH | | | $220.00 |
| Custom AMX | 6267 | | USA | M-PK-H | | WH | | | $220.00 |
| Custom AMX | 6267 | | USA | M-PK-S | | WH | | | $220.00 |
| Custom AMX | 6267 | | USA | M-PR | | WH | | | $200.00 |
| Custom AMX | 6267 | | USA | M-RD | | WH | | | $70.00 |
| Custom AMX | 6267 | | USA | M-RD-R | | WH | | | $75.00 |
| Custom AMX | 6267 | | USA | M-YW | | WH | | | $85.00 |
| Custom AMX | 6267 | | USA | M-YW-L | | WH | | | $140.00 |
| Custom Charger | 6268 | | USA | E-OR | | WH | | | $300.00 |
| Custom Charger | 6268 | | USA | M-AQ | | WH | | | $150.00 |
| Custom Charger | 6268 | | USA | M-BL | | WH | | | $150.00 |
| Custom Charger | 6268 | | USA | M-BL-I | | WH | | | $300.00 |
| Custom Charger | 6268 | | USA | M-BL-P | | WH | | | $300.00 |
| Custom Charger | 6268 | | USA | M-BR-D | | WH | | | $460.00 |
| Custom Charger | 6268 | | USA | M-BR-P | | WH | | | $420.00 |
| Custom Charger | 6268 | | USA | M-GD | | WH | | | $180.00 |
| Custom Charger | 6268 | | USA | M-GR | | WH | | | $260.00 |
| Custom Charger | 6268 | | USA | M-GR-E | | WH | | | $280.00 |
| Custom Charger | 6268 | | USA | M-GR-L | | WH | | | $200.00 |
| Custom Charger | 6268 | | USA | M-GR-O | | WH | | | $260.00 |
| Custom Charger | 6268 | | USA | M-MG | | WH | | | $260.00 |
| Custom Charger | 6268 | | USA | M-OR | | WH | | | $260.00 |
| Custom Charger | 6268 | | USA | M-PK | | WH | | | $190.00 |
| Custom Charger | 6268 | | USA | M-PK-H | | WH | | | $190.00 |
| Custom Charger | 6268 | | USA | M-PK-S | | WH | | | $190.00 |
| Custom Charger | 6268 | | USA | M-PR | | WH | | | $240.00 |

## 1969 Variations

| Name | Number | Casting | Country | Color | Windows | Interior | Paint | Other | Value |
|---|---|---|---|---|---|---|---|---|---|
| Custom Charger | 6268 | | USA | M-RD | | WH | | | $180.00 |
| Custom Charger | 6268 | | USA | M-RD-R | | WH | | | $200.00 |
| Custom Charger | 6268 | | USA | M-YW | | WH | | | $180.00 |
| Custom Charger | 6268 | | USA | M-YW-L | | WH | | | $230.00 |
| Police Cruiser | 6269 | | USA | WH/BK | | WH | | Transparent RD light | $120.00 |
| Police Cruiser | 6269 | | USA | WH/BK | | WH | | Opaque RD light | $120.00 |
| Volks Beach Bomb | 6274 | | HK | M-AQ | BL | WH | | | $140.00 |
| Volks Beach Bomb | 6274 | | HK | M-AQ | BL | BK | | | $130.00 |
| Volks Beach Bomb | 6274 | | HK | M-AQ | BL | GY | | | $130.00 |
| Volks Beach Bomb | 6274 | | HK | M-AQ | BL | BR-L | | | $130.00 |
| Volks Beach Bomb | 6274 | | HK | M-AQ | BL | BR-D | | | $130.00 |
| Volks Beach Bomb | 6274 | | HK | M-BL | BL | WH | | | $140.00 |
| Volks Beach Bomb | 6274 | | HK | M-BL | BL | BK | | | $130.00 |
| Volks Beach Bomb | 6274 | | HK | M-BL | BL | GY | | | $130.00 |
| Volks Beach Bomb | 6274 | | HK | M-BL | BL | BR-L | | | $130.00 |
| Volks Beach Bomb | 6274 | | HK | M-BL | BL | BR-D | | | $130.00 |
| Volks Beach Bomb | 6274 | Rear boards | HK | M-BL | BL | WH | | | $10,000.00 |
| Volks Beach Bomb | 6274 | Rear boards | HK | M-BL | BL | BK | | | $10,000.00 |
| Volks Beach Bomb | 6274 | Rear boards | HK | M-BL | BL | GY | | | $10,000.00 |
| Volks Beach Bomb | 6274 | Rear boards | HK | M-BL | BL | BR-L | | | $10,000.00 |
| Volks Beach Bomb | 6274 | Rear boards | HK | M-BL | BL | BR-D | | | $10,000.00 |
| Volks Beach Bomb | 6274 | Rear boards | HK | M-BL-I | BL | WH | | | $10,000.00 |
| Volks Beach Bomb | 6274 | Rear boards | HK | M-BL-I | BL | BK | | | $10,000.00 |
| Volks Beach Bomb | 6274 | Rear boards | HK | M-BL-I | BL | GY | | | $10,000.00 |
| Volks Beach Bomb | 6274 | Rear boards | HK | M-BL-I | BL | BR-L | | | $10,000.00 |
| Volks Beach Bomb | 6274 | Rear boards | HK | M-BL-I | BL | BR-D | | | $10,000.00 |
| Volks Beach Bomb | 6274 | Rear boards | HK | M-BL-P | RI | WH | | | $10,000.00 |
| Volks Beach Bomb | 6274 | Rear boards | HK | M-BL-P | BL | BK | | | $10,000.00 |
| Volks Beach Bomb | 6274 | Rear boards | HK | M-BL-P | BL | GY | | | $10,000.00 |
| Volks Beach Bomb | 6274 | Rear boards | HK | M-BL-P | BL | BR-L | | | $10,000.00 |
| Volks Beach Bomb | 6274 | Rear boards | HK | M-BL-P | BL | BR-D | | | $10,000.00 |
| Volks Beach Bomb | 6274 | | HK | M-BR-D | BL | WH | | | $200.00 |
| Volks Beach Bomb | 6274 | | HK | M-BR-D | BL | BK | | | $180.00 |
| Volks Beach Bomb | 6274 | | HK | M-BR-D | BL | GY | | | $180.00 |
| Volks Beach Bomb | 6274 | | HK | M-BR-D | BL | BR-L | | | $180.00 |
| Volks Beach Bomb | 6274 | | HK | M-BR-D | BL | BR-D | | | $180.00 |
| Volks Beach Bomb | 6274 | | HK | M-BR-P | BL | WH | | | $180.00 |
| Volks Beach Bomb | 6274 | | HK | M-BR-P | BL | BK | | | $160.00 |
| Volks Beach Bomb | 6274 | | HK | M-BR-P | BL | GY | | | $160.00 |
| Volks Beach Bomb | 6274 | | HK | M-BR-P | BL | BR-L | | | $160.00 |
| Volks Beach Bomb | 6274 | | HK | M-BR-P | BL | BR-D | | | $160.00 |
| Volks Beach Bomb | 6274 | | HK | M-GD | BL | WH | | | $140.00 |
| Volks Beach Bomb | 6274 | | HK | M-GD | BL | BK | | | $130.00 |
| Volks Beach Bomb | 6274 | | HK | M-GD | BL | GY | | | $130.00 |
| Volks Beach Bomb | 6274 | | HK | M-GD | BL | BR-L | | | $130.00 |
| Volks Beach Bomb | 6274 | | HK | M-GD | BL | BR-D | | | $130.00 |
| Volks Beach Bomb | 6274 | Rear boards | HK | M-GD | BL | WH | | | $10,000.00 |
| Volks Beach Bomb | 6274 | Rear boards | HK | M-GD | BL | BK | | | $10,000.00 |
| Volks Beach Bomb | 6274 | Rear boards | HK | M-GD | BL | GY | | | $10,000.00 |
| Volks Beach Bomb | 6274 | Rear boards | HK | M-GD | BL | BR-L | | | $10,000.00 |
| Volks Beach Bomb | 6274 | Rear boards | HK | M-GD | BL | BR-D | | | $10,000.00 |
| Volks Beach Bomb | 6274 | | HK | M-GR | BL | WH | | | $70.00 |
| Volks Beach Bomb | 6274 | | HK | M-GR | BL | BK | | | $65.00 |
| Volks Beach Bomb | 6274 | | HK | M-GR | BL | GY | | | $65.00 |
| Volks Beach Bomb | 6274 | | HK | M-GR | BL | BR-L | | | $65.00 |
| Volks Beach Bomb | 6274 | | HK | M-GR | BL | BR-D | | | $65.00 |
| Volks Beach Bomb | 6274 | Rear boards | HK | M-GR | BL | WH | | | $10,000.00 |
| Volks Beach Bomb | 6274 | Rear boards | HK | M-GR | BL | BK | | | $10,000.00 |
| Volks Beach Bomb | 6274 | Rear boards | HK | M-GR | BL | GY | | | $10,000.00 |
| Volks Beach Bomb | 6274 | Rear boards | HK | M-GR | BL | BR-L | | | $10,000.00 |
| Volks Beach Bomb | 6274 | Rear boards | HK | M-GR | BL | BR-D | | | $10,000.00 |
| Volks Beach Bomb | 6274 | | HK | M-GR-E | BL | WH | | | $160.00 |
| Volks Beach Bomb | 6274 | | HK | M-GR-E | BL | BK | | | $150.00 |
| Volks Beach Bomb | 6274 | | HK | M-GR-E | BL | GY | | | $150.00 |
| Volks Beach Bomb | 6274 | | HK | M-GR-E | BL | BR-L | | | $150.00 |
| Volks Beach Bomb | 6274 | | HK | M-GR-E | BL | BR-D | | | $150.00 |
| Volks Beach Bomb | 6274 | Rear boards | HK | M-GR-E | BL | WH | | | $10,000.00 |
| Volks Beach Bomb | 6274 | Rear boards | HK | M-GR-E | BL | BK | | | $10,000.00 |

## 1969 Variations

| Name | Number | Casting | Country | Color | Windows | Interior | Paint | Other | Value |
|---|---|---|---|---|---|---|---|---|---|
| Volks Beach Bomb | 6274 | Rear boards | HK | M-GR-E | BL | GY | | | $10,000.00 |
| Volks Beach Bomb | 6274 | Rear boards | HK | M-GR-E | BL | BR-L | | | $10,000.00 |
| Volks Beach Bomb | 6274 | Rear boards | HK | M-GR-E | BL | BR-D | | | $10,000.00 |
| Volks Beach Bomb | 6274 | | HK | M-GR-L | BL | WH | | | $90.00 |
| Volks Beach Bomb | 6274 | | HK | M-GR-L | BL | BK | | | $80.00 |
| Volks Beach Bomb | 6274 | | HK | M-GR-L | BL | GY | | | $80.00 |
| Volks Beach Bomb | 6274 | | HK | M-GR-L | BL | BR-L | | | $80.00 |
| Volks Beach Bomb | 6274 | | HK | M-GR-L | BL | BR-D | | | $80.00 |
| Volks Beach Bomb | 6274 | Rear boards | HK | M-GR-L | BL | WH | | | $10,000.00 |
| Volks Beach Bomb | 6274 | Rear boards | HK | M-GR-L | BL | BK | | | $10,000.00 |
| Volks Beach Bomb | 6274 | Rear boards | HK | M-GR-L | BL | GY | | | $10,000.00 |
| Volks Beach Bomb | 6274 | Rear boards | HK | M-GR-L | BL | BR-L | | | $10,000.00 |
| Volks Beach Bomb | 6274 | Rear boards | HK | M-GR-L | BL | BR-D | | | $10,000.00 |
| Volks Beach Bomb | 6274 | | HK | M-GR-O | BL | WH | | | $140.00 |
| Volks Beach Bomb | 6274 | | HK | M-GR-O | BL | BK | | | $130.00 |
| Volks Beach Bomb | 6274 | | HK | M-GR-O | BL | GY | | | $130.00 |
| Volks Beach Bomb | 6274 | | HK | M-GR-O | BL | BR-L | | | $130.00 |
| Volks Beach Bomb | 6274 | | HK | M-GR-O | BL | BR-D | | | $130.00 |
| Volks Beach Bomb | 6274 | Rear boards | HK | M-PK-H | BL | WH | | | $70,000.00 |
| Volks Beach Bomb | 6274 | | HK | M-OR | BL | WH | | | $140.00 |
| Volks Beach Bomb | 6274 | | HK | M-OR | BL | BK | | | $130.00 |
| Volks Beach Bomb | 6274 | | HK | M-OR | BL | GY | | | $130.00 |
| Volks Beach Bomb | 6274 | | HK | M-OR | BL | BR-L | | | $130.00 |
| Volks Beach Bomb | 6274 | | HK | M-OR | BL | BR-D | | | $130.00 |
| Volks Beach Bomb | 6274 | | HK | M-PR | BL | WH | | | $160.00 |
| Volks Beach Bomb | 6274 | | HK | M-PR | BL | BK | | | $140.00 |
| Volks Beach Bomb | 6274 | | HK | M-PR | BL | GY | | | $140.00 |
| Volks Beach Bomb | 6274 | | HK | M-PR | BL | BR-L | | | $140.00 |
| Volks Beach Bomb | 6274 | | HK | M-PR | BL | BR-D | | | $140.00 |
| Volks Beach Bomb | 6274 | Rear boards | HK | M-PR | BL | WH | | | $10,000.00 |
| Volks Beach Bomb | 6274 | Rear boards | HK | M-PR | BL | BK | | | $10,000.00 |
| Volks Beach Bomb | 6274 | Rear boards | HK | M-PR | BL | GY | | | $10,000.00 |
| Volks Beach Bomb | 6274 | Rear boards | HK | M-PR | BL | BR-L | | | $10,000.00 |
| Volks Beach Bomb | 6274 | Rear boards | HK | M-PR | BL | BR-D | | | $10,000.00 |
| Volks Beach Bomb | 6274 | | HK | M-RD | BL | WH | | | $140.00 |
| Volks Beach Bomb | 6274 | | HK | M-RD | BL | BK | | | $130.00 |
| Volks Beach Bomb | 6274 | | HK | M-RD | BL | GY | | | $130.00 |
| Volks Beach Bomb | 6274 | | HK | M-RD | BL | BR-L | | | $130.00 |
| Volks Beach Bomb | 6274 | | HK | M-RD | BL | BR-D | | | $130.00 |
| Volks Beach Bomb | 6274 | Rear boards | HK | M-RD | BL | WH | | | $10,000.00 |
| Volks Beach Bomb | 6274 | Rear boards | HK | M-RD | BL | BK | | | $10,000.00 |
| Volks Beach Bomb | 6274 | Rear boards | HK | M-RD | BL | GY | | | $10,000.00 |
| Volks Beach Bomb | 6274 | Rear boards | HK | M-RD | BL | BR-L | | | $10,000.00 |
| Volks Beach Bomb | 6274 | Rear boards | HK | M-RD | BL | BR-D | | | $10,000.00 |
| Volks Beach Bomb | 6274 | | HK | M-RD-R | BL | WH | | | $160.00 |
| Volks Beach Bomb | 6274 | | HK | M-RD-R | BL | BK | | | $150.00 |
| Volks Beach Bomb | 6274 | | HK | M-RD-R | BL | GY | | | $150.00 |
| Volks Beach Bomb | 6274 | | HK | M-RD-R | BL | BR-L | | | $150.00 |
| Volks Beach Bomb | 6274 | | HK | M-RD-R | BL | BR-D | | | $150.00 |
| Volks Beach Bomb | 6274 | | HK | M-YW | BL | WH | | | $140.00 |
| Volks Beach Bomb | 6274 | | HK | M-YW | BL | BK | | | $130.00 |
| Volks Beach Bomb | 6274 | | HK | M-YW | BL | GY | | | $130.00 |
| Volks Beach Bomb | 6274 | | HK | M-YW | BL | BR-L | | | $130.00 |
| Volks Beach Bomb | 6274 | | HK | M-YW | BL | BR-D | | | $130.00 |
| Volks Beach Bomb | 6274 | Rear boards | HK | M-YW | BL | WH | | | $10,000.00 |
| Volks Beach Bomb | 6274 | Rear boards | HK | M-YW | BL | BK | | | $10,000.00 |
| Volks Beach Bomb | 6274 | Rear boards | HK | M-YW | BL | GY | | | $10,000.00 |
| Volks Beach Bomb | 6274 | Rear boards | HK | M-YW | BL | BR-L | | | $10,000.00 |
| Volks Beach Bomb | 6274 | Rear boards | HK | M-YW | BL | BR-D | | | $10,000.00 |
| Volks Beach Bomb | 6274 | | HK | M-YW-L | BL | WH | | | $200.00 |
| Volks Beach Bomb | 6274 | | HK | M-YW-L | BL | BK | | | $180.00 |
| Volks Beach Bomb | 6274 | | HK | M-YW-L | BL | GY | | | $180.00 |
| Volks Beach Bomb | 6274 | | HK | M-YW-L | BL | BR-L | | | $180.00 |
| Volks Beach Bomb | 6274 | | HK | M-YW-L | BL | BR-D | | | $180.00 |
| Volks Beach Bomb | 6274 | | HK | M-YW-L | BL | WH | | | $10,000.00 |
| Volks Beach Bomb | 6274 | | HK | M-YW-L | BL | BK | | | $10,000.00 |
| Volks Beach Bomb | 6274 | | HK | M-YW-L | BL | GY | | | $10,000.00 |
| Volks Beach Bomb | 6274 | | HK | M-YW-L | BL | BR-L | | | $10,000.00 |
| Volks Beach Bomb | 6274 | | HK | M-YW-L | BL | BR-D | | | $10,000.00 |
| | | | | | | | | | |
| Mercedes 280 SL | 6275 | | HK | M-AQ | BL | WH | BK-RF | | $60.00 |

## 1969 Variations

| Name | Number | Casting | Country | Color | Windows | Interior | Paint | Other | Value |
|---|---|---|---|---|---|---|---|---|---|
| Mercedes 280 SL | 6275 | | HK | M-AQ | BL | WH | | | $55.00 |
| Mercedes 280 SL | 6275 | | HK | M-AQ | BL | BK | BK-RF | | $55.00 |
| Mercedes 280 SL | 6275 | | HK | M-AQ | BL | BK | | | $40.00 |
| Mercedes 280 SL | 6275 | | HK | M-AQ | BL | GY | BK-RF | | $55.00 |
| Mercedes 280 SL | 6275 | | HK | M-AQ | BL | GY | | | $50.00 |
| Mercedes 280 SL | 6275 | | HK | M-AQ | BL | BR-L | BK-RF | | $55.00 |
| Mercedes 280 SL | 6275 | | HK | M-AQ | BL | BR-L | | | $50.00 |
| Mercedes 280 SL | 6275 | | HK | M-AQ | BL | BR-D | BK-RF | | $55.00 |
| Mercedes 280 SL | 6275 | | HK | M-AQ | BL | BR-D | | | $50.00 |
| Mercedes 280 SL | 6275 | | HK | M-BL | BL | WH | BK-RF | | $65.00 |
| Mercedes 280 SL | 6275 | | HK | M-BL | BL | WH | | | $60.00 |
| Mercedes 280 SL | 6275 | | HK | M-BL | BL | BK | BK-RF | | $60.00 |
| Mercedes 280 SL | 6275 | | HK | M-BL | BL | BK | | | $55.00 |
| Mercedes 280 SL | 6275 | | HK | M-BL | BL | GY | BK-RF | | $60.00 |
| Mercedes 280 SL | 6275 | | HK | M-BL | BL | GY | | | $55.00 |
| Mercedes 280 SL | 6275 | | HK | M-BL | BL | BR-L | BK-RF | | $60.00 |
| Mercedes 280 SL | 6275 | | HK | M-BL | BL | BR-L | | | $55.00 |
| Mercedes 280 SL | 6275 | | HK | M-BL | BL | BR-D | BK-RF | | $60.00 |
| Mercedes 280 SL | 6275 | | HK | M-BL | BL | BR-D | | | $55.00 |
| Mercedes 280 SL | 6275 | | HK | M-BL/GY | CL | BK | | | $300.00 |
| Mercedes 280 SL | 6275 | | HK | M-BL/GY | TNT | BK | | | $300.00 |
| Mercedes 280 SL | 6275 | | HK | M-BL-I | BL | WH | BK-RF | | $100.00 |
| Mercedes 280 SL | 6275 | | HK | M-BL-I | BL | WH | | | $95.00 |
| Mercedes 280 SL | 6275 | | HK | M-BL-I | BL | BK | BK-RF | | $95.00 |
| Mercedes 280 SL | 6275 | | HK | M-BL-I | BL | BK | | | $90.00 |
| Mercedes 280 SL | 6275 | | HK | M-BL-I | BL | GY | BK-RF | | $95.00 |
| Mercedes 280 SL | 6275 | | HK | M-BL-I | BL | GY | | | $90.00 |
| Mercedes 280 SL | 6275 | | HK | M-BL-I | BL | BR-L | BK-RF | | $95.00 |
| Mercedes 280 SL | 6275 | | HK | M-BL-I | BL | BR-L | | | $90.00 |
| Mercedes 280 SL | 6275 | | HK | M-BL-I | BL | BR-D | BK-RF | | $95.00 |
| Mercedes 280 SL | 0275 | | HK | M-BL-I | BL | BR-D | | | $90.00 |
| Mercedes 280 SL | 6275 | | HK | M-BL-P | BL | WH | BK-RF | | $90.00 |
| Mercedes 280 SL | 6275 | | HK | M-BL-P | BL | WH | | | $85.00 |
| Mercedes 280 SL | 6275 | | HK | M-BL-P | BL | BK | BK-RF | | $90.00 |
| Mercedes 280 SL | 6275 | | HK | M-BL-P | BL | BK | | | $85.00 |
| Mercedes 280 SL | 6275 | | HK | M-BL-P | BL | GY | BK-RF | | $90.00 |
| Mercedes 280 SL | 6275 | | HK | M-BL-P | BL | GY | | | $85.00 |
| Mercedes 280 SL | 6275 | | HK | M-BL-P | BL | BR-L | BK-RF | | $90.00 |
| Mercedes 280 SL | 6275 | | HK | M-BL-P | BL | BR-L | | | $85.00 |
| Mercedes 280 SL | 6275 | | HK | M-BL-P | BL | BR-D | BK-RF | | $90.00 |
| Mercedes 280 SL | 6275 | | HK | M-BL-P | BL | BR-D | | | $85.00 |
| Mercedes 280 SL | 6275 | | HK | M-BR-D | BL | WH | BK-RF | | $65.00 |
| Mercedes 280 SL | 6275 | | HK | M-BR-D | BL | WH | | | $60.00 |
| Mercedes 280 SL | 6275 | | HK | M-BR-D | BL | BK | BK-RF | | $60.00 |
| Mercedes 280 SL | 6275 | | HK | M-BR-D | BL | BK | | | $55.00 |
| Mercedes 280 SL | 6275 | | HK | M-BR-D | BL | GY | BK-RF | | $60.00 |
| Mercedes 280 SL | 6275 | | HK | M-BR-D | BL | GY | | | $55.00 |
| Mercedes 280 SL | 6275 | | HK | M-BR-D | BL | BR-L | BK-RF | | $60.00 |
| Mercedes 280 SL | 6275 | | HK | M-BR-D | BL | BR-L | | | $55.00 |
| Mercedes 280 SL | 6275 | | HK | M-BR-D | BL | BR-D | BK-RF | | $60.00 |
| Mercedes 280 SL | 6275 | | HK | M-BR-D | BL | BR-D | | | $55.00 |
| Mercedes 280 SL | 6275 | | HK | M-BR-P | BL | WH | BK-RF | | $60.00 |
| Mercedes 280 SL | 6275 | | HK | M-BR-P | BL | WH | | | $55.00 |
| Mercedes 280 SL | 6275 | | HK | M-BR-P | BL | BK | BK-RF | | $55.00 |
| Mercedes 280 SL | 6275 | | HK | M-BR-P | BL | BK | | | $50.00 |
| Mercedes 280 SL | 6275 | | HK | M-BR-P | BL | GY | BK-RF | | $55.00 |
| Mercedes 280 SL | 6275 | | HK | M-BR-P | BL | GY | | | $50.00 |
| Mercedes 280 SL | 6275 | | HK | M-BR-P | BL | BR-L | BK-RF | | $55.00 |
| Mercedes 280 SL | 6275 | | HK | M-BR-P | BL | BR-L | | | $50.00 |
| Mercedes 280 SL | 6275 | | HK | M-BR-P | BL | BR-D | BK-RF | | $55.00 |
| Mercedes 280 SL | 6275 | | HK | M-BR-P | BL | BR-D | | | $50.00 |
| Mercedes 280 SL | 6275 | | HK | M-GR | BL | WH | BK-RF | | $60.00 |
| Mercedes 280 SL | 6275 | | HK | M-GR | BL | WH | | | $55.00 |
| Mercedes 280 SL | 6275 | | HK | M-GR | BL | BK | BK-RF | | $55.00 |
| Mercedes 280 SL | 6275 | | HK | M-GR | BL | BK | | | $50.00 |
| Mercedes 280 SL | 6275 | | HK | M-GR | BL | GY | BK-RF | | $55.00 |
| Mercedes 280 SL | 6275 | | HK | M-GR | BL | GY | | | $50.00 |
| Mercedes 280 SL | 6275 | | HK | M-GR | BL | BR-L | BK-RF | | $55.00 |
| Mercedes 280 SL | 6275 | | HK | M-GR | BL | BR-L | | | $50.00 |
| Mercedes 280 SL | 6275 | | HK | M-GR | BL | BR-D | BK-RF | | $55.00 |
| Mercedes 280 SL | 6275 | | HK | M-GR | BL | BR-D | | | $50.00 |
| Mercedes 280 SL | 6275 | | HK | M-GR-E | BL | WH | BK-RF | | $65.00 |

## 1969 Variations

| Name | Number | Casting | Country | Color | Windows | Interior | Paint | Other | Value |
|---|---|---|---|---|---|---|---|---|---|
| Mercedes 280 SL | 6275 | | HK | M-GR-E | BL | WH | | | $50.00 |
| Mercedes 280 SL | 6275 | | HK | M-GR-E | BL | BK | BK-RF | | $60.00 |
| Mercedes 280 SL | 6275 | | HK | M-GR-E | BL | BK | | | $55.00 |
| Mercedes 280 SL | 6275 | | HK | M-GR-E | BL | GY | BK-RF | | $60.00 |
| Mercedes 280 SL | 6275 | | HK | M-GR-E | BL | GY | | | $55.00 |
| Mercedes 280 SL | 6275 | | HK | M-GR-E | BL | BR-L | BK-RF | | $60.00 |
| Mercedes 280 SL | 6275 | | HK | M-GR-E | BL | BR-L | | | $55.00 |
| Mercedes 280 SL | 6275 | | HK | M-GR-E | BL | BR-D | BK-RF | | $60.00 |
| Mercedes 280 SL | 6275 | | HK | M-GR-E | BL | BR-D | | | $55.00 |
| Mercedes 280 SL | 6275 | | HK | M-GR-O | BL | WH | BK-RF | | $65.00 |
| Mercedes 280 SL | 6275 | | HK | M-GR-O | BL | WH | | | $60.00 |
| Mercedes 280 SL | 6275 | | HK | M-GR-O | BL | BK | BK-RF | | $60.00 |
| Mercedes 280 SL | 6275 | | HK | M-GR-O | BL | BK | | | $55.00 |
| Mercedes 280 SL | 6275 | | HK | M-GR-O | BL | GY | BK-RF | | $60.00 |
| Mercedes 280 SL | 6275 | | HK | M-GR-O | BL | GY | | | $55.00 |
| Mercedes 280 SL | 6275 | | HK | M-GR-O | BL | BR-L | BK-RF | | $60.00 |
| Mercedes 280 SL | 6275 | | HK | M-GR-O | BL | BR-L | | | $55.00 |
| Mercedes 280 SL | 6275 | | HK | M-GR-O | BL | BR-D | BK-RF | | $60.00 |
| Mercedes 280 SL | 6275 | | HK | M-GR-O | BL | BR-D | | | $55.00 |
| Mercedes 280 SL | 6275 | | HK | M-OR | BL | WH | BK-RF | | $60.00 |
| Mercedes 280 SL | 6275 | | HK | M-OR | BL | WH | | | $55.00 |
| Mercedes 280 SL | 6275 | | HK | M-OR | BL | BK | BK-RF | | $60.00 |
| Mercedes 280 SL | 6275 | | HK | M-OR | BL | BK | | | $50.00 |
| Mercedes 280 SL | 6275 | | HK | M-OR | BL | GY | BK-RF | | $55.00 |
| Mercedes 280 SL | 6275 | | HK | M-OR | BL | GY | | | $40.00 |
| Mercedes 280 SL | 6275 | | HK | M-OR | BL | BR-L | BK-RF | | $55.00 |
| Mercedes 280 SL | 6275 | | HK | M-OR | BL | BR-L | | | $50.00 |
| Mercedes 280 SL | 6275 | | HK | M-OR | BL | BR-D | BK-RF | | $55.00 |
| Mercedes 280 SL | 6275 | | HK | M-OR | BL | BR-D | | | $50.00 |
| Mercedes 280 SL | 6275 | | HK | M-PR | BL | WH | BK-RF | | $65.00 |
| Mercedes 280 SL | 6275 | | HK | M-PR | BL | WH | | | $60.00 |
| Mercedes 280 SL | 6275 | | HK | M-PR | BL | BK | BK-RF | | $60.00 |
| Mercedes 280 SL | 6275 | | HK | M-PR | BL | BK | | | $55.00 |
| Mercedes 280 SL | 6275 | | HK | M-PR | BL | GY | BK-RF | | $60.00 |
| Mercedes 280 SL | 6275 | | HK | M-PR | BL | GY | | | $55.00 |
| Mercedes 280 SL | 6275 | | HK | M-PR | BL | BR-L | BK-RF | | $60.00 |
| Mercedes 280 SL | 6275 | | HK | M-PR | BL | BR-L | | | $55.00 |
| Mercedes 280 SL | 6275 | | HK | M-PR | BL | BR-D | BK-RF | | $60.00 |
| Mercedes 280 SL | 6275 | | HK | M-PR | BL | BR-D | | | $55.00 |
| Mercedes 280 SL | 6275 | | HK | M-RD | BL | WH | BK-RF | | $60.00 |
| Mercedes 280 SL | 6275 | | HK | M-RD | BL | WH | | | $55.00 |
| Mercedes 280 SL | 6275 | | HK | M-RD | BL | BK | BK-RF | | $55.00 |
| Mercedes 280 SL | 6275 | | HK | M-RD | BL | BK | | | $50.00 |
| Mercedes 280 SL | 6275 | | HK | M-RD | BL | GY | BK-RF | | $55.00 |
| Mercedes 280 SL | 6275 | | HK | M-RD | BL | GY | | | $50.00 |
| Mercedes 280 SL | 6275 | | HK | M-RD | BL | BR-L | BK-RF | | $55.00 |
| Mercedes 280 SL | 6275 | | HK | M-RD | BL | BR-L | | | $50.00 |
| Mercedes 280 SL | 6275 | | HK | M-RD | BL | BR-D | BK-RF | | $55.00 |
| Mercedes 280 SL | 6275 | | HK | M-RD | BL | BR-D | | | $50.00 |
| Mercedes 280 SL | 6275 | | HK | M-RD | BL | BK | | | $300.00 |
| Mercedes 280 SL | 6275 | | HK | M-RD-R | BL | WH | BK-RF | | $65.00 |
| Mercedes 280 SL | 6275 | | HK | M-RD-R | BL | WH | | | $60.00 |
| Mercedes 280 SL | 6275 | | HK | M-RD-R | BL | BK | BK-RF | | $60.00 |
| Mercedes 280 SL | 6275 | | HK | M-RD-R | BL | BK | | | $55.00 |
| Mercedes 280 SL | 6275 | | HK | M-RD-R | BL | GY | BK-RF | | $60.00 |
| Mercedes 280 SL | 6275 | | HK | M-RD-R | BL | GY | | | $55.00 |
| Mercedes 280 SL | 6275 | | HK | M-RD-R | BL | BR-L | BK-RF | | $60.00 |
| Mercedes 280 SL | 6275 | | HK | M-RD-R | BL | BR-L | | | $55.00 |
| Mercedes 280 SL | 6275 | | HK | M-RD-R | BL | BR-D | BK-RF | | $60.00 |
| Mercedes 280 SL | 6275 | | HK | M-RD-R | BL | BR-D | | | $55.00 |
| Mercedes 280 SL | 6275 | | HK | SL | BL | WH | | | $300.00 |
| | | | | | | | | | |
| Rolls Royce Silver Shadow | 6276 | | HK | E-GY | BL | WH | BK-RF | | $50.00 |
| Rolls Royce Silver Shadow | 6276 | | HK | E-GY | BL | WH | | | $45.00 |
| Rolls Royce Silver Shadow | 6276 | | HK | E-GY | BL | BK | BK-RF | | $45.00 |
| Rolls Royce Silver Shadow | 6276 | | HK | E-GY | BL | BK | | | $40.00 |
| Rolls Royce Silver Shadow | 6276 | | HK | E-GY | BL | GY | BK-RF | | $45.00 |
| Rolls Royce Silver Shadow | 6276 | | HK | E-GY | BL | GY | | | $40.00 |
| Rolls Royce Silver Shadow | 6276 | | HK | E-GY | BL | BR-L | BK-RF | | $45.00 |
| Rolls Royce Silver Shadow | 6276 | | HK | E-GY | BL | BR-L | | | $40.00 |
| Rolls Royce Silver Shadow | 6276 | | HK | E-GY | BL | BR-D | BK-RF | | $45.00 |

## 1969 Variations

| Name | Number | Casting | Country | Color | Windows | Interior | Paint | Other | Value |
|---|---|---|---|---|---|---|---|---|---|
| Rolls Royce Silver Shadow | 6276 | | HK | E-GY | BL | BR-D | | | $40.00 |
| Rolls Royce Silver Shadow | 6276 | | HK | M-AQ | BL | WH | BK-RF | | $95.00 |
| Rolls Royce Silver Shadow | 6276 | | HK | M-AQ | BL | WH | | | $90.00 |
| Rolls Royce Silver Shadow | 6276 | | HK | M-AQ | BL | BK | BK-RF | | $90.00 |
| Rolls Royce Silver Shadow | 6276 | | HK | M-AQ | BL | BK | | | $85.00 |
| Rolls Royce Silver Shadow | 6276 | | HK | M-AQ | BL | GY | BK-RF | | $90.00 |
| Rolls Royce Silver Shadow | 6276 | | HK | M-AQ | BL | GY | | | $85.00 |
| Rolls Royce Silver Shadow | 6276 | | HK | M-AQ | BL | BR-L | BK-RF | | $90.00 |
| Rolls Royce Silver Shadow | 6276 | | HK | M-AQ | BL | BR-L | | | $85.00 |
| Rolls Royce Silver Shadow | 6276 | | HK | M-AQ | BL | BR-D | BK-RF | | $90.00 |
| Rolls Royce Silver Shadow | 6276 | | HK | M-AQ | BL | BR-D | | | $85.00 |
| Rolls Royce Silver Shadow | 6276 | | HK | M-BL | BL | WH | BK-RF | | $95.00 |
| Rolls Royce Silver Shadow | 6276 | | HK | M-BL | BL | WH | | | $90.00 |
| Rolls Royce Silver Shadow | 6276 | | HK | M-BL | BL | BK | BK-RF | | $90.00 |
| Rolls Royce Silver Shadow | 6276 | | HK | M-BL | BL | BK | | | $85.00 |
| Rolls Royce Silver Shadow | 6276 | | HK | M-BL | BL | GY | BK-RF | | $90.00 |
| Rolls Royce Silver Shadow | 6276 | | HK | M-BL | BL | GY | | | $85.00 |
| Rolls Royce Silver Shadow | 6276 | | HK | M-BL | BL | BR-L | BK-RF | | $90.00 |
| Rolls Royce Silver Shadow | 6276 | | HK | M-BL | BL | BR-L | | | $85.00 |
| Rolls Royce Silver Shadow | 6276 | | HK | M-BL | BL | BR-D | BK-RF | | $90.00 |
| Rolls Royce Silver Shadow | 6276 | | HK | M-BL | BL | BR-D | | | $85.00 |
| Rolls Royce Silver Shadow | 6276 | | HK | M-GD | BL | WH | BK-RF | | $95.00 |
| Rolls Royce Silver Shadow | 6276 | | HK | M-GD | BL | WH | | | $90.00 |
| Rolls Royce Silver Shadow | 6276 | | HK | M-GD | BL | BK | BK-RF | | $90.00 |
| Rolls Royce Silver Shadow | 6276 | | HK | M-GD | BL | BK | | | $85.00 |
| Rolls Royce Silver Shadow | 6276 | | HK | M-GD | BL | GY | BK-RF | | $90.00 |
| Rolls Royce Silver Shadow | 6276 | | HK | M-GD | BL | GY | | | $85.00 |
| Rolls Royce Silver Shadow | 6276 | | HK | M-GD | BL | BR-L | BK-RF | | $90.00 |
| Rolls Royce Silver Shadow | 6276 | | HK | M-GD | BL | BR-L | | | $85.00 |
| Rolls Royce Silver Shadow | 6276 | | HK | M-GD | BL | BR-D | DK-RF | | $90.00 |
| Rolls Royce Silver Shadow | 6276 | | HK | M-GD | BL | BR-D | | | $85.00 |
| Rolls Royce Silver Shadow | 6276 | | HK | M-GR | BL | WH | BK-RF | | $95.00 |
| Rolls Royce Silver Shadow | 6276 | | HK | M-GR | BL | WH | | | $90.00 |
| Rolls Royce Silver Shadow | 6276 | | HK | M-GR | BL | BK | BK-RF | | $90.00 |
| Rolls Royce Silver Shadow | 6276 | | HK | M-GR | BL | BK | | | $85.00 |
| Rolls Royce Silver Shadow | 6276 | | HK | M-GR | BL | GY | BK-RF | | $90.00 |
| Rolls Royce Silver Shadow | 6276 | | HK | M-GR | BL | GY | | | $85.00 |
| Rolls Royce Silver Shadow | 6276 | | HK | M-GR | BL | BR-L | BK-RF | | $90.00 |
| Rolls Royce Silver Shadow | 6276 | | HK | M-GR | BL | BR-L | | | $85.00 |
| Rolls Royce Silver Shadow | 6276 | | HK | M-GR | BL | BR-D | BK-RF | | $90.00 |
| Rolls Royce Silver Shadow | 6276 | | HK | M-GR | BL | BR-D | | | $85.00 |
| Rolls Royce Silver Shadow | 6276 | | HK | M-GR-E | BL | WH | BK-RF | | $110.00 |
| Rolls Royce Silver Shadow | 6276 | | HK | M-GR-E | BL | WH | | | $100.00 |
| Rolls Royce Silver Shadow | 6276 | | HK | M-GR-E | BL | BK | BK-RF | | $100.00 |
| Rolls Royce Silver Shadow | 6276 | | HK | M-GR-E | BL | BK | | | $95.00 |
| Rolls Royce Silver Shadow | 6276 | | HK | M-GR-E | BL | GY | BK-RF | | $100.00 |
| Rolls Royce Silver Shadow | 6276 | | HK | M-GR-E | BL | GY | | | $95.00 |
| Rolls Royce Silver Shadow | 6276 | | HK | M-GR-E | BL | BR-L | BK-RF | | $90.00 |
| Rolls Royce Silver Shadow | 6276 | | HK | M-GR-E | BL | BR-L | | | $95.00 |
| Rolls Royce Silver Shadow | 6276 | | HK | M-GR-E | BL | BR-D | BK-RF | | $100.00 |
| Rolls Royce Silver Shadow | 6276 | | HK | M-GR-E | BL | BR-D | | | $95.00 |
| Rolls Royce Silver Shadow | 6276 | | HK | M-GR-L | BL | WH | BK-RF | | $120.00 |
| Rolls Royce Silver Shadow | 6276 | | HK | M-GR-L | BL | WH | | | $110.00 |
| Rolls Royce Silver Shadow | 6276 | | HK | M-GR-L | BL | BK | BK-RF | | $110.00 |
| Rolls Royce Silver Shadow | 6276 | | HK | M-GR-L | BL | BK | | | $110.00 |
| Rolls Royce Silver Shadow | 6276 | | HK | M-GR-L | BL | GY | BK-RF | | $110.00 |
| Rolls Royce Silver Shadow | 6276 | | HK | M-GR-L | BL | GY | | | $110.00 |
| Rolls Royce Silver Shadow | 6276 | | HK | M-GR-L | BL | BR-L | BK-RF | | $110.00 |
| Rolls Royce Silver Shadow | 6276 | | HK | M-GR-L | BL | BR-L | | | $110.00 |
| Rolls Royce Silver Shadow | 6276 | | HK | M-GR-L | BL | BR-D | BK-RF | | $110.00 |
| Rolls Royce Silver Shadow | 6276 | | HK | M-GR-L | BL | BR-D | | | $110.00 |
| Rolls Royce Silver Shadow | 6276 | | HK | M-MG | BL | WH | BK-RF | | $180.00 |
| Rolls Royce Silver Shadow | 6276 | | HK | M-MG | BL | WH | | | $160.00 |
| Rolls Royce Silver Shadow | 6276 | | HK | M-MG | BL | BK | BK-RF | | $170.00 |
| Rolls Royce Silver Shadow | 6276 | | HK | M-MG | BL | BK | | | $150.00 |
| Rolls Royce Silver Shadow | 6276 | | HK | M-MG | BL | GY | BK-RF | | $170.00 |
| Rolls Royce Silver Shadow | 6276 | | HK | M-MG | BL | GY | | | $150.00 |
| Rolls Royce Silver Shadow | 6276 | | HK | M-MG | BL | BR-L | BK-RF | | $170.00 |
| Rolls Royce Silver Shadow | 6276 | | HK | M-MG | BL | BR-L | | | $150.00 |
| Rolls Royce Silver Shadow | 6276 | | HK | M-MG | BL | BR-D | BK-RF | | $170.00 |
| Rolls Royce Silver Shadow | 6276 | | HK | M-MG | BL | BR-D | | | $150.00 |
| Rolls Royce Silver Shadow | 6276 | | HK | M-OR | BL | WH | BK-RF | | $95.00 |

## 1969 Variations

| Name | Number | Casting | Country | Color | Windows | Interior | Paint | Other | Value |
|---|---|---|---|---|---|---|---|---|---|
| Rolls Royce Silver Shadow | 6276 | | HK | M-OR | BL | WH | | | $90.00 |
| Rolls Royce Silver Shadow | 6276 | | HK | M-OR | BL | BK | BK-RF | | $90.00 |
| Rolls Royce Silver Shadow | 6276 | | HK | M-OR | BL | BK | | | $85.00 |
| Rolls Royce Silver Shadow | 6276 | | HK | M-OR | BL | GY | BK-RF | | $90.00 |
| Rolls Royce Silver Shadow | 6276 | | HK | M-OR | BL | GY | | | $85.00 |
| Rolls Royce Silver Shadow | 6276 | | HK | M-OR | BL | BR-L | BK-RF | | $90.00 |
| Rolls Royce Silver Shadow | 6276 | | HK | M-OR | BL | BR-L | | | $85.00 |
| Rolls Royce Silver Shadow | 6276 | | HK | M-OR | BL | BR-D | BK-RF | | $90.00 |
| Rolls Royce Silver Shadow | 6276 | | HK | M-OR | BL | BR-D | | | $85.00 |
| Rolls Royce Silver Shadow | 6276 | | HK | M-PK | BL | WH | BK-RF | | $460.00 |
| Rolls Royce Silver Shadow | 6276 | | HK | M-PK | BL | WH | | | $440.00 |
| Rolls Royce Silver Shadow | 6276 | | HK | M-PK | BL | BK | BK-RF | | $440.00 |
| Rolls Royce Silver Shadow | 6276 | | HK | M-PK | BL | BK | | | $420.00 |
| Rolls Royce Silver Shadow | 6276 | | HK | M-PK | BL | GY | BK-RF | | $440.00 |
| Rolls Royce Silver Shadow | 6276 | | HK | M-PK | BL | GY | | | $420.00 |
| Rolls Royce Silver Shadow | 6276 | | HK | M-PK | BL | BR-L | BK-RF | | $440.00 |
| Rolls Royce Silver Shadow | 6276 | | HK | M-PK | BL | BR-L | | | $420.00 |
| Rolls Royce Silver Shadow | 6276 | | HK | M-PK | BL | BR-D | BK-RF | | $440.00 |
| Rolls Royce Silver Shadow | 6276 | | HK | M-PK | BL | BR-D | | | $420.00 |
| Rolls Royce Silver Shadow | 6276 | | HK | M-PK-H | BL | WH | BK-RF | | $460.00 |
| Rolls Royce Silver Shadow | 6276 | | HK | M-PK-H | BL | WH | | | $440.00 |
| Rolls Royce Silver Shadow | 6276 | | HK | M-PK-H | BL | BK | BK-RF | | $440.00 |
| Rolls Royce Silver Shadow | 6276 | | HK | M-PK-H | BL | BK | | | $420.00 |
| Rolls Royce Silver Shadow | 6276 | | HK | M-PK-H | BL | GY | BK-RF | | $440.00 |
| Rolls Royce Silver Shadow | 6276 | | HK | M-PK-H | BL | GY | | | $420.00 |
| Rolls Royce Silver Shadow | 6276 | | HK | M-PK-H | BL | BR-L | BK-RF | | $440.00 |
| Rolls Royce Silver Shadow | 6276 | | HK | M-PK-H | BL | BR-L | | | $420.00 |
| Rolls Royce Silver Shadow | 6276 | | HK | M-PK-H | BL | BR-D | BK-RF | | $440.00 |
| Rolls Royce Silver Shadow | 6276 | | HK | M-PK-H | BL | BR-D | | | $420.00 |
| Rolls Royce Silver Shadow | 6276 | | HK | M-PK-S | BL | WH | BK-RF | | $460.00 |
| Rolls Royce Silver Shadow | 6276 | | HK | M-PK-S | BL | WH | | | $440.00 |
| Rolls Royce Silver Shadow | 6276 | | HK | M-PK-S | BL | BK | BK-RF | | $440.00 |
| Rolls Royce Silver Shadow | 6276 | | HK | M-PK-S | BL | BK | | | $420.00 |
| Rolls Royce Silver Shadow | 6276 | | HK | M-PK-S | BL | GY | BK-RF | | $440.00 |
| Rolls Royce Silver Shadow | 6276 | | HK | M-PK-S | BL | GY | | | $420.00 |
| Rolls Royce Silver Shadow | 6276 | | HK | M-PK-S | BL | BR-L | BK-RF | | $440.00 |
| Rolls Royce Silver Shadow | 6276 | | HK | M-PK-S | BL | BR-L | | | $420.00 |
| Rolls Royce Silver Shadow | 6276 | | HK | M-PK-S | BL | BR-D | BK-RF | | $440.00 |
| Rolls Royce Silver Shadow | 6276 | | HK | M-PK-S | BL | BR-D | | | $420.00 |
| Rolls Royce Silver Shadow | 6276 | | HK | M-PR | BL | WH | BK-RF | | $220.00 |
| Rolls Royce Silver Shadow | 6276 | | HK | M-PR | BL | WH | | | $210.00 |
| Rolls Royce Silver Shadow | 6276 | | HK | M-PR | BL | BK | BK-RF | | $210.00 |
| Rolls Royce Silver Shadow | 6276 | | HK | M-PR | BL | BK | | | $200.00 |
| Rolls Royce Silver Shadow | 6276 | | HK | M-PR | BL | GY | BK-RF | | $210.00 |
| Rolls Royce Silver Shadow | 6276 | | HK | M-PR | BL | GY | | | $200.00 |
| Rolls Royce Silver Shadow | 6276 | | HK | M-PR | BL | BR-L | BK-RF | | $210.00 |
| Rolls Royce Silver Shadow | 6276 | | HK | M-PR | BL | BR-L | | | $200.00 |
| Rolls Royce Silver Shadow | 6276 | | HK | M-PR | BL | BR-D | BK-RF | | $210.00 |
| Rolls Royce Silver Shadow | 6276 | | HK | M-PR | BL | BR-D | | | $200.00 |
| Rolls Royce Silver Shadow | 6276 | | HK | M-RD | BL | WH | BK-RF | | $95.00 |
| Rolls Royce Silver Shadow | 6276 | | HK | M-RD | BL | WH | | | $90.00 |
| Rolls Royce Silver Shadow | 6276 | | HK | M-RD | BL | BK | BK-RF | | $90.00 |
| Rolls Royce Silver Shadow | 6276 | | HK | M-RD | BL | BK | | | $85.00 |
| Rolls Royce Silver Shadow | 6276 | | HK | M-RD | BL | GY | BK-RF | | $90.00 |
| Rolls Royce Silver Shadow | 6276 | | HK | M-RD | BL | GY | | | $85.00 |
| Rolls Royce Silver Shadow | 6276 | | HK | M-RD | BL | BR-L | BK-RF | | $90.00 |
| Rolls Royce Silver Shadow | 6276 | | HK | M-RD | BL | BR-L | | | $85.00 |
| Rolls Royce Silver Shadow | 6276 | | HK | M-RD | BL | BR-D | BK-RF | | $90.00 |
| Rolls Royce Silver Shadow | 6276 | | HK | M-RD | BL | BR-D | | | $85.00 |
| Rolls Royce Silver Shadow | 6276 | | HK | M-RD-R | BL | WH | BK-RF | | $90.00 |
| Rolls Royce Silver Shadow | 6276 | | HK | M-RD-R | BL | WH | | | $85.00 |
| Rolls Royce Silver Shadow | 6276 | | HK | M-RD-R | BL | BK | BK-RF | | $85.00 |
| Rolls Royce Silver Shadow | 6276 | | HK | M-RD-R | BL | BK | | | $80.00 |
| Rolls Royce Silver Shadow | 6276 | | HK | M-RD-R | BL | GY | BK-RF | | $85.00 |
| Rolls Royce Silver Shadow | 6276 | | HK | M-RD-R | BL | GY | | | $80.00 |
| Rolls Royce Silver Shadow | 6276 | | HK | M-RD-R | BL | BR-L | BK-RF | | $85.00 |
| Rolls Royce Silver Shadow | 6276 | | HK | M-RD-R | BL | BR-L | | | $80.00 |
| Rolls Royce Silver Shadow | 6276 | | HK | M-RD-R | BL | BR-D | BK-RF | | $85.00 |
| Rolls Royce Silver Shadow | 6276 | | HK | M-RD-R | BL | BR-D | | | $80.00 |
| Rolls Royce Silver Shadow | 6276 | | HK | M-YW | BL | WH | BK-RF | | $105.00 |
| Rolls Royce Silver Shadow | 6276 | | HK | M-YW | BL | WH | | | $100.00 |
| Rolls Royce Silver Shadow | 6276 | | HK | M-YW | BL | BK | BK-RF | | $100.00 |

## 1969 Variations

| Name | Number | Casting | Country | Color | Windows | Interior | Paint | Other | Value |
|---|---|---|---|---|---|---|---|---|---|
| Rolls Royce Silver Shadow | 6276 | | HK | M-YW | BL | BK | | | $95.00 |
| Rolls Royce Silver Shadow | 6276 | | HK | M-YW | BL | GY | BK-RF | | $100.00 |
| Rolls Royce Silver Shadow | 6276 | | HK | M-YW | BL | GY | | | $95.00 |
| Rolls Royce Silver Shadow | 6276 | | HK | M-YW | BL | BR-L | BK-RF | | $100.00 |
| Rolls Royce Silver Shadow | 6276 | | HK | M-YW | BL | BR-L | | | $95.00 |
| Rolls Royce Silver Shadow | 6276 | | HK | M-YW | BL | BR-D | BK-RF | | $100.00 |
| Rolls Royce Silver Shadow | 6276 | | HK | M-YW | BL | BR-D | | | $95.00 |
| Rolls Royce Silver Shadow | 6276 | | HK | M-YW-L | BL | WH | BK-RF | | $120.00 |
| Rolls Royce Silver Shadow | 6276 | | HK | M-YW-L | BL | WH | | | $110.00 |
| Rolls Royce Silver Shadow | 6276 | | HK | M-YW-L | BL | BK | BK-RF | | $110.00 |
| Rolls Royce Silver Shadow | 6276 | | HK | M-YW-L | BL | BK | | | $100.00 |
| Rolls Royce Silver Shadow | 6276 | | HK | M-YW-L | BL | GY | BK-RF | | $110.00 |
| Rolls Royce Silver Shadow | 6276 | | HK | M-YW-L | BL | GY | | | $100.00 |
| Rolls Royce Silver Shadow | 6276 | | HK | M-YW-L | BL | BR-L | BK-RF | | $110.00 |
| Rolls Royce Silver Shadow | 6276 | | HK | M-YW-L | BL | BR-L | | | $100.00 |
| Rolls Royce Silver Shadow | 6276 | | HK | M-YW-L | BL | BR-D | BK-RF | | $110.00 |
| Rolls Royce Silver Shadow | 6276 | | HK | M-YW-L | BL | BR-D | | | $100.00 |
| | | | | | | | | | |
| Maserati Mistral | 6277 | | HK | M-AQ | BL | WH | | | $90.00 |
| Maserati Mistral | 6277 | | HK | M-AQ | BL | BK | | | $85.00 |
| Maserati Mistral | 6277 | | HK | M-AQ | BL | GY | | | $85.00 |
| Maserati Mistral | 6277 | | HK | M-AQ | BL | BR-L | | | $85.00 |
| Maserati Mistral | 6277 | | HK | M-AQ | BL | BR-D | | | $85.00 |
| Maserati Mistral | 6277 | | HK | M-AQ | BL | WH | BK-RF | | $95.00 |
| Maserati Mistral | 6277 | | HK | M-AQ | BL | BK | BK-RF | | $90.00 |
| Maserati Mistral | 6277 | | HK | M-AQ | BL | GY | BK-RF | | $90.00 |
| Maserati Mistral | 6277 | | HK | M-AQ | BL | BR-L | BK-RF | | $90.00 |
| Maserati Mistral | 6277 | | HK | M-AQ | BL | BR-D | BK-RF | | $90.00 |
| Maserati Mistral | 6277 | | HK | M-BL | BL | WH | | | $90.00 |
| Maserati Mistral | 6277 | | HK | M-BL | BL | BK | | | $85.00 |
| Maserati Mistral | 6277 | | HK | M-BL | BL | GY | | | $85.00 |
| Maserati Mistral | 6277 | | HK | M-BL | BL | BR-L | | | $85.00 |
| Maserati Mistral | 6277 | | HK | M-BL | BL | BR-D | | | $85.00 |
| Maserati Mistral | 6277 | | HK | M-BL | BL | WH | BK-RF | | $95.00 |
| Maserati Mistral | 6277 | | HK | M-BL | BL | BK | BK-RF | | $90.00 |
| Maserati Mistral | 6277 | | HK | M-BL | BL | GY | BK-RF | | $90.00 |
| Maserati Mistral | 6277 | | HK | M-BL | BL | BR-L | BK-RF | | $90.00 |
| Maserati Mistral | 6277 | | HK | M-BL | BL | BR-D | BK-RF | | $90.00 |
| Maserati Mistral | 6277 | | HK | M-BL/GY | TNT | WH | | | $200.00 |
| Maserati Mistral | 6277 | | HK | M-BL-I | BL | WH | | | $130.00 |
| Maserati Mistral | 6277 | | HK | M-BL-I | BL | BK | | | $125.00 |
| Maserati Mistral | 6277 | | HK | M-BL-I | BL | GY | | | $125.00 |
| Maserati Mistral | 6277 | | HK | M-BL-I | BL | BR-L | | | $125.00 |
| Maserati Mistral | 6277 | | HK | M-BL-I | BL | BR-D | | | $125.00 |
| Maserati Mistral | 6277 | | HK | M-BL-I | BL | WH | BK-RF | | $140.00 |
| Maserati Mistral | 6277 | | HK | M-BL-I | BL | BK | BK-RF | | $135.00 |
| Maserati Mistral | 6277 | | HK | M-BL-I | BL | GY | BK-RF | | $135.00 |
| Maserati Mistral | 6277 | | HK | M-BL-I | BL | BR-L | BK-RF | | $135.00 |
| Maserati Mistral | 6277 | | HK | M-BL-I | BL | BR-D | BK-RF | | $135.00 |
| Maserati Mistral | 6277 | | HK | M-BL-P | BL | WH | | | $120.00 |
| Maserati Mistral | 6277 | | HK | M-BL-P | BL | BK | | | $115.00 |
| Maserati Mistral | 6277 | | HK | M-BL-P | BL | GY | | | $115.00 |
| Maserati Mistral | 6277 | | HK | M-BL-P | BL | BR-L | | | $115.00 |
| Maserati Mistral | 6277 | | HK | M-BL-P | BL | BR-D | | | $115.00 |
| Maserati Mistral | 6277 | | HK | M-BL-P | BL | WH | BK-RF | | $130.00 |
| Maserati Mistral | 6277 | | HK | M-BL-P | BL | BK | BK-RF | | $125.00 |
| Maserati Mistral | 6277 | | HK | M-BL-P | BL | GY | BK-RF | | $125.00 |
| Maserati Mistral | 6277 | | HK | M-BL-P | BL | BR-L | BK-RF | | $125.00 |
| Maserati Mistral | 6277 | | HK | M-BL-P | BL | BR-D | BK-RF | | $125.00 |
| Maserati Mistral | 6277 | | HK | M-BR-D | BL | WH | | | $100.00 |
| Maserati Mistral | 6277 | | HK | M-BR-D | BL | BK | | | $95.00 |
| Maserati Mistral | 6277 | | HK | M-BR-D | BL | GY | | | $95.00 |
| Maserati Mistral | 6277 | | HK | M-BR-D | BL | BR-L | | | $95.00 |
| Maserati Mistral | 6277 | | HK | M-BR-D | BL | BR-D | | | $95.00 |
| Maserati Mistral | 6277 | | HK | M-BR-D | BL | WH | BK-RF | | $105.00 |
| Maserati Mistral | 6277 | | HK | M-BR-D | BL | BK | BK-RF | | $100.00 |
| Maserati Mistral | 6277 | | HK | M-BR-D | BL | GY | BK-RF | | $100.00 |
| Maserati Mistral | 6277 | | HK | M-BR-D | BL | BR-L | BK-RF | | $100.00 |
| Maserati Mistral | 6277 | | HK | M-BR-D | BL | BR-D | BK-RF | | $100.00 |
| Maserati Mistral | 6277 | | HK | M-BR-P | BL | WH | | | $90.00 |
| Maserati Mistral | 6277 | | HK | M-BR-P | BL | BK | | | $85.00 |

## 1969 Variations

| Name | Number | Casting | Country | Color | Windows | Interior | Paint | Other | Value |
|---|---|---|---|---|---|---|---|---|---|
| Maserati Mistral | 6277 | | HK | M-BR-P | BL | GY | | | $85.00 |
| Maserati Mistral | 6277 | | HK | M-BR-P | BL | BR-L | | | $85.00 |
| Maserati Mistral | 6277 | | HK | M-BR-P | BL | BR-D | | | $85.00 |
| Maserati Mistral | 6277 | | HK | M-BR-P | BL | WH | BK-RF | | $95.00 |
| Maserati Mistral | 6277 | | HK | M-BR-P | BL | BK | BK-RF | | $90.00 |
| Maserati Mistral | 6277 | | HK | M-BR-P | BL | GY | BK-RF | | $90.00 |
| Maserati Mistral | 6277 | | HK | M-BR-P | BL | BR-L | BK-RF | | $90.00 |
| Maserati Mistral | 6277 | | HK | M-BR-P | BL | BR-D | BK-RF | | $90.00 |
| Maserati Mistral | 6277 | | HK | M-GD | BL | WH | | | $140.00 |
| Maserati Mistral | 6277 | | HK | M-GD | BL | BK | | | $130.00 |
| Maserati Mistral | 6277 | | HK | M-GD | BL | GY | | | $130.00 |
| Maserati Mistral | 6277 | | HK | M-GD | BL | BR-L | | | $130.00 |
| Maserati Mistral | 6277 | | HK | M-GD | BL | BR-D | | | $130.00 |
| Maserati Mistral | 6277 | | HK | M-GD | BL | WH | BK-RF | | $160.00 |
| Maserati Mistral | 6277 | | HK | M-GD | BL | BK | BK-RF | | $150.00 |
| Maserati Mistral | 6277 | | HK | M-GD | BL | GY | BK-RF | | $150.00 |
| Maserati Mistral | 6277 | | HK | M-GD | BL | BR-L | BK-RF | | $150.00 |
| Maserati Mistral | 6277 | | HK | M-GD | BL | BR-D | BK-RF | | $150.00 |
| Maserati Mistral | 6277 | | HK | M-GR | BL | WH | | | $90.00 |
| Maserati Mistral | 6277 | | HK | M-GR | BL | BK | | | $85.00 |
| Maserati Mistral | 6277 | | HK | M-GR | BL | GY | | | $85.00 |
| Maserati Mistral | 6277 | | HK | M-GR | BL | BR-L | | | $85.00 |
| Maserati Mistral | 6277 | | HK | M-GR | BL | BR-D | | | $85.00 |
| Maserati Mistral | 6277 | | HK | M-GR | BL | WH | BK-RF | | $95.00 |
| Maserati Mistral | 6277 | | HK | M-GR | BL | BK | BK-RF | | $90.00 |
| Maserati Mistral | 6277 | | HK | M-GR | BL | GY | BK-RF | | $90.00 |
| Maserati Mistral | 6277 | | HK | M-GR | BL | BR-L | BK-RF | | $90.00 |
| Maserati Mistral | 6277 | | HK | M-GR | BL | BR-D | BK-RF | | $90.00 |
| Maserati Mistral | 6277 | | HK | M-GR-E | BL | WH | | | $100.00 |
| Maserati Mistral | 6277 | | HK | M-GR-E | BL | BK | | | $95.00 |
| Maserati Mistral | 6277 | | HK | M-GR-E | BL | GY | | | $95.00 |
| Maserati Mistral | 6277 | | HK | M-GR-E | BL | BR-L | | | $95.00 |
| Maserati Mistral | 6277 | | HK | M-GR-E | BL | BR-D | | | $95.00 |
| Maserati Mistral | 6277 | | HK | M-GR-E | BL | WH | BK-RF | | $105.00 |
| Maserati Mistral | 6277 | | HK | M-GR-E | BL | BK | BK-RF | | $100.00 |
| Maserati Mistral | 6277 | | HK | M-GR-E | BL | GY | BK-RF | | $100.00 |
| Maserati Mistral | 6277 | | HK | M-GR-E | BL | BR-L | BK-RF | | $100.00 |
| Maserati Mistral | 6277 | | HK | M-GR-E | BL | BR-D | BK-RF | | $100.00 |
| Maserati Mistral | 6277 | | HK | M-GR-L | BL | WH | | | $140.00 |
| Maserati Mistral | 6277 | | HK | M-GR-L | BL | BK | | | $130.00 |
| Maserati Mistral | 6277 | | HK | M-GR-L | BL | GY | | | $130.00 |
| Maserati Mistral | 6277 | | HK | M-GR-L | BL | BR-L | | | $130.00 |
| Maserati Mistral | 6277 | | HK | M-GR-L | BL | BR-D | | | $130.00 |
| Maserati Mistral | 6277 | | HK | M-GR-L | BL | WH | BK-RF | | $160.00 |
| Maserati Mistral | 6277 | | HK | M-GR-L | BL | BK | BK-RF | | $150.00 |
| Maserati Mistral | 6277 | | HK | M-GR-L | BL | GY | BK-RF | | $150.00 |
| Maserati Mistral | 6277 | | HK | M-GR-L | BL | BR-L | BK-RF | | $150.00 |
| Maserati Mistral | 6277 | | HK | M-GR-L | BL | BR-D | BK-RF | | $150.00 |
| Maserati Mistral | 6277 | | HK | M-GR-O | BL | WH | | | $105.00 |
| Maserati Mistral | 6277 | | HK | M-GR-O | BL | BK | | | $100.00 |
| Maserati Mistral | 6277 | | HK | M-GR-O | BL | GY | | | $100.00 |
| Maserati Mistral | 6277 | | HK | M-GR-O | BL | BR-L | | | $100.00 |
| Maserati Mistral | 6277 | | HK | M-GR-O | BL | BR-D | | | $100.00 |
| Maserati Mistral | 6277 | | HK | M-GR-O | BL | WH | BK-RF | | $110.00 |
| Maserati Mistral | 6277 | | HK | M-GR-O | BL | BK | BK-RF | | $105.00 |
| Maserati Mistral | 6277 | | HK | M-GR-O | BL | GY | BK-RF | | $105.00 |
| Maserati Mistral | 6277 | | HK | M-GR-O | BL | BR-L | BK-RF | | $105.00 |
| Maserati Mistral | 6277 | | HK | M-GR-O | BL | BR-D | BK-RF | | $105.00 |
| Maserati Mistral | 6277 | | HK | M-MG | BL | WH | | | $120.00 |
| Maserati Mistral | 6277 | | HK | M-MG | BL | BK | | | $115.00 |
| Maserati Mistral | 6277 | | HK | M-MG | BL | GY | | | $115.00 |
| Maserati Mistral | 6277 | | HK | M-MG | BL | BR-L | | | $115.00 |
| Maserati Mistral | 6277 | | HK | M-MG | BL | BR-D | | | $115.00 |
| Maserati Mistral | 6277 | | HK | M-MG | BL | WH | BK-RF | | $130.00 |
| Maserati Mistral | 6277 | | HK | M-MG | BL | BK | BK-RF | | $125.00 |
| Maserati Mistral | 6277 | | HK | M-MG | BL | GY | BK-RF | | $125.00 |
| Maserati Mistral | 6277 | | HK | M-MG | BL | BR-L | BK-RF | | $125.00 |
| Maserati Mistral | 6277 | | HK | M-MG | BL | BR-D | BK-RF | | $125.00 |
| Maserati Mistral | 6277 | | HK | M-OR | BL | WH | | | $90.00 |
| Maserati Mistral | 6277 | | HK | M-OR | BL | BK | | | $85.00 |
| Maserati Mistral | 6277 | | HK | M-OR | BL | GY | | | $85.00 |
| Maserati Mistral | 6277 | | HK | M-OR | BL | BR-L | | | $85.00 |

## 1969 Variations

| Name | Number | Casting | Country | Color | Windows | Interior | Paint | Other | Value |
|---|---|---|---|---|---|---|---|---|---|
| Maserati Mistral | 6277 | | HK | M-OR | BL | BR-D | | | $85.00 |
| Maserati Mistral | 6277 | | HK | M-OR | BL | WH | BK-RF | | $95.00 |
| Maserati Mistral | 6277 | | HK | M-OR | BL | BK | BK-RF | | $90.00 |
| Maserati Mistral | 6277 | | HK | M-OR | BL | GY | BK-RF | | $90.00 |
| Maserati Mistral | 6277 | | HK | M-OR | BL | BR-L | BK-RF | | $90.00 |
| Maserati Mistral | 6277 | | HK | M-OR | BL | BR-D | BK-RF | | $90.00 |
| Maserati Mistral | 6277 | | HK | M-PR | BL | WH | | | $90.00 |
| Maserati Mistral | 6277 | | HK | M-PR | BL | BK | | | $85.00 |
| Maserati Mistral | 6277 | | HK | M-PR | BL | GY | | | $85.00 |
| Maserati Mistral | 6277 | | HK | M-PR | BL | BR-L | | | $85.00 |
| Maserati Mistral | 6277 | | HK | M-PR | BL | BR-D | | | $85.00 |
| Maserati Mistral | 6277 | | HK | M-PR | BL | WH | BK-RF | | $95.00 |
| Maserati Mistral | 6277 | | HK | M-PR | BL | BK | BK-RF | | $90.00 |
| Maserati Mistral | 6277 | | HK | M-PR | BL | GY | BK-RF | | $90.00 |
| Maserati Mistral | 6277 | | HK | M-PR | BL | BR-L | BK-RF | | $90.00 |
| Maserati Mistral | 6277 | | HK | M-PR | BL | BR-D | BK-RF | | $90.00 |
| Maserati Mistral | 6277 | | HK | M-RD | BL | WH | | | $100.00 |
| Maserati Mistral | 6277 | | HK | M-RD | BL | BK | | | $95.00 |
| Maserati Mistral | 6277 | | HK | M-RD | BL | GY | | | $95.00 |
| Maserati Mistral | 6277 | | HK | M-RD | BL | BR-L | | | $95.00 |
| Maserati Mistral | 6277 | | HK | M-RD | BL | BR-D | | | $95.00 |
| Maserati Mistral | 6277 | | HK | M-RD | BL | WH | BK-RF | | $105.00 |
| Maserati Mistral | 6277 | | HK | M-RD | BL | BK | BK-RF | | $100.00 |
| Maserati Mistral | 6277 | | HK | M-RD | BL | GY | BK-RF | | $100.00 |
| Maserati Mistral | 6277 | | HK | M-RD | BL | BR-L | BK-RF | | $100.00 |
| Maserati Mistral | 6277 | | HK | M-RD | BL | BR-D | BK-RF | | $100.00 |
| Maserati Mistral | 6277 | | HK | M-RD-R | BL | WH | | | $110.00 |
| Maserati Mistral | 6277 | | HK | M-RD-R | BL | BK | | | $106.00 |
| Maserati Mistral | 6277 | | HK | M-RD-R | BL | GY | | | $105.00 |
| Maserati Mistral | 6277 | | HK | M-RD-R | BL | BR-L | | | $105.00 |
| Maserati Mistral | 0277 | | HK | M-RD-R | BL | BR-D | | | $105.00 |
| Maserati Mistral | 6277 | | HK | M-RD-R | BL | WH | BK-RF | | $115.00 |
| Maserati Mistral | 6277 | | HK | M-RD-R | BL | BK | BK-RF | | $110.00 |
| Maserati Mistral | 6277 | | HK | M-RD-R | BL | GY | BK-RF | | $110.00 |
| Maserati Mistral | 6277 | | HK | M-RD-R | BL | BR-L | BK-RF | | $110.00 |
| Maserati Mistral | 6277 | | HK | M-RD-R | BL | BR-D | BK-RF | | $110.00 |
| Maserati Mistral | 6277 | | HK | M-YW | BL | WH | | | $140.00 |
| Maserati Mistral | 6277 | | HK | M-YW | BL | BK | | | $130.00 |
| Maserati Mistral | 6277 | | HK | M-YW | BL | GY | | | $130.00 |
| Maserati Mistral | 6277 | | HK | M-YW | BL | BR-L | | | $130.00 |
| Maserati Mistral | 6277 | | HK | M-YW | BL | BR-D | | | $130.00 |
| Maserati Mistral | 6277 | | HK | M-YW | BL | WH | BK-RF | | $160.00 |
| Maserati Mistral | 6277 | | HK | M-YW | BL | BK | BK-RF | | $150.00 |
| Maserati Mistral | 6277 | | HK | M-YW | BL | GY | BK-RF | | $150.00 |
| Maserati Mistral | 6277 | | HK | M-YW | BL | BR-L | BK-RF | | $150.00 |
| Maserati Mistral | 6277 | | HK | M-YW | BL | BR-D | BK-RF | | $150.00 |
| Maserati Mistral | 6277 | | HK | M-YW-L | BL | WH | | | $140.00 |
| Maserati Mistral | 6277 | | HK | M-YW-L | BL | BK | | | $130.00 |
| Maserati Mistral | 6277 | | HK | M-YW-L | BL | GY | | | $130.00 |
| Maserati Mistral | 6277 | | HK | M-YW-L | BL | BR-L | | | $130.00 |
| Maserati Mistral | 6277 | | HK | M-YW-L | BL | BR-D | | | $130.00 |
| Maserati Mistral | 6277 | | HK | M-YW-L | BL | WH | BK-RF | | $160.00 |
| Maserati Mistral | 6277 | | HK | M-YW-L | BL | BK | BK-RF | | $150.00 |
| Maserati Mistral | 6277 | | HK | M-YW-L | BL | GY | BK-RF | | $150.00 |
| Maserati Mistral | 6277 | | HK | M-YW-L | BL | BR-L | BK-RF | | $150.00 |
| Maserati Mistral | 6277 | | HK | M-YW-L | BL | BR-D | BK-RF | | $150.00 |

## 1970 Variations

| Name | Number | Casting | Country | Color | Windows | Interior | Paint | Other | Value |
|---|---|---|---|---|---|---|---|---|---|
| Heavy Chevy | 6189 | | HK | CH | | WH | BK-STR | | $100.00 |
| Heavy Chevy | 6189 | | HK | CH | | GY | BK-STR | | $100.00 |
| | | | | | | | | | |
| King Kuda | 6190 | | HK | CH | BL | WH | | | $100.00 |
| King Kuda | 6190 | | HK | CH | BL | GY | | | $100.00 |
| | | | | | | | | | |
| Red Baron | 6400 | | HK | M-RD | | BK | | | $35.00 |
| Red Baron | 6400 | | HK | M-RD | | WH | | | $250.00 |
| Red Baron | 6400 | | HK | M-RD-R | | BK | | | $400.00 |
| | | | | | | | | | |
| The Demon | 6401 | | HK | M-AQ | | WH | | | $60.00 |
| The Demon | 6401 | | HK | M-AQ | | BK | | | $35.00 |
| The Demon | 6401 | | HK | M-BL | | WH | | | $60.00 |
| The Demon | 6401 | | HK | M-BL | | BK | | | $35.00 |
| The Demon | 6401 | | HK | M-BR-D | | WH | | | $80.00 |
| The Demon | 6401 | | HK | M-BR-D | | BK | | | $55.00 |
| The Demon | 6401 | | HK | M-BR-P | | WH | | | $60.00 |
| The Demon | 6401 | | HK | M-BR-P | | BK | | | $45.00 |
| The Demon | 6401 | | HK | M-GD | | WH | | | $75.00 |
| The Demon | 6401 | | HK | M-GD | | BK | | | $45.00 |
| The Demon | 6401 | | HK | M-GR | | WH | | | $60.00 |
| The Demon | 6401 | | HK | M-GR | | BK | | | $45.00 |
| The Demon | 6401 | | HK | M-GR-E | | WH | | | $70.00 |
| The Demon | 6401 | | HK | M-GR-E | | BK | | | $35.00 |
| The Demon | 6401 | | HK | M-GR-L | | WH | | | $80.00 |
| The Demon | 6401 | | HK | M-GR-L | | BK | | | $40.00 |
| The Demon | 6401 | | HK | M-GR-O | | WH | | | $80.00 |
| The Demon | 6401 | | HK | M-GR-O | | BK | | | $40.00 |
| The Demon | 6401 | | HK | M-MG | | WH | | | $60.00 |
| The Demon | 6401 | | HK | M-MG | | BK | | | $45.00 |
| The Demon | 6401 | | HK | M-OR | | WH | | | $60.00 |
| The Demon | 6401 | | HK | M-OR | | BK | | | $45.00 |
| The Demon | 6401 | | HK | M-PR | | WH | | | $60.00 |
| The Demon | 6401 | | HK | M-PR | | BK | | | $45.00 |
| The Demon | 6401 | | HK | M-RD | | WH | | | $60.00 |
| The Demon | 6401 | | HK | M-RD | | BK | | | $45.00 |
| The Demon | 6401 | | HK | M-RD-R | | WH | | | $70.00 |
| The Demon | 6401 | | HK | M-RD-R | | BK | | | $35.00 |
| The Demon | 6401 | | HK | M-YW | | WH | | | $60.00 |
| The Demon | 6401 | | HK | M-YW | | BK | | | $30.00 |
| The Demon | 6401 | | HK | M-YW-L | | WH | | | $90.00 |
| The Demon | 6401 | | HK | M-YW-L | | BK | | | $45.00 |
| | | | | | | | | | |
| Paddy Wagon | 6402 | | USA | BL-D | | BR | | BL top | $30.00 |
| Paddy Wagon | 6402 | | HK | BL-D | | BR | | BL top | $30.00 |
| Paddy Wagon | 6402 | Low top | USA | BL-D | | | | BK top | $500.00 |
| | | | | | | | | | |
| Sand Crab | 6403 | | USA | M-AQ | TNT-RF | BK | | | $50.00 |
| Sand Crab | 6403 | | HK | M-AQ | TNT-RF | WH | | | $50.00 |
| Sand Crab | 6403 | | USA | M-BL | TNT-RF | BK | | | $45.00 |
| Sand Crab | 6403 | | HK | M-BL | TNT-RF | WH | | | $45.00 |
| Sand Crab | 6403 | | USA | M-BL-I | TNT-RF | BK | | | $65.00 |
| Sand Crab | 6403 | | HK | M-BL-I | TNT-RF | WH | | | $65.00 |
| Sand Crab | 6403 | | USA | M-BL-P | TNT-RF | BK | | | $55.00 |
| Sand Crab | 6403 | | HK | M-BL-P | TNT-RF | WH | | | $55.00 |
| Sand Crab | 6403 | | USA | M-GD | TNT-RF | BK | | | $45.00 |
| Sand Crab | 6403 | | HK | M-GD | TNT-RF | WH | | | $45.00 |
| Sand Crab | 6403 | | USA | M-GR | TNT-RF | BK | | | $45.00 |
| Sand Crab | 6403 | | HK | M-GR | TNT-RF | WH | | | $45.00 |
| Sand Crab | 6403 | | USA | M-GR-E | TNT-RF | BK | | | $35.00 |
| Sand Crab | 6403 | | HK | M-GR-E | TNT-RF | WH | | | $35.00 |
| Sand Crab | 6403 | | USA | M-GR-L | TNT-RF | BK | | | $45.00 |
| Sand Crab | 6403 | | HK | M-GR-L | TNT-RF | WH | | | $45.00 |
| Sand Crab | 6403 | | USA | M-GR-O | TNT-RF | BK | | | $50.00 |
| Sand Crab | 6403 | | HK | M-GR-O | TNT-RF | WH | | | $50.00 |
| Sand Crab | 6403 | | USA | M-MG | TNT-RF | BK | | | $35.00 |
| Sand Crab | 6403 | | HK | M-MG | TNT-RF | WH | | | $35.00 |
| Sand Crab | 6403 | | USA | M-OR | TNT-RF | BK | | | $45.00 |
| Sand Crab | 6403 | | HK | M-OR | TNT-RF | WH | | | $45.00 |

## 1970 Variations

| Name | Number | Casting | Country | Color | Windows | Interior | Paint | Other | Value |
|---|---|---|---|---|---|---|---|---|---|
| Sand Crab | 6403 | | USA | M-PK | TNT-RF | BK | | | $110.00 |
| Sand Crab | 6403 | | HK | M-PK | TNT-RF | WH | | | $110.00 |
| Sand Crab | 6403 | | USA | M-PK-H | TNT-RF | BK | | | $110.00 |
| Sand Crab | 6403 | | HK | M-PK-H | TNT-RF | WH | | | $110.00 |
| Sand Crab | 6403 | | USA | M-PK-S | TNT-RF | BK | | | $110.00 |
| Sand Crab | 6403 | | HK | M-PK-S | TNT-RF | WH | | | $110.00 |
| Sand Crab | 6403 | | USA | M-RD | TNT-RF | BK | | | $45.00 |
| Sand Crab | 6403 | | HK | M-RD | TNT-RF | WH | | | $45.00 |
| Sand Crab | 6403 | | USA | M-RD-R | TNT-RF | BK | | | $50.00 |
| Sand Crab | 6403 | | HK | M-RD-R | TNT-RF | WH | | | $50.00 |
| Sand Crab | 6403 | | USA | M-YW | TNT-RF | BK | | | $45.00 |
| Sand Crab | 6403 | | HK | M-YW | TNT-RF | WH | | | $45.00 |
| Sand Crab | 6403 | | USA | M-YW-L | TNT-RF | BK | | | $40.00 |
| Sand Crab | 6403 | | HK | M-YW-L | TNT-RF | WH | | | $40.00 |
| | | | | | | | | | |
| Classic Nomad | 6404 | | USA | M-AQ | CL | WH | | | $100.00 |
| Classic Nomad | 6404 | | USA | M-BL | CL | WH | | | $95.00 |
| Classic Nomad | 6404 | | USA | M-BL-I | CL | WH | | | $90.00 |
| Classic Nomad | 6404 | | USA | M-BL-P | CL | WH | | | $90.00 |
| Classic Nomad | 6404 | | USA | M-BR-D | CL | WH | | | $75.00 |
| Classic Nomad | 6404 | | USA | M-BR-P | CL | WH | | | $150.00 |
| Classic Nomad | 6404 | | USA | M-GD | CL | WH | | | $120.00 |
| Classic Nomad | 6404 | | USA | M-GR | CL | WH | | | $80.00 |
| Classic Nomad | 6404 | | USA | M-GR-E | CL | WH | | | $80.00 |
| Classic Nomad | 6404 | | USA | M-GR-L | CL | WH | | | $75.00 |
| Classic Nomad | 6404 | | USA | M-GR-O | CL | WH | | | $85.00 |
| Classic Nomad | 6404 | | USA | M-MG | CL | WH | | | $100.00 |
| Classic Nomad | 6404 | | USA | M-OR | CL | WH | | | $95.00 |
| Classic Nomad | 6404 | | USA | M-PK | CL | WH | | | $220.00 |
| Classic Nomad | 6404 | | USA | M-PK-H | CL | WH | | | $220.00 |
| Classic Nomad | 6404 | | USA | M-PK-S | CL | WH | | | $220.00 |
| Classic Nomad | 6404 | | USA | M-PR | CL | WH | | | $140.00 |
| Classic Nomad | 6404 | | USA | M-RD | CL | WH | | | $75.00 |
| Classic Nomad | 6404 | | USA | M-RD-R | CL | WH | | | $80.00 |
| Classic Nomad | 6404 | | USA | M-YW | CL | WH | | | $75.00 |
| Classic Nomad | 6404 | | USA | M-YW-L | CL | WH | | | $85.00 |
| | | | | | | | | | |
| Nitty Gritty Kitty | 6405 | | HK | M-AQ | BL | WH | | | $85.00 |
| Nitty Gritty Kitty | 6405 | | HK | M-AQ | BL | BK | | | $90.00 |
| Nitty Gritty Kitty | 6405 | | HK | M-AQ | BL | GY | | | $75.00 |
| Nitty Gritty Kitty | 6405 | | HK | M-AQ | BL | BR-L | | | $75.00 |
| Nitty Gritty Kitty | 6405 | | HK | M-AQ | BL | BR-D | | | $75.00 |
| Nitty Gritty Kitty | 6405 | | HK | M-BL | BL | WH | | | $85.00 |
| Nitty Gritty Kitty | 6405 | | HK | M-BL | BL | BK | | | $75.00 |
| Nitty Gritty Kitty | 6405 | | HK | M-BL | BL | GY | | | $75.00 |
| Nitty Gritty Kitty | 6405 | | HK | M-BL | BL | BR-L | | | $75.00 |
| Nitty Gritty Kitty | 6405 | | HK | M-BL | BL | BR-D | | | $75.00 |
| Nitty Gritty Kitty | 6405 | | HK | M-BR-D | BL | WH | | | $110.00 |
| Nitty Gritty Kitty | 6405 | | HK | M-BR-D | BL | BK | | | $100.00 |
| Nitty Gritty Kitty | 6405 | | HK | M-BR-D | BL | GY | | | $100.00 |
| Nitty Gritty Kitty | 6405 | | HK | M-BR-D | BL | BR-L | | | $100.00 |
| Nitty Gritty Kitty | 6405 | | HK | M-BR-D | BL | BR-D | | | $100.00 |
| Nitty Gritty Kitty | 6405 | | HK | M-BR-P | BL | WH | | | $95.00 |
| Nitty Gritty Kitty | 6405 | | HK | M-BR-P | BL | BK | | | $85.00 |
| Nitty Gritty Kitty | 6405 | | HK | M-BR-P | BL | GY | | | $85.00 |
| Nitty Gritty Kitty | 6405 | | HK | M-BR-P | BL | BR-L | | | $85.00 |
| Nitty Gritty Kitty | 6405 | | HK | M-BR-P | BL | BR-D | | | $85.00 |
| Nitty Gritty Kitty | 6405 | | HK | M-GD | BL | WH | | | $80.00 |
| Nitty Gritty Kitty | 6405 | | HK | M-GD | BL | BK | | | $70.00 |
| Nitty Gritty Kitty | 6405 | | HK | M-GD | BL | GY | | | $70.00 |
| Nitty Gritty Kitty | 6405 | | HK | M-GD | BL | BR-L | | | $70.00 |
| Nitty Gritty Kitty | 6405 | | HK | M-GD | BL | BR-D | | | $70.00 |
| Nitty Gritty Kitty | 6405 | | HK | M-GR | BL | WH | | | $75.00 |
| Nitty Gritty Kitty | 6405 | | HK | M-GR | BL | BK | | | $65.00 |
| Nitty Gritty Kitty | 6405 | | HK | M-GR | BL | GY | | | $65.00 |
| Nitty Gritty Kitty | 6405 | | HK | M-GR | BL | BR-L | | | $65.00 |
| Nitty Gritty Kitty | 6405 | | HK | M-GR | BL | BR-D | | | $65.00 |
| Nitty Gritty Kitty | 6405 | | HK | M-GR-E | BL | WH | | | $80.00 |
| Nitty Gritty Kitty | 6405 | | HK | M-GR-E | BL | BK | | | $70.00 |
| Nitty Gritty Kitty | 6405 | | HK | M-GR-E | BL | GY | | | $70.00 |

## 1970 Variations

| Name | Number | Casting | Country | Color | Windows | Interior | Paint | Other | Value |
|---|---|---|---|---|---|---|---|---|---|
| Nitty Gritty Kitty | 6405 | | HK | M-GR-E | BL | BR-L | | | $70.00 |
| Nitty Gritty Kitty | 6405 | | HK | M-GR-E | BL | BR-D | | | $70.00 |
| Nitty Gritty Kitty | 6405 | | HK | M-GR-O | BL | WH | | | $95.00 |
| Nitty Gritty Kitty | 6405 | | HK | M-GR-O | BL | BK | | | $80.00 |
| Nitty Gritty Kitty | 6405 | | HK | M-GR-O | BL | GY | | | $80.00 |
| Nitty Gritty Kitty | 6405 | | HK | M-GR-O | BL | BR-L | | | $80.00 |
| Nitty Gritty Kitty | 6405 | | HK | M-GR-O | BL | BR-D | | | $80.00 |
| Nitty Gritty Kitty | 6405 | | HK | M-OR | BL | WH | | | $85.00 |
| Nitty Gritty Kitty | 6405 | | HK | M-OR | BL | BK | | | $75.00 |
| Nitty Gritty Kitty | 6405 | | HK | M-OR | BL | GY | | | $75.00 |
| Nitty Gritty Kitty | 6405 | | HK | M-OR | BL | BR-L | | | $75.00 |
| Nitty Gritty Kitty | 6405 | | HK | M-OR | BL | BR-D | | | $75.00 |
| Nitty Gritty Kitty | 6405 | | HK | M-PR | BL | WH | | | $95.00 |
| Nitty Gritty Kitty | 6405 | | HK | M-PR | BL | BK | | | $85.00 |
| Nitty Gritty Kitty | 6405 | | HK | M-PR | BL | GY | | | $85.00 |
| Nitty Gritty Kitty | 6405 | | HK | M-PR | BL | BR-L | | | $85.00 |
| Nitty Gritty Kitty | 6405 | | HK | M-PR | BL | BR-D | | | $85.00 |
| Nitty Gritty Kitty | 6405 | | HK | M-RD | BL | WH | | | $100.00 |
| Nitty Gritty Kitty | 6405 | | HK | M-RD | BL | BK | | | $90.00 |
| Nitty Gritty Kitty | 6405 | | HK | M-RD | BL | GY | | | $90.00 |
| Nitty Gritty Kitty | 6405 | | HK | M-RD | BL | BR-L | | | $90.00 |
| Nitty Gritty Kitty | 6405 | | HK | M-RD | BL | BR-D | | | $90.00 |
| Nitty Gritty Kitty | 6405 | | HK | M-RD-R | BL | WH | | | $110.00 |
| Nitty Gritty Kitty | 6405 | | HK | M-RD-R | BL | BK | | | $100.00 |
| Nitty Gritty Kitty | 6405 | | HK | M-RD-R | BL | GY | | | $100.00 |
| Nitty Gritty Kitty | 6405 | | HK | M-RD-R | BL | BR-L | | | $100.00 |
| Nitty Gritty Kitty | 6405 | | HK | M-RD-R | BL | BR-D | | | $100.00 |
| | | | | | | | | | |
| TNT Bird | 6407 | | HK | M-AQ | | WH | | | $65.00 |
| TNT Bird | 6407 | | HK | M-AQ | | BK | | | $55.00 |
| TNT Bird | 6407 | | HK | M-AQ | | GY | | | $55.00 |
| TNT Bird | 6407 | | HK | M-AQ | | BR-L | | | $55.00 |
| TNT Bird | 6407 | | HK | M-AQ | | BR-D | | | $55.00 |
| TNT Bird | 6407 | | HK | M-BL | | WH | | | $65.00 |
| TNT Bird | 6407 | | HK | M-BL | | BK | | | $55.00 |
| TNT Bird | 6407 | | HK | M-BL | | GY | | | $55.00 |
| TNT Bird | 6407 | | HK | M-BL | | BR-L | | | $55.00 |
| TNT Bird | 6407 | | HK | M-BL | | BR-D | | | $55.00 |
| TNT Bird | 6407 | | HK | M-BR-D | | WH | | | $65.00 |
| TNT Bird | 6407 | | HK | M-BR-D | | BK | | | $55.00 |
| TNT Bird | 6407 | | HK | M-BR-D | | GY | | | $55.00 |
| TNT Bird | 6407 | | HK | M-BR-D | | BR-L | | | $55.00 |
| TNT Bird | 6407 | | HK | M-BR-D | | BR-D | | | $55.00 |
| TNT Bird | 6407 | | HK | M-BR-P | | WH | | | $65.00 |
| TNT Bird | 6407 | | HK | M-BR-P | | BK | | | $55.00 |
| TNT Bird | 6407 | | HK | M-BR-P | | GY | | | $55.00 |
| TNT Bird | 6407 | | HK | M-BR-P | | BR-L | | | $55.00 |
| TNT Bird | 6407 | | HK | M-BR-P | | BR-D | | | $55.00 |
| TNT Bird | 6407 | | HK | M-GR | | WH | | | $65.00 |
| TNT Bird | 6407 | | HK | M-GR | | BK | | | $55.00 |
| TNT Bird | 6407 | | HK | M-GR | | GY | | | $55.00 |
| TNT Bird | 6407 | | HK | M-GR | | BR-L | | | $55.00 |
| TNT Bird | 6407 | | HK | M-GR | | BR-D | | | $55.00 |
| TNT Bird | 6407 | | HK | M-GR-E | | WH | | | $70.00 |
| TNT Bird | 6407 | | HK | M-GR-E | | BK | | | $60.00 |
| TNT Bird | 6407 | | HK | M-GR-E | | GY | | | $60.00 |
| TNT Bird | 6407 | | HK | M-GR-E | | BR-L | | | $60.00 |
| TNT Bird | 6407 | | HK | M-GR-E | | BR-D | | | $60.00 |
| TNT Bird | 6407 | | HK | M-GR-O | | WH | | | $80.00 |
| TNT Bird | 6407 | | HK | M-GR-O | | BK | | | $70.00 |
| TNT Bird | 6407 | | HK | M-GR-O | | GY | | | $70.00 |
| TNT Bird | 6407 | | HK | M-GR-O | | BR-L | | | $70.00 |
| TNT Bird | 6407 | | HK | M-GR-O | | BR-D | | | $70.00 |
| TNT Bird | 6407 | | HK | M-OR | | WH | | | $65.00 |
| TNT Bird | 6407 | | HK | M-OR | | BK | | | $55.00 |
| TNT Bird | 6407 | | HK | M-OR | | GY | | | $55.00 |
| TNT Bird | 6407 | | HK | M-OR | | BR-L | | | $55.00 |
| TNT Bird | 6407 | | HK | M-OR | | BR-D | | | $55.00 |
| TNT Bird | 6407 | | HK | M-PR | | WH | | | $80.00 |
| TNT Bird | 6407 | | HK | M-PR | | BK | | | $70.00 |
| TNT Bird | 6407 | | HK | M-PR | | GY | | | $70.00 |

## 1970 Variations

| Name | Number | Casting | Country | Color | Windows | Interior | Paint | Other | Value |
|---|---|---|---|---|---|---|---|---|---|
| TNT Bird | 6407 | | HK | M-PR | | BR-L | | | $70.00 |
| TNT Bird | 6407 | | HK | M-PR | | BR-D | | | $70.00 |
| TNT Bird | 6407 | | HK | M-RD | | WH | | | $65.00 |
| TNT Bird | 6407 | | HK | M-RD | | BK | | | $55.00 |
| TNT Bird | 6407 | | HK | M-RD | | GY | | | $55.00 |
| TNT Bird | 6407 | | HK | M-RD | | BR-L | | | $55.00 |
| TNT Bird | 6407 | | HK | M-RD | | BR-D | | | $55.00 |
| TNT Bird | 6407 | | HK | M-RD-R | | WH | | | $80.00 |
| TNT Bird | 6407 | | HK | M-RD-R | | BK | | | $70.00 |
| TNT Bird | 6407 | | HK | M-RD-R | | GY | | | $70.00 |
| TNT Bird | 6407 | | HK | M-RD-R | | BR-L | | | $70.00 |
| TNT Bird | 6407 | | HK | M-RD-R | | BR-D | | | $70.00 |
| | | | | | | | | | |
| Heavy Chevy | 6408 | | HK | M-AQ | | WH | | | $80.00 |
| Heavy Chevy | 6408 | | HK | M-AQ | | BK | | | $70.00 |
| Heavy Chevy | 6408 | | HK | M-AQ | | GY | | | $70.00 |
| Heavy Chevy | 6408 | | HK | M-AQ | | BR-L | | | $70.00 |
| Heavy Chevy | 6408 | | HK | M-AQ | | BR-D | | | $70.00 |
| Heavy Chevy | 6408 | | HK | M-BL | | WH | | | $80.00 |
| Heavy Chevy | 6408 | | HK | M-BL | | BK | | | $70.00 |
| Heavy Chevy | 6408 | | HK | M-BL | | GY | | | $70.00 |
| Heavy Chevy | 6408 | | HK | M-BL | | BR-L | | | $70.00 |
| Heavy Chevy | 6408 | | HK | M-BL | | BR-D | | | $70.00 |
| Heavy Chevy | 6408 | | HK | M-BL-I | | WH | | | $130.00 |
| Heavy Chevy | 6408 | | HK | M-BL-I | | BK | | | $120.00 |
| Heavy Chevy | 6408 | | HK | M-BL-I | | GY | | | $120.00 |
| Heavy Chevy | 6408 | | HK | M-BL-I | | BR-L | | | $120.00 |
| Heavy Chevy | 6408 | | HK | M-BL-I | | BR-D | | | $120.00 |
| Heavy Chevy | 6408 | | HK | M-BL-P | | WH | | | $100.00 |
| Heavy Chevy | 6408 | | HK | M-BL-P | | BK | | | $90.00 |
| Heavy Chevy | 6408 | | HK | M-BL-P | | GY | | | $90.00 |
| Heavy Chevy | 6408 | | HK | M-BL-P | | BR-L | | | $90.00 |
| Heavy Chevy | 6408 | | HK | M-BL-P | | BR-D | | | $90.00 |
| Heavy Chevy | 6408 | | HK | M-BR-D | | WH | | | $90.00 |
| Heavy Chevy | 6408 | | HK | M-BR-D | | BK | | | $80.00 |
| Heavy Chevy | 6408 | | HK | M-BR-D | | GY | | | $80.00 |
| Heavy Chevy | 6408 | | HK | M-BR-D | | BR-L | | | $80.00 |
| Heavy Chevy | 6408 | | HK | M-BR-D | | BR-D | | | $80.00 |
| Heavy Chevy | 6408 | | HK | M-BR-P | | WH | | | $80.00 |
| Heavy Chevy | 6408 | | HK | M-BR-P | | BK | | | $70.00 |
| Heavy Chevy | 6408 | | HK | M-BR-P | | GY | | | $70.00 |
| Heavy Chevy | 6408 | | HK | M-BR-P | | BR-L | | | $70.00 |
| Heavy Chevy | 6408 | | HK | M-BR-P | | BR-D | | | $70.00 |
| Heavy Chevy | 6408 | | HK | M-GR | | WH | | | $80.00 |
| Heavy Chevy | 6408 | | HK | M-GR | | BK | | | $70.00 |
| Heavy Chevy | 6408 | | HK | M-GR | | GY | | | $70.00 |
| Heavy Chevy | 6408 | | HK | M-GR | | BR-L | | | $70.00 |
| Heavy Chevy | 6408 | | HK | M-GR | | BR-D | | | $70.00 |
| Heavy Chevy | 6408 | | HK | M-GR-E | | WH | | | $75.00 |
| Heavy Chevy | 6408 | | HK | M-GR-E | | BK | | | $65.00 |
| Heavy Chevy | 6408 | | HK | M-GR-E | | GY | | | $65.00 |
| Heavy Chevy | 6408 | | HK | M-GR-E | | BR-L | | | $65.00 |
| Heavy Chevy | 6408 | | HK | M-GR-E | | BR-D | | | $65.00 |
| Heavy Chevy | 6408 | | HK | M-GR-O | | WH | | | $105.00 |
| Heavy Chevy | 6408 | | HK | M-GR-O | | BK | | | $95.00 |
| Heavy Chevy | 6408 | | HK | M-GR-O | | GY | | | $95.00 |
| Heavy Chevy | 6408 | | HK | M-GR-O | | BR-L | | | $95.00 |
| Heavy Chevy | 6408 | | HK | M-GR-O | | BR-D | | | $95.00 |
| Heavy Chevy | 6408 | | HK | M-OR | | WH | | | $85.00 |
| Heavy Chevy | 6408 | | HK | M-OR | | BK | | | $75.00 |
| Heavy Chevy | 6408 | | HK | M-OR | | GY | | | $75.00 |
| Heavy Chevy | 6408 | | HK | M-OR | | BR-L | | | $75.00 |
| Heavy Chevy | 6408 | | HK | M-OR | | BR-D | | | $75.00 |
| Heavy Chevy | 6408 | | HK | M-PR | | WH | | | $90.00 |
| Heavy Chevy | 6408 | | HK | M-PR | | BK | | | $80.00 |
| Heavy Chevy | 6408 | | HK | M-PR | | GY | | | $80.00 |
| Heavy Chevy | 6408 | | HK | M-PR | | BR-L | | | $80.00 |
| Heavy Chevy | 6408 | | HK | M-PR | | BR-D | | | $80.00 |
| Heavy Chevy | 6408 | | HK | M-RD | | WH | | | $80.00 |
| Heavy Chevy | 6408 | | HK | M-RD | | BK | | | $70.00 |
| Heavy Chevy | 6408 | | HK | M-RD | | GY | | | $70.00 |

## 1970 Variations

| Name | Number | Casting | Country | Color | Windows | Interior | Paint | Other | Value |
|---|---|---|---|---|---|---|---|---|---|
| Heavy Chevy | 6408 | | HK | M-RD | | BR-L | | | $70.00 |
| Heavy Chevy | 6408 | | HK | M-RD | | BR-D | | | $70.00 |
| Heavy Chevy | 6408 | | HK | M-RD-R | | WH | | | $90.00 |
| Heavy Chevy | 6408 | | HK | M-RD-R | | BK | | | $80.00 |
| Heavy Chevy | 6408 | | HK | M-RD-R | | GY | | | $80.00 |
| Heavy Chevy | 6408 | | HK | M-RD-R | | BR-L | | | $80.00 |
| Heavy Chevy | 6408 | | HK | M-RD-R | | BR-D | | | $80.00 |
| Snake | 6409 | | USA | E-YW | CL | | | | $200.00 |
| Snake | 6409 | | HK | E-YW | BL | | | | $200.00 |
| Mongoose | 6410 | | USA | E-RD | CL | | | | $200.00 |
| Mongoose | 6410 | | HK | E-RD | BL | | | | $200.00 |
| King Kuda | 6411 | | HK | M-AQ | BL | WH | | | $80.00 |
| King Kuda | 6411 | | HK | M-AQ | BL | WH | BK-RF | | $90.00 |
| King Kuda | 6411 | | HK | M-AQ | BL | BK | | | $70.00 |
| King Kuda | 6411 | | HK | M-AQ | BL | BK | BK-RF | | $80.00 |
| King Kuda | 6411 | | HK | M-AQ | BL | GY | | | $70.00 |
| King Kuda | 6411 | | HK | M-AQ | BL | GY | BK-RF | | $80.00 |
| King Kuda | 6411 | | HK | M-AQ | BL | BR-L | | | $70.00 |
| King Kuda | 6411 | | HK | M-AQ | BL | BR-L | BK-RF | | $80.00 |
| King Kuda | 6411 | | HK | M-AQ | BL | BR-D | | | $70.00 |
| King Kuda | 6411 | | HK | M-AQ | BL | BR-D | BK-RF | | $80.00 |
| King Kuda | 6411 | | HK | M-BL | BL | WH | | | $80.00 |
| King Kuda | 6411 | | HK | M-BL | BL | WH | BK-RF | | $90.00 |
| King Kuda | 6411 | | HK | M-BL | BL | BK | | | $70.00 |
| King Kuda | 6411 | | HK | M-BL | BL | BK | BK-RF | | $80.00 |
| King Kuda | 6411 | | HK | M-BL | BL | GY | | | $70.00 |
| King Kuda | 6411 | | HK | M-BL | BL | GY | BK-RF | | $80.00 |
| King Kuda | 6411 | | HK | M-BL | BL | BR-L | | | $70.00 |
| King Kuda | 6411 | | HK | M-BL | BL | BR-L | BK-RF | | $80.00 |
| King Kuda | 6411 | | HK | M-BL | BL | BR-D | | | $70.00 |
| King Kuda | 6411 | | HK | M-BL | BL | BR-D | BK-RF | | $80.00 |
| King Kuda | 6411 | | HK | M-BR-D | BL | WH | | | $95.00 |
| King Kuda | 6411 | | HK | M-BR-D | BL | WH | BK-RF | | $105.00 |
| King Kuda | 6411 | | HK | M-BR-D | BL | BK | | | $85.00 |
| King Kuda | 6411 | | HK | M-BR-D | BL | BK | BK-RF | | $95.00 |
| King Kuda | 6411 | | HK | M-BR-D | BL | GY | | | $85.00 |
| King Kuda | 6411 | | HK | M-BR-D | BL | GY | BK-RF | | $95.00 |
| King Kuda | 6411 | | HK | M-BR-D | BL | BR-L | | | $85.00 |
| King Kuda | 6411 | | HK | M-BR-D | BL | BR-L | BK-RF | | $95.00 |
| King Kuda | 6411 | | HK | M-BR-D | BL | BR-D | | | $85.00 |
| King Kuda | 6411 | | HK | M-BR-D | BL | BR-D | BK-RF | | $95.00 |
| King Kuda | 6411 | | HK | M-BR-P | BL | WH | | | $85.00 |
| King Kuda | 6411 | | HK | M-BR-P | BL | WH | BK-RF | | $95.00 |
| King Kuda | 6411 | | HK | M-BR-P | BL | BK | | | $75.00 |
| King Kuda | 6411 | | HK | M-BR-P | BL | BK | BK-RF | | $85.00 |
| King Kuda | 6411 | | HK | M-BR-P | BL | GY | | | $75.00 |
| King Kuda | 6411 | | HK | M-BR-P | BL | GY | BK-RF | | $85.00 |
| King Kuda | 6411 | | HK | M-BR-P | BL | BR-L | | | $75.00 |
| King Kuda | 6411 | | HK | M-BR-P | BL | BR-L | BK-RF | | $85.00 |
| King Kuda | 6411 | | HK | M-BR-P | BL | BR-D | | | $75.00 |
| King Kuda | 6411 | | HK | M-BR-P | BL | BR-D | BK-RF | | $85.00 |
| King Kuda | 6411 | | HK | M-GD | BL | WH | | | $75.00 |
| King Kuda | 6411 | | HK | M-GD | BL | WH | BK-RF | | $85.00 |
| King Kuda | 6411 | | HK | M-GD | BL | BK | | | $65.00 |
| King Kuda | 6411 | | HK | M-GD | BL | BK | BK-RF | | $75.00 |
| King Kuda | 6411 | | HK | M-GD | BL | GY | | | $65.00 |
| King Kuda | 6411 | | HK | M-GD | BL | GY | BK-RF | | $75.00 |
| King Kuda | 6411 | | HK | M-GD | BL | BR-L | | | $65.00 |
| King Kuda | 6411 | | HK | M-GD | BL | BR-L | BK-RF | | $75.00 |
| King Kuda | 6411 | | HK | M-GD | BL | BR-D | | | $65.00 |
| King Kuda | 6411 | | HK | M-GD | BL | BR-D | BK-RF | | $75.00 |
| King Kuda | 6411 | | HK | M-GR | BL | WH | | | $65.00 |
| King Kuda | 6411 | | HK | M-GR | BL | WH | BK-RF | | $75.00 |
| King Kuda | 6411 | | HK | M-GR | BL | BK | | | $55.00 |
| King Kuda | 6411 | | HK | M-GR | BL | BK | BK-RF | | $65.00 |
| King Kuda | 6411 | | HK | M-GR | BL | GY | | | $55.00 |
| King Kuda | 6411 | | HK | M-GR | BL | GY | BK-RF | | $65.00 |

## 1970 Variations

| Name | Number | Casting | Country | Color | Windows | Interior | Paint | Other | Value |
|---|---|---|---|---|---|---|---|---|---|
| King Kuda | 6411 | | HK | M-GR | BL | BR-L | | | $55.00 |
| King Kuda | 6411 | | HK | M-GR | BL | BR-L | BK-RF | | $65.00 |
| King Kuda | 6411 | | HK | M-GR | BL | BR-D | | | $55.00 |
| King Kuda | 6411 | | HK | M-GR | BL | BR-D | BK-RF | | $65.00 |
| King Kuda | 6411 | | HK | M-GR-E | BL | WH | | | $70.00 |
| King Kuda | 6411 | | HK | M-GR-E | BL | WH | BK-RF | | $80.00 |
| King Kuda | 6411 | | HK | M-GR-E | BL | BK | | | $60.00 |
| King Kuda | 6411 | | HK | M-GR-E | BL | BK | BK-RF | | $70.00 |
| King Kuda | 6411 | | HK | M-GR-E | BL | GY | | | $60.00 |
| King Kuda | 6411 | | HK | M-GR-E | BL | GY | BK-RF | | $70.00 |
| King Kuda | 6411 | | HK | M-GR-E | BL | BR-L | | | $60.00 |
| King Kuda | 6411 | | HK | M-GR-E | BL | BR-L | BK-RF | | $70.00 |
| King Kuda | 6411 | | HK | M-GR-E | BL | BR-D | | | $60.00 |
| King Kuda | 6411 | | HK | M-GR-E | BL | BR-D | BK-RF | | $70.00 |
| King Kuda | 6411 | | HK | M-GR-L | BL | WH | | | $95.00 |
| King Kuda | 6411 | | HK | M-GR-L | BL | WH | BK-RF | | $105.00 |
| King Kuda | 6411 | | HK | M-GR-L | BL | BK | | | $85.00 |
| King Kuda | 6411 | | HK | M-GR-L | BL | BK | BK-RF | | $95.00 |
| King Kuda | 6411 | | HK | M-GR-L | BL | GY | | | $85.00 |
| King Kuda | 6411 | | HK | M-GR-L | BL | GY | BK-RF | | $95.00 |
| King Kuda | 6411 | | HK | M-GR-L | BL | BR-L | | | $85.00 |
| King Kuda | 6411 | | HK | M-GR-L | BL | BR-L | BK-RF | | $95.00 |
| King Kuda | 6411 | | HK | M-GR-L | BL | BR-D | | | $85.00 |
| King Kuda | 6411 | | HK | M-GR-L | BL | BR-D | BK-RF | | $95.00 |
| King Kuda | 6411 | | HK | M-GR-O | BL | WH | | | $90.00 |
| King Kuda | 6411 | | HK | M-GR-O | BL | WH | BK-RF | | $100.00 |
| King Kuda | 6411 | | HK | M-GR-O | BL | BK | | | $80.00 |
| King Kuda | 6411 | | HK | M-GR-O | BL | BK | BK-RF | | $90.00 |
| King Kuda | 6411 | | HK | M-GR-O | BL | GY | | | $80.00 |
| King Kuda | 6411 | | HK | M-GR-O | BL | GY | BK-RF | | $90.00 |
| King Kuda | 6411 | | HK | M-GR-O | BL | BR-L | | | $80.00 |
| King Kuda | 6411 | | HK | M-GR-O | BL | BR-L | BK-RF | | $90.00 |
| King Kuda | 6411 | | HK | M-GR-O | BL | BR-D | | | $80.00 |
| King Kuda | 6411 | | HK | M-GR-O | BL | BR-D | BK-RF | | $90.00 |
| King Kuda | 6411 | | HK | M-OR | BL | WH | | | $80.00 |
| King Kuda | 6411 | | HK | M-OR | BL | WH | BK-RF | | $90.00 |
| King Kuda | 6411 | | HK | M-OR | BL | BK | | | $70.00 |
| King Kuda | 6411 | | HK | M-OR | BL | BK | BK-RF | | $80.00 |
| King Kuda | 6411 | | HK | M-OR | BL | GY | | | $70.00 |
| King Kuda | 6411 | | HK | M-OR | BL | GY | BK-RF | | $80.00 |
| King Kuda | 6411 | | HK | M-OR | BL | BR-L | | | $70.00 |
| King Kuda | 6411 | | HK | M-OR | BL | BR-L | BK-RF | | $70.00 |
| King Kuda | 6411 | | HK | M-OR | BL | BR-D | | | $70.00 |
| King Kuda | 6411 | | HK | M-OR | BL | BR-D | BK-RF | | $80.00 |
| King Kuda | 6411 | | HK | M-PR | BL | WH | | | $85.00 |
| King Kuda | 6411 | | HK | M-PR | BL | WH | BK-RF | | $95.00 |
| King Kuda | 6411 | | HK | M-PR | BL | BK | | | $75.00 |
| King Kuda | 6411 | | HK | M-PR | BL | BK | BK-RF | | $85.00 |
| King Kuda | 6411 | | HK | M-PR | BL | GY | | | $75.00 |
| King Kuda | 6411 | | HK | M-PR | BL | GY | BK-RF | | $85.00 |
| King Kuda | 6411 | | HK | M-PR | BL | PR | | | $100.00 |
| King Kuda | 6411 | | HK | M-PR | BL | PR | BK-RF | | $120.00 |
| King Kuda | 6411 | | HK | M-PR | BL | BR-L | | | $75.00 |
| King Kuda | 6411 | | HK | M-PR | BL | BR-L | BK-RF | | $85.00 |
| King Kuda | 6411 | | HK | M-PR | BL | BR-D | | | $85.00 |
| King Kuda | 6411 | | HK | M-PR | BL | BR-D | BK-RF | | $85.00 |
| King Kuda | 6411 | | HK | M-RD | BL | WH | | | $80.00 |
| King Kuda | 6411 | | HK | M-RD | BL | WH | BK-RF | | $90.00 |
| King Kuda | 6411 | | HK | M-RD | BL | BK | | | $70.00 |
| King Kuda | 6411 | | HK | M-RD | BL | BK | BK-RF | | $80.00 |
| King Kuda | 6411 | | HK | M-RD | BL | GY | | | $70.00 |
| King Kuda | 6411 | | HK | M-RD | BL | GY | BK-RF | | $80.00 |
| King Kuda | 6411 | | HK | M-RD | BL | BR-L | | | $70.00 |
| King Kuda | 6411 | | HK | M-RD | BL | BR-L | BK-RF | | $80.00 |
| King Kuda | 6411 | | HK | M-RD | BL | BR-D | | | $70.00 |
| King Kuda | 6411 | | HK | M-RD | BL | BR-D | BK-RF | | $80.00 |
| King Kuda | 6411 | | HK | M-RD-R | BL | WH | | | $90.00 |
| King Kuda | 6411 | | HK | M-RD-R | BL | WH | BK-RF | | $85.00 |
| King Kuda | 6411 | | HK | M-RD-R | BL | BK | | | $65.00 |
| King Kuda | 6411 | | HK | M-RD-R | BL | BK | BK-RF | | $75.00 |
| King Kuda | 6411 | | HK | M-RD-R | BL | GY | | | $65.00 |
| King Kuda | 6411 | | HK | M-RD-R | BL | GY | BK-RF | | $75.00 |

## 1970 Variations

| Name | Number | Casting | Country | Color | Windows | Interior | Paint | Other | Value |
|---|---|---|---|---|---|---|---|---|---|
| King Kuda | 6411 | | HK | M-RD-R | BL | BR-L | | | $65.00 |
| King Kuda | 6411 | | HK | M-RD-R | BL | BR-L | BK-RF | | $75.00 |
| King Kuda | 6411 | | HK | M-RD-R | BL | BR-D | | | $65.00 |
| King Kuda | 6411 | | HK | M-RD-R | BL | BR-D | BK-RF | | $75.00 |
| King Kuda | 6411 | | HK | M-YW | BL | WH | | | $80.00 |
| King Kuda | 6411 | | HK | M-YW | BL | WH | BK-RF | | $90.00 |
| King Kuda | 6411 | | HK | M-YW | BL | BK | | | $70.00 |
| King Kuda | 6411 | | HK | M-YW | BL | BK | BK-RF | | $80.00 |
| King Kuda | 6411 | | HK | M-YW | BL | GY | | | $70.00 |
| King Kuda | 6411 | | HK | M-YW | BL | GY | BK-RF | | $80.00 |
| King Kuda | 6411 | | HK | M-YW | BL | BR-L | | | $70.00 |
| King Kuda | 6411 | | HK | M-YW | BL | BR-L | BK-RF | | $80.00 |
| King Kuda | 6411 | | HK | M-YW | BL | BR-D | | | $70.00 |
| King Kuda | 6411 | | HK | M-YW | BL | BR-D | BK-RF | | $80.00 |
| King Kuda | 6411 | | HK | M-YW-L | BL | WH | | | $110.00 |
| King Kuda | 6411 | | HK | M-YW-L | BL | WH | BK-RF | | $120.00 |
| King Kuda | 6411 | | HK | M-YW-L | BL | BK | | | $100.00 |
| King Kuda | 6411 | | HK | M-YW-L | BL | BK | BK-RF | | $110.00 |
| King Kuda | 6411 | | HK | M-YW-L | BL | GY | | | $100.00 |
| King Kuda | 6411 | | HK | M-YW-L | BL | GY | BK-RF | | $110.00 |
| King Kuda | 6411 | | HK | M-YW-L | BL | BR-L | | | $100.00 |
| King Kuda | 6411 | | HK | M-YW-L | BL | BR-L | BK-RF | | $110.00 |
| King Kuda | 6411 | | HK | M-YW-L | BL | BR-D | | | $100.00 |
| King Kuda | 6411 | | HK | M-YW-L | BL | BR-D | BK-RF | | $110.00 |
| | | | | | | | | | |
| Light My Firebird | 6412 | | HK | M-AQ | | WH | | | $45.00 |
| Light My Firebird | 6412 | | HK | M-AQ | | BK | | | $45.00 |
| Light My Firebird | 6412 | | HK | M-AQ | | GY | | | $45.00 |
| Light My Firebird | 6412 | | HK | M-AQ | | BR-L | | | $45.00 |
| Light My Firebird | 6412 | | HK | M-AQ | | BR-D | | | $45.00 |
| Light My Firebird | 6412 | | HK | M-BL | | WH | | | $45.00 |
| Light My Firebird | 6412 | | HK | M-BL | | BK | | | $45.00 |
| Light My Firebird | 6412 | | HK | M-BL | | GY | | | $45.00 |
| Light My Firebird | 6412 | | HK | M-BL | | BR-L | | | $45.00 |
| Light My Firebird | 6412 | | HK | M-BL | | BR-D | | | $45.00 |
| Light My Firebird | 6412 | | HK | M-BR-D | | WH | | | $75.00 |
| Light My Firebird | 6412 | | HK | M-BR-D | | BK | | | $75.00 |
| Light My Firebird | 6412 | | HK | M-BR-D | | GY | | | $75.00 |
| Light My Firebird | 6412 | | HK | M-BR-D | | BR-L | | | $75.00 |
| Light My Firebird | 6412 | | HK | M-BR-D | | BR-D | | | $75.00 |
| Light My Firebird | 6412 | | HK | M-BR-P | | WH | | | $65.00 |
| Light My Firebird | 6412 | | HK | M-BR-P | | BK | | | $65.00 |
| Light My Firebird | 6412 | | HK | M-BR-P | | GY | | | $65.00 |
| Light My Firebird | 6412 | | HK | M-BR-P | | BR-L | | | $65.00 |
| Light My Firebird | 6412 | | HK | M-BR-P | | BR-D | | | $65.00 |
| Light My Firebird | 6412 | | HK | M-GR | | WH | | | $45.00 |
| Light My Firebird | 6412 | | HK | M-GR | | BK | | | $45.00 |
| Light My Firebird | 6412 | | HK | M-GR | | GY | | | $45.00 |
| Light My Firebird | 6412 | | HK | M-GR | | BR-L | | | $45.00 |
| Light My Firebird | 6412 | | HK | M-GR | | BR-D | | | $45.00 |
| Light My Firebird | 6412 | | HK | M-GR-E | | WH | | | $45.00 |
| Light My Firebird | 6412 | | HK | M-GR-E | | BK | | | $45.00 |
| Light My Firebird | 6412 | | HK | M-GR-E | | GY | | | $45.00 |
| Light My Firebird | 6412 | | HK | M-GR-E | | BR-L | | | $45.00 |
| Light My Firebird | 6412 | | HK | M-GR-E | | BR-D | | | $45.00 |
| Light My Firebird | 6412 | | HK | M-GR-L | | WH | | | $70.00 |
| Light My Firebird | 6412 | | HK | M-GR-L | | BK | | | $60.00 |
| Light My Firebird | 6412 | | HK | M-GR-L | | GY | | | $60.00 |
| Light My Firebird | 6412 | | HK | M-GR-L | | BR-L | | | $60.00 |
| Light My Firebird | 6412 | | HK | M-GR-L | | BR-D | | | $60.00 |
| Light My Firebird | 6412 | | HK | M-GR-O | | WH | | | $60.00 |
| Light My Firebird | 6412 | | HK | M-GR-O | | BK | | | $60.00 |
| Light My Firebird | 6412 | | HK | M-GR-O | | GY | | | $60.00 |
| Light My Firebird | 6412 | | HK | M-GR-O | | BR-L | | | $60.00 |
| Light My Firebird | 6412 | | HK | M-GR-O | | BR-D | | | $60.00 |
| Light My Firebird | 6412 | | HK | M-OR | | WH | | | $45.00 |
| Light My Firebird | 6412 | | HK | M-OR | | BK | | | $45.00 |
| Light My Firebird | 6412 | | HK | M-OR | | GY | | | $45.00 |
| Light My Firebird | 6412 | | HK | M-OR | | BR-L | | | $45.00 |
| Light My Firebird | 6412 | | HK | M-OR | | BR-D | | | $45.00 |
| Light My Firebird | 6412 | | HK | M-PR | | WH | | | $45.00 |

## 1970 Variations

| Name | Number | Casting | Country | Color | Windows | Interior | Paint | Other | Value |
|---|---|---|---|---|---|---|---|---|---|
| Light My Firebird | 6412 | | HK | M-PR | | BK | | | $45.00 |
| Light My Firebird | 6412 | | HK | M-PR | | GY | | | $45.00 |
| Light My Firebird | 6412 | | HK | M-PR | | BR-L | | | $45.00 |
| Light My Firebird | 6412 | | HK | M-PR | | BR-D | | | $45.00 |
| Light My Firebird | 6412 | | HK | M-RD | | WH | | | $45.00 |
| Light My Firebird | 6412 | | HK | M-RD | | BK | | | $45.00 |
| Light My Firebird | 6412 | | HK | M-RD | | GY | | | $45.00 |
| Light My Firebird | 6412 | | HK | M-RD | | BR-L | | | $45.00 |
| Light My Firebird | 6412 | | HK | M-RD | | BR-D | | | $45.00 |
| Light My Firebird | 6412 | | HK | M-RD-R | | WH | | | $55.00 |
| Light My Firebird | 6412 | | HK | M-RD-R | | BK | | | $55.00 |
| Light My Firebird | 6412 | | HK | M-RD-R | | GY | | | $55.00 |
| Light My Firebird | 6412 | | HK | M-RD-R | | BR-L | | | $55.00 |
| Light My Firebird | 6412 | | HK | M-RD-R | | BR-D | | | $55.00 |
| Light My Firebird | 6412 | | HK | M-YW-L | | WH | | | $70.00 |
| Light My Firebird | 6412 | | HK | M-YW-L | | BK | | | $60.00 |
| Light My Firebird | 6412 | | HK | M-YW-L | | GY | | | $60.00 |
| Light My Firebird | 6412 | | HK | M-YW-L | | BR-L | | | $60.00 |
| Light My Firebird | 6412 | | HK | M-YW-L | | BR-D | | | $60.00 |
| Seasider | 6413 | | USA | M-AQ | CL | WH | | RD top WH bottom boat | $125.00 |
| Seasider | 6413 | | USA | M-AQ | CL | WH | | WH top RD bottom boat | $125.00 |
| Seasider | 6413 | | USA | M-AQ | CL | BK | | RD top WH bottom boat | $110.00 |
| Seasider | 6413 | | USA | M-AQ | CL | BK | | WH top RD bottom boat | $110.00 |
| Seasider | 6413 | | USA | M-AQ | CL | GY | | RD top WH bottom boat | $110.00 |
| Seasider | 6413 | | USA | M-AQ | CL | GY | | WH top RD bottom boat | $110.00 |
| Seasider | 6413 | | USA | M-AQ | CL | BR-L | | RD top WH bottom boat | $110.00 |
| Seasider | 6413 | | USA | M-AQ | CL | BR-L | | WH top RD bottom boat | $110.00 |
| Seasider | 6413 | | USA | M-AQ | CL | BR-D | | RD top WH bottom boat | $110.00 |
| Seasider | 6413 | | USA | M-AQ | CL | BR-D | | WH top RD bottom boat | $110.00 |
| Seasider | 6413 | | USA | M-BL | CL | WH | | RD top WH bottom boat | $110.00 |
| Seasider | 6413 | | USA | M-BL | CL | WH | | WH top RD bottom boat | $110.00 |
| Seasider | 6413 | | USA | M-BL | CL | BK | | RD top WH bottom boat | $100.00 |
| Seasider | 6413 | | USA | M-BL | CL | BK | | WH top RD bottom boat | $100.00 |
| Seasider | 6413 | | USA | M-BL | CL | GY | | RD top WH bottom boat | $100.00 |
| Seasider | 6413 | | USA | M-BL | CL | GY | | WH top RD bottom boat | $100.00 |
| Seasider | 6413 | | USA | M-BL | CL | BR-L | | RD top WH bottom boat | $100.00 |
| Seasider | 6413 | | USA | M-BL | CL | BR-L | | WH top RD bottom boat | $100.00 |
| Seasider | 6413 | | USA | M-BL | CL | BR-D | | RD top WH bottom boat | $100.00 |
| Seasider | 6413 | | USA | M-BL | CL | BR-D | | WH top RD bottom boat | $100.00 |
| Seasider | 6413 | | USA | M-GD | CL | WH | | RD top WH bottom boat | $110.00 |
| Seasider | 6413 | | USA | M-GD | CL | WH | | WH top RD bottom boat | $110.00 |
| Seasider | 6413 | | USA | M-GD | CL | BK | | RD top WH bottom boat | $100.00 |
| Seasider | 6413 | | USA | M-GD | CL | BK | | WH top RD bottom boat | $100.00 |
| Seasider | 6413 | | USA | M-GD | CL | GY | | RD top WH bottom boat | $100.00 |
| Seasider | 6413 | | USA | M-GD | CL | GY | | WH top RD bottom boat | $100.00 |
| Seasider | 6413 | | USA | M-GD | CL | BR-L | | RD top WH bottom boat | $100.00 |
| Seasider | 6413 | | USA | M-GD | CL | BR-L | | WH top RD bottom boat | $100.00 |
| Seasider | 6413 | | USA | M-GD | CL | BR-D | | RD top WH bottom boat | $100.00 |
| Seasider | 6413 | | USA | M-GD | CL | BR-D | | WH top RD bottom boat | $100.00 |
| Seasider | 6413 | | USA | M-GR | CL | WH | | RD top WH bottom boat | $110.00 |
| Seasider | 6413 | | USA | M-GR | CL | WH | | WH top RD bottom boat | $110.00 |
| Seasider | 6413 | | USA | M-GR | CL | BK | | RD top WH bottom boat | $100.00 |
| Seasider | 6413 | | USA | M-GR | CL | BK | | WH top RD bottom boat | $100.00 |
| Seasider | 6413 | | USA | M-GR | CL | GY | | RD top WH bottom boat | $100.00 |
| Seasider | 6413 | | USA | M-GR | CL | GY | | WH top RD bottom boat | $100.00 |
| Seasider | 6413 | | USA | M-GR | CL | BR-L | | RD top WH bottom boat | $100.00 |
| Seasider | 6413 | | USA | M-GR | CL | BR-L | | WH top RD bottom boat | $100.00 |
| Seasider | 6413 | | USA | M-GR | CL | BR-D | | RD top WH bottom boat | $100.00 |
| Seasider | 6413 | | USA | M-GR | CL | BR-D | | WH top RD bottom boat | $100.00 |
| Seasider | 6413 | | USA | M-GR-E | CL | WH | | RD top WH bottom boat | $125.00 |
| Seasider | 6413 | | USA | M-GR-E | CL | WH | | WH top RD bottom boat | $125.00 |
| Seasider | 6413 | | USA | M-GR-E | CL | BK | | RD top WH bottom boat | $110.00 |
| Seasider | 6413 | | USA | M-GR-E | CL | BK | | WH top RD bottom boat | $110.00 |
| Seasider | 6413 | | USA | M-GR-E | CL | GY | | RD top WH bottom boat | $110.00 |
| Seasider | 6413 | | USA | M-GR-E | CL | GY | | WH top RD bottom boat | $110.00 |
| Seasider | 6413 | | USA | M-GR-E | CL | BR-L | | RD top WH bottom boat | $110.00 |
| Seasider | 6413 | | USA | M-GR-E | CL | BR-L | | WH top RD bottom boat | $110.00 |
| Seasider | 6413 | | USA | M-GR-E | CL | BR-D | | RD top WH bottom boat | $110.00 |
| Seasider | 6413 | | USA | M-GR-E | CL | BR-D | | WH top RD bottom boat | $110.00 |
| Seasider | 6413 | | USA | M-GR-L | CL | WH | | RD top WH bottom boat | $125.00 |

## 1970 Variations

| Name | Number | Casting | Country | Color | Windows | Interior | Paint | Other | Value |
|---|---|---|---|---|---|---|---|---|---|
| Seasider | 6413 | | USA | M-GR-L | CL | WH | | WH top RD bottom boat | $125.00 |
| Seasider | 6413 | | USA | M-GR-L | CL | BK | | RD top WH bottom boat | $110.00 |
| Seasider | 6413 | | USA | M-GR-L | CL | BK | | WH top RD bottom boat | $110.00 |
| Seasider | 6413 | | USA | M-GR-L | CL | GY | | RD top WH bottom boat | $110.00 |
| Seasider | 6413 | | USA | M-GR-L | CL | GY | | WH top RD bottom boat | $110.00 |
| Seasider | 6413 | | USA | M-GR-L | CL | BR-L | | RD top WH bottom boat | $110.00 |
| Seasider | 6413 | | USA | M-GR-L | CL | BR-L | | WH top RD bottom boat | $110.00 |
| Seasider | 6413 | | USA | M-GR-L | CL | BR-D | | RD top WH bottom boat | $110.00 |
| Seasider | 6413 | | USA | M-GR-L | CL | BR-D | | WH top RD bottom boat | $110.00 |
| Seasider | 6413 | | USA | M-GR-L | CL | | | YW top WH bottom boat | $300.00 |
| Seasider | 6413 | | USA | M-GR-O | CL | WH | | YW top WH bottom boat | $300.00 |
| Seasider | 6413 | | USA | M-MG | CL | WH | | RD top WH bottom boat | $110.00 |
| Seasider | 6413 | | USA | M-MG | CL | WH | | WH top RD bottom boat | $110.00 |
| Seasider | 6413 | | USA | M-MG | CL | BK | | RD top WH bottom boat | $110.00 |
| Seasider | 6413 | | USA | M-MG | CL | BK | | WH top RD bottom boat | $110.00 |
| Seasider | 6413 | | USA | M-MG | CL | GY | | RD top WH bottom boat | $110.00 |
| Seasider | 6413 | | USA | M-MG | CL | GY | | WH top RD bottom boat | $110.00 |
| Seasider | 6413 | | USA | M-MG | CL | BR-L | | RD top WH bottom boat | $100.00 |
| Seasider | 6413 | | USA | M-MG | CL | BR-L | | WH top RD bottom boat | $100.00 |
| Seasider | 6413 | | USA | M-MG | CL | BR-D | | RD top WH bottom boat | $100.00 |
| Seasider | 6413 | | USA | M-MG | CL | BR-D | | WH top RD bottom boat | $100.00 |
| Seasider | 6413 | | USA | M-OR | CL | WH | | RD top WH bottom boat | $125.00 |
| Seasider | 6413 | | USA | M-OR | CL | WH | | WH top RD bottom boat | $125.00 |
| Seasider | 6413 | | USA | M-OR | CL | BK | | RD top WH bottom boat | $115.00 |
| Seasider | 6413 | | USA | M-OR | CL | BK | | WH top RD bottom boat | $115.00 |
| Seasider | 6413 | | USA | M-OR | CL | GY | | RD top WH bottom boat | $115.00 |
| Seasider | 6413 | | USA | M-OR | CL | GY | | WH top RD bottom boat | $115.00 |
| Seasider | 6413 | | USA | M-OR | CL | BR-L | | RD top WH bottom boat | $115.00 |
| Seasider | 6413 | | USA | M-OR | CL | BR-L | | WH top RD bottom boat | $115.00 |
| Seasider | 6413 | | USA | M-OR | CL | BR-D | | RD top WH bottom boat | $115.00 |
| Seasider | 6413 | | USA | M-OR | CL | BR-D | | WH top RD bottom boat | $115.00 |
| Seasider | 6413 | | USA | M-PK | CL | WH | | RD top WH bottom boat | $150.00 |
| Seasider | 6413 | | USA | M-PK | CL | WH | | WH top RD bottom boat | $150.00 |
| Seasider | 6413 | | USA | M-PK | CL | BK | | RD top WH bottom boat | $140.00 |
| Seasider | 6413 | | USA | M-PK | CL | BK | | WH top RD bottom boat | $140.00 |
| Seasider | 6413 | | USA | M-PK | CL | GY | | RD top WH bottom boat | $140.00 |
| Seasider | 6413 | | USA | M-PK | CL | GY | | WH top RD bottom boat | $140.00 |
| Seasider | 6413 | | USA | M-PK | CL | BR-L | | RD top WH bottom boat | $140.00 |
| Seasider | 6413 | | USA | M-PK | CL | BR-L | | WH top RD bottom boat | $140.00 |
| Seasider | 6413 | | USA | M-PK | CL | BR-D | | RD top WH bottom boat | $140.00 |
| Seasider | 6413 | | USA | M-PK | CL | BR-D | | WH top RD bottom boat | $140.00 |
| Seasider | 6413 | | USA | M-PK-H | CL | WH | | RD top WH bottom boat | $140.00 |
| Seasider | 6413 | | USA | M-PK-H | CL | WH | | WH top RD bottom boat | $140.00 |
| Seasider | 6413 | | USA | M-PK-H | CL | BK | | RD top WH bottom boat | $140.00 |
| Seasider | 6413 | | USA | M-PK-H | CL | BK | | WH top RD bottom boat | $140.00 |
| Seasider | 6413 | | USA | M-PK-H | CL | GY | | RD top WH bottom boat | $140.00 |
| Seasider | 6413 | | USA | M-PK-H | CL | GY | | WH top RD bottom boat | $140.00 |
| Seasider | 6413 | | USA | M-PK-H | CL | BR-L | | RD top WH bottom boat | $140.00 |
| Seasider | 6413 | | USA | M-PK-H | CL | BR-L | | WH top RD bottom boat | $140.00 |
| Seasider | 6413 | | USA | M-PK-H | CL | BR-D | | RD top WH bottom boat | $140.00 |
| Seasider | 6413 | | USA | M-PK-H | CL | BR-D | | WH top RD bottom boat | $140.00 |
| Seasider | 6413 | | USA | M-PK-S | CL | WH | | RD top WH bottom boat | $140.00 |
| Seasider | 6413 | | USA | M-PK-S | CL | WH | | WH top RD bottom boat | $140.00 |
| Seasider | 6413 | | USA | M-PK-S | CL | BK | | RD top WH bottom boat | $140.00 |
| Seasider | 6413 | | USA | M-PK-S | CL | BK | | WH top RD bottom boat | $140.00 |
| Seasider | 6413 | | USA | M-PK-S | CL | GY | | RD top WH bottom boat | $140.00 |
| Seasider | 6413 | | USA | M-PK-S | CL | GY | | WH top RD bottom boat | $140.00 |
| Seasider | 6413 | | USA | M-PK-S | CL | BR-L | | RD top WH bottom boat | $140.00 |
| Seasider | 6413 | | USA | M-PK-S | CL | BR-L | | WH top RD bottom boat | $140.00 |
| Seasider | 6413 | | USA | M-PK-S | CL | BR-D | | RD top WH bottom boat | $140.00 |
| Seasider | 6413 | | USA | M-PK-S | CL | BR-D | | WH top RD bottom boat | $140.00 |
| Seasider | 6413 | | USA | M-PR | CL | WH | | RD top WH bottom boat | $260.00 |
| Seasider | 6413 | | USA | M-PR | CL | WH | | WH top RD bottom boat | $260.00 |
| Seasider | 6413 | | USA | M-PR | CL | BK | | RD top WH bottom boat | $220.00 |
| Seasider | 6413 | | USA | M-PR | CL | BK | | WH top RD bottom boat | $220.00 |
| Seasider | 6413 | | USA | M-PR | CL | GY | | RD top WH bottom boat | $220.00 |
| Seasider | 6413 | | USA | M-PR | CL | GY | | WH top RD bottom boat | $220.00 |
| Seasider | 6413 | | USA | M-PR | CL | BR-L | | RD top WH bottom boat | $220.00 |
| Seasider | 6413 | | USA | M-PR | CL | BR-L | | WH top RD bottom boat | $220.00 |
| Seasider | 6413 | | USA | M-PR | CL | BR-D | | RD top WH bottom boat | $220.00 |
| Seasider | 6413 | | USA | M-PR | CL | BR-D | | WH top RD bottom boat | $220.00 |
| Seasider | 6413 | | USA | M-RD | CL | WH | | RD top WH bottom boat | $120.00 |

## 1970 Variations

| Name | Number | Casting | Country | Color | Windows | Interior | Paint | Other | Value |
|---|---|---|---|---|---|---|---|---|---|
| Seasider | 6413 | | USA | M-RD | CL | WH | | WH top RD bottom boat | $120.00 |
| Seasider | 6413 | | USA | M-RD | CL | BK | | RD top WH bottom boat | $100.00 |
| Seasider | 6413 | | USA | M-RD | CL | BK | | WH top RD bottom boat | $100.00 |
| Seasider | 6413 | | USA | M-RD | CL | GY | | RD top WH bottom boat | $100.00 |
| Seasider | 6413 | | USA | M-RD | CL | GY | | WH top RD bottom boat | $100.00 |
| Seasider | 6413 | | USA | M-RD | CL | BR-L | | RD top WH bottom boat | $100.00 |
| Seasider | 6413 | | USA | M-RD | CL | BR-L | | WH top RD bottom boat | $100.00 |
| Seasider | 6413 | | USA | M-RD | CL | BR-D | | RD top WH bottom boat | $100.00 |
| Seasider | 6413 | | USA | M-RD | CL | BR-D | | WH top RD bottom boat | $100.00 |
| Seasider | 6413 | | USA | M-RD-R | CL | WH | | RD top WH bottom boat | $100.00 |
| Seasider | 6413 | | USA | M-RD-R | CL | WH | | WH top RD bottom boat | $100.00 |
| Seasider | 6413 | | USA | M-RD-R | CL | BK | | RD top WH bottom boat | $90.00 |
| Seasider | 6413 | | USA | M-RD-R | CL | BK | | WH top RD bottom boat | $90.00 |
| Seasider | 6413 | | USA | M-RD-R | CL | GY | | RD top WH bottom boat | $90.00 |
| Seasider | 6413 | | USA | M-RD-R | CL | GY | | WH top RD bottom boat | $90.00 |
| Seasider | 6413 | | USA | M-RD-R | CL | BR-L | | RD top WH bottom boat | $90.00 |
| Seasider | 6413 | | USA | M-RD-R | CL | BR-L | | WH top RD bottom boat | $90.00 |
| Seasider | 6413 | | USA | M-RD-R | CL | BR-D | | RD top WH bottom boat | $90.00 |
| Seasider | 6413 | | USA | M-RD-R | CL | BR-D | | WH top RD bottom boat | $90.00 |
| Seasider | 6413 | | USA | M-YW | CL | WH | | RD top WH bottom boat | $90.00 |
| Seasider | 6413 | | USA | M-YW | CL | WH | | WH top RD bottom boat | $90.00 |
| Seasider | 6413 | | USA | M-YW | CL | BK | | RD top WH bottom boat | $100.00 |
| Seasider | 6413 | | USA | M-YW | CL | BK | | WH top RD bottom boat | $100.00 |
| Seasider | 6413 | | USA | M-YW | CL | GY | | RD top WH bottom boat | $100.00 |
| Seasider | 6413 | | USA | M-YW | CL | GY | | WH top RD bottom boat | $100.00 |
| Seasider | 6413 | | USA | M-YW | CL | BR-L | | RD top WH bottom boat | $100.00 |
| Seasider | 6413 | | USA | M-YW | CL | BR-L | | WH top RD bottom boat | $100.00 |
| Seasider | 6413 | | USA | M-YW | CL | BR-D | | RD top WH bottom boat | $100.00 |
| Seasider | 6413 | | USA | M-YW | CL | BR-D | | WH top RD bottom boat | $100.00 |
| Seasider | 6413 | | USA | M-YW-L | CL | WH | | RD top WH bottom boat | $120.00 |
| Seasider | 6413 | | USA | M-YW-L | CL | WH | | WH top HD bottom boat | $120.00 |
| Seasider | 6413 | | USA | M-YW-L | CL | BK | | RD top WH bottom boat | $110.00 |
| Seasider | 6413 | | USA | M-YW-L | CL | BK | | WH top RD bottom boat | $110.00 |
| Seasider | 6413 | | USA | M-YW-L | CL | GY | | RD top WH bottom boat | $110.00 |
| Seasider | 6413 | | USA | M-YW-L | CL | GY | | WH top RD bottom boat | $110.00 |
| Seasider | 6413 | | USA | M-YW-L | CL | BR-L | | RD top WH bottom boat | $110.00 |
| Seasider | 6413 | | USA | M-YW-L | CL | BR-L | | WH top RD bottom boat | $110.00 |
| Seasider | 6413 | | USA | M-YW-L | CL | BR-D | | RD top WH bottom boat | $110.00 |
| Seasider | 6413 | | USA | M-YW-L | CL | BR-D | | WH top RD bottom boat | $110.00 |
| | | | | | | | | | |
| Mighty Maverick | 6414 | | USA | M-AQ | | BK | | Rear wing & thick WH stripe | $70.00 |
| Mighty Maverick | 6414 | | HK | M-AQ | | BK | | Rear wing & thin WH stripe | $70.00 |
| Mighty Maverick | 6414 | | USA | M-AQ | | BK | | Rear wing & thick BK stripe | $110.00 |
| Mighty Maverick | 6414 | | USA | M-BL | | BK | | Rear wing & thick WH stripe | $60.00 |
| Mighty Maverick | 6414 | | HK | M-BL | | BK | | Rear wing & thin WH stripe | $60.00 |
| Mighty Maverick | 6414 | | USA | M-BL | | BK | | Rear wing & thick BK stripe | $110.00 |
| Mighty Maverick | 6414 | | USA | M-BR-D | | BK | | Rear wing & thick WH stripe | $80.00 |
| Mighty Maverick | 6414 | | HK | M-BR-D | | BK | | Rear wing & thin WH stripe | $80.00 |
| Mighty Maverick | 6414 | | USA | M-BR-D | | BK | | Rear wing & thick BK stripe | $130.00 |
| Mighty Maverick | 6414 | | USA | M-BR-P | | BK | | Rear wing & thick WH stripe | $70.00 |
| Mighty Maverick | 6414 | | HK | M-BR-P | | BK | | Rear wing & thin WH stripe | $70.00 |
| Mighty Maverick | 6414 | | USA | M-BR-P | | BK | | Rear wing & thick BK stripe | $95.00 |
| Mighty Maverick | 6414 | | USA | M-GD | | BK | | Rear wing & thick WH stripe | $60.00 |
| Mighty Maverick | 6414 | | HK | M-GD | | BK | | Rear wing & thin WH stripe | $60.00 |
| Mighty Maverick | 6414 | | USA | M-GD | | BK | | Rear wing & thick BK stripe | $110.00 |
| Mighty Maverick | 6414 | | USA | M-GR | | BK | | Rear wing & thick WH stripe | $60.00 |
| Mighty Maverick | 6414 | | HK | M-GR | | BK | | Rear wing & thin WH stripe | $60.00 |
| Mighty Maverick | 6414 | | USA | M-GR | | BK | | Rear wing & thick BK stripe | $110.00 |
| Mighty Maverick | 6414 | | USA | M-GR-E | | BK | | Rear wing & thick WH stripe | $70.00 |
| Mighty Maverick | 6414 | | HK | M-GR-E | | BK | | Rear wing & thin WH stripe | $70.00 |
| Mighty Maverick | 6414 | | USA | M-GR-E | | BK | | Rear wing & thick BK stripe | $95.00 |
| Mighty Maverick | 6414 | | USA | M-GR-L | | BK | | Rear wing & thick WH stripe | $60.00 |
| Mighty Maverick | 6414 | | HK | M-GR-L | | BK | | Rear wing & thin WH stripe | $60.00 |
| Mighty Maverick | 6414 | | USA | M-GR-L | | BK | | Rear wing & thick BK stripe | $100.00 |
| Mighty Maverick | 6414 | | USA | M-GR-O | | BK | | Rear wing & thick WH stripe | $100.00 |
| Mighty Maverick | 6414 | | HK | M-GR-O | | BK | | Rear wing & thin WH stripe | $100.00 |
| Mighty Maverick | 6414 | | USA | M-GR-O | | BK | | Rear wing & thick BK stripe | $130.00 |
| Mighty Maverick | 6414 | | USA | M-MG | | BK | | Rear wing & thick WH stripe | $70.00 |
| Mighty Maverick | 6414 | | HK | M-MG | | BK | | Rear wing & thin WH stripe | $70.00 |
| Mighty Maverick | 6414 | | USA | M-MG | | BK | | Rear wing & thick BK stripe | $95.00 |
| Mighty Maverick | 6414 | | USA | M-OR | | BK | | Rear wing & thick WH stripe | $60.00 |

## 1970 Variations

| Name | Number | Casting | Country | Color | Windows | Interior | Paint | Other | Value |
|---|---|---|---|---|---|---|---|---|---|
| Mighty Maverick | 6414 | | HK | M-OR | | BK | | Rear wing & thin WH stripe | $60.00 |
| Mighty Maverick | 6414 | | USA | M-OR | | BK | | Rear wing & thick BK stripe | $100.00 |
| Mighty Maverick | 6414 | | USA | M-PK | | BK | | Rear wing & thick WH stripe | $130.00 |
| Mighty Maverick | 6414 | | HK | M-PK | | BK | | Rear wing & thin WH stripe | $130.00 |
| Mighty Maverick | 6414 | | USA | M-PK | | BK | | Rear wing & thick BK stripe | $260.00 |
| Mighty Maverick | 6414 | | USA | M-PK-H | | BK | | Rear wing & thick WH stripe | $130.00 |
| Mighty Maverick | 6414 | | HK | M-PK-H | | BK | | Rear wing & thin WH stripe | $130.00 |
| Mighty Maverick | 6414 | | USA | M-PK-H | | BK | | Rear wing & thick BK stripe | $260.00 |
| Mighty Maverick | 6414 | | USA | M-PK-S | | BK | | Rear wing & thick WH stripe | $130.00 |
| Mighty Maverick | 6414 | | HK | M-PK-S | | BK | | Rear wing & thin WH stripe | $130.00 |
| Mighty Maverick | 6414 | | USA | M-PK-S | | BK | | Rear wing & thick BK stripe | $260.00 |
| Mighty Maverick | 6414 | | USA | M-PR | | BK | | Rear wing & thick WH stripe | $60.00 |
| Mighty Maverick | 6414 | | HK | M-PR | | BK | | Rear wing & thin WH stripe | $60.00 |
| Mighty Maverick | 6414 | | USA | M-PR | | BK | | Rear wing & thick BK stripe | $100.00 |
| Mighty Maverick | 6414 | | USA | M-RD | | BK | | Rear wing & thick WH stripe | $60.00 |
| Mighty Maverick | 6414 | | HK | M-RD | | BK | | Rear wing & thin WH stripe | $60.00 |
| Mighty Maverick | 6414 | | USA | M-RD | | BK | | Rear wing & thick BK stripe | $100.00 |
| Mighty Maverick | 6414 | | USA | M-RD-R | | BK | | Rear wing & thick WH stripe | $70.00 |
| Mighty Maverick | 6414 | | HK | M-RD-R | | BK | | Rear wing & thin WH stripe | $70.00 |
| Mighty Maverick | 6414 | | USA | M-RD-R | | BK | | Rear wing & thick BK stripe | $95.00 |
| Mighty Maverick | 6414 | | USA | M-YW | | BK | | Rear wing & thick WH stripe | $60.00 |
| Mighty Maverick | 6414 | | HK | M-YW | | BK | | Rear wing & thin WH stripe | $60.00 |
| Mighty Maverick | 6414 | | USA | M-YW | | BK | | Rear wing & thick BK stripe | $100.00 |
| Mighty Maverick | 6414 | | USA | M-YW-L | | BK | | Rear wing & thick WH stripe | $70.00 |
| Mighty Maverick | 6414 | | HK | M-YW-L | | BK | | Rear wing & thin WH stripe | $70.00 |
| Mighty Maverick | 6414 | | USA | M-YW-L | | BK | | Rear wing & thick BK stripe | $95.00 |
| Porsche 917 | 6416 | | USA | E-GY | | WH | | | $55.00 |
| Porsche 917 | 6416 | | HK | E-GY | | BK | | | $50.00 |
| Porsche 917 | 6416 | | USA | M-AQ | | WH | | | $65.00 |
| Porsche 917 | 6416 | | HK | M-AQ | | BK | | | $60.00 |
| Porsche 917 | 6416 | | USA | M-BL | | WH | | | $45.00 |
| Porsche 917 | 6416 | | HK | M-BL | | BK | | | $40.00 |
| Porsche 917 | 6416 | | USA | M-GD | | WH | | | $45.00 |
| Porsche 917 | 6416 | | HK | M-GD | | BK | | | $40.00 |
| Porsche 917 | 6416 | | USA | M-GR | | WH | | | $45.00 |
| Porsche 917 | 6416 | | HK | M-GR | | BK | | | $40.00 |
| Porsche 917 | 6416 | | USA | M-GR-E | | WH | | | $50.00 |
| Porsche 917 | 6416 | | HK | M-GR-E | | BK | | | $45.00 |
| Porsche 917 | 6416 | | USA | M-GR-L | | WH | | | $45.00 |
| Porsche 917 | 6416 | | HK | M-GR-L | | BK | | | $40.00 |
| Porsche 917 | 6416 | | USA | M-MG | | WH | | | $50.00 |
| Porsche 917 | 6416 | | HK | M-MG | | BK | | | $45.00 |
| Porsche 917 | 6416 | | USA | M-OR | | WH | | | $50.00 |
| Porsche 917 | 6416 | | HK | M-OR | | BK | | | $45.00 |
| Porsche 917 | 6416 | | USA | M-PK | | WH | | | $120.00 |
| Porsche 917 | 6416 | | HK | M-PK | | BK | | | $110.00 |
| Porsche 917 | 6416 | | USA | M-PK-H | | WH | | | $120.00 |
| Porsche 917 | 6416 | | HK | M-PK-H | | BK | | | $110.00 |
| Porsche 917 | 6416 | | USA | M-PK-S | | WH | | | $90.00 |
| Porsche 917 | 6416 | | HK | M-PK-S | | BK | | | $85.00 |
| Porsche 917 | 6416 | | USA | M-PR | | WH | | | $125.00 |
| Porsche 917 | 6416 | | HK | M-PR | | BK | | | $125.00 |
| Porsche 917 | 6416 | | USA | M-RD | | WH | | | $45.00 |
| Porsche 917 | 6416 | | HK | M-RD | | BK | | | $40.00 |
| Porsche 917 | 6416 | | USA | M-RD-R | | WH | | | $50.00 |
| Porsche 917 | 6416 | | HK | M-RD-R | | BK | | | $45.00 |
| Porsche 917 | 6416 | | USA | M-YW | | WH | | | $45.00 |
| Porsche 917 | 6416 | | HK | M-YW | | BK | | | $40.00 |
| Porsche 917 | 6416 | | USA | M-YW-L | | WH | | | $50.00 |
| Porsche 917 | 6416 | | HK | M-YW-L | | BK | | | $50.00 |
| Ferrari 312P | 6417 | | USA | E-RD | CL | WH | | | $200.00 |
| Ferrari 312P | 6417 | | HK | E-RD | BL | WH | | | $200.00 |
| Ferrari 312P | 6417 | | USA | E-RD | CL | BK | | | $40.00 |
| Ferrari 312P | 6417 | | HK | E-RD | BL | BK | | | $40.00 |
| Ferrari 312P | 6417 | | USA | M-AQ | CL | WH | | | $225.00 |
| Ferrari 312P | 6417 | | HK | M-AQ | BL | WH | | | $225.00 |
| Ferrari 312P | 6417 | | USA | M-AQ | CL | BK | | | $45.00 |
| Ferrari 312P | 6417 | | HK | M-AQ | BL | BK | | | $45.00 |

## 1970 Variations

| Name | Number | Casting | Country | Color | Windows | Interior | Paint | Other | Value |
|---|---|---|---|---|---|---|---|---|---|
| Ferrari 312P | 6417 | | USA | M-BL | CL | WH | | | $200.00 |
| Ferrari 312P | 6417 | | HK | M-BL | BL | WH | | | $200.00 |
| Ferrari 312P | 6417 | | USA | M-BL | CL | BK | | | $45.00 |
| Ferrari 312P | 6417 | | HK | M-BL | BL | BK | | | $45.00 |
| Ferrari 312P | 6417 | | USA | M-BR-D | CL | WH | | | $300.00 |
| Ferrari 312P | 6417 | | HK | M-BR-D | BL | WH | | | $300.00 |
| Ferrari 312P | 6417 | | USA | M-BR-D | CL | BK | | | $60.00 |
| Ferrari 312P | 6417 | | HK | M-BR-D | BL | BK | | | $60.00 |
| Ferrari 312P | 6417 | | USA | M-BR-P | CL | WH | | | $250.00 |
| Ferrari 312P | 6417 | | HK | M-BR-P | BL | WH | | | $250.00 |
| Ferrari 312P | 6417 | | USA | M-BR-P | CL | BK | | | $60.00 |
| Ferrari 312P | 6417 | | HK | M-BR-P | BL | BK | | | $60.00 |
| Ferrari 312P | 6417 | | USA | M-GD | CL | WH | | | $200.00 |
| Ferrari 312P | 6417 | | HK | M-GD | BL | WH | | | $200.00 |
| Ferrari 312P | 6417 | | USA | M-GD | CL | BK | | | $40.00 |
| Ferrari 312P | 6417 | | HK | M-GD | BL | BK | | | $40.00 |
| Ferrari 312P | 6417 | | USA | M-GR | CL | WH | | | $200.00 |
| Ferrari 312P | 6417 | | HK | M-GR | BL | WH | | | $200.00 |
| Ferrari 312P | 6417 | | USA | M-GR | CL | BK | | | $40.00 |
| Ferrari 312P | 6417 | | HK | M-GR | BL | BK | | | $40.00 |
| Ferrari 312P | 6417 | | USA | M-GR-E | CL | WH | | | $225.00 |
| Ferrari 312P | 6417 | | HK | M-GR-E | BL | WH | | | $225.00 |
| Ferrari 312P | 6417 | | USA | M-GR-E | CL | BK | | | $45.00 |
| Ferrari 312P | 6417 | | HK | M-GR-E | BL | BK | | | $45.00 |
| Ferrari 312P | 6417 | | USA | M-GR-L | CL | WH | | | $225.00 |
| Ferrari 312P | 6417 | | HK | M-GR-L | BL | WH | | | $225.00 |
| Ferrari 312P | 6417 | | USA | M-GR-L | CL | BK | | | $45.00 |
| Ferrari 312P | 6417 | | HK | M-GR-L | BL | BK | | | $45.00 |
| Ferrari 312P | 6417 | | USA | M-GR-O | CL | WH | | | $250.00 |
| Ferrari 312P | 6417 | | HK | M-GR-O | BL | WH | | | $250.00 |
| Ferrari 312P | 6417 | | USA | M-GR-O | CL | BK | | | $50.00 |
| Ferrari 312P | 6417 | | HK | M-GR-O | BL | BK | | | $50.00 |
| Ferrari 312P | 6417 | | USA | M-MG | CL | WH | | | $225.00 |
| Ferrari 312P | 6417 | | HK | M-MG | BL | WH | | | $225.00 |
| Ferrari 312P | 6417 | | USA | M-MG | CL | BK | | | $45.00 |
| Ferrari 312P | 6417 | | HK | M-MG | BL | BK | | | $45.00 |
| Ferrari 312P | 6417 | | USA | M-OR | CL | WH | | | $200.00 |
| Ferrari 312P | 6417 | | HK | M-OR | BL | WH | | | $200.00 |
| Ferrari 312P | 6417 | | USA | M-OR | CL | BK | | | $40.00 |
| Ferrari 312P | 6417 | | HK | M-OR | BL | BK | | | $40.00 |
| Ferrari 312P | 6417 | | USA | M-PK | CL | WH | | | $300.00 |
| Ferrari 312P | 6417 | | HK | M-PK | BL | WH | | | $300.00 |
| Ferrari 312P | 6417 | | USA | M-PK | CL | BK | | | $90.00 |
| Ferrari 312P | 6417 | | HK | M-PK | BL | BK | | | $90.00 |
| Ferrari 312P | 6417 | | USA | M-PK-H | CL | WH | | | $300.00 |
| Ferrari 312P | 6417 | | HK | M-PK-H | BL | WH | | | $300.00 |
| Ferrari 312P | 6417 | | USA | M-PK-H | CL | BK | | | $90.00 |
| Ferrari 312P | 6417 | | HK | M-PK-H | BL | BK | | | $90.00 |
| Ferrari 312P | 6417 | | USA | M-PK-S | CL | WH | | | $300.00 |
| Ferrari 312P | 6417 | | HK | M-PK-S | BL | WH | | | $300.00 |
| Ferrari 312P | 6417 | | USA | M-PK-S | CL | BK | | | $90.00 |
| Ferrari 312P | 6417 | | HK | M-PK-S | BL | BK | | | $90.00 |
| Ferrari 312P | 6417 | | USA | M-PR | CL | WH | | | $225.00 |
| Ferrari 312P | 6417 | | HK | M-PR | BL | WH | | | $225.00 |
| Ferrari 312P | 6417 | | USA | M-PR | CL | BK | | | $90.00 |
| Ferrari 312P | 6417 | | HK | M-PR | BL | BK | | | $90.00 |
| Ferrari 312P | 6417 | | USA | M-RD | CL | WH | | | $200.00 |
| Ferrari 312P | 6417 | | HK | M-RD | BL | WH | | | $200.00 |
| Ferrari 312P | 6417 | | HK | M-RD | CL | BK | | | $40.00 |
| Ferrari 312P | 6417 | | USA | M-RD | BL | BK | | | $40.00 |
| Ferrari 312P | 6417 | | USA | M-RD-R | CL | WH | | | $225.00 |
| Ferrari 312P | 6417 | | HK | M-RD-R | BL | WH | | | $225.00 |
| Ferrari 312P | 6417 | | USA | M-RD-R | CL | BK | | | $45.00 |
| Ferrari 312P | 6417 | | HK | M-RD-R | BL | BK | | | $45.00 |
| Ferrari 312P | 6417 | | USA | M-YW | CL | WH | | | $200.00 |
| Ferrari 312P | 6417 | | HK | M-YW | BL | WH | | | $200.00 |
| Ferrari 312P | 6417 | | USA | M-YW | CL | BK | | | $40.00 |
| Ferrari 312P | 6417 | | HK | M-YW | BL | BK | | | $40.00 |
| Ferrari 312P | 6417 | | USA | M-YW-L | CL | WH | | | $250.00 |
| Ferrari 312P | 6417 | | HK | M-YW-L | BL | WH | | | $250.00 |
| Ferrari 312P | 6417 | | USA | M-YW-L | CL | BK | | | $50.00 |
| Ferrari 312P | 6417 | | HK | M-YW-L | BL | BK | | | $50.00 |

## 1970 Variations

| Name | Number | Casting | Country | Color | Windows | Interior | Paint | Other | Value |
|---|---|---|---|---|---|---|---|---|---|
| Peepin' Bomb | 6419 | | USA | M-AQ | | BK | | SL headlights | $40.00 |
| Peepin' Bomb | 6419 | | HK | M-AQ | | BK | | SL headlights | $50.00 |
| Peepin' Bomb | 6419 | | USA | M-AQ | | BK | | OR headlights | $60.00 |
| Peepin' Bomb | 6419 | | HK | M-AQ | | BK | | OR headlights | $75.00 |
| Peepin' Bomb | 6419 | | USA | M-BL | | BK | | SL headlights | $40.00 |
| Peepin' Bomb | 6419 | | HK | M-BL | | BK | | SL headlights | $50.00 |
| Peepin' Bomb | 6419 | | USA | M-BL | | BK | | OR headlights | $60.00 |
| Peepin' Bomb | 6419 | | HK | M-BL | | BK | | OR headlights | $75.00 |
| Peepin' Bomb | 6419 | | USA | M-GD | | BK | | SL headlights | $40.00 |
| Peepin' Bomb | 6419 | | HK | M-GD | | BK | | SL headlights | $50.00 |
| Peepin' Bomb | 6419 | | USA | M-GD | | BK | | OR headlights | $60.00 |
| Peepin' Bomb | 6419 | | HK | M-GD | | BK | | OR headlights | $75.00 |
| Peepin' Bomb | 6419 | | USA | M-GR | | BK | | SL headlights | $40.00 |
| Peepin' Bomb | 6419 | | HK | M-GR | | BK | | SL headlights | $50.00 |
| Peepin' Bomb | 6419 | | USA | M-GR | | BK | | OR headlights | $60.00 |
| Peepin' Bomb | 6419 | | HK | M-GR | | BK | | OR headlights | $75.00 |
| Peepin' Bomb | 6419 | | USA | M-GR-E | | BK | | SL headlights | $45.00 |
| Peepin' Bomb | 6419 | | HK | M-GR-E | | BK | | SL headlights | $55.00 |
| Peepin' Bomb | 6419 | | USA | M-GR-E | | BK | | OR headlights | $70.00 |
| Peepin' Bomb | 6419 | | HK | M-GR-E | | BK | | OR headlights | $85.00 |
| Peepin' Bomb | 6419 | | USA | M-GR-L | | BK | | SL headlights | $40.00 |
| Peepin' Bomb | 6419 | | HK | M-GR-L | | BK | | SL headlights | $50.00 |
| Peepin' Bomb | 6419 | | USA | M-GR-L | | BK | | OR headlights | $60.00 |
| Peepin' Bomb | 6419 | | HK | M-GR-L | | BK | | OR headlights | $75.00 |
| Peepin' Bomb | 6419 | | USA | M-GR-O | | BK | | SL headlights | $50.00 |
| Peepin' Bomb | 6419 | | HK | M-GR-O | | BK | | SL headlights | $55.00 |
| Peepin' Bomb | 6419 | | USA | M-GR-O | | BK | | OR headlights | $80.00 |
| Peepin' Bomb | 6419 | | HK | M-GR-O | | BK | | OR headlights | $95.00 |
| Peepin' Bomb | 6419 | | USA | M-MG | | BK | | SL headlights | $45.00 |
| Peepin' Bomb | 6419 | | HK | M-MG | | BK | | SL headlights | $55.00 |
| Peepin' Bomb | 6419 | | USA | M-MG | | BK | | OR headlights | $70.00 |
| Peepin' Bomb | 6419 | | HK | M-MG | | BK | | OR headlights | $85.00 |
| Peepin' Bomb | 6419 | | USA | M-OR | | BK | | SL headlights | $40.00 |
| Peepin' Bomb | 6419 | | HK | M-OR | | BK | | SL headlights | $50.00 |
| Peepin' Bomb | 6419 | | USA | M-OR | | BK | | OR headlights | $60.00 |
| Peepin' Bomb | 6419 | | HK | M-OR | | BK | | OR headlights | $75.00 |
| Peepin' Bomb | 6419 | | USA | M-PK | | BK | | SL headlights | $50.00 |
| Peepin' Bomb | 6419 | | HK | M-PK | | BK | | SL headlights | $55.00 |
| Peepin' Bomb | 6419 | | USA | M-PK | | BK | | OR headlights | $80.00 |
| Peepin' Bomb | 6419 | | HK | M-PK | | BK | | OR headlights | $95.00 |
| Peepin' Bomb | 6419 | | USA | M-PK-H | | BK | | SL headlights | $50.00 |
| Peepin' Bomb | 6419 | | HK | M-PK-H | | BK | | SL headlights | $55.00 |
| Peepin' Bomb | 6419 | | USA | M-PK-H | | BK | | OR headlights | $80.00 |
| Peepin' Bomb | 6419 | | HK | M-PK-H | | BK | | OR headlights | $95.00 |
| Peepin' Bomb | 6419 | | USA | M-PK-S | | BK | | SL headlights | $50.00 |
| Peepin' Bomb | 6419 | | HK | M-PK-S | | BK | | SL headlights | $55.00 |
| Peepin' Bomb | 6419 | | USA | M-PK-S | | BK | | OR headlights | $80.00 |
| Peepin' Bomb | 6419 | | HK | M-PK-S | | BK | | OR headlights | $95.00 |
| Peepin' Bomb | 6419 | | USA | M-PR | | BK | | SL headlights | $50.00 |
| Peepin' Bomb | 6419 | | HK | M-PR | | BK | | SL headlights | $55.00 |
| Peepin' Bomb | 6419 | | USA | M-PR | | BK | | OR headlights | $80.00 |
| Peepin' Bomb | 6419 | | HK | M-PR | | BK | | OR headlights | $95.00 |
| Peepin' Bomb | 6419 | | USA | M-RD | | BK | | SL headlights | $40.00 |
| Peepin' Bomb | 6419 | | HK | M-RD | | BK | | SL headlights | $50.00 |
| Peepin' Bomb | 6419 | | USA | M-RD | | BK | | OR headlights | $60.00 |
| Peepin' Bomb | 6419 | | HK | M-RD | | BK | | OR headlights | $75.00 |
| Peepin' Bomb | 6419 | | USA | M-RD-R | | BK | | SL headlights | $45.00 |
| Peepin' Bomb | 6419 | | HK | M-RD-R | | BK | | SL headlights | $55.00 |
| Peepin' Bomb | 6419 | | USA | M-RD-R | | BK | | OR headlights | $70.00 |
| Peepin' Bomb | 6419 | | HK | M-RD-R | | BK | | OR headlights | $85.00 |
| Peepin' Bomb | 6419 | | USA | M-YW | | BK | | SL headlights | $40.00 |
| Peepin' Bomb | 6419 | | HK | M-YW | | BK | | SL headlights | $40.00 |
| Peepin' Bomb | 6419 | | USA | M-YW | | BK | | OR headlights | $60.00 |
| Peepin' Bomb | 6419 | | HK | M-YW | | BK | | OR headlights | $75.00 |
| Peepin' Bomb | 6419 | | USA | M-YW-L | | BK | | SL headlights | $45.00 |
| Peepin' Bomb | 6419 | | HK | M-YW-L | | BK | | SL headlights | $45.00 |
| Peepin' Bomb | 6419 | | USA | M-YW-L | | BK | | OR headlights | $55.00 |
| Peepin' Bomb | 6419 | | HK | M-YW-L | | BK | | OR headlights | $65.00 |

## 1970 Variations

| Name | Number | Casting | Country | Color | Windows | Interior | Paint | Other | Value |
|---|---|---|---|---|---|---|---|---|---|
| Carabo | 6420 | | USA | M-AQ | CL | WH | | | $45.00 |
| Carabo | 6420 | | HK | M-AQ | BL | WH | | | $45.00 |
| Carabo | 6420 | | USA | M-AQ | CL | BK | | | $40.00 |
| Carabo | 6420 | | HK | M-AQ | BL | BK | | | $40.00 |
| Carabo | 6420 | | USA | M-AQ | CL | GY | | | $40.00 |
| Carabo | 6420 | | HK | M-AQ | BL | GY | | | $40.00 |
| Carabo | 6420 | | USA | M-AQ | CL | BR-L | | | $40.00 |
| Carabo | 6420 | | HK | M-AQ | BL | BR-L | | | $40.00 |
| Carabo | 6420 | | USA | M-AQ | CL | BR-D | | | $40.00 |
| Carabo | 6420 | | HK | M-AQ | BL | BR-D | | | $40.00 |
| Carabo | 6420 | | USA | M-BL | CL | WH | | | $55.00 |
| Carabo | 6420 | | HK | M-BL | BL | WH | | | $55.00 |
| Carabo | 6420 | | USA | M-BL | CL | BK | | | $50.00 |
| Carabo | 6420 | | HK | M-BL | BL | BK | | | $50.00 |
| Carabo | 6420 | | USA | M-BL | CL | GY | | | $50.00 |
| Carabo | 6420 | | HK | M-BL | BL | GY | | | $50.00 |
| Carabo | 6420 | | USA | M-BL | CL | BR-L | | | $50.00 |
| Carabo | 6420 | | HK | M-BL | BL | BR-L | | | $50.00 |
| Carabo | 6420 | | USA | M-BL | CL | BR-D | | | $50.00 |
| Carabo | 6420 | | HK | M-BL | BL | BR-D | | | $50.00 |
| Carabo | 6420 | | USA | M-GD | CL | WH | | | $55.00 |
| Carabo | 6420 | | HK | M-GD | BL | WH | | | $55.00 |
| Carabo | 6420 | | USA | M-GD | CL | BK | | | $40.00 |
| Carabo | 6420 | | HK | M-GD | BL | BK | | | $40.00 |
| Carabo | 6420 | | USA | M-GD | CL | GY | | | $40.00 |
| Carabo | 6420 | | HK | M-GD | BL | GY | | | $40.00 |
| Carabo | 6420 | | USA | M-GD | CL | BR-L | | | $50.00 |
| Carabo | 6420 | | HK | M-GD | BL | BR-L | | | $50.00 |
| Carabo | 6420 | | USA | M-GD | CL | BR-D | | | $50.00 |
| Carabo | 6420 | | HK | M-GD | BL | BR-D | | | $50.00 |
| Carabo | 6420 | | USA | M-GR | CL | WH | | | $55.00 |
| Carabo | 6420 | | HK | M-GR | BL | WH | | | $55.00 |
| Carabo | 6420 | | USA | M-GR | CL | BK | | | $50.00 |
| Carabo | 6420 | | HK | M-GR | BL | BK | | | $50.00 |
| Carabo | 6420 | | USA | M-GR | CL | GY | | | $50.00 |
| Carabo | 6420 | | HK | M-GR | BL | GY | | | $50.00 |
| Carabo | 6420 | | USA | M-GR | CL | BR-L | | | $50.00 |
| Carabo | 6420 | | HK | M-GR | BL | BR-L | | | $50.00 |
| Carabo | 6420 | | USA | M-GR | CL | BR-D | | | $50.00 |
| Carabo | 6420 | | HK | M-GR | BL | BR-D | | | $50.00 |
| Carabo | 6420 | | USA | M-GR-E | CL | WH | | | $60.00 |
| Carabo | 6420 | | HK | M-GR-E | BL | WH | | | $60.00 |
| Carabo | 6420 | | USA | M-GR-E | CL | BK | | | $55.00 |
| Carabo | 6420 | | HK | M-GR-E | BL | BK | | | $55.00 |
| Carabo | 6420 | | USA | M-GR-E | CL | GY | | | $55.00 |
| Carabo | 6420 | | HK | M-GR-E | BL | GY | | | $55.00 |
| Carabo | 6420 | | USA | M-GR-E | CL | BR-L | | | $55.00 |
| Carabo | 6420 | | HK | M-GR-E | BL | BR-L | | | $55.00 |
| Carabo | 6420 | | USA | M-GR-E | CL | BR-D | | | $55.00 |
| Carabo | 6420 | | HK | M-GR-E | BL | BR-D | | | $55.00 |
| Carabo | 6420 | | USA | M-GR-L | CL | WH | | | $55.00 |
| Carabo | 6420 | | HK | M-GR-L | BL | WH | | | $55.00 |
| Carabo | 6420 | | USA | M-GR-L | CL | BK | | | $50.00 |
| Carabo | 6420 | | HK | M-GR-L | BL | BK | | | $50.00 |
| Carabo | 6420 | | USA | M-GR-L | CL | GY | | | $50.00 |
| Carabo | 6420 | | HK | M-GR-L | BL | GY | | | $50.00 |
| Carabo | 6420 | | USA | M-GR-L | CL | BR-L | | | $50.00 |
| Carabo | 6420 | | HK | M-GR-L | BL | BR-L | | | $50.00 |
| Carabo | 6420 | | USA | M-GR-L | CL | BR-D | | | $50.00 |
| Carabo | 6420 | | HK | M-GR-L | BL | BR-D | | | $50.00 |
| Carabo | 6420 | | USA | M-MG | CL | WH | | | $55.00 |
| Carabo | 6420 | | HK | M-MG | BL | WH | | | $55.00 |
| Carabo | 6420 | | USA | M-MG | CL | BK | | | $50.00 |
| Carabo | 6420 | | HK | M-MG | BL | BK | | | $50.00 |
| Carabo | 6420 | | USA | M-MG | CL | GY | | | $50.00 |
| Carabo | 6420 | | HK | M-MG | BL | GY | | | $50.00 |
| Carabo | 6420 | | USA | M-MG | CL | BR-L | | | $50.00 |
| Carabo | 6420 | | HK | M-MG | BL | BR-L | | | $50.00 |
| Carabo | 6420 | | USA | M-MG | CL | BR-D | | | $50.00 |
| Carabo | 6420 | | HK | M-MG | BL | BR-D | | | $50.00 |
| Carabo | 6420 | | USA | M-PK | CL | WH | | | $240.00 |
| Carabo | 6420 | | HK | M-PK | BL | WH | | | $240.00 |

## 1970 Variations

| Name | Number | Casting | Country | Color | Windows | Interior | Paint | Other | Value |
|---|---|---|---|---|---|---|---|---|---|
| Carabo | 6420 | | USA | M-PK | CL | BK | | | $220.00 |
| Carabo | 6420 | | HK | M-PK | BL | BK | | | $220.00 |
| Carabo | 6420 | | USA | M-PK | CL | GY | | | $220.00 |
| Carabo | 6420 | | HK | M-PK | BL | GY | | | $220.00 |
| Carabo | 6420 | | USA | M-PK | CL | BR-L | | | $220.00 |
| Carabo | 6420 | | HK | M-PK | BL | BR-L | | | $220.00 |
| Carabo | 6420 | | USA | M-PK | CL | BR-D | | | $220.00 |
| Carabo | 6420 | | HK | M-PK | BL | BR-D | | | $220.00 |
| Carabo | 6420 | | USA | M-PK-H | CL | WH | | | $240.00 |
| Carabo | 6420 | | HK | M-PK-H | BL | WH | | | $240.00 |
| Carabo | 6420 | | USA | M-PK-H | CL | BK | | | $220.00 |
| Carabo | 6420 | | HK | M-PK-H | BL | BK | | | $220.00 |
| Carabo | 6420 | | USA | M-PK-H | CL | GY | | | $220.00 |
| Carabo | 6420 | | HK | M-PK-H | BL | GY | | | $220.00 |
| Carabo | 6420 | | USA | M-PK-H | CL | BR-L | | | $220.00 |
| Carabo | 6420 | | HK | M-PK-H | BL | BR-L | | | $220.00 |
| Carabo | 6420 | | USA | M-PK-H | CL | BR-D | | | $220.00 |
| Carabo | 6420 | | HK | M-PK-H | BL | BR-D | | | $220.00 |
| Carabo | 6420 | | USA | M-PK-S | CL | WH | | | $240.00 |
| Carabo | 6420 | | HK | M-PK-S | BL | WH | | | $240.00 |
| Carabo | 6420 | | USA | M-PK-S | CL | BK | | | $220.00 |
| Carabo | 6420 | | HK | M-PK-S | BL | BK | | | $220.00 |
| Carabo | 6420 | | USA | M-PK-S | CL | GY | | | $220.00 |
| Carabo | 6420 | | HK | M-PK-S | BL | GY | | | $220.00 |
| Carabo | 6420 | | USA | M-PK-S | CL | BR-L | | | $220.00 |
| Carabo | 6420 | | HK | M-PK-S | BL | BR-L | | | $220.00 |
| Carabo | 6420 | | USA | M-PK-S | CL | BR-D | | | $220.00 |
| Carabo | 6420 | | HK | M-PK-S | BL | BR-D | | | $220.00 |
| Carabo | 6420 | | USA | M-RD | CL | WH | | | $55.00 |
| Carabo | 6420 | | HK | M-RD | BL | WH | | | $55.00 |
| Carabo | 6420 | | USA | M-RD | CL | BK | | | $50.00 |
| Carabo | 6420 | | HK | M-RD | BL | BK | | | $50.00 |
| Carabo | 6420 | | USA | M-RD | CL | GY | | | $50.00 |
| Carabo | 6420 | | HK | M-RD | BL | GY | | | $50.00 |
| Carabo | 6420 | | USA | M-RD | CL | BR-L | | | $50.00 |
| Carabo | 6420 | | HK | M-RD | BL | BR-L | | | $50.00 |
| Carabo | 6420 | | USA | M-RD | CL | BR-D | | | $50.00 |
| Carabo | 6420 | | HK | M-RD | BL | BR-D | | | $50.00 |
| Carabo | 6420 | | USA | M-RD-R | CL | WH | | | $60.00 |
| Carabo | 6420 | | HK | M-RD-R | BL | WH | | | $60.00 |
| Carabo | 6420 | | USA | M-RD-R | CL | BK | | | $55.00 |
| Carabo | 6420 | | HK | M-RD-R | BL | BK | | | $55.00 |
| Carabo | 6420 | | USA | M-RD-R | CL | GY | | | $55.00 |
| Carabo | 6420 | | HK | M-RD-R | BL | GY | | | $55.00 |
| Carabo | 6420 | | USA | M-RD-R | CL | BR-L | | | $55.00 |
| Carabo | 6420 | | HK | M-RD-R | BL | BR-L | | | $55.00 |
| Carabo | 6420 | | USA | M-RD-R | CL | BR-D | | | $55.00 |
| Carabo | 6420 | | HK | M-RD-R | BL | BR-D | | | $55.00 |
| Carabo | 6420 | | USA | M-YW | CL | WH | | | $55.00 |
| Carabo | 6420 | | HK | M-YW | BL | WH | | | $55.00 |
| Carabo | 6420 | | USA | M-YW | CL | BK | | | $50.00 |
| Carabo | 6420 | | HK | M-YW | BL | BK | | | $50.00 |
| Carabo | 6420 | | USA | M-YW | CL | GY | | | $50.00 |
| Carabo | 6420 | | HK | M-YW | BL | GY | | | $50.00 |
| Carabo | 6420 | | USA | M-YW | CL | BR-L | | | $50.00 |
| Carabo | 6420 | | HK | M-YW | BL | BR-L | | | $50.00 |
| Carabo | 6420 | | USA | M-YW | CL | BR-D | | | $50.00 |
| Carabo | 6420 | | HK | M-YW | BL | BR-D | | | $50.00 |
| Carabo | 6420 | | USA | M-YW-L | CL | WH | | | $60.00 |
| Carabo | 6420 | | HK | M-YW-L | BL | WH | | | $60.00 |
| Carabo | 6420 | | USA | M-YW-L | CL | BK | | | $55.00 |
| Carabo | 6420 | | HK | M-YW-L | BL | BK | | | $55.00 |
| Carabo | 6420 | | USA | M-YW-L | CL | GY | | | $55.00 |
| Carabo | 6420 | | HK | M-YW-L | BL | GY | | | $55.00 |
| Carabo | 6420 | | USA | M-YW-L | CL | BR-L | | | $55.00 |
| Carabo | 6420 | | HK | M-YW-L | BL | BR-L | | | $55.00 |
| Carabo | 6420 | | USA | M-YW-L | CL | BR-D | | | $55.00 |
| Carabo | 6420 | | HK | M-YW-L | BL | BR-D | | | $55.00 |
| | | | | | | | | | |
| Jack "Rabbit" Special | 6421 | | USA | E-WH | TNT | WH | BL-STR | | $40.00 |
| Jack "Rabbit" Special | 6421 | | USA | E-WH | TNT | BK | BL-STR | | $40.00 |

## 1970 Variations

| Name | Number | Casting | Country | Color | Windows | Interior | Paint | Other | Value |
|---|---|---|---|---|---|---|---|---|---|
| Jack "Rabbit" Special | 6421 | | USA | E-WH | TNT | GY | BL-STR | | $40.00 |
| Jack "Rabbit" Special | 6421 | | USA | E-WH | CL | WH | BL-STR | | $40.00 |
| Jack "Rabbit" Special | 6421 | | USA | E-WH | CL | BK | BL-STR | | $40.00 |
| Jack "Rabbit" Special | 6421 | | USA | E-WH | CL | GY | BL-STR | | $40.00 |
| Jack "Rabbit" Special | 6421 | | USA | E-WH | TNT | WH | BL&RD-STR | | $400.00 |
| Jack "Rabbit" Special | 6421 | | USA | E-WH | TNT | BK | BL&RD-STR | | $400.00 |
| Jack "Rabbit" Special | 6421 | | USA | E-WH | TNT | GY | BL&RD-STR | | $400.00 |
| Jack "Rabbit" Special | 6421 | | USA | E-WH | CL | WH | BL&RD-STR | | $400.00 |
| Jack "Rabbit" Special | 6421 | | USA | E-WH | CL | BK | BL&RD-STR | | $400.00 |
| Jack "Rabbit" Special | 6421 | | USA | E-WH | CL | GY | BL&RD-STR | | $400.00 |
| Swingin' Wing | 6422 | | USA | M-AQ | CL | WH | | | $65.00 |
| Swingin' Wing | 6422 | | HK | M-AQ | CL | WH | | | $65.00 |
| Swingin' Wing | 6422 | | USA | M-AQ | CL | BK | | | $60.00 |
| Swingin' Wing | 6422 | | HK | M-AQ | CL | BK | | | $60.00 |
| Swingin' Wing | 6422 | | USA | M-AQ | CL | GY | | | $60.00 |
| Swingin' Wing | 6422 | | HK | M-AQ | CL | GY | | | $60.00 |
| Swingin' Wing | 6422 | | USA | M-AQ | CL | BR-L | | | $60.00 |
| Swingin' Wing | 6422 | | HK | M-AQ | CL | BR-L | | | $60.00 |
| Swingin' Wing | 6422 | | USA | M-AQ | CL | BR-D | | | $60.00 |
| Swingin' Wing | 6422 | | HK | M-AQ | CL | BR-D | | | $60.00 |
| Swingin' Wing | 6422 | | USA | M-BL | CL | WH | | | $50.00 |
| Swingin' Wing | 6422 | | HK | M-BL | CL | WH | | | $50.00 |
| Swingin' Wing | 6422 | | USA | M-BL | CL | BK | | | $45.00 |
| Swingin' Wing | 6422 | | HK | M-BL | CL | BK | | | $45.00 |
| Swingin' Wing | 6422 | | USA | M-BL | CL | GY | | | $45.00 |
| Swingin' Wing | 6422 | | HK | M-BL | CL | GY | | | $45.00 |
| Swingin' Wing | 6422 | | USA | M-BL | CL | BR-L | | | $45.00 |
| Swingin' Wing | 6422 | | HK | M-BL | CL | BR-L | | | $45.00 |
| Swingin' Wing | 6422 | | USA | M-BL | CL | BR-D | | | $45.00 |
| Swingin' Wing | 6422 | | HK | M-BL | CL | BR-D | | | $45.00 |
| Swingin' Wing | 6422 | | USA | M-GD | CL | WH | | | $50.00 |
| Swingin' Wing | 6422 | | HK | M-GD | CL | WH | | | $50.00 |
| Swingin' Wing | 6422 | | USA | M-GD | CL | BK | | | $45.00 |
| Swingin' Wing | 6422 | | HK | M-GD | CL | BK | | | $45.00 |
| Swingin' Wing | 6422 | | USA | M-GD | CL | GY | | | $45.00 |
| Swingin' Wing | 6422 | | HK | M-GD | CL | GY | | | $45.00 |
| Swingin' Wing | 6422 | | USA | M-GD | CL | BR-L | | | $45.00 |
| Swingin' Wing | 6422 | | HK | M-GD | CL | BR-L | | | $45.00 |
| Swingin' Wing | 6422 | | USA | M-GD | CL | BR-D | | | $45.00 |
| Swingin' Wing | 6422 | | HK | M-GD | CL | BR-D | | | $45.00 |
| Swingin' Wing | 6422 | | USA | M-GR | CL | WH | | | $50.00 |
| Swingin' Wing | 6422 | | HK | M-GR | CL | WH | | | $50.00 |
| Swingin' Wing | 6422 | | USA | M-GR | CL | BK | | | $45.00 |
| Swingin' Wing | 6422 | | HK | M-GR | CL | BK | | | $45.00 |
| Swingin' Wing | 6422 | | USA | M-GR | CL | GY | | | $45.00 |
| Swingin' Wing | 6422 | | HK | M-GR | CL | GY | | | $45.00 |
| Swingin' Wing | 6422 | | USA | M-GR | CL | BR-L | | | $45.00 |
| Swingin' Wing | 6422 | | HK | M-GR | CL | BR-L | | | $45.00 |
| Swingin' Wing | 6422 | | USA | M-GR | CL | BR-D | | | $45.00 |
| Swingin' Wing | 6422 | | HK | M-GR | CL | BR-D | | | $45.00 |
| Swingin' Wing | 6422 | | USA | M-GR-E | CL | WH | | | $55.00 |
| Swingin' Wing | 6422 | | HK | M-GR-E | CL | WH | | | $55.00 |
| Swingin' Wing | 6422 | | USA | M-GR-E | CL | BK | | | $50.00 |
| Swingin' Wing | 6422 | | HK | M-GR-E | CL | BK | | | $50.00 |
| Swingin' Wing | 6422 | | USA | M-GR-E | CL | GY | | | $50.00 |
| Swingin' Wing | 6422 | | HK | M-GR-E | CL | GY | | | $50.00 |
| Swingin' Wing | 6422 | | USA | M-GR-E | CL | BR-L | | | $50.00 |
| Swingin' Wing | 6422 | | HK | M-GR-E | CL | BR-L | | | $50.00 |
| Swingin' Wing | 6422 | | USA | M-GR-E | CL | BR-D | | | $50.00 |
| Swingin' Wing | 6422 | | HK | M-GR-E | CL | BR-D | | | $50.00 |
| Swingin' Wing | 6422 | | USA | M-GR-L | CL | WH | | | $50.00 |
| Swingin' Wing | 6422 | | HK | M-GR-L | CL | WH | | | $50.00 |
| Swingin' Wing | 6422 | | USA | M-GR-L | CL | BK | | | $45.00 |
| Swingin' Wing | 6422 | | HK | M-GR-L | CL | BK | | | $45.00 |
| Swingin' Wing | 6422 | | USA | M-GR-L | CL | GY | | | $45.00 |
| Swingin' Wing | 6422 | | HK | M-GR-L | CL | GY | | | $45.00 |
| Swingin' Wing | 6422 | | USA | M-GR-L | CL | BR-L | | | $45.00 |
| Swingin' Wing | 6422 | | HK | M-GR-L | CL | BR-L | | | $45.00 |
| Swingin' Wing | 6422 | | USA | M-GR-L | CL | BR-D | | | $45.00 |
| Swingin' Wing | 6422 | | HK | M-GR-L | CL | BR-D | | | $45.00 |

## 1970 Variations

| Name | Number | Casting | Country | Color | Windows | Interior | Paint | Other | Value |
|---|---|---|---|---|---|---|---|---|---|
| Swingin' Wing | 6422 | | USA | M-MG | CL | WH | | | $50.00 |
| Swingin' Wing | 6422 | | HK | M-MG | CL | WH | | | $50.00 |
| Swingin' Wing | 6422 | | USA | M-MG | CL | BK | | | $45.00 |
| Swingin' Wing | 6422 | | HK | M-MG | CL | BK | | | $45.00 |
| Swingin' Wing | 6422 | | USA | M-MG | CL | GY | | | $45.00 |
| Swingin' Wing | 6422 | | HK | M-MG | CL | GY | | | $45.00 |
| Swingin' Wing | 6422 | | USA | M-MG | CL | BR-L | | | $45.00 |
| Swingin' Wing | 6422 | | HK | M-MG | CL | BR-L | | | $45.00 |
| Swingin' Wing | 6422 | | USA | M-MG | CL | BR-D | | | $45.00 |
| Swingin' Wing | 6422 | | HK | M-MG | CL | BR-D | | | $45.00 |
| Swingin' Wing | 6422 | | USA | M-OR | CL | WH | | | $65.00 |
| Swingin' Wing | 6422 | | HK | M-OR | CL | WH | | | $65.00 |
| Swingin' Wing | 6422 | | USA | M-OR | CL | BK | | | $60.00 |
| Swingin' Wing | 6422 | | HK | M-OR | CL | BK | | | $60.00 |
| Swingin' Wing | 6422 | | USA | M-OR | CL | GY | | | $60.00 |
| Swingin' Wing | 6422 | | HK | M-OR | CL | GY | | | $60.00 |
| Swingin' Wing | 6422 | | USA | M-OR | CL | BR-L | | | $60.00 |
| Swingin' Wing | 6422 | | HK | M-OR | CL | BR-L | | | $60.00 |
| Swingin' Wing | 6422 | | USA | M-OR | CL | BR-D | | | $60.00 |
| Swingin' Wing | 6422 | | HK | M-OR | CL | BR-D | | | $60.00 |
| Swingin' Wing | 6422 | | USA | M-PK | CL | WH | | | $120.00 |
| Swingin' Wing | 6422 | | HK | M-PK | CL | WH | | | $120.00 |
| Swingin' Wing | 6422 | | USA | M-PK | CL | BK | | | $110.00 |
| Swingin' Wing | 6422 | | HK | M-PK | CL | BK | | | $110.00 |
| Swingin' Wing | 6422 | | USA | M-PK | CL | GY | | | $110.00 |
| Swingin' Wing | 6422 | | HK | M-PK | CL | GY | | | $110.00 |
| Swingin' Wing | 6422 | | USA | M-PK | CL | BR-L | | | $110.00 |
| Swingin' Wing | 6422 | | HK | M-PK | CL | BR-L | | | $110.00 |
| Swingin' Wing | 6422 | | USA | M-PK | CL | BR-D | | | $110.00 |
| Swingin' Wing | 6422 | | HK | M-PK | CL | BR-D | | | $110.00 |
| Swingin' Wing | 6422 | | USA | M-PK-H | CL | WH | | | $120.00 |
| Swingin' Wing | 6422 | | HK | M-PK-H | CL | WH | | | $120.00 |
| Swingin' Wing | 6422 | | USA | M-PK-H | CL | BK | | | $110.00 |
| Swingin' Wing | 6422 | | HK | M-PK-H | CL | BK | | | $110.00 |
| Swingin' Wing | 6422 | | USA | M-PK-H | CL | GY | | | $110.00 |
| Swingin' Wing | 6422 | | HK | M-PK-H | CL | GY | | | $110.00 |
| Swingin' Wing | 6422 | | USA | M-PK-H | CL | BR-L | | | $110.00 |
| Swingin' Wing | 6422 | | HK | M-PK-H | CL | BR-L | | | $110.00 |
| Swingin' Wing | 6422 | | USA | M-PK-H | CL | BR-D | | | $110.00 |
| Swingin' Wing | 6422 | | HK | M-PK-H | CL | BR-D | | | $110.00 |
| Swingin' Wing | 6422 | | USA | M-PK-S | CL | WH | | | $120.00 |
| Swingin' Wing | 6422 | | HK | M-PK-S | CL | WH | | | $120.00 |
| Swingin' Wing | 6422 | | USA | M-PK-S | CL | BK | | | $110.00 |
| Swingin' Wing | 6422 | | HK | M-PK-S | CL | BK | | | $110.00 |
| Swingin' Wing | 6422 | | USA | M-PK-S | CL | GY | | | $110.00 |
| Swingin' Wing | 6422 | | HK | M-PK-S | CL | GY | | | $110.00 |
| Swingin' Wing | 6422 | | USA | M-PK-S | CL | BR-L | | | $110.00 |
| Swingin' Wing | 6422 | | HK | M-PK-S | CL | BR-L | | | $110.00 |
| Swingin' Wing | 6422 | | USA | M-PK-S | CL | BR-D | | | $110.00 |
| Swingin' Wing | 6422 | | HK | M-PK-S | CL | BR-D | | | $110.00 |
| Swingin' Wing | 6422 | | USA | M-PR | CL | WH | | | $65.00 |
| Swingin' Wing | 6422 | | HK | M-PR | CL | WH | | | $65.00 |
| Swingin' Wing | 6422 | | USA | M-PR | CL | BK | | | $60.00 |
| Swingin' Wing | 6422 | | HK | M-PR | CL | BK | | | $60.00 |
| Swingin' Wing | 6422 | | USA | M-PR | CL | GY | | | $60.00 |
| Swingin' Wing | 6422 | | HK | M-PR | CL | GY | | | $60.00 |
| Swingin' Wing | 6422 | | USA | M-PR | CL | BR-L | | | $60.00 |
| Swingin' Wing | 6422 | | HK | M-PR | CL | BR-L | | | $60.00 |
| Swingin' Wing | 6422 | | USA | M-PR | CL | BR-D | | | $60.00 |
| Swingin' Wing | 6422 | | HK | M-PR | CL | BR-D | | | $60.00 |
| Swingin' Wing | 6422 | | USA | M-RD | CL | WH | | | $50.00 |
| Swingin' Wing | 6422 | | HK | M-RD | CL | WH | | | $50.00 |
| Swingin' Wing | 6422 | | USA | M-RD | CL | BK | | | $45.00 |
| Swingin' Wing | 6422 | | HK | M-RD | CL | BK | | | $45.00 |
| Swingin' Wing | 6422 | | USA | M-RD | CL | GY | | | $45.00 |
| Swingin' Wing | 6422 | | HK | M-RD | CL | GY | | | $45.00 |
| Swingin' Wing | 6422 | | USA | M-RD | CL | BR-L | | | $45.00 |
| Swingin' Wing | 6422 | | HK | M-RD | CL | BR-L | | | $45.00 |
| Swingin' Wing | 6422 | | USA | M-RD | CL | BR-D | | | $45.00 |
| Swingin' Wing | 6422 | | HK | M-RD | CL | BR-D | | | $45.00 |
| Swingin' Wing | 6422 | | USA | M-RD-R | CL | WH | | | $55.00 |
| Swingin' Wing | 6422 | | HK | M-RD-R | CL | WH | | | $55.00 |

## 1970 Variations

| Name | Number | Casting | Country | Color | Windows | Interior | Paint | Other | Value |
|---|---|---|---|---|---|---|---|---|---|
| Swingin' Wing | 6422 | | USA | M-RD-R | CL | BK | | | $50.00 |
| Swingin' Wing | 6422 | | HK | M RD R | CL | BK | | | $50.00 |
| Swingin' Wing | 6422 | | USA | M-RD-R | CL | GY | | | $50.00 |
| Swingin' Wing | 6422 | | HK | M-RD-R | CL | GY | | | $50.00 |
| Swingin' Wing | 6422 | | USA | M-RD-R | CL | BR-L | | | $50.00 |
| Swingin' Wing | 6422 | | HK | M-RD-R | CL | BR-L | | | $50.00 |
| Swingin' Wing | 6422 | | USA | M-RD-R | CL | BR-D | | | $50.00 |
| Swingin' Wing | 6422 | | HK | M-RD-R | CL | BR-D | | | $50.00 |
| Swingin' Wing | 6422 | | USA | M-YW | CL | WH | | | $50.00 |
| Swingin' Wing | 6422 | | HK | M-YW | CL | WH | | | $50.00 |
| Swingin' Wing | 6422 | | USA | M-YW | CL | BK | | | $45.00 |
| Swingin' Wing | 6422 | | HK | M-YW | CL | BK | | | $45.00 |
| Swingin' Wing | 6422 | | USA | M-YW | CL | GY | | | $45.00 |
| Swingin' Wing | 6422 | | HK | M-YW | CL | GY | | | $45.00 |
| Swingin' Wing | 6422 | | USA | M-YW | CL | BR-L | | | $45.00 |
| Swingin' Wing | 6422 | | HK | M-YW | CL | BR-L | | | $45.00 |
| Swingin' Wing | 6422 | | USA | M-YW | CL | BR-D | | | $45.00 |
| Swingin' Wing | 6422 | | HK | M-YW | CL | BR-D | | | $45.00 |
| Swingin' Wing | 6422 | | USA | M-YW-L | CL | WH | | | $55.00 |
| Swingin' Wing | 6422 | | HK | M-YW-L | CL | WH | | | $55.00 |
| Swingin' Wing | 6422 | | USA | M-YW-L | CL | BK | | | $50.00 |
| Swingin' Wing | 6422 | | HK | M-YW-L | CL | BK | | | $50.00 |
| Swingin' Wing | 6422 | | USA | M-YW-L | CL | GY | | | $50.00 |
| Swingin' Wing | 6422 | | HK | M-YW-L | CL | GY | | | $50.00 |
| Swingin' Wing | 6422 | | USA | M-YW-L | CL | BR-L | | | $50.00 |
| Swingin' Wing | 6422 | | HK | M-YW-L | CL | BR-L | | | $50.00 |
| Swingin' Wing | 6422 | | USA | M-YW-L | CL | BR-D | | | $50.00 |
| Swingin' Wing | 6422 | | HK | M-YW-L | CL | BR-D | | | $50.00 |
| Mantis | 6423 | | USA | M-AQ | CL | WH | | | $50.00 |
| Mantis | 6423 | | HK | M-AQ | BL | WH | | | $50.00 |
| Mantis | 6423 | | USA | M-AQ | CL | BK | | | $45.00 |
| Mantis | 6423 | | HK | M-AQ | BL | BK | | | $45.00 |
| Mantis | 6423 | | USA | M-AQ | CL | GY | | | $45.00 |
| Mantis | 6423 | | HK | M-AQ | BL | GY | | | $45.00 |
| Mantis | 6423 | | USA | M-AQ | CL | BR-L | | | $45.00 |
| Mantis | 6423 | | HK | M-AQ | BL | BR-L | | | $45.00 |
| Mantis | 6423 | | USA | M-AQ | CL | BR-D | | | $45.00 |
| Mantis | 6423 | | HK | M-AQ | BL | BR-D | | | $45.00 |
| Mantis | 6423 | | USA | M-BL | CL | WH | | | $45.00 |
| Mantis | 6423 | | HK | M-BL | BL | WH | | | $45.00 |
| Mantis | 6423 | | USA | M-BL | CL | BK | | | $40.00 |
| Mantis | 6423 | | HK | M-BL | BL | BK | | | $40.00 |
| Mantis | 6423 | | USA | M-BL | CL | GY | | | $40.00 |
| Mantis | 6423 | | HK | M-BL | BL | GY | | | $40.00 |
| Mantis | 6423 | | USA | M-BL | CL | BR-L | | | $40.00 |
| Mantis | 6423 | | HK | M-BL | BL | BR-L | | | $40.00 |
| Mantis | 6423 | | USA | M-BL | CL | BR-D | | | $40.00 |
| Mantis | 6423 | | HK | M-BL | BL | BR-D | | | $40.00 |
| Mantis | 6423 | | USA | M-BR-D | CL | WH | | | $55.00 |
| Mantis | 6423 | | HK | M-BR-D | BL | WH | | | $55.00 |
| Mantis | 6423 | | USA | M-BR-D | CL | BK | | | $50.00 |
| Mantis | 6423 | | HK | M-BR-D | BL | BK | | | $50.00 |
| Mantis | 6423 | | USA | M-BR-D | CL | GY | | | $50.00 |
| Mantis | 6423 | | HK | M-BR-D | BL | GY | | | $50.00 |
| Mantis | 6423 | | USA | M-BR-D | CL | BR-L | | | $50.00 |
| Mantis | 6423 | | HK | M-BR-D | BL | BR-L | | | $50.00 |
| Mantis | 6423 | | USA | M-BR-D | CL | BR-D | | | $50.00 |
| Mantis | 6423 | | HK | M-BR-D | BL | BR-D | | | $50.00 |
| Mantis | 6423 | | USA | M-BR-P | CL | WH | | | $50.00 |
| Mantis | 6423 | | HK | M-BR-P | BL | WH | | | $50.00 |
| Mantis | 6423 | | USA | M-BR-P | CL | BK | | | $45.00 |
| Mantis | 6423 | | HK | M-BR-P | BL | BK | | | $45.00 |
| Mantis | 6423 | | USA | M-BR-P | CL | GY | | | $45.00 |
| Mantis | 6423 | | HK | M-BR-P | BL | GY | | | $45.00 |
| Mantis | 6423 | | USA | M-BR-P | CL | BR-L | | | $45.00 |
| Mantis | 6423 | | HK | M-BR-P | BL | BR-L | | | $45.00 |
| Mantis | 6423 | | USA | M-BR-P | CL | BR-D | | | $45.00 |
| Mantis | 6423 | | HK | M-BR-P | BL | BR-D | | | $45.00 |
| Mantis | 6423 | | USA | M-GD | CL | WH | | | $45.00 |
| Mantis | 6423 | | HK | M-GD | BL | WH | | | $45.00 |

## 1970 Variations

| Name | Number | Casting | Country | Color | Windows | Interior | Paint | Other | Value |
|---|---|---|---|---|---|---|---|---|---|
| Mantis | 6423 | | USA | M-GD | CL | BK | | | $40.00 |
| Mantis | 6423 | | HK | M-GD | BL | BK | | | $40.00 |
| Mantis | 6423 | | USA | M-GD | CL | GY | | | $40.00 |
| Mantis | 6423 | | HK | M-GD | BL | GY | | | $40.00 |
| Mantis | 6423 | | USA | M-GD | CL | BR-L | | | $40.00 |
| Mantis | 6423 | | HK | M-GD | BL | BR-L | | | $40.00 |
| Mantis | 6423 | | USA | M-GD | CL | BR-D | | | $40.00 |
| Mantis | 6423 | | HK | M-GD | BL | BR-D | | | $40.00 |
| Mantis | 6423 | | USA | M-GR | CL | WH | | | $45.00 |
| Mantis | 6423 | | HK | M-GR | BL | WH | | | $45.00 |
| Mantis | 6423 | | USA | M-GR | CL | BK | | | $40.00 |
| Mantis | 6423 | | HK | M-GR | BL | BK | | | $40.00 |
| Mantis | 6423 | | USA | M-GR | CL | GY | | | $40.00 |
| Mantis | 6423 | | HK | M-GR | BL | GY | | | $40.00 |
| Mantis | 6423 | | USA | M-GR | CL | BR-L | | | $40.00 |
| Mantis | 6423 | | HK | M-GR | BL | BR-L | | | $40.00 |
| Mantis | 6423 | | USA | M-GR | CL | BR-D | | | $40.00 |
| Mantis | 6423 | | HK | M-GR | BL | BR-D | | | $40.00 |
| Mantis | 6423 | | USA | M-GR-E | CL | WH | | | $50.00 |
| Mantis | 6423 | | HK | M-GR-E | BL | WH | | | $50.00 |
| Mantis | 6423 | | USA | M-GR-E | CL | BK | | | $45.00 |
| Mantis | 6423 | | HK | M-GR-E | BL | BK | | | $45.00 |
| Mantis | 6423 | | USA | M-GR-E | CL | GY | | | $45.00 |
| Mantis | 6423 | | HK | M-GR-E | BL | GY | | | $45.00 |
| Mantis | 6423 | | USA | M-GR-E | CL | BR-L | | | $45.00 |
| Mantis | 6423 | | HK | M-GR-E | BL | BR-L | | | $45.00 |
| Mantis | 6423 | | USA | M-GR-E | CL | BR-D | | | $45.00 |
| Mantis | 6423 | | HK | M-GR-E | BL | BR-D | | | $45.00 |
| Mantis | 6423 | | USA | M-GR-L | CL | WH | | | $50.00 |
| Mantis | 6423 | | HK | M-GR-L | BL | WH | | | $50.00 |
| Mantis | 6423 | | USA | M-GR-L | CL | BK | | | $45.00 |
| Mantis | 6423 | | HK | M-GR-L | BL | BK | | | $45.00 |
| Mantis | 6423 | | USA | M-GR-L | CL | GY | | | $45.00 |
| Mantis | 6423 | | HK | M-GR-L | BL | GY | | | $45.00 |
| Mantis | 6423 | | USA | M-GR-L | CL | BR-L | | | $45.00 |
| Mantis | 6423 | | HK | M-GR-L | BL | BR-L | | | $45.00 |
| Mantis | 6423 | | USA | M-GR-L | CL | BR-D | | | $45.00 |
| Mantis | 6423 | | HK | M-GR-L | BL | BR-D | | | $45.00 |
| Mantis | 6423 | | USA | M-GR-O | CL | WH | | | $45.00 |
| Mantis | 6423 | | HK | M-GR-O | BL | WH | | | $45.00 |
| Mantis | 6423 | | USA | M-GR-O | CL | BK | | | $40.00 |
| Mantis | 6423 | | HK | M-GR-O | BL | BK | | | $40.00 |
| Mantis | 6423 | | USA | M-GR-O | CL | GY | | | $40.00 |
| Mantis | 6423 | | HK | M-GR-O | BL | GY | | | $40.00 |
| Mantis | 6423 | | USA | M-GR-O | CL | BR-L | | | $40.00 |
| Mantis | 6423 | | HK | M-GR-O | BL | BR-L | | | $40.00 |
| Mantis | 6423 | | USA | M-GR-O | CL | BR-D | | | $40.00 |
| Mantis | 6423 | | HK | M-GR-O | BL | BR-D | | | $40.00 |
| Mantis | 6423 | | USA | M-MG | CL | WH | | | $55.00 |
| Mantis | 6423 | | HK | M-MG | BL | WH | | | $55.00 |
| Mantis | 6423 | | USA | M-MG | CL | BK | | | $50.00 |
| Mantis | 6423 | | HK | M-MG | BL | BK | | | $50.00 |
| Mantis | 6423 | | USA | M-MG | CL | GY | | | $50.00 |
| Mantis | 6423 | | HK | M-MG | BL | GY | | | $50.00 |
| Mantis | 6423 | | USA | M-MG | CL | BR-L | | | $50.00 |
| Mantis | 6423 | | HK | M-MG | BL | BR-L | | | $50.00 |
| Mantis | 6423 | | USA | M-MG | CL | BR-D | | | $50.00 |
| Mantis | 6423 | | HK | M-MG | BL | BR-D | | | $50.00 |
| Mantis | 6423 | | USA | M-OR | CL | WH | | | $45.00 |
| Mantis | 6423 | | HK | M-OR | BL | WH | | | $45.00 |
| Mantis | 6423 | | USA | M-OR | CL | BK | | | $40.00 |
| Mantis | 6423 | | HK | M-OR | BL | BK | | | $40.00 |
| Mantis | 6423 | | USA | M-OR | CL | GY | | | $40.00 |
| Mantis | 6423 | | HK | M-OR | BL | GY | | | $40.00 |
| Mantis | 6423 | | USA | M-OR | CL | BR-L | | | $40.00 |
| Mantis | 6423 | | HK | M-OR | BL | BR-L | | | $40.00 |
| Mantis | 6423 | | USA | M-OR | CL | BR-D | | | $40.00 |
| Mantis | 6423 | | HK | M-OR | BL | BR-D | | | $40.00 |
| Mantis | 6423 | | USA | M-PK | CL | WH | | | $100.00 |
| Mantis | 6423 | | HK | M-PK | BL | WH | | | $100.00 |
| Mantis | 6423 | | USA | M-PK | CL | BK | | | $90.00 |
| Mantis | 6423 | | HK | M-PK | BL | BK | | | $90.00 |

## 1970 Variations

| Name | Number | Casting | Country | Color | Windows | Interior | Paint | Other | Value |
|---|---|---|---|---|---|---|---|---|---|
| Mantis | 6423 | | USA | M-PK | CL | GY | | | $90.00 |
| Mantis | 0423 | | HK | M-PK | BL | GY | | | $90.00 |
| Mantis | 6423 | | USA | M-PK | CL | BR-L | | | $90.00 |
| Mantis | 6423 | | HK | M-PK | BL | BR-L | | | $90.00 |
| Mantis | 6423 | | USA | M-PK | CL | BR-D | | | $90.00 |
| Mantis | 6423 | | HK | M-PK | BL | BR-D | | | $90.00 |
| Mantis | 6423 | | USA | M-PK-H | CL | WH | | | $100.00 |
| Mantis | 6423 | | HK | M-PK-H | BL | WH | | | $100.00 |
| Mantis | 6423 | | USA | M-PK-H | CL | BK | | | $90.00 |
| Mantis | 6423 | | HK | M-PK-H | BL | BK | | | $90.00 |
| Mantis | 6423 | | USA | M-PK-H | CL | GY | | | $90.00 |
| Mantis | 6423 | | HK | M-PK-H | BL | GY | | | $90.00 |
| Mantis | 6423 | | USA | M-PK-H | CL | BR-L | | | $90.00 |
| Mantis | 6423 | | HK | M-PK-H | BL | BR-L | | | $90.00 |
| Mantis | 6423 | | USA | M-PK-H | CL | BR-D | | | $90.00 |
| Mantis | 6423 | | HK | M-PK-H | BL | BR-D | | | $90.00 |
| Mantis | 6423 | | USA | M-PK-S | CL | WH | | | $100.00 |
| Mantis | 6423 | | HK | M-PK-S | BL | WH | | | $100.00 |
| Mantis | 6423 | | USA | M-PK-S | CL | BK | | | $90.00 |
| Mantis | 6423 | | HK | M-PK-S | BL | BK | | | $90.00 |
| Mantis | 6423 | | USA | M-PK-S | CL | GY | | | $90.00 |
| Mantis | 6423 | | HK | M-PK-S | BL | GY | | | $90.00 |
| Mantis | 6423 | | USA | M-PK-S | CL | BR-L | | | $90.00 |
| Mantis | 6423 | | HK | M-PK-S | BL | BR-L | | | $90.00 |
| Mantis | 6423 | | USA | M-PK-S | CL | BR-D | | | $90.00 |
| Mantis | 6423 | | HK | M-PK-S | BL | BR-D | | | $90.00 |
| Mantis | 6423 | | USA | M-PR | CL | WH | | | $120.00 |
| Mantis | 6423 | | HK | M-PR | BL | WH | | | $120.00 |
| Mantis | 6423 | | USA | M-PR | CL | BK | | | $110.00 |
| Mantis | 6423 | | HK | M-PR | BL | BK | | | $110.00 |
| Mantis | 6423 | | USA | M-PR | CL | GY | | | $110.00 |
| Mantis | 6423 | | HK | M-PR | BL | GY | | | $110.00 |
| Mantis | 6423 | | USA | M-PR | CL | BR-L | | | $110.00 |
| Mantis | 6423 | | HK | M-PR | BL | BR-L | | | $110.00 |
| Mantis | 6423 | | USA | M-PR | CL | BR-D | | | $110.00 |
| Mantis | 6423 | | HK | M-PR | BL | BR-D | | | $110.00 |
| Mantis | 6423 | | USA | M-RD | CL | WH | | | $45.00 |
| Mantis | 6423 | | HK | M-RD | BL | WH | | | $45.00 |
| Mantis | 6423 | | USA | M-RD | CL | BK | | | $40.00 |
| Mantis | 6423 | | HK | M-RD | BL | BK | | | $40.00 |
| Mantis | 6423 | | USA | M-RD | CL | GY | | | $40.00 |
| Mantis | 6423 | | HK | M-RD | BL | GY | | | $40.00 |
| Mantis | 6423 | | USA | M-RD | CL | BR-L | | | $40.00 |
| Mantis | 6423 | | HK | M-RD | BL | BR-L | | | $40.00 |
| Mantis | 6423 | | USA | M-RD | CL | BR-D | | | $40.00 |
| Mantis | 6423 | | HK | M-RD | BL | BR-D | | | $40.00 |
| Mantis | 6423 | | USA | M-RD-R | CL | WH | | | $50.00 |
| Mantis | 6423 | | HK | M-RD-R | BL | WH | | | $50.00 |
| Mantis | 6423 | | USA | M-RD-R | CL | BK | | | $45.00 |
| Mantis | 6423 | | HK | M-RD-R | BL | BK | | | $45.00 |
| Mantis | 6423 | | USA | M-RD-R | CL | GY | | | $45.00 |
| Mantis | 6423 | | HK | M-RD-R | BL | GY | | | $45.00 |
| Mantis | 6423 | | USA | M-RD-R | CL | BR-L | | | $45.00 |
| Mantis | 6423 | | HK | M-RD-R | BL | BR-L | | | $45.00 |
| Mantis | 6423 | | USA | M-RD-R | CL | BR-D | | | $45.00 |
| Mantis | 6423 | | HK | M-RD-R | BL | BR-D | | | $45.00 |
| Mantis | 6423 | | USA | M-YW | CL | WH | | | $45.00 |
| Mantis | 6423 | | HK | M-YW | BL | WH | | | $45.00 |
| Mantis | 6423 | | USA | M-YW | CL | BK | | | $40.00 |
| Mantis | 6423 | | HK | M-YW | BL | BK | | | $40.00 |
| Mantis | 6423 | | USA | M-YW | CL | GY | | | $40.00 |
| Mantis | 6423 | | HK | M-YW | BL | GY | | | $40.00 |
| Mantis | 6423 | | USA | M-YW | CL | BR-L | | | $40.00 |
| Mantis | 6423 | | HK | M-YW | BL | BR-L | | | $40.00 |
| Mantis | 6423 | | USA | M-YW | CL | BR-D | | | $40.00 |
| Mantis | 6423 | | HK | M-YW | BL | BR-D | | | $40.00 |
| Mantis | 6423 | | USA | M-YW-L | CL | WH | | | $55.00 |
| Mantis | 6423 | | HK | M-YW-L | BL | WH | | | $55.00 |
| Mantis | 6423 | | USA | M-YW-L | CL | BK | | | $50.00 |
| Mantis | 6423 | | HK | M-YW-L | BL | BK | | | $50.00 |
| Mantis | 6423 | | USA | M-YW-L | CL | GY | | | $50.00 |
| Mantis | 6423 | | HK | M-YW-L | BL | GY | | | $50.00 |

## 1970 Variations

| Name | Number | Casting | Country | Color | Windows | Interior | Paint | Other | Value |
|---|---|---|---|---|---|---|---|---|---|
| Mantis | 6423 | | USA | M-YW-L | CL | BR-L | | | $50.00 |
| Mantis | 6423 | | HK | M-YW-L | BL | BR-L | | | $50.00 |
| Mantis | 6423 | | USA | M-YW-L | CL | BR-D | | | $50.00 |
| Mantis | 6423 | | HK | M-YW-L | BL | BR-D | | | $50.00 |
| | | | | | | | | | |
| Tri-Baby | 6424 | | USA | M-AQ | | WH | | | $80.00 |
| Tri-Baby | 6424 | | HK | M-AQ | | BK | | | $90.00 |
| Tri-Baby | 6424 | | HK | M-AQ | | GY | | | $90.00 |
| Tri-Baby | 6424 | | HK | M-AQ | | BR-L | | | $90.00 |
| Tri-Baby | 6424 | | HK | M-AQ | | BR-D | | | $90.00 |
| Tri-Baby | 6424 | | USA | M-BL | | WH | | | $50.00 |
| Tri-Baby | 6424 | | HK | M-BL | | BK | | | $95.00 |
| Tri-Baby | 6424 | | HK | M-BL | | GY | | | $95.00 |
| Tri-Baby | 6424 | | HK | M-BL | | BR-L | | | $95.00 |
| Tri-Baby | 6424 | | HK | M-BL | | BR-D | | | $95.00 |
| Tri-Baby | 6424 | | USA | M-GD | | WH | | | $50.00 |
| Tri-Baby | 6424 | | HK | M-GD | | BK | | | $95.00 |
| Tri-Baby | 6424 | | HK | M-GD | | GY | | | $95.00 |
| Tri-Baby | 6424 | | HK | M-GD | | BR-L | | | $95.00 |
| Tri-Baby | 6424 | | HK | M-GD | | BR-D | | | $95.00 |
| Tri-Baby | 6424 | | USA | M-GR | | WH | | | $50.00 |
| Tri-Baby | 6424 | | HK | M-GR | | BK | | | $95.00 |
| Tri-Baby | 6424 | | HK | M-GR | | GY | | | $95.00 |
| Tri-Baby | 6424 | | HK | M-GR | | BR-L | | | $95.00 |
| Tri-Baby | 6424 | | HK | M-GR | | BR-D | | | $95.00 |
| Tri-Baby | 6424 | | USA | M-GR-E | | WH | | | $55.00 |
| Tri-Baby | 6424 | | HK | M-GR-E | | BK | | | $90.00 |
| Tri-Baby | 6424 | | HK | M-GR-E | | GY | | | $90.00 |
| Tri-Baby | 6424 | | HK | M-GR-E | | BR-L | | | $90.00 |
| Tri-Baby | 6424 | | HK | M-GR-E | | BR-D | | | $90.00 |
| Tri-Baby | 6424 | | USA | M-GR-L | | WH | | | $50.00 |
| Tri-Baby | 6424 | | HK | M-GR-L | | BK | | | $95.00 |
| Tri-Baby | 6424 | | HK | M-GR-L | | GY | | | $95.00 |
| Tri-Baby | 6424 | | HK | M-GR-L | | BR-L | | | $95.00 |
| Tri-Baby | 6424 | | HK | M-GR-L | | BR-D | | | $95.00 |
| Tri-Baby | 6424 | | USA | M-MG | | WH | | | $55.00 |
| Tri-Baby | 6424 | | HK | M-MG | | BK | | | $90.00 |
| Tri-Baby | 6424 | | HK | M-MG | | GY | | | $90.00 |
| Tri-Baby | 6424 | | HK | M-MG | | BR-L | | | $90.00 |
| Tri-Baby | 6424 | | HK | M-MG | | BR-D | | | $90.00 |
| Tri-Baby | 6424 | | USA | M-PK | | WH | | | $110.00 |
| Tri-Baby | 6424 | | HK | M-PK | | BK | | | $150.00 |
| Tri-Baby | 6424 | | HK | M-PK | | GY | | | $150.00 |
| Tri-Baby | 6424 | | HK | M-PK | | BR-L | | | $150.00 |
| Tri-Baby | 6424 | | HK | M-PK | | BR-D | | | $150.00 |
| Tri-Baby | 6424 | | USA | M-PK-H | | WH | | | $100.00 |
| Tri-Baby | 6424 | | HK | M-PK-H | | BK | | | $150.00 |
| Tri-Baby | 6424 | | HK | M-PK-H | | GY | | | $150.00 |
| Tri-Baby | 6424 | | HK | M-PK-H | | BR-L | | | $150.00 |
| Tri-Baby | 6424 | | HK | M-PK-H | | BR-D | | | $150.00 |
| Tri-Baby | 6424 | | USA | M-PK-S | | WH | | | $90.00 |
| Tri-Baby | 6424 | | HK | M-PK-S | | BK | | | $110.00 |
| Tri-Baby | 6424 | | HK | M-PK-S | | GY | | | $110.00 |
| Tri-Baby | 6424 | | HK | M-PK-S | | BR-L | | | $110.00 |
| Tri-Baby | 6424 | | HK | M-PK-S | | BR-D | | | $110.00 |
| Tri-Baby | 6424 | | USA | M-RD | | WH | | | $50.00 |
| Tri-Baby | 6424 | | HK | M-RD | | BK | | | $80.00 |
| Tri-Baby | 6424 | | HK | M-RD | | GY | | | $80.00 |
| Tri-Baby | 6424 | | HK | M-RD | | BR-L | | | $80.00 |
| Tri-Baby | 6424 | | HK | M-RD | | BR-D | | | $80.00 |
| Tri-Baby | 6424 | | USA | M-RD-R | | WH | | | $55.00 |
| Tri-Baby | 6424 | | HK | M-RD-R | | BK | | | $90.00 |
| Tri-Baby | 6424 | | HK | M-RD-R | | GY | | | $90.00 |
| Tri-Baby | 6424 | | HK | M-RD-R | | BR-L | | | $90.00 |
| Tri-Baby | 6424 | | HK | M-RD-R | | BR-D | | | $90.00 |
| Tri-Baby | 6424 | | USA | M-YW | | WH | | | $50.00 |
| Tri-Baby | 6424 | | HK | M-YW | | BK | | | $80.00 |
| Tri-Baby | 6424 | | HK | M-YW | | GY | | | $80.00 |
| Tri-Baby | 6424 | | HK | M-YW | | BR-L | | | $80.00 |
| Tri-Baby | 6424 | | HK | M-YW | | BR-D | | | $80.00 |
| Tri-Baby | 6424 | | USA | M-YW-L | | WH | | | $55.00 |

## 1970 Variations

| Name | Number | Casting | Country | Color | Windows | Interior | Paint | Other | Value |
|---|---|---|---|---|---|---|---|---|---|
| Tri-Baby | 6424 | | HK | M-YW-L | | BK | | | $90.00 |
| Tri-Baby | 6424 | | HK | M-YW-L | | GY | | | $90.00 |
| Tri-Baby | 6424 | | HK | M-YW-L | | BR-L | | | $90.00 |
| Tri-Baby | 6424 | | HK | M-YW-L | | BR-D | | | $90.00 |
| | | | | | | | | | |
| Sky Show Fleetside | 6436 | | USA | M-AQ | CL | | | | $550.00 |
| Sky Show Fleetside | 6436 | | USA | M-BL | CL | | | | $550.00 |
| Sky Show Fleetside | 6436 | | USA | M-BL-I | CL | | | | $600.00 |
| Sky Show Fleetside | 6436 | | USA | M-BL-P | CL | | | | $640.00 |
| Sky Show Fleetside | 6436 | | USA | M-GD | CL | | | | $550.00 |
| Sky Show Fleetside | 6436 | | USA | M-GR | CL | | | | $550.00 |
| Sky Show Fleetside | 6436 | | USA | M-GR-E | CL | | | | $640.00 |
| Sky Show Fleetside | 6436 | | USA | M-GR-L | CL | | | | $550.00 |
| Sky Show Fleetside | 6436 | | USA | M-GR-O | CL | | | | $550.00 |
| Sky Show Fleetside | 6436 | | USA | M-MG | CL | | | | $550.00 |
| Sky Show Fleetside | 6436 | | USA | M-OR | CL | | | | $550.00 |
| Sky Show Fleetside | 6436 | | USA | M-PK | CL | | | | $640.00 |
| Sky Show Fleetside | 6436 | | USA | M-PK-H | CL | | | | $550.00 |
| Sky Show Fleetside | 6436 | | USA | M-PK-S | CL | | | | $550.00 |
| Sky Show Fleetside | 6436 | | USA | M-PR | CL | | | | $550.00 |
| Sky Show Fleetside | 6436 | | USA | M-RD | CL | | | | $550.00 |
| Sky Show Fleetside | 6436 | | USA | M-RD-R | CL | | | | $640.00 |
| Sky Show Fleetside | 6436 | | USA | M-YW | CL | | | | $550.00 |
| Sky Show Fleetside | 6436 | | USA | M-YW-L | CL | | | | $650.00 |
| | | | | | | | | | |
| Sky Show Deora | *6436 | | USA | M-AQ | CL | WH | | | $2,500.00 |
| Sky Show Deora | *6436 | | HK | M-AQ | BL | WH | | | $2,500.00 |
| Sky Show Deora | *6436 | | USA | M-AQ | CL | BK | | | $2,500.00 |
| Sky Show Deora | *6436 | | HK | M-AQ | BL | BK | | | $2,500.00 |
| Sky Show Deora | *6436 | | USA | M-AQ | CL | GY | | | $2,500.00 |
| Sky Show Deora | *6436 | | HK | M-AQ | BL | GY | | | $2,500.00 |
| Sky Show Deora | *6436 | | USA | M-AQ | CL | BR-L | | | $2,500.00 |
| Sky Show Deora | *6436 | | HK | M-AQ | BL | BR-L | | | $2,500.00 |
| Sky Show Deora | *6436 | | USA | M-AQ | CL | BR-D | | | $2,500.00 |
| Sky Show Deora | *6436 | | HK | M-AQ | BL | BR-D | | | $2,500.00 |
| Sky Show Deora | *6436 | | USA | M-PR | CL | WH | | | $3,000.00 |
| Sky Show Deora | *6436 | | HK | M-PR | BL | WH | | | $3,000.00 |
| Sky Show Deora | *6436 | | USA | M-PR | CL | BK | | | $3,000.00 |
| Sky Show Deora | *6436 | | HK | M-PR | BL | BK | | | $3,000.00 |
| Sky Show Deora | *6436 | | USA | M-PR | CL | GY | | | $3,000.00 |
| Sky Show Deora | *6436 | | HK | M-PR | BL | GY | | | $3,000.00 |
| Sky Show Deora | *6436 | | USA | M-PR | CL | BR-L | | | $3,000.00 |
| Sky Show Deora | *6436 | | HK | M-PR | BL | BR-L | | | $3,000.00 |
| Sky Show Deora | *6436 | | USA | M-PR | CL | BR-D | | | $3,000.00 |
| Sky Show Deora | *6436 | | HK | M-PR | BL | BR-D | | | $3,000.00 |
| | | | | | | | | | |
| Tow Truck | 6450 | | HK | M-AQ | | WH | | | $60.00 |
| Tow Truck | 6450 | | HK | M-AQ | | BK | | | $55.00 |
| Tow Truck | 6450 | | HK | M-AQ | | GY | | | $55.00 |
| Tow Truck | 6450 | | HK | M-AQ | | BR-L | | | $55.00 |
| Tow Truck | 6450 | | HK | M-AQ | | BR-D | | | $55.00 |
| Tow Truck | 6450 | | HK | M-BL | | WH | | | $60.00 |
| Tow Truck | 6450 | | HK | M-BL | | BK | | | $55.00 |
| Tow Truck | 6450 | | HK | M-BL | | GY | | | $55.00 |
| Tow Truck | 6450 | | HK | M-BL | | BR-L | | | $55.00 |
| Tow Truck | 6450 | | HK | M-BL | | BR-D | | | $55.00 |
| Tow Truck | 6450 | | HK | M-BR-D | | WH | | | $85.00 |
| Tow Truck | 6450 | | HK | M-BR-D | | BK | | | $80.00 |
| Tow Truck | 6450 | | HK | M-BR-D | | GY | | | $80.00 |
| Tow Truck | 6450 | | HK | M-BR-D | | BR-L | | | $80.00 |
| Tow Truck | 6450 | | HK | M-BR-D | | BR-D | | | $80.00 |
| Tow Truck | 6450 | | HK | M-BR-P | | WH | | | $80.00 |
| Tow Truck | 6450 | | HK | M-BR-P | | BK | | | $75.00 |
| Tow Truck | 6450 | | HK | M-BR-P | | GY | | | $75.00 |
| Tow Truck | 6450 | | HK | M-BR-P | | BR-L | | | $75.00 |
| Tow Truck | 6450 | | HK | M-BR-P | | BR-D | | | $75.00 |
| Tow Truck | 6450 | | HK | M-GD | | WH | | | $60.00 |
| Tow Truck | 6450 | | HK | M-GD | | BK | | | $55.00 |
| Tow Truck | 6450 | | HK | M-GD | | GY | | | $55.00 |
| Tow Truck | 6450 | | HK | M-GD | | BR-L | | | $55.00 |

## 1970 Variations

| Name | Number | Casting | Country | Color | Windows | Interior | Paint | Other | Value |
|---|---|---|---|---|---|---|---|---|---|
| Tow Truck | 6450 | | HK | M-GD | | BR-D | | | $55.00 |
| Tow Truck | 6450 | | HK | M-GR | | WH | | | $60.00 |
| Tow Truck | 6450 | | HK | M-GR | | BK | | | $55.00 |
| Tow Truck | 6450 | | HK | M-GR | | GY | | | $55.00 |
| Tow Truck | 6450 | | HK | M-GR | | BR-L | | | $55.00 |
| Tow Truck | 6450 | | HK | M-GR | | BR-D | | | $55.00 |
| Tow Truck | 6450 | | HK | M-GR-E | | WH | | | $65.00 |
| Tow Truck | 6450 | | HK | M-GR-E | | BK | | | $60.00 |
| Tow Truck | 6450 | | HK | M-GR-E | | GY | | | $60.00 |
| Tow Truck | 6450 | | HK | M-GR-E | | BR-L | | | $60.00 |
| Tow Truck | 6450 | | HK | M-GR-E | | BR-D | | | $60.00 |
| Tow Truck | 6450 | | HK | M-GR-L | | WH | | | $65.00 |
| Tow Truck | 6450 | | HK | M-GR-L | | BK | | | $60.00 |
| Tow Truck | 6450 | | HK | M-GR-L | | GY | | | $60.00 |
| Tow Truck | 6450 | | HK | M-GR-L | | BR-L | | | $60.00 |
| Tow Truck | 6450 | | HK | M-GR-L | | BR-D | | | $60.00 |
| Tow Truck | 6450 | | HK | M-GR-O | | WH | | | $65.00 |
| Tow Truck | 6450 | | HK | M-GR-O | | BK | | | $60.00 |
| Tow Truck | 6450 | | HK | M-GR-O | | GY | | | $60.00 |
| Tow Truck | 6450 | | HK | M-GR-O | | BR-L | | | $60.00 |
| Tow Truck | 6450 | | HK | M-GR-O | | BR-D | | | $60.00 |
| Tow Truck | 6450 | | HK | M-MG | | WH | | | $60.00 |
| Tow Truck | 6450 | | HK | M-MG | | BK | | | $55.00 |
| Tow Truck | 6450 | | HK | M-MG | | GY | | | $55.00 |
| Tow Truck | 6450 | | HK | M-MG | | BR-L | | | $55.00 |
| Tow Truck | 6450 | | HK | M-MG | | BR-D | | | $55.00 |
| Tow Truck | 6450 | | HK | M-OR | | WH | | | $60.00 |
| Tow Truck | 6450 | | HK | M-OR | | BK | | | $55.00 |
| Tow Truck | 6450 | | HK | M-OR | | GY | | | $55.00 |
| Tow Truck | 6450 | | HK | M-OR | | BR-L | | | $55.00 |
| Tow Truck | 6450 | | HK | M-OR | | BR-D | | | $55.00 |
| Tow Truck | 6450 | | HK | M-PK | | WH | | | $160.00 |
| Tow Truck | 6450 | | HK | M-PK | | BK | | | $150.00 |
| Tow Truck | 6450 | | HK | M-PK | | GY | | | $150.00 |
| Tow Truck | 6450 | | HK | M-PK | | BR-L | | | $150.00 |
| Tow Truck | 6450 | | HK | M-PK | | BR-D | | | $150.00 |
| Tow Truck | 6450 | | HK | M-PK-H | | WH | | | $160.00 |
| Tow Truck | 6450 | | HK | M-PK-H | | BK | | | $150.00 |
| Tow Truck | 6450 | | HK | M-PK-H | | GY | | | $150.00 |
| Tow Truck | 6450 | | HK | M-PK-H | | BR-L | | | $150.00 |
| Tow Truck | 6450 | | HK | M-PK-H | | BR-D | | | $150.00 |
| Tow Truck | 6450 | | HK | M-PK-S | | WH | | | $125.00 |
| Tow Truck | 6450 | | HK | M-PK-S | | BK | | | $120.00 |
| Tow Truck | 6450 | | HK | M-PK-S | | GY | | | $120.00 |
| Tow Truck | 6450 | | HK | M-PK-S | | BR-L | | | $120.00 |
| Tow Truck | 6450 | | HK | M-PK-S | | BR-D | | | $120.00 |
| Tow Truck | 6450 | | HK | M-PR | | WH | | | $60.00 |
| Tow Truck | 6450 | | HK | M-PR | | BK | | | $55.00 |
| Tow Truck | 6450 | | HK | M-PR | | GY | | | $55.00 |
| Tow Truck | 6450 | | HK | M-PR | | BR-L | | | $55.00 |
| Tow Truck | 6450 | | HK | M-PR | | BR-D | | | $55.00 |
| Tow Truck | 6450 | | HK | M-RD | | WH | | | $60.00 |
| Tow Truck | 6450 | | HK | M-RD | | BK | | | $55.00 |
| Tow Truck | 6450 | | HK | M-RD | | GY | | | $55.00 |
| Tow Truck | 6450 | | HK | M-RD | | BR-L | | | $55.00 |
| Tow Truck | 6450 | | HK | M-RD | | BR-D | | | $55.00 |
| Tow Truck | 6450 | | HK | M-RD-R | | WH | | | $65.00 |
| Tow Truck | 6450 | | HK | M-RD-R | | BK | | | $60.00 |
| Tow Truck | 6450 | | HK | M-RD-R | | GY | | | $60.00 |
| Tow Truck | 6450 | | HK | M-RD-R | | BR-L | | | $60.00 |
| Tow Truck | 6450 | | HK | M-RD-R | | BR-D | | | $60.00 |
| Tow Truck | 6450 | | HK | M-YW | | WH | | | $60.00 |
| Tow Truck | 6450 | | HK | M-YW | | BK | | | $55.00 |
| Tow Truck | 6450 | | HK | M-YW | | GY | | | $55.00 |
| Tow Truck | 6450 | | HK | M-YW | | BR-L | | | $55.00 |
| Tow Truck | 6450 | | HK | M-YW | | BR-D | | | $55.00 |
| Tow Truck | 6450 | | HK | M-YW-L | | WH | | | $70.00 |
| Tow Truck | 6450 | | HK | M-YW-L | | BK | | | $65.00 |
| Tow Truck | 6450 | | HK | M-YW-L | | GY | | | $65.00 |
| Tow Truck | 6450 | | HK | M-YW-L | | BR-L | | | $65.00 |
| Tow Truck | 6450 | | HK | M-YW-L | | BR-D | | | $65.00 |

## 1970 Variations

| Name | Number | Casting | Country | Color | Windows | Interior | Paint | Other | Value |
|---|---|---|---|---|---|---|---|---|---|
| Ambulance | 6451 | | HK | E-WH | | WH | | | $300.00 |
| Ambulance | 6451 | | HK | E-WH | | BK | | | $260.00 |
| Ambulance | 6451 | | HK | E-WH | | GY | | | $260.00 |
| Ambulance | 6451 | | HK | E-WH | | BR-L | | | $260.00 |
| Ambulance | 6451 | | HK | E-WH | | BR-D | | | $260.00 |
| Ambulance | 6451 | | HK | M-AQ | | WH | | | $75.00 |
| Ambulance | 6451 | | HK | M-AQ | | BK | | | $70.00 |
| Ambulance | 6451 | | HK | M-AQ | | GY | | | $70.00 |
| Ambulance | 6451 | | HK | M-AQ | | BR-L | | | $70.00 |
| Ambulance | 6451 | | HK | M-AQ | | BR-D | | | $70.00 |
| Ambulance | 6451 | | HK | M-BL | | WH | | | $75.00 |
| Ambulance | 6451 | | HK | M-BL | | BK | | | $70.00 |
| Ambulance | 6451 | | HK | M-BL | | GY | | | $70.00 |
| Ambulance | 6451 | | HK | M-BL | | BR-L | | | $70.00 |
| Ambulance | 6451 | | HK | M-BL | | BR-D | | | $70.00 |
| Ambulance | 6451 | | HK | M-BR-D | | WH | | | $85.00 |
| Ambulance | 6451 | | HK | M-BR-D | | BK | | | $80.00 |
| Ambulance | 6451 | | HK | M-BR-D | | GY | | | $80.00 |
| Ambulance | 6451 | | HK | M-BR-D | | BR-L | | | $80.00 |
| Ambulance | 6451 | | HK | M-BR-D | | BR-D | | | $80.00 |
| Ambulance | 6451 | | HK | M-BR-P | | WH | | | $80.00 |
| Ambulance | 6451 | | HK | M-BR-P | | BK | | | $75.00 |
| Ambulance | 6451 | | HK | M-BR-P | | GY | | | $75.00 |
| Ambulance | 6451 | | HK | M-BR-P | | BR-L | | | $75.00 |
| Ambulance | 6451 | | HK | M-BR-P | | BR-D | | | $75.00 |
| Ambulance | 6451 | | HK | M-GD | | WH | | | $75.00 |
| Ambulance | 6451 | | HK | M-GD | | BK | | | $70.00 |
| Ambulance | 6451 | | HK | M-GD | | GY | | | $70.00 |
| Ambulance | 6451 | | HK | M-GD | | BR-L | | | $70.00 |
| Ambulance | 6451 | | HK | M-GD | | BR-D | | | $70.00 |
| Ambulance | 6451 | | HK | M-GR | | WH | | | $75.00 |
| Ambulance | 6451 | | HK | M-GR | | BK | | | $70.00 |
| Ambulance | 6451 | | HK | M-GR | | GY | | | $70.00 |
| Ambulance | 6451 | | HK | M-GR | | BR-L | | | $70.00 |
| Ambulance | 6451 | | HK | M-GR | | BR-D | | | $70.00 |
| Ambulance | 6451 | | HK | M-GR-E | | WH | | | $80.00 |
| Ambulance | 6451 | | HK | M-GR-E | | BK | | | $75.00 |
| Ambulance | 6451 | | HK | M-GR-E | | GY | | | $75.00 |
| Ambulance | 6451 | | HK | M-GR-E | | BR-L | | | $75.00 |
| Ambulance | 6451 | | HK | M-GR-E | | BR-D | | | $75.00 |
| Ambulance | 6451 | | HK | M-GR-L | | WH | | | $75.00 |
| Ambulance | 6451 | | HK | M-GR-L | | BK | | | $70.00 |
| Ambulance | 6451 | | HK | M-GR-L | | GY | | | $70.00 |
| Ambulance | 6451 | | HK | M-GR-L | | BR-L | | | $70.00 |
| Ambulance | 6451 | | HK | M-GR-L | | BR-D | | | $70.00 |
| Ambulance | 6451 | | HK | M-GR-O | | WH | | | $80.00 |
| Ambulance | 6451 | | HK | M-GR-O | | BK | | | $75.00 |
| Ambulance | 6451 | | HK | M-GR-O | | GY | | | $75.00 |
| Ambulance | 6451 | | HK | M-GR-O | | BR-L | | | $75.00 |
| Ambulance | 6451 | | HK | M-GR-O | | BR-D | | | $75.00 |
| Ambulance | 6451 | | HK | M-MG | | WH | | | $80.00 |
| Ambulance | 6451 | | HK | M-MG | | BK | | | $75.00 |
| Ambulance | 6451 | | HK | M-MG | | GY | | | $75.00 |
| Ambulance | 6451 | | HK | M-MG | | BR-L | | | $75.00 |
| Ambulance | 6451 | | HK | M-MG | | BR-D | | | $75.00 |
| Ambulance | 6451 | | HK | M-OR | | WH | | | $95.00 |
| Ambulance | 6451 | | HK | M-OR | | BK | | | $90.00 |
| Ambulance | 6451 | | HK | M-OR | | GY | | | $90.00 |
| Ambulance | 6451 | | HK | M-OR | | BR-L | | | $90.00 |
| Ambulance | 6451 | | HK | M-OR | | BR-D | | | $90.00 |
| Ambulance | 6451 | | HK | M-PK | | WH | | | $180.00 |
| Ambulance | 6451 | | HK | M-PK | | BK | | | $160.00 |
| Ambulance | 6451 | | HK | M-PK | | GY | | | $160.00 |
| Ambulance | 6451 | | HK | M-PK | | BR-L | | | $160.00 |
| Ambulance | 6451 | | HK | M-PK | | BR-D | | | $160.00 |
| Ambulance | 6451 | | HK | M-PK-H | | WH | | | $180.00 |
| Ambulance | 6451 | | HK | M-PK-H | | BK | | | $160.00 |
| Ambulance | 6451 | | HK | M-PK-H | | GY | | | $160.00 |
| Ambulance | 6451 | | HK | M-PK-H | | BR-L | | | $160.00 |
| Ambulance | 6451 | | HK | M-PK-H | | BR-D | | | $160.00 |

## 1970 Variations

| Name | Number | Casting | Country | Color | Windows | Interior | Paint | Other | Value |
|---|---|---|---|---|---|---|---|---|---|
| Ambulance | 6451 | | HK | M-PK-S | | WH | | | $180.00 |
| Ambulance | 6451 | | HK | M-PK-S | | BK | | | $160.00 |
| Ambulance | 6451 | | HK | M-PK-S | | GY | | | $160.00 |
| Ambulance | 6451 | | HK | M-PK-S | | BR-L | | | $160.00 |
| Ambulance | 6451 | | HK | M-PK-S | | BR-D | | | $160.00 |
| Ambulance | 6451 | | HK | M-PR | | WH | | | $75.00 |
| Ambulance | 6451 | | HK | M-PR | | BK | | | $70.00 |
| Ambulance | 6451 | | HK | M-PR | | GY | | | $70.00 |
| Ambulance | 6451 | | HK | M-PR | | BR-L | | | $70.00 |
| Ambulance | 6451 | | HK | M-PR | | BR-D | | | $70.00 |
| Ambulance | 6451 | | HK | M-RD | | WH | | | $75.00 |
| Ambulance | 6451 | | HK | M-RD | | BK | | | $70.00 |
| Ambulance | 6451 | | HK | M-RD | | GY | | | $70.00 |
| Ambulance | 6451 | | HK | M-RD | | BR-L | | | $70.00 |
| Ambulance | 6451 | | HK | M-RD | | BR-D | | | $70.00 |
| Ambulance | 6451 | | HK | M-RD-R | | WH | | | $80.00 |
| Ambulance | 6451 | | HK | M-RD-R | | BK | | | $75.00 |
| Ambulance | 6451 | | HK | M-RD-R | | GY | | | $75.00 |
| Ambulance | 6451 | | HK | M-RD-R | | BR-L | | | $75.00 |
| Ambulance | 6451 | | HK | M-RD-R | | BR-D | | | $75.00 |
| Ambulance | 6451 | | HK | M-YW | | WH | | | $75.00 |
| Ambulance | 6451 | | HK | M-YW | | BK | | | $70.00 |
| Ambulance | 6451 | | HK | M-YW | | GY | | | $70.00 |
| Ambulance | 6451 | | HK | M-YW | | BR-L | | | $70.00 |
| Ambulance | 6451 | | HK | M-YW | | BR-D | | | $70.00 |
| Ambulance | 6451 | | HK | M-YW-L | | WH | | | $70.00 |
| Ambulance | 6451 | | HK | M-YW-L | | BK | | | $65.00 |
| Ambulance | 6451 | | HK | M-YW-L | | GY | | | $65.00 |
| Ambulance | 6451 | | HK | M-YW-L | | BR-L | | | $65.00 |
| Ambulance | 6451 | | HK | M-YW-L | | BR-D | | | $65.00 |
| | | | | | | | | | |
| Cement Mixer | 6452 | | HK | E-WH | | WH | | OR drum/OR truck bed | $260.00 |
| Cement Mixer | 6452 | | HK | E-WH | | WH | | OR drum/BR truck bed | $260.00 |
| Cement Mixer | 6452 | | HK | E-WH | | BK | | OR drum/OR truck bed | $240.00 |
| Cement Mixer | 6452 | | HK | E-WH | | BK | | OR drum/BR truck bed | $340.00 |
| Cement Mixer | 6452 | | HK | E-WH | | GY | | OR drum/OR truck bed | $240.00 |
| Cement Mixer | 6452 | | HK | E-WH | | GY | | OR drum/BR truck bed | $240.00 |
| Cement Mixer | 6452 | | HK | E-WH | | BR-L | | OR drum/OR truck bed | $240.00 |
| Cement Mixer | 6452 | | HK | E-WH | | BR-L | | OR drum/BR truck bed | $240.00 |
| Cement Mixer | 6452 | | HK | E-WH | | BR-D | | OR drum/OR truck bed | $240.00 |
| Cement Mixer | 6452 | | HK | E-WH | | BR-D | | OR drum/BR truck bed | $240.00 |
| Cement Mixer | 6452 | | HK | M-AQ | | WH | | OR drum/OR truck bed | $45.00 |
| Cement Mixer | 6452 | | HK | M-AQ | | WH | | OR drum/BR truck bed | $60.00 |
| Cement Mixer | 6452 | | HK | M-AQ | | BK | | OR drum/OR truck bed | $55.00 |
| Cement Mixer | 6452 | | HK | M-AQ | | BK | | OR drum/BR truck bed | $55.00 |
| Cement Mixer | 6452 | | HK | M-AQ | | GY | | OR drum/OR truck bed | $55.00 |
| Cement Mixer | 6452 | | HK | M-AQ | | GY | | OR drum/BR truck bed | $55.00 |
| Cement Mixer | 6452 | | HK | M-AQ | | BR-L | | OR drum/OR truck bed | $55.00 |
| Cement Mixer | 6452 | | HK | M-AQ | | BR-L | | OR drum/BR truck bed | $55.00 |
| Cement Mixer | 6452 | | HK | M-AQ | | BR-D | | OR drum/OR truck bed | $55.00 |
| Cement Mixer | 6452 | | HK | M-AQ | | BR-D | | OR drum/BR truck bed | $55.00 |
| Cement Mixer | 6452 | | HK | M-BL | | WH | | OR drum/OR truck bed | $60.00 |
| Cement Mixer | 6452 | | HK | M-BL | | WH | | OR drum/BR truck bed | $60.00 |
| Cement Mixer | 6452 | | HK | M-BL | | BK | | OR drum/OR truck bed | $55.00 |
| Cement Mixer | 6452 | | HK | M-BL | | BK | | OR drum/BR truck bed | $55.00 |
| Cement Mixer | 6452 | | HK | M-BL | | GY | | OR drum/OR truck bed | $55.00 |
| Cement Mixer | 6452 | | HK | M-BL | | GY | | OR drum/BR truck bed | $55.00 |
| Cement Mixer | 6452 | | HK | M-BL | | BR-L | | OR drum/OR truck bed | $55.00 |
| Cement Mixer | 6452 | | HK | M-BL | | BR-L | | OR drum/BR truck bed | $55.00 |
| Cement Mixer | 6452 | | HK | M-BL | | BR-D | | OR drum/OR truck bed | $55.00 |
| Cement Mixer | 6452 | | HK | M-BL | | BR-D | | OR drum/BR truck bed | $55.00 |
| Cement Mixer | 6452 | | HK | M-BR-D | | WH | | OR drum/OR truck bed | $60.00 |
| Cement Mixer | 6452 | | HK | M-BR-D | | WH | | OR drum/BR truck bed | $60.00 |
| Cement Mixer | 6452 | | HK | M-BR-D | | BK | | OR drum/OR truck bed | $55.00 |
| Cement Mixer | 6452 | | HK | M-BR-D | | BK | | OR drum/BR truck bed | $55.00 |
| Cement Mixer | 6452 | | HK | M-BR-D | | GY | | OR drum/OR truck bed | $55.00 |
| Cement Mixer | 6452 | | HK | M-BR-D | | GY | | OR drum/BR truck bed | $55.00 |
| Cement Mixer | 6452 | | HK | M-BR-D | | BR-L | | OR drum/OR truck bed | $55.00 |
| Cement Mixer | 6452 | | HK | M-BR-D | | BR-L | | OR drum/BR truck bed | $55.00 |
| Cement Mixer | 6452 | | HK | M-BR-D | | BR-D | | OR drum/OR truck bed | $55.00 |
| Cement Mixer | 6452 | | HK | M-BR-D | | BR-D | | OR drum/BR truck bed | $55.00 |

## 1970 Variations

| Name | Number | Casting | Country | Color | Windows | Interior | Paint | Other | Value |
|---|---|---|---|---|---|---|---|---|---|
| Cement Mixer | 6452 | | HK | M-BR-P | | WH | | OR drum/OR truck bed | $60.00 |
| Cement Mixer | 6452 | | HK | M-BR-P | | WH | | OR drum/BR truck bed | $60.00 |
| Cement Mixer | 6452 | | HK | M-BR-P | | BK | | OR drum/OR truck bed | $55.00 |
| Cement Mixer | 6452 | | HK | M-BR-P | | BK | | OR drum/BR truck bed | $55.00 |
| Cement Mixer | 6452 | | HK | M-BR-P | | GY | | OR drum/OR truck bed | $55.00 |
| Cement Mixer | 6452 | | HK | M-BR-P | | GY | | OR drum/BR truck bed | $55.00 |
| Cement Mixer | 6452 | | HK | M-BR-P | | BR-L | | OR drum/OR truck bed | $55.00 |
| Cement Mixer | 6452 | | HK | M-BR-P | | BR-L | | OR drum/BR truck bed | $55.00 |
| Cement Mixer | 6452 | | HK | M-BR-P | | BR-D | | OR drum/OR truck bed | $55.00 |
| Cement Mixer | 6452 | | HK | M-BR-P | | BR-D | | OR drum/BR truck bed | $55.00 |
| Cement Mixer | 6452 | | HK | M-GD | | WH | | OR drum/OR truck bed | $60.00 |
| Cement Mixer | 6452 | | HK | M-GD | | WH | | OR drum/BR truck bed | $60.00 |
| Cement Mixer | 6452 | | HK | M-GD | | BK | | OR drum/OR truck bed | $55.00 |
| Cement Mixer | 6452 | | HK | M-GD | | BK | | OR drum/BR truck bed | $55.00 |
| Cement Mixer | 6452 | | HK | M-GD | | GY | | OR drum/OR truck bed | $55.00 |
| Cement Mixer | 6452 | | HK | M-GD | | GY | | OR drum/BR truck bed | $55.00 |
| Cement Mixer | 6452 | | HK | M-GD | | BR-L | | OR drum/OR truck bed | $55.00 |
| Cement Mixer | 6452 | | HK | M-GD | | BR-L | | OR drum/BR truck bed | $55.00 |
| Cement Mixer | 6452 | | HK | M-GD | | BR-D | | OR drum/OR truck bed | $55.00 |
| Cement Mixer | 6452 | | HK | M-GD | | BR-D | | OR drum/BR truck bed | $55.00 |
| Cement Mixer | 6452 | | HK | M-GR | | WH | | OR drum/OR truck bed | $60.00 |
| Cement Mixer | 6452 | | HK | M-GR | | WH | | OR drum/BR truck bed | $60.00 |
| Cement Mixer | 6452 | | HK | M-GR | | BK | | OR drum/OR truck bed | $55.00 |
| Cement Mixer | 6452 | | HK | M-GR | | BK | | OR drum/BR truck bed | $55.00 |
| Cement Mixer | 6452 | | HK | M-GR | | GY | | OR drum/OR truck bed | $55.00 |
| Cement Mixer | 6452 | | HK | M-GR | | GY | | OR drum/BR truck bed | $55.00 |
| Cement Mixer | 6452 | | HK | M-GR | | BR-L | | OR drum/OR truck bed | $55.00 |
| Cement Mixer | 6452 | | HK | M-GR | | BR-L | | OR drum/BR truck bed | $55.00 |
| Cement Mixer | 6452 | | HK | M-GR | | BR-D | | OR drum/OR truck bed | $55.00 |
| Cement Mixer | 6452 | | HK | M-GR | | BR-D | | OR drum/BR truck bed | $55.00 |
| Cement Mixer | 6452 | | HK | M-GR-E | | WH | | OR drum/OR truck bed | $65.00 |
| Cement Mixer | 6452 | | HK | M-GR-E | | WH | | OR drum/BR truck bed | $65.00 |
| Cement Mixer | 6452 | | HK | M-GR-E | | BK | | OR drum/OR truck bed | $60.00 |
| Cement Mixer | 6452 | | HK | M-GR-E | | BK | | OR drum/BR truck bed | $60.00 |
| Cement Mixer | 6452 | | HK | M-GR-E | | GY | | OR drum/OR truck bed | $60.00 |
| Cement Mixer | 6452 | | HK | M-GR-E | | GY | | OR drum/BR truck bed | $60.00 |
| Cement Mixer | 6452 | | HK | M-GR-E | | BR-L | | OR drum/OR truck bed | $60.00 |
| Cement Mixer | 6452 | | HK | M-GR-E | | BR-L | | OR drum/BR truck bed | $60.00 |
| Cement Mixer | 6452 | | HK | M-GR-E | | BR-D | | OR drum/OR truck bed | $60.00 |
| Cement Mixer | 6452 | | HK | M-GR-E | | BR-D | | OR drum/BR truck bed | $60.00 |
| Cement Mixer | 6452 | | HK | M-GR-L | | WH | | OR drum/OR truck bed | $60.00 |
| Cement Mixer | 6452 | | HK | M-GR-L | | WH | | OR drum/BR truck bed | $60.00 |
| Cement Mixer | 6452 | | HK | M-GR-L | | BK | | OR drum/OR truck bed | $55.00 |
| Cement Mixer | 6452 | | HK | M-GR-L | | BK | | OR drum/BR truck bed | $55.00 |
| Cement Mixer | 6452 | | HK | M-GR-L | | GY | | OR drum/OR truck bed | $55.00 |
| Cement Mixer | 6452 | | HK | M-GR-L | | GY | | OR drum/BR truck bed | $55.00 |
| Cement Mixer | 6452 | | HK | M-GR-L | | BR-L | | OR drum/OR truck bed | $55.00 |
| Cement Mixer | 6452 | | HK | M-GR-L | | BR-L | | OR drum/BR truck bed | $55.00 |
| Cement Mixer | 6452 | | HK | M-GR-L | | BR-D | | OR drum/OR truck bed | $55.00 |
| Cement Mixer | 6452 | | HK | M-GR-L | | BR-D | | OR drum/BR truck bed | $55.00 |
| Cement Mixer | 6452 | | HK | M-GR-O | | WH | | OR drum/OR truck bed | $65.00 |
| Cement Mixer | 6452 | | HK | M-GR-O | | WH | | OR drum/BR truck bed | $65.00 |
| Cement Mixer | 6452 | | HK | M-GR-O | | BK | | OR drum/OR truck bed | $60.00 |
| Cement Mixer | 6452 | | HK | M-GR-O | | BK | | OR drum/BR truck bed | $60.00 |
| Cement Mixer | 6452 | | HK | M-GR-O | | GY | | OR drum/OR truck bed | $60.00 |
| Cement Mixer | 6452 | | HK | M-GR-O | | GY | | OR drum/BR truck bed | $60.00 |
| Cement Mixer | 6452 | | HK | M-GR-O | | BR-L | | OR drum/OR truck bed | $60.00 |
| Cement Mixer | 6452 | | HK | M-GR-O | | BR-L | | OR drum/BR truck bed | $60.00 |
| Cement Mixer | 6452 | | HK | M-GR-O | | BR-D | | OR drum/OR truck bed | $60.00 |
| Cement Mixer | 6452 | | HK | M-GR-O | | BR-D | | OR drum/BR truck bed | $60.00 |
| Cement Mixer | 6452 | | HK | M-OR | | WH | | OR drum/OR truck bed | $60.00 |
| Cement Mixer | 6452 | | HK | M-OR | | WH | | OR drum/BR truck bed | $60.00 |
| Cement Mixer | 6452 | | HK | M-OR | | BK | | OR drum/OR truck bed | $55.00 |
| Cement Mixer | 6452 | | HK | M-OR | | BK | | OR drum/BR truck bed | $55.00 |
| Cement Mixer | 6452 | | HK | M-OR | | GY | | OR drum/OR truck bed | $55.00 |
| Cement Mixer | 6452 | | HK | M-OR | | GY | | OR drum/BR truck bed | $55.00 |
| Cement Mixer | 6452 | | HK | M-OR | | BR-L | | OR drum/OR truck bed | $55.00 |
| Cement Mixer | 6452 | | HK | M-OR | | BR-L | | OR drum/BR truck bed | $55.00 |
| Cement Mixer | 6452 | | HK | M-OR | | BR-D | | OR drum/OR truck bed | $55.00 |
| Cement Mixer | 6452 | | HK | M-OR | | BR-D | | OR drum/BR truck bed | $55.00 |
| Cement Mixer | 6452 | | HK | M-PR | | WH | | OR drum/OR truck bed | $70.00 |
| Cement Mixer | 6452 | | HK | M-PR | | WH | | OR drum/BR truck bed | $70.00 |

## 1970 Variations

| Name | Number | Casting | Country | Color | Windows | Interior | Paint | Other | Value |
|---|---|---|---|---|---|---|---|---|---|
| Cement Mixer | 6452 | | HK | M-PR | | BK | | OR drum/OR truck bed | $65.00 |
| Cement Mixer | 6452 | | HK | M-PR | | BK | | OR drum/BR truck bed | $65.00 |
| Cement Mixer | 6452 | | HK | M-PR | | GY | | OR drum/OR truck bed | $65.00 |
| Cement Mixer | 6452 | | HK | M-PR | | GY | | OR drum/BR truck bed | $65.00 |
| Cement Mixer | 6452 | | HK | M-PR | | BR-L | | OR drum/OR truck bed | $65.00 |
| Cement Mixer | 6452 | | HK | M-PR | | BR-L | | OR drum/BR truck bed | $65.00 |
| Cement Mixer | 6452 | | HK | M-PR | | BR-D | | OR drum/OR truck bed | $65.00 |
| Cement Mixer | 6452 | | HK | M-PR | | BR-D | | OR drum/BR truck bed | $65.00 |
| Cement Mixer | 6452 | | HK | M-RD | | WH | | OR drum/OR truck bed | $60.00 |
| Cement Mixer | 6452 | | HK | M-RD | | WH | | OR drum/BR truck bed | $60.00 |
| Cement Mixer | 6452 | | HK | M-RD | | BK | | OR drum/OR truck bed | $55.00 |
| Cement Mixer | 6452 | | HK | M-RD | | BK | | OR drum/BR truck bed | $55.00 |
| Cement Mixer | 6452 | | HK | M-RD | | GY | | OR drum/OR truck bed | $55.00 |
| Cement Mixer | 6452 | | HK | M-RD | | GY | | OR drum/BR truck bed | $55.00 |
| Cement Mixer | 6452 | | HK | M-RD | | BR-L | | OR drum/OR truck bed | $55.00 |
| Cement Mixer | 6452 | | HK | M-RD | | BR-L | | OR drum/BR truck bed | $55.00 |
| Cement Mixer | 6452 | | HK | M-RD | | BR-D | | OR drum/OR truck bed | $55.00 |
| Cement Mixer | 6452 | | HK | M-RD | | BR-D | | OR drum/BR truck bed | $55.00 |
| Cement Mixer | 6452 | | HK | M-RD-R | | WH | | OR drum/OR truck bed | $65.00 |
| Cement Mixer | 6452 | | HK | M-RD-R | | WH | | OR drum/BR truck bed | $65.00 |
| Cement Mixer | 6452 | | HK | M-RD-R | | BK | | OR drum/OR truck bed | $60.00 |
| Cement Mixer | 6452 | | HK | M-RD-R | | BK | | OR drum/BR truck bed | $60.00 |
| Cement Mixer | 6452 | | HK | M-RD-R | | GY | | OR drum/OR truck bed | $60.00 |
| Cement Mixer | 6452 | | HK | M-RD-R | | GY | | OR drum/BR truck bed | $60.00 |
| Cement Mixer | 6452 | | HK | M-RD-R | | BR-L | | OR drum/OR truck bed | $60.00 |
| Cement Mixer | 6452 | | HK | M-RD-R | | BR-L | | OR drum/BR truck bed | $60.00 |
| Cement Mixer | 6452 | | HK | M-RD-R | | BR-D | | OR drum/OR truck bed | $60.00 |
| Cement Mixer | 6452 | | HK | M-RD-R | | BR-D | | OR drum/BR truck bed | $60.00 |
| Cement Mixer | 6452 | | HK | M-YW | | WH | | OR drum/OR truck bed | $60.00 |
| Cement Mixer | 6452 | | HK | M-YW | | WH | | OR drum/BR truck bed | $60.00 |
| Cement Mixer | 6452 | | HK | M-YW | | BK | | OR drum/OR truck bed | $55.00 |
| Cement Mixer | 6452 | | HK | M-YW | | BK | | OR drum/BR truck bed | $55.00 |
| Cement Mixer | 6452 | | HK | M-YW | | GY | | OR drum/OR truck bed | $55.00 |
| Cement Mixer | 6452 | | HK | M-YW | | GY | | OR drum/BR truck bed | $55.00 |
| Cement Mixer | 6452 | | HK | M-YW | | BR-L | | OR drum/OR truck bed | $55.00 |
| Cement Mixer | 6452 | | HK | M-YW | | BR-L | | OR drum/BR truck bed | $55.00 |
| Cement Mixer | 6452 | | HK | M-YW | | BR-D | | OR drum/OR truck bed | $55.00 |
| Cement Mixer | 6452 | | HK | M-YW | | BR-D | | OR drum/BR truck bed | $55.00 |
| Cement Mixer | 6452 | | HK | M-YW-L | | WH | | OR drum/OR truck bed | $55.00 |
| Cement Mixer | 6452 | | HK | M-YW-L | | WH | | OR drum/BR truck bed | $55.00 |
| Cement Mixer | 6452 | | HK | M-YW-L | | BK | | OR drum/OR truck bed | $50.00 |
| Cement Mixer | 6452 | | HK | M-YW-L | | BK | | OR drum/BR truck bed | $50.00 |
| Cement Mixer | 6452 | | HK | M-YW-L | | GY | | OR drum/OR truck bed | $50.00 |
| Cement Mixer | 6452 | | HK | M-YW-L | | GY | | OR drum/BR truck bed | $50.00 |
| Cement Mixer | 6452 | | HK | M-YW-L | | BR-L | | OR drum/OR truck bed | $50.00 |
| Cement Mixer | 6452 | | HK | M-YW-L | | BR-L | | OR drum/BR truck bed | $50.00 |
| Cement Mixer | 6452 | | HK | M-YW-L | | BR-D | | OR drum/OR truck bed | $50.00 |
| Cement Mixer | 6452 | | HK | M-YW-L | | BR-D | | OR drum/BR truck bed | $50.00 |
| | | | | | | | | | |
| Dump Truck | 6453 | | HK | E-WH | | WH | | YW tipper/OR truck bed | $260.00 |
| Dump Truck | 6453 | | HK | E-WH | | WH | | YW tipper/BR truck bed | $260.00 |
| Dump Truck | 6453 | | HK | E-WH | | WH | | OR tipper/BR truck bed | $260.00 |
| Dump Truck | 6453 | | HK | E-WH | | BK | | YW tipper/OR truck bed | $240.00 |
| Dump Truck | 6453 | | HK | E-WH | | BK | | YW tipper/BR truck bed | $240.00 |
| Dump Truck | 6453 | | HK | E-WH | | BK | | OR tipper/BR truck bed | $240.00 |
| Dump Truck | 6453 | | HK | E-WH | | GY | | YW tipper/OR truck bed | $240.00 |
| Dump Truck | 6453 | | HK | E-WH | | GY | | YW tipper/BR truck bed | $240.00 |
| Dump Truck | 6453 | | HK | E-WH | | GY | | OR tipper/BR truck bed | $240.00 |
| Dump Truck | 6453 | | HK | E-WH | | BR-L | | YW tipper/OR truck bed | $240.00 |
| Dump Truck | 6453 | | HK | E-WH | | BR-L | | YW tipper/BR truck bed | $240.00 |
| Dump Truck | 6453 | | HK | E-WH | | BR-L | | OR tipper/BR truck bed | $240.00 |
| Dump Truck | 6453 | | HK | E-WH | | BR-D | | YW tipper/OR truck bed | $240.00 |
| Dump Truck | 6453 | | HK | E-WH | | BR-D | | YW tipper/BR truck bed | $240.00 |
| Dump Truck | 6453 | | HK | E-WH | | BR-D | | OR tipper/BR truck bed | $240.00 |
| Dump Truck | 6453 | | HK | M-AQ | | WH | | YW tipper/OR truck bed | $50.00 |
| Dump Truck | 6453 | | HK | M-AQ | | WH | | YW tipper/BR truck bed | $50.00 |
| Dump Truck | 6453 | | HK | M-AQ | | WH | | OR tipper/BR truck bed | $50.00 |
| Dump Truck | 6453 | | HK | M-AQ | | BK | | YW tipper/OR truck bed | $45.00 |
| Dump Truck | 6453 | | HK | M-AQ | | BK | | YW tipper/BR truck bed | $45.00 |
| Dump Truck | 6453 | | HK | M-AQ | | BK | | OR tipper/BR truck bed | $45.00 |
| Dump Truck | 6453 | | HK | M-AQ | | GY | | YW tipper/OR truck bed | $45.00 |

**1970 Variations**

| Name | Number | Casting | Country | Color | Windows | Interior | Paint | Other | Value |
|---|---|---|---|---|---|---|---|---|---|
| Dump Truck | 6453 | | HK | M-AQ | | GY | | YW tipper/BR truck bed | $45.00 |
| Dump Truck | 6453 | | HK | M-AQ | | GY | | OR tipper/BR truck bed | $45.00 |
| Dump Truck | 6453 | | HK | M-AQ | | BR-L | | YW tipper/OR truck bed | $45.00 |
| Dump Truck | 6453 | | HK | M-AQ | | BR-L | | YW tipper/BR truck bed | $45.00 |
| Dump Truck | 6453 | | HK | M-AQ | | BR-L | | OR tipper/BR truck bed | $45.00 |
| Dump Truck | 6453 | | HK | M-AQ | | BR-D | | YW tipper/OR truck bed | $45.00 |
| Dump Truck | 6453 | | HK | M-AQ | | BR-D | | YW tipper/BR truck bed | $45.00 |
| Dump Truck | 6453 | | HK | M-AQ | | BR-D | | OR tipper/BR truck bed | $45.00 |
| Dump Truck | 6453 | | HK | M-BL | | WH | | YW tipper/OR truck bed | $50.00 |
| Dump Truck | 6453 | | HK | M-BL | | WH | | YW tipper/BR truck bed | $50.00 |
| Dump Truck | 6453 | | HK | M-BL | | WH | | OR tipper/BR truck bed | $50.00 |
| Dump Truck | 6453 | | HK | M-BL | | BK | | YW tipper/OR truck bed | $45.00 |
| Dump Truck | 6453 | | HK | M-BL | | BK | | YW tipper/BR truck bed | $45.00 |
| Dump Truck | 6453 | | HK | M-BL | | BK | | OR tipper/BR truck bed | $45.00 |
| Dump Truck | 6453 | | HK | M-BL | | GY | | YW tipper/OR truck bed | $45.00 |
| Dump Truck | 6453 | | HK | M-BL | | GY | | YW tipper/BR truck bed | $45.00 |
| Dump Truck | 6453 | | HK | M-BL | | GY | | OR tipper/BR truck bed | $45.00 |
| Dump Truck | 6453 | | HK | M-BL | | BR-L | | YW tipper/OR truck bed | $45.00 |
| Dump Truck | 6453 | | HK | M-BL | | BR-L | | YW tipper/BR truck bed | $45.00 |
| Dump Truck | 6453 | | HK | M-BL | | BR-L | | OR tipper/BR truck bed | $45.00 |
| Dump Truck | 6453 | | HK | M-BL | | BR-D | | YW tipper/OR truck bed | $45.00 |
| Dump Truck | 6453 | | HK | M-BL | | BR-D | | YW tipper/BR truck bed | $45.00 |
| Dump Truck | 6453 | | HK | M-BL | | BR-D | | OR tipper/BR truck bed | $45.00 |
| Dump Truck | 6453 | | HK | M-BR-D | | WH | | YW tipper/OR truck bed | $55.00 |
| Dump Truck | 6453 | | HK | M-BR-D | | WH | | YW tipper/BR truck bed | $55.00 |
| Dump Truck | 6453 | | HK | M-BR-D | | WH | | OR tipper/BR truck bed | $55.00 |
| Dump Truck | 6453 | | HK | M-BR-D | | BK | | YW tipper/OR truck bed | $50.00 |
| Dump Truck | 6453 | | HK | M-BR-D | | BK | | YW tipper/BR truck bed | $50.00 |
| Dump Truck | 6453 | | HK | M-BR-D | | BK | | OR tipper/BR truck bed | $50.00 |
| Dump Truck | 6453 | | HK | M-BR-D | | GY | | YW tipper/OR truck bed | $50.00 |
| Dump Truck | 6453 | | HK | M-BR-D | | GY | | YW tipper/BR truck bed | $50.00 |
| Dump Truck | 6453 | | HK | M-BR-D | | GY | | OR tipper/BR truck bed | $50.00 |
| Dump Truck | 6453 | | HK | M-BR-D | | BR-L | | YW tipper/OR truck bed | $50.00 |
| Dump Truck | 6453 | | HK | M-BR-D | | BR-L | | YW tipper/BR truck bed | $50.00 |
| Dump Truck | 6453 | | HK | M-BR-D | | BR-L | | OR tipper/BR truck bed | $50.00 |
| Dump Truck | 6453 | | HK | M-BR-D | | BR-D | | YW tipper/OR truck bed | $50.00 |
| Dump Truck | 6453 | | HK | M-BR-D | | BR-D | | YW tipper/BR truck bed | $50.00 |
| Dump Truck | 6453 | | HK | M-BR-D | | BR-D | | OR tipper/BR truck bed | $50.00 |
| Dump Truck | 6453 | | HK | M-BR-P | | WH | | YW tipper/OR truck bed | $50.00 |
| Dump Truck | 6453 | | HK | M-BR-P | | WH | | YW tipper/BR truck bed | $50.00 |
| Dump Truck | 6453 | | HK | M-BR-P | | WH | | OR tipper/BR truck bed | $50.00 |
| Dump Truck | 6453 | | HK | M-BR-P | | BK | | YW tipper/OR truck bed | $45.00 |
| Dump Truck | 6453 | | HK | M-BR-P | | BK | | YW tipper/BR truck bed | $45.00 |
| Dump Truck | 6453 | | HK | M-BR-P | | BK | | OR tipper/BR truck bed | $45.00 |
| Dump Truck | 6453 | | HK | M-BR-P | | GY | | YW tipper/OR truck bed | $45.00 |
| Dump Truck | 6453 | | HK | M-BR-P | | GY | | YW tipper/BR truck bed | $45.00 |
| Dump Truck | 6453 | | HK | M-BR-P | | GY | | OR tipper/BR truck bed | $45.00 |
| Dump Truck | 6453 | | HK | M-BR-P | | BR-L | | YW tipper/OR truck bed | $45.00 |
| Dump Truck | 6453 | | HK | M-BR-P | | BR-L | | YW tipper/BR truck bed | $45.00 |
| Dump Truck | 6453 | | HK | M-BR-P | | BR-L | | OR tipper/BR truck bed | $45.00 |
| Dump Truck | 6453 | | HK | M-BR-P | | BR-D | | YW tipper/OR truck bed | $45.00 |
| Dump Truck | 6453 | | HK | M-BR-P | | BR-D | | YW tipper/BR truck bed | $45.00 |
| Dump Truck | 6453 | | HK | M-BR-P | | BR-D | | OR tipper/BR truck bed | $45.00 |
| Dump Truck | 6453 | | HK | M-GD | | WH | | YW tipper/OR truck bed | $50.00 |
| Dump Truck | 6453 | | HK | M-GD | | WH | | YW tipper/BR truck bed | $50.00 |
| Dump Truck | 6453 | | HK | M-GD | | WH | | OR tipper/BR truck bed | $50.00 |
| Dump Truck | 6453 | | HK | M-GD | | BK | | YW tipper/OR truck bed | $45.00 |
| Dump Truck | 6453 | | HK | M-GD | | BK | | YW tipper/BR truck bed | $45.00 |
| Dump Truck | 6453 | | HK | M-GD | | BK | | OR tipper/BR truck bed | $45.00 |
| Dump Truck | 6453 | | HK | M-GD | | GY | | YW tipper/OR truck bed | $45.00 |
| Dump Truck | 6453 | | HK | M-GD | | GY | | YW tipper/BR truck bed | $45.00 |
| Dump Truck | 6453 | | HK | M-GD | | GY | | OR tipper/BR truck bed | $45.00 |
| Dump Truck | 6453 | | HK | M-GD | | BR-L | | YW tipper/OR truck bed | $45.00 |
| Dump Truck | 6453 | | HK | M-GD | | BR-L | | YW tipper/BR truck bed | $45.00 |
| Dump Truck | 6453 | | HK | M-GD | | BR-L | | OR tipper/BR truck bed | $45.00 |
| Dump Truck | 6453 | | HK | M-GD | | BR-D | | YW tipper/OR truck bed | $45.00 |
| Dump Truck | 6453 | | HK | M-GD | | BR-D | | YW tipper/BR truck bed | $45.00 |
| Dump Truck | 6453 | | HK | M-GD | | BR-D | | OR tipper/BR truck bed | $45.00 |
| Dump Truck | 6453 | | HK | M-GR | | WH | | YW tipper/OR truck bed | $50.00 |
| Dump Truck | 6453 | | HK | M-GR | | WH | | YW tipper/BR truck bed | $50.00 |
| Dump Truck | 6453 | | HK | M-GR | | WH | | OR tipper/BR truck bed | $50.00 |
| Dump Truck | 6453 | | HK | M-GR | | BK | | YW tipper/OR truck bed | $45.00 |

## 1970 Variations

| Name | Number | Casting | Country | Color | Windows | Interior | Paint | Other | Value |
|---|---|---|---|---|---|---|---|---|---|
| Dump Truck | 6453 | | HK | M-GR | | BK | | YW tipper/BR truck bed | $45.00 |
| Dump Truck | 6453 | | HK | M-GR | | BK | | OR tipper/BR truck bed | $45.00 |
| Dump Truck | 6453 | | HK | M-GR | | GY | | YW tipper/OR truck bed | $45.00 |
| Dump Truck | 6453 | | HK | M-GR | | GY | | YW tipper/BR truck bed | $45.00 |
| Dump Truck | 6453 | | HK | M-GR | | GY | | OR tipper/BR truck bed | $45.00 |
| Dump Truck | 6453 | | HK | M-GR | | BR-L | | YW tipper/OR truck bed | $45.00 |
| Dump Truck | 6453 | | HK | M-GR | | BR-L | | YW tipper/BR truck bed | $45.00 |
| Dump Truck | 6453 | | HK | M-GR | | BR-L | | OR tipper/BR truck bed | $45.00 |
| Dump Truck | 6453 | | HK | M-GR | | BR-D | | YW tipper/OR truck bed | $45.00 |
| Dump Truck | 6453 | | HK | M-GR | | BR-D | | YW tipper/BR truck bed | $45.00 |
| Dump Truck | 6453 | | HK | M-GR | | BR-D | | OR tipper/BR truck bed | $45.00 |
| Dump Truck | 6453 | | HK | M-GR-E | | WH | | YW tipper/OR truck bed | $55.00 |
| Dump Truck | 6453 | | HK | M-GR-E | | WH | | YW tipper/BR truck bed | $55.00 |
| Dump Truck | 6453 | | HK | M-GR-E | | WH | | OR tipper/BR truck bed | $55.00 |
| Dump Truck | 6453 | | HK | M-GR-E | | BK | | YW tipper/OR truck bed | $50.00 |
| Dump Truck | 6453 | | HK | M-GR-E | | BK | | YW tipper/BR truck bed | $50.00 |
| Dump Truck | 6453 | | HK | M-GR-E | | BK | | OR tipper/BR truck bed | $50.00 |
| Dump Truck | 6453 | | HK | M-GR-E | | GY | | YW tipper/OR truck bed | $50.00 |
| Dump Truck | 6453 | | HK | M-GR-E | | GY | | YW tipper/BR truck bed | $50.00 |
| Dump Truck | 6453 | | HK | M-GR-E | | GY | | OR tipper/BR truck bed | $50.00 |
| Dump Truck | 6453 | | HK | M-GR-E | | BR-L | | YW tipper/OR truck bed | $50.00 |
| Dump Truck | 6453 | | HK | M-GR-E | | BR-L | | YW tipper/BR truck bed | $50.00 |
| Dump Truck | 6453 | | HK | M-GR-E | | BR-L | | OR tipper/BR truck bed | $50.00 |
| Dump Truck | 6453 | | HK | M-GR-E | | BR-D | | YW tipper/OR truck bed | $50.00 |
| Dump Truck | 6453 | | HK | M-GR-E | | BR-D | | YW tipper/BR truck bed | $50.00 |
| Dump Truck | 6453 | | HK | M-GR-E | | BR-D | | OR tipper/BR truck bed | $50.00 |
| Dump Truck | 6453 | | HK | M-GR-L | | WH | | YW tipper/OR truck bed | $50.00 |
| Dump Truck | 6453 | | HK | M-GR-L | | WH | | YW tipper/BR truck bed | $50.00 |
| Dump Truck | 6453 | | HK | M-GR-L | | WH | | OR tipper/BR truck bed | $50.00 |
| Dump Truck | 6453 | | HK | M-GR-L | | BK | | YW tipper/OR truck bed | $45.00 |
| Dump Truck | 6453 | | HK | M-GR-L | | BK | | YW tipper/BR truck bed | $45.00 |
| Dump Truck | 6453 | | HK | M-GR-L | | BK | | OR tipper/BR truck bed | $45.00 |
| Dump Truck | 6453 | | HK | M-GR-L | | GY | | YW tipper/OR truck bed | $45.00 |
| Dump Truck | 6453 | | HK | M-GR-L | | GY | | YW tipper/BR truck bed | $45.00 |
| Dump Truck | 6453 | | HK | M-GR-L | | GY | | OR tipper/BR truck bed | $45.00 |
| Dump Truck | 6453 | | HK | M-GR-L | | BR-L | | YW tipper/OR truck bed | $45.00 |
| Dump Truck | 6453 | | HK | M-GR-L | | BR-L | | YW tipper/BR truck bed | $45.00 |
| Dump Truck | 6453 | | HK | M-GR-L | | BR-L | | OR tipper/BR truck bed | $45.00 |
| Dump Truck | 6453 | | HK | M-GR-L | | BR-D | | YW tipper/OR truck bed | $45.00 |
| Dump Truck | 6453 | | HK | M-GR-L | | BR-D | | YW tipper/BR truck bed | $45.00 |
| Dump Truck | 6453 | | HK | M-GR-L | | BR-D | | OR tipper/BR truck bed | $45.00 |
| Dump Truck | 6453 | | HK | M-GR-O | | WH | | YW tipper/OR truck bed | $45.00 |
| Dump Truck | 6453 | | HK | M-GR-O | | WH | | YW tipper/BR truck bed | $50.00 |
| Dump Truck | 6453 | | HK | M-GR-O | | WH | | OR tipper/BR truck bed | $50.00 |
| Dump Truck | 6453 | | HK | M-GR-O | | BK | | YW tipper/OR truck bed | $45.00 |
| Dump Truck | 6453 | | HK | M-GR-O | | BK | | YW tipper/BR truck bed | $45.00 |
| Dump Truck | 6453 | | HK | M-GR-O | | BK | | OR tipper/BR truck bed | $45.00 |
| Dump Truck | 6453 | | HK | M-GR-O | | GY | | YW tipper/OR truck bed | $45.00 |
| Dump Truck | 6453 | | HK | M-GR-O | | GY | | YW tipper/BR truck bed | $45.00 |
| Dump Truck | 6453 | | HK | M-GR-O | | GY | | OR tipper/BR truck bed | $45.00 |
| Dump Truck | 6453 | | HK | M-GR-O | | BR-L | | YW tipper/OR truck bed | $45.00 |
| Dump Truck | 6453 | | HK | M-GR-O | | BR-L | | YW tipper/BR truck bed | $45.00 |
| Dump Truck | 6453 | | HK | M-GR-O | | BR-L | | OR tipper/BR truck bed | $45.00 |
| Dump Truck | 6453 | | HK | M-GR-O | | BR-D | | YW tipper/OR truck bed | $45.00 |
| Dump Truck | 6453 | | HK | M-GR-O | | BR-D | | YW tipper/BR truck bed | $45.00 |
| Dump Truck | 6453 | | HK | M-GR-O | | BR-D | | OR tipper/BR truck bed | $45.00 |
| Dump Truck | 6453 | | HK | M-OR | | WH | | YW tipper/OR truck bed | $50.00 |
| Dump Truck | 6453 | | HK | M-OR | | WH | | YW tipper/BR truck bed | $50.00 |
| Dump Truck | 6453 | | HK | M-OR | | WH | | OR tipper/BR truck bed | $50.00 |
| Dump Truck | 6453 | | HK | M-OR | | BK | | YW tipper/OR truck bed | $45.00 |
| Dump Truck | 6453 | | HK | M-OR | | BK | | YW tipper/BR truck bed | $45.00 |
| Dump Truck | 6453 | | HK | M-OR | | BK | | OR tipper/BR truck bed | $45.00 |
| Dump Truck | 6453 | | HK | M-OR | | GY | | YW tipper/OR truck bed | $45.00 |
| Dump Truck | 6453 | | HK | M-OR | | GY | | YW tipper/BR truck bed | $45.00 |
| Dump Truck | 6453 | | HK | M-OR | | GY | | OR tipper/BR truck bed | $45.00 |
| Dump Truck | 6453 | | HK | M-OR | | BR-L | | YW tipper/OR truck bed | $45.00 |
| Dump Truck | 6453 | | HK | M-OR | | BR-L | | YW tipper/BR truck bed | $45.00 |
| Dump Truck | 6453 | | HK | M-OR | | BR-L | | OR tipper/BR truck bed | $45.00 |
| Dump Truck | 6453 | | HK | M-OR | | BR-D | | YW tipper/OR truck bed | $45.00 |
| Dump Truck | 6453 | | HK | M-OR | | BR-D | | YW tipper/BR truck bed | $45.00 |
| Dump Truck | 6453 | | HK | M-OR | | BR-D | | OR tipper/BR truck bed | $45.00 |
| Dump Truck | 6453 | | HK | M-PR | | WH | | YW tipper/OR truck bed | $50.00 |

## 1970 Variations

| Name | Number | Casting | Country | Color | Windows | Interior | Paint | Other | Value |
|---|---|---|---|---|---|---|---|---|---|
| Dump Truck | 6453 | | HK | M-PR | | WH | | YW tipper/BR truck bed | $50.00 |
| Dump Truck | 6453 | | HK | M-PR | | WH | | OR tipper/BR truck bed | $50.00 |
| Dump Truck | 6453 | | HK | M-PR | | BK | | YW tipper/OR truck bed | $45.00 |
| Dump Truck | 6453 | | HK | M-PR | | BK | | YW tipper/BR truck bed | $45.00 |
| Dump Truck | 6453 | | HK | M-PR | | BK | | OR tipper/BR truck bed | $45.00 |
| Dump Truck | 6453 | | HK | M-PR | | GY | | YW tipper/OR truck bed | $45.00 |
| Dump Truck | 6453 | | HK | M-PR | | GY | | YW tipper/BR truck bed | $45.00 |
| Dump Truck | 6453 | | HK | M-PR | | GY | | OR tipper/BR truck bed | $45.00 |
| Dump Truck | 6453 | | HK | M-PR | | BR-L | | YW tipper/OR truck bed | $45.00 |
| Dump Truck | 6453 | | HK | M-PR | | BR-L | | YW tipper/BR truck bed | $45.00 |
| Dump Truck | 6453 | | HK | M-PR | | BR-L | | OR tipper/BR truck bed | $45.00 |
| Dump Truck | 6453 | | HK | M-PR | | BR-D | | YW tipper/OR truck bed | $45.00 |
| Dump Truck | 6453 | | HK | M-PR | | BR-D | | YW tipper/BR truck bed | $45.00 |
| Dump Truck | 6453 | | HK | M-PR | | BR-D | | OR tipper/BR truck bed | $45.00 |
| Dump Truck | 6453 | | HK | M-RD | | WH | | YW tipper/OR truck bed | $55.00 |
| Dump Truck | 6453 | | HK | M-RD | | WH | | YW tipper/BR truck bed | $55.00 |
| Dump Truck | 6453 | | HK | M-RD | | WH | | OR tipper/BR truck bed | $55.00 |
| Dump Truck | 6453 | | HK | M-RD | | BK | | YW tipper/OR truck bed | $50.00 |
| Dump Truck | 6453 | | HK | M-RD | | BK | | YW tipper/BR truck bed | $50.00 |
| Dump Truck | 6453 | | HK | M-RD | | BK | | OR tipper/BR truck bed | $50.00 |
| Dump Truck | 6453 | | HK | M-RD | | GY | | YW tipper/OR truck bed | $50.00 |
| Dump Truck | 6453 | | HK | M-RD | | GY | | YW tipper/BR truck bed | $50.00 |
| Dump Truck | 6453 | | HK | M-RD | | GY | | OR tipper/BR truck bed | $50.00 |
| Dump Truck | 6453 | | HK | M-RD | | BR-L | | YW tipper/OR truck bed | $50.00 |
| Dump Truck | 6453 | | HK | M-RD | | BR-L | | YW tipper/BR truck bed | $50.00 |
| Dump Truck | 6453 | | HK | M-RD | | BR-L | | OR tipper/BR truck bed | $50.00 |
| Dump Truck | 6453 | | HK | M-RD | | BR-D | | YW tipper/OR truck bed | $50.00 |
| Dump Truck | 6453 | | HK | M-RD | | BR-D | | YW tipper/BR truck bed | $50.00 |
| Dump Truck | 6453 | | HK | M-RD | | BR-D | | OR tipper/BR truck bed | $50.00 |
| Dump Truck | 6453 | | HK | M-RD-R | | WH | | YW tipper/OR truck bod | $60.00 |
| Dump Truck | 6453 | | HK | M-RD-R | | WH | | YW tipper/BR truck bed | $60.00 |
| Dump Truck | 6453 | | HK | M-RD-R | | WH | | OR tipper/BR truck bed | $60.00 |
| Dump Truck | 6453 | | HK | M-RD-R | | BK | | YW tipper/OR truck bed | $55.00 |
| Dump Truck | 6453 | | HK | M-RD-R | | BK | | YW tipper/BR truck bed | $55.00 |
| Dump Truck | 6453 | | HK | M-RD-R | | BK | | OR tipper/BR truck bed | $55.00 |
| Dump Truck | 6453 | | HK | M-RD-R | | GY | | YW tipper/OR truck bed | $55.00 |
| Dump Truck | 6453 | | HK | M-RD-R | | GY | | YW tipper/BR truck bed | $55.00 |
| Dump Truck | 6453 | | HK | M-RD-R | | GY | | OR tipper/BR truck bed | $55.00 |
| Dump Truck | 6453 | | HK | M-RD-R | | BR-L | | YW tipper/OR truck bed | $55.00 |
| Dump Truck | 6453 | | HK | M-RD-R | | BR-L | | YW tipper/BR truck bed | $55.00 |
| Dump Truck | 6453 | | HK | M-RD-R | | BR-L | | OR tipper/BR truck bed | $55.00 |
| Dump Truck | 6453 | | HK | M-RD-R | | BR-D | | YW tipper/OR truck bed | $55.00 |
| Dump Truck | 6453 | | HK | M-RD-R | | BR-D | | YW tipper/BR truck bed | $55.00 |
| Dump Truck | 6453 | | HK | M-RD-R | | BR-D | | OR tipper/BR truck bed | $55.00 |
| Dump Truck | 6453 | | HK | M-YW | | WH | | YW tipper/OR truck bed | $50.00 |
| Dump Truck | 6453 | | HK | M-YW | | WH | | YW tipper/BR truck bed | $50.00 |
| Dump Truck | 6453 | | HK | M-YW | | WH | | OR tipper/BR truck bed | $50.00 |
| Dump Truck | 6453 | | HK | M-YW | | BK | | YW tipper/OR truck bed | $45.00 |
| Dump Truck | 6453 | | HK | M-YW | | BK | | YW tipper/BR truck bed | $45.00 |
| Dump Truck | 6453 | | HK | M-YW | | BK | | OR tipper/BR truck bed | $45.00 |
| Dump Truck | 6453 | | HK | M-YW | | GY | | YW tipper/OR truck bed | $45.00 |
| Dump Truck | 6453 | | HK | M-YW | | GY | | YW tipper/BR truck bed | $45.00 |
| Dump Truck | 6453 | | HK | M-YW | | GY | | OR tipper/BR truck bed | $45.00 |
| Dump Truck | 6453 | | HK | M-YW | | BR-L | | YW tipper/OR truck bed | $45.00 |
| Dump Truck | 6453 | | HK | M-YW | | BR-L | | YW tipper/BR truck bed | $45.00 |
| Dump Truck | 6453 | | HK | M-YW | | BR-L | | OR tipper/BR truck bed | $45.00 |
| Dump Truck | 6453 | | HK | M-YW | | BR-D | | YW tipper/OR truck bed | $45.00 |
| Dump Truck | 6453 | | HK | M-YW | | BR-D | | YW tipper/BR truck bed | $45.00 |
| Dump Truck | 6453 | | HK | M-YW | | BR-D | | OR tipper/BR truck bed | $45.00 |
| Dump Truck | 6453 | | HK | M-YW-L | | WH | | YW tipper/OR truck bed | $55.00 |
| Dump Truck | 6453 | | HK | M-YW-L | | WH | | YW tipper/BR truck bed | $55.00 |
| Dump Truck | 6453 | | HK | M-YW-L | | WH | | OR tipper/BR truck bed | $55.00 |
| Dump Truck | 6453 | | HK | M-YW-L | | BK | | YW tipper/OR truck bed | $50.00 |
| Dump Truck | 6453 | | HK | M-YW-L | | BK | | YW tipper/BR truck bed | $50.00 |
| Dump Truck | 6453 | | HK | M-YW-L | | BK | | OR tipper/BR truck bed | $50.00 |
| Dump Truck | 6453 | | HK | M-YW-L | | GY | | YW tipper/OR truck bed | $50.00 |
| Dump Truck | 6453 | | HK | M-YW-L | | GY | | YW tipper/BR truck bed | $50.00 |
| Dump Truck | 6453 | | HK | M-YW-L | | GY | | OR tipper/BR truck bed | $50.00 |
| Dump Truck | 6453 | | HK | M-YW-L | | BR-L | | YW tipper/OR truck bed | $50.00 |
| Dump Truck | 6453 | | HK | M-YW-L | | BR-L | | YW tipper/BR truck bed | $50.00 |
| Dump Truck | 6453 | | HK | M-YW-L | | BR-L | | OR tipper/BR truck bed | $50.00 |
| Dump Truck | 6453 | | HK | M-YW-L | | BR-D | | YW tipper/OR truck bed | $50.00 |

## 1970 Variations

| Name | Number | Casting | Country | Color | Windows | Interior | Paint | Other | Value |
|---|---|---|---|---|---|---|---|---|---|
| Dump Truck | 6453 | | HK | M-YW-L | | BR-D | | YW tipper/BR truck bed | $50.00 |
| Dump Truck | 6453 | | HK | M-YW-L | | BR-D | | OR tipper/BR truck bed | $50.00 |
| | | | | | | | | | |
| Fire Engine | 6454 | | HK | E-RD | | WH | | BK ladder | $200.00 |
| Fire Engine | 6454 | | HK | E-RD | | BK | | BK ladder | $180.00 |
| Fire Engine | 6454 | | HK | M-RD | | WH | | WH ladder | $400.00 |
| Fire Engine | 6454 | | HK | M-RD | | WH | | BK ladder | $75.00 |
| Fire Engine | 6454 | | HK | M-RD | | BK | | BK ladder | $70.00 |
| | | | | | | | | | |
| Moving Van | 6455 | | HK | E-RD | | WH | | WH trailer w/ smooth door | $240.00 |
| Moving Van | 6455 | | HK | E-RD | | WH | | WH trailer w/ ridged door | $250.00 |
| Moving Van | 6455 | | HK | E-RD | | WH | | GY trailer w/ smooth door | $120.00 |
| Moving Van | 6455 | | HK | E-RD | | WH | | GY trailer w/ ridged door | $130.00 |
| Moving Van | 6455 | | HK | E-RD | | BK | | WH trailer w/ smooth door | $200.00 |
| Moving Van | 6455 | | HK | E-RD | | BK | | WH trailer w/ ridged door | $110.00 |
| Moving Van | 6455 | | HK | E-RD | | BK | | GY trailer w/ smooth door | $160.00 |
| Moving Van | 6455 | | HK | E-RD | | BK | | GY trailer w/ ridged door | $190.00 |
| Moving Van | 6455 | | HK | E-RD | | GY | | WH trailer w/ smooth door | $200.00 |
| Moving Van | 6455 | | HK | E-RD | | GY | | WH trailer w/ ridged door | $210.00 |
| Moving Van | 6455 | | HK | E-RD | | GY | | GY trailer w/ smooth door | $180.00 |
| Moving Van | 6455 | | HK | E-RD | | GY | | GY trailer w/ ridged door | $190.00 |
| Moving Van | 6455 | | HK | E-RD | | BR-L | | WH trailer w/ smooth door | $200.00 |
| Moving Van | 6455 | | HK | E-RD | | BR-L | | WH trailer w/ ridged door | $110.00 |
| Moving Van | 6455 | | HK | E-RD | | BR-L | | GY trailer w/ smooth door | $180.00 |
| Moving Van | 6455 | | HK | E-RD | | BR-L | | GY trailer w/ ridged door | $190.00 |
| Moving Van | 6455 | | HK | E-RD | | BR-D | | WH trailer w/ smooth door | $200.00 |
| Moving Van | 6455 | | HK | E-RD | | BR-D | | WH trailer w/ ridged door | $110.00 |
| Moving Van | 6455 | | HK | E-RD | | BR-D | | GY trailer w/ smooth door | $180.00 |
| Moving Van | 6455 | | HK | E-RD | | BR-D | | GY trailer w/ ridged door | $190.00 |
| Moving Van | 6455 | | HK | E-WH | | WH | | WH trailer w/ smooth door | $300.00 |
| Moving Van | 6455 | | HK | E-WH | | WH | | WH trailer w/ ridged door | $310.00 |
| Moving Van | 6455 | | HK | E-WH | | WH | | GY trailer w/ smooth door | $280.00 |
| Moving Van | 6455 | | HK | E-WH | | WH | | GY trailer w/ ridged door | $190.00 |
| Moving Van | 6455 | | HK | E-WH | | BK | | WH trailer w/ smooth door | $260.00 |
| Moving Van | 6455 | | HK | E-WH | | BK | | WH trailer w/ ridged door | $270.00 |
| Moving Van | 6455 | | HK | E-WH | | BK | | GY trailer w/ smooth door | $240.00 |
| Moving Van | 6455 | | HK | E-WH | | BK | | GY trailer w/ ridged door | $250.00 |
| Moving Van | 6455 | | HK | E-WH | | GY | | WH trailer w/ smooth door | $260.00 |
| Moving Van | 6455 | | HK | E-WH | | GY | | WH trailer w/ ridged door | $270.00 |
| Moving Van | 6455 | | HK | E-WH | | GY | | GY trailer w/ smooth door | $240.00 |
| Moving Van | 6455 | | HK | E-WH | | GY | | GY trailer w/ ridged door | $250.00 |
| Moving Van | 6455 | | HK | E-WH | | BR-L | | WH trailer w/ smooth door | $260.00 |
| Moving Van | 6455 | | HK | E-WH | | BR-L | | WH trailer w/ ridged door | $270.00 |
| Moving Van | 6455 | | HK | E-WH | | BR-L | | GY trailer w/ smooth door | $240.00 |
| Moving Van | 6455 | | HK | E-WH | | BR-L | | GY trailer w/ ridged door | $250.00 |
| Moving Van | 6455 | | HK | E-WH | | BR-D | | WH trailer w/ smooth door | $260.00 |
| Moving Van | 6455 | | HK | E-WH | | BR-D | | WH trailer w/ ridged door | $270.00 |
| Moving Van | 6455 | | HK | E-WH | | BR-D | | GY trailer w/ smooth door | $240.00 |
| Moving Van | 6455 | | HK | E-WH | | BR-D | | GY trailer w/ ridged door | $250.00 |
| Moving Van | 6455 | | HK | M-AQ | | WH | | WH trailer w/ smooth door | $70.00 |
| Moving Van | 6455 | | HK | M-AQ | | WH | | WH trailer w/ ridged door | $75.00 |
| Moving Van | 6455 | | HK | M-AQ | | WH | | GY trailer w/ smooth door | $65.00 |
| Moving Van | 6455 | | HK | M-AQ | | WH | | GY trailer w/ ridged door | $70.00 |
| Moving Van | 6455 | | HK | M-AQ | | BK | | WH trailer w/ smooth door | $65.00 |
| Moving Van | 6455 | | HK | M-AQ | | BK | | WH trailer w/ ridged door | $70.00 |
| Moving Van | 6455 | | HK | M-AQ | | BK | | GY trailer w/ smooth door | $60.00 |
| Moving Van | 6455 | | HK | M-AQ | | BK | | GY trailer w/ ridged door | $65.00 |
| Moving Van | 6455 | | HK | M-AQ | | GY | | WH trailer w/ smooth door | $65.00 |
| Moving Van | 6455 | | HK | M-AQ | | GY | | WH trailer w/ ridged door | $70.00 |
| Moving Van | 6455 | | HK | M-AQ | | GY | | GY trailer w/ smooth door | $60.00 |
| Moving Van | 6455 | | HK | M-AQ | | GY | | GY trailer w/ ridged door | $65.00 |
| Moving Van | 6455 | | HK | M-AQ | | BR-L | | WH trailer w/ smooth door | $65.00 |
| Moving Van | 6455 | | HK | M-AQ | | BR-L | | WH trailer w/ ridged door | $70.00 |
| Moving Van | 6455 | | HK | M-AQ | | BR-L | | GY trailer w/ smooth door | $60.00 |
| Moving Van | 6455 | | HK | M-AQ | | BR-L | | GY trailer w/ ridged door | $65.00 |
| Moving Van | 6455 | | HK | M-AQ | | BR-D | | WH trailer w/ smooth door | $65.00 |
| Moving Van | 6455 | | HK | M-AQ | | BR-D | | WH trailer w/ ridged door | $70.00 |
| Moving Van | 6455 | | HK | M-AQ | | BR-D | | GY trailer w/ smooth door | $60.00 |
| Moving Van | 6455 | | HK | M-AQ | | BR-D | | GY trailer w/ ridged door | $65.00 |
| Moving Van | 6455 | | HK | M-BL | | WH | | WH trailer w/ smooth door | $70.00 |

**1970 Variations**

| Name | Number | Casting | Country | Color | Windows | Interior | Paint | Other | Value |
|---|---|---|---|---|---|---|---|---|---|
| Moving Van | 6455 | | HK | M-BL | | WH | | WH trailer w/ ridged door | $75.00 |
| Moving Van | 6455 | | HK | M-BL | | WH | | GY trailer w/ smooth door | $65.00 |
| Moving Van | 6455 | | HK | M-BL | | WH | | GY trailer w/ ridged door | $70.00 |
| Moving Van | 6455 | | HK | M-BL | | BK | | WH trailer w/ smooth door | $65.00 |
| Moving Van | 6455 | | HK | M-BL | | BK | | WH trailer w/ ridged door | $70.00 |
| Moving Van | 6455 | | HK | M-BL | | BK | | GY trailer w/ smooth door | $60.00 |
| Moving Van | 6455 | | HK | M-BL | | BK | | GY trailer w/ ridged door | $65.00 |
| Moving Van | 6455 | | HK | M-BL | | GY | | WH trailer w/ smooth door | $65.00 |
| Moving Van | 6455 | | HK | M-BL | | GY | | WH trailer w/ ridged door | $70.00 |
| Moving Van | 6455 | | HK | M-BL | | GY | | GY trailer w/ smooth door | $60.00 |
| Moving Van | 6455 | | HK | M-BL | | GY | | GY trailer w/ ridged door | $65.00 |
| Moving Van | 6455 | | HK | M-BL | | BR-L | | WH trailer w/ smooth door | $65.00 |
| Moving Van | 6455 | | HK | M-BL | | BR-L | | WH trailer w/ ridged door | $70.00 |
| Moving Van | 6455 | | HK | M-BL | | BR-L | | GY trailer w/ smooth door | $60.00 |
| Moving Van | 6455 | | HK | M-BL | | BR-L | | GY trailer w/ ridged door | $65.00 |
| Moving Van | 6455 | | HK | M-BL | | BR-D | | WH trailer w/ smooth door | $65.00 |
| Moving Van | 6455 | | HK | M-BL | | BR-D | | WH trailer w/ ridged door | $70.00 |
| Moving Van | 6455 | | HK | M-BL | | BR-D | | GY trailer w/ smooth door | $60.00 |
| Moving Van | 6455 | | HK | M-BL | | BR-D | | GY trailer w/ ridged door | $65.00 |
| Moving Van | 6455 | | HK | M-BR-D | | WH | | WH trailer w/ smooth door | $105.00 |
| Moving Van | 6455 | | HK | M-BR-D | | WH | | WH trailer w/ ridged door | $110.00 |
| Moving Van | 6455 | | HK | M-BR-D | | WH | | GY trailer w/ smooth door | $100.00 |
| Moving Van | 6455 | | HK | M-BR-D | | WH | | GY trailer w/ ridged door | $105.00 |
| Moving Van | 6455 | | HK | M-BR-D | | BK | | WH trailer w/ smooth door | $95.00 |
| Moving Van | 6455 | | HK | M-BR-D | | BK | | WH trailer w/ ridged door | $100.00 |
| Moving Van | 6455 | | HK | M-BR-D | | BK | | GY trailer w/ smooth door | $90.00 |
| Moving Van | 6455 | | HK | M-BR-D | | BK | | GY trailer w/ ridged door | $95.00 |
| Moving Van | 6455 | | HK | M-BR-D | | GY | | WH trailer w/ smooth door | $95.00 |
| Moving Van | 6455 | | HK | M-BR-D | | GY | | WH trailer w/ ridged door | $100.00 |
| Moving Van | 6455 | | HK | M-BR-D | | GY | | GY trailer w/ smooth door | $90.00 |
| Moving Van | 6455 | | HK | M-BR-D | | GY | | GY trailer w/ ridged door | $95.00 |
| Moving Van | 6455 | | HK | M-BR-D | | BR-L | | WH trailer w/ smooth door | $95.00 |
| Moving Van | 6455 | | HK | M-BR-D | | BR-L | | WH trailer w/ ridged door | $100.00 |
| Moving Van | 6455 | | HK | M-BR-D | | BR-L | | GY trailer w/ smooth door | $90.00 |
| Moving Van | 6455 | | HK | M-BR-D | | BR-L | | GY trailer w/ ridged door | $95.00 |
| Moving Van | 6455 | | HK | M-BR-D | | BR-D | | WH trailer w/ smooth door | $95.00 |
| Moving Van | 6455 | | HK | M-BR-D | | BR-D | | WH trailer w/ ridged door | $100.00 |
| Moving Van | 6455 | | HK | M-BR-D | | BR-D | | GY trailer w/ smooth door | $90.00 |
| Moving Van | 6455 | | HK | M-BR-D | | BR-D | | GY trailer w/ ridged door | $95.00 |
| Moving Van | 6455 | | HK | M-BR-P | | WH | | WH trailer w/ smooth door | $95.00 |
| Moving Van | 6455 | | HK | M-BR-P | | WH | | WH trailer w/ ridged door | $100.00 |
| Moving Van | 6455 | | HK | M-BR-P | | WH | | GY trailer w/ smooth door | $90.00 |
| Moving Van | 6455 | | HK | M-BR-P | | WH | | GY trailer w/ ridged door | $95.00 |
| Moving Van | 6455 | | HK | M-BR-P | | BK | | WH trailer w/ smooth door | $85.00 |
| Moving Van | 6455 | | HK | M-BR-P | | BK | | WH trailer w/ ridged door | $90.00 |
| Moving Van | 6455 | | HK | M-BR-P | | BK | | GY trailer w/ smooth door | $80.00 |
| Moving Van | 6455 | | HK | M-BR-P | | BK | | GY trailer w/ ridged door | $85.00 |
| Moving Van | 6455 | | HK | M-BR-P | | GY | | WH trailer w/ smooth door | $85.00 |
| Moving Van | 6455 | | HK | M-BR-P | | GY | | WH trailer w/ ridged door | $90.00 |
| Moving Van | 6455 | | HK | M-BR-P | | GY | | GY trailer w/ smooth door | $80.00 |
| Moving Van | 6455 | | HK | M-BR-P | | GY | | GY trailer w/ ridged door | $85.00 |
| Moving Van | 6455 | | HK | M-BR-P | | BR-L | | WH trailer w/ smooth door | $85.00 |
| Moving Van | 6455 | | HK | M-BR-P | | BR-L | | WH trailer w/ ridged door | $90.00 |
| Moving Van | 6455 | | HK | M-BR-P | | BR-L | | GY trailer w/ smooth door | $80.00 |
| Moving Van | 6455 | | HK | M-BR-P | | BR-L | | GY trailer w/ ridged door | $85.00 |
| Moving Van | 6455 | | HK | M-BR-P | | BR-D | | WH trailer w/ smooth door | $85.00 |
| Moving Van | 6455 | | HK | M-BR-P | | BR-D | | WH trailer w/ ridged door | $90.00 |
| Moving Van | 6455 | | HK | M-BR-P | | BR-D | | GY trailer w/ smooth door | $80.00 |
| Moving Van | 6455 | | HK | M-BR-P | | BR-D | | GY trailer w/ ridged door | $85.00 |
| Moving Van | 6455 | | HK | M-GD | | WH | | WH trailer w/ smooth door | $70.00 |
| Moving Van | 6455 | | HK | M-GD | | WH | | WH trailer w/ ridged door | $75.00 |
| Moving Van | 6455 | | HK | M-GD | | WH | | GY trailer w/ smooth door | $65.00 |
| Moving Van | 6455 | | HK | M-GD | | WH | | GY trailer w/ ridged door | $70.00 |
| Moving Van | 6455 | | HK | M-GD | | BK | | WH trailer w/ smooth door | $65.00 |
| Moving Van | 6455 | | HK | M-GD | | BK | | WH trailer w/ ridged door | $70.00 |
| Moving Van | 6455 | | HK | M-GD | | BK | | GY trailer w/ smooth door | $60.00 |
| Moving Van | 6455 | | HK | M-GD | | BK | | GY trailer w/ ridged door | $65.00 |
| Moving Van | 6455 | | HK | M-GD | | GY | | WH trailer w/ smooth door | $65.00 |
| Moving Van | 6455 | | HK | M-GD | | GY | | WH trailer w/ ridged door | $70.00 |
| Moving Van | 6455 | | HK | M-GD | | GY | | GY trailer w/ smooth door | $60.00 |
| Moving Van | 6455 | | HK | M-GD | | GY | | GY trailer w/ ridged door | $65.00 |
| Moving Van | 6455 | | HK | M-GD | | BR-L | | WH trailer w/ smooth door | $65.00 |

## 1970 Variations

| Name | Number | Casting | Country | Color | Windows | Interior | Paint | Other | Value |
|---|---|---|---|---|---|---|---|---|---|
| Moving Van | 6455 | | HK | M-GD | | BR-L | | WH trailer w/ ridged door | $70.00 |
| Moving Van | 6455 | | HK | M-GD | | BR-L | | GY trailer w/ smooth door | $60.00 |
| Moving Van | 6455 | | HK | M-GD | | BR-L | | GY trailer w/ ridged door | $65.00 |
| Moving Van | 6455 | | HK | M-GD | | BR-D | | WH trailer w/ smooth door | $65.00 |
| Moving Van | 6455 | | HK | M-GD | | BR-D | | WH trailer w/ ridged door | $70.00 |
| Moving Van | 6455 | | HK | M-GD | | BR-D | | GY trailer w/ smooth door | $60.00 |
| Moving Van | 6455 | | HK | M-GD | | BR-D | | GY trailer w/ ridged door | $65.00 |
| Moving Van | 6455 | | HK | M-GR | | WH | | WH trailer w/ smooth door | $70.00 |
| Moving Van | 6455 | | HK | M-GR | | WH | | WH trailer w/ ridged door | $75.00 |
| Moving Van | 6455 | | HK | M-GR | | WH | | GY trailer w/ smooth door | $65.00 |
| Moving Van | 6455 | | HK | M-GR | | WH | | GY trailer w/ ridged door | $70.00 |
| Moving Van | 6455 | | HK | M-GR | | BK | | WH trailer w/ smooth door | $65.00 |
| Moving Van | 6455 | | HK | M-GR | | BK | | WH trailer w/ ridged door | $70.00 |
| Moving Van | 6455 | | HK | M-GR | | BK | | GY trailer w/ smooth door | $60.00 |
| Moving Van | 6455 | | HK | M-GR | | BK | | GY trailer w/ ridged door | $65.00 |
| Moving Van | 6455 | | HK | M-GR | | GY | | WH trailer w/ smooth door | $65.00 |
| Moving Van | 6455 | | HK | M-GR | | GY | | WH trailer w/ ridged door | $70.00 |
| Moving Van | 6455 | | HK | M-GR | | GY | | GY trailer w/ smooth door | $60.00 |
| Moving Van | 6455 | | HK | M-GR | | GY | | GY trailer w/ ridged door | $65.00 |
| Moving Van | 6455 | | HK | M-GR | | BR-L | | WH trailer w/ smooth door | $65.00 |
| Moving Van | 6455 | | HK | M-GR | | BR-L | | WH trailer w/ ridged door | $70.00 |
| Moving Van | 6455 | | HK | M-GR | | BR-L | | GY trailer w/ smooth door | $60.00 |
| Moving Van | 6455 | | HK | M-GR | | BR-L | | GY trailer w/ ridged door | $65.00 |
| Moving Van | 6455 | | HK | M-GR | | BR-D | | WH trailer w/ smooth door | $65.00 |
| Moving Van | 6455 | | HK | M-GR | | BR-D | | WH trailer w/ ridged door | $70.00 |
| Moving Van | 6455 | | HK | M-GR | | BR-D | | GY trailer w/ smooth door | $60.00 |
| Moving Van | 6455 | | HK | M-GR | | BR-D | | GY trailer w/ ridged door | $65.00 |
| Moving Van | 6455 | | HK | M-GR-E | | WH | | WH trailer w/ smooth door | $75.00 |
| Moving Van | 6455 | | HK | M-GR-E | | WH | | WH trailer w/ ridged door | $80.00 |
| Moving Van | 6455 | | HK | M-GR-E | | WH | | GY trailer w/ smooth door | $70.00 |
| Moving Van | 6455 | | HK | M-GR-E | | WH | | GY trailer w/ ridged door | $75.00 |
| Moving Van | 6455 | | HK | M-GR-E | | BK | | WH trailer w/ smooth door | $70.00 |
| Moving Van | 6455 | | HK | M-GR-E | | BK | | WH trailer w/ ridged door | $75.00 |
| Moving Van | 6455 | | HK | M-GR-E | | BK | | GY trailer w/ smooth door | $65.00 |
| Moving Van | 6455 | | HK | M-GR-E | | BK | | GY trailer w/ ridged door | $70.00 |
| Moving Van | 6455 | | HK | M-GR-E | | GY | | WH trailer w/ smooth door | $70.00 |
| Moving Van | 6455 | | HK | M-GR-E | | GY | | WH trailer w/ ridged door | $75.00 |
| Moving Van | 6455 | | HK | M-GR-E | | GY | | GY trailer w/ smooth door | $65.00 |
| Moving Van | 6455 | | HK | M-GR-E | | GY | | GY trailer w/ ridged door | $70.00 |
| Moving Van | 6455 | | HK | M-GR-E | | BR-L | | WH trailer w/ smooth door | $70.00 |
| Moving Van | 6455 | | HK | M-GR-E | | BR-L | | WH trailer w/ ridged door | $75.00 |
| Moving Van | 6455 | | HK | M-GR-E | | BR-L | | GY trailer w/ smooth door | $65.00 |
| Moving Van | 6455 | | HK | M-GR-E | | BR-L | | GY trailer w/ ridged door | $70.00 |
| Moving Van | 6455 | | HK | M-GR-E | | BR-D | | WH trailer w/ smooth door | $70.00 |
| Moving Van | 6455 | | HK | M-GR-E | | BR-D | | WH trailer w/ ridged door | $75.00 |
| Moving Van | 6455 | | HK | M-GR-E | | BR-D | | GY trailer w/ smooth door | $65.00 |
| Moving Van | 6455 | | HK | M-GR-E | | BR-D | | GY trailer w/ ridged door | $70.00 |
| Moving Van | 6455 | | HK | M-GR-L | | WH | | WH trailer w/ smooth door | $75.00 |
| Moving Van | 6455 | | HK | M-GR-L | | WH | | WH trailer w/ ridged door | $80.00 |
| Moving Van | 6455 | | HK | M-GR-L | | WH | | GY trailer w/ smooth door | $70.00 |
| Moving Van | 6455 | | HK | M-GR-L | | WH | | GY trailer w/ ridged door | $75.00 |
| Moving Van | 6455 | | HK | M-GR-L | | BK | | WH trailer w/ smooth door | $70.00 |
| Moving Van | 6455 | | HK | M-GR-L | | BK | | WH trailer w/ ridged door | $75.00 |
| Moving Van | 6455 | | HK | M-GR-L | | BK | | GY trailer w/ smooth door | $65.00 |
| Moving Van | 6455 | | HK | M-GR-L | | BK | | GY trailer w/ ridged door | $70.00 |
| Moving Van | 6455 | | HK | M-GR-L | | GY | | WH trailer w/ smooth door | $70.00 |
| Moving Van | 6455 | | HK | M-GR-L | | GY | | WH trailer w/ ridged door | $75.00 |
| Moving Van | 6455 | | HK | M-GR-L | | GY | | GY trailer w/ smooth door | $65.00 |
| Moving Van | 6455 | | HK | M-GR-L | | GY | | GY trailer w/ ridged door | $70.00 |
| Moving Van | 6455 | | HK | M-GR-L | | BR-L | | WH trailer w/ smooth door | $70.00 |
| Moving Van | 6455 | | HK | M-GR-L | | BR-L | | WH trailer w/ ridged door | $75.00 |
| Moving Van | 6455 | | HK | M-GR-L | | BR-L | | GY trailer w/ smooth door | $65.00 |
| Moving Van | 6455 | | HK | M-GR-L | | BR-L | | GY trailer w/ ridged door | $70.00 |
| Moving Van | 6455 | | HK | M-GR-L | | BR-D | | WH trailer w/ smooth door | $70.00 |
| Moving Van | 6455 | | HK | M-GR-L | | BR-D | | WH trailer w/ ridged door | $75.00 |
| Moving Van | 6455 | | HK | M-GR-L | | BR-D | | GY trailer w/ smooth door | $65.00 |
| Moving Van | 6455 | | HK | M-GR-L | | BR-D | | GY trailer w/ ridged door | $70.00 |
| Moving Van | 6455 | | HK | M-GR-O | | WH | | WH trailer w/ smooth door | $75.00 |
| Moving Van | 6455 | | HK | M-GR-O | | WH | | WH trailer w/ ridged door | $80.00 |
| Moving Van | 6455 | | HK | M-GR-O | | WH | | GY trailer w/ smooth door | $70.00 |
| Moving Van | 6455 | | HK | M-GR-O | | WH | | GY trailer w/ ridged door | $75.00 |
| Moving Van | 6455 | | HK | M-GR-O | | BK | | WH trailer w/ smooth door | $70.00 |

## 1970 Variations

| Name | Number | Casting | Country | Color | Windows | Interior | Paint | Other | Value |
|---|---|---|---|---|---|---|---|---|---|
| Moving Van | 6455 | | HK | M-GR-O | | BK | | WH trailer w/ ridged door | $75.00 |
| Moving Van | 6455 | | HK | M-GR-O | | BK | | GY trailer w/ smooth door | $65.00 |
| Moving Van | 6455 | | HK | M-GR-O | | BK | | GY trailer w/ ridged door | $70.00 |
| Moving Van | 6455 | | HK | M-GR-O | | GY | | WH trailer w/ smooth door | $70.00 |
| Moving Van | 6455 | | HK | M-GR-O | | GY | | WH trailer w/ ridged door | $75.00 |
| Moving Van | 6455 | | HK | M-GR-O | | GY | | GY trailer w/ smooth door | $65.00 |
| Moving Van | 6455 | | HK | M-GR-O | | GY | | GY trailer w/ ridged door | $70.00 |
| Moving Van | 6455 | | HK | M-GR-O | | BR-L | | WH trailer w/ smooth door | $70.00 |
| Moving Van | 6455 | | HK | M-GR-O | | BR-L | | WH trailer w/ ridged door | $75.00 |
| Moving Van | 6455 | | HK | M-GR-O | | BR-L | | GY trailer w/ smooth door | $65.00 |
| Moving Van | 6455 | | HK | M-GR-O | | BR-L | | GY trailer w/ ridged door | $70.00 |
| Moving Van | 6455 | | HK | M-GR-O | | BR-D | | WH trailer w/ smooth door | $70.00 |
| Moving Van | 6455 | | HK | M-GR-O | | BR-D | | WH trailer w/ ridged door | $75.00 |
| Moving Van | 6455 | | HK | M-GR-O | | BR-D | | GY trailer w/ smooth door | $65.00 |
| Moving Van | 6455 | | HK | M-GR-O | | BR-D | | GY trailer w/ ridged door | $70.00 |
| Moving Van | 6455 | | HK | M-PR | | WH | | WH trailer w/ smooth door | $105.00 |
| Moving Van | 6455 | | HK | M-PR | | WH | | WH trailer w/ ridged door | $110.00 |
| Moving Van | 6455 | | HK | M-PR | | WH | | GY trailer w/ smooth door | $100.00 |
| Moving Van | 6455 | | HK | M-PR | | WH | | GY trailer w/ ridged door | $105.00 |
| Moving Van | 6455 | | HK | M-PR | | BK | | WH trailer w/ smooth door | $95.00 |
| Moving Van | 6455 | | HK | M-PR | | BK | | WH trailer w/ ridged door | $100.00 |
| Moving Van | 6455 | | HK | M-PR | | BK | | GY trailer w/ smooth door | $90.00 |
| Moving Van | 6455 | | HK | M-PR | | BK | | GY trailer w/ ridged door | $95.00 |
| Moving Van | 6455 | | HK | M-PR | | GY | | WH trailer w/ smooth door | $95.00 |
| Moving Van | 6455 | | HK | M-PR | | GY | | WH trailer w/ ridged door | $100.00 |
| Moving Van | 6455 | | HK | M-PR | | GY | | GY trailer w/ smooth door | $90.00 |
| Moving Van | 6455 | | HK | M-PR | | GY | | GY trailer w/ ridged door | $95.00 |
| Moving Van | 6455 | | HK | M-PR | | BR-L | | WH trailer w/ smooth door | $95.00 |
| Moving Van | 6455 | | HK | M-PR | | BR-L | | WH trailer w/ ridged door | $100.00 |
| Moving Van | 6455 | | HK | M-PR | | BR-L | | GY trailer w/ smooth door | $90.00 |
| Moving Van | 6455 | | HK | M-PR | | BR-L | | GY trailer w/ ridged door | $95.00 |
| Moving Van | 6455 | | HK | M-PR | | BR-D | | WH trailer w/ smooth door | $95.00 |
| Moving Van | 6455 | | HK | M-PR | | BR-D | | WH trailer w/ ridged door | $100.00 |
| Moving Van | 6455 | | HK | M-PR | | BR-D | | GY trailer w/ smooth door | $90.00 |
| Moving Van | 6455 | | HK | M-PR | | BR-D | | GY trailer w/ ridged door | $95.00 |
| Moving Van | 6455 | | HK | M-RD | | WH | | WH trailer w/ smooth door | $70.00 |
| Moving Van | 6455 | | HK | M-RD | | WH | | WH trailer w/ ridged door | $75.00 |
| Moving Van | 6455 | | HK | M-RD | | WH | | GY trailer w/ smooth door | $65.00 |
| Moving Van | 6455 | | HK | M-RD | | WH | | GY trailer w/ ridged door | $70.00 |
| Moving Van | 6455 | | HK | M-RD | | BK | | WH trailer w/ smooth door | $65.00 |
| Moving Van | 6455 | | HK | M-RD | | BK | | WH trailer w/ ridged door | $70.00 |
| Moving Van | 6455 | | HK | M-RD | | BK | | GY trailer w/ smooth door | $60.00 |
| Moving Van | 6455 | | HK | M-RD | | BK | | GY trailer w/ ridged door | $65.00 |
| Moving Van | 6455 | | HK | M-RD | | GY | | WH trailer w/ smooth door | $65.00 |
| Moving Van | 6455 | | HK | M-RD | | GY | | WH trailer w/ ridged door | $70.00 |
| Moving Van | 6455 | | HK | M-RD | | GY | | GY trailer w/ smooth door | $60.00 |
| Moving Van | 6455 | | HK | M-RD | | GY | | GY trailer w/ ridged door | $65.00 |
| Moving Van | 6455 | | HK | M-RD | | BR-L | | WH trailer w/ smooth door | $65.00 |
| Moving Van | 6455 | | HK | M-RD | | BR-L | | WH trailer w/ ridged door | $70.00 |
| Moving Van | 6455 | | HK | M-RD | | BR-L | | GY trailer w/ smooth door | $60.00 |
| Moving Van | 6455 | | HK | M-RD | | BR-L | | GY trailer w/ ridged door | $65.00 |
| Moving Van | 6455 | | HK | M-RD | | BR-D | | WH trailer w/ smooth door | $65.00 |
| Moving Van | 6455 | | HK | M-RD | | BR-D | | WH trailer w/ ridged door | $70.00 |
| Moving Van | 6455 | | HK | M-RD | | BR-D | | GY trailer w/ smooth door | $60.00 |
| Moving Van | 6455 | | HK | M-RD | | BR-D | | GY trailer w/ ridged door | $65.00 |
| Moving Van | 6455 | | HK | M-RD-R | | WH | | WH trailer w/ smooth door | $75.00 |
| Moving Van | 6455 | | HK | M-RD-R | | WH | | WH trailer w/ ridged door | $80.00 |
| Moving Van | 6455 | | HK | M-RD-R | | WH | | GY trailer w/ smooth door | $70.00 |
| Moving Van | 6455 | | HK | M-RD-R | | WH | | GY trailer w/ ridged door | $75.00 |
| Moving Van | 6455 | | HK | M-RD-R | | BK | | WH trailer w/ smooth door | $70.00 |
| Moving Van | 6455 | | HK | M-RD-R | | BK | | WH trailer w/ ridged door | $75.00 |
| Moving Van | 6455 | | HK | M-RD-R | | BK | | GY trailer w/ smooth door | $65.00 |
| Moving Van | 6455 | | HK | M-RD-R | | BK | | GY trailer w/ ridged door | $70.00 |
| Moving Van | 6455 | | HK | M-RD-R | | GY | | WH trailer w/ smooth door | $70.00 |
| Moving Van | 6455 | | HK | M-RD-R | | GY | | WH trailer w/ ridged door | $75.00 |
| Moving Van | 6455 | | HK | M-RD-R | | GY | | GY trailer w/ smooth door | $65.00 |
| Moving Van | 6455 | | HK | M-RD-R | | GY | | GY trailer w/ ridged door | $70.00 |
| Moving Van | 6455 | | HK | M-RD-R | | BR-L | | WH trailer w/ smooth door | $70.00 |
| Moving Van | 6455 | | HK | M-RD-R | | BR-L | | WH trailer w/ ridged door | $75.00 |
| Moving Van | 6455 | | HK | M-RD-R | | BR-L | | GY trailer w/ smooth door | $65.00 |
| Moving Van | 6455 | | HK | M-RD-R | | BR-L | | GY trailer w/ ridged door | $70.00 |
| Moving Van | 6455 | | HK | M-RD-R | | BR-D | | WH trailer w/ smooth door | $70.00 |

**1970 Variations**

| Name | Number | Casting | Country | Color | Windows | Interior | Paint | Other | Value |
|---|---|---|---|---|---|---|---|---|---|
| Moving Van | 6455 | | HK | M-RD-R | | BR-D | | WH trailer w/ ridged door | $75.00 |
| Moving Van | 6455 | | HK | M-RD-R | | BR-D | | GY trailer w/ smooth door | $65.00 |
| Moving Van | 6455 | | HK | M-RD-R | | BR-D | | GY trailer w/ ridged door | $70.00 |
| Moving Van | 6455 | | HK | M-YW | | WH | | WH trailer w/ ridged door | $70.00 |
| Moving Van | 6455 | | HK | M-YW | | WH | | WH trailer w/ ridged door | $75.00 |
| Moving Van | 6455 | | HK | M-YW | | WH | | GY trailer w/ smooth door | $65.00 |
| Moving Van | 6455 | | HK | M-YW | | WH | | GY trailer w/ ridged door | $70.00 |
| Moving Van | 6455 | | HK | M-YW | | BK | | WH trailer w/ smooth door | $65.00 |
| Moving Van | 6455 | | HK | M-YW | | BK | | WH trailer w/ ridged door | $70.00 |
| Moving Van | 6455 | | HK | M-YW | | BK | | GY trailer w/ smooth door | $60.00 |
| Moving Van | 6455 | | HK | M-YW | | BK | | GY trailer w/ ridged door | $65.00 |
| Moving Van | 6455 | | HK | M-YW | | GY | | WH trailer w/ smooth door | $65.00 |
| Moving Van | 6455 | | HK | M-YW | | GY | | WH trailer w/ ridged door | $70.00 |
| Moving Van | 6455 | | HK | M-YW | | GY | | GY trailer w/ smooth door | $60.00 |
| Moving Van | 6455 | | HK | M-YW | | GY | | GY trailer w/ ridged door | $65.00 |
| Moving Van | 6455 | | HK | M-YW | | BR-L | | WH trailer w/ smooth door | $65.00 |
| Moving Van | 6455 | | HK | M-YW | | BR-L | | WH trailer w/ ridged door | $70.00 |
| Moving Van | 6455 | | HK | M-YW | | BR-L | | GY trailer w/ smooth door | $60.00 |
| Moving Van | 6455 | | HK | M-YW | | BR-L | | GY trailer w/ ridged door | $65.00 |
| Moving Van | 6455 | | HK | M-YW | | BR-D | | WH trailer w/ smooth door | $65.00 |
| Moving Van | 6455 | | HK | M-YW | | BR-D | | WH trailer w/ ridged door | $70.00 |
| Moving Van | 6455 | | HK | M-YW | | BR-D | | GY trailer w/ smooth door | $60.00 |
| Moving Van | 6455 | | HK | M-YW | | BR-D | | GY trailer w/ ridged door | $65.00 |
| Moving Van | 6455 | | HK | M-YW-L | | WH | | WH trailer w/ smooth door | $85.00 |
| Moving Van | 6455 | | HK | M-YW-L | | WH | | WH trailer w/ ridged door | $90.00 |
| Moving Van | 6455 | | HK | M-YW-L | | WH | | GY trailer w/ smooth door | $80.00 |
| Moving Van | 6455 | | HK | M-YW-L | | WH | | GY trailer w/ ridged door | $85.00 |
| Moving Van | 6455 | | HK | M-YW-L | | BK | | WH trailer w/ smooth door | $80.00 |
| Moving Van | 6455 | | HK | M-YW-L | | BK | | WH trailer w/ ridged door | $85.00 |
| Moving Van | 6455 | | HK | M-YW-L | | BK | | GY trailer w/ smooth door | $75.00 |
| Moving Van | 6455 | | HK | M-YW-L | | BK | | GY trailer w/ ridged door | $80.00 |
| Moving Van | 6455 | | HK | M-YW-L | | GY | | WH trailer w/ smooth door | $80.00 |
| Moving Van | 6455 | | HK | M-YW-L | | GY | | WH trailer w/ ridged door | $85.00 |
| Moving Van | 6455 | | HK | M-YW-L | | GY | | GY trailer w/ smooth door | $75.00 |
| Moving Van | 6455 | | HK | M-YW-L | | GY | | GY trailer w/ ridged door | $80.00 |
| Moving Van | 6455 | | HK | M-YW-L | | BR-L | | WH trailer w/ smooth door | $80.00 |
| Moving Van | 6455 | | HK | M-YW-L | | BR-L | | WH trailer w/ ridged door | $85.00 |
| Moving Van | 6455 | | HK | M-YW-L | | BR-L | | GY trailer w/ smooth door | $75.00 |
| Moving Van | 6455 | | HK | M-YW-L | | BR-L | | GY trailer w/ ridged door | $80.00 |
| Moving Van | 6455 | | HK | M-YW-L | | BR-D | | WH trailer w/ smooth door | $80.00 |
| Moving Van | 6455 | | HK | M-YW-L | | BR-D | | WH trailer w/ ridged door | $85.00 |
| Moving Van | 6455 | | HK | M-YW-L | | BR-D | | GY trailer w/ smooth door | $75.00 |
| Moving Van | 6455 | | HK | M-YW-L | | BR-D | | GY trailer w/ ridged door | $80.00 |
| Mod Quad | 6456 | | USA | M-AQ | CL | WH | | | $80.00 |
| Mod Quad | 6456 | | HK | M-AQ | BL | WH | | | $80.00 |
| Mod Quad | 6456 | | USA | M-AQ | CL | BK | | | $70.00 |
| Mod Quad | 6456 | | HK | M-AQ | BL | BK | | | $70.00 |
| Mod Quad | 6456 | | USA | M-AQ | CL | GY | | | $70.00 |
| Mod Quad | 6456 | | HK | M-AQ | BL | GY | | | $70.00 |
| Mod Quad | 6456 | | USA | M-AQ | CL | BR-L | | | $70.00 |
| Mod Quad | 6456 | | HK | M-AQ | BL | BR-L | | | $70.00 |
| Mod Quad | 6456 | | USA | M-AQ | CL | BR-D | | | $70.00 |
| Mod Quad | 6456 | | HK | M-AQ | BL | BR-D | | | $70.00 |
| Mod Quad | 6456 | | USA | M-BL | CL | WH | | | $50.00 |
| Mod Quad | 6456 | | HK | M-BL | BL | WH | | | $50.00 |
| Mod Quad | 6456 | | USA | M-BL | CL | BK | | | $45.00 |
| Mod Quad | 6456 | | HK | M-BL | BL | BK | | | $45.00 |
| Mod Quad | 6456 | | USA | M-BL | CL | GY | | | $45.00 |
| Mod Quad | 6456 | | HK | M-BL | BL | GY | | | $45.00 |
| Mod Quad | 6456 | | USA | M-BL | CL | BR-L | | | $45.00 |
| Mod Quad | 6456 | | HK | M-BL | BL | BR-L | | | $45.00 |
| Mod Quad | 6456 | | USA | M-BL | CL | BR-D | | | $45.00 |
| Mod Quad | 6456 | | HK | M-BL | BL | BR-D | | | $45.00 |
| Mod Quad | 6456 | | USA | M-GD | CL | WH | | | $50.00 |
| Mod Quad | 6456 | | HK | M-GD | BL | WH | | | $50.00 |
| Mod Quad | 6456 | | USA | M-GD | CL | BK | | | $45.00 |
| Mod Quad | 6456 | | HK | M-GD | BL | BK | | | $45.00 |
| Mod Quad | 6456 | | USA | M-GD | CL | GY | | | $45.00 |
| Mod Quad | 6456 | | HK | M-GD | BL | GY | | | $45.00 |
| Mod Quad | 6456 | | USA | M-GD | CL | BR-L | | | $45.00 |

## 1970 Variations

| Name | Number | Casting | Country | Color | Windows | Interior | Paint | Other | Value |
|---|---|---|---|---|---|---|---|---|---|
| Mod Quad | 6456 | | HK | M-GD | BL | BR-L | | | $45.00 |
| Mod Quad | 6456 | | USA | M-GD | CL | BR-D | | | $45.00 |
| Mod Quad | 6456 | | HK | M-GD | BL | BR-D | | | $45.00 |
| Mod Quad | 6456 | | USA | M-GR | CL | WH | | | $50.00 |
| Mod Quad | 6456 | | HK | M-GR | BL | WH | | | $50.00 |
| Mod Quad | 6456 | | USA | M-GR | CL | BK | | | $45.00 |
| Mod Quad | 6456 | | HK | M-GR | BL | BK | | | $45.00 |
| Mod Quad | 6456 | | USA | M-GR | CL | GY | | | $45.00 |
| Mod Quad | 6456 | | HK | M-GR | BL | GY | | | $45.00 |
| Mod Quad | 6456 | | USA | M-GR | CL | BR-L | | | $45.00 |
| Mod Quad | 6456 | | HK | M-GR | BL | BR-L | | | $45.00 |
| Mod Quad | 6456 | | USA | M-GR | CL | BR-D | | | $45.00 |
| Mod Quad | 6456 | | HK | M-GR | BL | BR-D | | | $45.00 |
| Mod Quad | 6456 | | USA | M-GR-E | CL | WH | | | $55.00 |
| Mod Quad | 6456 | | HK | M-GR-E | BL | WH | | | $55.00 |
| Mod Quad | 6456 | | USA | M-GR-E | CL | BK | | | $50.00 |
| Mod Quad | 6456 | | HK | M-GR-E | BL | BK | | | $50.00 |
| Mod Quad | 6456 | | USA | M-GR-E | CL | GY | | | $50.00 |
| Mod Quad | 6456 | | HK | M-GR-E | BL | GY | | | $50.00 |
| Mod Quad | 6456 | | USA | M-GR-E | CL | BR-L | | | $50.00 |
| Mod Quad | 6456 | | HK | M-GR-E | BL | BR-L | | | $50.00 |
| Mod Quad | 6456 | | USA | M-GR-E | CL | BR-D | | | $50.00 |
| Mod Quad | 6456 | | HK | M-GR-E | BL | BR-D | | | $50.00 |
| Mod Quad | 6456 | | USA | M-GR-L | CL | WH | | | $50.00 |
| Mod Quad | 6456 | | HK | M-GR-L | BL | WH | | | $50.00 |
| Mod Quad | 6456 | | USA | M-GR-L | CL | BK | | | $45.00 |
| Mod Quad | 6456 | | HK | M-GR-L | BL | BK | | | $45.00 |
| Mod Quad | 6456 | | USA | M-GR-L | CL | GY | | | $45.00 |
| Mod Quad | 6456 | | HK | M-GR-L | BL | GY | | | $45.00 |
| Mod Quad | 6456 | | USA | M-GR-L | CL | RR-L | | | $45.00 |
| Mod Quad | 6456 | | HK | M-GR-L | BL | BR-L | | | $45.00 |
| Mod Quad | 6456 | | USA | M-GR-L | CL | BR-D | | | $45.00 |
| Mod Quad | 6456 | | HK | M-GR-L | BL | BR-D | | | $45.00 |
| Mod Quad | 6456 | | USA | M-GR-O | CL | WH | | | $50.00 |
| Mod Quad | 6456 | | HK | M-GR-O | BL | WH | | | $50.00 |
| Mod Quad | 6456 | | USA | M-GR-O | CL | BK | | | $45.00 |
| Mod Quad | 6456 | | HK | M-GR-O | BL | BK | | | $45.00 |
| Mod Quad | 6456 | | USA | M-GR-O | CL | GY | | | $45.00 |
| Mod Quad | 6456 | | HK | M-GR-O | BL | GY | | | $45.00 |
| Mod Quad | 6456 | | USA | M-GR-O | CL | BR-L | | | $45.00 |
| Mod Quad | 6456 | | HK | M-GR-O | BL | BR-L | | | $45.00 |
| Mod Quad | 6456 | | USA | M-GR-O | CL | BR-D | | | $45.00 |
| Mod Quad | 6456 | | HK | M-GR-O | BL | BR-D | | | $45.00 |
| Mod Quad | 6456 | | USA | M-MG | CL | WH | | | $80.00 |
| Mod Quad | 6456 | | HK | M-MG | BL | WH | | | $80.00 |
| Mod Quad | 6456 | | USA | M-MG | CL | BK | | | $70.00 |
| Mod Quad | 6456 | | HK | M-MG | BL | BK | | | $70.00 |
| Mod Quad | 6456 | | USA | M-MG | CL | GY | | | $70.00 |
| Mod Quad | 6456 | | HK | M-MG | BL | GY | | | $70.00 |
| Mod Quad | 6456 | | USA | M-MG | CL | BR-L | | | $70.00 |
| Mod Quad | 6456 | | HK | M-MG | BL | BR-L | | | $70.00 |
| Mod Quad | 6456 | | USA | M-MG | CL | BR-D | | | $70.00 |
| Mod Quad | 6456 | | HK | M-MG | BL | BR-D | | | $70.00 |
| Mod Quad | 6456 | | USA | M-OR | CL | WH | | | $50.00 |
| Mod Quad | 6456 | | HK | M-OR | BL | WH | | | $50.00 |
| Mod Quad | 6456 | | USA | M-OR | CL | BK | | | $45.00 |
| Mod Quad | 6456 | | HK | M-OR | BL | BK | | | $45.00 |
| Mod Quad | 6456 | | USA | M-OR | CL | GY | | | $45.00 |
| Mod Quad | 6456 | | HK | M-OR | BL | GY | | | $45.00 |
| Mod Quad | 6456 | | USA | M-OR | CL | BR-L | | | $45.00 |
| Mod Quad | 6456 | | HK | M-OR | BL | BR-L | | | $45.00 |
| Mod Quad | 6456 | | USA | M-OR | CL | BR-D | | | $45.00 |
| Mod Quad | 6456 | | HK | M-OR | BL | BR-D | | | $45.00 |
| Mod Quad | 6456 | | USA | M-PK | CL | WH | | | $220.00 |
| Mod Quad | 6456 | | HK | M-PK | BL | WH | | | $220.00 |
| Mod Quad | 6456 | | USA | M-PK | CL | BK | | | $200.00 |
| Mod Quad | 6456 | | HK | M-PK | BL | BK | | | $200.00 |
| Mod Quad | 6456 | | USA | M-PK | CL | GY | | | $200.00 |
| Mod Quad | 6456 | | HK | M-PK | BL | GY | | | $200.00 |
| Mod Quad | 6456 | | USA | M-PK | CL | BR-L | | | $200.00 |
| Mod Quad | 6456 | | HK | M-PK | BL | BR-L | | | $200.00 |
| Mod Quad | 6456 | | USA | M-PK | CL | BR-D | | | $200.00 |

## 1970 Variations

| Name | Number | Casting | Country | Color | Windows | Interior | Paint | Other | Value |
|---|---|---|---|---|---|---|---|---|---|
| Mod Quad | 6456 | | HK | M-PK | BL | BR-D | | | $300.00 |
| Mod Quad | 6456 | | USA | M-PK-H | CL | WH | | | $220.00 |
| Mod Quad | 6456 | | HK | M-PK-H | BL | WH | | | $220.00 |
| Mod Quad | 6456 | | USA | M-PK-H | CL | BK | | | $200.00 |
| Mod Quad | 6456 | | HK | M-PK-H | BL | BK | | | $200.00 |
| Mod Quad | 6456 | | USA | M-PK-H | CL | GY | | | $200.00 |
| Mod Quad | 6456 | | HK | M-PK-H | BL | GY | | | $200.00 |
| Mod Quad | 6456 | | USA | M-PK-H | CL | BR-L | | | $200.00 |
| Mod Quad | 6456 | | HK | M-PK-H | BL | BR-L | | | $200.00 |
| Mod Quad | 6456 | | USA | M-PK-H | CL | BR-D | | | $200.00 |
| Mod Quad | 6456 | | HK | M-PK-H | BL | BR-D | | | $200.00 |
| Mod Quad | 6456 | | USA | M-PK-S | CL | WH | | | $180.00 |
| Mod Quad | 6456 | | HK | M-PK-S | BL | WH | | | $180.00 |
| Mod Quad | 6456 | | USA | M-PK-S | CL | BK | | | $170.00 |
| Mod Quad | 6456 | | HK | M-PK-S | BL | BK | | | $170.00 |
| Mod Quad | 6456 | | USA | M-PK-S | CL | GY | | | $170.00 |
| Mod Quad | 6456 | | HK | M-PK-S | BL | GY | | | $170.00 |
| Mod Quad | 6456 | | USA | M-PK-S | CL | BR-L | | | $170.00 |
| Mod Quad | 6456 | | HK | M-PK-S | BL | BR-L | | | $170.00 |
| Mod Quad | 6456 | | USA | M-PK-S | CL | BR-D | | | $170.00 |
| Mod Quad | 6456 | | HK | M-PK-S | BL | BR-D | | | $170.00 |
| Mod Quad | 6456 | | USA | M-PL | CL | WH | | | $80.00 |
| Mod Quad | 6456 | | HK | M-PL | BL | WH | | | $80.00 |
| Mod Quad | 6456 | | USA | M-PL | CL | BK | | | $80.00 |
| Mod Quad | 6456 | | HK | M-PL | BL | BK | | | $80.00 |
| Mod Quad | 6456 | | USA | M-PL | CL | GY | | | $80.00 |
| Mod Quad | 6456 | | HK | M-PL | BL | GY | | | $80.00 |
| Mod Quad | 6456 | | USA | M-PL | CL | BR-L | | | $80.00 |
| Mod Quad | 6456 | | HK | M-PL | BL | BR-L | | | $80.00 |
| Mod Quad | 6456 | | USA | M-PL | CL | BR-D | | | $80.00 |
| Mod Quad | 6456 | | HK | M-PL | BL | BR-D | | | $80.00 |
| Mod Quad | 6456 | | USA | M-PR | CL | WH | | | $80.00 |
| Mod Quad | 6456 | | HK | M-PR | BL | WH | | | $80.00 |
| Mod Quad | 6456 | | USA | M-PR | CL | BK | | | $70.00 |
| Mod Quad | 6456 | | HK | M-PR | BL | BK | | | $70.00 |
| Mod Quad | 6456 | | USA | M-PR | CL | GY | | | $70.00 |
| Mod Quad | 6456 | | HK | M-PR | BL | GY | | | $70.00 |
| Mod Quad | 6456 | | USA | M-PR | CL | BR-L | | | $70.00 |
| Mod Quad | 6456 | | HK | M-PR | BL | BR-L | | | $70.00 |
| Mod Quad | 6456 | | USA | M-PR | CL | BR-D | | | $70.00 |
| Mod Quad | 6456 | | HK | M-PR | BL | BR-D | | | $70.00 |
| Mod Quad | 6456 | | USA | M-RD | CL | WH | | | $70.00 |
| Mod Quad | 6456 | | HK | M-RD | BL | WH | | | $70.00 |
| Mod Quad | 6456 | | USA | M-RD | CL | BK | | | $45.00 |
| Mod Quad | 6456 | | HK | M-RD | BL | BK | | | $45.00 |
| Mod Quad | 6456 | | USA | M-RD | CL | GY | | | $45.00 |
| Mod Quad | 6456 | | HK | M-RD | BL | GY | | | $45.00 |
| Mod Quad | 6456 | | USA | M-RD | CL | BR-L | | | $45.00 |
| Mod Quad | 6456 | | HK | M-RD | BL | BR-L | | | $45.00 |
| Mod Quad | 6456 | | USA | M-RD | CL | BR-D | | | $45.00 |
| Mod Quad | 6456 | | HK | M-RD | BL | BR-D | | | $45.00 |
| Mod Quad | 6456 | | USA | M-RD-R | CL | WH | | | $55.00 |
| Mod Quad | 6456 | | HK | M-RD-R | BL | WH | | | $55.00 |
| Mod Quad | 6456 | | USA | M-RD-R | CL | BK | | | $50.00 |
| Mod Quad | 6456 | | HK | M-RD-R | BL | BK | | | $50.00 |
| Mod Quad | 6456 | | USA | M-RD-R | CL | GY | | | $50.00 |
| Mod Quad | 6456 | | HK | M-RD-R | BL | GY | | | $50.00 |
| Mod Quad | 6456 | | USA | M-RD-R | CL | BR-L | | | $50.00 |
| Mod Quad | 6456 | | HK | M-RD-R | BL | BR-L | | | $50.00 |
| Mod Quad | 6456 | | USA | M-RD-R | CL | BR-D | | | $50.00 |
| Mod Quad | 6456 | | HK | M-RD-R | BL | BR-D | | | $50.00 |
| Mod Quad | 6456 | | USA | M-YW | CL | WH | | | $50.00 |
| Mod Quad | 6456 | | HK | M-YW | BL | WH | | | $50.00 |
| Mod Quad | 6456 | | USA | M-YW | CL | BK | | | $45.00 |
| Mod Quad | 6456 | | HK | M-YW | BL | BK | | | $45.00 |
| Mod Quad | 6456 | | USA | M-YW | CL | GY | | | $45.00 |
| Mod Quad | 6456 | | HK | M-YW | BL | GY | | | $45.00 |
| Mod Quad | 6456 | | USA | M-YW | CL | BR-L | | | $45.00 |
| Mod Quad | 6456 | | HK | M-YW | BL | BR-L | | | $45.00 |
| Mod Quad | 6456 | | USA | M-YW | CL | BR-D | | | $45.00 |
| Mod Quad | 6456 | | HK | M-YW | BL | BR-D | | | $45.00 |
| Mod Quad | 6456 | | USA | M-YW-L | CL | WH | | | $55.00 |

## 1970 Variations

| Name | Number | Casting | Country | Color | Windows | Interior | Paint | Other | Value |
|---|---|---|---|---|---|---|---|---|---|
| Mod Quad | 6456 | | HK | M-YW-L | BL | WH | | | $55.00 |
| Mod Quad | 6456 | | USA | M-YW-L | CL | BK | | | $50.00 |
| Mod Quad | 6456 | | HK | M-YW-L | BL | BK | | | $50.00 |
| Mod Quad | 6456 | | USA | M-YW-L | CL | GY | | | $50.00 |
| Mod Quad | 6456 | | HK | M-YW-L | BL | GY | | | $50.00 |
| Mod Quad | 6456 | | USA | M-YW-L | CL | BR-L | | | $50.00 |
| Mod Quad | 6456 | | HK | M-YW-L | BL | BR-L | | | $50.00 |
| Mod Quad | 6456 | | USA | M-YW-L | CL | BR-D | | | $50.00 |
| Mod Quad | 6456 | | HK | M-YW-L | BL | BR-D | | | $50.00 |
| Whip Creamer | 6457 | | USA | M-AQ | CL | WH | | | $90.00 |
| Whip Creamer | 6457 | | HK | M-AQ | GY-TNT | WH | | | $90.00 |
| Whip Creamer | 6457 | | USA | M-AQ | CL | BK | | | $60.00 |
| Whip Creamer | 6457 | | HK | M-AQ | GY-TNT | BK | | | $60.00 |
| Whip Creamer | 6457 | | USA | M-AQ | CL | GY | | | $60.00 |
| Whip Creamer | 6457 | | HK | M-AQ | GY-TNT | GY | | | $60.00 |
| Whip Creamer | 6457 | | USA | M-AQ | CL | BR-L | | | $60.00 |
| Whip Creamer | 6457 | | HK | M-AQ | GY-TNT | BR-L | | | $60.00 |
| Whip Creamer | 6457 | | USA | M-AQ | CL | BR-D | | | $60.00 |
| Whip Creamer | 6457 | | HK | M-AQ | GY-TNT | BR-D | | | $60.00 |
| Whip Creamer | 6457 | | USA | M-BL | CL | WH | | | $90.00 |
| Whip Creamer | 6457 | | HK | M-BL | GY-TNT | WH | | | $90.00 |
| Whip Creamer | 6457 | | USA | M-BL | CL | BK | | | $60.00 |
| Whip Creamer | 6457 | | HK | M-BL | GY-TNT | BK | | | $60.00 |
| Whip Creamer | 6457 | | USA | M-BL | CL | GY | | | $60.00 |
| Whip Creamer | 6457 | | HK | M-BL | GY-TNT | GY | | | $60.00 |
| Whip Creamer | 6457 | | USA | M-BL | CL | BR-L | | | $60.00 |
| Whip Creamer | 6457 | | HK | M-BL | GY-TNT | BR-L | | | $60.00 |
| Whip Creamer | 6457 | | USA | M-BL | CL | BR-D | | | $60.00 |
| Whip Creamer | 6457 | | HK | M-BL | GY-INT | BR-D | | | $60.00 |
| Whip Creamer | 6457 | | USA | M-GD | CL | WH | | | $65.00 |
| Whip Creamer | 6457 | | HK | M-GD | GY-TNT | WH | | | $65.00 |
| Whip Creamer | 6457 | | USA | M-GD | CL | BK | | | $45.00 |
| Whip Creamer | 6457 | | HK | M-GD | GY-TNT | BK | | | $45.00 |
| Whip Creamer | 6457 | | USA | M-GD | CL | GY | | | $45.00 |
| Whip Creamer | 6457 | | HK | M-GD | GY-TNT | GY | | | $45.00 |
| Whip Creamer | 6457 | | USA | M-GD | CL | BR-L | | | $45.00 |
| Whip Creamer | 6457 | | HK | M-GD | GY-TNT | BR-L | | | $45.00 |
| Whip Creamer | 6457 | | USA | M-GD | CL | BR-D | | | $45.00 |
| Whip Creamer | 6457 | | HK | M-GD | GY-TNT | BR-D | | | $45.00 |
| Whip Creamer | 6457 | | USA | M-GR | CL | WH | | | $50.00 |
| Whip Creamer | 6457 | | HK | M-GR | GY-TNT | WH | | | $65.00 |
| Whip Creamer | 6457 | | USA | M-GR | CL | BK | | | $45.00 |
| Whip Creamer | 6457 | | HK | M-GR | GY-TNT | BK | | | $45.00 |
| Whip Creamer | 6457 | | USA | M-GR | CL | GY | | | $45.00 |
| Whip Creamer | 6457 | | HK | M-GR | GY-TNT | GY | | | $45.00 |
| Whip Creamer | 6457 | | USA | M-GR | CL | BR-L | | | $45.00 |
| Whip Creamer | 6457 | | HK | M-GR | GY-TNT | BR-L | | | $45.00 |
| Whip Creamer | 6457 | | USA | M-GR | CL | BR-D | | | $45.00 |
| Whip Creamer | 6457 | | HK | M-GR | GY-TNT | BR-D | | | $45.00 |
| Whip Creamer | 6457 | | USA | M-GR-E | CL | WH | | | $60.00 |
| Whip Creamer | 6457 | | HK | M-GR-E | GY-TNT | WH | | | $75.00 |
| Whip Creamer | 6457 | | USA | M-GR-E | CL | BK | | | $50.00 |
| Whip Creamer | 6457 | | HK | M-GR-E | GY-TNT | BK | | | $50.00 |
| Whip Creamer | 6457 | | USA | M-GR-E | CL | GY | | | $50.00 |
| Whip Creamer | 6457 | | HK | M-GR-E | GY-TNT | GY | | | $50.00 |
| Whip Creamer | 6457 | | USA | M-GR-E | CL | BR-L | | | $50.00 |
| Whip Creamer | 6457 | | HK | M-GR-E | GY-TNT | BR-L | | | $50.00 |
| Whip Creamer | 6457 | | USA | M-GR-E | CL | BR-D | | | $50.00 |
| Whip Creamer | 6457 | | HK | M-GR-E | GY-TNT | BR-D | | | $50.00 |
| Whip Creamer | 6457 | | USA | M-GR-L | CL | WH | | | $65.00 |
| Whip Creamer | 6457 | | HK | M-GR-L | GY-TNT | WH | | | $65.00 |
| Whip Creamer | 6457 | | USA | M-GR-L | CL | BK | | | $45.00 |
| Whip Creamer | 6457 | | HK | M-GR-L | GY-TNT | BK | | | $45.00 |
| Whip Creamer | 6457 | | USA | M-GR-L | CL | GY | | | $45.00 |
| Whip Creamer | 6457 | | HK | M-GR-L | GY-TNT | GY | | | $45.00 |
| Whip Creamer | 6457 | | USA | M-GR-L | CL | BR-L | | | $45.00 |
| Whip Creamer | 6457 | | HK | M-GR-L | GY-TNT | BR-L | | | $45.00 |
| Whip Creamer | 6457 | | USA | M-GR-L | CL | BR-D | | | $45.00 |
| Whip Creamer | 6457 | | HK | M-GR-L | GY-TNT | BR-D | | | $45.00 |
| Whip Creamer | 6457 | | USA | M-MG | CL | WH | | | $75.00 |

## 1970 Variations

| Name | Number | Casting | Country | Color | Windows | Interior | Paint | Other | Value |
|---|---|---|---|---|---|---|---|---|---|
| Whip Creamer | 6457 | | HK | M-MG | GY-TNT | WH | | | $90.00 |
| Whip Creamer | 6457 | | USA | M-MG | CL | BK | | | $60.00 |
| Whip Creamer | 6457 | | HK | M-MG | GY-TNT | BK | | | $60.00 |
| Whip Creamer | 6457 | | USA | M-MG | CL | GY | | | $60.00 |
| Whip Creamer | 6457 | | HK | M-MG | GY-TNT | GY | | | $60.00 |
| Whip Creamer | 6457 | | USA | M-MG | CL | BR-L | | | $60.00 |
| Whip Creamer | 6457 | | HK | M-MG | GY-TNT | BR-L | | | $60.00 |
| Whip Creamer | 6457 | | USA | M-MG | CL | BR-D | | | $60.00 |
| Whip Creamer | 6457 | | HK | M-MG | GY-TNT | BR-D | | | $60.00 |
| Whip Creamer | 6457 | | USA | M-OR | CL | WH | | | $80.00 |
| Whip Creamer | 6457 | | HK | M-OR | GY-TNT | WH | | | $80.00 |
| Whip Creamer | 6457 | | USA | M-OR | CL | BK | | | $60.00 |
| Whip Creamer | 6457 | | HK | M-OR | GY-TNT | BK | | | $65.00 |
| Whip Creamer | 6457 | | USA | M-OR | CL | GY | | | $65.00 |
| Whip Creamer | 6457 | | HK | M-OR | GY-TNT | GY | | | $65.00 |
| Whip Creamer | 6457 | | USA | M-OR | CL | BR-L | | | $65.00 |
| Whip Creamer | 6457 | | HK | M-OR | GY-TNT | BR-L | | | $65.00 |
| Whip Creamer | 6457 | | USA | M-OR | CL | BR-D | | | $65.00 |
| Whip Creamer | 6457 | | HK | M-OR | GY-TNT | BR-D | | | $65.00 |
| Whip Creamer | 6457 | | USA | M-PK | CL | WH | | | $75.00 |
| Whip Creamer | 6457 | | HK | M-PK | GY-TNT | WH | | | $150.00 |
| Whip Creamer | 6457 | | USA | M-PK | CL | BK | | | $90.00 |
| Whip Creamer | 6457 | | HK | M-PK | GY-TNT | BK | | | $90.00 |
| Whip Creamer | 6457 | | USA | M-PK | CL | GY | | | $90.00 |
| Whip Creamer | 6457 | | HK | M-PK | GY-TNT | GY | | | $90.00 |
| Whip Creamer | 6457 | | USA | M-PK | CL | BR-L | | | $90.00 |
| Whip Creamer | 6457 | | HK | M-PK | GY-TNT | BR-L | | | $90.00 |
| Whip Creamer | 6457 | | USA | M-PK | CL | BR-D | | | $90.00 |
| Whip Creamer | 6457 | | HK | M-PK | GY-TNT | BR-D | | | $90.00 |
| Whip Creamer | 6457 | | USA | M-PK-H | CL | WH | | | $150.00 |
| Whip Creamer | 6457 | | HK | M-PK-H | GY-TNT | WH | | | $150.00 |
| Whip Creamer | 6457 | | USA | M-PK-H | CL | BK | | | $90.00 |
| Whip Creamer | 6457 | | HK | M-PK-H | GY-TNT | BK | | | $90.00 |
| Whip Creamer | 6457 | | USA | M-PK-H | CL | GY | | | $90.00 |
| Whip Creamer | 6457 | | HK | M-PK-H | GY-TNT | GY | | | $90.00 |
| Whip Creamer | 6457 | | USA | M-PK-H | CL | BR-L | | | $90.00 |
| Whip Creamer | 6457 | | HK | M-PK-H | GY-TNT | BR-L | | | $90.00 |
| Whip Creamer | 6457 | | USA | M-PK-H | CL | BR-D | | | $90.00 |
| Whip Creamer | 6457 | | HK | M-PK-H | GY-TNT | BR-D | | | $90.00 |
| Whip Creamer | 6457 | | USA | M-PK-S | CL | WH | | | $90.00 |
| Whip Creamer | 6457 | | HK | M-PK-S | GY-TNT | WH | | | $90.00 |
| Whip Creamer | 6457 | | USA | M-PK-S | CL | BK | | | $75.00 |
| Whip Creamer | 6457 | | HK | M-PK-S | GY-TNT | BK | | | $75.00 |
| Whip Creamer | 6457 | | USA | M-PK-S | CL | GY | | | $75.00 |
| Whip Creamer | 6457 | | HK | M-PK-S | GY-TNT | GY | | | $75.00 |
| Whip Creamer | 6457 | | USA | M-PK-S | CL | BR-L | | | $75.00 |
| Whip Creamer | 6457 | | HK | M-PK-S | GY-TNT | BR-L | | | $75.00 |
| Whip Creamer | 6457 | | USA | M-PK-S | CL | BR-D | | | $75.00 |
| Whip Creamer | 6457 | | HK | M-PK-S | GY-TNT | BR-D | | | $75.00 |
| Whip Creamer | 6457 | | USA | M-PR | CL | WH | | | $100.00 |
| Whip Creamer | 6457 | | HK | M-PR | GY-TNT | WH | | | $100.00 |
| Whip Creamer | 6457 | | USA | M-PR | CL | BK | | | $90.00 |
| Whip Creamer | 6457 | | HK | M-PR | GY-TNT | BK | | | $90.00 |
| Whip Creamer | 6457 | | USA | M-PR | CL | GY | | | $90.00 |
| Whip Creamer | 6457 | | HK | M-PR | GY-TNT | GY | | | $90.00 |
| Whip Creamer | 6457 | | USA | M-PR | CL | BR-L | | | $90.00 |
| Whip Creamer | 6457 | | HK | M-PR | GY-TNT | BR-L | | | $90.00 |
| Whip Creamer | 6457 | | USA | M-PR | CL | BR-D | | | $90.00 |
| Whip Creamer | 6457 | | HK | M-PR | GY-TNT | BR-D | | | $90.00 |
| Whip Creamer | 6457 | | USA | M-RD | CL | WH | | | $75.00 |
| Whip Creamer | 6457 | | HK | M-RD | GY-TNT | WH | | | $90.00 |
| Whip Creamer | 6457 | | USA | M-RD | CL | BK | | | $60.00 |
| Whip Creamer | 6457 | | HK | M-RD | GY-TNT | BK | | | $60.00 |
| Whip Creamer | 6457 | | USA | M-RD | CL | GY | | | $60.00 |
| Whip Creamer | 6457 | | HK | M-RD | GY-TNT | GY | | | $60.00 |
| Whip Creamer | 6457 | | USA | M-RD | CL | BR-L | | | $60.00 |
| Whip Creamer | 6457 | | HK | M-RD | GY-TNT | BR-L | | | $60.00 |
| Whip Creamer | 6457 | | USA | M-RD | CL | BR-D | | | $60.00 |
| Whip Creamer | 6457 | | HK | M-RD | GY-TNT | BR-D | | | $60.00 |
| Whip Creamer | 6457 | | USA | M-RD-R | CL | WH | | | $80.00 |
| Whip Creamer | 6457 | | HK | M-RD-R | GY-TNT | WH | | | $80.00 |
| Whip Creamer | 6457 | | USA | M-RD-R | CL | BK | | | $50.00 |

## 1970 Variations

| Name | Number | Casting | Country | Color | Windows | Interior | Paint | Other | Value |
|---|---|---|---|---|---|---|---|---|---|
| Whip Creamer | 6457 | | HK | M-RD-R | GY-TNT | BK | | | $50.00 |
| Whip Creamer | 0457 | | USA | M-RD-R | CL | GY | | | $50.00 |
| Whip Creamer | 6457 | | HK | M-RD-R | GY-TNT | GY | | | $50.00 |
| Whip Creamer | 6457 | | USA | M-RD-R | CL | BR-L | | | $50.00 |
| Whip Creamer | 6457 | | HK | M-RD-R | GY-TNT | BR-L | | | $50.00 |
| Whip Creamer | 6457 | | USA | M-RD-R | CL | BR-D | | | $50.00 |
| Whip Creamer | 6457 | | HK | M-RD-R | GY-TNT | BR-D | | | $50.00 |
| Whip Creamer | 6457 | | USA | M-YW | CL | WH | | | $65.00 |
| Whip Creamer | 6457 | | HK | M-YW | GY-TNT | WH | | | $65.00 |
| Whip Creamer | 6457 | | USA | M-YW | CL | BK | | | $45.00 |
| Whip Creamer | 6457 | | HK | M-YW | GY-TNT | BK | | | $45.00 |
| Whip Creamer | 6457 | | USA | M-YW | CL | GY | | | $45.00 |
| Whip Creamer | 6457 | | HK | M-YW | GY-TNT | GY | | | $45.00 |
| Whip Creamer | 6457 | | USA | M-YW | CL | BR-L | | | $45.00 |
| Whip Creamer | 6457 | | HK | M-YW | GY-TNT | BR-L | | | $45.00 |
| Whip Creamer | 6457 | | USA | M-YW | CL | BR-D | | | $45.00 |
| Whip Creamer | 6457 | | HK | M-YW | GY-TNT | BR-D | | | $45.00 |
| Whip Creamer | 6457 | | USA | M-YW-L | CL | WH | | | $60.00 |
| Whip Creamer | 6457 | | HK | M-YW-L | GY-TNT | WH | | | $75.00 |
| Whip Creamer | 6457 | | USA | M-YW-L | CL | BK | | | $50.00 |
| Whip Creamer | 6457 | | HK | M-YW-L | GY-TNT | BK | | | $50.00 |
| Whip Creamer | 6457 | | USA | M-YW-L | CL | GY | | | $50.00 |
| Whip Creamer | 6457 | | HK | M-YW-L | GY-TNT | GY | | | $50.00 |
| Whip Creamer | 6457 | | USA | M-YW-L | CL | BR-L | | | $50.00 |
| Whip Creamer | 6457 | | HK | M-YW-L | GY-TNT | BR-L | | | $50.00 |
| Whip Creamer | 6457 | | USA | M-YW-L | CL | BR-D | | | $50.00 |
| Whip Creamer | 6457 | | HK | M-YW-L | GY-TNT | BR-D | | | $50.00 |
| | | | | | | | | | |
| Power Pad | 6459 | | USA | M-AQ | | BK | | | $95 |
| Power Pad | 6459 | | USA | M-BL | | BK | | | $125.00 |
| Power Pad | 6459 | | USA | M-BL-I | | BK | | | $95.00 |
| Power Pad | 6459 | | USA | M-BL-P | | BK | | | $95.00 |
| Power Pad | 6459 | | USA | M-GD | | BK | | | $70.00 |
| Power Pad | 6459 | | USA | M-GR | | BK | | | $70.00 |
| Power Pad | 6459 | | USA | M-GR-E | | BK | | | $75.00 |
| Power Pad | 6459 | | USA | M-GR-L | | BK | | | $70.00 |
| Power Pad | 6459 | | USA | M-MG | | BK | | | $70.00 |
| Power Pad | 6459 | | USA | M-PK | | BK | | | $150.00 |
| Power Pad | 6459 | | USA | M-PK-H | | BK | | | $150.00 |
| Power Pad | 6459 | | USA | M-PK-S | | BK | | | $150.00 |
| Power Pad | 6459 | | USA | M-RD | | BK | | | $75.00 |
| Power Pad | 6459 | | USA | M-RD-R | | BK | | | $90.00 |
| Power Pad | 6459 | | USA | M-YW | | BK | | | $80.00 |
| Power Pad | 6459 | | USA | M-YW-L | | BK | | | $75.00 |
| | | | | | | | | | |
| Fire Chief Cruiser | 6469 | | USA | M-RD | | WH | WH-TR | | $55.00 |
| Fire Chief Cruiser | 6469 | | USA | M-RD-D | | WH | WH-TR | | $55.00 |
| | | | | | | | | | |
| Boss Hoss | 6499 | | HK | CH | | WH | | | $100.00 |
| Boss Hoss | 6499 | | HK | CH | | BK | | | $90.00 |

## 1971 Variations

| Name | Number | Casting | Country | Color | Windows | Interior | Paint | Other | Value |
|---|---|---|---|---|---|---|---|---|---|
| Bugeye | 5178 | scoop | USA | M-AQ | CL | WH | | | $70.00 |
| Bugeye | 5178 | scoop | USA | M-AQ | CL | WH | | | $70.00 |
| Bugeye | 5178 | scoop | HK | M-AQ | BL | BK | | | $65.00 |
| Bugeye | 5178 | scoop | HK | M-AQ | BL | BK | | | $65.00 |
| Bugeye | 5178 | scoop | USA | M-AQ | CL | WH | BK-EC | | $80.00 |
| Bugeye | 5178 | scoop | USA | M-AQ | CL | WH | BK-EC | | $80.00 |
| Bugeye | 5178 | scoop | HK | M-AQ | BL | BK | BK-EC | | $75.00 |
| Bugeye | 5178 | scoop | HK | M-AQ | BL | BK | BK-EC | | $75.00 |
| Bugeye | 5178 | scoop | USA | M-BL | CL | WH | | | $70.00 |
| Bugeye | 5178 | scoop | USA | M-BL | CL | WH | | | $70.00 |
| Bugeye | 5178 | scoop | HK | M-BL | BL | BK | | | $65.00 |
| Bugeye | 5178 | scoop | HK | M-BL | BL | BK | | | $65.00 |
| Bugeye | 5178 | scoop | USA | M-BL | CL | WH | BK-EC | | $80.00 |
| Bugeye | 5178 | scoop | USA | M-BL | CL | WH | BK-EC | | $80.00 |
| Bugeye | 5178 | scoop | HK | M-BL | BL | BK | BK-EC | | $75.00 |
| Bugeye | 5178 | scoop | HK | M-BL | BL | BK | BK-EC | | $75.00 |
| Bugeye | 5178 | scoop | USA | M-GD | CL | WH | | | $75.00 |
| Bugeye | 5178 | scoop | USA | M-GD | CL | WH | | | $75.00 |
| Bugeye | 5178 | scoop | HK | M-GD | BL | BK | | | $70.00 |
| Bugeye | 5178 | scoop | HK | M-GD | BL | BK | | | $70.00 |
| Bugeye | 5178 | scoop | USA | M-GD | CL | WH | BK-EC | | $85.00 |
| Bugeye | 5178 | scoop | USA | M-GD | CL | WH | BK-EC | | $85.00 |
| Bugeye | 5178 | scoop | HK | M-GD | BL | BK | BK-EC | | $80.00 |
| Bugeye | 5178 | scoop | HK | M-GD | BL | BK | BK-EC | | $80.00 |
| Bugeye | 5178 | scoop | USA | M-GR | CL | WH | | | $75.00 |
| Bugeye | 5178 | scoop | USA | M-GR | CL | WH | | | $75.00 |
| Bugeye | 5178 | scoop | HK | M-GR | BL | BK | | | $70.00 |
| Bugeye | 5178 | scoop | HK | M-GR | BL | BK | | | $70.00 |
| Bugeye | 5178 | scoop | USA | M-GR | CL | WH | BK-EC | | $85.00 |
| Bugeye | 5178 | scoop | USA | M-GR | CL | WH | BK-EC | | $85.00 |
| Bugeye | 5178 | scoop | HK | M-GR | BL | BK | BK-EC | | $80.00 |
| Bugeye | 5178 | scoop | HK | M-GR | BL | BK | BK-EC | | $80.00 |
| Bugeye | 5178 | scoop | USA | M-GR-E | CL | WH | | | $80.00 |
| Bugeye | 5178 | scoop | USA | M-GR-E | CL | WH | | | $80.00 |
| Bugeye | 5178 | scoop | HK | M-GR-E | BL | BK | | | $75.00 |
| Bugeye | 5178 | scoop | HK | M-GR-E | BL | BK | | | $75.00 |
| Bugeye | 5178 | scoop | USA | M-GR-E | CL | WH | BK-EC | | $90.00 |
| Bugeye | 5178 | scoop | USA | M-GR-E | CL | WH | BK-EC | | $90.00 |
| Bugeye | 5178 | scoop | HK | M-GR-E | BL | BK | BK-EC | | $85.00 |
| Bugeye | 5178 | scoop | HK | M-GR-E | BL | BK | BK-EC | | $85.00 |
| Bugeye | 5178 | scoop | USA | M-GR-L | CL | WH | | | $70.00 |
| Bugeye | 5178 | scoop | USA | M-GR-L | CL | WH | | | $70.00 |
| Bugeye | 5178 | scoop | HK | M-GR-L | BL | BK | | | $65.00 |
| Bugeye | 5178 | scoop | HK | M-GR-L | BL | BK | | | $65.00 |
| Bugeye | 5178 | scoop | USA | M-GR-L | CL | WH | BK-EC | | $80.00 |
| Bugeye | 5178 | scoop | USA | M-GR-L | CL | WH | BK-EC | | $80.00 |
| Bugeye | 5178 | scoop | HK | M-GR-L | BL | BK | BK-EC | | $75.00 |
| Bugeye | 5178 | scoop | HK | M-GR-L | BL | BK | BK-EC | | $75.00 |
| Bugeye | 5178 | scoop | USA | M-MG | CL | WH | | | $70.00 |
| Bugeye | 5178 | scoop | USA | M-MG | CL | WH | | | $70.00 |
| Bugeye | 5178 | scoop | HK | M-MG | BL | BK | | | $65.00 |
| Bugeye | 5178 | scoop | HK | M-MG | BL | BK | | | $65.00 |
| Bugeye | 5178 | scoop | USA | M-MG | CL | WH | BK-EC | | $80.00 |
| Bugeye | 5178 | scoop | USA | M-MG | CL | WH | BK-EC | | $80.00 |
| Bugeye | 5178 | scoop | HK | M-MG | BL | BK | BK-EC | | $75.00 |
| Bugeye | 5178 | scoop | HK | M-MG | BL | BK | BK-EC | | $75.00 |
| Bugeye | 5178 | scoop | USA | M-OR | CL | WH | | | $90.00 |
| Bugeye | 5178 | scoop | USA | M-OR | CL | WH | | | $90.00 |
| Bugeye | 5178 | scoop | HK | M-OR | BL | BK | | | $85.00 |
| Bugeye | 5178 | scoop | HK | M-OR | BL | BK | | | $85.00 |
| Bugeye | 5178 | scoop | USA | M-OR | CL | WH | BK-EC | | $100.00 |
| Bugeye | 5178 | scoop | USA | M-OR | CL | WH | BK-EC | | $100.00 |
| Bugeye | 5178 | scoop | HK | M-OR | BL | BK | BK-EC | | $95.00 |
| Bugeye | 5178 | scoop | HK | M-OR | BL | BK | BK-EC | | $95.00 |
| Bugeye | 5178 | scoop | USA | M-PK | CL | WH | | | $280.00 |
| Bugeye | 5178 | scoop | USA | M-PK | CL | WH | | | $280.00 |
| Bugeye | 5178 | scoop | HK | M-PK | BL | BK | | | $260.00 |
| Bugeye | 5178 | scoop | HK | M-PK | BL | BK | | | $260.00 |
| Bugeye | 5178 | scoop | USA | M-PK | CL | WH | BK-EC | | $300.00 |
| Bugeye | 5178 | scoop | USA | M-PK | CL | WH | BK-EC | | $300.00 |
| Bugeye | 5178 | scoop | HK | M-PK | BL | BK | BK-EC | | $280.00 |
| Bugeye | 5178 | scoop | HK | M-PK | BL | BK | BK-EC | | $280.00 |

## 1971 Variations

| Name | Number | Casting | Country | Color | Windows | Interior | Paint | Other | Value |
|---|---|---|---|---|---|---|---|---|---|
| Bugeye | 5178 | scoop | USA | M-PK-H | CL | WH | | | $280.00 |
| Bugeye | 5178 | scoop | USA | M-PK-H | CL | WH | | | $280.00 |
| Bugeye | 5178 | scoop | HK | M-PK-H | BL | BK | | | $260.00 |
| Bugeye | 5178 | scoop | HK | M-PK-H | BL | BK | | | $260.00 |
| Bugeye | 5178 | scoop | USA | M-PK-H | CL | WH | BK-EC | | $300.00 |
| Bugeye | 5178 | scoop | USA | M-PK-H | CL | WH | BK-EC | | $300.00 |
| Bugeye | 5178 | scoop | HK | M-PK-H | BL | BK | BK-EC | | $280.00 |
| Bugeye | 5178 | scoop | HK | M-PK-H | BL | BK | BK-EC | | $280.00 |
| Bugeye | 5178 | scoop | USA | M-PK-S | CL | WH | | | $280.00 |
| Bugeye | 5178 | scoop | USA | M-PK-S | CL | WH | | | $280.00 |
| Bugeye | 5178 | scoop | HK | M-PK-S | BL | BK | | | $260.00 |
| Bugeye | 5178 | scoop | HK | M-PK-S | BL | BK | | | $260.00 |
| Bugeye | 5178 | scoop | USA | M-PK-S | CL | WH | BK-EC | | $300.00 |
| Bugeye | 5178 | scoop | USA | M-PK-S | CL | WH | BK-EC | | $300.00 |
| Bugeye | 5178 | scoop | HK | M-PK-S | BL | BK | BK-EC | | $280.00 |
| Bugeye | 5178 | scoop | HK | M-PK-S | BL | BK | BK-EC | | $280.00 |
| Bugeye | 5178 | scoop | USA | M-RD | CL | WH | | | $70.00 |
| Bugeye | 5178 | scoop | USA | M-RD | CL | WH | | | $70.00 |
| Bugeye | 5178 | scoop | HK | M-RD | BL | BK | | | $65.00 |
| Bugeye | 5178 | scoop | HK | M-RD | BL | BK | | | $65.00 |
| Bugeye | 5178 | scoop | USA | M-RD | CL | WH | BK-EC | | $80.00 |
| Bugeye | 5178 | scoop | USA | M-RD | CL | WH | BK-EC | | $80.00 |
| Bugeye | 5178 | scoop | HK | M-RD | BL | BK | BK-EC | | $75.00 |
| Bugeye | 5178 | scoop | HK | M-RD | BL | BK | BK-EC | | $75.00 |
| Bugeye | 5178 | scoop | USA | M-RD-R | CL | WH | | | $75.00 |
| Bugeye | 5178 | scoop | USA | M-RD-R | CL | WH | | | $75.00 |
| Bugeye | 5178 | scoop | HK | M-RD-R | BL | BK | | | $70.00 |
| Bugeye | 5178 | scoop | HK | M-RD-R | BL | BK | | | $70.00 |
| Bugeye | 5178 | scoop | USA | M-RD-R | CL | WH | BK-EC | | $85.00 |
| Bugeye | 5178 | scoop | USA | M-RD-R | CL | WH | BK-EC | | $85.00 |
| Bugeye | 5178 | scoop | HK | M-RD-R | BL | BK | BK-EC | | $80.00 |
| Bugeye | 5178 | scoop | HK | M-RD-R | BL | BK | BK-EC | | $80.00 |
| Bugeye | 5178 | scoop | USA | M-YW | CL | WH | | | $75.00 |
| Bugeye | 5178 | scoop | USA | M-YW | CL | WH | | | $75.00 |
| Bugeye | 5178 | scoop | HK | M-YW | BL | BK | | | $70.00 |
| Bugeye | 5178 | scoop | HK | M-YW | BL | BK | | | $70.00 |
| Bugeye | 5178 | scoop | USA | M-YW | CL | WH | BK-EC | | $70.00 |
| Bugeye | 5178 | scoop | USA | M-YW | CL | WH | BK-EC | | $70.00 |
| Bugeye | 5178 | scoop | HK | M-YW | BL | BK | BK-EC | | $65.00 |
| Bugeye | 5178 | scoop | HK | M-YW | BL | BK | BK-EC | | $65.00 |
| Bugeye | 5178 | scoop | USA | M-YW-L | CL | WH | | | $65.00 |
| Bugeye | 5178 | scoop | USA | M-YW-L | CL | WH | | | $65.00 |
| Bugeye | 5178 | scoop | HK | M-YW-L | BL | BK | | | $60.00 |
| Bugeye | 5178 | scoop | HK | M-YW-L | BL | BK | | | $60.00 |
| Bugeye | 5178 | scoop | USA | M-YW-L | CL | WH | BK-EC | | $75.00 |
| Bugeye | 5178 | scoop | USA | M-YW-L | CL | WH | BK-EC | | $75.00 |
| Bugeye | 5178 | scoop | HK | M-YW-L | BL | BK | BK-EC | | $70.00 |
| Bugeye | 5178 | scoop | HK | M-YW-L | BL | BK | BK-EC | | $70.00 |
| Snake Dragster | 5951 | | USA | E-WH | | | | BK front wheels | $140.00 |
| Snake Dragster | 5951 | | USA | E-WH | | | | CL front wheels | $130.00 |
| Mongoose Dragster | 5952 | | USA | M-BL | | | | BK front wheels | $130.00 |
| Mongoose Dragster | 5952 | | USA | M-BL | | | | CL front wheels | $130.00 |
| Snake 2 | 5953 | | USA | E-WH | | | | | $130.00 |
| Snake 2 | 5953 | | HK | E-WH | | | | | $130.00 |
| Mongoose 2 | 5954 | | HK | M-BL | | | | | $150.00 |
| Mongoose2 | 5954 | | USA | M-BL | | | | | $150.00 |
| Noodle Head | 6000 | | USA | M-AQ | | WH | | | $100.00 |
| Noodle Head | 6000 | | HK | M-AQ | | WH | | | $100.00 |
| Noodle Head | 6000 | | USA | M-AQ | | BK | | | $95.00 |
| Noodle Head | 6000 | | HK | M-AQ | | BK | | | $95.00 |
| Noodle Head | 6000 | | USA | M-AQ | | GY | | | $95.00 |
| Noodle Head | 6000 | | HK | M-AQ | | GY | | | $95.00 |
| Noodle Head | 6000 | | USA | M-AQ | | BR-L | | | $95.00 |
| Noodle Head | 6000 | | HK | M-AQ | | BR-L | | | $95.00 |
| Noodle Head | 6000 | | USA | M-AQ | | BR-D | | | $95.00 |
| Noodle Head | 6000 | | HK | M-AQ | | BR-D | | | $95.00 |

## 1971 Variations

| Name | Number | Casting | Country | Color | Windows | Interior | Paint | Other | Value |
|---|---|---|---|---|---|---|---|---|---|
| Noodle Head | 6000 | | USA | M-BL | | WH | | | $100.00 |
| Noodle Head | 6000 | | HK | M-BL | | WH | | | $100.00 |
| Noodle Head | 6000 | | USA | M-BL | | BK | | | $95.00 |
| Noodle Head | 6000 | | HK | M-BL | | BK | | | $95.00 |
| Noodle Head | 6000 | | USA | M-BL | | GY | | | $95.00 |
| Noodle Head | 6000 | | HK | M-BL | | GY | | | $95.00 |
| Noodle Head | 6000 | | USA | M-BL | | BR-L | | | $95.00 |
| Noodle Head | 6000 | | HK | M-BL | | BR-L | | | $95.00 |
| Noodle Head | 6000 | | USA | M-BL | | BR-D | | | $95.00 |
| Noodle Head | 6000 | | HK | M-BL | | BR-D | | | $95.00 |
| Noodle Head | 6000 | | USA | M-BL-I | | WH | | | $140.00 |
| Noodle Head | 6000 | | HK | M-BL-I | | WH | | | $140.00 |
| Noodle Head | 6000 | | USA | M-BL-I | | BK | | | $130.00 |
| Noodle Head | 6000 | | HK | M-BL-I | | BK | | | $130.00 |
| Noodle Head | 6000 | | USA | M-BL-I | | GY | | | $130.00 |
| Noodle Head | 6000 | | HK | M-BL-I | | GY | | | $130.00 |
| Noodle Head | 6000 | | USA | M-BL-I | | BR-L | | | $130.00 |
| Noodle Head | 6000 | | HK | M-BL-I | | BR-L | | | $130.00 |
| Noodle Head | 6000 | | USA | M-BL-I | | BR-D | | | $130.00 |
| Noodle Head | 6000 | | HK | M-BL-I | | BR-D | | | $130.00 |
| Noodle Head | 6000 | | USA | M-BL-P | | WH | | | $130.00 |
| Noodle Head | 6000 | | HK | M-BL-P | | WH | | | $130.00 |
| Noodle Head | 6000 | | USA | M-BL-P | | BK | | | $120.00 |
| Noodle Head | 6000 | | HK | M-BL-P | | BK | | | $120.00 |
| Noodle Head | 6000 | | USA | M-BL-P | | GY | | | $120.00 |
| Noodle Head | 6000 | | HK | M-BL-P | | GY | | | $120.00 |
| Noodle Head | 6000 | | USA | M-BL-P | | BR-L | | | $120.00 |
| Noodle Head | 6000 | | HK | M-BL-P | | BR-L | | | $120.00 |
| Noodle Head | 6000 | | USA | M-BL-P | | BR-D | | | $120.00 |
| Noodle Head | 6000 | | HK | M-BL-P | | BR-D | | | $120.00 |
| Noodle Head | 6000 | | USA | M-GD | | WH | | | $70.00 |
| Noodle Head | 6000 | | HK | M-GD | | WH | | | $70.00 |
| Noodle Head | 6000 | | USA | M-GD | | BK | | | $65.00 |
| Noodle Head | 6000 | | HK | M-GD | | BK | | | $65.00 |
| Noodle Head | 6000 | | USA | M-GD | | GY | | | $65.00 |
| Noodle Head | 6000 | | HK | M-GD | | GY | | | $65.00 |
| Noodle Head | 6000 | | USA | M-GD | | BR-L | | | $65.00 |
| Noodle Head | 6000 | | HK | M-GD | | BR-L | | | $65.00 |
| Noodle Head | 6000 | | USA | M-GD | | BR-D | | | $65.00 |
| Noodle Head | 6000 | | HK | M-GD | | BR-D | | | $65.00 |
| Noodle Head | 6000 | | USA | M-GR | | WH | | | $100.00 |
| Noodle Head | 6000 | | HK | M-GR | | WH | | | $100.00 |
| Noodle Head | 6000 | | USA | M-GR | | BK | | | $95.00 |
| Noodle Head | 6000 | | HK | M-GR | | BK | | | $95.00 |
| Noodle Head | 6000 | | USA | M-GR | | GY | | | $95.00 |
| Noodle Head | 6000 | | HK | M-GR | | GY | | | $95.00 |
| Noodle Head | 6000 | | USA | M-GR | | BR-L | | | $95.00 |
| Noodle Head | 6000 | | HK | M-GR | | BR-L | | | $95.00 |
| Noodle Head | 6000 | | USA | M-GR | | BR-D | | | $95.00 |
| Noodle Head | 6000 | | HK | M-GR | | BR-D | | | $95.00 |
| Noodle Head | 6000 | | USA | M-GR-E | | WH | | | $110.00 |
| Noodle Head | 6000 | | HK | M-GR-E | | WH | | | $110.00 |
| Noodle Head | 6000 | | USA | M-GR-E | | BK | | | $100.00 |
| Noodle Head | 6000 | | HK | M-GR-E | | BK | | | $100.00 |
| Noodle Head | 6000 | | USA | M-GR-E | | GY | | | $100.00 |
| Noodle Head | 6000 | | HK | M-GR-E | | GY | | | $100.00 |
| Noodle Head | 6000 | | USA | M-GR-E | | BR-L | | | $100.00 |
| Noodle Head | 6000 | | HK | M-GR-E | | BR-L | | | $100.00 |
| Noodle Head | 6000 | | USA | M-GR-E | | BR-D | | | $100.00 |
| Noodle Head | 6000 | | HK | M-GR-E | | BR-D | | | $100.00 |
| Noodle Head | 6000 | | USA | M-GR-L | | WH | | | $95.00 |
| Noodle Head | 6000 | | HK | M-GR-L | | WH | | | $95.00 |
| Noodle Head | 6000 | | USA | M-GR-L | | BK | | | $85.00 |
| Noodle Head | 6000 | | HK | M-GR-L | | BK | | | $85.00 |
| Noodle Head | 6000 | | USA | M-GR-L | | GY | | | $85.00 |
| Noodle Head | 6000 | | HK | M-GR-L | | GY | | | $85.00 |
| Noodle Head | 6000 | | USA | M-GR-L | | BR-L | | | $85.00 |
| Noodle Head | 6000 | | HK | M-GR-L | | BR-L | | | $85.00 |
| Noodle Head | 6000 | | USA | M-GR-L | | BR-D | | | $85.00 |
| Noodle Head | 6000 | | HK | M-GR-L | | BR-D | | | $85.00 |
| Noodle Head | 6000 | | USA | M-GR-O | | WH | | | $90.00 |
| Noodle Head | 6000 | | HK | M-GR-O | | WH | | | $90.00 |

## 1971 Variations

| Name | Number | Casting | Country | Color | Windows | Interior | Paint | Other | Value |
|---|---|---|---|---|---|---|---|---|---|
| Noodle Head | 6000 | | USA | M-GR-O | | BK | | | $85.00 |
| Noodle Head | 6000 | | HK | M-GR-O | | BK | | | $85.00 |
| Noodle Head | 6000 | | USA | M-GR-O | | GY | | | $85.00 |
| Noodle Head | 6000 | | HK | M-GR-O | | GY | | | $85.00 |
| Noodle Head | 6000 | | USA | M-GR-O | | BR-L | | | $85.00 |
| Noodle Head | 6000 | | HK | M-GR-O | | BR-L | | | $85.00 |
| Noodle Head | 6000 | | USA | M-GR-O | | BR-D | | | $85.00 |
| Noodle Head | 6000 | | HK | M-GR-O | | BR-D | | | $85.00 |
| Noodle Head | 6000 | | USA | M-MG | | WH | | | $70.00 |
| Noodle Head | 6000 | | HK | M-MG | | WH | | | $70.00 |
| Noodle Head | 6000 | | USA | M-MG | | BK | | | $65.00 |
| Noodle Head | 6000 | | HK | M-MG | | BK | | | $65.00 |
| Noodle Head | 6000 | | USA | M-MG | | GY | | | $65.00 |
| Noodle Head | 6000 | | HK | M-MG | | GY | | | $65.00 |
| Noodle Head | 6000 | | USA | M-MG | | BR-L | | | $65.00 |
| Noodle Head | 6000 | | HK | M-MG | | BR-L | | | $65.00 |
| Noodle Head | 6000 | | USA | M-MG | | BR-D | | | $65.00 |
| Noodle Head | 6000 | | HK | M-MG | | BR-D | | | $65.00 |
| Noodle Head | 6000 | | USA | M-PK | | WH | | | $280.00 |
| Noodle Head | 6000 | | HK | M-PK | | WH | | | $280.00 |
| Noodle Head | 6000 | | USA | M-PK | | BK | | | $260.00 |
| Noodle Head | 6000 | | HK | M-PK | | BK | | | $260.00 |
| Noodle Head | 6000 | | USA | M-PK | | GY | | | $260.00 |
| Noodle Head | 6000 | | HK | M-PK | | GY | | | $260.00 |
| Noodle Head | 6000 | | USA | M-PK | | BR-L | | | $260.00 |
| Noodle Head | 6000 | | HK | M-PK | | BR-L | | | $260.00 |
| Noodle Head | 6000 | | USA | M-PK | | BR-D | | | $260.00 |
| Noodle Head | 6000 | | HK | M-PK | | BR-D | | | $260.00 |
| Noodle Head | 6000 | | USA | M-PK-H | | WH | | | $280.00 |
| Noodle Head | 6000 | | HK | M-PK-H | | WH | | | $280.00 |
| Noodle Head | 6000 | | USA | M-PK-H | | BK | | | $260.00 |
| Noodle Head | 6000 | | HK | M-PK-H | | BK | | | $260.00 |
| Noodle Head | 6000 | | USA | M-PK-H | | GY | | | $260.00 |
| Noodle Head | 6000 | | HK | M-PK-H | | GY | | | $260.00 |
| Noodle Head | 6000 | | USA | M-PK-H | | BR-L | | | $260.00 |
| Noodle Head | 6000 | | HK | M-PK-H | | BR-L | | | $260.00 |
| Noodle Head | 6000 | | USA | M-PK-H | | BR-D | | | $260.00 |
| Noodle Head | 6000 | | HK | M-PK-H | | BR-D | | | $260.00 |
| Noodle Head | 6000 | | USA | M-PK-S | | WH | | | $140.00 |
| Noodle Head | 6000 | | HK | M-PK-S | | WH | | | $140.00 |
| Noodle Head | 6000 | | USA | M-PK-S | | BK | | | $130.00 |
| Noodle Head | 6000 | | HK | M-PK-S | | BK | | | $130.00 |
| Noodle Head | 6000 | | USA | M-PK-S | | GY | | | $130.00 |
| Noodle Head | 6000 | | HK | M-PK-S | | GY | | | $130.00 |
| Noodle Head | 6000 | | USA | M-PK-S | | BR-L | | | $130.00 |
| Noodle Head | 6000 | | HK | M-PK-S | | BR-L | | | $130.00 |
| Noodle Head | 6000 | | USA | M-PK-S | | BR-D | | | $130.00 |
| Noodle Head | 6000 | | HK | M-PK-S | | BR-D | | | $130.00 |
| Noodle Head | 6000 | | USA | M-RD | | WH | | | $85.00 |
| Noodle Head | 6000 | | HK | M-RD | | WH | | | $85.00 |
| Noodle Head | 6000 | | USA | M-RD | | BK | | | $80.00 |
| Noodle Head | 6000 | | HK | M-RD | | BK | | | $80.00 |
| Noodle Head | 6000 | | USA | M-RD | | GY | | | $80.00 |
| Noodle Head | 6000 | | HK | M-RD | | GY | | | $80.00 |
| Noodle Head | 6000 | | USA | M-RD | | BR-L | | | $80.00 |
| Noodle Head | 6000 | | HK | M-RD | | BR-L | | | $80.00 |
| Noodle Head | 6000 | | USA | M-RD | | BR-D | | | $80.00 |
| Noodle Head | 6000 | | HK | M-RD | | BR-D | | | $80.00 |
| Noodle Head | 6000 | | USA | M-RD-R | | WH | | | $90.00 |
| Noodle Head | 6000 | | HK | M-RD-R | | WH | | | $90.00 |
| Noodle Head | 6000 | | USA | M-RD-R | | BK | | | $85.00 |
| Noodle Head | 6000 | | HK | M-RD-R | | BK | | | $85.00 |
| Noodle Head | 6000 | | USA | M-RD-R | | GY | | | $85.00 |
| Noodle Head | 6000 | | HK | M-RD-R | | GY | | | $85.00 |
| Noodle Head | 6000 | | USA | M-RD-R | | BR-L | | | $85.00 |
| Noodle Head | 6000 | | HK | M-RD-R | | BR-L | | | $85.00 |
| Noodle Head | 6000 | | USA | M-RD-R | | BR-D | | | $85.00 |
| Noodle Head | 6000 | | HK | M-RD-R | | BR-D | | | $85.00 |
| Noodle Head | 6000 | | USA | M-YW | | WH | | | $85.00 |
| Noodle Head | 6000 | | HK | M-YW | | WH | | | $85.00 |
| Noodle Head | 6000 | | USA | M-YW | | BK | | | $80.00 |
| Noodle Head | 6000 | | HK | M-YW | | BK | | | $80.00 |

## 1971 Variations

| Name | Number | Casting | Country | Color | Windows | Interior | Paint | Other | Value |
|---|---|---|---|---|---|---|---|---|---|
| Noodle Head | 6000 | | USA | M-YW | | GY | | | $80.00 |
| Noodle Head | 6000 | | HK | M-YW | | GY | | | $80.00 |
| Noodle Head | 6000 | | USA | M-YW | | BR-L | | | $80.00 |
| Noodle Head | 6000 | | HK | M-YW | | BR-L | | | $80.00 |
| Noodle Head | 6000 | | USA | M-YW | | BR-D | | | $80.00 |
| Noodle Head | 6000 | | HK | M-YW | | BR-D | | | $80.00 |
| Noodle Head | 6000 | | USA | M-YW-L | | WH | | | $80.00 |
| Noodle Head | 6000 | | HK | M-YW-L | | WH | | | $80.00 |
| Noodle Head | 6000 | | USA | M-YW-L | | BK | | | $75.00 |
| Noodle Head | 6000 | | HK | M-YW-L | | BK | | | $75.00 |
| Noodle Head | 6000 | | USA | M-YW-L | | GY | | | $75.00 |
| Noodle Head | 6000 | | HK | M-YW-L | | GY | | | $75.00 |
| Noodle Head | 6000 | | USA | M-YW-L | | BR-L | | | $75.00 |
| Noodle Head | 6000 | | HK | M-YW-L | | BR-L | | | $75.00 |
| Noodle Head | 6000 | | USA | M-YW-L | | BR-D | | | $75.00 |
| Noodle Head | 6000 | | HK | M-YW-L | | BR-D | | | $75.00 |
| | | | | | | | | | |
| What-4 | 6001 | | HK | M-AQ | CL | WH | | | $150.00 |
| What-4 | 6001 | | HK | M-AQ | BL | WH | | | $150.00 |
| What-4 | 6001 | | HK | M-AQ | CL | BK | | | $150.00 |
| What-4 | 6001 | | HK | M-AQ | BL | BK | | | $150.00 |
| What-4 | 6001 | | HK | M-AQ | CL | GY | | | $150.00 |
| What-4 | 6001 | | HK | M-AQ | BL | GY | | | $150.00 |
| What-4 | 6001 | | HK | M-AQ | CL | BR-L | | | $150.00 |
| What-4 | 6001 | | HK | M-AQ | BL | BR-L | | | $150.00 |
| What-4 | 6001 | | HK | M-AQ | CL | BR-D | | | $150.00 |
| What-4 | 6001 | | HK | M-AQ | BL | BR-D | | | $150.00 |
| What-4 | 6001 | | HK | M-BL | CL | WH | | | $160.00 |
| What-4 | 6001 | | HK | M-BL | BL | WH | | | $160.00 |
| What-4 | 6001 | | HK | M-BL | CL | BK | | | $150.00 |
| What-4 | 6001 | | HK | M-BL | BL | BK | | | $150.00 |
| What-4 | 6001 | | HK | M-BL | CL | GY | | | $150.00 |
| What-4 | 6001 | | HK | M-BL | BL | GY | | | $150.00 |
| What-4 | 6001 | | HK | M-BL | CL | BR-L | | | $150.00 |
| What-4 | 6001 | | HK | M-BL | BL | BR-L | | | $150.00 |
| What-4 | 6001 | | HK | M-BL | CL | BR-D | | | $150.00 |
| What-4 | 6001 | | HK | M-BL | BL | BR-D | | | $150.00 |
| What-4 | 6001 | | HK | M-BL-I | CL | WH | | | $200.00 |
| What-4 | 6001 | | HK | M-BL-I | BL | WH | | | $200.00 |
| What-4 | 6001 | | HK | M-BL-I | CL | BK | | | $200.00 |
| What-4 | 6001 | | HK | M-BL-I | BL | BK | | | $200.00 |
| What-4 | 6001 | | HK | M-BL-I | CL | GY | | | $200.00 |
| What-4 | 6001 | | HK | M-BL-I | BL | GY | | | $200.00 |
| What-4 | 6001 | | HK | M-BL-I | CL | BR-L | | | $200.00 |
| What-4 | 6001 | | HK | M-BL-I | BL | BR-L | | | $200.00 |
| What-4 | 6001 | | HK | M-BL-I | CL | BR-D | | | $200.00 |
| What-4 | 6001 | | HK | M-BL-I | BL | BR-D | | | $200.00 |
| What-4 | 6001 | | HK | M-BL-P | CL | WH | | | $200.00 |
| What-4 | 6001 | | HK | M-BL-P | BL | WH | | | $200.00 |
| What-4 | 6001 | | HK | M-BL-P | CL | BK | | | $200.00 |
| What-4 | 6001 | | HK | M-BL-P | BL | BK | | | $200.00 |
| What-4 | 6001 | | HK | M-BL-P | CL | GY | | | $200.00 |
| What-4 | 6001 | | HK | M-BL-P | BL | GY | | | $200.00 |
| What-4 | 6001 | | HK | M-BL-P | CL | BR-L | | | $200.00 |
| What-4 | 6001 | | HK | M-BL-P | BL | BR-L | | | $200.00 |
| What-4 | 6001 | | HK | M-BL-P | CL | BR-D | | | $200.00 |
| What-4 | 6001 | | HK | M-BL-P | BL | BR-D | | | $200.00 |
| What-4 | 6001 | | HK | M-GD | CL | WH | | | $165.00 |
| What-4 | 6001 | | HK | M-GD | BL | WH | | | $165.00 |
| What-4 | 6001 | | HK | M-GD | CL | BK | | | $155.00 |
| What-4 | 6001 | | HK | M-GD | BL | BK | | | $155.00 |
| What-4 | 6001 | | HK | M-GD | CL | GY | | | $155.00 |
| What-4 | 6001 | | HK | M-GD | BL | GY | | | $155.00 |
| What-4 | 6001 | | HK | M-GD | CL | BR-L | | | $155.00 |
| What-4 | 6001 | | HK | M-GD | BL | BR-L | | | $155.00 |
| What-4 | 6001 | | HK | M-GD | CL | BR-D | | | $155.00 |
| What-4 | 6001 | | HK | M-GD | BL | BR-D | | | $155.00 |
| What-4 | 6001 | | HK | M-GR | CL | WH | | | $150.00 |
| What-4 | 6001 | | HK | M-GR | BL | WH | | | $150.00 |
| What-4 | 6001 | | HK | M-GR | CL | BK | | | $140.00 |
| What-4 | 6001 | | HK | M-GR | BL | BK | | | $140.00 |

## 1971 Variations

| Name | Number | Casting | Country | Color | Windows | Interior | Paint | Other | Value |
|---|---|---|---|---|---|---|---|---|---|
| What-4 | 6001 | | HK | M-GR | CL | GY | | | $140.00 |
| What-4 | 6001 | | HK | M-GR | BL | GY | | | $140.00 |
| What-4 | 6001 | | HK | M-GR | CL | BR-L | | | $140.00 |
| What-4 | 6001 | | HK | M-GR | BL | BR-L | | | $140.00 |
| What-4 | 6001 | | HK | M-GR | CL | BR-D | | | $140.00 |
| What-4 | 6001 | | HK | M-GR | BL | BR-D | | | $140.00 |
| What-4 | 6001 | | HK | M-GR-E | CL | WH | | | $160.00 |
| What-4 | 6001 | | HK | M-GR-E | BL | WH | | | $160.00 |
| What-4 | 6001 | | HK | M-GR-E | CL | BK | | | $150.00 |
| What-4 | 6001 | | HK | M-GR-E | BL | BK | | | $150.00 |
| What-4 | 6001 | | HK | M-GR-E | CL | GY | | | $150.00 |
| What-4 | 6001 | | HK | M-GR-E | BL | GY | | | $150.00 |
| What-4 | 6001 | | HK | M-GR-E | CL | BR-L | | | $150.00 |
| What-4 | 6001 | | HK | M-GR-E | BL | BR-L | | | $150.00 |
| What-4 | 6001 | | HK | M-GR-E | CL | BR-D | | | $150.00 |
| What-4 | 6001 | | HK | M-GR-E | BL | BR-D | | | $150.00 |
| What-4 | 6001 | | HK | M-GR-L | CL | WH | | | $150.00 |
| What-4 | 6001 | | HK | M-GR-L | BL | WH | | | $150.00 |
| What-4 | 6001 | | HK | M-GR-L | CL | BK | | | $140.00 |
| What-4 | 6001 | | HK | M-GR-L | BL | BK | | | $140.00 |
| What-4 | 6001 | | HK | M-GR-L | CL | GY | | | $140.00 |
| What-4 | 6001 | | HK | M-GR-L | BL | GY | | | $140.00 |
| What-4 | 6001 | | HK | M-GR-L | CL | BR-L | | | $140.00 |
| What-4 | 6001 | | HK | M-GR-L | BL | BR-L | | | $140.00 |
| What-4 | 6001 | | HK | M-GR-L | CL | BR-D | | | $140.00 |
| What-4 | 6001 | | HK | M-GR-L | BL | BR-D | | | $140.00 |
| What-4 | 6001 | | HK | M-MG | CL | WH | | | $220.00 |
| What-4 | 6001 | | HK | M-MG | BL | WH | | | $220.00 |
| What-4 | 6001 | | HK | M-MG | CL | BK | | | $210.00 |
| What-4 | 6001 | | HK | M-MG | BL | BK | | | $210.00 |
| What-4 | 6001 | | HK | M-MG | CL | GY | | | $210.00 |
| What-4 | 6001 | | HK | M-MG | BL | GY | | | $210.00 |
| What-4 | 6001 | | HK | M-MG | CL | BR-L | | | $210.00 |
| What-4 | 6001 | | HK | M-MG | BL | BR-L | | | $210.00 |
| What-4 | 6001 | | HK | M-MG | CL | BR-D | | | $210.00 |
| What-4 | 6001 | | HK | M-MG | BL | BR-D | | | $210.00 |
| What-4 | 6001 | | HK | M-PR | CL | WH | | | $330.00 |
| What-4 | 6001 | | HK | M-PR | BL | WH | | | $330.00 |
| What-4 | 6001 | | HK | M-PR | CL | BK | | | $310.00 |
| What-4 | 6001 | | HK | M-PR | BL | BK | | | $310.00 |
| What-4 | 6001 | | HK | M-PR | CL | GY | | | $310.00 |
| What-4 | 6001 | | HK | M-PR | BL | GY | | | $310.00 |
| What-4 | 6001 | | HK | M-PR | CL | BR-L | | | $310.00 |
| What-4 | 6001 | | HK | M-PR | BL | BR-L | | | $310.00 |
| What-4 | 6001 | | HK | M-PR | CL | BR-D | | | $310.00 |
| What-4 | 6001 | | HK | M-PR | BL | BR-D | | | $310.00 |
| What-4 | 6001 | | HK | M-RD | CL | WH | | | $330.00 |
| What-4 | 6001 | | HK | M-RD | BL | WH | | | $330.00 |
| What-4 | 6001 | | HK | M-RD | CL | BK | | | $310.00 |
| What-4 | 6001 | | HK | M-RD | BL | BK | | | $310.00 |
| What-4 | 6001 | | HK | M-RD | CL | GY | | | $310.00 |
| What-4 | 6001 | | HK | M-RD | BL | GY | | | $310.00 |
| What-4 | 6001 | | HK | M-RD | CL | BR-L | | | $310.00 |
| What-4 | 6001 | | HK | M-RD | BL | BR-L | | | $310.00 |
| What-4 | 6001 | | HK | M-RD | CL | BR-D | | | $310.00 |
| What-4 | 6001 | | HK | M-RD | BL | BR-D | | | $310.00 |
| What-4 | 6001 | | HK | M-RD-R | CL | WH | | | $175.00 |
| What-4 | 6001 | | HK | M-RD-R | BL | WH | | | $175.00 |
| What-4 | 6001 | | HK | M-RD-R | CL | BK | | | $165.00 |
| What-4 | 6001 | | HK | M-RD-R | BL | BK | | | $165.00 |
| What-4 | 6001 | | HK | M-RD-R | CL | GY | | | $165.00 |
| What-4 | 6001 | | HK | M-RD-R | BL | GY | | | $165.00 |
| What-4 | 6001 | | HK | M-RD-R | CL | BR-L | | | $165.00 |
| What-4 | 6001 | | HK | M-RD-R | BL | BR-L | | | $165.00 |
| What-4 | 6001 | | HK | M-RD-R | CL | BR-D | | | $165.00 |
| What-4 | 6001 | | HK | M-RD-R | BL | BR-D | | | $165.00 |
| What-4 | 6001 | | HK | M-YW | CL | WH | | | $165.00 |
| What-4 | 6001 | | HK | M-YW | BL | WH | | | $165.00 |
| What-4 | 6001 | | HK | M-YW | CL | BK | | | $155.00 |
| What-4 | 6001 | | HK | M-YW | BL | BK | | | $155.00 |
| What-4 | 6001 | | HK | M-YW | CL | GY | | | $155.00 |
| What-4 | 6001 | | HK | M-YW | BL | GY | | | $155.00 |

## 1971 Variations

| Name | Number | Casting | Country | Color | Windows | Interior | Paint | Other | Value |
|---|---|---|---|---|---|---|---|---|---|
| What-4 | 6001 | | HK | M-YW | CL | BR-L | | | $155.00 |
| What-4 | 6001 | | HK | M-YW | BL | BR-L | | | $155.00 |
| What-4 | 6001 | | HK | M-YW | CL | BR-D | | | $155.00 |
| What-4 | 6001 | | HK | M-YW | BL | BR-D | | | $155.00 |
| What-4 | 6001 | | HK | M-YW-L | CL | WH | | | $170.00 |
| What-4 | 6001 | | HK | M-YW-L | BL | WH | | | $170.00 |
| What-4 | 6001 | | HK | M-YW-L | CL | BK | | | $160.00 |
| What-4 | 6001 | | HK | M-YW-L | BL | BK | | | $160.00 |
| What-4 | 6001 | | HK | M-YW-L | CL | GY | | | $160.00 |
| What-4 | 6001 | | HK | M-YW-L | BL | GY | | | $160.00 |
| What-4 | 6001 | | HK | M-YW-L | CL | BR-L | | | $160.00 |
| What-4 | 6001 | | HK | M-YW-L | BL | BR-L | | | $160.00 |
| What-4 | 6001 | | HK | M-YW-L | CL | BR-D | | | $160.00 |
| What-4 | 6001 | | HK | M-YW-L | BL | BR-D | | | $160.00 |
| | | | | | | | | | |
| Six Shooter | 6003 | | HK | M-AQ | | WH | | | $115.00 |
| Six Shooter | 6003 | | HK | M-AQ | | BK | | | $100.00 |
| Six Shooter | 6003 | | HK | M-AQ | | GY | | | $100.00 |
| Six Shooter | 6003 | | HK | M-AQ | | BR-L | | | $100.00 |
| Six Shooter | 6003 | | HK | M-AQ | | BR-D | | | $100.00 |
| Six Shooter | 6003 | | HK | M-BL | | WH | | | $115.00 |
| Six Shooter | 6003 | | HK | M-BL | | BK | | | $100.00 |
| Six Shooter | 6003 | | HK | M-BL | | GY | | | $100.00 |
| Six Shooter | 6003 | | HK | M-BL | | BR-L | | | $100.00 |
| Six Shooter | 6003 | | HK | M-BL | | BR-D | | | $100.00 |
| Six Shooter | 6003 | | HK | M-BL-I | | WH | | | $125.00 |
| Six Shooter | 6003 | | HK | M-BL-I | | BK | | | $115.00 |
| Six Shooter | 6003 | | HK | M-BL-I | | GY | | | $115.00 |
| Six Shooter | 6003 | | HK | M-BL-I | | BR-L | | | $115.00 |
| Six Shooter | 6003 | | HK | M-BL-I | | BR-D | | | $115.00 |
| Six Shooter | 6003 | | HK | M-BL-P | | WH | | | $115.00 |
| Six Shooter | 6003 | | HK | M-BL-P | | BK | | | $100.00 |
| Six Shooter | 6003 | | HK | M-BL-P | | GY | | | $100.00 |
| Six Shooter | 6003 | | HK | M-BL-P | | BR-L | | | $100.00 |
| Six Shooter | 6003 | | HK | M-BL-P | | BR-D | | | $100.00 |
| Six Shooter | 6003 | | HK | M-GD | | WH | | | $90.00 |
| Six Shooter | 6003 | | HK | M-GD | | BK | | | $80.00 |
| Six Shooter | 6003 | | HK | M-GD | | GY | | | $80.00 |
| Six Shooter | 6003 | | HK | M-GD | | BR-L | | | $80.00 |
| Six Shooter | 6003 | | HK | M-GD | | BR-D | | | $80.00 |
| Six Shooter | 6003 | | HK | M-MG | | WH | | | $160.00 |
| Six Shooter | 6003 | | HK | M-MG | | BK | | | $150.00 |
| Six Shooter | 6003 | | HK | M-MG | | GY | | | $150.00 |
| Six Shooter | 6003 | | HK | M-MG | | BR-L | | | $150.00 |
| Six Shooter | 6003 | | HK | M-MG | | BR-D | | | $150.00 |
| Six Shooter | 6003 | | HK | M-YW | | WH | | | $90.00 |
| Six Shooter | 6003 | | HK | M-YW | | BK | | | $80.00 |
| Six Shooter | 6003 | | HK | M-YW | | GY | | | $80.00 |
| Six Shooter | 6003 | | HK | M-YW | | BR-L | | | $80.00 |
| Six Shooter | 6003 | | HK | M-YW | | BR-D | | | $80.00 |
| | | | | | | | | | |
| Special Delivery | 6006 | | HK | M-BL | | | | | $90.00 |
| Special Delivery | 6006 | | HK | M-BL-P | | | | | $90.00 |
| | | | | | | | | | |
| Fuel Tanker | 6018 | | HK | E-WH | | WH | | | $110.00 |
| Fuel Tanker | 6018 | | HK | E-WH | | BK | | | $100.00 |
| Fuel Tanker | 6018 | | HK | E-WH | | GY | | | $100.00 |
| Fuel Tanker | 6018 | | HK | E-WH | | BR-L | | | $100.00 |
| Fuel Tanker | 6018 | | HK | E-WH | | BR-D | | | $100.00 |
| | | | | | | | | | |
| Team Trailer | 6019 | | HK | E-WH | BL-CLT | WH | | | $160.00 |
| Team Trailer | 6019 | | HK | E-WH | BL | WH | | | $140.00 |
| Team Trailer | 6019 | | HK | E-WH | BL-CLT | BK | | | $155.00 |
| Team Trailer | 6019 | | HK | E-WH | BL | BK | | | $135.00 |
| Team Trailer | 6019 | | HK | E-WH | BL | BK | | BL trailer | $400.00 |
| Team Trailer | 6019 | | HK | E-WH | BL-CLT | GY | | | $155.00 |
| Team Trailer | 6019 | | HK | E-WH | BL | GY | | | $135.00 |
| Team Trailer | 6019 | | HK | E-WH | BL-CLT | BR-L | | | $155.00 |
| Team Trailer | 6019 | | HK | E-WH | BL | BR-L | | | $135.00 |

## 1971 Variations

| Name | Number | Casting | Country | Color | Windows | Interior | Paint | Other | Value |
|---|---|---|---|---|---|---|---|---|---|
| Team Trailer | 6019 | | HK | E-WH | BL-CLT | BR-D | | | $155.00 |
| Team Trailer | 6019 | | HK | E-WH | BL | BR-D | | | $135.00 |
| Team Trailer | 6019 | | HK | M-BL | BL-CLT | WH | | | $160.00 |
| Team Trailer | 6019 | | HK | M-BL | BL | WH | | | $140.00 |
| Team Trailer | 6019 | | HK | M-BL | BL-CLT | BK | | | $155.00 |
| Team Trailer | 6019 | | HK | M-BL | BL | BK | | | $135.00 |
| Team Trailer | 6019 | | HK | M-BL | BL-CLT | GY | | | $155.00 |
| Team Trailer | 6019 | | HK | M-BL | BL | GY | | | $135.00 |
| Team Trailer | 6019 | | HK | M-BL | BL-CLT | BR-L | | | $155.00 |
| Team Trailer | 6019 | | HK | M-BL | BL | BR-L | | | $135.00 |
| Team Trailer | 6019 | | HK | M-BL | BL-CLT | BR-D | | | $155.00 |
| Team Trailer | 6019 | | HK | M-BL | BL | BR-D | | | $135.00 |
| Team Trailer | 6019 | | HK | M-RD | BL-CLT | WH | | | $160.00 |
| Team Trailer | 6019 | | HK | M-RD | BL | WH | | | $140.00 |
| Team Trailer | 6019 | | HK | M-RD | BL-CLT | BK | | | $155.00 |
| Team Trailer | 6019 | | HK | M-RD | BL | BK | | | $135.00 |
| Team Trailer | 6019 | | HK | M-RD | BL-CLT | GY | | | $155.00 |
| Team Trailer | 6019 | | HK | M-RD | BL | GY | | | $135.00 |
| Team Trailer | 6019 | | HK | M-RD | BL-CLT | BR-L | | | $155.00 |
| Team Trailer | 6019 | | HK | M-RD | BL | BR-L | | | $135.00 |
| Team Trailer | 6019 | | HK | M-RD | BL-CLT | BR-D | | | $155.00 |
| Team Trailer | 6019 | | HK | M-RD | BL | BR-D | | | $135.00 |
| Snorkel | 6020 | | HK | E-WH | | WH | | | $170.00 |
| Snorkel | 6020 | | HK | E-WH | | BK | | | $160.00 |
| Snorkel | 6020 | | HK | E-WH | | GY | | | $160.00 |
| Snorkel | 6020 | | HK | E-WH | | BR-L | | | $160.00 |
| Snorkel | 6020 | | HK | E-WH | | BR-D | | | $160.00 |
| Snorkel | 6020 | | HK | M-AQ | | WH | | | $110.00 |
| Snorkel | 6020 | | HK | M-AQ | | BK | | | $100.00 |
| Snorkel | 6020 | | HK | M-AQ | | GY | | | $100.00 |
| Snorkel | 6020 | | HK | M-AQ | | BR-L | | | $100.00 |
| Snorkel | 6020 | | HK | M-AQ | | BR-D | | | $100.00 |
| Snorkel | 6020 | | HK | M-BL | | WH | | | $100.00 |
| Snorkel | 6020 | | HK | M-BL | | BK | | | $90.00 |
| Snorkel | 6020 | | HK | M-BL | | GY | | | $90.00 |
| Snorkel | 6020 | | HK | M-BL | | BR-L | | | $90.00 |
| Snorkel | 6020 | | HK | M-BL | | BR-D | | | $90.00 |
| Snorkel | 6020 | | HK | M-BR-D | | WH | | | $120.00 |
| Snorkel | 6020 | | HK | M-BR-D | | BK | | | $110.00 |
| Snorkel | 6020 | | HK | M-BR-D | | GY | | | $110.00 |
| Snorkel | 6020 | | HK | M-BR-D | | BR-L | | | $110.00 |
| Snorkel | 6020 | | HK | M-BR-D | | BR-D | | | $110.00 |
| Snorkel | 6020 | | HK | M-BR-P | | WH | | | $110.00 |
| Snorkel | 6020 | | HK | M-BR-P | | BK | | | $100.00 |
| Snorkel | 6020 | | HK | M-BR-P | | GY | | | $100.00 |
| Snorkel | 6020 | | HK | M-BR-P | | BR-L | | | $100.00 |
| Snorkel | 6020 | | HK | M-BR-P | | BR-D | | | $100.00 |
| Snorkel | 6020 | | HK | M-GD | | WH | | | $120.00 |
| Snorkel | 6020 | | HK | M-GD | | BK | | | $110.00 |
| Snorkel | 6020 | | HK | M-GD | | GY | | | $110.00 |
| Snorkel | 6020 | | HK | M-GD | | BR-L | | | $110.00 |
| Snorkel | 6020 | | HK | M-GD | | BR-D | | | $110.00 |
| Snorkel | 6020 | | HK | M-GR | | WH | | | $110.00 |
| Snorkel | 6020 | | HK | M-GR | | BK | | | $100.00 |
| Snorkel | 6020 | | HK | M-GR | | GY | | | $100.00 |
| Snorkel | 6020 | | HK | M-GR | | BR-L | | | $100.00 |
| Snorkel | 6020 | | HK | M-GR | | BR-D | | | $100.00 |
| Snorkel | 6020 | | HK | M-GR-E | | WH | | | $120.00 |
| Snorkel | 6020 | | HK | M-GR-E | | BK | | | $110.00 |
| Snorkel | 6020 | | HK | M-GR-E | | GY | | | $110.00 |
| Snorkel | 6020 | | HK | M-GR-E | | BR-L | | | $110.00 |
| Snorkel | 6020 | | HK | M-GR-E | | BR-D | | | $110.00 |
| Snorkel | 6020 | | HK | M-GR-L | | WH | | | $130.00 |
| Snorkel | 6020 | | HK | M-GR-L | | BK | | | $120.00 |
| Snorkel | 6020 | | HK | M-GR-L | | GY | | | $120.00 |
| Snorkel | 6020 | | HK | M-GR-L | | BR-L | | | $120.00 |
| Snorkel | 6020 | | HK | M-GR-L | | BR-D | | | $120.00 |
| Snorkel | 6020 | | HK | M-GR-O | | WH | | | $130.00 |
| Snorkel | 6020 | | HK | M-GR-O | | BK | | | $120.00 |
| Snorkel | 6020 | | HK | M-GR-O | | GY | | | $120.00 |

## 1971 Variations

| Name | Number | Casting | Country | Color | Windows | Interior | Paint | Other | Value |
|---|---|---|---|---|---|---|---|---|---|
| Snorkel | 6020 | | HK | M-GR-O | | BR-L | | | $120.00 |
| Snorkel | 6020 | | HK | M-GR-O | | BR-D | | | $120.00 |
| Snorkel | 6020 | | HK | M-MG | | WH | | | $130.00 |
| Snorkel | 6020 | | HK | M-MG | | BK | | | $120.00 |
| Snorkel | 6020 | | HK | M-MG | | GY | | | $120.00 |
| Snorkel | 6020 | | HK | M-MG | | BR-L | | | $120.00 |
| Snorkel | 6020 | | HK | M-MG | | BR-D | | | $120.00 |
| Snorkel | 6020 | | HK | M-PK | | WH | | | $150.00 |
| Snorkel | 6020 | | HK | M-PK | | BK | | | $140.00 |
| Snorkel | 6020 | | HK | M-PK | | GY | | | $140.00 |
| Snorkel | 6020 | | HK | M-PK | | BR-L | | | $150.00 |
| Snorkel | 6020 | | HK | M-PK | | BR-D | | | $140.00 |
| Snorkel | 6020 | | HK | M-PK-H | | WH | | | $150.00 |
| Snorkel | 6020 | | HK | M-PK-H | | BK | | | $140.00 |
| Snorkel | 6020 | | HK | M-PK-H | | GY | | | $140.00 |
| Snorkel | 6020 | | HK | M-PK-H | | BR-L | | | $140.00 |
| Snorkel | 6020 | | HK | M-PK-H | | BR-D | | | $140.00 |
| Snorkel | 6020 | | HK | M-PK-S | | WH | | | $130.00 |
| Snorkel | 6020 | | HK | M-PK-S | | BK | | | $120.00 |
| Snorkel | 6020 | | HK | M-PK-S | | GY | | | $120.00 |
| Snorkel | 6020 | | HK | M-PK-S | | BR-L | | | $120.00 |
| Snorkel | 6020 | | HK | M-PK-S | | BR-D | | | $120.00 |
| Snorkel | 6020 | | HK | M-RD | | WH | | | $110.00 |
| Snorkel | 6020 | | HK | M-RD | | BK | | | $100.00 |
| Snorkel | 6020 | | HK | M-RD | | GY | | | $100.00 |
| Snorkel | 6020 | | HK | M-RD | | BR-L | | | $100.00 |
| Snorkel | 6020 | | HK | M-RD | | BR-D | | | $100.00 |
| Snorkel | 6020 | | HK | M-RD-R | | WH | | | $120.00 |
| Snorkel | 6020 | | HK | M-RD-R | | BK | | | $110.00 |
| Snorkel | 6020 | | HK | M-RD-R | | GY | | | $110.00 |
| Snorkel | 6020 | | HK | M-RD-R | | BR-L | | | $110.00 |
| Snorkel | 6020 | | HK | M-RD-R | | BR-D | | | $110.00 |
| Snorkel | 6020 | | HK | M-YW | | WH | | | $120.00 |
| Snorkel | 6020 | | HK | M-YW | | BK | | | $110.00 |
| Snorkel | 6020 | | HK | M-YW | | GY | | | $110.00 |
| Snorkel | 6020 | | HK | M-YW | | BR-L | | | $110.00 |
| Snorkel | 6020 | | HK | M-YW | | BR-D | | | $110.00 |
| Snorkel | 6020 | | HK | M-YW-L | | WH | | | $140.00 |
| Snorkel | 6020 | | HK | M-YW-L | | BK | | | $130.00 |
| Snorkel | 6020 | | HK | M-YW-L | | GY | | | $130.00 |
| Snorkel | 6020 | | HK | M-YW-L | | BR-L | | | $130.00 |
| Snorkel | 6020 | | HK | M-YW-L | | BR-D | | | $130.00 |
| The Hood | 6175 | | USA | M-AQ | | BK | | | $60.00 |
| The Hood | 6175 | | HK | M-AQ | | BK | | | $60.00 |
| The Hood | 6175 | | USA | M-AQ | | BK | BK-RF | | $65.00 |
| The Hood | 6175 | | HK | M-AQ | | BK | BK-RF | | $65.00 |
| The Hood | 6175 | | USA | M-AQ | | GY | | | $60.00 |
| The Hood | 6175 | | HK | M-AQ | | GY | | | $60.00 |
| The Hood | 6175 | | USA | M-AQ | | GY | BK-RF | | $65.00 |
| The Hood | 6175 | | HK | M-AQ | | GY | BK-RF | | $65.00 |
| The Hood | 6175 | | USA | M-AQ | | BR-D | | | $60.00 |
| The Hood | 6175 | | HK | M-AQ | | BR-D | | | $60.00 |
| The Hood | 6175 | | USA | M-AQ | | BR-D | BK-RF | | $65.00 |
| The Hood | 6175 | | HK | M-AQ | | BR-D | BK-RF | | $65.00 |
| The Hood | 6175 | | USA | M-BL | | BK | | | $60.00 |
| The Hood | 6175 | | HK | M-BL | | BK | | | $60.00 |
| The Hood | 6175 | | USA | M-BL | | BK | BK-RF | | $65.00 |
| The Hood | 6175 | | HK | M-BL | | BK | BK-RF | | $65.00 |
| The Hood | 6175 | | USA | M-BL | | GY | | | $60.00 |
| The Hood | 6175 | | HK | M-BL | | GY | | | $60.00 |
| The Hood | 6175 | | USA | M-BL | | GY | BK-RF | | $65.00 |
| The Hood | 6175 | | HK | M-BL | | GY | BK-RF | | $65.00 |
| The Hood | 6175 | | USA | M-BL | | BR-D | | | $60.00 |
| The Hood | 6175 | | HK | M-BL | | BR-D | | | $60.00 |
| The Hood | 6175 | | USA | M-BL | | BR-D | BK-RF | | $65.00 |
| The Hood | 6175 | | HK | M-BL | | BR-D | BK-RF | | $65.00 |
| The Hood | 6175 | | USA | M-BL-I | | BK | | | $90.00 |
| The Hood | 6175 | | HK | M-BL-I | | BK | | | $90.00 |
| The Hood | 6175 | | USA | M-BL-I | | BK | BK-RF | | $100.00 |
| The Hood | 6175 | | HK | M-BL-I | | BK | BK-RF | | $100.00 |

## 1971 Variations

| Name | Number | Casting | Country | Color | Windows | Interior | Paint | Other | Value |
|---|---|---|---|---|---|---|---|---|---|
| The Hood | 6175 | | USA | M-BL-I | | GY | | | $90.00 |
| The Hood | 6175 | | HK | M-BL-I | | GY | | | $90.00 |
| The Hood | 6175 | | USA | M-BL-I | | GY | BK-RF | | $100.00 |
| The Hood | 6175 | | HK | M-BL-I | | GY | BK-RF | | $100.00 |
| The Hood | 6175 | | USA | M-BL-I | | BR-D | | | $90.00 |
| The Hood | 6175 | | HK | M-BL-I | | BR-D | | | $90.00 |
| The Hood | 6175 | | USA | M-BL-I | | BR-D | BK-RF | | $100.00 |
| The Hood | 6175 | | HK | M-BL-I | | BR-D | BK-RF | | $100.00 |
| The Hood | 6175 | | USA | M-BL-P | | BK | | | $70.00 |
| The Hood | 6175 | | HK | M-BL-P | | BK | | | $70.00 |
| The Hood | 6175 | | USA | M-BL-P | | BK | BK-RF | | $80.00 |
| The Hood | 6175 | | HK | M-BL-P | | BK | BK-RF | | $80.00 |
| The Hood | 6175 | | USA | M-BL-P | | GY | | | $70.00 |
| The Hood | 6175 | | HK | M-BL-P | | GY | | | $70.00 |
| The Hood | 6175 | | USA | M-BL-P | | GY | BK-RF | | $80.00 |
| The Hood | 6175 | | HK | M-BL-P | | GY | BK-RF | | $80.00 |
| The Hood | 6175 | | USA | M-BL-P | | BR-D | | | $70.00 |
| The Hood | 6175 | | HK | M-BL-P | | BR-D | | | $70.00 |
| The Hood | 6175 | | USA | M-BL-P | | BR-D | BK-RF | | $80.00 |
| The Hood | 6175 | | HK | M-BL-P | | BR-D | BK-RF | | $80.00 |
| The Hood | 6175 | | USA | M-GD | | BK | | | $50.00 |
| The Hood | 6175 | | HK | M-GD | | BK | | | $50.00 |
| The Hood | 6175 | | USA | M-GD | | BK | BK-RF | | $55.00 |
| The Hood | 6175 | | HK | M-GD | | BK | BK-RF | | $55.00 |
| The Hood | 6175 | | USA | M-GD | | GY | | | $50.00 |
| The Hood | 6175 | | HK | M-GD | | GY | | | $50.00 |
| The Hood | 6175 | | USA | M-GD | | GY | BK-RF | | $55.00 |
| The Hood | 6175 | | HK | M-GD | | GY | BK-RF | | $55.00 |
| The Hood | 6175 | | USA | M-GD | | BR-D | | | $50.00 |
| The Hood | 6175 | | HK | M-GD | | BR-D | | | $50.00 |
| The Hood | 6175 | | USA | M-GD | | BR-D | BK-RF | | $55.00 |
| The Hood | 6175 | | HK | M-GD | | BR-D | BK-RF | | $55.00 |
| The Hood | 6175 | | USA | M-GR | | BK | | | $70.00 |
| The Hood | 6175 | | HK | M-GR | | BK | | | $70.00 |
| The Hood | 6175 | | USA | M-GR | | BK | BK-RF | | $80.00 |
| The Hood | 6175 | | HK | M-GR | | BK | BK-RF | | $80.00 |
| The Hood | 6175 | | USA | M-GR | | GY | | | $70.00 |
| The Hood | 6175 | | HK | M-GR | | GY | | | $70.00 |
| The Hood | 6175 | | USA | M-GR | | GY | BK-RF | | $80.00 |
| The Hood | 6175 | | HK | M-GR | | GY | BK-RF | | $80.00 |
| The Hood | 6175 | | USA | M-GR | | BR-D | | | $70.00 |
| The Hood | 6175 | | HK | M-GR | | BR-D | | | $70.00 |
| The Hood | 6175 | | USA | M-GR | | BR-D | BK-RF | | $80.00 |
| The Hood | 6175 | | HK | M-GR | | BR-D | BK-RF | | $80.00 |
| The Hood | 6175 | | USA | M-GR-E | | BK | | | $80.00 |
| The Hood | 6175 | | HK | M-GR-E | | BK | | | $80.00 |
| The Hood | 6175 | | USA | M-GR-E | | BK | BK-RF | | $90.00 |
| The Hood | 6175 | | HK | M-GR-E | | BK | BK-RF | | $90.00 |
| The Hood | 6175 | | USA | M-GR-E | | GY | | | $80.00 |
| The Hood | 6175 | | HK | M-GR-E | | GY | | | $80.00 |
| The Hood | 6175 | | USA | M-GR-E | | GY | BK-RF | | $90.00 |
| The Hood | 6175 | | HK | M-GR-E | | GY | BK-RF | | $90.00 |
| The Hood | 6175 | | USA | M-GR-E | | BR-D | | | $80.00 |
| The Hood | 6175 | | HK | M-GR-E | | BR-D | | | $80.00 |
| The Hood | 6175 | | USA | M-GR-E | | BR-D | BK-RF | | $90.00 |
| The Hood | 6175 | | HK | M-GR-E | | BR-D | BK-RF | | $90.00 |
| The Hood | 6175 | | USA | M-GR-L | | BK | | | $50.00 |
| The Hood | 6175 | | HK | M-GR-L | | BK | | | $50.00 |
| The Hood | 6175 | | USA | M-GR-L | | BK | BK-RF | | $55.00 |
| The Hood | 6175 | | HK | M-GR-L | | BK | BK-RF | | $55.00 |
| The Hood | 6175 | | USA | M-GR-L | | GY | | | $50.00 |
| The Hood | 6175 | | HK | M-GR-L | | GY | | | $50.00 |
| The Hood | 6175 | | USA | M-GR-L | | GY | BK-RF | | $55.00 |
| The Hood | 6175 | | HK | M-GR-L | | GY | BK-RF | | $55.00 |
| The Hood | 6175 | | USA | M-GR-L | | BR-D | | | $50.00 |
| The Hood | 6175 | | HK | M-GR-L | | BR-D | | | $50.00 |
| The Hood | 6175 | | USA | M-GR-L | | BR-D | BK-RF | | $55.00 |
| The Hood | 6175 | | HK | M-GR-L | | BR-D | BK-RF | | $55.00 |
| The Hood | 6175 | | USA | M-GR-O | | BK | | | $110.00 |
| The Hood | 6175 | | HK | M-GR-O | | BK | | | $110.00 |
| The Hood | 6175 | | USA | M-GR-O | | BK | BK-RF | | $130.00 |
| The Hood | 6175 | | HK | M-GR-O | | BK | BK-RF | | $130.00 |

## 1971 Variations

| Name | Number | Casting | Country | Color | Windows | Interior | Paint | Other | Value |
|---|---|---|---|---|---|---|---|---|---|
| The Hood | 6175 | | USA | M-GR-O | | GY | | | $110.00 |
| The Hood | 6175 | | HK | M-GR-O | | GY | | | $110.00 |
| The Hood | 6175 | | USA | M-GR-O | | GY | BK-RF | | $130.00 |
| The Hood | 6175 | | HK | M-GR-O | | GY | BK-RF | | $130.00 |
| The Hood | 6175 | | USA | M-GR-O | | BR-D | | | $110.00 |
| The Hood | 6175 | | HK | M-GR-O | | BR-D | | | $110.00 |
| The Hood | 6175 | | USA | M-GR-O | | BR-D | BK-RF | | $130.00 |
| The Hood | 6175 | | HK | M-GR-O | | BR-D | BK-RF | | $130.00 |
| The Hood | 6175 | | USA | M-MG | | BK | | | $50.00 |
| The Hood | 6175 | | HK | M-MG | | BK | | | $50.00 |
| The Hood | 6175 | | USA | M-MG | | BK | BK-RF | | $55.00 |
| The Hood | 6175 | | HK | M-MG | | BK | BK-RF | | $55.00 |
| The Hood | 6175 | | USA | M-MG | | GY | | | $50.00 |
| The Hood | 6175 | | HK | M-MG | | GY | | | $50.00 |
| The Hood | 6175 | | USA | M-MG | | GY | BK-RF | | $55.00 |
| The Hood | 6175 | | HK | M-MG | | GY | BK-RF | | $55.00 |
| The Hood | 6175 | | USA | M-MG | | BR-D | | | $50.00 |
| The Hood | 6175 | | HK | M-MG | | BR-D | | | $50.00 |
| The Hood | 6175 | | USA | M-MG | | BR-D | BK-RF | | $55.00 |
| The Hood | 6175 | | HK | M-MG | | BR-D | BK-RF | | $55.00 |
| The Hood | 6175 | | USA | M-PL | | BK | | | $230.00 |
| The Hood | 6175 | | HK | M-PL | | BK | | | $230.00 |
| The Hood | 6175 | | USA | M-PL | | BK | BK-RF | | $230.00 |
| The Hood | 6175 | | HK | M-PL | | BK | BK-RF | | $230.00 |
| The Hood | 6175 | | USA | M-PL | | GY | | | $230.00 |
| The Hood | 6175 | | HK | M-PL | | GY | | | $230.00 |
| The Hood | 6175 | | USA | M-PL | | GY | BK-RF | | $230.00 |
| The Hood | 6175 | | HK | M-PL | | GY | BK-RF | | $230.00 |
| The Hood | 6175 | | USA | M-PL | | BR-D | | | $230.00 |
| The Hood | 6175 | | HK | M-PL | | BR-D | | | $230.00 |
| The Hood | 6175 | | USA | M-PL | | BR-D | BK-RF | | $230.00 |
| The Hood | 6175 | | HK | M-PL | | BR-D | BK-RF | | $230.00 |
| The Hood | 6175 | | USA | M-PK | | BK | | | $230.00 |
| The Hood | 6175 | | HK | M-PK | | BK | | | $230.00 |
| The Hood | 6175 | | USA | M-PK | | BK | BK-RF | | $250.00 |
| The Hood | 6175 | | HK | M-PK | | BK | BK-RF | | $250.00 |
| The Hood | 6175 | | USA | M-PK | | GY | | | $230.00 |
| The Hood | 6175 | | HK | M-PK | | GY | | | $230.00 |
| The Hood | 6175 | | USA | M-PK | | GY | BK-RF | | $250.00 |
| The Hood | 6175 | | HK | M-PK | | GY | BK-RF | | $250.00 |
| The Hood | 6175 | | USA | M-PK | | BR-D | | | $230.00 |
| The Hood | 6175 | | HK | M-PK | | BR-D | | | $230.00 |
| The Hood | 6175 | | USA | M-PK | | BR-D | BK-RF | | $250.00 |
| The Hood | 6175 | | HK | M-PK | | BR-D | BK-RF | | $250.00 |
| The Hood | 6175 | | USA | M-PK-H | | BK | | | $230.00 |
| The Hood | 6175 | | HK | M-PK-H | | BK | | | $230.00 |
| The Hood | 6175 | | USA | M-PK-H | | BK | BK-RF | | $250.00 |
| The Hood | 6175 | | HK | M-PK-H | | BK | BK-RF | | $250.00 |
| The Hood | 6175 | | USA | M-PK-H | | GY | | | $230.00 |
| The Hood | 6175 | | HK | M-PK-H | | GY | | | $230.00 |
| The Hood | 6175 | | USA | M-PK-H | | GY | BK-RF | | $250.00 |
| The Hood | 6175 | | HK | M-PK-H | | GY | BK-RF | | $250.00 |
| The Hood | 6175 | | USA | M-PK-H | | BR-D | | | $230.00 |
| The Hood | 6175 | | HK | M-PK-H | | BR-D | | | $230.00 |
| The Hood | 6175 | | USA | M-PK-H | | BR-D | BK-RF | | $250.00 |
| The Hood | 6175 | | HK | M-PK-H | | BR-D | BK-RF | | $250.00 |
| The Hood | 6175 | | USA | M-PK-S | | BK | | | $230.00 |
| The Hood | 6175 | | HK | M-PK-S | | BK | | | $230.00 |
| The Hood | 6175 | | USA | M-PK-S | | BK | BK-RF | | $250.00 |
| The Hood | 6175 | | HK | M-PK-S | | BK | BK-RF | | $250.00 |
| The Hood | 6175 | | USA | M-PK-S | | GY | | | $230.00 |
| The Hood | 6175 | | HK | M-PK-S | | GY | | | $230.00 |
| The Hood | 6175 | | USA | M-PK-S | | GY | BK-RF | | $250.00 |
| The Hood | 6175 | | HK | M-PK-S | | GY | BK-RF | | $250.00 |
| The Hood | 6175 | | USA | M-PK-S | | BR-D | | | $230.00 |
| The Hood | 6175 | | HK | M-PK-S | | BR-D | | | $230.00 |
| The Hood | 6175 | | USA | M-PK-S | | BR-D | BK-RF | | $250.00 |
| The Hood | 6175 | | HK | M-PK-S | | BR-D | BK-RF | | $250.00 |
| The Hood | 6175 | | USA | M-PL | | BK | | | $80.00 |
| The Hood | 6175 | | HK | M-PL | | BK | | | $80.00 |
| The Hood | 6175 | | USA | M-PL | | BK | BK-RF | | $90.00 |
| The Hood | 6175 | | HK | M-PL | | BK | BK-RF | | $90.00 |

## 1971 Variations

| Name | Number | Casting | Country | Color | Windows | Interior | Paint | Other | Value |
|---|---|---|---|---|---|---|---|---|---|
| The Hood | 6175 | | USA | M-PL | | GY | | | $80.00 |
| The Hood | 6175 | | HK | M-PL | | GY | | | $80.00 |
| The Hood | 6175 | | USA | M-PL | | GY | BK-RF | | $90.00 |
| The Hood | 6175 | | HK | M-PL | | GY | BK-RF | | $90.00 |
| The Hood | 6175 | | USA | M-PL | | BR-D | | | $80.00 |
| The Hood | 6175 | | HK | M-PL | | BR-D | | | $80.00 |
| The Hood | 6175 | | USA | M-PL | | BR-D | BK-RF | | $90.00 |
| The Hood | 6175 | | HK | M-PL | | BR-D | BK-RF | | $90.00 |
| The Hood | 6175 | | USA | M-PR | | BK | | | $80.00 |
| The Hood | 6175 | | HK | M-PR | | BK | | | $80.00 |
| The Hood | 6175 | | USA | M-PR | | BK | BK-RF | | $90.00 |
| The Hood | 6175 | | HK | M-PR | | BK | BK-RF | | $90.00 |
| The Hood | 6175 | | USA | M-PR | | GY | | | $80.00 |
| The Hood | 6175 | | HK | M-PR | | GY | | | $80.00 |
| The Hood | 6175 | | USA | M-PR | | GY | BK-RF | | $90.00 |
| The Hood | 6175 | | HK | M-PR | | GY | BK-RF | | $90.00 |
| The Hood | 6175 | | USA | M-PR | | BR-D | | | $80.00 |
| The Hood | 6175 | | HK | M-PR | | BR-D | | | $80.00 |
| The Hood | 6175 | | USA | M-PR | | BR-D | BK-RF | | $90.00 |
| The Hood | 6175 | | HK | M-PR | | BR-D | BK-RF | | $90.00 |
| The Hood | 6175 | | USA | M-RD | | BK | | | $50.00 |
| The Hood | 6175 | | HK | M-RD | | BK | | | $50.00 |
| The Hood | 6175 | | USA | M-RD | | BK | BK-RF | | $55.00 |
| The Hood | 6175 | | HK | M-RD | | BK | BK-RF | | $55.00 |
| The Hood | 6175 | | USA | M-RD | | GY | | | $50.00 |
| The Hood | 6175 | | HK | M-RD | | GY | | | $50.00 |
| The Hood | 6175 | | USA | M-RD | | GY | BK-RF | | $55.00 |
| The Hood | 6175 | | HK | M-RD | | GY | BK-RF | | $55.00 |
| The Hood | 6175 | | USA | M-RD | | BR-D | | | $50.00 |
| The Hood | 6175 | | HK | M-RD | | BR-D | | | $50.00 |
| The Hood | 6175 | | USA | M-RD | | BR-D | BK-RF | | $55.00 |
| The Hood | 6175 | | HK | M-RD | | BR-D | BK-RF | | $55.00 |
| The Hood | 6175 | | USA | M-RD-R | | BK | | | $55.00 |
| The Hood | 6175 | | HK | M-RD-R | | BK | | | $55.00 |
| The Hood | 6175 | | USA | M-RD-R | | BK | BK-RF | | $60.00 |
| The Hood | 6175 | | HK | M-RD-R | | BK | BK-RF | | $60.00 |
| The Hood | 6175 | | USA | M-RD-R | | GY | | | $55.00 |
| The Hood | 6175 | | HK | M-RD-R | | GY | | | $55.00 |
| The Hood | 6175 | | USA | M-RD-R | | GY | BK-RF | | $60.00 |
| The Hood | 6175 | | HK | M-RD-R | | GY | BK-RF | | $60.00 |
| The Hood | 6175 | | USA | M-RD-R | | BR-D | | | $55.00 |
| The Hood | 6175 | | HK | M-RD-R | | BR-D | | | $55.00 |
| The Hood | 6175 | | USA | M-RD-R | | BR-D | BK-RF | | $60.00 |
| The Hood | 6175 | | HK | M-RD-R | | BR-D | BK-RF | | $60.00 |
| The Hood | 6175 | | USA | M-YW | | BK | | | $50.00 |
| The Hood | 6175 | | HK | M-YW | | BK | | | $50.00 |
| The Hood | 6175 | | USA | M-YW | | BK | BK-RF | | $55.00 |
| The Hood | 6175 | | HK | M-YW | | BK | BK-RF | | $55.00 |
| The Hood | 6175 | | USA | M-YW | | GY | | | $50.00 |
| The Hood | 6175 | | HK | M-YW | | GY | | | $50.00 |
| The Hood | 6175 | | USA | M-YW | | GY | BK-RF | | $55.00 |
| The Hood | 6175 | | HK | M-YW | | GY | BK-RF | | $55.00 |
| The Hood | 6175 | | USA | M-YW | | BR-D | | | $50.00 |
| The Hood | 6175 | | HK | M-YW | | BR-D | | | $50.00 |
| The Hood | 6175 | | USA | M-YW | | BR-D | BK-RF | | $55.00 |
| The Hood | 6175 | | HK | M-YW | | BR-D | BK-RF | | $55.00 |
| The Hood | 6175 | | USA | M-YW-L | | BK | | | $55.00 |
| The Hood | 6175 | | HK | M-YW-L | | BK | | | $55.00 |
| The Hood | 6175 | | USA | M-YW-L | | BK | BK-RF | | $60.00 |
| The Hood | 6175 | | HK | M-YW-L | | BK | BK-RF | | $60.00 |
| The Hood | 6175 | | USA | M-YW-L | | GY | | | $55.00 |
| The Hood | 6175 | | HK | M-YW-L | | GY | | | $55.00 |
| The Hood | 6175 | | USA | M-YW-L | | GY | BK-RF | | $60.00 |
| The Hood | 6175 | | HK | M-YW-L | | GY | BK-RF | | $60.00 |
| The Hood | 6175 | | USA | M-YW-L | | BR-D | | | $55.00 |
| The Hood | 6175 | | HK | M-YW-L | | BR-D | | | $55.00 |
| The Hood | 6175 | | USA | M-YW-L | | BR-D | BK-RF | | $60.00 |
| The Hood | 6175 | | HK | M-YW-L | | BR-D | BK-RF | | $60.00 |
| | | | | | | | | | |
| Short Order | 6176 | | HK | M-AQ | | BK | | | $75.00 |
| Short Order | 6176 | | HK | M-BL | | BK | | | $125.00 |

## 1971 Variations

| Name | Number | Casting | Country | Color | Windows | Interior | Paint | Other | Value |
|---|---|---|---|---|---|---|---|---|---|
| Short Order | 6176 | | HK | M-GD | | BK | | | $75.00 |
| Short Order | 6176 | | HK | M-GR | | BK | | | $75.00 |
| Short Order | 6176 | | HK | M-GR-E | | BK | | | $80.00 |
| Short Order | 6176 | | HK | M-GR-L | | BK | | | $75.00 |
| Short Order | 6176 | | HK | M-GR-O | | BK | | | $75.00 |
| Short Order | 6176 | | HK | M-MG | | BK | | | $110.00 |
| Short Order | 6176 | | HK | M-OR | | BK | | | $110.00 |
| Short Order | 6176 | | HK | M-PR | | BK | | | $250.00 |
| Short Order | 6176 | | HK | M-RD | | BK | | | $75.00 |
| Short Order | 6176 | | HK | M-RD-R | | BK | | | $80.00 |
| Short Order | 6176 | | HK | M-YW | | BK | | | $75.00 |
| Short Order | 6176 | | HK | M-YW-L | | BK | | | $80.00 |
| | | | | | | | | | |
| T-4-2 | 6177 | | HK | M-AQ | | BK | | | $80.00 |
| T-4-2 | 6177 | | HK | M-AQ | | GY | | | $80.00 |
| T-4-2 | 6177 | | HK | M-AQ | | BR-D | | | $80.00 |
| T-4-2 | 6177 | | HK | M-BL | | BK | | | $75.00 |
| T-4-2 | 6177 | | HK | M-BL | | GY | | | $75.00 |
| T-4-2 | 6177 | | HK | M-BL | | BR-D | | | $75.00 |
| T-4-2 | 6177 | | HK | M-BL-I | | BK | | | $80.00 |
| T-4-2 | 6177 | | HK | M-BL-I | | GY | | | $80.00 |
| T-4-2 | 6177 | | HK | M-BL-I | | BR-D | | | $80.00 |
| T-4-2 | 6177 | | HK | M-BL-P | | BK | | | $80.00 |
| T-4-2 | 6177 | | HK | M-BL-P | | GY | | | $80.00 |
| T-4-2 | 6177 | | HK | M-BL-P | | BR-D | | | $80.00 |
| T-4-2 | 6177 | | HK | M-GD | | BK | | | $75.00 |
| T-4-2 | 6177 | | HK | M-GD | | GY | | | $75.00 |
| T-4-2 | 6177 | | HK | M-GD | | BR-D | | | $75.00 |
| T-4-2 | 6177 | | HK | M-GR | | BK | | | $80.00 |
| T-4-2 | 6177 | | HK | M-GR | | GY | | | $80.00 |
| T-4-2 | 6177 | | HK | M-GR | | BR-D | | | $80.00 |
| T-4-2 | 6177 | | HK | M-GR-E | | BK | | | $90.00 |
| T-4-2 | 6177 | | HK | M-GR-E | | GY | | | $90.00 |
| T-4-2 | 6177 | | HK | M-GR-E | | BR-D | | | $90.00 |
| T-4-2 | 6177 | | HK | M-GR-L | | BK | | | $60.00 |
| T-4-2 | 6177 | | HK | M-GR-L | | GY | | | $60.00 |
| T-4-2 | 6177 | | HK | M-GR-L | | BR-D | | | $60.00 |
| T-4-2 | 6177 | | HK | M-MG | | BK | | | $140.00 |
| T-4-2 | 6177 | | HK | M-MG | | GY | | | $140.00 |
| T-4-2 | 6177 | | HK | M-MG | | BR-D | | | $140.00 |
| T-4-2 | 6177 | | HK | M-RD | | BK | | | $85.00 |
| T-4-2 | 6177 | | HK | M-RD | | GY | | | $85.00 |
| T-4-2 | 6177 | | HK | M-RD | | BR-D | | | $85.00 |
| T-4-2 | 6177 | | HK | M-RD-R | | BK | | | $95.00 |
| T-4-2 | 6177 | | HK | M-RD-R | | GY | | | $95.00 |
| T-4-2 | 6177 | | HK | M-RD-R | | BR-D | | | $95.00 |
| T-4-2 | 6177 | | HK | M-YW | | BK | | | $60.00 |
| T-4-2 | 6177 | | HK | M-YW | | GY | | | $60.00 |
| T-4-2 | 6177 | | HK | M-YW | | BR-D | | | $60.00 |
| T-4-2 | 6177 | | HK | M-YW-L | | BK | | | $70.00 |
| T-4-2 | 6177 | | HK | M-YW-L | | GY | | | $70.00 |
| T-4-2 | 6177 | | HK | M-YW-L | | BR-D | | | $70.00 |
| | | | | | | | | | |
| Jet Threat | 6179 | | HK | E-RD | | | | | $110.00 |
| Jet Threat | 6179 | | HK | M-AQ | | | | | $80.00 |
| Jet Threat | 6179 | | HK | M-BL | | | | | $85.00 |
| Jet Threat | 6179 | | HK | M-BL-I | | | | | $95.00 |
| Jet Threat | 6179 | | HK | M-BL-P | | | | | $95.00 |
| Jet Threat | 6179 | | HK | M-GD | | | | | $70.00 |
| Jet Threat | 6179 | | HK | M-GR | | | | | $85.00 |
| Jet Threat | 6179 | | HK | M-GR-E | | | | | $90.00 |
| Jet Threat | 6179 | | HK | M-GR-L | | | | | $80.00 |
| Jet Threat | 6179 | | HK | M-GR-O | | | | | $90.00 |
| Jet Threat | 6179 | | HK | M-MG | | | | | $110.00 |
| Jet Threat | 6179 | | HK | M-PR | | | | | $150.00 |
| Jet Threat | 6179 | | HK | M-RD | | | | | $110.00 |
| Jet Threat | 6179 | | HK | M-RD-R | | | | | $120.00 |
| Jet Threat | 6179 | | HK | M-YW | | | | | $70.00 |
| Jet Threat | 6179 | | HK | M-YW-L | | | | | $75.00 |

## 1971 Variations

| Name | Number | Casting | Country | Color | Windows | Interior | Paint | Other | Value |
|---|---|---|---|---|---|---|---|---|---|
| Pit Crew Car | 6183 | | HK | E-WH | | WH | | | $150.00 |
| Pit Crew Car | 6183 | | HK | E-WH | | BK | | | $150.00 |
| | | | | | | | | | |
| Ice "T" | 6184 | | HK | YW | | | | | $75.00 |
| | | | | | | | | | |
| Mutt Mobile | 6185 | | HK | M-AQ | | BK | | | $80.00 |
| Mutt Mobile | 6185 | | HK | M-BL | | BK | | | $400.00 |
| Mutt Mobile | 6185 | | HK | M-BL-I | | BK | | | $120.00 |
| Mutt Mobile | 6185 | | HK | M-BL-P | | BK | | | $110.00 |
| Mutt Mobile | 6185 | | HK | M-GD | | BK | | | $110.00 |
| Mutt Mobile | 6185 | | HK | M-MG | | BK | | | $150.00 |
| Mutt Mobile | 6185 | | HK | M-PK | | BK | | | $340.00 |
| Mutt Mobile | 6185 | | HK | M-PK-H | | BK | | | $340.00 |
| Mutt Mobile | 6185 | | HK | M-PK-S | | BK | | | $340.00 |
| Mutt Mobile | 6185 | | HK | M-PL | | BK | | | $140.00 |
| Mutt Mobile | 6185 | | HK | M-RD | | BK | | | $150.00 |
| Mutt Mobile | 6185 | | HK | M-RD-R | | BK | | | $160.00 |
| Mutt Mobile | 6185 | | HK | M-YW | | BK | | | $110.00 |
| | | | | | | | | | |
| Rocket Bye Baby | 6186 | | HK | M-AQ | | WH | | | $80.00 |
| Rocket Bye Baby | 6186 | | HK | M-AQ | | BK | | | $70.00 |
| Rocket Bye Baby | 6186 | | HK | M-AQ | | GY | | | $70.00 |
| Rocket Bye Baby | 6186 | | HK | M-AQ | | BR-L | | | $70.00 |
| Rocket Bye Baby | 6186 | | HK | M-AQ | | BR-D | | | $70.00 |
| Rocket Bye Baby | 6186 | | HK | M-BL | | WH | | | $80.00 |
| Rocket Bye Baby | 6186 | | HK | M-BL | | BK | | | $70.00 |
| Rocket Bye Baby | 6186 | | HK | M-BL | | GY | | | $70.00 |
| Rocket Bye Baby | 6186 | | HK | M-BL | | BR-L | | | $70.00 |
| Rocket Bye Baby | 6186 | | HK | M-BL | | BR-D | | | $70.00 |
| Rocket Bye Baby | 6186 | | HK | M-GD | | WH | | | $140.00 |
| Rocket Bye Baby | 6186 | | HK | M-GD | | BK | | | $130.00 |
| Rocket Bye Baby | 6186 | | HK | M-GD | | GY | | | $130.00 |
| Rocket Bye Baby | 6186 | | HK | M-GD | | BR-L | | | $130.00 |
| Rocket Bye Baby | 6186 | | HK | M-GD | | BR-D | | | $130.00 |
| Rocket Bye Baby | 6186 | | HK | M-GR | | WH | | | $85.00 |
| Rocket Bye Baby | 6186 | | HK | M-GR | | BK | | | $75.00 |
| Rocket Bye Baby | 6186 | | HK | M-GR | | GY | | | $75.00 |
| Rocket Bye Baby | 6186 | | HK | M-GR | | BR-L | | | $75.00 |
| Rocket Bye Baby | 6186 | | HK | M-GR | | BR-D | | | $75.00 |
| Rocket Bye Baby | 6186 | | HK | M-GR-E | | WH | | | $95.00 |
| Rocket Bye Baby | 6186 | | HK | M-GR-E | | BK | | | $85.00 |
| Rocket Bye Baby | 6186 | | HK | M-GR-E | | GY | | | $85.00 |
| Rocket Bye Baby | 6186 | | HK | M-GR-E | | BR-L | | | $85.00 |
| Rocket Bye Baby | 6186 | | HK | M-GR-E | | BR-D | | | $85.00 |
| Rocket Bye Baby | 6186 | | HK | M-GR-L | | WH | | | $150.00 |
| Rocket Bye Baby | 6186 | | HK | M-GR-L | | BK | | | $140.00 |
| Rocket Bye Baby | 6186 | | HK | M-GR-L | | GY | | | $140.00 |
| Rocket Bye Baby | 6186 | | HK | M-GR-L | | BR-L | | | $140.00 |
| Rocket Bye Baby | 6186 | | HK | M-GR-L | | BR-D | | | $140.00 |
| Rocket Bye Baby | 6186 | | HK | M-GR-O | | WH | | | $95.00 |
| Rocket Bye Baby | 6186 | | HK | M-GR-O | | BK | | | $95.00 |
| Rocket Bye Baby | 6186 | | HK | M-GR-O | | GY | | | $95.00 |
| Rocket Bye Baby | 6186 | | HK | M-GR-O | | BR-L | | | $95.00 |
| Rocket Bye Baby | 6186 | | HK | M-GR-O | | BR-D | | | $95.00 |
| Rocket Bye Baby | 6186 | | HK | M-MG | | WH | | | $150.00 |
| Rocket Bye Baby | 6186 | | HK | M-MG | | BK | | | $140.00 |
| Rocket Bye Baby | 6186 | | HK | M-MG | | GY | | | $140.00 |
| Rocket Bye Baby | 6186 | | HK | M-MG | | BR-L | | | $140.00 |
| Rocket Bye Baby | 6186 | | HK | M-MG | | BR-D | | | $140.00 |
| Rocket Bye Baby | 6186 | | HK | M-RD | | WH | | | $150.00 |
| Rocket Bye Baby | 6186 | | HK | M-RD | | BK | | | $140.00 |
| Rocket Bye Baby | 6186 | | HK | M-RD | | GY | | | $140.00 |
| Rocket Bye Baby | 6186 | | HK | M-RD | | BR-L | | | $140.00 |
| Rocket Bye Baby | 6186 | | HK | M-RD | | BR-D | | | $140.00 |
| Rocket Bye Baby | 6186 | | HK | M-RD-R | | WH | | | $160.00 |
| Rocket Bye Baby | 6186 | | HK | M-RD-R | | BK | | | $150.00 |
| Rocket Bye Baby | 6186 | | HK | M-RD-R | | GY | | | $150.00 |
| Rocket Bye Baby | 6186 | | HK | M-RD-R | | BR-L | | | $150.00 |
| Rocket Bye Baby | 6186 | | HK | M-RD-R | | BR-D | | | $150.00 |
| Rocket Bye Baby | 6186 | | HK | M-YW | | WH | | | $140.00 |

## 1971 Variations

| Name | Number | Casting | Country | Color | Windows | Interior | Paint | Other | Value |
|---|---|---|---|---|---|---|---|---|---|
| Rocket Bye Baby | 6186 | | HK | M-YW | | BK | | | $130.00 |
| Rocket Bye Baby | 6186 | | HK | M-YW | | GY | | | $130.00 |
| Rocket Bye Baby | 6186 | | HK | M-YW | | BR-L | | | $130.00 |
| Rocket Bye Baby | 6186 | | HK | M-YW | | BR-D | | | $130.00 |
| Rocket Bye Baby | 6186 | | HK | M-YW-L | | WH | | | $160.00 |
| Rocket Bye Baby | 6186 | | HK | M-YW-L | | BK | | | $150.00 |
| Rocket Bye Baby | 6186 | | HK | M-YW-L | | GY | | | $150.00 |
| Rocket Bye Baby | 6186 | | HK | M-YW-L | | BR-L | | | $150.00 |
| Rocket Bye Baby | 6186 | | HK | M-YW-L | | BR-D | | | $150.00 |
| Bye-Focal | 6187 | | HK | M-AQ | CL-HD | BR-L | | Rear air intake | $125.00 |
| Bye-Focal | 6187 | | HK | M-AQ | CL-HD | BR-D | | Rear air intake | $125.00 |
| Bye-Focal | 6187 | | HK | M-AQ | CL-HD | BR-L | | Front air intake | $130.00 |
| Bye-Focal | 6187 | | HK | M-AQ | CL-HD | BR-D | | Front air intake | $130.00 |
| Bye-Focal | 6187 | | HK | M-AQ | TNT-HD | BR-L | | Rear air intake | $115.00 |
| Bye-Focal | 6187 | | HK | M-AQ | TNT-HD | BR-D | | Rear air intake | $115.00 |
| Bye-Focal | 6187 | | HK | M-AQ | TNT-HD | BR-L | | Front air intake | $125.00 |
| Bye-Focal | 6187 | | HK | M-AQ | TNT-HD | BR-D | | Front air intake | $125.00 |
| Bye-Focal | 6187 | | HK | M-BL | CL-HD | BR-L | | Rear air intake | $130.00 |
| Bye-Focal | 6187 | | HK | M-BL | CL-HD | BR-D | | Rear air intake | $130.00 |
| Bye-Focal | 6187 | | HK | M-BL | CL-HD | BR-L | | Front air intake | $140.00 |
| Bye-Focal | 6187 | | HK | M-BL | CL-HD | BR-D | | Front air intake | $140.00 |
| Bye-Focal | 6187 | | HK | M-BL | TNT-HD | BR-L | | Rear air intake | $125.00 |
| Bye-Focal | 6187 | | HK | M-BL | TNT-HD | BR-D | | Rear air intake | $125.00 |
| Bye-Focal | 6187 | | HK | M-BL | TNT-HD | BR-L | | Front air intake | $130.00 |
| Bye-Focal | 6187 | | HK | M-BL | TNT-HD | BR-D | | Front air intake | $130.00 |
| Bye-Focal | 6187 | | HK | M-BL-I | CL-HD | BR-L | | Rear air intake | $150.00 |
| Bye-Focal | 6187 | | HK | M-BL-I | CL-HD | BR-D | | Rear air intake | $150.00 |
| Bye-Focal | 6187 | | HK | M-BL-I | CL-HD | BR-L | | Front air intake | $160.00 |
| Bye-Focal | 6187 | | HK | M-BL-I | CL-HD | BR-D | | Front air intake | $160.00 |
| Bye-Focal | 6187 | | HK | M-BL-I | TNT-HD | BR-L | | Rear air intake | $140.00 |
| Bye-Focal | 6187 | | HK | M-BL-I | TNT-HD | BR-D | | Rear air intake | $140.00 |
| Bye-Focal | 6187 | | HK | M-BL-I | TNT-HD | BR-L | | Front air intake | $150.00 |
| Bye-Focal | 6187 | | HK | M-BL-I | TNT-HD | BR-D | | Front air intake | $150.00 |
| Bye-Focal | 6187 | | HK | M-BL-P | CL-HD | BR-L | | Rear air intake | $135.00 |
| Bye-Focal | 6187 | | HK | M-BL-P | CL-HD | BR-D | | Rear air intake | $135.00 |
| Bye-Focal | 6187 | | HK | M-BL-P | CL-HD | BR-L | | Front air intake | $145.00 |
| Bye-Focal | 6187 | | HK | M-BL-P | CL-HD | BR-D | | Front air intake | $145.00 |
| Bye-Focal | 6187 | | HK | M-BL-P | TNT-HD | BR-L | | Rear air intake | $125.00 |
| Bye-Focal | 6187 | | HK | M-BL-P | TNT-HD | BR-D | | Rear air intake | $125.00 |
| Bye-Focal | 6187 | | HK | M-BL-P | TNT-HD | BR-L | | Front air intake | $135.00 |
| Bye-Focal | 6187 | | HK | M-BL-P | TNT-HD | BR-D | | Front air intake | $135.00 |
| Bye-Focal | 6187 | | HK | M-GD | CL-HD | BR-L | | Rear air intake | $100.00 |
| Bye-Focal | 6187 | | HK | M-GD | CL-HD | BR-D | | Rear air intake | $100.00 |
| Bye-Focal | 6187 | | HK | M-GD | CL-HD | BR-L | | Front air intake | $100.00 |
| Bye-Focal | 6187 | | HK | M-GD | TNT-HD | BR-D | | Front air intake | $100.00 |
| Bye-Focal | 6187 | | HK | M-GD | TNT-HD | BR-L | | Rear air intake | $100.00 |
| Bye-Focal | 6187 | | HK | M-GD | TNT-HD | BR-D | | Rear air intake | $100.00 |
| Bye-Focal | 6187 | | HK | M-GD | TNT-HD | BR-L | | Front air intake | $100.00 |
| Bye-Focal | 6187 | | HK | M-GD | TNT-HD | BR-D | | Front air intake | $100.00 |
| Bye-Focal | 6187 | | HK | M-GR | CL-HD | BR-L | | Rear air intake | $135.00 |
| Bye-Focal | 6187 | | HK | M-GR | CL-HD | BR-D | | Rear air intake | $135.00 |
| Bye-Focal | 6187 | | HK | M-GR | CL-HD | BR-L | | Front air intake | $140.00 |
| Bye-Focal | 6187 | | HK | M-GR | CL-HD | BR-D | | Front air intake | $140.00 |
| Bye-Focal | 6187 | | HK | M-GR | TNT-HD | BR-L | | Rear air intake | $125.00 |
| Bye-Focal | 6187 | | HK | M-GR | TNT-HD | BR-D | | Rear air intake | $125.00 |
| Bye-Focal | 6187 | | HK | M-GR | TNT-HD | BR-L | | Front air intake | $130.00 |
| Bye-Focal | 6187 | | HK | M-GR | TNT-HD | BR-D | | Front air intake | $140.00 |
| Bye-Focal | 6187 | | HK | M-GR-E | CL-HD | BR-L | | Rear air intake | $145.00 |
| Bye-Focal | 6187 | | HK | M-GR-E | CL-HD | BR-D | | Rear air intake | $145.00 |
| Bye-Focal | 6187 | | HK | M-GR-E | CL-HD | BR-L | | Front air intake | $155.00 |
| Bye-Focal | 6187 | | HK | M-GR-E | CL-HD | BR-D | | Front air intake | $145.00 |
| Bye-Focal | 6187 | | HK | M-GR-E | TNT-HD | BR-L | | Rear air intake | $125.00 |
| Bye-Focal | 6187 | | HK | M-GR-E | TNT-HD | BR-D | | Rear air intake | $125.00 |
| Bye-Focal | 6187 | | HK | M-GR-E | TNT-HD | BR-L | | Front air intake | $130.00 |
| Bye-Focal | 6187 | | HK | M-GR-E | TNT-HD | BR-D | | Front air intake | $130.00 |
| Bye-Focal | 6187 | | HK | M-GR-L | CL-HD | BR-L | | Rear air intake | $145.00 |
| Bye-Focal | 6187 | | HK | M-GR-L | CL-HD | BR-D | | Rear air intake | $145.00 |
| Bye-Focal | 6187 | | HK | M-GR-L | CL-HD | BR-L | | Front air intake | $155.00 |
| Bye-Focal | 6187 | | HK | M-GR-L | CL-HD | BR-D | | Front air intake | $155.00 |
| Bye-Focal | 6187 | | HK | M-GR-L | TNT-HD | BR-L | | Rear air intake | $135.00 |

## 1971 Variations

| Name | Number | Casting | Country | Color | Windows | Interior | Paint | Other | Value |
|---|---|---|---|---|---|---|---|---|---|
| Bye-Focal | 6187 | | HK | M-GR-L | TNT-HD | BR-D | | Rear air intake | $135.00 |
| Bye-Focal | 6187 | | HK | M-GR-L | TNT-HD | BR-L | | Front air intake | $145.00 |
| Bye-Focal | 6187 | | HK | M-GR-L | TNT-HD | BR-D | | Front air intake | $145.00 |
| Bye-Focal | 6187 | | HK | M-GR-O | CL-HD | BR-L | | Rear air intake | $260.00 |
| Bye-Focal | 6187 | | HK | M-GR-O | CL-HD | BR-D | | Rear air intake | $260.00 |
| Bye-Focal | 6187 | | HK | M-GR-O | CL-HD | BR-L | | Front air intake | $280.00 |
| Bye-Focal | 6187 | | HK | M-GR-O | CL-HD | BR-D | | Front air intake | $280.00 |
| Bye-Focal | 6187 | | HK | M-GR-O | TNT-HD | BR-L | | Rear air intake | $240.00 |
| Bye-Focal | 6187 | | HK | M-GR-O | TNT-HD | BR-D | | Rear air intake | $240.00 |
| Bye-Focal | 6187 | | HK | M-GR-O | TNT-HD | BR-L | | Front air intake | $260.00 |
| Bye-Focal | 6187 | | HK | M-GR-O | TNT-HD | BR-D | | Front air intake | $260.00 |
| Bye-Focal | 6187 | | HK | M-MG | CL-HD | BR-L | | Rear air intake | $150.00 |
| Bye-Focal | 6187 | | HK | M-MG | CL-HD | BR-D | | Rear air intake | $150.00 |
| Bye-Focal | 6187 | | HK | M-MG | CL-HD | BR-L | | Front air intake | $155.00 |
| Bye-Focal | 6187 | | HK | M-MG | CL-HD | BR-D | | Front air intake | $155.00 |
| Bye-Focal | 6187 | | HK | M-MG | TNT-HD | BR-L | | Rear air intake | $145.00 |
| Bye-Focal | 6187 | | HK | M-MG | TNT-HD | BR-D | | Rear air intake | $145.00 |
| Bye-Focal | 6187 | | HK | M-MG | TNT-HD | BR-L | | Front air intake | $150.00 |
| Bye-Focal | 6187 | | HK | M-MG | TNT-HD | BR-D | | Front air intake | $150.00 |
| Bye-Focal | 6187 | | HK | M-PK | CL-HD | BR-L | | Rear air intake | $300.00 |
| Bye-Focal | 6187 | | HK | M-PK | CL-HD | BR-D | | Rear air intake | $300.00 |
| Bye-Focal | 6187 | | HK | M-PK | CL-HD | BR-L | | Front air intake | $320.00 |
| Bye-Focal | 6187 | | HK | M-PK | CL-HD | BR-D | | Front air intake | $320.00 |
| Bye-Focal | 6187 | | HK | M-PK | TNT-HD | BR-L | | Rear air intake | $280.00 |
| Bye-Focal | 6187 | | HK | M-PK | TNT-HD | BR-D | | Rear air intake | $280.00 |
| Bye-Focal | 6187 | | HK | M-PK | TNT-HD | BR-L | | Front air intake | $300.00 |
| Bye-Focal | 6187 | | HK | M-PK | TNT-HD | BR-D | | Front air intake | $300.00 |
| Bye-Focal | 6187 | | HK | M-PK-H | CL-HD | BR-L | | Rear air intake | $300.00 |
| Bye-Focal | 6187 | | HK | M-PK-H | CL-HD | BR-D | | Rear air intake | $300.00 |
| Bye-Focal | 6187 | | HK | M-PK-H | CL-IID | BR-L | | Front air intake | $320.00 |
| Bye-Focal | 6187 | | HK | M-PK-H | CL-HD | BR-D | | Front air intake | $320.00 |
| Bye-Focal | 6187 | | HK | M-PK-H | TNT-HD | BR-L | | Rear air intake | $280.00 |
| Bye-Focal | 6187 | | HK | M-PK-H | TNT-HD | BR-D | | Rear air intake | $280.00 |
| Bye-Focal | 6187 | | HK | M-PK-H | TNT-HD | BR-L | | Front air intake | $300.00 |
| Bye-Focal | 6187 | | HK | M-PK-H | TNT-HD | BR-D | | Front air intake | $300.00 |
| Bye-Focal | 6187 | | HK | M-PK-S | CL-HD | BR-L | | Rear air intake | $300.00 |
| Bye-Focal | 6187 | | HK | M-PK-S | CL-HD | BR-D | | Rear air intake | $300.00 |
| Bye-Focal | 6187 | | HK | M-PK-S | CL-HD | BR-L | | Front air intake | $320.00 |
| Bye-Focal | 6187 | | HK | M-PK-S | CL-HD | BR-D | | Front air intake | $320.00 |
| Bye-Focal | 6187 | | HK | M-PK-S | TNT-HD | BR-L | | Rear air intake | $280.00 |
| Bye-Focal | 6187 | | HK | M-PK-S | TNT-HD | BR-D | | Rear air intake | $280.00 |
| Bye-Focal | 6187 | | HK | M-PK-S | TNT-HD | BR-L | | Front air intake | $300.00 |
| Bye-Focal | 6187 | | HK | M-PK-S | TNT-HD | BR-D | | Front air intake | $300.00 |
| Bye-Focal | 6187 | | HK | M-PR | CL-HD | BR-L | | Rear air intake | $95.00 |
| Bye-Focal | 6187 | | HK | M-PR | CL-HD | BR-D | | Rear air intake | $95.00 |
| Bye-Focal | 6187 | | HK | M-PR | CL-HD | BR-L | | Front air intake | $105.00 |
| Bye-Focal | 6187 | | HK | M-PR | CL-HD | BR-D | | Front air intake | $105.00 |
| Bye-Focal | 6187 | | HK | M-PR | TNT-HD | BR-L | | Rear air intake | $85.00 |
| Bye-Focal | 6187 | | HK | M-PR | TNT-HD | BR-D | | Rear air intake | $85.00 |
| Bye-Focal | 6187 | | HK | M-PR | TNT-HD | BR-L | | Front air intake | $95.00 |
| Bye-Focal | 6187 | | HK | M-PR | TNT-HD | BR-D | | Front air intake | $95.00 |
| Bye-Focal | 6187 | | HK | M-RD | CL-HD | BR-L | | Rear air intake | $100.00 |
| Bye-Focal | 6187 | | HK | M-RD | CL-HD | BR-D | | Rear air intake | $100.00 |
| Bye-Focal | 6187 | | HK | M-RD | CL-HD | BR-L | | Front air intake | $100.00 |
| Bye-Focal | 6187 | | HK | M-RD | CL-HD | BR-D | | Front air intake | $100.00 |
| Bye-Focal | 6187 | | HK | M-RD | TNT-HD | BR-L | | Rear air intake | $100.00 |
| Bye-Focal | 6187 | | HK | M-RD | TNT-HD | BR-D | | Rear air intake | $100.00 |
| Bye-Focal | 6187 | | HK | M-RD | TNT-HD | BR-L | | Front air intake | $100.00 |
| Bye-Focal | 6187 | | HK | M-RD | TNT-HD | BR-D | | Front air intake | $100.00 |
| Bye-Focal | 6187 | | HK | M-RD-R | CL-HD | BR-L | | Rear air intake | $100.00 |
| Bye-Focal | 6187 | | HK | M-RD-R | CL-HD | BR-D | | Rear air intake | $100.00 |
| Bye-Focal | 6187 | | HK | M-RD-R | CL-HD | BR-L | | Front air intake | $100.00 |
| Bye-Focal | 6187 | | HK | M-RD-R | CL-HD | BR-D | | Front air intake | $100.00 |
| Bye-Focal | 6187 | | HK | M-RD-R | TNT-HD | BR-L | | Rear air intake | $100.00 |
| Bye-Focal | 6187 | | HK | M-RD-R | TNT-HD | BR-D | | Rear air intake | $100.00 |
| Bye-Focal | 6187 | | HK | M-RD-R | TNT-HD | BR-L | | Front air intake | $100.00 |
| Bye-Focal | 6187 | | HK | M-RD-R | TNT-HD | BR-D | | Front air intake | $100.00 |
| Bye-Focal | 6187 | | HK | M-YW-L | CL-HD | BR-L | | Rear air intake | $140.00 |
| Bye-Focal | 6187 | | HK | M-YW-L | CL-HD | BR-D | | Rear air intake | $140.00 |
| Bye-Focal | 6187 | | HK | M-YW-L | CL-HD | BR-L | | Front air intake | $150.00 |
| Bye-Focal | 6187 | | HK | M-YW-L | CL-HD | BR-D | | Front air intake | $150.00 |
| Bye-Focal | 6187 | | HK | M-YW-L | TNT-HD | BR-L | | Rear air intake | $130.00 |

## 1971 Variations

| Name | Number | Casting | Country | Color | Windows | Interior | Paint | Other | Value |
|---|---|---|---|---|---|---|---|---|---|
| Bye-Focal | 6187 | | HK | M-YW-L | TNT-HD | BR-D | | Rear air intake | $130.00 |
| Bye-Focal | 6187 | | HK | M-YW-L | TNT-HD | BR-L | | Front air intake | $140.00 |
| Bye-Focal | 6187 | | HK | M-YW-L | TNT-HD | BR-D | | Front air intake | $140.00 |
| | | | | | | | | | |
| Strip Teaser | 6188 | | HK | M-AQ | | BK | | | $95.00 |
| Strip Teaser | 6188 | | HK | M-BL | | BK | | | $110.00 |
| Strip Teaser | 6188 | | HK | M-BL-I | | BK | | | $160.00 |
| Strip Teaser | 6188 | | HK | M-BL-P | | BK | | | $150.00 |
| Strip Teaser | 6188 | | HK | M-GD | | BK | | | $110.00 |
| Strip Teaser | 6188 | | HK | M-GR | | BK | | | $110.00 |
| Strip Teaser | 6188 | | HK | M-GR-E | | BK | | | $110.00 |
| Strip Teaser | 6188 | | HK | M-GR-L | | BK | | | $130.00 |
| Strip Teaser | 6188 | | HK | M-GR-O | | BK | | | $110.00 |
| Strip Teaser | 6188 | | HK | M-MG | | BK | | | $220.00 |
| Strip Teaser | 6188 | | HK | M-RD | | BK | | | $110.00 |
| Strip Teaser | 6188 | | HK | M-RD-R | | BK | | | $110.00 |
| Strip Teaser | 6188 | | HK | M-YW | | BK | | | $110.00 |
| Strip Teaser | 6188 | | HK | M-YW-L | | BK | | | $140.00 |
| | | | | | | | | | |
| Waste Wagon | 6192 | | HK | M-AQ | | WH | | YW container | $130.00 |
| Waste Wagon | 6192 | | HK | M-AQ | | WH | | OR container | $130.00 |
| Waste Wagon | 6192 | | HK | M-AQ | | BK | | YW container | $120.00 |
| Waste Wagon | 6192 | | HK | M-AQ | | BK | | OR container | $120.00 |
| Waste Wagon | 6192 | | HK | M-AQ | | GY | | YW container | $120.00 |
| Waste Wagon | 6192 | | HK | M-AQ | | GY | | OR container | $120.00 |
| Waste Wagon | 6192 | | HK | M-AQ | | BR-L | | YW container | $120.00 |
| Waste Wagon | 6192 | | HK | M-AQ | | BR-L | | OR container | $120.00 |
| Waste Wagon | 6192 | | HK | M-AQ | | BR-D | | YW container | $120.00 |
| Waste Wagon | 6192 | | HK | M-AQ | | BR-D | | OR container | $120.00 |
| Waste Wagon | 6192 | | HK | M-BL | | WH | | YW container | $120.00 |
| Waste Wagon | 6192 | | HK | M-BL | | WH | | OR container | $120.00 |
| Waste Wagon | 6192 | | HK | M-BL | | BK | | YW container | $110.00 |
| Waste Wagon | 6192 | | HK | M-BL | | BK | | OR container | $110.00 |
| Waste Wagon | 6192 | | HK | M-BL | | GY | | YW container | $110.00 |
| Waste Wagon | 6192 | | HK | M-BL | | GY | | OR container | $110.00 |
| Waste Wagon | 6192 | | HK | M-BL | | BR-L | | YW container | $110.00 |
| Waste Wagon | 6192 | | HK | M-BL | | BR-L | | OR container | $110.00 |
| Waste Wagon | 6192 | | HK | M-BL | | BR-D | | YW container | $110.00 |
| Waste Wagon | 6192 | | HK | M-BL | | BR-D | | OR container | $110.00 |
| Waste Wagon | 6192 | | HK | M-BR-D | | WH | | YW container | $140.00 |
| Waste Wagon | 6192 | | HK | M-BR-D | | WH | | OR container | $140.00 |
| Waste Wagon | 6192 | | HK | M-BR-D | | BK | | YW container | $130.00 |
| Waste Wagon | 6192 | | HK | M-BR-D | | BK | | OR container | $130.00 |
| Waste Wagon | 6192 | | HK | M-BR-D | | GY | | YW container | $130.00 |
| Waste Wagon | 6192 | | HK | M-BR-D | | GY | | OR container | $130.00 |
| Waste Wagon | 6192 | | HK | M-BR-D | | BR-L | | YW container | $130.00 |
| Waste Wagon | 6192 | | HK | M-BR-D | | BR-L | | OR container | $130.00 |
| Waste Wagon | 6192 | | HK | M-BR-D | | BR-D | | YW container | $130.00 |
| Waste Wagon | 6192 | | HK | M-BR-D | | BR-D | | OR container | $130.00 |
| Waste Wagon | 6192 | | HK | M-BR-P | | WH | | YW container | $130.00 |
| Waste Wagon | 6192 | | HK | M-BR-P | | WH | | OR container | $130.00 |
| Waste Wagon | 6192 | | HK | M-BR-P | | BK | | YW container | $120.00 |
| Waste Wagon | 6192 | | HK | M-BR-P | | BK | | OR container | $120.00 |
| Waste Wagon | 6192 | | HK | M-BR-P | | GY | | YW container | $120.00 |
| Waste Wagon | 6192 | | HK | M-BR-P | | GY | | OR container | $120.00 |
| Waste Wagon | 6192 | | HK | M-BR-P | | BR-L | | YW container | $120.00 |
| Waste Wagon | 6192 | | HK | M-BR-P | | BR-L | | OR container | $120.00 |
| Waste Wagon | 6192 | | HK | M-BR-P | | BR-D | | YW container | $120.00 |
| Waste Wagon | 6192 | | HK | M-BR-P | | BR-D | | OR container | $120.00 |
| Waste Wagon | 6192 | | HK | M-GD | | WH | | YW container | $120.00 |
| Waste Wagon | 6192 | | HK | M-GD | | WH | | OR container | $120.00 |
| Waste Wagon | 6192 | | HK | M-GD | | BK | | YW container | $110.00 |
| Waste Wagon | 6192 | | HK | M-GD | | BK | | OR container | $110.00 |
| Waste Wagon | 6192 | | HK | M-GD | | GY | | YW container | $110.00 |
| Waste Wagon | 6192 | | HK | M-GD | | GY | | OR container | $110.00 |
| Waste Wagon | 6192 | | HK | M-GD | | BR-L | | YW container | $110.00 |
| Waste Wagon | 6192 | | HK | M-GD | | BR-L | | OR container | $110.00 |
| Waste Wagon | 6192 | | HK | M-GD | | BR-D | | YW container | $110.00 |
| Waste Wagon | 6192 | | HK | M-GD | | BR-D | | OR container | $110.00 |
| Waste Wagon | 6192 | | HK | M-GR | | WH | | YW container | $120.00 |
| Waste Wagon | 6192 | | HK | M-GR | | WH | | OR container | $120.00 |

## 1971 Variations

| Name | Number | Casting | Country | Color | Windows | Interior | Paint | Other | Value |
|---|---|---|---|---|---|---|---|---|---|
| Waste Wagon | 6192 | | HK | M-GR | | BK | | YW container | $110.00 |
| Waste Wagon | 6192 | | HK | M-GR | | BK | | OR container | $110.00 |
| Waste Wagon | 6192 | | HK | M-GR | | GY | | YW container | $110.00 |
| Waste Wagon | 6192 | | HK | M-GR | | GY | | OR container | $110.00 |
| Waste Wagon | 6192 | | HK | M-GR | | BR-L | | YW container | $110.00 |
| Waste Wagon | 6192 | | HK | M-GR | | BR-L | | OR container | $110.00 |
| Waste Wagon | 6192 | | HK | M-GR | | BR-D | | YW container | $110.00 |
| Waste Wagon | 6192 | | HK | M-GR | | BR-D | | OR container | $110.00 |
| Waste Wagon | 6192 | | HK | M-GR-E | | WH | | YW container | $130.00 |
| Waste Wagon | 6192 | | HK | M-GR-E | | WH | | OR container | $130.00 |
| Waste Wagon | 6192 | | HK | M-GR-E | | BK | | YW container | $120.00 |
| Waste Wagon | 6192 | | HK | M-GR-E | | BK | | OR container | $120.00 |
| Waste Wagon | 6192 | | HK | M-GR-E | | GY | | YW container | $120.00 |
| Waste Wagon | 6192 | | HK | M-GR-E | | GY | | OR container | $120.00 |
| Waste Wagon | 6192 | | HK | M-GR-E | | BR-L | | YW container | $120.00 |
| Waste Wagon | 6192 | | HK | M-GR-E | | BR-L | | OR container | $120.00 |
| Waste Wagon | 6192 | | HK | M-GR-E | | BR-D | | YW container | $120.00 |
| Waste Wagon | 6192 | | HK | M-GR-E | | BR-D | | OR container | $120.00 |
| Waste Wagon | 6192 | | HK | M-GR-L | | WH | | YW container | $120.00 |
| Waste Wagon | 6192 | | HK | M-GR-L | | WH | | OR container | $120.00 |
| Waste Wagon | 6192 | | HK | M-GR-L | | BK | | YW container | $110.00 |
| Waste Wagon | 6192 | | HK | M-GR-L | | BK | | OR container | $110.00 |
| Waste Wagon | 6192 | | HK | M-GR-L | | GY | | YW container | $110.00 |
| Waste Wagon | 6192 | | HK | M-GR-L | | GY | | OR container | $110.00 |
| Waste Wagon | 6192 | | HK | M-GR-L | | BR-L | | YW container | $110.00 |
| Waste Wagon | 6192 | | HK | M-GR-L | | BR-L | | OR container | $110.00 |
| Waste Wagon | 6192 | | HK | M-GR-L | | BR-D | | YW container | $110.00 |
| Waste Wagon | 6192 | | HK | M-GR-L | | BR-D | | OR container | $110.00 |
| Waste Wagon | 6192 | | HK | M-MG | | WH | | YW container | $120.00 |
| Waste Wagon | 6192 | | HK | M-MG | | WH | | OR container | $120.00 |
| Waste Wagon | 6192 | | HK | M-MG | | BK | | YW container | $110.00 |
| Waste Wagon | 6192 | | HK | M-MG | | BK | | OR container | $110.00 |
| Waste Wagon | 6192 | | HK | M-MG | | GY | | YW container | $110.00 |
| Waste Wagon | 6192 | | HK | M-MG | | GY | | OR container | $110.00 |
| Waste Wagon | 6192 | | HK | M-MG | | BR-L | | YW container | $110.00 |
| Waste Wagon | 6192 | | HK | M-MG | | BR-L | | OR container | $110.00 |
| Waste Wagon | 6192 | | HK | M-MG | | BR-D | | YW container | $110.00 |
| Waste Wagon | 6192 | | HK | M-MG | | BR-D | | OR container | $110.00 |
| Waste Wagon | 6192 | | HK | M-OR | | WH | | YW container | $130.00 |
| Waste Wagon | 6192 | | HK | M-OR | | WH | | OR container | $130.00 |
| Waste Wagon | 6192 | | HK | M-OR | | BK | | YW container | $120.00 |
| Waste Wagon | 6192 | | HK | M-OR | | BK | | OR container | $120.00 |
| Waste Wagon | 6192 | | HK | M-OR | | GY | | YW container | $120.00 |
| Waste Wagon | 6192 | | HK | M-OR | | GY | | OR container | $120.00 |
| Waste Wagon | 6192 | | HK | M-OR | | BR-L | | YW container | $120.00 |
| Waste Wagon | 6192 | | HK | M-OR | | BR-L | | OR container | $120.00 |
| Waste Wagon | 6192 | | HK | M-OR | | BR-D | | YW container | $120.00 |
| Waste Wagon | 6192 | | HK | M-OR | | BR-D | | OR container | $120.00 |
| Waste Wagon | 6192 | | HK | M-PK | | WH | | YW container | $180.00 |
| Waste Wagon | 6192 | | HK | M-PK | | WH | | OR container | $180.00 |
| Waste Wagon | 6192 | | HK | M-PK | | BK | | YW container | $170.00 |
| Waste Wagon | 6192 | | HK | M-PK | | BK | | OR container | $170.00 |
| Waste Wagon | 6192 | | HK | M-PK | | GY | | YW container | $170.00 |
| Waste Wagon | 6192 | | HK | M-PK | | GY | | OR container | $170.00 |
| Waste Wagon | 6192 | | HK | M-PK | | BR-L | | YW container | $170.00 |
| Waste Wagon | 6192 | | HK | M-PK | | BR-L | | OR container | $170.00 |
| Waste Wagon | 6192 | | HK | M-PK | | BR-D | | YW container | $170.00 |
| Waste Wagon | 6192 | | HK | M-PK | | BR-D | | OR container | $170.00 |
| Waste Wagon | 6192 | | HK | M-PK-H | | WH | | YW container | $180.00 |
| Waste Wagon | 6192 | | HK | M-PK-H | | WH | | OR container | $180.00 |
| Waste Wagon | 6192 | | HK | M-PK-H | | BK | | YW container | $170.00 |
| Waste Wagon | 6192 | | HK | M-PK-H | | BK | | OR container | $170.00 |
| Waste Wagon | 6192 | | HK | M-PK-H | | GY | | YW container | $170.00 |
| Waste Wagon | 6192 | | HK | M-PK-H | | GY | | OR container | $170.00 |
| Waste Wagon | 6192 | | HK | M-PK-H | | BR-L | | YW container | $170.00 |
| Waste Wagon | 6192 | | HK | M-PK-H | | BR-L | | OR container | $170.00 |
| Waste Wagon | 6192 | | HK | M-PK-H | | BR-D | | YW container | $170.00 |
| Waste Wagon | 6192 | | HK | M-PK-H | | BR-D | | OR container | $170.00 |
| Waste Wagon | 6192 | | HK | M-PK-S | | WH | | YW container | $180.00 |
| Waste Wagon | 6192 | | HK | M-PK-S | | WH | | OR container | $180.00 |
| Waste Wagon | 6192 | | HK | M-PK-S | | BK | | YW container | $170.00 |
| Waste Wagon | 6192 | | HK | M-PK-S | | BK | | OR container | $160.00 |

## 1971 Variations

| Name | Number | Casting | Country | Color | Windows | Interior | Paint | Other | Value |
|---|---|---|---|---|---|---|---|---|---|
| Waste Wagon | 6192 | | HK | M-PK-S | | GY | | YW container | $160.00 |
| Waste Wagon | 6192 | | HK | M-PK-S | | GY | | OR container | $160.00 |
| Waste Wagon | 6192 | | HK | M-PK-S | | BR-L | | YW container | $160.00 |
| Waste Wagon | 6192 | | HK | M-PK-S | | BR-L | | OR container | $160.00 |
| Waste Wagon | 6192 | | HK | M-PK-S | | BR-D | | YW container | $160.00 |
| Waste Wagon | 6192 | | HK | M-PK-S | | BR-D | | OR container | $160.00 |
| Waste Wagon | 6192 | | HK | M-PR | | WH | | YW container | $130.00 |
| Waste Wagon | 6192 | | HK | M-PR | | WH | | OR container | $130.00 |
| Waste Wagon | 6192 | | HK | M-PR | | BK | | YW container | $120.00 |
| Waste Wagon | 6192 | | HK | M-PR | | BK | | OR container | $120.00 |
| Waste Wagon | 6192 | | HK | M-PR | | GY | | YW container | $120.00 |
| Waste Wagon | 6192 | | HK | M-PR | | GY | | OR container | $120.00 |
| Waste Wagon | 6192 | | HK | M-PR | | BR-L | | YW container | $120.00 |
| Waste Wagon | 6192 | | HK | M-PR | | BR-L | | OR container | $120.00 |
| Waste Wagon | 6192 | | HK | M-PR | | BR-D | | YW container | $120.00 |
| Waste Wagon | 6192 | | HK | M-PR | | BR-D | | OR container | $120.00 |
| Waste Wagon | 6192 | | HK | M-RD | | WH | | YW container | $120.00 |
| Waste Wagon | 6192 | | HK | M-RD | | WH | | OR container | $120.00 |
| Waste Wagon | 6192 | | HK | M-RD | | BK | | YW container | $110.00 |
| Waste Wagon | 6192 | | HK | M-RD | | BK | | OR container | $110.00 |
| Waste Wagon | 6192 | | HK | M-RD | | GY | | YW container | $110.00 |
| Waste Wagon | 6192 | | HK | M-RD | | GY | | OR container | $110.00 |
| Waste Wagon | 6192 | | HK | M-RD | | BR-L | | YW container | $110.00 |
| Waste Wagon | 6192 | | HK | M-RD | | BR-L | | OR container | $110.00 |
| Waste Wagon | 6192 | | HK | M-RD | | BR-D | | YW container | $110.00 |
| Waste Wagon | 6192 | | HK | M-RD | | BR-D | | OR container | $110.00 |
| Waste Wagon | 6192 | | HK | M-RD-R | | WH | | YW container | $130.00 |
| Waste Wagon | 6192 | | HK | M-RD-R | | WH | | OR container | $130.00 |
| Waste Wagon | 6192 | | HK | M-RD-R | | BK | | YW container | $120.00 |
| Waste Wagon | 6192 | | HK | M-RD-R | | BK | | OR container | $120.00 |
| Waste Wagon | 6192 | | HK | M-RD-R | | GY | | YW container | $120.00 |
| Waste Wagon | 6192 | | HK | M-RD-R | | GY | | OR container | $120.00 |
| Waste Wagon | 6192 | | HK | M-RD-R | | BR-L | | YW container | $120.00 |
| Waste Wagon | 6192 | | HK | M-RD-R | | BR-L | | OR container | $120.00 |
| Waste Wagon | 6192 | | HK | M-RD-R | | BR-D | | YW container | $120.00 |
| Waste Wagon | 6192 | | HK | M-RD-R | | BR-D | | OR container | $120.00 |
| Waste Wagon | 6192 | | HK | M-YW | | WH | | YW container | $120.00 |
| Waste Wagon | 6192 | | HK | M-YW | | WH | | OR container | $120.00 |
| Waste Wagon | 6192 | | HK | M-YW | | BK | | YW container | $110.00 |
| Waste Wagon | 6192 | | HK | M-YW | | BK | | OR container | $110.00 |
| Waste Wagon | 6192 | | HK | M-YW | | GY | | YW container | $110.00 |
| Waste Wagon | 6192 | | HK | M-YW | | GY | | OR container | $110.00 |
| Waste Wagon | 6192 | | HK | M-YW | | BR-L | | YW container | $110.00 |
| Waste Wagon | 6192 | | HK | M-YW | | BR-L | | OR container | $110.00 |
| Waste Wagon | 6192 | | HK | M-YW | | BR-D | | YW container | $110.00 |
| Waste Wagon | 6192 | | HK | M-YW | | BR-D | | OR container | $110.00 |
| Waste Wagon | 6192 | | HK | M-YW-L | | WH | | YW container | $130.00 |
| Waste Wagon | 6192 | | HK | M-YW-L | | WH | | OR container | $130.00 |
| Waste Wagon | 6192 | | HK | M-YW-L | | BK | | YW container | $120.00 |
| Waste Wagon | 6192 | | HK | M-YW-L | | BK | | OR container | $120.00 |
| Waste Wagon | 6192 | | HK | M-YW-L | | GY | | YW container | $120.00 |
| Waste Wagon | 6192 | | HK | M-YW-L | | GY | | OR container | $120.00 |
| Waste Wagon | 6192 | | HK | M-YW-L | | BR-L | | YW container | $120.00 |
| Waste Wagon | 6192 | | HK | M-YW-L | | BR-L | | OR container | $120.00 |
| Waste Wagon | 6192 | | HK | M-YW-L | | BR-D | | YW container | $120.00 |
| Waste Wagon | 6192 | | HK | M-YW-L | | BR-D | | OR container | $120.00 |
| | | | | | | | | | |
| Scooper | 6193 | | HK | M-AQ | | WH | | | $130.00 |
| Scooper | 6193 | | HK | M-AQ | | BK | | | $120.00 |
| Scooper | 6193 | | HK | M-AQ | | GY | | | $120.00 |
| Scooper | 6193 | | HK | M-AQ | | BR-L | | | $120.00 |
| Scooper | 6193 | | HK | M-AQ | | BR-D | | | $120.00 |
| Scooper | 6193 | | HK | M-BL | | WH | | | $120.00 |
| Scooper | 6193 | | HK | M-BL | | BK | | | $110.00 |
| Scooper | 6193 | | HK | M-BL | | GY | | | $110.00 |
| Scooper | 6193 | | HK | M-BL | | BR-L | | | $110.00 |
| Scooper | 6193 | | HK | M-BL | | BR-D | | | $110.00 |
| Scooper | 6193 | | HK | M-GD | | WH | | | $120.00 |
| Scooper | 6193 | | HK | M-GD | | BK | | | $110.00 |
| Scooper | 6193 | | HK | M-GD | | GY | | | $110.00 |
| Scooper | 6193 | | HK | M-GD | | BR-L | | | $110.00 |

## 1971 Variations

| Name | Number | Casting | Country | Color | Windows | Interior | Paint | Other | Value |
|---|---|---|---|---|---|---|---|---|---|
| Scooper | 6193 | | HK | M-GD | | BR-D | | | $110.00 |
| Scooper | 6193 | | HK | M-GR | | WH | | | $120.00 |
| Scooper | 6193 | | HK | M-GR | | BK | | | $110.00 |
| Scooper | 6193 | | HK | M-GR | | GY | | | $110.00 |
| Scooper | 6193 | | HK | M-GR | | BR-L | | | $110.00 |
| Scooper | 6193 | | HK | M-GR | | BR-D | | | $110.00 |
| Scooper | 6193 | | HK | M-GR-E | | WH | | | $130.00 |
| Scooper | 6193 | | HK | M-GR-E | | BK | | | $120.00 |
| Scooper | 6193 | | HK | M-GR-E | | GY | | | $120.00 |
| Scooper | 6193 | | HK | M-GR-E | | BR-L | | | $120.00 |
| Scooper | 6193 | | HK | M-GR-E | | BR-D | | | $120.00 |
| Scooper | 6193 | | HK | M-GR-L | | WH | | | $120.00 |
| Scooper | 6193 | | HK | M-GR-L | | BK | | | $110.00 |
| Scooper | 6193 | | HK | M-GR-L | | GY | | | $110.00 |
| Scooper | 6193 | | HK | M-GR-L | | BR-L | | | $110.00 |
| Scooper | 6193 | | HK | M-GR-L | | BR-D | | | $110.00 |
| Scooper | 6193 | | HK | M-GR-O | | WH | | | $120.00 |
| Scooper | 6193 | | HK | M-GR-O | | BK | | | $110.00 |
| Scooper | 6193 | | HK | M-GR-O | | GY | | | $110.00 |
| Scooper | 6193 | | HK | M-GR-O | | BR-L | | | $110.00 |
| Scooper | 6193 | | HK | M-GR-O | | BR-D | | | $110.00 |
| Scooper | 6193 | | HK | M-MG | | WH | | | $130.00 |
| Scooper | 6193 | | HK | M-MG | | BK | | | $120.00 |
| Scooper | 6193 | | HK | M-MG | | GY | | | $120.00 |
| Scooper | 6193 | | HK | M-MG | | BR-L | | | $120.00 |
| Scooper | 6193 | | HK | M-MG | | BR-D | | | $120.00 |
| Scooper | 6193 | | HK | M-PR | | BK | | Back/Scooper same color | $300.00 |
| Scooper | 6193 | | HK | M-RD | | WH | | | $130.00 |
| Scooper | 6193 | | HK | M-RD | | BK | | | $120.00 |
| Scooper | 6193 | | HK | M-RD | | GY | | | $120.00 |
| Scooper | 6193 | | HK | M-RD | | BR-L | | | $120.00 |
| Scooper | 6193 | | HK | M-RD | | BR-D | | | $120.00 |
| Scooper | 6193 | | HK | M-RD-R | | WH | | | $140.00 |
| Scooper | 6193 | | HK | M-RD-R | | BK | | | $130.00 |
| Scooper | 6193 | | HK | M-RD-R | | GY | | | $130.00 |
| Scooper | 6193 | | HK | M-RD-R | | BR-L | | | $130.00 |
| Scooper | 6193 | | HK | M-RD-R | | BR-D | | | $130.00 |
| Scooper | 6193 | | HK | M-YW | | WH | | | $120.00 |
| Scooper | 6193 | | HK | M-YW | | BK | | | $110.00 |
| Scooper | 6193 | | HK | M-YW | | GY | | | $110.00 |
| Scooper | 6193 | | HK | M-YW | | BR-L | | | $110.00 |
| Scooper | 6193 | | HK | M-YW | | BR-D | | | $110.00 |
| Scooper | 6193 | | HK | M-YW-L | | WH | | | $130.00 |
| Scooper | 6193 | | HK | M-YW-L | | BK | | | $120.00 |
| Scooper | 6193 | | HK | M-YW-L | | GY | | | $120.00 |
| Scooper | 6193 | | HK | M-YW-L | | BR-L | | | $120.00 |
| Scooper | 6193 | | HK | M-YW-L | | BR-D | | | $120.00 |
| Racer Rig | 6194 | | HK | E-WH | | WH | | | $150.00 |
| Racer Rig | 6194 | | HK | E-WH | | BK | | | $140.00 |
| Racer Rig | 6194 | | HK | E-WH | | GY | | | $140.00 |
| Racer Rig | 6194 | | HK | E-WH | | BR-L | | | $140.00 |
| Racer Rig | 6194 | | HK | E-WH | | BR-D | | | $140.00 |
| Racer Rig | 6194 | | HK | M-RD | | WH | | | $135.00 |
| Racer Rig | 6194 | | HK | M-RD | | BK | | | $125.00 |
| Racer Rig | 6194 | | HK | M-RD | | GY | | | $125.00 |
| Racer Rig | 6194 | | HK | M-RD | | BR-L | | | $125.00 |
| Racer Rig | 6194 | | HK | M-RD | | BR-D | | | $125.00 |
| Boss Hoss | 6407 | | HK | M-AQ | | WH | | | $125.00 |
| Boss Hoss | 6407 | | HK | M-AQ | | WH | BK-RF | | | $145.00 |
| Boss Hoss | 6407 | | HK | M-AQ | | BK | | | $115.00 |
| Boss Hoss | 6407 | | HK | M-AQ | | BK | BK-RF | | | $135.00 |
| Boss Hoss | 6407 | | HK | M-AQ | | GY | | | $115.00 |
| Boss Hoss | 6407 | | HK | M-AQ | | GY | BK-RF | | | $135.00 |
| Boss Hoss | 6407 | | HK | M-AQ | | BR-L | | | $115.00 |
| Boss Hoss | 6407 | | HK | M-AQ | | BR-L | BK-RF | | | $135.00 |
| Boss Hoss | 6407 | | HK | M-AQ | | BR-D | | | $115.00 |
| Boss Hoss | 6407 | | HK | M-AQ | | BR-D | BK-RF | | | $135.00 |
| Boss Hoss | 6407 | | HK | M-BL | | WH | | | $125.00 |
| Boss Hoss | 6407 | | HK | M-BL | | WH | BK-RF | | | $145.00 |

## 1971 Variations

| Name | Number | Casting | Country | Color | Windows | Interior | Paint | Other | Value |
|---|---|---|---|---|---|---|---|---|---|
| Boss Hoss | 6407 | | HK | M-BL | | BK | | | $115.00 |
| Boss Hoss | 6407 | | HK | M-BL | | BK | BK-RF | | $135.00 |
| Boss Hoss | 6407 | | HK | M-BL | | GY | | | $115.00 |
| Boss Hoss | 6407 | | HK | M-BL | | GY | BK-RF | | $135.00 |
| Boss Hoss | 6407 | | HK | M-BL | | BR-L | | | $115.00 |
| Boss Hoss | 6407 | | HK | M-BL | | BR-L | BK-RF | | $135.00 |
| Boss Hoss | 6407 | | HK | M-BL | | BR-D | | | $115.00 |
| Boss Hoss | 6407 | | HK | M-BL | | BR-D | BK-RF | | $135.00 |
| Boss Hoss | 6407 | | HK | M-BR-P | | WH | | | $125.00 |
| Boss Hoss | 6407 | | HK | M-BR-P | | WH | BK-RF | | $145.00 |
| Boss Hoss | 6407 | | HK | M-BR-P | | BK | | | $115.00 |
| Boss Hoss | 6407 | | HK | M-BR-P | | BK | BK-RF | | $135.00 |
| Boss Hoss | 6407 | | HK | M-BR-P | | GY | | | $115.00 |
| Boss Hoss | 6407 | | HK | M-BR-P | | GY | BK-RF | | $135.00 |
| Boss Hoss | 6407 | | HK | M-BR-P | | BR-L | | | $115.00 |
| Boss Hoss | 6407 | | HK | M-BR-P | | BR-L | BK-RF | | $135.00 |
| Boss Hoss | 6407 | | HK | M-BR-P | | BR-D | | | $115.00 |
| Boss Hoss | 6407 | | HK | M-BR-P | | BR-D | BK-RF | | $135.00 |
| Boss Hoss | 6407 | | HK | M-GR | | WH | | | $135.00 |
| Boss Hoss | 6407 | | HK | M-GR | | WH | BK-RF | | $155.00 |
| Boss Hoss | 6407 | | HK | M-GR | | BK | | | $125.00 |
| Boss Hoss | 6407 | | HK | M-GR | | BK | BK-RF | | $145.00 |
| Boss Hoss | 6407 | | HK | M-GR | | GY | | | $125.00 |
| Boss Hoss | 6407 | | HK | M-GR | | GY | BK-RF | | $145.00 |
| Boss Hoss | 6407 | | HK | M-GR | | BR-L | | | $125.00 |
| Boss Hoss | 6407 | | HK | M-GR | | BR-L | BK-RF | | $145.00 |
| Boss Hoss | 6407 | | HK | M-GR | | BR-D | | | $125.00 |
| Boss Hoss | 6407 | | HK | M-GR | | BR-D | BK-RF | | $145.00 |
| Boss Hoss | 6407 | | HK | M-GR-E | | WH | | | $135.00 |
| Boss Hoss | 6407 | | HK | M-GR-E | | WH | BK-RF | | $155.00 |
| Boss Hoss | 6407 | | HK | M-GR-E | | BK | | | $125.00 |
| Boss Hoss | 6407 | | HK | M-GR-E | | BK | BK-RF | | $145.00 |
| Boss Hoss | 6407 | | HK | M-GR-E | | GY | | | $125.00 |
| Boss Hoss | 6407 | | HK | M-GR-E | | GY | BK-RF | | $145.00 |
| Boss Hoss | 6407 | | HK | M-GR-E | | BR-L | | | $125.00 |
| Boss Hoss | 6407 | | HK | M-GR-E | | BR-L | BK-RF | | $145.00 |
| Boss Hoss | 6407 | | HK | M-GR-E | | BR-D | | | $125.00 |
| Boss Hoss | 6407 | | HK | M-GR-E | | BR-D | BK-RF | | $145.00 |
| Boss Hoss | 6407 | | HK | M-GR-O | | WH | | | $200.00 |
| Boss Hoss | 6407 | | HK | M-GR-O | | WH | BK-RF | | $225.00 |
| Boss Hoss | 6407 | | HK | M-GR-O | | BK | | | $200.00 |
| Boss Hoss | 6407 | | HK | M-GR-O | | BK | BK-RF | | $200.00 |
| Boss Hoss | 6407 | | HK | M-GR-O | | GY | | | $190.00 |
| Boss Hoss | 6407 | | HK | M-GR-O | | GY | BK-RF | | $225.00 |
| Boss Hoss | 6407 | | HK | M-GR-O | | BR-L | | | $190.00 |
| Boss Hoss | 6407 | | HK | M-GR-O | | BR-L | BK-RF | | $225.00 |
| Boss Hoss | 6407 | | HK | M-GR-O | | BR-D | | | $190.00 |
| Boss Hoss | 6407 | | HK | M-GR-O | | BR-D | BK-RF | | $225.00 |
| Boss Hoss | 6407 | | HK | M-MG | | WH | | | $140.00 |
| Boss Hoss | 6407 | | HK | M-MG | | WH | BK-RF | | $160.00 |
| Boss Hoss | 6407 | | HK | M-MG | | BK | | | $130.00 |
| Boss Hoss | 6407 | | HK | M-MG | | BK | BK-RF | | $150.00 |
| Boss Hoss | 6407 | | HK | M-MG | | GY | | | $130.00 |
| Boss Hoss | 6407 | | HK | M-MG | | GY | BK-RF | | $150.00 |
| Boss Hoss | 6407 | | HK | M-MG | | BR-L | | | $130.00 |
| Boss Hoss | 6407 | | HK | M-MG | | BR-L | BK-RF | | $150.00 |
| Boss Hoss | 6407 | | HK | M-MG | | BR-D | | | $130.00 |
| Boss Hoss | 6407 | | HK | M-MG | | BR-D | BK-RF | | $150.00 |
| Boss Hoss | 6407 | | HK | M-OR | | WH | | | $120.00 |
| Boss Hoss | 6407 | | HK | M-OR | | WH | BK-RF | | $140.00 |
| Boss Hoss | 6407 | | HK | M-OR | | BK | | | $110.00 |
| Boss Hoss | 6407 | | HK | M-OR | | BK | BK-RF | | $130.00 |
| Boss Hoss | 6407 | | HK | M-OR | | GY | | | $110.00 |
| Boss Hoss | 6407 | | HK | M-OR | | GY | BK-RF | | $130.00 |
| Boss Hoss | 6407 | | HK | M-OR | | BR-L | | | $110.00 |
| Boss Hoss | 6407 | | HK | M-OR | | BR-L | BK-RF | | $130.00 |
| Boss Hoss | 6407 | | HK | M-OR | | BR-D | | | $110.00 |
| Boss Hoss | 6407 | | HK | M-OR | | BR-D | BK-RF | | $130.00 |
| Boss Hoss | 6407 | | HK | M-PK | | WH | | | $150.00 |
| Boss Hoss | 6407 | | HK | M-PK | | WH | BK-RF | | $440.00 |
| Boss Hoss | 6407 | | HK | M-PK | | BK | | | $380.00 |
| Boss Hoss | 6407 | | HK | M-PK | | BK | BK-RF | | $420.00 |

## 1971 Variations

| Name | Number | Casting | Country | Color | Windows | Interior | Paint | Other | Value |
|---|---|---|---|---|---|---|---|---|---|
| Boss Hoss | 6407 | | HK | M-PK | | GY | | | $380.00 |
| Boss Hoss | 6407 | | HK | M-PK | | GY | BK-RF | | $420.00 |
| Boss Hoss | 6407 | | HK | M-PK | | BR-L | | | $380.00 |
| Boss Hoss | 6407 | | HK | M-PK | | BR-L | BK-RF | | $320.00 |
| Boss Hoss | 6407 | | HK | M-PK | | BR-D | | | $380.00 |
| Boss Hoss | 6407 | | HK | M-PK | | BR-D | BK-RF | | $420.00 |
| Boss Hoss | 6407 | | HK | M-PK-H | | WH | | | $400.00 |
| Boss Hoss | 6407 | | HK | M-PK-H | | WH | BK-RF | | $340.00 |
| Boss Hoss | 6407 | | HK | M-PK-H | | BK | | | $380.00 |
| Boss Hoss | 6407 | | HK | M-PK-H | | BK | BK-RF | | $420.00 |
| Boss Hoss | 6407 | | HK | M-PK-H | | GY | | | $380.00 |
| Boss Hoss | 6407 | | HK | M-PK-H | | GY | BK-RF | | $420.00 |
| Boss Hoss | 6407 | | HK | M-PK-H | | BR-L | | | $380.00 |
| Boss Hoss | 6407 | | HK | M-PK-H | | BR-L | BK-RF | | $420.00 |
| Boss Hoss | 6407 | | HK | M-PK-H | | BR-D | | | $380.00 |
| Boss Hoss | 6407 | | HK | M-PK-H | | BR-D | BK-RF | | $420.00 |
| Boss Hoss | 6407 | | HK | M-PK-S | | WH | | | $400.00 |
| Boss Hoss | 6407 | | HK | M-PK-S | | WH | BK-RF | | $440.00 |
| Boss Hoss | 6407 | | HK | M-PK-S | | BK | | | $380.00 |
| Boss Hoss | 6407 | | HK | M-PK-S | | BK | BK-RF | | $420.00 |
| Boss Hoss | 6407 | | HK | M-PK-S | | GY | | | $380.00 |
| Boss Hoss | 6407 | | HK | M-PK-S | | GY | BK-RF | | $420.00 |
| Boss Hoss | 6407 | | HK | M-PK-S | | BR-L | | | $380.00 |
| Boss Hoss | 6407 | | HK | M-PK-S | | BR-L | BK-RF | | $420.00 |
| Boss Hoss | 6407 | | HK | M-PK-S | | BR-D | | | $380.00 |
| Boss Hoss | 6407 | | HK | M-PK-S | | BR-D | BK-RF | | $420.00 |
| Boss Hoss | 6407 | | HK | M-PR | | WH | | | $260.00 |
| Boss Hoss | 6407 | | HK | M-PR | | WH | BK-RF | | $300.00 |
| Boss Hoss | 6407 | | HK | M-PR | | BK | | | $240.00 |
| Boss Hoss | 6407 | | HK | M-PR | | BK | BK-RF | | $280.00 |
| Boss Hoss | 6407 | | HK | M-PR | | GY | | | $240.00 |
| Boss Hoss | 6407 | | HK | M-PR | | GY | BK-RF | | $280.00 |
| Boss Hoss | 6407 | | HK | M-PR | | BR-L | | | $240.00 |
| Boss Hoss | 6407 | | HK | M-PR | | BR-L | BK-RF | | $280.00 |
| Boss Hoss | 6407 | | HK | M-PR | | BR-D | | | $240.00 |
| Boss Hoss | 6407 | | HK | M-PR | | BR-D | BK-RF | | $280.00 |
| Boss Hoss | 6407 | | HK | M-RD | | WH | | | $110.00 |
| Boss Hoss | 6407 | | HK | M-RD | | WH | BK-RF | | $130.00 |
| Boss Hoss | 6407 | | HK | M-RD | | BK | | | $100.00 |
| Boss Hoss | 6407 | | HK | M-RD | | BK | BK-RF | | $120.00 |
| Boss Hoss | 6407 | | HK | M-RD | | RD | | | $110.00 |
| Boss Hoss | 6407 | | HK | M-RD | | RD | BK-RF | | $130.00 |
| Boss Hoss | 6407 | | HK | M-RD | | GY | | | $100.00 |
| Boss Hoss | 6407 | | HK | M-RD | | GY | BK-RF | | $120.00 |
| Boss Hoss | 6407 | | HK | M-RD | | BR-L | | | $100.00 |
| Boss Hoss | 6407 | | HK | M-RD | | BR-L | BK-RF | | $120.00 |
| Boss Hoss | 6407 | | HK | M-RD | | BR-D | | | $100.00 |
| Boss Hoss | 6407 | | HK | M-RD | | BR-D | BK-RF | | $120.00 |
| Boss Hoss | 6407 | | HK | M-RD-R | | WH | | | $130.00 |
| Boss Hoss | 6407 | | HK | M-RD-R | | WH | BK-RF | | $150.00 |
| Boss Hoss | 6407 | | HK | M-RD-R | | BK | | | $120.00 |
| Boss Hoss | 6407 | | HK | M-RD-R | | BK | BK-RF | | $140.00 |
| Boss Hoss | 6407 | | HK | M-RD-R | | RD | | | $130.00 |
| Boss Hoss | 6407 | | HK | M-RD-R | | RD | BK-RF | | $150.00 |
| Boss Hoss | 6407 | | HK | M-RD-R | | GY | | | $100.00 |
| Boss Hoss | 6407 | | HK | M-RD-R | | GY | BK-RF | | $120.00 |
| Boss Hoss | 6407 | | HK | M-RD-R | | BR-L | | | $100.00 |
| Boss Hoss | 6407 | | HK | M-RD-R | | BR-L | BK-RF | | $120.00 |
| Boss Hoss | 6407 | | HK | M-RD-R | | BR-D | | | $100.00 |
| Boss Hoss | 6407 | | HK | M-RD-R | | BR-D | BK-RF | | $120.00 |
| Sugar Caddy | 6418 | | HK | M-AQ | BL | WH | | | $50.00 |
| Sugar Caddy | 6418 | | HK | M-AQ | BL | BK | | | $40.00 |
| Sugar Caddy | 6418 | | HK | M-AQ | BL | GY | | | $40.00 |
| Sugar Caddy | 6418 | | HK | M-AQ | BL | BR-L | | | $40.00 |
| Sugar Caddy | 6418 | | HK | M-AQ | BL | BR-D | | | $40.00 |
| Sugar Caddy | 6418 | | HK | M-BL | BL | WH | | | $50.00 |
| Sugar Caddy | 6418 | | HK | M-BL | BL | BK | | | $40.00 |
| Sugar Caddy | 6418 | | HK | M-BL | BL | GY | | | $40.00 |
| Sugar Caddy | 6418 | | HK | M-BL | BL | BR-L | | | $40.00 |
| Sugar Caddy | 6418 | | HK | M-BL | BL | BR-D | | | $40.00 |

## 1971 Variations

| Name | Number | Casting | Country | Color | Windows | Interior | Paint | Other | Value |
|---|---|---|---|---|---|---|---|---|---|
| Sugar Caddy | 6418 | | HK | M-BR-D | BL | WH | | | $70.00 |
| Sugar Caddy | 6418 | | HK | M-BR-D | BL | BK | | | $60.00 |
| Sugar Caddy | 6418 | | HK | M-BR-D | BL | GY | | | $60.00 |
| Sugar Caddy | 6418 | | HK | M-BR-D | BL | BR-L | | | $60.00 |
| Sugar Caddy | 6418 | | HK | M-BR-D | BL | BR-D | | | $60.00 |
| Sugar Caddy | 6418 | | HK | M-BR-P | BL | WH | | | $60.00 |
| Sugar Caddy | 6418 | | HK | M-BR-P | BL | BK | | | $50.00 |
| Sugar Caddy | 6418 | | HK | M-BR-P | BL | GY | | | $50.00 |
| Sugar Caddy | 6418 | | HK | M-BR-P | BL | BR-L | | | $50.00 |
| Sugar Caddy | 6418 | | HK | M-BR-P | BL | BR-D | | | $50.00 |
| Sugar Caddy | 6418 | | HK | M-GD | BL | WH | | | $50.00 |
| Sugar Caddy | 6418 | | HK | M-GD | BL | BK | | | $40.00 |
| Sugar Caddy | 6418 | | HK | M-GD | BL | GY | | | $40.00 |
| Sugar Caddy | 6418 | | HK | M-GD | BL | BR-L | | | $40.00 |
| Sugar Caddy | 6418 | | HK | M-GD | BL | BR-D | | | $40.00 |
| Sugar Caddy | 6418 | | HK | M-GR | BL | WH | | | $50.00 |
| Sugar Caddy | 6418 | | HK | M-GR | BL | BK | | | $40.00 |
| Sugar Caddy | 6418 | | HK | M-GR | BL | GY | | | $40.00 |
| Sugar Caddy | 6418 | | HK | M-GR | BL | BR-L | | | $40.00 |
| Sugar Caddy | 6418 | | HK | M-GR | BL | BR-D | | | $40.00 |
| Sugar Caddy | 6418 | | HK | M-GR-E | BL | WH | | | $60.00 |
| Sugar Caddy | 6418 | | HK | M-GR-E | BL | BK | | | $50.00 |
| Sugar Caddy | 6418 | | HK | M-GR-E | BL | GY | | | $50.00 |
| Sugar Caddy | 6418 | | HK | M-GR-E | BL | BR-L | | | $50.00 |
| Sugar Caddy | 6418 | | HK | M-GR-E | BL | BR-D | | | $50.00 |
| Sugar Caddy | 6418 | | HK | M-GR-L | BL | WH | | | $50.00 |
| Sugar Caddy | 6418 | | HK | M-GR-L | BL | BK | | | $40.00 |
| Sugar Caddy | 6418 | | HK | M-GR-L | BL | GY | | | $40.00 |
| Sugar Caddy | 6418 | | HK | M-GR-L | BL | BR-L | | | $40.00 |
| Sugar Caddy | 6418 | | HK | M-GR-L | BL | BR-D | | | $40.00 |
| Sugar Caddy | 6418 | | HK | M-GR-O | BL | WH | | | $60.00 |
| Sugar Caddy | 6418 | | HK | M-GR-O | BL | BK | | | $50.00 |
| Sugar Caddy | 6418 | | HK | M-GR-O | BL | GY | | | $50.00 |
| Sugar Caddy | 6418 | | HK | M-GR-O | BL | BR-L | | | $50.00 |
| Sugar Caddy | 6418 | | HK | M-GR-O | BL | BR-D | | | $50.00 |
| Sugar Caddy | 6418 | | HK | M-OR | BL | WH | | | $75.00 |
| Sugar Caddy | 6418 | | HK | M-OR | BL | BK | | | $65.00 |
| Sugar Caddy | 6418 | | HK | M-OR | BL | GY | | | $65.00 |
| Sugar Caddy | 6418 | | HK | M-OR | BL | BR-L | | | $65.00 |
| Sugar Caddy | 6418 | | HK | M-OR | BL | BR-D | | | $65.00 |
| Sugar Caddy | 6418 | | HK | M-PK | BL | WH | | | $130.00 |
| Sugar Caddy | 6418 | | HK | M-PK | BL | BK | | | $120.00 |
| Sugar Caddy | 6418 | | HK | M-PK | BL | GY | | | $120.00 |
| Sugar Caddy | 6418 | | HK | M-PK | BL | BR-L | | | $120.00 |
| Sugar Caddy | 6418 | | HK | M-PK | BL | BR-D | | | $120.00 |
| Sugar Caddy | 6418 | | HK | M-PK-H | BL | WH | | | $130.00 |
| Sugar Caddy | 6418 | | HK | M-PK-H | BL | BK | | | $120.00 |
| Sugar Caddy | 6418 | | HK | M-PK-H | BL | GY | | | $120.00 |
| Sugar Caddy | 6418 | | HK | M-PK-H | BL | BR-L | | | $120.00 |
| Sugar Caddy | 6418 | | HK | M-PK-H | BL | BR-D | | | $120.00 |
| Sugar Caddy | 6418 | | HK | M-PK-S | BL | WH | | | $130.00 |
| Sugar Caddy | 6418 | | HK | M-PK-S | BL | BK | | | $120.00 |
| Sugar Caddy | 6418 | | HK | M-PK-S | BL | GY | | | $120.00 |
| Sugar Caddy | 6418 | | HK | M-PK-S | BL | BR-L | | | $120.00 |
| Sugar Caddy | 6418 | | HK | M-PK-S | BL | BR-D | | | $120.00 |
| Sugar Caddy | 6418 | | HK | M-PR | BL | WH | | | $50.00 |
| Sugar Caddy | 6418 | | HK | M-PR | BL | BK | | | $40.00 |
| Sugar Caddy | 6418 | | HK | M-PR | BL | GY | | | $40.00 |
| Sugar Caddy | 6418 | | HK | M-PR | BL | BR-L | | | $40.00 |
| Sugar Caddy | 6418 | | HK | M-PR | BL | BR-D | | | $40.00 |
| Sugar Caddy | 6418 | | HK | M-RD | BL | WH | | | $50.00 |
| Sugar Caddy | 6418 | | HK | M-RD | BL | BK | | | $40.00 |
| Sugar Caddy | 6418 | | HK | M-RD | BL | GY | | | $40.00 |
| Sugar Caddy | 6418 | | HK | M-RD | BL | BR-L | | | $40.00 |
| Sugar Caddy | 6418 | | HK | M-RD | BL | BR-D | | | $40.00 |
| Sugar Caddy | 6418 | | HK | M-RD-R | BL | WH | | | $60.00 |
| Sugar Caddy | 6418 | | HK | M-RD-R | BL | BK | | | $50.00 |
| Sugar Caddy | 6418 | | HK | M-RD-R | BL | GY | | | $50.00 |
| Sugar Caddy | 6418 | | HK | M-RD-R | BL | BR-L | | | $50.00 |
| Sugar Caddy | 6418 | | HK | M-RD-R | BL | BR-D | | | $50.00 |
| Sugar Caddy | 6418 | | HK | M-YW | BL | WH | | | $50.00 |
| Sugar Caddy | 6418 | | HK | M-YW | BL | BK | | | $40.00 |

## 1971 Variations

| Name | Number | Casting | Country | Color | Windows | Interior | Paint | Other | Value |
|---|---|---|---|---|---|---|---|---|---|
| Sugar Caddy | 6418 | | HK | M-YW | BL | GY | | | $40.00 |
| Sugar Caddy | 6418 | | HK | M-YW | BL | BR-L | | | $40.00 |
| Sugar Caddy | 6418 | | HK | M-YW | BL | BR-D | | | $40.00 |
| Sugar Caddy | 6418 | | HK | M-YW-L | BL | WH | | | $60.00 |
| Sugar Caddy | 6418 | | HK | M-YW-L | BL | BK | | | $50.00 |
| Sugar Caddy | 6418 | | HK | M-YW-L | BL | GY | | | $50.00 |
| Sugar Caddy | 6418 | | HK | M-YW-L | BL | BR-L | | | $50.00 |
| Sugar Caddy | 6418 | | HK | M-YW-L | BL | BR-D | | | $50.00 |
| | | | | | | | | | |
| Hairy Hauler | 6458 | | USA | M-AQ | | WH | | | $60.00 |
| Hairy Hauler | 6458 | | USA | M-BL | | WH | | | $65.00 |
| Hairy Hauler | 6458 | | USA | M-BL-I | | WH | | | $100.00 |
| Hairy Hauler | 6458 | | USA | M-BL-P | | WH | | | $90.00 |
| Hairy Hauler | 6458 | | USA | M-GD | | WH | | | $65.00 |
| Hairy Hauler | 6458 | | USA | M-GR | | WH | | | $65.00 |
| Hairy Hauler | 6458 | | USA | M-GR-E | | WH | | | $70.00 |
| Hairy Hauler | 6458 | | USA | M-GR-L | | WH | | | $65.00 |
| Hairy Hauler | 6458 | | USA | M-GR-O | | WH | | | $65.00 |
| Hairy Hauler | 6458 | | USA | M-MG | | WH | | | $65.00 |
| Hairy Hauler | 6458 | | USA | M-PK | | WH | | | $150.00 |
| Hairy Hauler | 6458 | | USA | M-PK-H | | WH | | | $150.00 |
| Hairy Hauler | 6458 | | USA | M-PK-S | | WH | | | $150.00 |
| Hairy Hauler | 6458 | | USA | M-PR | | WH | | | $150.00 |
| Hairy Hauler | 6458 | | USA | M-RD | | WH | | | $65.00 |
| Hairy Hauler | 6458 | | USA | M-RD-R | | WH | | | $70.00 |
| Hairy Hauler | 6458 | | USA | M-YW | | WH | | | $65.00 |
| Hairy Hauler | 6458 | | USA | M-YW-L | | WH | | | $70.00 |
| | | | | | | | | | |
| AMX/2 | 6460 | | USA | M-AQ | | BK | | | $65.00 |
| AMX/2 | 6460 | | USA | M-BL | | BK | | | $110.00 |
| AMX/2 | 6460 | | USA | M-GD | | BK | | | $55.00 |
| AMX/2 | 6460 | | USA | M-GR | | BK | | | $55.00 |
| AMX/2 | 6460 | | USA | M-GR-E | | BK | | | $60.00 |
| AMX/2 | 6460 | | USA | M-GR-L | | BK | | | $55.00 |
| AMX/2 | 6460 | | USA | M-GR-O | | BK | | | $70.00 |
| AMX/2 | 6460 | | USA | M-MG | | BK | | | $55.00 |
| AMX/2 | 6460 | | USA | M-OR | | BK | | | $70.00 |
| AMX/2 | 6460 | | USA | M-PK | | BK | | | $65.00 |
| AMX/2 | 6460 | | USA | M-PK-H | | BK | | | $65.00 |
| AMX/2 | 6460 | | USA | M-PK-S | | BK | | | $65.00 |
| AMX/2 | 6460 | | USA | M-PL | | BK | | | $95.00 |
| AMX/2 | 6460 | | USA | M-PR | | BK | | | $95.00 |
| AMX/2 | 6460 | | USA | M-RD | | BK | | | $55.00 |
| AMX/2 | 6460 | | USA | M-RD-R | | BK | | | $60.00 |
| AMX/2 | 6460 | | USA | M-YW | | BK | | | $55.00 |
| AMX/2 | 6460 | | USA | M-YW-L | | BK | | | $60.00 |
| | | | | | | | | | |
| Grass Hopper | 6461 | | HK | M-AQ | | BK | | | $45.00 |
| Grass Hopper | 6461 | | HK | M-BL | | BK | | | $50.00 |
| Grass Hopper | 6461 | | HK | M-BR-D | | BK | | | $65.00 |
| Grass Hopper | 6461 | | HK | M-BR-P | | BK | | | $60.00 |
| Grass Hopper | 6461 | | HK | M-GD | | BK | | | $45.00 |
| Grass Hopper | 6461 | | HK | M-GR | | BK | | | $45.00 |
| Grass Hopper | 6461 | | HK | M-GR-E | | BK | | | $50.00 |
| Grass Hopper | 6461 | | HK | M-GR-L | | BK | | | $45.00 |
| Grass Hopper | 6461 | | HK | M-GR-O | | BK | | | $45.00 |
| Grass Hopper | 6461 | | HK | M-MG | | BK | | | $45.00 |
| Grass Hopper | 6461 | | HK | M-PK | | BK | | | $70.00 |
| Grass Hopper | 6461 | | HK | M-PK-H | | BK | | | $70.00 |
| Grass Hopper | 6461 | | HK | M-PK-S | | BK | | | $70.00 |
| Grass Hopper | 6461 | | HK | M-PR | | BK | | | $65.00 |
| Grass Hopper | 6461 | | HK | M-RD | | BK | | | $45.00 |
| Grass Hopper | 6461 | | HK | M-RD-R | | BK | | | $50.00 |
| Grass Hopper | 6461 | | HK | M-YW | | BK | | | $45.00 |
| Grass Hopper | 6461 | | HK | M-YW-L | | BK | | | $50.00 |
| | | | | | | | | | |
| Cockney Cab | 6466 | | USA | M-AQ | | BK | | | $60.00 |
| Cockney Cab | 6466 | | HK | M-AQ | | BK | | | $60.00 |
| Cockney Cab | 6466 | | USA | M-AQ | | GY | | | $60.00 |

## 1971 Variations

| Name | Number | Casting | Country | Color | Windows | Interior | Paint | Other | Value |
|---|---|---|---|---|---|---|---|---|---|
| Cockney Cab | 6466 | | HK | M-AQ | | GY | | | $60.00 |
| Cockney Cab | 6466 | | USA | M-BL | | BK | | | $60.00 |
| Cockney Cab | 6466 | | HK | M-BL | | BK | | | $60.00 |
| Cockney Cab | 6466 | | USA | M-BL | | GY | | | $60.00 |
| Cockney Cab | 6466 | | HK | M-BL | | GY | | | $60.00 |
| Cockney Cab | 6466 | | USA | M-BR-D | | BK | | | $70.00 |
| Cockney Cab | 6466 | | HK | M-BR-D | | BK | | | $70.00 |
| Cockney Cab | 6466 | | USA | M-BR-D | | GY | | | $70.00 |
| Cockney Cab | 6466 | | HK | M-BR-D | | GY | | | $70.00 |
| Cockney Cab | 6466 | | USA | M-BR-P | | BK | | | $65.00 |
| Cockney Cab | 6466 | | HK | M-BR-P | | BK | | | $65.00 |
| Cockney Cab | 6466 | | USA | M-BR-P | | GY | | | $65.00 |
| Cockney Cab | 6466 | | HK | M-BR-P | | GY | | | $65.00 |
| Cockney Cab | 6466 | | USA | M-GD | | BK | | | $55.00 |
| Cockney Cab | 6466 | | HK | M-GD | | BK | | | $55.00 |
| Cockney Cab | 6466 | | USA | M-GD | | GY | | | $55.00 |
| Cockney Cab | 6466 | | HK | M-GD | | GY | | | $55.00 |
| Cockney Cab | 6466 | | USA | M-GR | | BK | | | $55.00 |
| Cockney Cab | 6466 | | HK | M-GR | | BK | | | $55.00 |
| Cockney Cab | 6466 | | USA | M-GR | | GY | | | $55.00 |
| Cockney Cab | 6466 | | HK | M-GR | | GY | | | $55.00 |
| Cockney Cab | 6466 | | USA | M-GR-E | | BK | | | $60.00 |
| Cockney Cab | 6466 | | HK | M-GR-E | | BK | | | $60.00 |
| Cockney Cab | 6466 | | USA | M-GR-E | | GY | | | $60.00 |
| Cockney Cab | 6466 | | HK | M-GR-E | | GY | | | $60.00 |
| Cockney Cab | 6466 | | USA | M-GR-L | | BK | | | $55.00 |
| Cockney Cab | 6466 | | HK | M-GR-L | | BK | | | $55.00 |
| Cockney Cab | 6466 | | USA | M-GR-L | | GY | | | $55.00 |
| Cockney Cab | 6466 | | HK | M-GR-L | | GY | | | $55.00 |
| Cockney Cab | 6466 | | USA | M-GR-O | | BK | | | $55.00 |
| Cockney Cab | 6466 | | HK | M-GR-O | | BK | | | $55.00 |
| Cockney Cab | 6466 | | USA | M-GR-O | | GY | | | $55.00 |
| Cockney Cab | 6466 | | HK | M-GR-O | | GY | | | $55.00 |
| Cockney Cab | 6466 | | USA | M-MG | | BK | | | $55.00 |
| Cockney Cab | 6466 | | HK | M-MG | | BK | | | $55.00 |
| Cockney Cab | 6466 | | USA | M-MG | | GY | | | $55.00 |
| Cockney Cab | 6466 | | HK | M-MG | | GY | | | $55.00 |
| Cockney Cab | 6466 | | USA | M-PK | | BK | | | $60.00 |
| Cockney Cab | 6466 | | HK | M-PK | | BK | | | $60.00 |
| Cockney Cab | 6466 | | USA | M-PK | | GY | | | $60.00 |
| Cockney Cab | 6466 | | HK | M-PK | | GY | | | $60.00 |
| Cockney Cab | 6466 | | USA | M-PK-H | | BK | | | $60.00 |
| Cockney Cab | 6466 | | HK | M-PK-H | | BK | | | $60.00 |
| Cockney Cab | 6466 | | USA | M-PK-H | | GY | | | $60.00 |
| Cockney Cab | 6466 | | HK | M-PK-H | | GY | | | $60.00 |
| Cockney Cab | 6466 | | USA | M-PK-S | | BK | | | $60.00 |
| Cockney Cab | 6466 | | HK | M-PK-S | | BK | | | $60.00 |
| Cockney Cab | 6466 | | USA | M-PK-S | | GY | | | $60.00 |
| Cockney Cab | 6466 | | HK | M-PK-S | | GY | | | $60.00 |
| Cockney Cab | 6466 | | USA | M-PL | | BK | | | $60.00 |
| Cockney Cab | 6466 | | HK | M-PL | | BK | | | $60.00 |
| Cockney Cab | 6466 | | USA | M-PL | | GY | | | $60.00 |
| Cockney Cab | 6466 | | HK | M-PL | | GY | | | $60.00 |
| Cockney Cab | 6466 | | USA | M-RD | | BK | | | $55.00 |
| Cockney Cab | 6466 | | HK | M-RD | | BK | | | $55.00 |
| Cockney Cab | 6466 | | USA | M-RD | | GY | | | $55.00 |
| Cockney Cab | 6466 | | HK | M-RD | | GY | | | $55.00 |
| Cockney Cab | 6466 | | USA | M-RD-R | | BK | | | $60.00 |
| Cockney Cab | 6466 | | HK | M-RD-R | | BK | | | $60.00 |
| Cockney Cab | 6466 | | USA | M-RD-R | | GY | | | $60.00 |
| Cockney Cab | 6466 | | HK | M-RD-R | | GY | | | $60.00 |
| Cockney Cab | 6466 | | USA | M-YW | | BK | | | $55.00 |
| Cockney Cab | 6466 | | HK | M-YW | | BK | | | $55.00 |
| Cockney Cab | 6466 | | USA | M-YW | | GY | | | $55.00 |
| Cockney Cab | 6466 | | HK | M-YW | | GY | | | $55.00 |
| Cockney Cab | 6466 | | USA | M-YW-L | | BK | | | $60.00 |
| Cockney Cab | 6466 | | HK | M-YW-L | | BK | | | $60.00 |
| Cockney Cab | 6466 | | USA | M-YW-L | | GY | | | $60.00 |
| Cockney Cab | 6466 | | HK | M-YW-L | | GY | | | $60.00 |
| | | | | | | | | | |
| Olds 442 | 6467 | | USA | M-AQ | | WH | | | $550.00 |

## 1971 Variations

| Name | Number | Casting | Country | Color | Windows | Interior | Paint | Other | Value |
|---|---|---|---|---|---|---|---|---|---|
| Olds 442 | 6467 | | USA | M-BL | | WH | | | $450.00 |
| Olds 442 | 6467 | | USA | M-BL-I | | WH | | | $650.00 |
| Olds 442 | 6467 | | USA | M-BL-P | | WH | | | $600.00 |
| Olds 442 | 6467 | | USA | M-GD | | WH | | | $450.00 |
| Olds 442 | 6467 | | USA | M-GR | | WH | | | $450.00 |
| Olds 442 | 6467 | | USA | M-GR-E | | WH | | | $500.00 |
| Olds 442 | 6467 | | USA | M-GR-L | | WH | | | $450.00 |
| Olds 442 | 6467 | | USA | M-GR-O | | WH | | | $550.00 |
| Olds 442 | 6467 | | USA | M-MG | | WH | | | $450.00 |
| Olds 442 | 6467 | | USA | M-OR | | WH | | | $550.00 |
| Olds 442 | 6467 | | USA | M-OR | | BK | | | $500.00 |
| Olds 442 | 6467 | | USA | M-PK | | WH | | | $700.00 |
| Olds 442 | 6467 | | USA | M-PK-H | | WH | | | $700.00 |
| Olds 442 | 6467 | | USA | M-PK-S | | WH | | | $700.00 |
| Olds 442 | 6467 | | USA | M-RD | | WH | | | $450.00 |
| Olds 442 | 6467 | | USA | M-RD-R | | WH | | | $450.00 |
| Olds 442 | 6467 | | USA | M-YW | | WH | | | $450.00 |
| Olds 442 | 6467 | | USA | M-YW-L | | WH | | | $500.00 |
| Sc'ool Bus | 6468 | | HK | YW | | | | | $300.00 |
| Evil Weevil | 6471 | | HK | M-AQ | | WH | | | $65.00 |
| Evil Weevil | 6471 | | HK | M-AQ | | BK | | | $55.00 |
| Evil Weevil | 6471 | | HK | M-AQ | | GY | | | $55.00 |
| Evil Weevil | 6471 | | HK | M-AQ | | BR-L | | | $55.00 |
| Evil Weevil | 6471 | | HK | M-AQ | | BR-D | | | $55.00 |
| Evil Weevil | 6471 | | HK | M-BL | | WH | | | $60.00 |
| Evil Weevil | 6471 | | HK | M-BL | | BK | | | $50.00 |
| Evil Weevil | 6471 | | HK | M BL | | GY | | | $50.00 |
| Evil Weevil | 6471 | | HK | M-BL | | BR-L | | | $50.00 |
| Evil Weevil | 6471 | | HK | M-BL | | BR-D | | | $50.00 |
| Evil Weevil | 6471 | | HK | M-GD | | WH | | | $60.00 |
| Evil Weevil | 6471 | | HK | M-GD | | BK | | | $50.00 |
| Evil Weevil | 6471 | | HK | M-GD | | GY | | | $50.00 |
| Evil Weevil | 6471 | | HK | M-GD | | BR-L | | | $50.00 |
| Evil Weevil | 6471 | | HK | M-GD | | BR-D | | | $50.00 |
| Evil Weevil | 6471 | | HK | M-GR | | WH | | | $60.00 |
| Evil Weevil | 6471 | | HK | M-GR | | BK | | | $50.00 |
| Evil Weevil | 6471 | | HK | M-GR | | GY | | | $50.00 |
| Evil Weevil | 6471 | | HK | M-GR | | BR-L | | | $50.00 |
| Evil Weevil | 6471 | | HK | M-GR | | BR-D | | | $50.00 |
| Evil Weevil | 6471 | | HK | M-GR-E | | WH | | | $65.00 |
| Evil Weevil | 6471 | | HK | M-GR-E | | BK | | | $55.00 |
| Evil Weevil | 6471 | | HK | M-GR-E | | GY | | | $55.00 |
| Evil Weevil | 6471 | | HK | M-GR-E | | BR-L | | | $55.00 |
| Evil Weevil | 6471 | | HK | M-GR-E | | BR-D | | | $55.00 |
| Evil Weevil | 6471 | | HK | M-GR-L | | WH | | | $60.00 |
| Evil Weevil | 6471 | | HK | M-GR-L | | BK | | | $50.00 |
| Evil Weevil | 6471 | | HK | M-GR-L | | GY | | | $50.00 |
| Evil Weevil | 6471 | | HK | M-GR-L | | BR-L | | | $50.00 |
| Evil Weevil | 6471 | | HK | M-GR-L | | BR-D | | | $50.00 |
| Evil Weevil | 6471 | | HK | M-GR-O | | WH | | | $65.00 |
| Evil Weevil | 6471 | | HK | M-GR-O | | BK | | | $55.00 |
| Evil Weevil | 6471 | | HK | M-GR-O | | GY | | | $55.00 |
| Evil Weevil | 6471 | | HK | M-GR-O | | BR-L | | | $55.00 |
| Evil Weevil | 6471 | | HK | M-GR-O | | BR-D | | | $55.00 |
| Evil Weevil | 6471 | | HK | M-MG | | WH | | | $65.00 |
| Evil Weevil | 6471 | | HK | M-MG | | BK | | | $55.00 |
| Evil Weevil | 6471 | | HK | M-MG | | GY | | | $55.00 |
| Evil Weevil | 6471 | | HK | M-MG | | BR-L | | | $55.00 |
| Evil Weevil | 6471 | | HK | M-MG | | BR-D | | | $55.00 |
| Evil Weevil | 6471 | | HK | M-PL | | WH | | | $75.00 |
| Evil Weevil | 6471 | | HK | M-PL | | BK | | | $65.00 |
| Evil Weevil | 6471 | | HK | M-PL | | GY | | | $65.00 |
| Evil Weevil | 6471 | | HK | M-PL | | BR-L | | | $65.00 |
| Evil Weevil | 6471 | | HK | M-PL | | BR-D | | | $65.00 |
| Evil Weevil | 6471 | | HK | M-PR | | WH | | | $65.00 |
| Evil Weevil | 6471 | | HK | M-PR | | BK | | | $55.00 |
| Evil Weevil | 6471 | | HK | M-PR | | GY | | | $55.00 |
| Evil Weevil | 6471 | | HK | M-PR | | BR-L | | | $55.00 |
| Evil Weevil | 6471 | | HK | M-PR | | BR-D | | | $55.00 |

## 1971 Variations

| Name | Number | Casting | Country | Color | Windows | Interior | Paint | Other | Value |
|---|---|---|---|---|---|---|---|---|---|
| Evil Weevil | 6471 | | HK | M-RD | | WH | | | $60.00 |
| Evil Weevil | 6471 | | HK | M-RD | | BK | | | $50.00 |
| Evil Weevil | 6471 | | HK | M-RD | | GY | | | $50.00 |
| Evil Weevil | 6471 | | HK | M-RD | | BR-L | | | $50.00 |
| Evil Weevil | 6471 | | HK | M-RD | | BR-D | | | $50.00 |
| Evil Weevil | 6471 | | HK | M-RD-R | | WH | | | $65.00 |
| Evil Weevil | 6471 | | HK | M-RD-R | | BK | | | $55.00 |
| Evil Weevil | 6471 | | HK | M-RD-R | | GY | | | $55.00 |
| Evil Weevil | 6471 | | HK | M-RD-R | | BR-L | | | $55.00 |
| Evil Weevil | 6471 | | HK | M-RD-R | | BR-D | | | $55.00 |
| Evil Weevil | 6471 | | HK | M-YW | | WH | | | $60.00 |
| Evil Weevil | 6471 | | HK | M-YW | | BK | | | $50.00 |
| Evil Weevil | 6471 | | HK | M-YW | | GY | | | $50.00 |
| Evil Weevil | 6471 | | HK | M-YW | | BR-L | | | $50.00 |
| Evil Weevil | 6471 | | HK | M-YW | | BR-D | | | $50.00 |
| Evil Weevil | 6471 | | HK | M-YW-L | | WH | | | $65.00 |
| Evil Weevil | 6471 | | HK | M-YW-L | | BK | | | $55.00 |
| Evil Weevil | 6471 | | HK | M-YW-L | | GY | | | $55.00 |
| Evil Weevil | 6471 | | HK | M-YW-L | | BR-L | | | $55.00 |
| Evil Weevil | 6471 | | HK | M-YW-L | | BR-D | | | $55.00 |
| Classic Cord | 6472 | | USA | M-AQ | | BK | | | $500.00 |
| Classic Cord | 6472 | | USA | M-BL | | BK | | | $190.00 |
| Classic Cord | 6472 | | USA | M-BL-I | | BK | | | $350.00 |
| Classic Cord | 6472 | | USA | M-BL-P | | BK | | | $300.00 |
| Classic Cord | 6472 | | USA | M-BR-D | | BK | | | $200.00 |
| Classic Cord | 6472 | | USA | M-BR-P | | BK | | | $190.00 |
| Classic Cord | 6472 | | USA | M-GD | | BK | | | $190.00 |
| Classic Cord | 6472 | | USA | M-GR | | BK | | | $190.00 |
| Classic Cord | 6472 | | USA | M-GR-E | | BK | | | $200.00 |
| Classic Cord | 6472 | | USA | M-GR-L | | BK | | | $170.00 |
| Classic Cord | 6472 | | USA | M-MG | | BK | | | $170.00 |
| Classic Cord | 6472 | | USA | M-PK | | BK | | | $400.00 |
| Classic Cord | 6472 | | USA | M-PK-H | | BK | | | $400.00 |
| Classic Cord | 6472 | | USA | M-PK-S | | BK | | | $400.00 |
| Classic Cord | 6472 | | USA | M-PL | | BK | | | $400.00 |
| Classic Cord | 6472 | | USA | M-PR | | BK | | | $300.00 |
| Classic Cord | 6472 | | USA | M-RD | | BK | | | $215.00 |
| Classic Cord | 6472 | | USA | M-RD-R | | BK | | | $225.00 |
| Classic Cord | 6472 | | USA | M-YW | | BK | | | $190.00 |
| Classic Cord | 6472 | | USA | M-YW-L | | BK | | | $180.00 |

## 1972 Variations

| Name | Number | Casting | Country | Color | Windows | Interior | Paint | Other | Value |
|---|---|---|---|---|---|---|---|---|---|
| Rear Engine Mongoose | 5699 | | HK | BL | | | | BK front wheels | $250.00 |
| Rear Engine Mongoose | 5699 | | HK | BL | | | | CL front wheels | $250.00 |
| Rear Engine Snake | 5856 | | HK | YW | | | | BK front wheels | $250.00 |
| Rear Engine Snake | 5856 | | HK | YW | | | | CL front wheels | $250.00 |
| Open Fire | 5881 | | HK | M-BL | | BK | | | $300.00 |
| Open Fire | 5881 | | HK | M-GD | | BK | | | $175.00 |
| Open Fire | 5881 | | HK | M-GR-L | | BK | | | $220.00 |
| Open Fire | 5881 | | HK | M-MG | | BK | | | $175.00 |
| Open Fire | 5881 | | HK | M-PR | | BK | | | $220.00 |
| Open Fire | 5881 | | HK | M-RD | | BK | | | $175.00 |
| Open Fire | 5881 | | HK | M-RS-R | | BK | | | $185.00 |
| Open Fire | 5881 | | HK | M-YW | | BK | | | $175.00 |
| Open Fire | 5881 | | HK | M-YW-L | | BK | | | $230.00 |
| Funny Money | 6005 | | HK | GY | | | BL/YW | | $90.00 |
| Funny Money | 6005 | | HK | GY | | | BL/OR | | $120.00 |
| Ferrari 512 | 6021 | | HK | M-AQ | | BK | | | $170.00 |
| Ferrari 512 | 6021 | | HK | M-BL | | BK | | | $170.00 |
| Ferrari 512 | 6021 | | HK | M-GD | | BK | | | $150.00 |
| Ferrari 512 | 6021 | | HK | M-GR | | BK | | | $150.00 |
| Ferrari 512 | 6021 | | HK | M-GR-E | | BK | | | $160.00 |
| Ferrari 512 | 6021 | | HK | M-GR-L | | BK | | | $150.00 |
| Ferrari 512 | 6021 | | HK | M-MG | | BK | | | $150.00 |
| Ferrari 512 | 6021 | | HK | M-RD | | BK | | | $150.00 |
| Ferrari 512 | 6021 | | HK | M-RS-R | | BK | | | $160.00 |
| Ferrari 512 | 6021 | | HK | M-YW | | BK | | | $150.00 |
| Ferrari 512 | 6021 | | HK | M-YW-L | | BK | | | $150.00 |
| Side Kick | 6022 | | HK | M-AQ | | | | | $150.00 |
| Side Kick | 6022 | | HK | M-BL | | | | | $150.00 |
| Side Kick | 6022 | | HK | M-GD | | | | | $140.00 |
| Side Kick | 6022 | | HK | M-GR | | | | | $140.00 |
| Side Kick | 6022 | | HK | M-GR-E | | | | | $150.00 |
| Side Kick | 6022 | | HK | M-GR-L | | | | | $140.00 |
| Side Kick | 6022 | | HK | M-MG | | | | | $140.00 |
| Side Kick | 6022 | | HK | M-PK | | | | | $180.00 |
| Side Kick | 6022 | | HK | M-PK-H | | | | | $180.00 |
| Side Kick | 6022 | | HK | M-PK-S | | | | | $180.00 |
| Side Kick | 6022 | | HK | M-PR | | | | | $220.00 |
| Side Kick | 6022 | | HK | M-RD | | | | | $150.00 |
| Side Kick | 6022 | | HK | M-RS-R | | | | | $160.00 |
| Side Kick | 6022 | | HK | M-YW | | | | | $140.00 |
| Side Kick | 6022 | | HK | M-YW-L | | | | | $150.00 |
| Mercedes-Benz C-111 | 6169 | | HK | M-AQ | | WH | | | $170.00 |
| Mercedes-Benz C-111 | 6169 | | HK | M-AQ | | BK | | | $160.00 |
| Mercedes-Benz C-111 | 6169 | | HK | M-AQ | | GY | | | $160.00 |
| Mercedes-Benz C-111 | 6169 | | HK | M-AQ | | BR-P | | | $160.00 |
| Mercedes-Benz C-111 | 6169 | | HK | M-AQ | | BR-D | | | $160.00 |
| Mercedes-Benz C-111 | 6169 | | HK | M-BL | | WH | | | $170.00 |
| Mercedes-Benz C-111 | 6169 | | HK | M-BL | | BK | | | $160.00 |
| Mercedes-Benz C-111 | 6169 | | HK | M-BL | | GY | | | $160.00 |
| Mercedes-Benz C-111 | 6169 | | HK | M-BL | | BR-P | | | $160.00 |
| Mercedes-Benz C-111 | 6169 | | HK | M-BL | | BR-D | | | $160.00 |
| Mercedes-Benz C-111 | 6169 | | HK | M-BL-I | | WH | | | $190.00 |
| Mercedes-Benz C-111 | 6169 | | HK | M-BL-I | | BK | | | $180.00 |
| Mercedes-Benz C-111 | 6169 | | HK | M-BL-I | | GY | | | $180.00 |
| Mercedes-Benz C-111 | 6169 | | HK | M-BL-I | | BR-P | | | $180.00 |
| Mercedes-Benz C-111 | 6169 | | HK | M-BL-I | | BR-D | | | $180.00 |
| Mercedes-Benz C-111 | 6169 | | HK | M-BL-P | | WH | | | $180.00 |
| Mercedes-Benz C-111 | 6169 | | HK | M-BL-P | | BK | | | $170.00 |
| Mercedes-Benz C-111 | 6169 | | HK | M-BL-P | | GY | | | $170.00 |
| Mercedes-Benz C-111 | 6169 | | HK | M-BL-P | | BR-P | | | $170.00 |
| Mercedes-Benz C-111 | 6169 | | HK | M-BL-P | | BR-D | | | $170.00 |
| Mercedes-Benz C-111 | 6169 | | HK | M-GD | | WH | | | $150.00 |

## 1972 Variations

| Name | Number | Casting | Country | Color | Windows | Interior | Paint | Other | Value |
|---|---|---|---|---|---|---|---|---|---|
| Mercedes-Benz C-111 | 6169 | | HK | M-GD | | BK | | | $140.00 |
| Mercedes-Benz C-111 | 6169 | | HK | M-GD | | GY | | | $140.00 |
| Mercedes-Benz C-111 | 6169 | | HK | M-GD | | BR-P | | | $140.00 |
| Mercedes-Benz C-111 | 6169 | | HK | M-GD | | BR-D | | | $140.00 |
| Mercedes-Benz C-111 | 6169 | | HK | M-GR | | WH | | | $150.00 |
| Mercedes-Benz C-111 | 6169 | | HK | M-GR | | BK | | | $140.00 |
| Mercedes-Benz C-111 | 6169 | | HK | M-GR | | GY | | | $140.00 |
| Mercedes-Benz C-111 | 6169 | | HK | M-GR | | BR-P | | | $140.00 |
| Mercedes-Benz C-111 | 6169 | | HK | M-GR | | BR-D | | | $140.00 |
| Mercedes-Benz C-111 | 6169 | | HK | M-GR-E | | WH | | | $160.00 |
| Mercedes-Benz C-111 | 6169 | | HK | M-GR-E | | BK | | | $150.00 |
| Mercedes-Benz C-111 | 6169 | | HK | M-GR-E | | GY | | | $150.00 |
| Mercedes-Benz C-111 | 6169 | | HK | M-GR-E | | BR-P | | | $150.00 |
| Mercedes-Benz C-111 | 6169 | | HK | M-GR-E | | BR-D | | | $150.00 |
| Mercedes-Benz C-111 | 6169 | | HK | M-GR-L | | WH | | | $150.00 |
| Mercedes-Benz C-111 | 6169 | | HK | M-GR-L | | BK | | | $140.00 |
| Mercedes-Benz C-111 | 6169 | | HK | M-GR-L | | GY | | | $140.00 |
| Mercedes-Benz C-111 | 6169 | | HK | M-GR-L | | BR-P | | | $140.00 |
| Mercedes-Benz C-111 | 6169 | | HK | M-GR-L | | BR-D | | | $140.00 |
| Mercedes-Benz C-111 | 6169 | | HK | M-MG | | WH | | | $150.00 |
| Mercedes-Benz C-111 | 6169 | | HK | M-MG | | BK | | | $140.00 |
| Mercedes-Benz C-111 | 6169 | | HK | M-MG | | GY | | | $140.00 |
| Mercedes-Benz C-111 | 6169 | | HK | M-MG | | BR-P | | | $140.00 |
| Mercedes-Benz C-111 | 6169 | | HK | M-MG | | BR-D | | | $140.00 |
| Mercedes-Benz C-111 | 6169 | | HK | M-PK | | WH | | | $190.00 |
| Mercedes-Benz C-111 | 6169 | | HK | M-PK | | BK | | | $180.00 |
| Mercedes-Benz C-111 | 6169 | | HK | M-PK | | GY | | | $180.00 |
| Mercedes-Benz C-111 | 6169 | | HK | M-PK | | BR-P | | | $180.00 |
| Mercedes-Benz C-111 | 6169 | | HK | M-PK | | BR-D | | | $180.00 |
| Mercedes-Benz C-111 | 6169 | | HK | M-PK-H | | WH | | | $190.00 |
| Mercedes-Benz C-111 | 6169 | | HK | M-PK-H | | BK | | | $180.00 |
| Mercedes-Benz C-111 | 6169 | | HK | M-PK-H | | GY | | | $180.00 |
| Mercedes-Benz C-111 | 6169 | | HK | M-PK-H | | BR-P | | | $180.00 |
| Mercedes-Benz C-111 | 6169 | | HK | M-PK-H | | BR-D | | | $180.00 |
| Mercedes-Benz C-111 | 6169 | | HK | M-PK-S | | WH | | | $190.00 |
| Mercedes-Benz C-111 | 6169 | | HK | M-PK-S | | BK | | | $180.00 |
| Mercedes-Benz C-111 | 6169 | | HK | M-PK-S | | GY | | | $180.00 |
| Mercedes-Benz C-111 | 6169 | | HK | M-PK-S | | BR-P | | | $180.00 |
| Mercedes-Benz C-111 | 6169 | | HK | M-PK-S | | BR-D | | | $180.00 |
| Mercedes-Benz C-111 | 6169 | | HK | M-RD | | WH | | | $170.00 |
| Mercedes-Benz C-111 | 6169 | | HK | M-RD | | BK | | | $160.00 |
| Mercedes-Benz C-111 | 6169 | | HK | M-RD | | GY | | | $160.00 |
| Mercedes-Benz C-111 | 6169 | | HK | M-RD | | BR-P | | | $160.00 |
| Mercedes-Benz C-111 | 6169 | | HK | M-RD | | BR-D | | | $160.00 |
| Mercedes-Benz C-111 | 6169 | | HK | M-RS-R | | WH | | | $180.00 |
| Mercedes-Benz C-111 | 6169 | | HK | M-RS-R | | BK | | | $170.00 |
| Mercedes-Benz C-111 | 6169 | | HK | M-RS-R | | GY | | | $170.00 |
| Mercedes-Benz C-111 | 6169 | | HK | M-RS-R | | BR-P | | | $170.00 |
| Mercedes-Benz C-111 | 6169 | | HK | M-RS-R | | BR-D | | | $170.00 |
| Mercedes-Benz C-111 | 6169 | | HK | M-YW | | WH | | | $150.00 |
| Mercedes-Benz C-111 | 6169 | | HK | M-YW | | BK | | | $140.00 |
| Mercedes-Benz C-111 | 6169 | | HK | M-YW | | GY | | | $140.00 |
| Mercedes-Benz C-111 | 6169 | | HK | M-YW | | BR-P | | | $140.00 |
| Mercedes-Benz C-111 | 6169 | | HK | M-YW | | BR-D | | | $140.00 |
| Mercedes-Benz C-111 | 6169 | | HK | M-YW-L | | WH | | | $160.00 |
| Mercedes-Benz C-111 | 6169 | | HK | M-YW-L | | BK | | | $150.00 |
| Mercedes-Benz C-111 | 6169 | | HK | M-YW-L | | GY | | | $150.00 |
| Mercedes-Benz C-111 | 6169 | | HK | M-YW-L | | BR-P | | | $150.00 |
| Mercedes-Benz C-111 | 6169 | | HK | M-YW-L | | BR-D | | | $150.00 |

### The Unauthorized Encyclopedia of Corgi Toys
Bill Manzke

The rise, fall and rebirth of Corgi Toys is explained and illustrated with hundreds of color photos of toy models and memorabilia never before seen in print. The smaller Husky and Corgi Juniors lines are also covered. Most importantly, this encylopedia presents the most complete variation listing and values guide for Corgi toys published to date.

Size: 8 1/2" x 11"  779 color photos
Price Guide  256 pp.
ISBN: 0-7643-0308-2  soft cover  $34.95

### Corgi Toys
Edward Force

Every model of Corgi toy is shown in 128 color group photos with the history supplemented by detailed descriptions of all the models and their known variations. Includes up-to-date price guide.

Size: 9" x 6"  128 color plates
Updated Price Guide  224 pp
ISBN: 0-7643-0253-1  soft cover  $16.95

### The Complete Book of Hot Wheels™
*Revised and Expanded 4th Edition*
Bob Parker

Wonderful color photographs cover nearly every casting from the first Hot Wheels toy cars through the 1999 model year. A complete visual guide with a listing of the many variations to help collectors sort through the vast and rapidly growing world of Hot Wheels.

Size: 8 1/2" x 11"  686 color photos
Price Guide  160 pp.
ISBN: 0-7643-1083-6  soft cover  $29.95

### Hot Wheels™
### A Collector's Guide
*Revised & Expanded 4th Edition*
Bob Parker

A revised and expanded edition with extensive information about all the die cast Hot Wheels toy vehicles. Over 100 color pictures display nearly all the Hot Wheels made up to 1968, and a complete variation guide and checklist covers all the cars through 1995. This book will be an essential reference for collectors of all types of die cast toy vehicles.

Size: 9" x 6"  654 cars, access. & photos
Price Guide  160 pp.
ISBN: 0-7643-1217-0  soft cover  $19.95

### Dinky Toys
*Revised 5th Edition*
Edward Force

Dinky Toys, produced from 1933 to 1980, are discussed with a concise history, detailed list of major variations, chronological list, and newly revised price guide. Included are all the Dinky Toys made in Britain, France, Spain and other parts of the world, from the earliest model railroad accessories to the first miniature cars to bear the name Dinky Toys.

Size: 9" x 6"  128 color photos
Price Guide/Index  224 pp.
ISBN: 0-7643-1372-X  soft cover  $19.95

### Classic Miniature Vehicles
### Made in Germany
Edward Force

German manufacturers produced interesting and superb miniature die cast toy vehicles which are described here. Color photos of over 2000 German toy vehicles make this a most useful book for die cast collectors and fanciers of miniatures.

Size: 9" x 6"  
Price Guide  
ISBN: 0-88740-251-8   soft cover

80 color photos  
256 pp.  
$16.95

### Classic Miniature Vehicles
### Made in Italy
Dr. Edward Force

America's foremost authority on miniature vehicles turns to Italy, where die cast miniature vehicles began to be manufactured after the end of World War II. Cars from Mercury, Lima, Nigam, PM, Ra-Ro, Rivarossi, Safar, SVP and other Italian companies are presented in color with informative vital facts about the cars detailed in an easy-to-use format.

Size: 9" x 6"  
Price Guide  
ISBN: 0-88740-433-2   soft cover

96 photos  
256 pp.  
$16.95

### Classic Miniature Vehicles
### Made In France
Dr. Edward Force

Miniature vehicle production in France by 39 manufacturers is represented here by nearly 2000 vehicles described and shown in color photos. Information provided in encyclopedic entries includes vehicles by the companies C.I.J., Cle, France Jouets, J.R.D., Minialuxe, Norev, Quiralu, Rami, and Safir.

Size: 9" x 6"  
Price Guide  
ISBN: 0-88740-316-6   soft cover

96 color plates  
280 pp.  
$16.95

### A World of Bus Toys and Models
Kurt M. Resch with photography by Richard Romagnoli

Toy and model buses are closely examined in this book. Bus transportation from the 1920s to the present appears in over 500 gorgeous color photos of over 1100 toy buses. This is the missing link in the transportation toy library, the book that bus lovers have been waiting for.

Size: 8 1/2" x 11"  
Price Guide  
ISBN: 0-7643-0814-9   soft cover

510 color photos  
160 pp.  
$29.95

### Cast Iron Automotive Toys
Myra Yellin Outwater & Eric B. Outwater with Stevie & Bill Weart

Rare and exquisite cast iron toys are coveted by collectors of *all* ages. There are the best from leading American cast iron toy manufacturers, including Kenton, Dent, Hubley, Arcade, Kilgore, Vindex, and A. C. Williams, along with pieces by Champion, Globe, and Grey Iron, and more. Original catalog advertisements, signage, manufacturers' marks, and over 850 magnificent toys are displayed in over 880 color photos, including automobiles, trucks, motorcycles, tractors, farm and construction equipment, and aeronautics.

Size: 8 1/2" x 11"  
Price Guide  
ISBN: 0-7643-1077-1   hard cover

880 color photos  
264 pp.  
$69.95

## Antique Motorcycle Toys
### Rich Bertoia.
Clockwork toy motorcyles from Europe, Japan and America possess beauty and complexity of design matched only by their extreme rarity. This reference book documents hundreds of motorcycle toys, including police chases, stunt riders, elegant cruisers, and spacemen, through over 150 color photographs and interesting text and values, making this a truly special edition for collectors of all levels.

| | |
|---|---|
| Size: 11" x 8 1/2" | 162 color photos |
| Price Guide | 160 pp. |
| ISBN: 0-7643-0862-9 hard cover | $49.95 |

## Collecting the Tin Toy Car, 1950-1970
### Dale Kelley
A beautiful tribute to those realistic and extremely collectible tin toy vehicles of the 1950s and '60s which are exact replicas of full size cars. The photos remind many of their youth and inspire collectors to extend their hunt for more. This book set a high standard by becoming influential on all the later books about collecting toy cars.

| | |
|---|---|
| Size: 8 1/2" x 11" | 360 color & b/w illus. |
| Rarity Guide | 200 pp. |
| ISBN: 0-88740-012-4 hard cover | $29.95 |

## Matchbox® Toys
*Revised 5th Edition*
### Nancy Schiffer
All the Matchbox toys made between 1947 and 1982 in color photos with history of the companies and descriptions of each toy and their variations. This a thorough study of the subject. The list of collector's clubs can lead one to fellow-enthusiasts, upcoming toy shows, and new toys as they are released. Above all, newly revised prices will give you an informed edge in the busy collector's market.

| | |
|---|---|
| Size: 9" x 6" | 1236 toys in color & b/w photos |
| Price Guide | 208 pp. |
| ISBN: 0-7643-0991-9 soft cover | $19.95 |

## Matchbox® and Lledo™ Toys
### Edward Force
Miniature vehicle Matchbox toys and Lledo toys made from 1983 to 1987 are illustrated in color with comprehensive text identifying all variations, helpful background information and price guide.

| | |
|---|---|
| Size: 9" x 6" | 96 photos of 1400 toys |
| Price Guide | 185 pp. |
| ISBN: 0-88740-127-9 soft cover | $14.95 |

## Lledo Toys
### Dr. Edward Force
Matchbox toys co-founder Jack Odell later founded Lledo (his name spelled backwards) toys and produced the first models in 1983. Since then, the fleet of Lledo miniature antique vehicles has grown to include thousands of models. Over 2000 are shown in color photos with an informative history, extensive list of variations, and a price guide.

| | |
|---|---|
| Size: 9" x 6" | 100 color photos |
| Price Guide | 160 pp. |
| ISBN: 0-7643-0013-X soft cover | $19.95 |

## Solido Toys
### Dr. Edward Force
1200 miniature Solido vehicle models, nearly all illustrated here in full color. With the company history and a detailed accounting of models and variations listed in an easy-to-use format, this book is a necessary reference for collectors of Solido and other die cast toy vehicles.

| | |
|---|---|
| Size: 9" x 6" | 80 color photos |
| Price Guide | 256 pp. |
| ISBN: 0-88740-532-0 soft cover | $16.95 |